International Marketing

Holt, Rinehart and Winston Marketing Series

Paul E. Green, Advisor
Wharton School, University of Pennsylvania

Philip Kotler, Advisor
Northwestern University

International Marketing

Vern Terpstra

The University of Michigan

HOLT, RINEHART AND WINSTON, INC.

NEW YORK   CHICAGO   SAN FRANCISCO   ATLANTA
DALLAS   TORONTO   MONTREAL   LONDON   SYDNEY

Copyright © 1972 by Holt, Rinehart and Winston, Inc.
All rights reserved
Library of Congress Catalog Card Number: 74–177491
ISBN: 0–03–085619–1
Printed in the United States of America
2   3   4   5   038   9   8   7   6   5   4   3   2   1

To Bonnie, Ben, Kathy, and Jim

FOREWORD

The subject of international marketing is attracting the increased interest of business firms and government officials throughout the world. Nations see in foreign markets major opportunities for their commercial expansion and prosperity. They are recognizing, too, that international expansion is more than a matter of understanding tariffs, foreign currencies, and international carriers. One of the key skills in going abroad is the ability of the seller to understand and measure markets, develop appropriate products and prices, arrange efficient distribution, and design effective promotion. The logic of the modern discipline of marketing is central to achieving good results in any market, whether national or international.

We are therefore pleased to publish Vern Terpstra's *International Marketing* in the Holt, Rinehart, and Winston Marketing Series. The reader will find in these pages an extremely knowledgeable and authoritative discussion of the major issues facing international marketing management. Professor Terpstra combines most effectively both an *environmental approach*—to give the reader an understanding of the setting of international marketing—and a *managerial approach*—to give the reader a feeling for the decisions faced by those companies that choose to venture abroad. His account is highly readable and comprehensive. The major concepts and tools of marketing are lucidly applied to the solution of problems faced in international marketing. This text is not only the latest to appear in this field but will, in our opinion, be the most notable in its excellence of organization, exposition, and analysis.

Paul E. Green
Philip Kotler

vii

PREFACE

This book endeavors to introduce the reader to the nature and practice of international marketing. It assumes a familiarity with general marketing management and builds on this knowledge to develop insight and understanding into the peculiar nature of *international* marketing management. The problems of marketing *across* national boundaries are analyzed, as well as those arising from marketing *within* a number of different national markets. The text covers not only the situation of the domestic firm which is exporting, but also the needs of those firms which assemble, license, or produce in foreign markets. In other words, *International Marketing* considers the full range of international marketing involvement from the exporter to the multinational firm.

The text is managerial in the sense that it focuses on the problems and decisions facing managers of international marketing in business enterprises. However, this does not mean that the interests of consumers and host countries are ignored. They are explicitly considered throughout the book as important determinants of the international marketing task. In that sense the book is socially conscious.

Part I studies in some depth the environments of international marketing. The reason for starting this way is that the problems and peculiarities of international marketing derive largely from the different environments in which it occurs. The potential international marketing manager must recognize the relevant aspects of these environments if he is to operate successfully. A market orientation obviously requires a knowledge of the market environment, and that of the international marketer tends to be quite different from that facing his domestic counterpart. Part I assists the international marketer in recognizing the nature and impact of his environment.

Part II deals specifically with the problems and decisions facing the international marketing manager. The organization of this part follows that of most marketing texts, that is, the chapters reflect the kinds of product, pricing, promotion, and other decisions that marketing managers must make. Part II assumes familiarity with general marketing principles and practice, and analyzes their application in an international and multinational context. These chapters, the core of the text, identify the distinctive nature of *international* marketing management. Numerous company examples are used in each chapter to show both the problems and the approaches used to solve them. Various analytical techniques used in decision making are also suggested.

Part III is a brief discussion of the ways of integrating and coordinating the firm's marketing programs in many diverse markets. Planning, organization, and control are examined as three principal means of coordinating the firm's international marketing activities.

International Marketing has received contributions from many sources. Ten years of living abroad (in Europe and Africa) have helped the author to understand environments outside the United States. Ten years of research and teaching in international business have helped me in the conceptualization and organization of the field of international business and marketing.

Individuals from many fields and countries have helped in ways I cannot identify. Certain groups have been especially helpful, however. One group is composed of the numerous international executives I have met in conducting research, seminars, or consulting work. Their always generous response has been an invaluable input.

I must admit also that I owe a debt to competing textbooks in international marketing. Over the years I have used in my classes all of the following texts: Kramer, *International Marketing*; Hess and Cateora, *International Marketing*; Fayerweather, *International Marketing*; Root, *Strategic Planning for Export Marketing*; Miracle and Albaum, *International Marketing Management*.

On the present text, many academic colleagues have helped me. Several professors in marketing or international business at the University of Michigan have reviewed parts of the manuscript. The publishers favored me with an exceptionally qualified group of reviewers: Professors Jean Boddewyn, New York University; Richard Clewett, Northwestern University; Paul Green, Wharton School, University of Pennsylvania; and Philip Kotler, Northwestern University. Their comments on the whole manuscript led to useful modifications and improvements. As the primary producer, however, I must stand behind my product as it is finally presented.

Ann Arbor, Michigan   V. T.
December 1971.

CONTENTS

PART I

THE INTERNATIONAL ENVIRONMENT

In Part I, we will look at the world environment in which international marketing takes place. Just as space scientists and astronauts must study the expected environment on the moon and other planets, so the international marketer must analyze the environment in which he will be operating. The kind of steps he can take and the adaptations he must make will be determined largely by this environment, just as the astronauts' actions are defined by the moon's environment. Therefore, in Part I we will attempt to gain some familiarity with the international marketer's sphere of operation, dwelling particularly on the uncontrollable variables and how they affect the international marketing task. Some of the variables discussed are completely new to the marketing manager; others he has encountered in his domestic marketing. However, even the variables he knows by name behave in less familiar and predictable ways in foreign markets.

1

INTRODUCTION TO INTERNATIONAL MARKETING

Technological advances in transportation and communication have made close neighbors of the world's nations. We are increasingly aware of our global interdependence in such areas as economics, ecology, and politics, including war and peace. Although this book deals with marketing, it discusses the significance of this international interdependence to the business firm. More precisely, this book deals with marketing internationally and with the management of international marketing. Before we consider management questions, however, we will identify the vocabulary and environment of international marketing.

SOME DEFINITIONS AND DISTINCTIONS

Marketing

Marketing has been defined in several ways. In this book, we define marketing broadly as the collection of activities undertaken by the firm to relate profitably to its market. Whereas the firm is, in some sense, master in its own house, its ultimate success depends primarily on how well it performs outside, in the marketplace. Successful performance requires knowledge of the market. Therefore, the first task of the firm is to study its prospective buyers. Who are they? Where are they? What factors influence their purchase (or nonpurchase) of its product? Incidentally, we might note that until recently the firm in the communist economies was not faced with this task. Today, however, with the impact of "Libermanism" and the increasing affluence of consumers, a marketing orientation and market intelligence activity are becoming necessary even for Soviet firms.

The second task of the firm is to develop products or services that satisfy customer needs and wants. In this regard, the firm must set prices and terms on these products that appear reasonable to buyers but that at the same time return what the firm considers a fair profit. The firm's third task concerns the distribution function, that is, making the products available when and where buyers can conveniently get them. As its fourth and final task, the firm must inform the market about its wares and will probably have to use some persuasion to get them to buy. Although the firm's marketing responsibility is often considered to end with the sale, this is not always true. An implied warranty of satisfaction goes with the product; thus the firm must occasionally reassure the buyer and, in many cases, perform after-sale service. Marketing in the firm, then, involves all these activities relating to the market. The marketing manager must plan and coordinate these activities in order to produce a successful integrated marketing program.

International Marketing

The collection of activities just described (market intelligence, product development, pricing, distribution, and promotion) constitutes the essence of marketing for the purpose of this book. What then is international marketing? At its simplest, it is the performance of one or more of these activities across national boundaries. At its most complete, it involves the performance of all these functions in many countries. In other words, *international* marketing is *marketing* carried on across national boundaries. Thus a small exporting firm can be an international marketer to a limited extent merely by distributing its products in foreign markets. That same firm becomes a more complete international marketer to the degree that it participates in the pricing, promotion, and other marketing activities for its products in foreign markets. An extra dimension in *international marketing management* is the planning, coordination, and control of all these functions to form an integrated multinational operation.

If the activities and goals of international marketing are the same as those of domestic marketing, one might well ask, Why a separate text and study of international marketing? The answer is that although the basic functions (product development, promotion, and so on) are the same in both markets, implementation of the firm's marketing programs can be very different; that is, managing international marketing can be significantly different from managing domestic marketing.

A major goal of this book is to analyze and illustrate the difference between international and domestic marketing management. Some of the reasons for difference are more obvious than others. For example, the parameters that determine the nature of a firm's marketing program are likely to be different in each of the firm's foreign markets. One can easily imagine that the "uncontrollable" factors would not be the same in, say, France, Brazil, India, and the United States. Among other things, the nature of demand, competition, and the distribution structure will have characteristics peculiar to each national market. The firm's marketing program must adapt to these market characteristics if it is to be successful.

What may be less obvious is that even the "controllable" elements in marketing may vary from market to market internationally. The controllable elements are considered to be price, product, channels of distribution, and promotion. However, the firm's cost and price structure, products and product line, and promotional capabilities are probably somewhat different in each of its foreign markets. Thus virtually all the determinants of the marketing program can vary, giving rise to complexities in international marketing management that are not encountered in the domestic market.

An added dimension of international marketing management is the problem of coordination and integration of the firm's many national marketing programs into an effective multinational program. Indeed, a principal rationale of multinational business operations, as opposed to the alternative of independent national companies, is that the division of labor and the transfer of know-how in international operations enable the whole to be greater than the sum of its parts.

A practical result of these differences is that one needs to acquire competence as an *international* marketing manager, a competence broader than that required for marketing in a specific foreign country and distinctly different from that demanded by domestic marketing management.[1]

In other words, the international marketing manager is concerned with *multinational marketing* (marketing in many countries) as well as with *international marketing* (marketing across national boundaries).

Foreign and Comparative Marketing

We will not discuss foreign domestic marketing per se, but we define foreign marketing here as national marketing conducted by national concerns without regard to international considerations. For example, a small French manufacturer of consumer goods selling to a regional market in France would probably give no thought to international parameters in his marketing decision making. But the multinational company, on the other hand, needs to be aware of domestic marketing practices in the countries where it is selling. It will even participate in such marketing through its national subsidiaries. The concern of the multinational firm, however, is not a broad general study of domestic marketing in many nations, but only those aspects that affect its own operations in particular countries.

The international firm needs to study foreign marketing primarily to answer questions such as the following: How can we best market our products in country X? Do we need to adapt our American marketing approach to the local market? Can we introduce marketing innovations to serve the market better and more profitably than it is being served by local concerns? What this book will try to present, therefore, will not be a survey of foreign domestic marketing, but rather the critical aspects of foreign marketing systems as they affect the marketing functions under discussion.

Another topic we touch on only briefly in this book is comparative marketing. Comparative marketing is the organized study of marketing systems in

[1] See also John Fayerweather, *International Business Management* (New York: McGraw-Hill Book Co., 1969), pp. 1–4.

many countries—the similarities, differences, and the reasons therefore. Such study is useful in broadening one's understanding of marketing and in helping one to develop generalized theories of marketing and, perhaps, useful classification systems. Thus knowledge of comparative marketing can be applied to international marketing. Although we discuss aspects of the subject in this text, a thorough study of comparative marketing requires approaches and analytical techniques different from those used in studying the management of international marketing, which is our major concern. Therefore, these related topics will enter our discussion only as they help us to understand the problems facing the international marketing manager.[2]

International Trade or International Marketing?

The truism that no man is an island unto himself applies as well to economics as to other kinds of human activity. Some form of economic exchange has characterized the history of mankind almost from the beginning. The relatively recent phenomenon called "internation trade" is related to the rise of the nation-state as the dominant form of political organization; it is the exchange of goods and services between one country (and its residents) and other countries (and their residents). Although international trade statistics do not go back very far into history, there is no doubt that the volume of world trade has risen greatly in absolute terms and has become an increasingly important component of world economic activity. World trade has grown especially rapidly since World War II, with the dollar volume doubling each decade since that time. The total in 1970 reached about $300 billion.[3]

There is a relationship between international trading and international marketing, but the terms are not synonymous. International trading involves several of the marketing functions, but much of such trading does not involve international marketing management. By the latter expression we mean the administration of an international marketing program by a firm, whereas much of world trade is a more simple exchange of goods—a buying or selling operation, with little or no active marketing management being practiced. For example, one large component of international exchange is the trade in commodities. Primary commodities are handled by a variety of specialized intermediaries, each performing a limited role. Although these intermediaries may perform their tasks efficiently, they do not do so under an overall marketing plan or program such as that developed by the marketing manager of a firm. One might say that commodities are sold and delivered, rather than marketed. The International Coffee Organization has tried to overcome this weakness by incorporating a marketing and promotional activity as part of its function.

---

[2] For studies in comparative marketing see Robert Bartels, ed., *Comparative Marketing: Wholesaling in Fifteen Countries* (Homewood, Ill.: Richard D. Irwin, 1963); Jean Boddewyn, *Comparative Management and Marketing* (Glenview, Ill.: Scott, Foresman and Co., 1969); David Carson, *International Marketing* (New York: John Wiley and Sons, 1967).

[3] *International Financial Statistics,* 1971.

Another important segment of international trade carried on without marketing management is the state trading done by governmental organizations. The American foreign-aid program, surplus food disposal, and strategic and offshore procurement are examples of this. The American government engages in buying and selling—or giving—but does little real marketing. This pattern is changing somewhat, as evidenced by American efforts to sell weapons and military equipment to NATO countries. The Department of Defense has undertaken active promotional efforts as well as other marketing activities to encourage foreign purchases of equipment developed in the United States.

Communist-bloc trade is another example. In communist trade, the emphasis is on procurement. The goods sold are seen primarily as a means of payment, rather than as products designed for particular market needs. In fact, much of communist-bloc trade is on a barter or swap basis rather than on a regular commercial basis. One of the major hindrances to an expansion of East–West trade is not American government restrictions but the marketing inadequacies of the communist economies. These inadequacies cause them some trouble internally, but their problem is much greater in international trade where there is competition and the buyers have alternatives.

As we will see in Chapter 2, there are good reasons for the international marketer to become familiar with the nature and patterns of world trade. It is misleading, however, to equate the volume of international trade with the volume of international marketing. We noted differences relating to commodities and state trading above. A further important distinction derives from the fact that much of international marketing activity takes place without the passage of goods between nations. Thus foreign subsidiaries of American companies, for example, could have all their sales within a national market (not entering international trade statistics) while several of their marketing functions are being performed internationally (for instance, marketing planning, product development, and promotion).

One implication of this distinction between international trade and international marketing is that if one wishes to learn about the latter, he will benefit more from studying basic marketing and the international marketing practices of companies than from studying international trade per se. (We will look briefly at international trade in Part I and extensively at the international marketing task in Part II, with frequent mention of companies' experiences and problems.) Table 1–1 highlights some of the differences in nature and emphasis between international trade and international marketing.

International Trade or International Business?

Another distinction to be noted is that between international trade and international business. Many of the differences between international trade and international marketing also apply here. International business involves the performance of one or more of the business functions across national boundaries. This need not always require a movement of goods between nations. For example, the foreign sales of American subsidiaries are several times larger than total American exports. Many of these foreign sales are within the country where the subsidiary is located, and thus not in international trade statistics. Of course, these subsidiaries also frequently export some of their output. For example, Ford of Britain is that country's second largest exporter.

Table 1–1 Comparison of International Trade and International Marketing

DIMENSION	INTERNATIONAL TRADE	INTERNATIONAL MARKETING
Actors	Nations	Firms
Goods move across frontiers	Yes	Not necessarily
Impetus	Comparative advantage	Company decisions (usually profit motivated)
Information source	Nation's balance of payments	Company records
Marketing activities:		
Buy and sell	Yes	Yes
Physical distribution	Yes	Yes
Pricing	Yes	Yes
Market research	Generally not	Yes
Product development	Generally not	Yes
Promotion	Generally not	Yes
Distribution channel management	No	Yes

An ambivalent relationship exists between international trade and international business. There is an intriguing possibility that international business may be replacing part of international trade; that is, international business may be a partial substitute for international trade. To illustrate this, let us note some trade-expanding aspects of international business. First, the foreign investment associated with it can have a twofold impact: (1) Investment in and equipping of the foreign plant may lead to an increase in world-trade figures; and (2) the new investment contributes to the growth of the host country and raises its imports. In addition, the experience of American companies shows that the existence of a foreign plant usually means an increase in their exports to that country. This happens because of the strong marketing support to company sales given by the firm's investment and physical presence in that country. Another force behind trade expansion is the desire of multinational firms to rationalize their production; these firms prefer to specialize by plant and export to other markets to gain economies of scale.

Offsetting the trade-expanding aspects of international business are other forces that tend to limit international trade. As a company invests in a foreign plant, it acquires foreign production capacity to replace some or all of the products it was exporting to that market. Once foreign subsidiaries are established, a variety of pressures cause them to become more and more self-contained, to produce more products locally and to depend less on imports from abroad. Balance of payments deficits in the host country may force that government to restrict imports and raise the percentage of the product or product line that is produced locally ("local content" requirements). National complaints about the "technology gap" may lead to local production of what are considered advanced products as well as standard items. Considerations of local marketing and the desires of the subsidiary management can both work together toward larger, more self-contained national operations.

The net effect of these trade-expanding and trade-contracting forces is uncertain. If nations generally follow liberal trading policies, the expansionary effects should be greater. In any case, the impact of international corporations will be critical. This is especially true if most of the world's future international business will be in the hands of a few hundred corporations, as seems possible. These corporations will be multinational operators concerned with international growth and profit maximization through the use of corporate skills and resources. They will not be merely international traders limiting themselves to export selling.

There is one further significant distinction between international business and international trade. International trade traditionally has involved arm's-length transactions between independent parties. By contrast, many of the foreign transactions of an international company are with affiliated parts of the firm. The parent company sells to the subsidiaries, and the subsidiaries sell to each other and to the parent. Even licensees can be involved, as "in-laws" of the corporate family. Thus many of the firm's international transactions are intracompany transactions, even though crossing national boundaries. Obviously, decision processes and influences, as well as trade flows, in internal company logistics are different from those in the arm's-length transactions of international trade.

The International Firm

Firms are incorporated by sovereign states. An incorporated firm is a citizen. There is no "internation" that can legally create or license international companies. (It has been suggested, however, that the United Nations should do this.) Of course, a firm can own companies incorporated in other nations. Although both the national and the international company are domiciled within a nation, the international firm is distinctive in that it has special interests outside that nation. In fact, part of its corporate family is domiciled in other nations. The firm's international interests can be identified in various ways, including the following: the percent of assets, personnel, sales, and/or profits outside of its home market; the number of countries in which it is operating and selling; and the extent to which company decision making considers international as well as domestic markets.

For purposes of this text, we will use a rather loose definition of the international enterprise. The international firm is a company with operations (production and sales) in more than one country. Of course, the more countries in which the firm is operating, the more international it is. We will use the term "multinational firm" interchangeably with "international firm." The foreign production operations of the multinational company may be through wholly owned subsidiaries, joint ventures, licensing, or contract manufacturing.

A firm that operates only through exports from its home country is not an international firm according to our definition. Such a firm could, of course, be an international marketer if it took an active role in the marketing of its products abroad. In other words, international marketing is not limited to international firms.

THE FIRM FACES THE WORLD MARKET

We have discussed the nature of international marketing and suggested that it involves the firm as the firm relates to foreign markets. For the firm to be an international marketer it must relate actively to one or more markets outside its own country. How important is this kind of relationship for the firm? To what degree should the American firm be concerned about the world market and international marketing? Many small firms and a number of large companies that limit activity to the American domestic market have satisfactory sales and profits. It is not suggested that a firm must market internationally to be successful or profitable. However, the time is passing when a manufacturing concern can safely ignore international influences on its business. A threat to a firm's domestic market may force the firm to reassess its role in the world market as well as nationally.

Already many firms are finding that to be competitive nationally, they must be competitive internationally. A number of factors are causing an increasing variety and quantity of foreign goods to enter the American market, destroying the isolation from foreign competition that firms had enjoyed previously. Some of these factors are increasing affluence, greater sophistication of consumers and purchasing agents, improved communication with the rest of the world, better transportation that lowers the costs of imported goods, lower tariffs on imports because of the Kennedy Round and other tariff negotiations, and increased aggressiveness of foreign businessmen.

Quite apart from an import threat, there may be other compelling reasons for even the small firm to "think international." If the firm is thinking positively about growth and profit maximization, again the answer and the best opportunities may be international. Some examples will illustrate how even small firms can be successful in exporting.

Tatum Farms of Georgia began exporting hatching eggs and baby chicks at the end of 1963 through an export broker. Subsequently the firm sold some 70 percent of its production abroad.[4]

After a 1967 trade show in Tokyo, Gudebrod Brothers of Philadelphia began averaging $4,000 per month in export sales to Japan of its Dacron fishing thread.[5]

Valley Forge Products Company of Brooklyn was originally a manufacturer of automotive parts for U.S.-made vehicles. In 1963, the firm began making

[4] From *International Commerce*, November 11, 1968, p. 8.
[5] *International Commerce*, August 5, 1968, p. 1.

replacement parts for foreign-made cars as well. By this action the company avoided being affected by the decrease in export of U.S.-made cars occurring at that time. Valley Forge now has more than seventy sales representatives in sixty-five countries and has received the presidential "E" award for increasing exports.[6]

There are several reasons marketing abroad may be an attractive option for a firm.

1. A product can be near the end of its life cycle in the United States at the same time it experiences a growth market abroad.
2. In some product lines, competition in foreign markets may be less intense than domestically. (Of course, sometimes the reverse is true.)
3. If the firm has excess capacity, it can produce for foreign markets at a favorable marginal cost per unit. This favorable cost situation applies whether the foreign price is a "full cost" price or an "incremental cost" price.
4. Geographical diversification, that is, going international, may be a more desirable alternative than product-line diversification. The most notable example of this is Wrigleys. The company still specializes in the production and marketing of a very narrow product line, chewing gum. Wrigleys' only diversification efforts have been to expand its market coverage internationally, both in production and in marketing. This diversification has been sufficient to keep Wrigleys in the *Fortune* 500.

The argument here is not that all manufacturing firms should go international (although over 15,000 American firms are engaged in some international marketing). For many of them, that would be an unwise decision. The point is rather that sound decision making requires consideration of all the feasible alternatives. Many companies do not consider adequately the international market as a major alternative road to growth and profits, if they consider it at all. Even among many companies marketing internationally, decision making has a domestic bias. Some domestic bias is justified by hard economic and political facts, but not all of it, by any means. As foreign markets become more important, decision making in the firm must become more truly international. Table 1–2 shows the importance of international markets to some of America's larger multinational marketers.

LEVELS OF INTERNATIONAL MARKETING INVOLVEMENT

When the firm chooses to become an international marketer, its degree of commitment to foreign markets can vary widely. The following sections give an overview of the range of possible levels of involvement.

Casual or Accidental Exporting

At this passive level of involvement, the firm may be selling abroad without even knowing it. Resident buyers for foreign companies or distributors may be buying the firm's goods and sending them overseas while the firm considers

[6] *International Commerce,* July 8, 1968, p. 8.

these typical domestic sales. Regular American customers of industrial goods producers may export the firm's goods as part of their supplies for their own foreign operations. In other cases the firm may be aware of its sales abroad but do nothing to encourage the occasional orders. The letter with the foreign stamps, and perhaps written in a foreign language, arouses interest and discussion in the office ("How did they find out about us?") but no follow up is made after the order is filled, if it is. (Unfortunately, it has happened that such letters did not even receive the courtesy of a response because of a disinterest in such business and the bother involved.) This sort of casual exporting probably occurs in a large number of firms but it does not represent any real commitment to or involvement in international marketing. Opportunistic firms may see such occasional exporting as a way to unload an unexpected surplus or some obsolete inventory.

Table 1–2 Importance of Foreign Markets to Some American Companies

COMPANY	PERCENT SALES ABROAD IN 1970
DuPont	17.5
General Motors	19.5*
Chrysler	24.3*
International Harvester	25.1
Abbott Laboratories	28.2
Warner Lambert Pharmaceuticals	36.0
Singer	36.5
I.B.M.	39.1
U.S.M. Corporation	43.2
Heinz (H.J.)	44.5
N.C.R.	45.2
Pfizer (Chas.)	47.3
Caterpillar Tractor	52.5
Colgate Palmolive	55.4
Massey Ferguson	73.6

* Excludes Canada.

Source: Compiled from each firm's 1970 Annual Report.

Active Exporting

Because of the number of unsolicited orders from abroad, an overseas move by a competitor, a company officer's hearing a speech or success story about exporting, or for any of several reasons, the firm may decide to seek export sales actively. This means that some resources must be allocated to exports. The company may either set up its own export operation in-house or hire some outside organization to handle its export marketing. For example, the combination export manager discussed in Chapter 11 can act as the company's own export department, giving it "instant" experience and market knowledge. There are also possibilities for cooperative exporting, as in a Webb-Pomerene association or in a "piggyback" operation. The key point here is that the firm is making a commitment to seek export business.

Foreign Licensing

The firm may license foreign manufacturers to produce its products, taking the place of exporting. This practice represents a somewhat greater degree of involvement than exporting in that the company's products are now being produced in foreign markets, even though by proxy. Licensing may prove more practical than exporting because of the high costs of shipping goods from America, high tariff barriers or quota restrictions, or nationalistic preferences for locally produced goods. Licensing may also be desirable because of marketing advantages gained, such as the local market knowledge and distribution capabilities of the licensee.

Overseas Marketing by the Firm

Establishment of a foreign sales office or marketing subsidiary abroad represents a further commitment to international business. The product may come from American plants, licensees, or contract manufacturing, but the foreign marketing is now controlled more directly by the firm through its physical presence in the market.

Foreign Production and Foreign Marketing

A firm reaches the utmost degree of international involvement when it engages in its own foreign manufacturing operations. Although foreign licensing means foreign production, this production is only through the licensee with little or no resource commitment by the licensor. Significant financial and managerial resources probably will be needed for foreign production, though these requirements may vary. For example, foreign assembly operations are less demanding than complete foreign manufacturing, and a joint venture will mean a sharing of costs and risks with the partner who is usually a national.

Acquisition of an existing producer in a foreign market is a popular and quick way of entering the market. Although this may be as costly—or more so—in financial terms as starting a plant from the ground up, the demands on management are apt to be much less. The truth of this depends on whether the firm is a "passive" or an "active" acquirer. For example, some American companies that have acquired going concerns in Europe have made very little change in their operations, except to add a financial or quality control man to the staff and a few of their leading American products to the existing line of the foreign company. Firms take this approach in part because they lack experience and familiarity with the foreign market and in part because they want to avoid spoiling a profitable operation.

The more passive the acquiring firm, the more the direct investment resembles a portfolio investment. Since the acquiring firm using a passive approach makes a relatively small contribution, it may be more vulnerable politically and have some difficulty justifying its takeover of the local company. (But of course the fewer changes it makes, the less obvious its presence.) The active acquirer tends to modernize (or "Americanize") and internationalize the acquired firm, trying to integrate it into a more effective multinational operation. Problems arise from this approach, too, resulting from inadequate consideration of local interests or failure to realize the desired effective multinational integration.

Whatever form its company-owned foreign manufacturing takes, the firm is nevertheless in the foreign market with both feet. Most of its business activities are being carried out in foreign markets as well as in the United States (except for R&D perhaps). Besides production, one of its major tasks is the management of the marketing program in the foreign markets concerned. The firm has become a full-fledged multinational marketer.

The preceding discussion has shown that as a firm considers the world market, it finds a wide range of possibilities for involvement in as well as profit from international marketing. Even the small firm can be a successful international marketer through a type of involvement appropriate to its own situation and resources. The billion-dollar corporations have a wider range of choices, but even for them the alternatives vary on the basis of division, product line, and country.

The classification of levels of involvement given here is not meant to be absolute nor the categories mutually exclusive. It does illustrate, however, that there are many alternatives open to the firm. The decision to go international is not an all-or-nothing decision. There is no necessary progression from casual exporting to foreign production and marketing, although there are many examples of this. A large diversified company is apt to be participating at all these levels of involvement for different products or in different countries.

For example, General Electric Company is the sole owner of several manufacturing plants overseas. It also has joint ventures in some countries, licensing in others, and a large export operation from the United States. The company even uses an export agent for foreign sales of its complete line of aircraft lamps. GE's variety of international marketing activities accounted for 1968 sales of $1.7 billion: $500 million in exports, and sales by consolidated foreign affiliates of $1,200 million.[7]

In addition to recognizing that the firm has alternative ways of going international, it is important to become familiar with the different kinds of foreign-market involvement because the marketing strategies that can be employed by the firm will depend in large part on the method of involvement it chooses. For example, the pricing problems facing the exporter will differ from those facing a foreign subsidiary or joint venture. The promotional options available to a licensor will be more restricted than those open to a firm that is the sole owner of an operation. These important managerial implications will be examined in Part II.

[7] Annual Report for 1968.

THE APPROACH OF THIS BOOK

The sources of the differences between international and domestic marketing are to be found not in the functions themselves but in the parameters that determine how the functions are performed. Therefore, a major task of the student of international marketing is to identify the relevant parameters and to understand how they affect the marketing program. To do this, he must first have a good grasp of the nature of marketing and marketing management. This book assumes that the reader has that grasp from other marketing courses. The text will endeavor to help the student recognize the international environmental parameters pertinent to marketing and the role they play in marketing management. Part I discusses the world environment in which international marketing is practiced, whereas Part II analyzes the management of marketing in this multinational context. Part III deals with planning and coordinating the international marketing program.

Part I: International Environment

We are not always aware of the importance of the environment in the behavior of the firm. However, in domestic business studies, consideration of the environment plays a critical though somewhat unrecognized role. A number of "environmental" courses in the curriculum deal with topics such as business and society, business and government, business conditions, and business law. In the functional courses, too, much attention is paid to the external environment of the firm. In marketing, for example, there will be discussions of buyer behavior, demographic trends, competition, laws regulating pricing or promotion, developments in retailing, and the like. Part I of this text attempts to do for international marketing what these courses and discussions do for domestic business studies.

An illustration from another business function, accounting, might help to highlight further the influence of environment. If we ask the question, What determines the practice of accounting in the United States today? we would answer with a number of factors including the following:

1. The Internal Revenue Service
2. The Securities and Exchange Commission
3. Requirements of state and local governments
4. Requirements of other organizations such as the New York Stock Exchange or the Interstate Commerce Commission
5. The role of business schools in teaching accounting and conducting research
6. The certification examinations, such as for the CPA
7. The role of professional organizations such as the American Accounting Association and the American Institute of Certified Public Accountants
8. The influence of the "Big Eight" accounting firms
9. The complex structure of American business enterprise and the separation of ownership from management
10. The historical influence of English accounting practice

If we then ask the question, What determines the practice of accounting in France or Brazil? we see immediately that there is a nearly complete lack of identity or uniformity of parameters in the different countries. There are important similarities, of course, but the differences are emphasized more strikingly. Asking the same questions about other business functions, such as marketing, can be equally revealing.

Part II: International Marketing Management

Part II of the book deals with the various functions of marketing as they are performed in the international environment. The discussion will focus on the problems peculiar to international marketing and therefore will be less comprehensive than in a regular marketing text. It should, however, help to broaden the student's understanding of marketing in general. The foreign environment dealt with in Part I will then be seen to be the key variable in comprehending the "international" in international marketing.

Part III: Coordination and Integration

A second critical international aspect of marketing management, considered in Part III, is the task of integrating and coordinating many individual national marketing programs into an effective multinational operation.

For purposes of this text, the principal actors in the international marketing drama are the practitioners, that is, the firms and managers who actually market internationally. This does not mean that consumers, governments, advertising agencies, and other participants are not involved. It merely means that our major focus will be on the problems and decisions facing management in international marketing.

A large part of our discussion will center on international marketing by manufacturers. However, most of the analysis and principles apply equally well to the international marketing problems of extractive, service, or other industries. We will discuss thoroughly and illustrate with many examples the large multinational firms' marketing practices and problems. By this we do not mean to exclude the smaller firms, even though they are not always explicitly mentioned. Much of the discussion will apply equally well to small firms as to large ones. Many of the problems peculiar to small firms in international marketing will be covered when the analysis is specifically directed to the export level of involvement, which includes most of the chapters in Part II.

Questions

1.1 What is international marketing?

1.2 Why does international marketing differ from domestic marketing?

1.3 How does the management of marketing in the international firm differ from the management of marketing in the domestic firm?

1.4 What are some of the distinctions between international trade and international marketing?

1.5 Discuss the impact of international business on international trade.

1.6 How would you define the "international firm"? Give examples of firms that fit and do not fit your definition.

1.7   What are some of the pressures encouraging a firm to "think international" in its operations?

1.8   What kinds of firms might be interested in international marketing?

1.9   Why does a study of international marketing include a study of the international environment?

1.10   What does it mean to say that a firm engages in "multinational marketing"? "foreign marketing"?

1.11   The sale of a Volkswagen in America and the gift of grain by the United States to India both enter international trade statistics. What differences are there in the international marketing of these two products?

Further Readings

Books:

Bartels, Robert, ed., *Comparative Marketing: Wholesaling in Fifteen Countries* (Homewood, Ill.: Richard D. Irwin, 1963).

Boddewyn, Jean, *Comparative Management and Marketing* (Glenview, Ill.: Scott, Foresman and Co., 1969).

Carson, David, *International Marketing—A Comparative Systems Approach* (New York: John Wiley and Sons, 1967).

Dowd, Laurence P., *Principles of World Business* (Boston: Allyn and Bacon, 1965), chap. 1.

Fayerweather, John, ed., *International Marketing,* 2nd ed. (Englewood Cliffs, N.J.: Prentice-Hall, 1970), chap. 1.

Hess, John M., and Philip R. Cateora, *International Marketing* (Homewood, Ill.: Richard D. Irwin, 1966), chap. 1.

Kramer, Roland L., *International Marketing,* 3rd ed. (Cincinnati, Ohio: South-Western Publishing Co., 1970), chap. 1.

Mulvihill, Donald F., *Domestic Marketing Systems Abroad: An Annotated Bibliography,* 2nd ed. (Kent, Ohio: The Kent State University Press, 1967).

Sommers, Montrose S., and Jerome B. Kernan, eds., *Comparative Marketing Systems—A Cultural Approach* (New York: Appleton-Century-Crofts, 1968).

2

ECONOMIC ENVIRONMENT:
THE WORLD ECONOMY

Marketing is an economic activity and is therefore affected by the economic environment in which it is conducted. International marketing has a twofold economic environment: (1) the global or world economy, and (2) the individual economies of countries. This chapter will discuss the international economy, and Chapter 3 will consider the relevant dimensions of foreign domestic economies.

It is reasonable to speak of the "world economy" because the nations of the world do relate to each other economically. Nations, of course, also relate to each other politically, diplomatically, militarily, and culturally. Many of these other elements of international relations are intertwined with economic considerations. For example, Marco Polo's travels and the Crusades had significant economic impact. The great voyages of discovery and the building of colonial empires were motivated by economic as well as political aspirations. More recently, economic considerations have played a role in international hostilities as well as in regional cooperative movements, such as the European Economic Community (EEC). International economic concerns are also frequent items on the agenda of the United Nations and its affiliated agencies.

The existence of this international or world economy is critical for the business firm. Because nations do relate to each other economically, international business and marketing operations are made possible. Today, in fact, international marketers are major participants in international economic relations. For that reason, it is necessary to examine the world economy to see how it aids and constrains international marketing. We will begin by considering international trade, a major element in international economic relations.

NATION TRADES WITH NATION

In Chapter 1, we noted the distinctions between international trade and international business and international marketing. Although our primary concern is international marketing rather than international trade, a brief survey of international trade will prove useful. Trading between groups has been going on for thousands of years, at least since the beginning of recorded history. Much early trade was economically motivated, carried on through barter or commercial transactions. However, a large part of the exchange of goods historically occurred through military conquest: "To the victor belong the spoils." Numerous examples can be cited from ancient history as well as modern. The predominant pattern of international trade today, however, is the voluntary exchange of goods and services.

The Legacy of Mercantilism

To understand international trade in today's world, it is useful to begin with the mercantilist era, which ran roughly from 1500 to 1750. The developments in this period laid the foundation for the modern practice of international trade. An important political development was the rise of nation-states and the consequent growth of a national consciousness and a feeling of national unity among the people in many European countries during this time. Groups formed relationships on a national basis as they do today. This marked a significant change from earlier relationship patterns which were on a tribal, religious, imperial, or feudal basis. The mercantilists, placing the economic interests of the nation foremost, created large internal markets, replacing the previous fragmentation. A key socioeconomic development was the rise of the commercial or capitalist class. Previously, the nobility, the clergy, and the military were the only powerful classes. Now the industrialist and trader assumed a large, and increasingly respected, role.

The importance of the Renaissance to the rise of mercantilism should not be overlooked. This period was not only one of intellectual awakening but also one of many technical discoveries and inventions, some of which aided the geographical discoveries so important to mercantilism. These geographical discoveries made residents of different continents aware that they were part of a global neighborhood; equally significant from our viewpoint was their effect on trade. First, the voyages led to the development of global trading networks and even trading companies, such as the Dutch East India Company. Second, the voyages effectively demonstrated to people what kinds of goods were available in different parts of the world and increased their desire for trade.

Nationalism

It is useful to look beyond these developments of the mercantilist period to the patterns of economic thought and action that accompanied them; much of today's thinking and action on international trade matters is strikingly similar to that of the mercantilists. Along with the rise of nation-states came the philosophy or ideology of nationalism. A positive element of nationalism was that it created a larger unity and loyalty to replace the fragmented rivalries of tribe and region. There were some less desirable elements of nationalist thought and practice, however.

To political leaders, nationalism implied that trade was for the national interest and thus should be conducted by the nation rather than by private companies—or, at the very least, there should be strong national control over it. The pervasive idea that what one nation gained from trade was to some extent at the expense of others resulted from a static view of the world's resources and productive capacity. It is perhaps one of the reasons for the extent and acceptance of piracy. For example, Sir Francis Drake was honored by Queen Elizabeth I for contributing to English wealth by pirating Spanish ships. Also inherent in much nationalist thought is the idea that one's own nation stands against others in a continuing rivalry. This is reflected in such a national anthem as Germany's *"Deutschland, Deutschland über Alles,"* of World War II fame. Although internationalism is increasing today, nationalism remains a potent determinant of international economic relations. We are not far removed from the mercantilists on this score.

Bullionism

Another mercantilist idea was that wealth consisted, above all else, in gold and silver. This bullionist idea was expressed by one Frenchman who said, "We live not so much from trade in raw materials as from gold and silver." An Englishman stated that it is "better to have plenty of gold and silver in the realm than plenty of merchants and merchandizes."[1] Although few would echo these sentiments today, they do provide a background for understanding the mystique of gold and its role in the modern international financial order.

"Favorable Balance of Trade"

Following logically the premise that gold or bullion represented wealth and the "sinews of war" was another mercantilist doctrine which has left a legacy for the modern world. This is the idea that a nation gains from foreign trade only if it has an excess in the value of exports over imports. The mercantilists called this excess a "favorable balance of trade" because it had to be paid for with gold and silver, thus adding to the wealth of the nation. Though the expression "a favorable balance of trade" has lost its bullionist significance today, it is still widely used to describe a country's trading situation. If imports are greater than exports, of course, the trade balance is "unfavorable."

If one does not accept the idea that gold and silver are the principal elements of a nation's wealth, it is rather hard to agree with the idea that it is economically good for a country to export more than it imports. A nation's giving away in exports more than it gets in imports may exemplify commendable altruism, but it does not increase the nation's wealth. The communist-bloc countries sensibly realize that their wealth consists of the goods they obtain, so their policy is to maximize imports but minimize exports. This was also Nazi Germany's policy in the 1930s.

The market economies of the West emphasize sales (exports) more than

---

[1] August Hecksher, *Mercantilism* (London: Allen & Unwin, 1936), vol. II, pp. 25, 26.

purchases (imports), thus transferring to the national level a concept that is more appropriate at the individual-firm level. For the firm it is generally true that it is profitable for sales to be greater than expenditures. A nation looking to its selfish interest would be better off to consume more than it is able to produce, that is, live beyond its means by importing more than it exports. Only if the creditor nations sending the excess imports wish to begin collecting for them might the receiving nation wish to develop a "favorable" balance of trade. This would not be done for its own sake, or for the purpose of accumulating gold, but merely to pay the nation's bills and maintain its international credit standing.

The Decline of Mercantilism

It is useful to note the mercantilist origin of some of today's thinking on international trade matters. However, it is important to remember that these ideas and practices have been modified by various intellectual and practical developments since 1750. Nationalism is still much in evidence, but some of its international trade aspects have changed. The idea that one nation's trade gains are at the expense of other nations is less strongly held. The more developed countries no longer adhere to the idea that strict national control and conduct of trade is essential; in this matter of control of foreign trade, however, the communist-bloc countries and the less developed nations are still quite close to mercantilist practice.

Nationlist trade practices have been modified in recent years by the development and activities of many international organizations. The United Nations has had a moderating effect on nationalist actions, although its recommendations are not always successful. Both the General Agreement on Tariffs and Trade (GATT) and the International Monetary Fund (IMF) have contributed greatly to limiting arbitrary national actions in international trade and finance. The rise of regional groupings in all parts of the world is also gradually encouraging multilateral action and cooperation in place of frequently hostile or "beggar my neighbor" unilateral action.

Bullionist thinking, or the emphasis on gold as the major form of wealth, received a major blow from the development of the quantity theory of money and the price-specie flow theory. The quantity theory showed that the amount of money (gold in this case) was not in itself an indicator of wealth but a determinant of the level of prices. Thus a country with a favorable balance of trade would receive gold, and its internal price level would rise. But as its prices rose, its exports would become more expensive and decline in volume. Its imports would increase as they became relatively cheaper. This would lead eventually to an unfavorable balance of trade and an outflow of gold (specie) to pay for the deficit.

Today additional factors contribute to the declining importance of gold, namely the failure of the gold supply to keep up with the demands of trading nations and the acceptance of other means of international payment, especially the dollar. The decline in the role of gold led in turn to less stress on a favorable balance of trade (which, we will recall, was supposed to bring gold into the country). Nevertheless, it is noteworthy that gold is still a key element of the international financial system. Many favor increasing its role rather than replacing or supplementing it with other kinds of money.

A major intellectual blow to mercantilist thought was Adam Smith's *Wealth of Nations*. Following up and extending some of the philosophical developments of the eighteenth century, Smith formulated cogent arguments against some principal tenets of mercantilism. His idea was that the selfish actions of individuals lead to the welfare of all through "the invisible hand" of market forces. This meant that laissez faire was better for the nation than government control of trade. Nor was his argument limited to internal trade. He strongly advocated free trade between nations. Smith's philosophy was in accord with the thinking of the rising commercial and industrial classes, so his free-trade philosophy gradually became the practice of the time, replacing a more rigid mercantilism.

A Picture of World Trade

Global Volume

The volume of world trade (world exports) in 1970 was about $300 billion, a figure larger than the gross national product (GNP) of every nation in the world except the United States and the Soviet Union, and about three times the GNP of all of South America. This is one indication of international trade's importance as part of world economic activity and the international division of labor. Not only does international trade loom large in the world economy, but also it is one of the fastest growing areas of economic activity. Since World War II, the volume of world trade has risen faster than most other indicators of economic activity, such as the index of industrial production; in fact, it has doubled each decade.

This growth trend suggests that internationalism is increasing as a way of economic life and that both nations and firms must consider its significance for their own well-being. Nations moving in the direction of trade expansion can enjoy the benefits of membership in the world economy and raise their real standard of living. Nations moving in the direction of trade restriction, such as China or Burma, might enhance their political separation and isolation, but usually at the expense of economic progress. Firms, like nations, become increasingly aware that they are in the world marketplace, in considering opportunities for growth as well as in facing new competition. The isolationist position today is difficult to maintain for firms as well as for nations.

The Nations' Foreign Trade

Another way of looking at the significance of international trade is to relate it to individual nations. In 1968, United States' exports of goods and services were over $50 billion. This was only about 6 percent of GNP, but a percentage figure cannot measure its importance to the economy. For one thing, exports in particular product lines represent much higher percentages of output, up to 50 percent in some cases. American exports of non-electric machinery were $6.5 billion in 1968, and of grains, $2.5 billion. Conversely, imports account for a large part of our supplies in many products; for example, 100 percent for coffee, crude rubber, diamonds, and bananas.

Imports of base metals and road motor vehicles were almost $4 billion respectively in 1968. Thus some industries are much more dependent on international trade than others.

Some nations are also more dependent on international trade than others. Although the United States is the world's leading importer and exporter, such trade is only a modest percent of its GNP. Belgium and the Netherlands, on the other hand, export well over one-third of their production, and Germany about 20 percent. Put another way, the four Scandinavian countries import goods each year to the value of $600 per capita. The corresponding figure for the United States is about $135. For the communist economies, the percentages are low because these countries desire self-sufficiency and independence from the outside world. In general, the percentages for less developed countries are likely to drop because many lack the wherewithal to trade. Though their needs are great, they have little to sell. This is less true of the oil-producing countries, of course.

The export involvement of the nation influences that of the firm. It is not surprising, therefore, that firms from heavy exporting countries tend to be more internationally oriented than those from other countries. For example, the average American manufacturer is less apt to be an exporter than is the average Belgian or Dutch firm.

Composition of World Trade

A look at the composition of world trade shows the market share obtained by different kinds of goods and services. Considering only the trade in products and commodities, as in Table 2–1, the striking development in the past few decades is the growing share held by manufactured goods exports, coupled with a relative decline in the share obtained by primary products. As recently as 1953, primary products made up over half of world trade. By 1968, however, manufactures constituted over 60 percent of such trade. The less developed countries are the principal exporters of primary products (food and raw materials) and their dissatisfaction with their declining market share is increased by the relatively adverse price trend for these products. From a base year 1960, primary products prices have just held their own, while prices on manufactures have risen steadily.

The table shows that for the less developed countries, it is a case of exporting more and enjoying it less. Their share of international trade roughly parallels the drop in the proportion of primary materials—from over 50 percent in 1953 to about 35 percent in 1968. There are several reasons for these changing market shares. One is the development of synthetics and other substitutes for primary products. Another is growing agricultural self-sufficiency in the industrialized countries. A third reason is the growth of manufacturing as compared to primary production in total world output. The implication for countries with falling market shares is to change their product line, that is, industrialize. This does not mean dropping existing primary exports but rather adding manufactures to them. Most less developed countries, of course, are trying to do just this. Diversification is thus a goal of nations as well as of business enterprises.

Table 2–1   World Export Shares by Products, 1960–1968

	1960	1961	1962	1963	1964	1965	1966	1967	1968
World exports									
Value (billion dollars f.o.b.)									
Total	127.9	133.9	141.4	153.9	172.2	186.4	203.4	214.3	238.2
Primary products	56.2	58.0	59.7	65.0	71.0	73.7	77.6	79.6	83.8
Manufactures	69.3	73.1	78.9	85.9	98.1	109.3	122.0	130.8	150.6
Unit value (1960 = 100)									
Total	100	99	99	100	102	103	106	105	104
Primary products	100	98	97	100	102	102	102	101	100
Manufactures	100	101	101	101	102	105	108	109	108
Volume (1960 = 100)									
Total	100	106	112	120	132	142	150	160	180
Primary products	100	105	109	116	124	129	135	140	150
Manufactures	100	105	112	123	139	150	163	173	200
World commodity output									
Volume (1960 = 100)									
All commodities	100	104	110	116	124	130	139	144	154
Agriculture	100	102	105	108	110	111	115	120	123
Industry	100	105	112	119	129	137	148	154	165

Note: The unit value indices do not include the Eastern trading area; the export volume indices are estimates.

Source: GATT, *International Trade 1968*, p. 1.

For international business concerns, a study of the composition of world trade shows what is being traded as well as who is buying and selling at the national level. Trend analysis will show which products are growing and which are fading, thus indicating some of the opportunities available to the firm. The interest of less developed countries in changing their international trade position through industrialization may also create investment opportunities for the firm in manufacturing or processing. Ventures such as these could help the less developed countries increase their manufactured exports by adding new items to their export line, or by further refining or processing the primary commodities already exported. If the cost situation does not allow exports to be competitive, the country may still encourage and protect certain manufacturing operations that replace imports in order to save their scarce foreign exchange.

Patterns of World Trade

Examining the patterns of international trade yields further practical information. Table 2–2 highlights the fact that the industrialized nations trade mostly with each other, accounting for almost half of total world trade in this way.

Table 2–2 Trade within and between Industrial and Developing Areas and the Eastern Trading Area, 1960–1968 (Billion dollars f.o.b. and percentages of world exports)

DESTINATION ORIGIN	YEAR	INDUSTRIAL AREAS		DEVELOPING AREAS		EASTERN TRADING AREA		TOTAL WORLD*	
		VALUE	%	VALUE	%	VALUE	%	VALUE	%
INDUSTRIAL AREAS	1960	54.14	42.3	21.00	16.4	2.83	2.2	81.50	63.7
	1961	58.44	43.7	21.53	16.1	2.99	2.2	86.03	64.3
	1962	62.98	44.5	21.10	14.9	3.21	2.3	90.57	64.0
	1963	69.36	45.1	22.10	14.4	3.42	2.2	98.64	64.1
	1964	78.65	45.7	24.23	14.0	4.29	2.5	111.81	64.9
	1965	87.18	46.8	25.68	13.8	4.70	2.5	122.78	65.9
	1966	96.94	47.7	28.23	13.9	5.59	2.7	135.64	66.7
	1967	103.10	48.1	28.60	13.4	6.00	2.8	143.07	66.8
	1968	117.39	49.3	32.04	13.4	6.33	2.7	161.29	67.7
DEVELOPING AREAS	1960	19.25	15.0	6.26	4.9	1.23	1.0	27.48	21.5
	1961	19.27	14.4	6.36	4.8	1.49	1.1	27.82	20.8
	1962	20.26	14.3	6.55	4.6	1.58	1.1	29.10	20.6
	1963	22.23	14.4	6.88	4.5	1.69	1.1	31.60	20.5
	1964	24.40	14.2	7.44	4.3	1.97	1.1	34.67	20.1
	1965	25.49	13.7	7.72	4.1	2.42	1.3	36.51	19.6
	1966	27.44	13.5	8.04	3.9	2.36	1.2	38.70	19.0
	1967	28.80	13.4	8.26	3.9	2.17	1.0	40.16	18.7
	1968	31.45	13.2	8.75	3.7	2.24	0.9	43.43	18.2
EASTERN TRADING AREA	1960	2.80	2.2	1.27	1.0	10.91	8.5	15.02	11.7
	1961	2.99	2.2	1.89	1.4	10.84	8.1	15.74	11.7
	1962	3.20	2.3	2.14	1.5	12.02	8.5	17.39	12.3
	1963	3.55	2.3	2.51	1.7	12.60	8.2	18.70	12.2
	1964	4.11	2.4	2.70	1.6	13.42	7.8	20.27	11.8
	1965	4.71	2.5	2.98	1.6	13.99	7.5	21.73	11.6
	1966	5.67	2.8	3.31	1.6	14.18	7.0	23.20	11.4
	1967	6.00	2.8	3.44	1.6	15.40	7.2	24.89	11.6
	1968	6.32	2.7	3.56	1.5	17.10	7.2	27.03	11.4
TOTAL WORLD*	1960	79.13	61.8	29.16	22.8	15.11	11.8	127.93	100.0
	1961	83.90	62.7	30.41	22.7	15.57	11.6	133.88	100.0
	1962	89.79	63.5	30.44	21.5	16.98	12.0	141.42	100.0
	1963	98.84	64.2	32.17	21.0	18.03	11.7	153.90	100.0
	1964	111.23	64.6	35.13	20.4	20.03	11.6	172.20	100.0
	1965	121.35	65.1	37.21	19.9	21.42	11.5	186.42	100.0
	1966	134.40	66.1	40.58	19.9	22.32	11.0	203.37	100.0
	1967	142.28	66.4	41.51	19.4	23.86	11.1	214.29	100.0
	1968	159.93	67.2	45.48	19.1	25.87	10.9	238.15	100.0

* Including Australia, New Zealand and South Africa.

Source: GATT, *International Trade 1968*, p. 2.

The developing nations too trade primarily with industrialized countries, rather than among themselves ($31 billion to $8.75 billion in 1968). As might be expected from the changing composition of trade, the role of industrialized nations is becoming more important and accounted for two-thirds of total world trade in 1968. The share of the developing areas dropped from 27 percent in 1953 to 18.2 percent in 1968, even though population has grown faster in these nations than in others. These comparisons help to illustrate what is called the growing gap between developed and developing areas. Also evident from the table is the relatively small world-trade role of the Eastern trading area (the communist countries).

The overall picture of world-trade patterns we have given provides necessary background for understanding world trade. However, it is often more important to the firm to identify the trading patterns of *particular* nations or areas it is concerned with in its business dealings. Table 2–3 shows the major trading partners of the United States. To complement this information, a firm might use a *product* breakdown by country to provide a more complete profile of a nation's trade.

Table 2–3   Leading Trading Partners of United States

	MAJOR SUPPLIERS	($ MILLIONS)		MAJOR CUSTOMERS	($ MILLIONS)
1.	Canada	11,093	1.	Canada	9,084
2.	Japan	5,875	2.	Japan	4,652
3.	West Germany	3,129	3.	West Germany	2,740
4.	United Kingdom	2,196	4.	United Kingdom	2,537
5.	Italy	1,316	5.	Mexico	1,703
6.	Mexico	1,222	6.	France	1,484
7.	Venezuela	1,082	7.	Italy	1,352
8.	France	942	8.	Netherlands	1,068
9.	Hong Kong	815	9.	Australia	1,003
10.	Belgium	682	10.	Brazil	841

Source: *Survey of Current Business,* March, 1971.

Similar tables can be prepared for most countries, and should be for the countries where the firm is considering operations. In these facts of international trade are some clues as to the "why" of a particular country's trade patterns. The general statement that most trade is with industrial countries is borne out by the United States' figures, of course, but the importance of other factors becomes evident as well. For example, the role of Canada and Mexico as United States' trading partners cannot be explained very well in terms of their size or degree of industrialization. Geographic proximity is an important consideration in this case. Countries that are neighbors are going to be better trading partners, other things being equal, than those distant from each other. The lower transport costs are accompanied by greater familiarity and ease of communication and control.

The political influences on trade can also be revealed in such a table. For example, although Cuba is also a close neighbor of the United States and not a terribly small country (population 8 million), there is practically no trade between Cuba and the United States. The East–West trade split among European neighbors shows similar patterns. (The overall question of East–West trade will be discussed below.) The point we make here is that an analysis of trade patterns both on an aggregate and on a national basis can be useful to the firm in planning its global marketing and logistics systems. Examination of the causes of trade patterns will suggest possible approaches either to adapting to the patterns, or to modifying them where feasible.

International Trade Theory

In domestic marketing, much emphasis is laid on the analysis of buyer behavior and motivation. For the international trader and marketer, some understanding of the "why" of international trade can be equally useful. A knowledge of the basic causes and nature of international trade can help the international marketer to see how his firm fits into the picture. It is easier and more profitable for the firm to work with the underlying economic forces than against them. But to work with them, the firm must understand them.

Essentially, international trade theory seeks the answers to a few basic questions: Why do nations trade? What goods do they trade? How are the gains from trade divided? Nations trade for economic, political, and cultural reasons, but the principal economic basis for internation trade is differences in price; that is, a nation can buy some goods more cheaply from other nations than it can make them itself. In a sense, the nation faces the same "make-or-buy" decision as does the firm. Just as most firms do not go for complete vertical integration but buy many materials and supplies from outside firms, so most nations decide against complete self-sufficiency (or autarky) in favor of buying cheaper goods from other countries.

Adam Smith has a famous example that helps to illustrate this. In discussing the advantages to England in trading manufactured goods for Portugal's wine, he notes that grapes could be grown "under glass" (in green houses) in England but that to do so would lead to England's having both less wine and fewer manufactures than if it specialized in manufactures. In fact, Smith's major conclusion was that the wealth of nations derived from the division of labor and specialization. Applied to the international picture, this means trade rather than autarky.

Comparative Costs—Comparative Advantage

It has been said that price differences are the immediate basis of international trade. The firm that decides whether to make or buy or chooses one supplier over another also considers price as a principal variable. The next question in trade theory is, Why do nations have different prices on goods? The answer is that prices differ because countries producing these goods have different comparative cost structures. Why do countries have different comparative costs? The Swedish economist Bertil Ohlin came up with an explanation that is generally held to be essentially valid. Ohlin said that different countries have dissimilar prices and costs on goods because different goods require a different mix of factors in their production, and because countries differ in their supply of these factors. Thus, in reference to Smith's example, Portugal's wine would be cheaper than wine made in England because Portugal has a relatively better endowment of wine-making factors (for example, land and climate) than does England.

What we have been discussing is the principle of comparative advantage. This principle says that a country will tend to produce and export those goods in which it has the greatest comparative advantage (or the least comparative disadvantage) and import those goods in which it has the least comparative advantage (or the greatest comparative disadvantage). The theory thus makes it possible to predict what goods a nation will trade, both its exports and imports. As Smith suggested, the nation maximizes its supply of goods by concentrating production in those areas where it is most efficient and trading some of these products for imported products where it is least efficient. An examination of the exports and imports of most trading nations tends to support the theory. Table 2–4 shows the leading exports and imports of the United States in 1970 as a case in point.

Table 2–4   Some Leading Commodities in U.S. Foreign Trade—1970 (in billions of dollars)

EXPORTS		IMPORTS	
1. Nonelectric machinery	$8.3	1. Motor vehicles and parts	$5.1
2. Chemicals	3.8	2. Metals and ores	4.8
3. Motor vehicles and parts	3.5	3. Nonelectric machinery	3.0
4. Electric apparatus	3.0	4. Petroleum and products	2.8
5. Coal, ores, base metals	2.9	5. Textiles and clothing	2.3
6. Grains, cereals	2.6	6. Electric apparatus	2.3
7. Aircraft	2.0	7. Chemicals	1.5
8. Soybeans	1.2	8. Coffee	1.2

Source: *Survey of Current Business,* 1971.

EXPORTS   The table shows how international trade theory helps to explain the composition of the United States' trade. The United States has a high ratio of arable land to population. This factor endowment combined with modern mechanized agricultural practices gives the United States a comparative advantage in temperate zone agricultural products, for example, grains and soybeans. The country's broad natural resource base is also reflected in exports of coal and metals. Because America is a capital-rich country and engages heavily in research and development, it is a leading exporter of all kinds of things that entail these factors, for example, machinery and equipment, chemicals and aircraft. The export item "motor vehicles" is misleading, because most of these go only to Canada and are part of the North American logistics network of the "Big Three" auto companies.

IMPORTS   On the import side, we see the items in which the United States is relatively inefficient and/or has a comparative disadvantage. Imports of such items as metals, petroleum, and coffee reflect areas where the United States' resource endowment is either inadequate or nonexistent (for example, coffee). The metals imported generally would be different from those exported. Textiles and clothing represent one of the simplest kinds of manufactured goods and, therefore, countries having low-cost labor tend to have a comparative advantage in their production.

Road motor vehicles again are a special case. Part of these are imported from the Canadian plants of American manufacturers. The other large component is, of course, Volkswagen. It is uncertain how much of this figure represents a comparative advantage of German and other suppliers, and how much this has been a market segment the major American producers chose to ignore. The American auto producers preferred to make larger cars with bigger profit margins. Only when imported cars attained a certain market share did the American manufacturers react strongly. In the early 1960s, American firms fought imports by introducing the "compact" cars. In 1969, they began to fight foreign competition with small cars, such as the Ford Maverick and the even smaller Pinto and Vega.

The Product Life Cycle and International Trade

A recent refinement in trade theory is related to the product life cycle concept. The product life cycle in marketing refers to the consumption pattern for a product. When applied to international trade theory, it refers primarily to international trade and production patterns. The model suggests that many products go through a trade cycle wherein the United States is initially an exporter, then loses its export markets, and finally may become an importer of the product. Empirical studies in several product areas have demonstrated the validity of the model.[2]

The production and trade cycle is as follows:

Phase 1. United States' export strength
Phase 2. Foreign production starts
Phase 3. Foreign production becomes competitive in export markets
Phase 4. Import competition begins

In phase 1, according to the theory, product-development activities and invention are likely to be related to the needs of the home market (the United States example has been studied most). The new product probably will be produced in the home market because it will have a comparative advantage, *not* because of the traditional reason, superior factor endowment, but because of the production learning curve on the new product, the need for communication with suppliers and customers, and lack of consumer concern with price on new products.

[2] Louis T. Wells, Jr., "A Product Life Cycle for International Trade?" *Journal of Marketing* (July 1968), pp. 1–6.

In phase 2, incomes and product familiarity in other countries increase. As foreign markets expand, manufacturers in wealthy countries begin producing for their own markets. The declining American exports of home dishwashers are an example of a product in phase 2.

In phase 3, foreign producers gain production experience. Because their labor costs are lower, their products become competitive with American exports in third countries. An example is the European export of ranges and refrigerators to Latin America.

In phase 4, the foreign producer has cost savings and economies of scale sufficient to allow him to export to the country where the product originated.

In phase 1 the product is "new." In phase 2 it is "maturing." In phases 3 and 4 it is "standardized." The product may become so standardized by phase 4 that it almost becomes a commodity. Textiles in general are an example of a product in phase 4, whereas large computers probably are still in phase 1. Products in phase 4 may be produced in less developed countries for export to the developed countries. This modification of the theory of comparative advantage gives further insight into patterns of international trade and production. It is helpful to the international company in planning logistics.

The Balance of Payments

In the study of international trade, the principal source of information is the balance of payments statements of the trading nations. The balance of payments is a summary statement of all the economic transactions between one country and all other countries over a period of time, usually one year. A nation's international trade is usually made up of millions of individual transactions. These transactions can be summarized and reported in a variety of ways, depending on the use to be made of the data. Usually they are organized to meet the needs of government decision makers. Table 2–5 is a very brief summary account of the United States' balance of payments for 1969.

In governmental reporting, the balance of payments is often broken down into a current account and one or more capital accounts, as in Table 2–5. The current account is a record of all the *goods and services* the nation exchanged with other nations. The capital account includes all kinds of international *financial transactions*, such as private foreign investment and government borrowing, lending, or payments. The international marketer usually is more interested in the details of current account transactions, that is, the nature of the goods being traded and their origin and destination. These details are often available for individual nations. The *Walker World Trade Annual*, in five volumes, contains an international summary based on United Nations data.

The balance of payments is an indicator of the international economic health of a country. Its data help government policy makers plan monetary, fiscal, foreign-exchange, and commercial policies. For example, in the late 1960s, the United States was either dealing with or considering such measures as an income tax surcharge, raising the rediscount rate to member banks in the Federal Reserve System, imposing an import surcharge, and restricting private money and capital flows abroad. All of these considerations were dictated primarily by the deficit in the United States' balance of payments.

The International Marketer and the Balance of Payments

Understanding balance of payment analysis can be useful to the international businessman also in his decision making. In the late 1960s, corporations engaged in international business had a special reason for interest. They had to maintain their own individual company balance of payments record to report to the U.S. Department of Commerce. This meant recording all money flows between the corporation and foreign countries. The principal outflows were direct investment overseas and payments for imports from foreign subsidiaries. The principal inflows were company export receipts, dividends, and royalties from abroad. The government wanted corporations to maximize the inflows of money from abroad to help in reducing or eliminating the nation's balance of payments deficit. (The continued United States balance of payments deficit meant that for many years the country had supplied more dollars to foreigners than they had spent in the United States for all their purchases of American goods and services. They were accumulating dollar claims against the United States.)

Table 2–5 U.S. Balance of Payments—1969 (in billions of dollars)

TRANSACTIONS	BALANCE OF PAYMENTS ACCOUNTS		
	RECEIPTS	PAYMENTS	BALANCE
Goods and services	55.4	53.3	+2.1
1. Mdse. trade (goods)	36.5	35.8	+ .7
2. Services	18.9	17.5	+1.4
Private capital	3.7	5.0	−1.3
1. Long term	3.7	4.4	− .7
2. Short term	0	.6	− .6
Government	1.5	5.5	−4.0
1. Loans	1.5	3.4	−1.9
2. Grants and transfers		2.1	−2.1
Other			
1. Private transfers		.8	− .8
2. Errors and omissions		3.0	−3.0
3. Changes in U.S. reserve assets	.8	2.0	−1.2
4. Changes in U.S. liquid liabilities	8.9	.7	+8.2
Total	70.3	70.3	.0

Source: Federal Reserve Bank of St. Louis.

Marketing Decisions

Balance of payments data, besides fulfilling a government requirement, have specific marketing applications. They can provide information for many decisions the firm faces in marketing internationally. In the discussion of international trade theory, we presented tables on trade which are useful in making international investment and marketing decisions. These tables are drawn from balance of payments data. Two important international marketing decisions are the choice of location of supply for foreign markets and the selection of markets to sell to. Balance of payments analysis can show which nations are importers and exporters of the products in question. The firm can thus identify its own best import and export targets, that is, countries to sell to and countries to sell from.

When the firm is considering foreign market opportunities, it will find a country's import statistics for its kind of products to be a preliminary indicator of market potential. By ranking a number of countries according to these statistics, the firm can get an ordering of market opportunities to help in its strategic planning. Furthermore, the firm can get an indication of the kind of competition it will encounter in these countries by noting the major supplying nations for the products in question. The statistics sometimes even permit identification of low-price supplying nations and high-price (high-quality?) suppliers. In all use of balance of payments data it is necessary to consider a period of several years to get an idea of trends.

Another marketing decision that can be aided by balance of payments analysis is selection of the firm's international product line. Although market characteristics within each national market will be important in choosing a product line, the international aspects or dimensions of the firm's product line will be determined in part by the balance of payments situation of all the relevant markets. In other words, products that are produced and consumed *within* one market can be selected primarily within a national context. When *international* logistics are involved and the firm supplies products to or from other foreign markets, balance of payments analysis is useful in deciding which products are most mobile.

An overall review of a country's balance of payments can also help the firm to decide on the nature of an appropriate operation there. For example: Should the firm export from the United States or produce locally? Should the local operation be a sales office, an assembly or processing plant, or a complete production facility? Should local production be for export, or should it substitute for imports? These are the kinds of questions a detailed analysis of a country's balance of payments can help to answer by identifying the country's international economic strengths and weaknesses.

Financial Considerations

Up to now, we have considered primarily the current account in the balance of payments, and especially the movement of goods as it provides information for the international marketer. A look at the capital account is also useful. A nation's international solvency can be evaluated by checking its capital account over several years. If the nation is steadily losing its gold and foreign exchange reserves, there is a strong likelihood of a currency devaluation or some kind of exchange control. Exchange control means that the government restricts the amount of money sent out of the country as well as the uses to which it can be put. With exchange control, the firm may have difficulty getting a foreign exchange allocation to repatriate profits or even to import its products. If the firm is importing products that are considered luxuries or not necessary to the nation's development, the scarce foreign exchange will go instead to capital goods and others on which the nation places a higher priority.

The firm's pricing policies too will be affected by balance of payments problems of the host country. If the firm cannot repatriate profits from a country, it will try to use its transfer-pricing to minimize the profits earned in that country, meanwhile increasing profits elsewhere where it can repatriate them. If the exporting firm fears devaluation of a currency, it will hesitate to quote prices in that currency, preferring to give terms in its home currency or another "safe" currency. Thus it can be seen that the balance of payments is an important information source for the international marketer. He should develop some skill in its analysis.

Commercial Policy

One of the reasons international trade is different from domestic trade is that it is carried on between different political units, each exercising sovereign control over its own trade. Although all nations control their foreign trade, they vary in the degree and particular implementation of such control. Each nation invariably establishes trade laws that favor its nationals and discriminate against traders from other countries. This means, for example, that an American firm trying to sell in the French market will face certain handicaps deriving from the French government's control over its trade. These handicaps to the American firm are in addition to any disadvantages resulting from distance or cultural differences. By the same token, the French firm trying to sell in the United States will face similar restrictions when competing with American firms selling in their home market.

Tariffs

Commercial policy is the term used to refer to government measures and regulations bearing on its foreign trade. The principal tools of commercial policy are tariffs, quantitative restrictions, exchange control, and administrative regulation, or the "invisible tariff." Each of these will be discussed in turn as it relates to the task of the international marketer. Tariffs are essentially a special tax on products imported from other countries. The tax may be levied on the quantity—such as 10 cents per pound, gallon, or yard—or on the value of the imported goods—such as 10 percent or 20 percent ad valorem. The former tax is called a specific duty and is used especially for primary or staple commodities. Ad valorem duties are used generally on manufactured products.

Governments may have two purposes in placing special taxes on goods coming from other countries. They may wish to earn revenue and/or make foreign goods more expensive in order to protect national producers. When the United States was a new nation, most of the government revenues came from tariffs. Many less developed countries today earn a large amount of their revenue from tariffs because it is one of the easiest taxes for them to collect. Today, however, the protective purpose generally outweighs revenue as a rationale for tariffs. One could argue that with a tariff a country penalizes its consumers by making them pay higher prices. This would be true for its producers too in the case of raw materials or components imported. The counterargument is that the nation is interested not only in its consumption but also in its gross national product and a high level of national employment. If the nation is too liberal with imports, it may hurt the output and employment in its own industries.

What are the implications of tariffs for the international marketer? There are several, and they affect the firm's pricing, product, and distribution policies as well as its foreign investment decisions. If the firm is supplying a market by exports, the tariff increases the price of its product and reduces the firm's competitiveness in that foreign market. This necessitates the design of a price structure that will tend to reduce or minimize the tariff barrier. A greater emphasis on marginal cost pricing as opposed to full cost pricing could result. This examination of price will be accompanied by a review of other aspects of the firm's approach to the foreign market. The product may be modified or stripped down to lower the price or perhaps to get a more favorable tariff classification. For example, watches going into a country could be taxed as timepieces at one rate, or as jewelry at a higher rate. The manufacturer might be able to adapt his product to meet requirements for the lower tariff.

Another way the manufacturer can minimize the tariff burden is to ship products ckd (completely knocked down) for assembly in the local market. The tariff on unassembled products or key ingredients is usually lower than that on completely finished goods. The country employs a differential tariff to reduce its foreign exchange outlay and to promote local employment and value added. This establishment of local assembly or compounding operations is a mild form of the phenomenon known as a "tariff factory." The term is used when the primary reason for the local plant is to get behind the tariff wall to protect markets that the firm can no longer serve by exports. In its strongest form, this would mean complete local production rather than just assembly.

In some circumstances, the firm may seek to turn the tariff to its own advantage. Assume that the host country is exerting strong pressure for local manufacture that will be noncompetitive with existing sources. The firm might acquiesce on the condition that the plant it sets up be protected, at least initially, by tariffs imposed against more efficient outside suppliers. It would seek this protection as an "infant industry" against mature companies abroad. Thus, if the firm becomes a local company by establishing a subsidiary there, it may benefit from the tariff protection but still dislike the tariffs it pays on imported supplies or parts.

Quotas

Quantitative restrictions or quotas are a barrier to imports by setting absolute limits on the amount of goods in particular product categories that may enter the country. An import quota can be a more serious restriction than a tariff because the firm has less flexibility in responding to it. Price or product modifications will not get around quotas the way they might get around tariffs. The government's goal in establishing quotas on certain classes of imports is obviously not revenue. It will get none, unless it sells import licenses to those favored to import up to the quota limit. Its goal is rather the conservation of scarce foreign exchange and/or the protection of local production and employment in the product lines affected. About the only response the firm can make to a quota is to assure itself a share of the quota or to set up local production, if the market size warrants it. Since the latter is in accord with the wishes of government, the firm might be regarded favorably for taking such action.

Exchange Control

Exchange control is the most complete tool for regulation of foreign trade, except for comprehensive state-trading as is practiced in the communist economies. Exchange control is a government monopoly of all dealings in foreign exchange. A national company earning foreign exchange from its exports must sell this foreign exchange to the control agency, usually the central bank. A company wishing to buy goods from abroad must buy its foreign exchange from the control agency rather than in the free market. Exchange control always means that foreign exchange is in scarce supply, and therefore the government is rationing it out according to its own priorities rather than letting higher prices ration it.

Firms producing within the country have to be on the government's favored list to get exchange for imported supplies; or, alternatively, they may try to develop local suppliers, running the risk of higher costs and indifferent quality control. The firms exporting to that nation must also be on the government's favored list. Otherwise they will lose their market if importers can get no foreign exchange to pay them. Generally, exchange control countries favor the import of capital goods and necessary consumer goods but avoid luxuries. The definition of "luxuries" will vary from country to country, but it usually includes cars, appliances, and cosmetics. If the exporter does lose his market through exchange control, about the only option he has is to produce within the country, if the market is large enough to be interesting.

Another important implication for the firm when foreign exchange is limited is that the government is unlikely to give high priority to a company's profit remittances as a way of using the country's scarce foreign earnings. In this situation, the firm will try to use the transfer-pricing mechanism to get some earnings out or to avoid accumulating earnings there. It accomplishes this by charging high transfer prices on supplies sold to the subsidiary and low transfer prices on goods sold by that subsidiary to other affiliates of the company in noncontrolled markets. The firm's ability to do this depends on the plan's acceptance by the tax and customs officials of the country with exchange control. They will not look kindly on attempts to make the subsidiary in their country a nonprofit operation.

The Invisible Tariff

There are other governmental barriers to international trade that are hard to classify. They have various names, for example, administrative protection, the invisible tariff, or nontariff barriers (NTBs). As traditional trade barriers have declined since World War II, the NTBs have taken on added significance. They include such things as customs documentation requirements, marks of origin, food and drug laws, labeling laws, "buy national" policies, and so on. Because these barriers are so diverse, their international marketing impact cannot be covered in a brief discussion. Their implications will be discussed in detail in the relevant chapters of Part II. For the present, it is sufficient to note that they can affect many elements of marketing strategy, including location of production, product and package design, and pricing.

OTHER DIMENSIONS AND INSTITUTIONS IN THE WORLD ECONOMY

GATT

Since each nation is sovereign in determining its own commercial policy, the danger is that unilateral and arbitrary national actions will minimize international trade and specialization. This was the situation in the 1930s when international trade was at a low ebb and each nation tried to maintain domestic employment while restricting imports which might help foreign rather than domestic employment. The bankruptcy of these unilateral "beggar my neighbor" policies was evident in the world-wide depression to which they contributed. This unhappy experience led the major trading nations to seek better solutions after World War II. One outcome of their efforts was the General Agreement on Tariffs and Trade (GATT).

At Bretton Woods, New Hampshire, in 1944, allied nations planned an International Trade Organization (ITO) which would be open to all trading countries. Its goal was to replace the unilateral actions of the 1930s with multilateral cooperation. ITO never came into being because the nations disagreed on certain points, particularly articles relating to foreign investment. Fortunately, several nations were engaged in trade negotiations in Geneva in 1947. In anticipation of the ITO formation, they made a general agreement (GATT) which was a looser, more informal arrangement. When ITO failed of ratification (the United States did not approve the final proposal), GATT became, by default, the world's trading club.

Though GATT's initial membership consisted of only twenty-three countries, these included the major trading nations of the Western world. Today GATT is more than ever the world's trading club; it counts over ninety members and associates. The member countries account for well over 80 percent of total world trade. There are about twenty members from the industrialized nations of the West, including Japan, and over sixty members or associates from the less developed countries. The communist countries are represented by four members.

The inception and growth of GATT have undoubtedly contributed to the expansion of world trade. Since 1947, GATT has sponsored six major tariff negotiations, the latest being the Kennedy Round of 1964–1967. As a result of these conferences, the tariff rates for tens of thousands of items have been reduced, and a high proportion of world trade has seen an easing of restrictions. To provide a framework for multilateral trade negotiations is a primary reason for GATT's existence, but there are other GATT principles that further trade expansion. One is the principle of nondiscrimination. Each contracting party must grant all others the same rate of import duty; that is, a tariff concession granted to one trading partner must be extended to all GATT members under the most-favored-nation clause.

Another GATT principle is the concept of consultation. When trade disagreements arise, GATT encourages and provides a forum for consultation. In such an atmosphere, disagreeing members are more likely to compromise than to resort to arbitrary trade-restricting actions. All in all, world-trade cooperation since World War II has led to an international open-door trading policy better than the world could have expected. GATT has been a major contributor to this.

UNCTAD

Although GATT has been an important force in world-trade expansion, results and benefits have not been distributed equally. The less developed countries have been dissatisfied with trade arrangements because their share of world trade has been declining, and the prices of their raw-material exports compare unfavorably with the prices of their manufactured-goods imports. Though many of these countries are members of GATT, they felt that GATT did more to further trade in goods of industrialized nations than it did to promote their own primary products. It is true that tariff negotiations and reductions have been far more important to manufactured goods than to primary products. The result of these countries' dissatisfaction was the formation of The United Nations Conference on Trade and Development (UNCTAD) in 1964. UNCTAD is a permanent organ of the UN General Assembly and counts 136 member countries (more than the UN itself).

The goal of UNCTAD is to further the development of emerging nations— by trade as well as other means. Under GATT trade expanded especially in manufactured goods, creating a growing trade gap between industrial and developing countries as well as unfavorable terms of trade for the poorer countries; that is, the price relationship between industrial and primary goods was strongly in favor of the former. UNCTAD seeks to improve the prices of primary-good exports through commodity agreements. If the commodity-producing countries could get together to control supply effectively, this would mean higher prices and, hopefully, higher total returns from commodity exports.

Commodity agreements sound good in theory but have not worked very well in practice, except perhaps for the international coffee agreement. The major problem in commodity agreements has been inability to control supply when there are many supplying nations. Each individual nation could increase its returns by exceeding its export quota, but if several do this, the agreement is ineffective. Some of the same difficulties that arise with price-support programs in domestic agriculture are encountered here. Furthermore, price supports encourage substitution of other materials or products.

UNCTAD is also attempting to establish a tariff preference system favoring the export of manufactured goods from less developed countries. Since these countries' export of commodities has not been sufficient to maintain their share of trade, they want to expand in the growth area of world trade, industrial exports. This aim might be accomplished if the industrialized countries were to place low or zero tariffs on these exports while allowing the developing countries to maintain high protective tariffs themselves. These "preferences" then would be unilateral tariff concessions by the industrialized countries in favor of the nonindustrialized countries.

Progress has been slow toward the granting of preferences. This is unfortunate because the potential benefit to less developed countries should be greater than that to be derived from commodity agreements. The industrialized countries of the West have agreed in principle to extend such preferences, even though this arrangement is contrary to the GATT principle of nondiscrimination. The major deterrent to any significant implementation of a preferential tariff system, however, is not the GATT principle. It is the practical political consideration that the industrialized countries' own "low technology" industries would be hurt by such imports. For example, textiles are one of the prime candidates for manufactured exports of less developed countries, but the developed nations excluded these from their list of preferential tariff concessions.

The major UNCTAD achievements have been modest. One is organizational. A new "club" for world-trade matters has been established with a large membership and financing from the UN budget. This means that there is a continuing lobby to press for attainment of UNCTAD goals, that is, the goals of the approximately ninety less developed countries who belong. A second UNCTAD achievement is all the publicity and attention given by so many countries to the trade aspects of a major world problem—the gap in economic development between the "have" and "have not" nations. In spite of the lack of more concrete achievements to date, it is likely that future trade relations will be designed to be more helpful to less developed nations. GATT already has undertaken several initiatives in line with goals expressed in UNCTAD. The industrial nations cannot afford to ignore the strongly expressed needs and desires of their neighbors.

GATT, UNCTAD, and the Firm

These two international trade organizations have an important impact on the international economic environment of the firm. GATT's success in reducing barriers to international trade has meant that the firm's global logistics can be more rational and international than in a world of tight trade restrictions. Further, the firm, through its national subsidiaries in various markets, can help to protect its interest in trade and tariff matters through discussions with governments in advance of trade negotiations. In the United States, for example, there is a Trade Information Committee that holds hearings at which businessmen can present their international trading problems. These problems are noted for consideration in GATT negotiations. Not many nations have established such a formal procedure, but usually there is an adequate means through which to present the company interest. If there is a significant overlap between company activities and host government interest, the firm may find the government a valuable supporter.

UNCTAD's activity and program could have even more direct impact on the firm's operations than GATT. If UNCTAD ever realizes its goal of having the industrialized nations grant major tariff and trade preferences for the manufactured goods of nonindustrialized countries, international firms could take a major role in achieving the desired results. In general the less developed countries would have difficulty being competitive in exports of many manufactured goods, in which case elimination of tariff barriers through a preference system would not be sufficient to enable them to export. At this point the international firm can be a potentially decisive factor. If the firm adds its technical and international know-how and resources to those of the host country, more competitive production will result. Included in the resources of the international firm is its global distribution network, which could be the critical factor in gaining foreign market access for the new manufactured goods. Not only does this distribution network facilitate market access; perhaps more important, it supplies the local market experience and marketing know-how lacked by most producers in the developing countries.

It appears that there can be a great complementarity of interest between the less developed countries and international business firms in the question of preferences. On the one hand, the marriage of these interests could help the nations achieve their industrialization and balance of payments goals; on the other, multinational companies could expand their international markets and participate more actively and profitably in the growth of the less developed nations, a majority of the world's population.

In addition to affecting growth, the achievement of a preferential system would have a significant impact on the logistics of the multinational firm. Such preferences, as opposed to the GATT principle of nondiscrimination, would mean that the export of some products to less developed countries would be almost impossible. Local production could be essential for the firm to retain these markets. On *some* products that the firm ships from one developed country to others, it might be necessary to change to a production source in an emerging country because of the tariff preference given to the latter source. Thus, the firm's internal logistics would have to be realigned with the new realities.

East–West Trade

We have been discussing the trading problems between developed and less developed nations, or what could be called the problems of North–South trade. There is another division in the world economy that also has a geographic designation, though the division is essentially political. That division is between the communist economies and the so-called Western nations. In this section we discuss the peculiar economic problems arising from this ideological split.

Before considering the nature of East–West trade, it is useful to identify "East" and "West." East means primarily the Soviet Union, the socialist economies of Eastern Europe, plus China. However, other countries have joined that group, such as North Korea, North Vietnam, and the former "Western" country, Cuba. Furthermore, there are degrees of "Eastern-ness" or separation from the West in this group of nations. From the American viewpoint, for example, the most Eastern of these countries are China, Cuba, Albania, North Korea, and North Vietnam. For many years, all trade was absolutely prohibited with this subgroup. At the other extreme, the most Western of these nations are Yugoslavia and Poland, with whom much more trade and business is permitted. Czechoslovakia was leaning West, too, till pulled back by the Soviet Union.

There are degrees of "Western-ness" also. Though the term "West" is often used to describe all noncommunist nations, for trade purposes it is more accurate to restrict it to NATO (North Atlantic Treaty Organization) members and/or OECD (Organization for Economic Cooperation and Development) members. This includes primarily the nations of Western Europe, the United States, Canada, and Japan. Australia, New Zealand, and the Union of South Africa might also be included along with some others.

What is significant for the international firm is that there are wide differences among Western nations in attitudes and controls on trade with the East. When the East–West Cold War was very cold, most of these nations were in general agreement on imposing severe trade restrictions. This cold war thawed during the decade of the 1960s, and many Western European nations began easing up on trade restrictions. In some cases, they actually encouraged trade with the East. The international firm will find itself owning subsidiaries in countries with differing controls on such trade. This both poses problems and offers opportunities.

Market Big, Business Small

The volume of East–West trade has always been very modest in terms of the economic size of the two groups. Exports of NATO members to the communist world were $4.5 billion in 1967, or only about 3 percent of their total exports. There are several reasons for this low volume of trade. One, already mentioned, is the Cold War. To some extent, NATO countries consider the communist countries to be the enemy. Though this attitude has been steadily weakening in the past decade, such incidents as the Russian invasion of Czechoslovakia tend to revive it.

Accompanying this negative attitude are Western government regulations and controls on trade with the East. The United States, for example, has a Trading with the Enemy Act, administered by the Treasury Department, which prohibits trade with Albania, China, North Vietnam, North Korea, and Cuba. The Export Control Act, administered by the Department of Commerce, requires special licenses on exports of certain products and technologies that might aid the communist nations. These laws are discussed further in Chapter 5. American controls have been easing, but continued progress depends primarily on military and political developments rather than on economic concerns.

Another reason for the low volume of trade is ideological. The centrally planned economies lean toward autarky or self-sufficiency rather than foreign-trade interdependence. The more an economy is opened to the outside world through trade, the more difficult it is to control that economy. Therefore much of the international trading that the communist countries do engage in is within the framework of the Council for Mutual Economic Assistance (CMEA), the Russian counterpart of the European Economic Community (EEC). CMEA includes most of the communist countries as members.

A further reason for limited East–West trade is lack of marketing orientation and skills within the communist economies. These economies are designed to meet the desires of the planners rather than to meet the needs of the market. The purpose of exports is to pay for imports, not to fulfill market demand. Because they deal within a budget or command economy at home, they are generally ill equipped with the marketing skills necessary for selling in the market economies of the West. Related to this problem is their difficulty in earning hard currencies to pay for their imports from the West. This financing problem causes them to try to barter goods for goods, an approach generally unwelcome to the Western trader who is used to selling for hard cash.

The Firm Looks East

With the relaxing of tensions and hostilities on each side, both East and West have made increasing efforts to expand trade across the rusting Iron Curtain. Eastern nations want the new goods and technology of the West. Western business looks longingly on the great market potential of the East. Yugoslavia is in the forefront of Eastern countries trading with the West, but she is not alone in expanding such trade. Italy has been the most aggressive Western nation in trading with the East. The most spectacular evidence is the $800-million Fiat plant built in the USSR, but there are many kinds of transactions, such as a contract for 14 fully equipped supermarkets won by the Milan-based SIRCE company.

In this improved climate and environment for trading with the East, the firm must seriously consider its own position regarding Eastern markets. Since most Western European governments have a liberal attitude toward such trade, the problem for the American firm is acute. Although the American government has eased up on trade restrictions with the East, regulations are still a hindrance, and the American people have been even more conservative in their attitude than the government. As a result, the firm may move slowly to avoid negative reactions in the large domestic market.

In spite of the various constraints, however, the potential market involved for many high-technology goods or even consumer products is so great that it demands American executive attention—all the more so because the early entry of European firms could preempt this market, making it more difficult or impossible to enter later. As an executive of one farm-equipment manufacturer said longingly: "They (the CMEA countries) have twice the population and three times the land area of the United States."

As consumer interests receive more attention in the Eastern economies (for example, the Fiat plant, supermarkets, and the like), significant market opportunities may appear for consumer-oriented Western firms. Industrial goods firms already have market opportunities. Their problem is to find ways to finance their sales, or to learn to use barter or switch trading effectively. Perhaps the key to expanded sales to CMEA countries lies in helping them to overcome their marketing weaknesses. Western firms could do this by integrating these countries into their international operations. There are two ways this can be done. One is to incorporate Eastern suppliers into the firm's operaticns; their supplies would pay for the firm's sales to the supplying country. Another is for the Western firm to include some Eastern country's related products in its own multinational marketing program. Again, these related products would pay for the firm's sales to the supplying country. These two approaches could be alternatives to barter or switch trading.

Regionalism

One of the major developments in the world economy since World War II is the growth of regional groupings. The EEC is the most famous and successful of these, but it is only one of many. Regional groupings are agreements between nations in the same region to cooperate in various economic matters. There may also be political ties between these same nations, but it is the economic aspect that concerns us here. Regionalism, or the tendency towards economic cooperation within regions, is an attempt by nations to attain goals they cannot achieve in isolation. NATO is a counterpart in the military field.

There arc costs to a nation in joining regional groupings, the chief one of which is giving up some of its sovereignty in economic matters. Nations do this only because they hope the benefits will be greater than the costs. A variety of benefits are sought through economic integration. One goal of many groupings is countervailing power. Thus the EEC sought a stronger position vis-à-vis the superpowers, the United States and the USSR. EFTA was formed largely as a means of gaining bargaining strength with the EEC. LAFTA in turn seeks countervailing power to both the EEC and the United States. Another objective of regional groupings is to achieve the benefits of free trade in a limited region. By getting together and trading freely among themselves, the member nations can get larger markets and economies of scale for their industries.

The reduction of trade barriers in the group provides further dynamism to the member economies by increasing competition. Sluggish national firms or monopolies lose their protective walls and are forced to change their behavior in a more competitive and innovative direction. Furthermore, the group of countries together may be able to afford an industry too large for any individual member country to support because of the scale of capital and other resources required. Thus industrialization can be aided by regional integration. All this could mean greater wealth, progress, and self-sufficiency for the region. If the region does become more self-sufficient, the member countries' balance of payments positions could improve, lessening their dependence on foreign exchange earnings. For less developed countries in perennial balance of payments difficulties, this point becomes very important. In reaching for these goals, there are varying forms and degrees of economic integration to choose from.

Free-Trade Areas

Although all regional groupings have economic goals, the various groups differ in organization and motivation. There are three basic kinds of organization for economic integration. The simplest is a free-trade area. In a free-trade area the member countries agree to have *free movement of goods among themselves*, that is, no tariffs or quotas against goods coming from other members. The European Free Trade Association (EFTA) and the Latin American Free Trade Area (LAFTA) are the major examples today. EFTA is only partly a free-trade area, as the members have agreed to free trade primarily in industrial goods. Agricultural products are still subject to many restrictions in trade between member countries. On the other hand, EFTA is somewhat more than a free-trade area as members are cooperating on other regulations and policies affecting trade, for example, government procurement and antitrust policy. LAFTA is aiming at a free-trade area but progress has been gradual—occasionally even invisible.

EFTA began with the Stockholm Convention in 1960. It aimed at the abolition by 1970 of tariffs on manufactures traded between the member countries. This goal was achieved three years early, on January 1, 1967. LAFTA began with the 1961 Treaty of Montevideo and aimed at free trade among members by 1973. Though trade among members doubled between 1961 and 1965, very little progress has been made since then. National producers are afraid of competition from other member countries. Some governments are afraid that the gains from integration will go primarily to other members. These fears have seriously affected the forward momentum, and the integration timetable will stretch well beyond the 1973 target; in fact, the members have advanced their target date for achieving integration to 1980.

Customs Union

A customs union goes beyond a free-trade area. It is similar in that it has no tariffs on trade among members. However, it has the more ambitious requirement that members also have a *uniform tariff on trade with nonmembers*. Thus a customs union is like a single nation not only in internal trade; it also presents a united front to the rest of the world with its common external tariff. A customs union is more difficult to achieve than a free-trade area because each member must yield its sovereignty in commercial-policy matters, not just concerning trade with a small number of member nations but with the whole world. Its advantage lies in making the economic integration stronger and avoiding the administrative problems of a free-trade area. For example, in a free-trade area, imports of a particular good would always enter the member country with the lowest tariff on that good, regardless of the country of destination. To avoid this waste and perversion of normal trade patterns, special regulations and administrative procedures are necessary.

The leading example of a customs union is the EEC. Although the EEC is often referred to as the Common Market, it is more accurately described as a customs union. In July 1968, the EEC achieved a full customs union, a goal they began working toward January 1, 1958. Though this is a slower timetable than EFTA's, it represents a much more ambitious endeavor, because it includes not only a free-trade area among members but also a common external tariff. In addition, it covers agricultural products, which are omitted by EFTA.

Common Markets or Economic Union

A true common market includes a customs union but goes significantly beyond it. A common market seeks to standardize or *harmonize all government regulations affecting trade*. These include all aspects of government economic policy that pertain to business, for example, corporation and excise taxes, labor laws, fringe benefits and social security programs, incorporation laws, and antitrust laws. In such an economic union, business and trade decisions would be based on geographic, cultural, and market factors but would be unaffected by the national laws of different members because they would be uniform. The United States is the best example of a common market. Even here, however, the example is not perfect because different states do have different laws and taxes pertaining to business. American business decisions therefore are somewhat influenced by differing state laws as well as by the usual geographic and market factors.

Even though true common markets are hard to find, it is important to understand their nature because economic union is a kind of guiding light for all kinds of regional groupings. For some groups, of course, the light is rather far away. The EEC, however, has made big strides toward economic union. Besides the successful customs union, they have achieved a common agricultural policy and made progress toward common policies for labor, antitrust law, excise taxes, transportation, and the like.

The Central American Common Market (CACM) is the most successful regional grouping in the less developed nations. The members have achieved or are working toward a customs union, free movement of labor among members, and coordination of monetary policies and national planning. They have also established a common Central American Bank for Economic Integration (CABEI). In addition to these groups that have "common market" as part of their name, many other regional groups are moving in the direction of a common market.

For example, EFTA is a free-trade area limited to industrial goods. It has nevertheless made modest progress on a number of other fronts "to ensure that trade between the member states takes place under conditions of fair competition on terms as nearly equal as possible," in the words of the Stockholm Convention. Consultation has been undertaken on many economic matters, such as rules of competition and government purchasing policies.

There is a continuing effort to harmonize economic and financial policies. Nations that seek the economies of scale and other benefits of economic integration tend to move in the direction of a common market because they find that free-trade areas and other such limited arrangements do not yield all the benefits they desire.

Historically, tariffs have been one of the most important determinants of international trade patterns. Once they disappear or are reduced, however, a host of nontariff factors takes their place in affecting trade. When members of regional groups attack these other governmental barriers, they are moving, however slowly, in the direction of economic union, beyond a free-trade area or customs union. This is true for any regional grouping that has made any progress, regardless of what name it calls itself. In looking at the implications of any regional grouping, the international marketer will be less concerned with the name it carries than with its goals, problems, and the method it plans to use to meet these.

Other Groupings

The best known regional groups are the EEC, EFTA, LAFTA, and the CACM. There are numerous other groups ranging from loose associations to arrangements of the common-market type. A common-market approach is being tried by Nordek (the Scandinavian countries), the countries maintaining simultaneous membership in EFTA. The situation is similar in Benelux, which counts three EEC members. Because of problems in LAFTA, several nations formed a smaller but stronger and closer grouping, the Andean Common Market. Kenya, Tanzania, and Uganda have formed the East African Common Market. There has been talk of an Arab Common Market but little activity thus far. The more groupings using common-market approaches, the more the changes that will occur in the environment of international business. The international marketer must be especially alert to these developments. Table 2–6 lists the major regional economic groupings with their members as of 1970.

Table 2–6 Regional Groups

MEMBERSHIP AND DATE OF ORIGIN
1. ANCOM: Andean Development Corporation (also called the Andean Common Market)—September, 1967   Bolivia, Colombia, Chile, Ecuador, Peru

2. Arab Economic Unity Agreement—April 30, 1964
    Iraq, Jordan, Kuwait, Syria, U.A.R. (Egypt)
    Other signatories—Sudan, Yemen

3. ASEAN: Association of South East Asian Nations—August, 1967   Indonesia, Malaysia, Philippines, Singapore, Thailand
4. Benelux—November, 1960   Belgium, Luxembourg, the Netherlands
5. CACM: Central American Common Market—1960   Costa Rica, El Salvador, Guatemala, Honduras, Nicaragua

6. CARIFTA: Caribbean Free Trade Area—January, 1966
    Antigua, Barbados, Dominica, Grenada, Guyana, Jamaica, Montserrat, St. Christopher-Nevis-Anguilla, St. Lucia, St. Vincent, Trinidad and Tobago

7. CMEA: Council for Mutual Economic Assistance (also called COMECON) —1949
    Albania, Bulgaria, Czechoslovakia, East Germany, Hungary, Mongolian People's Republic, Poland, Romania, USSR
    Partial participant—Yugoslavia

8. East African Community—December, 1967
    Kenya, Tanzania, Uganda

9. EEC: European Economic Community—January 1, 1958
    Belgium, France, West Germany, Italy, Luxembourg, the Netherlands
    Associated members—(in Europe) Greece, Turkey, Israel, Spain; (in Africa) Burundi, Cameroon, Central African Republic, Chad, Congo (Brazzaville), Congo (Democratic Republic), Dahomey, Gabon, Ivory Coast, Madagascar, Mali, Mauritania, Niger, Rwanda, Senegal, Somalia, Togo, Upper Volta

10. EFTA: European Free Trade Area—May, 1960
    Austria, Denmark, Norway, Portugal, Sweden, Switzerland, United Kingdom
    Associate member—Finland

11. LAFTA: Latin American Free Trade Association (also called ALALC)— February, 1960
    Argentina, Bolivia, Brazil, Chile, Colombia, Ecuador, Mexico, Paraguay, Peru, Uruguay, Venezuela

12. Nordek: The Nordic Council—1953
    Denmark, Finland, Iceland, Norway, Sweden

13. OCAM: *Organisation Commune Africaine et Malgache*—February, 1965
    Cameroon, Central African Republic, Chad, Congo (Brazzaville), Congo (Democratic Republic), Dahomey, Gabon, Ivory Coast, Madagascar, Niger, Rwanda, Senegal, Togo, Upper Volta

---

There are a number of examples of looser forms of economic cooperation. Many of these are of interest because they give rise to developments that can affect the operations of the firm, though less significantly than the more ambitious forms of economic integration. Many nations of black Africa are associated with the EEC and enjoy preferential entry of their goods into EEC countries. EEC producers in turn have an advantage over non-EEC producers in selling to the associated states. Greece and Turkey are also associate members of EEC, and Spain and Israel signed agreements in 1970.

In Asia, there have been various halting steps toward regional cooperation. The latest is the Association of Southeast Asian Nations (ASEAN, pronounced Asian). Though the agreement makes no mention of a common market or free-trade area, it does mention more effective collaboration in industry and agriculture, "including the study of the problems of international commodity trade." A very specialized example of regional integration is the automobile agreement between Canada and the United States, allowing free trade in automobiles between the two countries. It has resulted in great changes in trade patterns and internal company logistics.

Regionalism and the Multinational Company

The rise of regional groupings is a major change in the economic environment that has several implications for the international firm. It means that fewer but larger economic entities are gradually replacing the multitude of national markets. When the firm is considering an investment decision, the relevant market area may include six or ten countries rather than just one national market. Part of the large American investment in Western Europe in the 1960s was a result of the attraction of the larger market offered by the EEC. The "United States of Europe" was one expression used to describe the new Europe.

The firm's logistics also will be modified by regional groupings. There will be strong pressures to supply from within a region rather than to export to it. The firm will have the added incentive of the larger market, but it will be pressured to get behind the common external tariff to compete with local producers. At the same time, these local producers will become stronger competitors because of the economies of scale they realize in the larger market, and because of the stronger competition in the free-trade area. A firm's operations within a regional group will tend to be more self-contained than they would be in ungrouped individual national markets. In the latter the firm would rely more on *international* than on *intragroup* logistics patterns.

The firm's marketing program will have to be modified in common-market areas. As the differences in markets diminish, there will be greater uniformity in the firm's marketing approach to the member countries. The firm will gain economies of scale in product development, pricing, distribution, and promotion. For example, as member nations harmonize their food, drug, and labeling laws, the firm can eliminate product and packaging differences which were required solely by the differences in national laws. Similar modifications would occur in the other functional areas of the firm, for instance, in personnel, financial management, accounting and control. Some examples will illustrate how firms have adapted to take advantage of the new market realities created by regional groupings.

A manufacturer of home-care products closed down eight national production sources in Europe soon after the Common Market was formed. The firm concentrated its continental European production in the Netherlands to gain economies of scale possible within the free-trade area. To further facilitate and benefit from centralized production, the firm standardized its package sizes and designs, including color, even though copy was continued in different national languages.

Eversharp was challenging Gillette's strong position in razor blades in Latin America. Gillette had plants in Argentina, Brazil, Mexico, and Colombia. Eversharp chose to begin production in Venezuela where it could purchase a local blade manufacturer. Here Eversharp could protect the local market while gaining entry into third markets in LAFTA where Gillette had already obtained concessions under the Montevideo Treaty. One of Eversharp's managers in Venezuela acted as LAFTA coordinator to search out opportunities for further concessions in LAFTA markets. With the help of the Venezuelan government, happy to see its exports expand, this effort has paid off. Two of Gillette's protected markets, Mexico and Colombia, were opened to Eversharp through the LAFTA negotiation process.[3]

Although LAFTA integration has been slow, complementation agreements have been one way to accelerate integration in certain product areas. A complementation agreement involves two or more LAFTA countries who grant each other tariff concessions on a few products in the same industry. This is a limited free-trade arrangement within the larger but incomplete free-trade area. A good example is the so-called IBM Agreement in which Argentina, Brazil, Chile, and Uruguay formed a free-trade area for data-processing equipment and punch cards. This means that for these products and these countries, the benefits of rationalization of production and distribution are already realized. IBM benefits also, though its competitors will eventually gain as well.

The International Financial System

A major goal of business is to make a profit, so firms pay close attention to financial matters. International business also is concerned with making a profit, but international companies must be even more concerned with financial matters than national firms are. One reason is that the international firm must deal with many currencies, and many national financial markets where conditions differ from one to the other. Some of the problems within foreign financial markets will be touched on in Chapter 3. Marketing across national boundaries requires other financial considerations which we will discuss here.

Exchange-Rate Instability

Dealing with many different currencies is not a serious problem in itself. The difficulty lies in the ever-present possibility that currencies may change in value vis-à-vis each other. Domestic inflation is a factor in many countries and affects the pricing policies of the national firm. Selling across national boundaries poses a different problem, however. In this case, there is no steady and predictable change in prices, as is usual with inflation; instead abrupt changes may take place in the exchange rate of one or more currencies.

The exchange rate is the domestic price of a foreign currency. For the United States, this means that there is a dollar rate, or price, for the British pound, the Swiss franc, the Brazilian cruzeiro, as well as every other currency. If one country changes the value of its currency, firms selling to or from that country may find that the altered exchange rate is sufficient to wipe out their profit, or, on the brighter side, give them a windfall gain. In any case, they must be on the alert for currency devaluations in order to optimize their financial performance. Unfortunately, currency devaluations are not rare in international finance.

[3] *Business Latin America,* September 11, 1969, p. 291.

In August 1969, France devalued its franc by about 12 percent. Following almost immediately was a similar devaluation by more than twelve African nations in the "franc zone" (former French colonies that maintained strong trade ties with France). Even the Belgian franc was threatened by speculative pressure. Foreign firms selling to French customers and quoting French franc prices at this time suffered losses of 12 percent, because the amount of French francs received in payment after the devaluation was equivalent to 12 percent less of their own currency. Firms in France selling to outside customers broke even or made a windfall gain, depending on whether they quoted in French francs or the customer's currency.

In the days of the gold standard, exchange rates did not change in value. The stability and certainty of the international gold standard came to an end, however, with the advent of World War I. The international financial system of the 1930s had no certainty, stability, or accepted rules. Instead there were frequent and arbitrary changes in exchange rates. This chaotic and uncertain situation contributed to the decline in international trade during that period. The world-wide depression of the thirties was reinforced by the added risks in international finance.

In 1944, some of the allied nations met at Bretton Woods to design a better international economic system for the postwar world. One element of this system dealt with international trade, namely, the ITO, which died but left us with an effective world-trade club in GATT. Another element concerned with the need for international capital led to the formation of the International Bank for Reconstruction and Development (IBRD), commonly called the World Bank. A third aspect involving the international monetary system resulted in the establishment of the International Monetary Fund (IMF).

The International Monetary Fund

Various kinds of international financial systems are possible. One system advocated by Milton Friedman and a number of academic economists is freely fluctuating exchange rates, whereby exchange rates would be like other market prices, determined by daily conditions of supply and demand. There are several advantages in this approach. Those who favor market prices over government-determined prices might favor them for the exchange rate also. With flexible exchange rates, a country never has a defict in its balance of payments; the market clears and balances every trading period through adjustments in the exchange rate. With no deficits to worry about, the nation can release its exchange reserves and put them to work. Furthermore, it can eliminate the costs and administrative burden of holding reserves and stabilizing its exchange rate.

A final advantage claimed for flexible rates is that domestic policies can be determined on the basis of domestic needs with less attention to balance of payments considerations. In spite of these attractions, there is little likelihood that we will soon see a world of flexible exchange rates. The major reason is that international businessmen, bankers, and government policy makers fear they would mean extra uncertainty and risk, and therefore a diminution of world trade. Nevertheless, unsettled conditions in international finance exert continued pressure for greater flexibility.

Another candidate for an international financial system is the gold standard as it was practiced in the nineteenth century. This would mean stable, even rigid, exchange rates with gold the principal, if not the only, international money. The advantages would be certainty and stability of exchange rates to encourage trade and the discipline afforded by gold, which is reassuring to bankers who tend to be more cautious when dealing in paper monies. Though the gold standard approach to international finance has some strong proponents, it is less likely to be realized than are freely fluctuating exchange rates.

Serious problems are involved in getting an adequate supply of gold to back the international monetary system because either new gold must be mined or the price of existing gold must be increased. Another major political drawback is that the discipline of the gold standard in the past forced countries with balance of payments deficits to take deflationary action domestically to make the system work. Governments dislike taking unpopular domestic actions in any case, but especially if they are forced to by an external factor such as the balance of payments deficit.

The current international financial system as it operates with IMF tries to avoid the drawbacks of the above approaches. Because stable exchange rates are desired by most of those concerned with international trade, the IMF provides for stable "pegged" rates. Because countries wish to isolate their domestic economic policies somewhat from their balance of payments problems, the IMF allows occasional adjustments or changes in the exchange rate as an alternative to unpopular domestic measures. To enable nations to maintain stable rates for relatively long periods and to enjoy a greater volume of trade, the IMF has contributed to world reserves and liquidity growth. With resources of over $28 billion in the monetary fund, the IMF through its pooled reserves and credit practices has allowed many nations to continue trading in spite of balance of payments setbacks. The remarkable growth of world trade since World War II is an indication that the IMF has had fair success in its goal of promoting trade expansion, particularly through its provision of international liquidity and encouragement of stable exchange rates.

Although no firm has dealings with the IMF, there are few organizations that have had a more significant impact on the environment of international business. The IMF emphasis on stable exchange rates has facilitated international trade and finance for the firm by reducing uncertainty. By providing international liquidity, the IMF has enabled exchange rates to remain stable longer, while at the same time permitting a greater volume of international trade. The IMF has exerted steady pressure on its member nations to eliminate exchange control and various other financial restrictions on trade. This has contributed not only to the growth of international trade, but to the greater ease with which it is conducted. Although there remain many problems and uncertainties in international finance, these are undoubtedly much less severe than they would be in the absence of IMF. Therefore, the firm can welcome IMF's continuing efforts to maintain a stable and expanding international financial system.

The World Bank

The International Bank for Reconstruction and Development (IBRD or World Bank) is another institution conceived at Bretton Woods. It has also had an important impact on the world economy in which international business operates. Whereas the IMF is concerned with the provision of short-term liquidity, the World Bank supplies long-term capital to aid economic development. The World Bank provides over $1 billion a year for this purpose, and its lending has expanded greatly under the presidency of Robert McNamara. IDA (International Development Association) is a daughter organization of the World Bank created for the purpose of giving "soft" loans to developing countries, that is, long-term loans at very low interest rates. Lending done by these two groups is for all aspects of development as, for example, improving infrastructure, industrial projects, agriculture, education, tourism, and population control. The total amount made available by these two organizations in 1969 was $1.8 billion.

World Bank activities have improved the international economic environment and aid the international businessman in several ways. The supply of capital has meant a higher level of economic activity and therefore better markets for firms. This is true not only in general terms but in specific instances as well. For example, many firms are suppliers to projects in developing countries for which the World Bank and IDA are lending billions of dollars. This often opens up new import markets that might have been impossible to enter if the World Bank had not given financial assistance to the country. Firms might also find themselves raising some local capital abroad from one of the 26 development-finance institutions aided by the World Bank.

There is yet another way in which the World Bank may help international business. The bank has established a center for the settlement of investment disputes between nations and companies. Because the World Bank realizes that private investment is needed in addition to its own lending, it seeks to encourage private lending and limit obstacles in its path. This encouragement includes not only arbitration facilities, but also efforts in behalf of investment agreements and multilateral investment insurance.

The United States in the World Economy

Although the international environment in which the firm operates is important, the global influence of the country in which the international firm has its home base cannot be ignored. In ways varying from country to country, the home government and nation are a constraint upon the international operations of the firm. A Swedish or Dutch multinational company has a different set of constraints from those that affect an American firm or a firm from one of the former colonial powers, England or France. Since most of the readers of this book will be Americans, we will examine the international constraints peculiar to an American multinational company. The pattern can be applied in general to international firms domiciled in other nations.

One obvious constraint on the firm's international operations is its home government's attitude and policies toward such business. Most governments encourage exports to maintain a strong balance of payments or to eliminate a deficit, accomplishing their aim sometimes through tax advantages, sometimes in other ways. The American government generally does not give tax incentives for exports, although this approach was recommended in a study done for the Department of Commerce. However, government assistance is given through the valuable information and promotional services of the Department of Commerce. Furthermore, the Export-Import Bank helps to finance many American exports, and there is a government assisted program of export credit insurance.

The United States foreign aid program has helped many American companies to make export sales to markets that otherwise would have been closed because of their lack of foreign exchange. If the foreign aid programs have a favorable effect on recipient nations' attitudes toward Americans, this will improve the host nation environment for the foreign operations of American firms. A critical determinant of the firm's ability to export is, of course, the resource endowment and comparative advantage of its home country. Furthermore, the business and competitive environment at home may have taught the firm skills that aid its performance abroad.

There are other American policies that relate to international business. The government has encouraged investment in less developed countries by its investment guaranty program. On the other hand, the government limited foreign investment in the late 1960s, first through a voluntary and later through a mandatory program controlling the outflow of private capital. Until 1962, government tax policy was favorable to foreign business. Firms did not pay United States tax on foreign earnings until remitted back to America. In effect while this money was being used abroad it was an interest-free loan. The 1962 tax law changed this, eliminating the so-called tax havens.

The government's posture in commercial policy can help or hinder the firm in selling internationally. A national free-trading posture will make it easier for the firm than a protectionist policy because of retaliation in foreign markets. The firm is often able to influence its nation's commercial policy in its industry through trade-association representation to the appropriate government bodies. In the United States, these include the Tariff Commission, the Trade Information Committee, and the relevant congressmen.

One direct restriction on the firm's foreign sales is the government's policy on trading with communist countries. For example, if the British or French government wanted to sell equipment to Cuba or Communist China, the American subsidiaries there could not supply components for this equipment. France lost aircraft sales to China for this reason. This caused trouble not only for the United States, but for American firms in France.

Government actions and national achievements quite apart from commercial or financial policy decisions can affect the firm internationally. American antitrust policy has constrained the actions of American companies abroad. American technological and space achievements aid American companies in foreign sales of high-technology products. In part, these technological advances are supported by government funds for research and development. On the other hand, foreign dissatisfaction with America's role in the world can threaten foreign operations of American firms. Dissatisfaction over the Vietnam war or some other American action may lead to a march on the United States Embassy—or the local Sears store or Coca-Cola bottler.

The very size and wealth of the American economy is a source of both envy and resentment. It affects the image of American companies abroad where they are often considered to have an unfair advantage over other firms, especially local companies. The United States is the world's leading exporter and also the world's largest importer. This fact lends weight to American objectives in commercial policy negotiations, which is favorable to the foreign sales of American firms. Since the American market is so attractive, other countries must open up their markets a bit if they wish to sell to the United States. In all these ways, a company's nationality affects its international marketing strategies and possibilities.

Questions

2.1 Nationalism, bullionism, and a "favorable balance of trade" were elements of mercantilism. In what way are these elements with us today?

2.2 World trade is large and growing rapidly. What is the significance of this for the firm?

2.3 How can a study of the patterns of world trade be useful to the international marketer?

2.4 How might the principle of comparative advantage be useful to the international marketing planner?

2.5 What is a balance of payments? Indicate several ways balance of payments analysis can be useful to the international marketer.

2.6 The Moonbeam Company, a producer of small consumer durables, had been exporting into Latinia for several years. Then Latinia imposed a 20-percent ad valorem duty on Moonbeam products. What can Moonbeam do?

2.7 What could Moonbeam do if Latinia had instead imposed a quota that reduced Moonbeam's exports by 60 percent?

2.8 What are some of the implications of exchange control for the international marketer?

2.9 What has been the impact of GATT on the environment of international marketing?

2.10 If UNCTAD is successful in getting the industrial nations to grant tariff preferences to less developed countries, what might this mean for the international firm?

2.11 Discuss the implications of the East–West split in world trade for the international marketer.

2.12 Why might the American exporter feel threatened by the growth of regional groups around the world? How might he react to this threat to his markets?

2.13 As the EEC develops into a true common market, what modifications could appear in the marketing program of an international firm with operations in all the member countries?

2.14 "A world in which exchange rates fluctuate constantly is a threat to international marketing." Discuss.

2.15 In what ways can the IMF be considered the friend of the international marketer?

2.16 How does the World Bank help the international marketer?

2.17 Discuss the impact of American nationality on the international marketing of United States firms.

Further Readings

Books:

For more extensive discussions of international economic questions and institutions, see standard texts in the field, such as the following:

Kindleberger, Charles P., *International Economics*, 4th ed. (Homewood, Ill.: Richard D. Irwin, 1968).

Kreinin, Mordechai E., *International Economics: A Policy Approach* (New York: Harcourt, Brace, Jovanovich, 1971).

Articles:

Wells, Louis T., Jr., "A Product Life Cycle for International Trade?" *Journal of Marketing* (July 1968), pp. 1–6.

Data Sources:

GATT, *International Trade* (annual).
International Financial Statistics (monthly).
International Monetary Fund, *Annual Reports,* Washington, D.C.
IBRD, *Annual Reports,* Washington, D.C.
Survey of Current Business (monthly).
United Nations, *Yearbook of International Trade Statistics,* New York: New York, United Nations (annual).
Walker World Trade Annual.

3

ECONOMIC ENVIRONMENT: THE FOREIGN ECONOMIES

The economic environment has long been recognized as an uncontrollable factor in the task of marketing management. The economic environment of international marketing is peculiar in two ways. First, it contains an *international* economic environment that affects marketing between nations. We looked at this international environment in Chapter 2. Second, the economic environment of international marketing includes the *domestic* economy of every nation in which the firm is selling. Thus the international marketer faces the traditional task of economic analysis but in a context that may include 100 countries or more. This chapter addresses itself to the identification of the relevant economic dimensions of individual world markets. The investigation will be directed toward answering two broad questions: How big is the market? and, What is the market like? Answers to the first question will help to determine the firms' market potentials and priorities abroad. Answers to the second question will help to determine the nature of the marketing task.

SIZE OF THE MARKET

The firm's initial concern in examining world markets is the potential they offer for sales of its products. If the firm already sells abroad, the international marketer must determine market size not only for present markets but also for potential markets. This helps him to allocate effort efficiently among present markets and to determine which new markets to enter next. Market size for any given product is a function of particular variables and indicators, and its determination requires an ad hoc analysis. However, there are certain general indicators of market size which are relevant for many goods. We will see how world markets are described by the following general indicators:

population, population growth, distribution of the population; distribution of income, income per capita, and gross national product.

Possible markets are numerous. The *United Nations Statistical Yearbook* lists data for 242 political entities. Of course, many of these are very small. United Nations membership itself counts just over 130 countries. On a more practical level, the World Bank counts 122 countries with a population of over one million. The number of these nations that are worthwhile markets will vary from firm to firm. However, many companies sell in over 100 different world markets. Singer, for example, sells in 180 countries.

Population

It takes people to make a market and, other things being equal, the greater the population in a country, the better the market. Of course, other things are never equal, so population figures in themselves are not usually a sufficient guide to market size. Nevertheless, the consumption of many products is correlated with population figures. For many "necessary" goods such as ethical drugs, health-care items, some food products, or educational supplies, population figures may be a very good first indicator of market potential. For other products which are low in price or which meet particular needs, population again may be a useful market indicator. Products in these latter categories include soft drinks, ball-point pens, bicycles, and sewing machines.

In analyzing foreign economies, population figures will be one of the first considerations of the international marketer. He will be struck by the tremendous differences in size of the sovereign nations of the world. For example, the largest nation in the world has over 10,000 times the population of some of the smallest countries. Well over half the people of the world live in the seven countries that have populations of more than 100 million. On the other hand, three-fourths of the countries have populations of less than 10 million, and over 30 have less than 1 million people.

Though the marketer is concerned primarily with individual markets, regional patterns are also important for regional logistics. For example, Asia includes five of the seven nations with populations over 100 million (six, if the USSR is considered Asian). By contrast, Africa, the Middle East, and Latin America are relatively thinly populated. Nigeria is the only large African nation, with 64 million people. Turkey is the largest country in the Middle East, with just 34 million people. Latin America counts just two relatively populous nations: Brazil with 92 million people and Mexico with 49 million. Europe is smaller in land area but more densely populated than any other region. Western Europe has four nations with populations over 50 million. These facts and others can be observed in Table 3–1 which lists the fifty nations having a population of 10 million or more as of 1970.

Population Growth Rates

The international marketer is concerned not only with the *current* population of a foreign market. Since many of his decisions have future effects, he must also know about population trends. Almost every nation is experiencing population growth, but the rate of increase varies from as low as 0.4 percent per year to ten times that, or about 4 percent a year. Ireland and Austria are examples of countries at the lower end of that range, while El Salvador, Nicaragua, and Libya are at the upper end.

Table 3–1   The World's Most Populous Nations (1970 estimates)

NATION	POPULATION (MILLIONS)	NATION	POPULATION (MILLIONS)
1. Mainland China	745	26. North Vietnam	21.6
2. India	543	27. Canada	21.2
3. USSR	241.3	28. Colombia	20.7
4. U.S.A.	204.3	29. Yugoslavia	20.5
5. Pakistan	129	30. Romania	20.2
6. Indonesia	116.8	31. South Africa	19.8
7. Japan	102.8	32. South Vietnam	18.1
8. Brazil	92	33. Congo	17.4
9. Nigeria	64	34. East Germany	17.1
10. West Germany	60.9	35. Afghanistan	16.6
11. United Kingdom	55.6	36. Sudan	15.4
12. Italy	53.3	37. Morocco	15.3
13. France	50.4	38. Czechoslovakia	14.4
14. Mexico	49.6	39. Taiwan	14
15. Philippines	38	40. Netherlands	13.5
16. Thailand	35.2	41. Peru	13.4
17. Turkey	34.8	42. North Korea	13.4
18. U.A.R.	32.8	43. Algeria	13.2
19. Spain	32.8	44. Tanzania	13
20. Poland	32.6	45. Australia	12.4
21. South Korea	31.5	46. Ceylon	12.3
22. Iran	28	47. Nepal	11
23. Burma	27.2	48. Malaysia	10.9
24. Ethiopia	24.2	49. Kenya	10.6
25. Argentina	24.1	50. Hungary	10.3

Source: *1970 Commercial Atlas and Marketing Guide* (New York: Rand McNally & Co.), pp. 584–587.

Here again regional patterns are observable. All the European and North American nations average only about 1 percent a year population increase. Their populations remain quite stable. Africa, the Middle East, and the Far East have an intermediate rate of population increase, averaging a growth of something over 2 percent a year, or a little more than twice as much as in Europe and North America. All the nations in these regions are quite close to the average for their region, except for some African countries which show rather wide differences in population growth rates. However, the most notable exception to its regional pattern is Japan, whose annual rate of population increase is only about 1 percent. Japan follows the European rather than the Asian pattern on this score. Mainland China is an unknown quantity.

Latin America is the region with the world's highest rate of population increase, averaging about 3 percent a year. Indeed, in Central America, the rate of increase is about 3.5 percent. The only exceptions to the regional pattern are Argentina and Uruguay, which have low rates closer to the European pattern than to that of their neighbors. This is to be expected perhaps, as both countries, especially Argentina, have populations almost entirely of European descent, in contrast to the rest of Latin America. Figure 3–1 illustrates graphically the differences in regional growth rates.

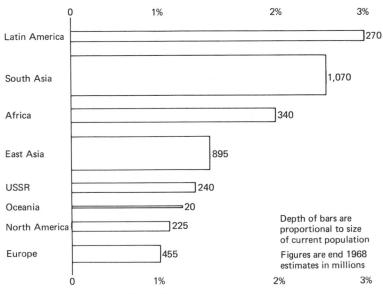

Figure 3–1   Growth in World Population
percent increase end 1967–end 1968

From *Finance and Development*, December, 1969, p. 50.

The picture of population growth in the foreign economy has important though sometimes contrary implications for the international marketer. On the favorable side, population growth often lends buoyancy to the economy. It can mean the formation of new households and increased demand for a whole range of goods. This has been the traditional attitude toward population growth in the United States. However, growing concern over the population explosion has highlighted the negative aspects of high rates of growth. High rates of population increase can hinder modernization and development of the economy by holding back per capita income, which can make a market less attractive to many firms rather than more attractive. But it is an ill wind that blows good for no one, and some firms could market profitably even to countries with population problems. Examples are producers of birth-control supplies, medicines, certain foods, or educational materials.

Distribution of the Population

Understanding population figures involves more than the mere counting of heads. Although two heads may be better than one, it does make a difference what kind of heads one is counting. The international marketer must organize the population figures for a foreign economy and classify them in ways that show him the relevant segments of the market. Classification may be by age group, sex, education, or occupation, for example. Religious, tribal, educational, and other socio-cultural attributes will be discussed in Chapter 4. Here we will consider such population characteristics as age and income distribution and population density. Occupational classifications will be covered under the section Nature of the Foreign Economy.

Age

People in different stages of life have different needs. In the American market, for example, many firms recognize distinct segments related to age groupings. The same information is useful in other economies. The economies of the world fall into three categories as to age distribution. Many of the developing nations are experiencing a population explosion because of declining infant mortality. Because of short life expectancy, this leads to a high percentage of inactive population in the 0 to 14 age group. Only 3 to 4 percent of the population is over sixty-five years of age in these countries, examples of which are Ghana and Ceylon.

Australia and the United States are examples of developed nations where life expectancy is long, but the population is still rather youthful, reflecting the relative youth of these nations' economies. A large proportion of both Australia's and the United States' population is over sixty-five years of age. At the same time, a much larger proportion are in the under-fifteen group. The third category of countries includes the mature industrial economies, such as those in Western Europe. In these countries, the number of people in the middle-age group is about the same as in the younger age group. Considered graphically, the age distribution takes more the shape of a rectangle than a triangle as in the other two categories. These countries have one-sixth of their population over sixty years of age. Figure 3–2 shows these different patterns.

Density and Concentration

The compactness or concentration of population is important to the marketer in evaluating distribution and communication problems. The United States had a population density of fifty-five persons per square mile in 1967. This is only about one-twentieth of the Netherland's population density. Even with a modern transportation network, distribution costs in the United States are likely to be higher than in the Netherlands. For example, many advertisements in the United States used to read "Slightly higher west of the Rockies." Promotion is also facilitated where the population is concentrated.

Other things being equal, the marketer prefers to operate in economies with concentrated populations. There is a great difference in population density between nations and regions of the world. On a regional basis the population densities range as follows: Oceania, 5 persons per square mile; South America, 25; Africa and the USSR, 29; North America, 33; Asia, 179; and Europe, 239.[1]

[1] All figures from *Statistical Abstract of the United States*, 1969.

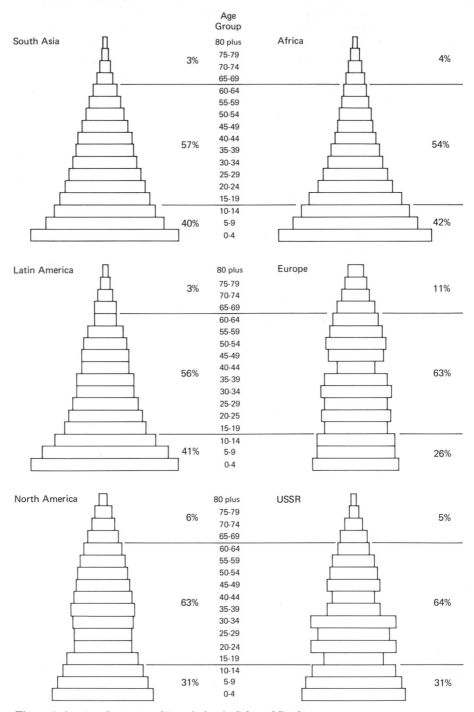

Figure 3–2   Age Structure of Population in Selected Regions

Source: *Finance and Development*, December, 1969, p. 51.

Regional figures on population density give generally good clues as to the densities of countries within the regions. However, there are some extremes around the regional average. For example, in Southeast Asia, the range is from ninety-nine persons per square mile in Burma to 949 in Taiwan. In Europe, the range is from thirty-one in Norway to 975 in the Netherlands. Nevertheless, in evaluating a particular country, the international marketer is interested in the figures not only for that country, but for a possible regional market that might be served by common production and distribution facilities.

Even when using the density figure for a given country, careful interpretation is necessary. For example, Egypt in 1967 was listed as having about eighty persons per square mile. That is very misleading, because Egypt's population is among the world's most concentrated, almost entirely located along the Nile River. The rest of the country is desert. Canada provides a similar example with a density of five but most of the population concentrated in a narrow band along the United States border and the major portion of the land mass unoccupied. In such cases, the population is very much more concentrated and reachable than the statistics indicate.

Income

Markets require not only people, but people with money. Therefore, it is necessary to examine various income measures in a country to go along with a population analysis. We will look at three important dimensions of income in foreign markets: the distribution of income among the population; the usefulness of per capita income figures; and gross national product.

Distribution of Income

One way of further understanding the size of a market is to look at the distribution of income within it. Per capita income figures are averages and are meaningful especially if most people of the country are near the average. Frequently, however, this is not the case. Among world nations, the United States has a rather equal distribution of income among her people. Even in the United States, however, marketers are very attentive to differences in income levels or classes when studying potential for their product, if the product is at all income-sensitive. Many economies have a much more skewed distribution of income than America has. Then the per capita figure is misleading because very few are at the average. Most are below it, with a certain group of wealthy people above it. Such economies are said to lack a middle class. They have a bimodal income distribution.

For the marketer, a bimodal income distribution means that he must analyze not a single economy but a dual economy within one country. The poorer group must be studied separately from the wealthy group. He might find that the two groups are not different segments of the same market, but are actually different markets. Brazil, India, and Mexico are three examples of countries with sizeable groups of affluent consumers alongside a majority of the population living in poverty. Italy is a notable example of a European country with a dual economy, that is, the impoverished south versus the affluent north. For many products, the affluent groups in these countries can be considered as strong a potential market as similar groups in North America.

Per Capita Income

The statistic most frequently used to describe a country economically is its per capita income. This figure is used as a shorthand expression not only for a country's level of economic development, but also for its degree of modernization, industrialization, and progress in health, education, and welfare. It is not surprising that international marketers usually begin with per capita income in evaluating a foreign economy. Partial justification for using this figure lies in the fact that it is commonly available and widely accepted. A more pertinent justification is that it is in fact a good indicator of the size or quality of a market. That is a question we will examine below.

There is a wide range in the per capita income figures of the world's nations. Table 3–2 shows this range, with the United States at the top with $3,600 and such nations as Burma and Malawi at the bottom with about one-sixtieth of that amount. From Table 3–2 emerges a rather grim picture of poverty in the majority of the nations of the world. Well over half the nations have a per capita income under $500, and over twenty-five under $100. If markets are people with money, it would appear that many nations are not attractive markets.

Per capita income figures are indeed valuable to the international marketer in evaluating foreign economies. Because they are relied on so extensively, however, the following words of caution are in order.

MAY NOT REFLECT PURCHASING POWER.   Per capita income comparisons are expressed in a common currency—usually United States dollars—through an exchange rate conversion. The dollar figure for a country is derived by dividing its per capita income figure in national currency by its rate of exchange against the dollar. The resulting dollar statistic for a country's per capita income is accurate only if the exchange rate reflects the relative domestic purchasing power of the two currencies. There is often reason for doubting that this is so.

The exchange rate is a price of one currency in terms of another. The supply and demand determinants of that price are the demand for and supply of foreign exchange, or a country's imports and exports. These exports and imports are only part of the total economic activity of a nation, for example, about 5 percent for the United States. Furthermore, the kinds of goods exported and imported are not usually typical of the goods exchanged within the country. Many countries export primary goods—for instance, coffee, oil, and copper—which are consumed only to a limited degree at home. They import industrial goods and capital equipment which are not produced at home. It would be surprising if the price resulting from the external exchange of such goods actually reflected the purchasing power within the country. To the degree that it does not, the per capita income figures are misleading.

The limitations of an exchange rate in indicating relative purchasing power can be illustrated further. Take the experience of the tourist. Anyone who has visited even one foreign country knows that his own currency does not have an "average" value in terms of his consumption in that country. Instead he will observe that some prices appear high, others low. In other words, the value of his own currency there depends on what he buys with it.

If one wishes to live in the same style abroad as he does at home, his expenses probably will be considerably higher than if he lives like the residents of the host country. For example, the price of white bread in Germany is over twice as much as it is in France. Of course, the Germans do not consume as much white bread as the French. This indicates another aspect of prices and purchasing power, that is, people tend to consume more of the things which are inexpensive in their country. However, the exchange rate reflects the *international* goods and services of a country, not its *domestic* consumption.

A further example is the case of devaluation. Britain devalued by 14.3 percent in November 1967. This certainly did not mean that the British market for any given product was down by 14 percent the day after the devaluation. Yet that is what is implied with the use of per capita income figures derived from an exchange rate conversion.

LACK OF COMPARABILITY.   Another limitation to the use of per capita income figures is that there is a twofold lack of comparability in the international income figures themselves. First, many goods entering into the national income totals of the developed economies are only partially in the money economy in less developed countries. A large part of an American's budget, for example, goes for food, clothing, and shelter. In many less developed nations, these items may be largely self-provided and therefore not reflected in national income totals.

Second, many goods that figure in the national income of developed nations do not figure in the national incomes of poorer countries. For example, a significant amount of United States national income is derived from such items as snow removal, heating of buildings and homes, pollution control, military and space expenditures, agricultural support programs, and winter vacations in Florida or other warmer states. Many less developed nations are in tropical areas, and their citizens are not necessarily poorer for not having any of the above-mentioned items of consumption. However, their national income figure is lower because of their absence. The author spent eight years in a rural area of Congo. Although not living entirely in the Congolese manner, he found his food, clothing, and housing expenses to be a fraction of those he incurred living in the northern part of the United States. This meant that a given income went much further for consumption of these basic items.

SALES MAY NOT BE RELATED TO PER CAPITA INCOME.   A third limitation to using per capita income figures to indicate market potential is that the sales of many goods show little correlation with per capita income. Many consumer goods sales correlate more closely with population or household figures

Table 3–2 Gross National Product per Capita (1967) and Average Annual Growth Rate (1961–1967) (Countries with populations of 1 million or more)

COUNTRY	GNP PER CAPITA (US DOLLARS)	GROWTH RATE (PER-CENT)	COUNTRY	GNP PER CAPITA (US DOLLARS)	GROWTH RATE (PER-CENT)
United States	3,670	3.3	Portugal	420	5.1
Sweden	2,500	3.8	Costa Rica	410	1.7
Canada	2,380	3.3	Mongolia†	410	—
Switzerland	2,310	2.5	Nicaragua	360	4.1
Australia	1,970	2.7	Peru	350	2.9
Denmark	1,950	3.8	Saudi Arabia	350	8.4
France	1,950	3.8	Cuba†	330	−0.8
New Zealand	1,890	1.8	Albania†	320	2.8
Norway	1,860	4.4	Guatemala	310	1.9
West Germany	1,750	2.8	Colombia	300	1.5
Belgium	1,740	3.9	Malaysia	290	2.7
United Kingdom	1,700	2.2	Turkey	290	3.1
Finland	1,660	3.6	Iran	280	4.8
Netherlands	1,520	3.2	El Salvador	270	2.4
East Germany†	1,300	3.8	Dominican Republic	260	−0.7
Austria	1,210	3.5	Algeria	250	−3.5
Puerto Rico	1,210	6.2	Brazil	250	1.2
Israel	1,200	4.2	Republic of China	250	6.7
Italy	1,120	4.5	Jordan	250	5.8
Czechoslovakia†	1,110	3.1	Honduras	240	1.9
Japan	1,000	9.3	Iraq	230	1.9
USSR†	970	5.2	Ivory Coast	230	5.4
Ireland	910	3.1	North Korea	230	—
Hungary†	900	5.3	Southern Rhodesia	230	0.2
Venezuela	880	1.1	Paraguay	220	1.5
Argentina	800	1.3	Ecuador	210	1.0
Trinidad and Tobago	790	4.3	Tunisia	210	1.4
Poland†	780	5.2	Ghana	200	−0.1
Libya	720	21.4	Papua and		
Romania†	720	8.1	New Guinea	200	3.0
Greece	700	6.7	Angola	190	2.1
Bulgaria†	690	6.8	Liberia	190	1.5
Spain	680	6.9	Morocco	190	0.3
Hong Kong	620	7.9	Senegal	190	−0.1
Singapore	600	2.9	Mozambique	180	3.3
South Africa			Philippines	180	0.8
(incl. South			Syria	180	3.9
West Africa)	590	3.9	Zambia	180	1.6
Panama	550	4.8	Bolivia	170	3.4
Uruguay	550	−1.1	Ceylon	160	1.3
Yugoslavia	530	5.4	Republic of Korea	160	4.8
Lebanon	520	2.3	United Arab		
Mexico	490	2.8	Republic	160	2.7
Chile	470	2.3	Sierra Leone	140	1.3
Jamaica	460	1.7	Cambodia	130	1.1

Table 3–2   (Continued)

COUNTRY	GNP PER CAPITA (US DOLLARS)	GROWTH RATE (PER-CENT)	COUNTRY	GNP PER CAPITA (US DOLLARS)	GROWTH RATE (PER-CENT)
Cameroon	130	0.6	Pakistan	90	2.9
Mauritania	130	6.9	Sudan	90	0.2
Southern Yemen	130	−1.1	Dahomey	80	0.2
Thailand	130	3.9	Mali	80	0.7
Central African			Nigeria	80	1.1
Republic	120	−1.0	Tanzania	80	1.9
Kenya	120	1.1	Afghanistan	70	−0.5
Republic of			Burma	70	0.6
Vietnam	120	1.8	Chad	70	−0.6
Indonesia	100	0.6	Haiti	70	−3.3
Malagasy Republic	100	−0.5	Nepal	70	0.1
Togo	100	0.5	Niger	70	0.1
Uganda	100	1.2	Yemen*	70	1.8
North Vietnam†	100	—	Ethiopia	60	2.7
Mainland China†	90	—	Malawi	60	3.2
Congo			Rwanda*	60	1.7
(Dem. Rep. of)	90	−0.5	Burundi	50	−0.1
Guinea	90	2.5	Somalia*	50	−1.6
India	90	0.9	Upper Volta	50	−0.6
Laos*	90	−0.1			

Note: In view of the usual errors inherent in this type of data and to avoid a misleading impression of accuracy, the figures for GNP per capita have been rounded to the nearest $10.

* Estimates of GNP per capita and its growth rate are tentative.

† Estimates of GNP per capita and its growth rate have a wide margin of error mainly because of the problems in deriving the GNP at factor cost from net material product and in converting the GNP estimate into U.S. dollars.

Source: *World Bank Atlas*, 1969.

than with per capita income. Some examples might be Coca Cola, ball-point pens, bicycles, sewing machines, and transistor radios. Industrial goods and capital equipment sales generally correlate better with the industrial structure or total national income than with per capita income. For example, the airport and office buildings in Kinshasa, Congo, are equipped in much the same way similar places in New York City are. Extractive or manufacturing industries tend to use similar equipment wherever they are located. Where governments run health and education programs, per capita income is not necessarily a useful guide to the national potential in goods supplied to the health and education industries.

UNEVEN INCOME DISTRIBUTION.   Finally, per capita figures are less meaningful if there is great unevenness of income distribution in the country. This has already been discussed above under income distribution.

Gross National Product

Another useful way to evaluate foreign markets is to compare their gross national products, or GNPs. As already discussed, for certain goods, total GNP is a better indicator of market potential than is per capita income. Where this is true, a ranking of countries by GNP is a useful starting point. Table 3–3 gives a listing of the thirty economies with a GNP of $10 billion or more in 1968. (Mainland China is omitted because of inadequate data.) This table gives another view of the poverty in the world, or the smallness of most economies. If only thirty nations can qualify for this list, that means that over 100 nations have a GNP of less than $10 billion.

Table 3–3   Countries With Gross National Product Over $10 Billion

COUNTRY	1968 GNP ($ BILLIONS)	COUNTRY	1968 GNP ($ BILLIONS)
1. United States	$861	16. Spain	$25
2. USSR	396	17. Czechoslovakia	23
3. Japan	142	18. Brazil	22
4. West Germany	132	19. Belgium	21
5. France	126	20. Romania	20
6. United Kingdom	102	21. Switzerland	17
7. Italy	75	22. Argentina	15
8. Canada	62	23. South Africa	14
9. India	43	24. Hungary	14
10. Poland	39	25. Pakistan	13
11. East Germany	33	26. Denmark	12
12. Mexico	27	27. Turkey	12
13. Australia	27	28. Indonesia	11
14. Sweden	26	29. Austria	11
15. Netherlands	25	30. Philippines	10

Source: *Business International*, December 5, 1969, p. 388, and December 12, 1969, p. 396.

It is helpful to contrast the GNP approach to measuring market potential with the per capita income approach. For example, Kuwait's per capita income was about $3,500 in 1968 and India's about $73. Judging by this, Kuwait is about fifty times as attractive as India. However, India's 1968 GNP was twenty-five times as great as Kuwait's and its population 1,000 times as large. This is obviously an extreme example, but it illustrates the need for proper comparisons.

At this point, we should balance our criticism of the per capita income approach. For those goods that do require high consumer incomes, it may be true that a small country like Belgium (about 10 million people) is a better market than India, even though Belgium's GNP is less than half that of India. For example, in 1968 there were four times as many passenger cars in use in Belgium as in India. Belgium's edge in TV sets was very much greater. On the other hand, in trucks, buses, and steel, India had at least 50 percent greater consumption than Belgium as well as twice as many radios. Thus the relevant income figure for evaluating a market will depend largely on the product.

NATURE OF THE ECONOMY

We have just considered varied indicators of the economic size and market potential of foreign economies and how they might be compared. There are other equally important characteristics of an economy that affect a marketing manager's program. Some of these are socio-cultural or political and will be discussed in following chapters. Here we will examine primarily other economic dimensions of nations as they relate to the task of international marketing management. The principal topics covered include the nation's physical endowment, the nature of its economic activity, its infrastructure, and its degree of urbanization.

The Nation's Physical Endowment

Natural Resources

A nation's natural resources include its actual and potential forms of wealth supplied by nature—for example, minerals and waterpower—as well as its land area, topography, and climate. The international marketer needs to understand the economic geography of a nation in relation to his marketing task there. Land area as such is not very important, except where it figures in population density and potential distribution problems. However, knowledge of local natural resources can be important to the international marketer in evaluating a country. Natural resources may provide raw materials for the local production of the international company. Even when a firm is exporting into a country, it might benefit from knowing the local resource endowment.

Merck built a compounding plant in India. The company received the Indian government's permission to ship key ingredients from the United States. This permission was later withdrawn, and Merck had to locate a new raw material source in India to keep the plant operating. Fortunately, the needed raw materials were eventually found in the country.

Another reason for exploring the country's resource base is to better evaluate its future economic prospects. Some countries that today have relatively weak markets might develop more rapidly than others because of their richer resource endowment. New technologies or discoveries can rapidly change a nation's economic prospects. Oil changed the outlook for Libya and Nigeria, for example. In Australia, it was the discovery of other minerals that started a boom in the late 1960s.

By the same token, technological change can also impoverish an economy that is depending largely on just one export commodity. For example, the development of rayon, nylon, and synthetic rubber did great damage to the countries exporting silk and natural rubber. What would be the impact on

Brazil if a good synthetic coffee were developed? A glance through the maps in any good atlas will give a picture of how the various natural resources are distributed among the nations and regions of the world. (See, for example, the *Oxford Economic Atlas of the World*.) Climate and the animal, vegetable, and mineral resources of regions are noted in an atlas. A nation's human resources are identified in other ways.

Topography

Topography refers to the surface features of the land, including rivers, lakes, forests, deserts, and mountains. These are the features that make a country different and interesting for the tourist. For the international marketer, they have more practical significance. The immediate significance of a nation's topography to him lies in its indication of possible physical distribution problems. Flat country generally means easy transportaton by road or rail. Mountains are always a barrier that raises transportation costs.

Mountains also may divide a nation into two or more distinct markets. For example, in many South American nations, the Andes Mountains divide the country into entirely separate areas. Although these areas are united politically, the marketer will often find that culturally and economically they are separate markets. Deserts and tropical forests are additional barriers to transportation and separaters of markets. When the international marketer analyzes a national or regional market, he must examine maps showing the topography, population, and transportation situation in order to anticipate marketing and logistical problems. Ordinary political outline maps are not useful for this purpose.

Navigable rivers are desirable in a country because they usually enable economical transportation. The Mississippi and St. Lawrence Seaway are North American examples. In Europe, river and canal transportation are more important than anywhere else in the world. Even landlocked Switzerland can ship by river barge to Atlantic ports. The accessibility of a market will also be determined by its ports and harbors, that is, its contact with sea transportation.

Landlocked countries such as Bolivia, Zambia, and Rhodesia are more costly to reach than neighboring countries with seaports. These countries have transportation problems other than cost if there are political differences with the neighbors whose seaports and railroads they must use. Both Rhodesia and Zambia are cases in point. Finally, the existence of lakes, seashore, rivers, and mountains can indicate particular marketing opportunities. Suppliers to the tourist, recreation, and sporting industries will find markets in countries endowed with places for boating, skiing, and similar recreational activities.

Climate

Climate is another important dimension of a nation's physical endowment. Climate includes not only the temperature range, but also wind, rain, snow, and dryness and humidity. The United States is a very large country and thus has great climatic variation within its borders. Most nations are smaller and have more uniform climatic patterns. Climate is an important determinant of the firm's product offerings. An obvious example is the heater or air conditioner in an automobile. However, it also affects a whole range of consumer goods from foods to clothing, and from housing to recreational supplies. Even medical needs in the tropics are different from those in temperate zones.

Extremes of climate may dictate modifications in product, packaging, or distribution requirements. For example, electrical equipment and many consumer packaged goods need special protection in hot, humid climates. There is great international variation on this score; for example, India has thirteen inches of rainfall in the month of July, Guinea has fifty-one inches, New York City has four inches. By contrast, the American military in Vietnam found that their transport vehicles required extra attention because of the very dry, dusty conditions in some parts of Vietnam at certain times of the year.

Climate has another, more subtle effect on the nature of the market. Although there is insufficient scientific evidence as to the nature of the climatic impact, there are a number of observable differences between tropical-country markets in general and temperate-zone countries in general. For example, almost all of the less developed countries are tropical or subtropical. Tropical countries generally have low per capita incomes and a high percentage of the population engaged in agriculture. Gunnar Myrdal's gloomy conclusions as to Asia's prospects for economic development[2] were based in part on his evaluation of the adverse effects of climate. The marketing manager needs to be aware of climate to the extent that it affects people as consumers or workers.

The Nature of Economic Activity

Rostow's View

The economist Walt Rostow gives a useful description of foreign economies in his famous stages of economic growth.[3] According to Rostow, all the nations of the world are in or passing through one of the following levels of economic development: (1) the traditional society; (2) the preconditons for take-off; (3) the take-off; (4) the drive to maturity; (5) the age of high mass consumption. Each level or stage represents a different type of economy, that is, differing production and marketing systems. The marketing opportunities and problems encountered by the international firm would vary according to the host country's stage of economic growth.

Although Rostow's classification was developed from the viewpoint of the economist, a similar type of analysis may be useful to the international marketer who sells in a large number of world markets. In Chapter 7 we give some suggestions as to how the international marketer might develop a classification system to meet his own needs. Here we will look at various specific aspects within foreign economies that affect the marketing task.

[2] Gunnar Myrdal, *Asian Drama* (New York: The Twentieth Century Fund, 1968).
[3] W. W. Rostow, *The Stages of Economic Growth* (New York: Cambridge University Press, 1960).

Farm or Factory?

One way to determine the kind of market a country offers is to look at the origin of its national product. Is the economy agricultural or industrial? What is the nature of its agricultural, manufacturing, and service or tertiary industries? Such a breakdown and analysis are especially useful to industrial marketers. However, even consumer-goods marketers will find that consumer demands and mentality are related to the nature of the economic activities in the country. One does not have to believe in Marx's economic determinism to recognize such influences. For example, there are invariably differences in the consumption patterns of the farmer compared with those of a factory worker, especially outside the United States.

Table 3–4   Economic Origin of Domestic Product (Percent)

	AGRICULTURE	INDUSTRIAL ACTIVITY*
United States	3%	32%
Europe		
United Kingdom	3	39
Germany—West	4	43
Netherlands	7	41
France	7	38
Norway	7	30
Italy	13	32
Greece	24	19
Latin America		
Argentina	15	37
Mexico	16	33
Bolivia	22	29
Guatemala	29	16
Brazil	30	27
Colombia	32	22
Ecuador	35	18
South East Asia		
Japan	12	29
Taiwan	26	23
Thailand	31	16
Philippines	33	20
Burma	34	10
Pakistan	47	12
India	49	16
Africa		
Insufficient data, though primarily agricultural.		

* Generally includes mining, manufacturing, and energy.

Source: *Statistical Abstract of the United States*, 1970.

Table 3–4 shows some of the international variations in the patterns of economic activity. In the Western European countries agriculture generally accounts for well under one-tenth of domestic product, whereas industrial activity (primarily manufacturing) accounts for over one-third. In Latin America, agriculture generally accounts for almost one-third of domestic product whereas industrial activity accounts for about one-fourth. Argentina and Mexico are the exceptions. Asia, excluding Japan, shows the extreme situation; agriculture accounts for from one-third to one-half of domestic product, whereas industry accounts for only about one-sixth. Figures for Africa would resemble those for Asia if data were available. These statistics succeed in showing significant differences between the economies of the world but actually they understate the real situation. In many nations, especially the poorer ones, agriculture is one of the least productive sectors of the economy. This means that the proportion of the population engaged in agriculture is often much higher than agriculture's percent of domestic product.

Input-Output Tables

Although it is useful to analyze an economy in terms of its agricultural-industrial sectors, frequently it is desirable to make a more detailed examination. Such sources as the *United Nations Statistical Yearbook* show national production in a wide range of products and commodities. Industrial marketers particularly are concerned about the industrial structure of an economy. A firm that sells to particular industries must know which economies contain those industries as well as the industries' size. Even beyond this, the firm would like to know the technology used in its client industries. For example, many nations have textile industries but not all use the same combinations of materials, labor, and equipment. The economist would say they do not all have the same production function.

If the firm could construct input-output tables for its industry for all relevant markets it would gain a better idea of how its supplies or equipment fit in with the industrial structure in given markets. Firms use input-output tables more and more in American marketing. A few firms are using them in international marketing also. Although the construction of such tables, even for one industry, can be difficult, it is a technique that the international marketer should be aware of. As our data and analytical skills improve, economic analysis through input-output tables will be less difficult and more available.[4]

Infrastructure

A manufacturing firm in the United States generally considers itself to perform two major kinds of activities in relation to its goods: production and marketing. Domestic management is not required to consider the extent to which its operations depend on supporting facilities and services outside the firm. These external facilities and services collectively are called the infrastructure of an economy. They include paved roads, railroads, energy supplies,

---

[4] Input-output tables give a detailed picture of the industrial structure of an economy, showing the interconnections between the various sectors. The input-output matrix shows what each industry bought from every other industry in a given year. For a discussion of input-output analysis, see Wassily Leontief, *Input-Output Economics* (New York: Oxford University Press, 1966).

and other communication and transport services. The commercial and financial infrastructure includes such things as advertising agencies and media, distributive organizations, marketing research companies, and credit and banking facilities. The more adequate the quantity and quality of all of these services in a country, the better the firm can perform its own production and marketing tasks there. Where these facilities and services are not adequate, the firm must adapt its operations, or perhaps avoid the market altogether.

Infrastructure is a critical variable in the analysis of a foreign economy. When considering the potential profitability of operations in a given country, the international marketer must evaluate the infrastructure constraints as well as the market potential for his products. As might be expected, there is great international variation in the quality of infrastructure available. Generally, the higher the level of economic development, the better the infrastructure. Table 3–5 gives some indication of the variation in transportation and energy services available. The United States figures are given as a basis for comparison. Although to yield the most accurate information the figures should be related to population size and land area, even the absolute figures are revealing. (Energy consumption is on a per capita basis.)

Transportation

The importance of transportation to business operations needs no elaboration. In Table 3–5 transportation facilities are indicated by rail-freight shipments, commercial vehicles in use, and international shipping by sea. Air-freight shipments, another possible indicator, are not given. Internal physical distribution possibilities are best indicated here by rail shipments and commercial vehicles in use. A number of interesting international comparisons can be made on the basis of both statistics.

For example, West Germany and Nigeria are reasonably similar in population size but Nigeria is much larger in land area. However, West Germany has twenty-eight times as much rail freight shipped and over thirty times as many commercial vehicles as Nigeria. Japan and Pakistan also are similar in population size, but Pakistan is larger in land area. Nevertheless, Japan has over five times the volume of rail freight shipped and ninety times as many commercial vehicles as Pakistan. India has almost three times the United States population in about one-third the land area. Even so, the United States has ten times as much rail freight shipped and over thirty times as many commercial vehicles as India. The internal logistics possibilites would vary greatly between these nations.

Although we are discussing the nature of the foreign domestic economy, a consideration of its international shipping is still useful (see Table 3–5, third column). Most foreign operations of an international company are not entirely self-contained within one country. Rather, they are linked on the supply and/or demand side to other markets of the firm. Thus it is important in planning the firm's global logistics to know how each of the firm's markets might relate to the others. One good indicator of this is the volume and frequency of international shipments by sea.

Table 3–5   Transportation and Energy Consumption*

	RAILWAYS NET TON-KILOMETERS (MILLIONS)	COMMER-CIAL VEHICLES (THOU-SANDS IN USE)	INTERNA-TIONAL SHIPPING BY SEA (VESSELS ENTERED, BY 1,000 TONS)	ENERGY PER CAPITA (KG COAL EQUIV.)
United States	1,087,000	16,300	172,700	10,300
Western Europe				
France	63,000	2,500	86,300	3,300
West Germany	59,000	900	79,500	4,500
Italy	17,200	800	106,900	2,220
Spain	8,200	600	42,700	1,300
Sweden	14,800	150	19,800	5,400
United Kingdom	24,000	1,700	122,700	5,000
Latin America				
Argentina	13,000	650	11,000	1,400
Brazil	22,000	950	67,600	450
Colombia	1,100	120	10,700	n.a.
Guatemala	75	21	3,760	240
Mexico	20,400	470	3,070	1,060
Peru	625	110	26,600	630
South East Asia				
India	101,000	460	17,330	184
Japan	60,000	7,200	160,000	2,520
Pakistan	7,600	67	8,600	96
Philippines	117	170	12,400	250
Taiwan	2,700	33	15,300	820
Thailand	2,100	155	7,200	200
Africa				
Congo	2,000	23	2,620	85
Ghana	272	21	5,300	130
Nigeria	1,800	30	4,800	30
Sudan	2,400	19	2,260	90
Tanzania	n.a.	12	5,970	53
U.A.R. (Egypt)	3,000	27	4,200	300

* Some of the numbers have been rounded in order to facilitate comparison.

Source: *United Nations Statistical Yearbook*, 1969.

Energy

The statistics on energy consumption per capita serve both as a guide to market potential and as a guide to the adequacy of the local infrastructure. Marketers of electrical machinery and equipment and consumer durables are concerned about the extent of electrification throughout the market. In countries with low figures for energy consumption, the marketer will find that power is available only in the cities and not in the villages or countryside where most of the population may live. Energy consumption is also closely related to the overall industrialization of an economy and thus is correlated to the market for industrial goods there. Finally, energy consumption per capita is probably the best single indicator as to the adequacy of a country's overall infrastructure. Table 3–5, fourth column, gives an idea of the international differences in energy consumption.

Communications

In addition to being able to move its goods a firm must be able to communicate with its various audiences, especially workers, suppliers, and customers. Communication with those outside the firm will depend on the communications infrastructure of the country. Intracompany communications between subsidiaries or with headquarters will be equally dependent on local facilities. Table 3–6 shows the distribution and availability of several communications media in the major regions of the world. Again, United States figures are given as a basis for comparison. Newspaper and movie statistics are on a per capita basis, but telephone and radio usage are given in absolute figures for each country. Movie attendance is included because movie theaters are an important advertising medium in many countries.

In general, international variations in communications infrastructure follow variations in level of economic development as indicated by per capita income. However, many nations have a communications infrastructure either much stronger or much weaker than per capita income would suggest. In Asia, for example, Japan is obviously outstanding in all dimensions—indeed surpasses several European countries—even on a per capita basis. Japan has a higher per capita consumption of newspapers, telephones, and radios than France. Taiwan is another country with much stronger communications facilities than most of its Asian neighbors. Argentina is well ahead of its Latin American neighbors, and Ghana is relatively strong among black African nations.

A more complete and detailed listing of countries in the manner of Table 3–6 would benefit the international marketing manager in two ways. First, it would help him to analyze the communication and promotional possibilities in different foreign markets. Second, it would help him locate marketing subsidiaries or regional headquarters offices where there are good internal and international communication facilities. Such a study would, of course, be more detailed than Table 3–6, covering also mail service, telex, and air transportation. Nevertheless, the table is indicative of the international variablity in communications infrastructure.

Commercial Infrastructure

Equally important to the firm as the transportation, communication, and energy capabilities of a nation is its commercial infrastructure. By this is meant the availability and quality of such supporting services as banks and financial institutions, advertising agencies, distribution channels, and marketing research organizations. American firms accustomed to strong supporting services in the United States will often find great differences in foreign markets. Wherever the commercial infrastructure is weak, or even very different from that in the

Table 3–6   Communications

	NEWSPAPERS (COPIES/ 1,000 POP.)	TELEPHONES (NUMBER IN USE)	RADIOS (NUMBER IN USE)	MOVIES PER CAPITA ANNUAL ATTENDANCE
United States	312	99,000	263,000	12
Western Europe				
France	245	6,600	6,600	5
Germany	332	9,600	18,800	5
Italy	113	6,500	11,700	12
Spain	153	3,000	3,400	13
Sweden	501	3,600	4,000	7
United Kingdom	488	11,300	12,100	5
Latin America				
Argentina	148	1,500	6,000	7
Brazil	33	1,400	5,600	4
Colombia	52	500	2,200	4
Guatemala	31	32	200	2
Mexico	116	928	4,800	9
Peru	47	143	1,800	6
Southeast Asia				
India	13	927	6,500	4
Japan	465	16,000	22,500	4
Pakistan	18	146	1,200	1
Philippines	27	188	1,200	1
Taiwan	64	192	1,400	6
Thailand	22	86	2,800	n.a.
Africa				
Congo	n.a.	21	60	1
Ghana	37	36	700	2
Nigeria	7	75	1,300	n.a.
Sudan	5	38	180	1
Tanzania	3	25	135	1
U.A.R. (Egypt)	n.a.	335	4,300	2

Source: *United Nations Statistical Yearbook*, 1967.

firm's domestic market, the firm must make adjustments in its operations that will affect costs and effectiveness.

No table on commercial infrastructure is available and comparable data are more difficult to find in this area. Nevertheless, a firm can get reasonably good information on the commercial infrastructure of a country. The best sources are commercial attachés and domestic service organizations with foreign operations, for example, banks, accounting firms, and advertising agencies.

Urbanization

One of the most significant characteristics of an economy is the extent to which it is urbanized. There are numerous cultural and economic differences between people living in cities and those living in villages or rural areas. In the United States, these differences are reflected in the vocabulary and attitudes of the people. For example, "urbane" and "urbanity" derive from "urban" and signify a sophistication of outlook. By contrast, the words "peasant" and "farmer" are often used to describe not just a vocation but a way of life and thought. Modern transportation and communication have greatly reduced the differences between urban and rural populations in the United States, but in most of the world the urban-rural differences persist. Because these differences are important determinants of consumer behavior, the international marketer needs to be aware of the situation particular to each of his markets.

Farm versus City

There are several reasons for the contrasting behavior of urban and rural populations. Urbanites tend to be dependent for all their material needs whereas rural dwellers often supply much of their food, clothing, and shelter through their own efforts. The city dweller must meet his needs through money payments to others. Cities are centers of industry and commerce. Because the city dweller deals constantly in money within a commercial-industrial framework, he becomes a more sophisticated consumer than the rural dweller, who often is unaware of the technical and economic complexities of modern society.

Cities are the places in an economy where communications media are most developed and effective; information contributes to the city dweller's sophistication. Cities also offer more possibilities for formal and informal education which affect the literacy, skills, and attitudes of their inhabitants. Urbanites therefore tend to be less conservative and tradition-oriented than rural dwellers. There is a stronger demonstration effect of new products and consumption patterns in urban areas, which leads to stronger markets there. All in all, there are many attitudinal and behavioral differences that are related to the urban-rural dichotomy in a given economy.

The international marketer must study carefully the relation of urbanization to the consumption and use of his products. For some products in some countries, he will find urban and rural populations to be distinct segments; in other cases, there will be no difference; in yet others, he may decide that urban areas provide the only feasible market. In the latter situation, there could be several reasons favoring the urban markets: income and consumption patterns, distribution facilities, or communications possibilities.

Table 3–7 shows the percent urban population for major world regions and forty leading nations. The United States figure is again given as a basis for comparison. The figures are not directly comparable as the data are based on different definitions; nevertheless, they are reasonable approximations. The United States has a very large land area with a low population density: Because 70 percent of the population is urban, however, distribution and communication are relatively easy and efficient. As can be seen from Table 3–7, very few countries are as urbanized as the United States. Therefore, very few offer the same kind of convenient, sophisticated markets for consumer goods.

African and Asian nations are particularly lacking in urbanization, with a few exceptions such as South Africa, Japan, and Taiwan. Combined with low incomes in these regions, the lack of urbanization makes these markets unat-

Table 3–7 Urbanization—Selected Countries

COUNTRY	% URBAN	COUNTRY	% URBAN
United States	70	*Europe*	
		Denmark	46
Africa		France	63
Algeria	39	East Germany	73
Congo (Kinshasa)	22	Greece	55
Egypt	41	Iceland	49
Ethiopia	12	Netherlands	78
Ghana	23	Norway	41
Kenya	8	Portugal	22
Nigeria	16	Sweden	77
South Africa	47	Swizerland	51
Tunisia	40	USSR	56
Zambia	20	United Kingdom	79
Asia		*Latin America*	
Cambodia	10	Argentina	75
Ceylon	19	Brazil	46
India	18	Chile	68
Indonesia	15	Colombia	52
Iran	39	Guatemala	34
Japan	68	Mexico	58
Korea	34	Panama	46
Nepal	4	Peru	46
Pakistan	13	Venezuela	67
Turkey	35		
		Australia	83

Source: *United Nations Demographic Yearbook*, 1968, 1969.

tractive to many consumer-goods marketers. These poor markets are not only small, they are also difficult to reach when most of the population is rural. Thus the degree of urbanization is an indicator of both the size of the market and the nature of the marketing task. Though this kind of data is especially significant for consumer-goods marketers, even industrial-goods firms will find a correlation between their market potential and urbanization. Because urbanization is a global trend, the marketer will need up-to-date figures.

Other Characteristics of Foreign Economies

Our survey of foreign economies has been introductory rather than exhaustive in nature. However, it should be helpful in giving the market analyst a feel for the relevant dimensions of national economies. Before concluding this chapter, we look briefly at a few other characteristics of foreign economies that can be important in decision making on operations there.

Tax Structure

No government can run without taxes. However, the impact of taxes on business operations varies from country to country. For example, corporation income tax rates will affect the firm's choice of location for foreign investment. Sales and excise taxes will affect the firm's prices. Since the incidence of such taxes varies, the firm will have a somewhat different rating or valuation for each function as related to each foreign market.

The following figures give some indication of the international differences in tax structure. Direct taxes on households account for 13 percent of total taxes in France, 35 percent in the United States, and over 44 percent in Sweden. Direct taxes on corporations account for 3 percent of total taxes in Denmark, 16 percent in the United States, and over 21 percent in Japan. Indirect taxes account for 30 percent of total taxes in the Netherlands, 31 percent in the United States, and over 48 percent in Denmark. These are comparisons of developed countries. The less developed countries present a generally different picture. The poorer countries rely about twice as heavily on direct corporate taxes for revenue as the industrialized countries. Conversely, they get a much smaller part of their revenue from personal income taxes. The kind of operation appropriate for a country will be determined in part by the country's tax structure.

Inflation

Each country has its own monetary system and an independent monetary policy. The result is differing kinds of financial environment and differing rates of inflation among nations. High rates of inflation characterize many less developed countries and complicate cost control and pricing. Differential rates of inflation also influence how the firm moves funds and goods among its various markets. The marketing implications of inflation are discussed in greater detail in Chapter 14.

Role of Government

The business environment and the nature of business operations in an economy are very dependent on the role government plays in that economy, as one can see by studying India and Egypt. If government has strong socialist leanings, it may restrict the sectors of the economy where private and foreign companies may be engaged. Where international companies are allowed to operate, governments will have a range of regulations restricting their operations. These regulations may affect the product, service, advertising, pricing, or any other marketing activities of the firm. Similar regulations restrict domestic operations also, but each country has its own pattern of regulation, so the international marketer must be informed and flexible.

In a number of countries, the international companies may have the government as a partner in a joint venture. This is especially true in less developed countries that want local partnership but lack a strong private sector to provide the capital. Such a partnership provides special constraints of its own on the international company. The role of government will be discussed in more detail in Chapter 5.

Foreign Investment in the Economy

When contemplating operations in a foreign economy, the international marketer will be interested to know what other international firms are operating there, whether they are just selling in the market or producing there too. This information will give useful clues as to the government's attitude toward foreign companies. It will also help to determine something about the competitive environment the firm will encounter.

That a country has few or no international companies operating in it could indicate a good opportunity for one to enter—or it could indicate that the environment is inhospitable or that the market is unprofitable for any but national companies. Conversely, an economy that has many interenational companies operating in it indicates an open market but one that may be very competitive for any newcomer. A distinction must be made, of course, between extractive industries and manufacturing or marketing subsidiaries. Extractive industries go into a country for raw material supply rather than for marketing reasons.

In Table 3–8, we see the number of United States companies with investments in selected foreign markets. The figures are for 1968. Canada is given as a basis for comparison. The companies include extractive and service

Table 3–8 Number of American Companies with Investment in Selected Foreign Markets 1968

COUNTRY	NUMBER OF FIRMS (APPROX.) 1968	COUNTRY	NUMBER OF FIRMS (APPROX.) 1968
Canada	1330	*Western Europe*	
		France	611
Africa		West Germany	594
Algeria	24	Italy	527
Congo (Kinshasa)	4	Netherlands	434
Egypt	35	Norway	65
Ethiopia	14	Spain	241
Ghana	13	Sweden	199
Kenya	54	Switzerland	437
Nigeria	49	United Kingdom	999
South Africa	214		
Tunisia	20	*Latin America*	
Zambia	12	Argentina	199
		Bolivia	22
Asia		Brazil	363
Afghanistan	6	Chile	96
Burma	12	Colombia	193
Ceylon	15	Ecuador	80
India	205	Guatemala	60
Indonesia	29	Mexico	650
Japan	555	Peru	158
Pakistan	78	Venezuela	313
Philippines	197		
Taiwan	58	*Australia*	509
Thailand	68		

Source: *Directory of American Firms Operating in Foreign Countries*, 7th ed. (New York: World Trade Academy Press, 1969).

industries as well as manufacturing. Though the data do not reveal the size of the investment in each country, they do indicate how American firms in general evaluated the different markets. After Canada with more than 1,300 companies, Western Europe and Latin America were the favorite markets of United States firms. Africa was very low in terms of American investment except for South Africa. This reflects not only the limited size of the markets but also the fact that Africa has been closely related to Europe, both economically and politically. The Asian nations also counted few American companies, except for Japan, the Philippines, and India.

The reader can go through Table 3–8 and evaluate for himself the role of geography, politics, and economics in determining the pattern of American foreign investment. The international marketer must be alert for trends. For example, in some Latin American nations with strong "anti-Yanqui" sentiments the marketer could see a leveling off, or even a decrease, in United States investment. Cuba is an extreme example. The international marketer could also determine growing economies with relatively stable political environments and an absence of strong anti-United States feeling. Australia, Japan, and Taiwan are examples of such improved or continually favorable investment climates. Such a table needs to be kept up to date, because changes in investment climate can occur rapidly.

Questions

3.1   Which foreign economies would the international marketer be interested in investigating?

3.2   How can the international marketer get an idea of the size and market potential of foreign economies?

3.3   For what kinds of products might population figures be a good indicator of market potential?

3.4   What is the significance of a nation's population growth rate for the international marketer?

3.5   What is the interest of the international marketer in the age distribution of foreign market populations?

3.6   What is the marketing significance of the population density figures for foreign markets? Why is caution needed in using such figures?

3.7   Discuss the influence of the dual economy phenomenon for the international marketer.

3.8   What are the uses and limitations of per capita income figures in evaluating foreign markets?

3.9   For what kinds of products might the total GNP of a nation be a reasonably good guide to market potential?

3.10 Why does the international marketer study the natural resource base of foreign markets?

3.11 What can a study of topography tell the international marketer about his foreign markets?

3.12 Discuss the role of climate in international market analysis.

3.13 "The marketing opportunities and problems encountered by the international firm vary according to the host country's level of economic development." Discuss.

3.14 How could the international marketer use input-output tables on foreign markets?

3.15 Discuss a nation's infrastructure as a constraint on marketing there. Discuss the commercial infrastructure also.

3.16 How does the degree of urbanization in a country affect the firm's marketing there?

3.17 Discuss briefly the following characteristics of foreign economies and their impact on international marketing: (a) inflation, (b) role of government in the economy, (c) amount of foreign investment.

Further Readings

Books:

Bennett, Peter D., ed., *Marketing and Economic Development* (Chicago: American Marketing Association, 1965), pp. 49–183.

Boesch, Hans, *A Geography of World Economy* (Princeton, N.J.: Van Nostrand, 1964).

Coale, Ansley J., and Edgar M. Hoover, *Population Growth and Economic Development in Low Income Countries* (Princeton, N.J.: Princeton University Press, 1958).

Cottrell, William Frederich, *Energy and Society: The Relation between Energy, Social Change and Economic Development* (New York: McGraw-Hill Book Co., 1955).

Dewhurst, J. Frederic, et al., *Europe's Needs and Resources* (New York: The Twentieth Century Fund, 1961).

Leontief, Wassily, *Input-Output Economics* (New York: Oxford University Press, 1966).

Moyer, Reed, *Marketing in Economic Development* (East Lansing, Mich.: Michigan State University Press, 1965).

Myrdal, Gunnar, *Asian Drama* (New York: The Twentieth Century Fund, 1968).

Rostow, W. W., *The Stages of Economic Growth* (Cambridge, Mass.: Cambridge University Press, 1960).

Data Sources:

Commercial Atlas and Marketing Guide (New York: Rand McNally and Co., 1970).

Oxford Economic Atlas of the World.

Statistical Abstract of the United States (annual).

United Nations, *United Nations Demographic Yearbook* (annual).

United Nations, *United Nations Statistical Yearbook* (annual).

4

CULTURAL ENVIRONMENT:
THE PEOPLE OF THE WORLD

Marketing has always been recognized as an economic activity involving the exchange of goods and services. However, it is only in recent years that socio-cultural influences have been identified as critical determinants of marketing behavior. In other words, marketing is a cultural as well as economic phenomenon. Because our understanding of marketing and our approach to it tend to be culture-bound, we must acquire a knowledge and appreciation of diverse cultural environments in order to achieve successful international marketing. We must, so to speak, remove our culturally-tinted glasses to study foreign markets.

Two major developments since World War II in the study and management of marketing have been the use of quantitative methods of analysis and the application of behavioral-science findings and approaches. The growing use of anthropology, sociology, and psychology in marketing analysis is explicit recognition of the noneconomic bases of marketing behavior. We now know that it is not enough to say that consumption is a function of income. Consumption is a function of many other cultural influences as well. Furthermore, only noneconomic factors can explain the different patterns of consumption of two individuals with identical incomes—or, by analogy, of two different countries with similar per capita incomes.

Table 4–1 illustrates the importance of nonincome factors in determining consumption patterns. It shows household appliance ownership in five neighboring Western European countries with similar levels of per capita income. The variations in consumption are obviously not attributable to differences in income. They can be explained only by differences in culture or patterns of living among the various nations. The differences in consumption behavior are striking. On almost every item, the degree of saturation in the highest country is at least 50 percent greater than in the lowest country. (The high and low consumption countries for each item are indicated in boldface type.) The same source shows that similar international variation can be found for many other products and services, such as canned foods, deodorants, dining in restaurants, and use of leisure time.

Table 4–1 Household Appliance Ownership in Five Western European Nations— 1969 (per 100 households)

APPLIANCE	FRANCE	WEST GERMANY	NETHER- LANDS	GREAT BRITAIN	BELGIUM
Telephone	**19**	31	**43**	34	33
Electric vacuum cleaner	**59**	87	**98**	83	61
Electric washing machine	60	66	**80**	**56**	62
Refrigerator	80	**87**	76	61	**53**
Deep freeze	5	**17**	7	**2**	11
Electric toaster	**8**	**38**	37	22	29
Television set	**69**	82	88	**92**	70
Transistor portable radio	**72**	**46**	50	67	48
Electric sewing machine	26	27	**48**	26	26

Source: *A Survey of Europe Today* (London: Readers Digest Association, 1970), tables 10–11, pp. 66–69.

WHAT IS CULTURE?

Culture is so pervasive yet complex that it is difficult to define in short, simple terms. It seems that each anthropologist has his own definition. One has called it "the integrated sum total of learned behavioral traits that are manifest and shared by members of a society."[1] It may be considered as the man-made part of our environment, or the distinctive way of life of a people. Culture is not biologically transmitted; any given culture or way of life is learned behavior which depends on the environment and not on heredity. This idea was fundamental in Aldous Huxley's *Brave New World* where the scientists were creating a new culture by conditioning and molding an environment which would lead to the "brave new world," or the planners' vision of utopia. Perhaps the easiest way to grasp the complexity of culture is to examine its varied aspects. We will proceed to this examination after we note the role that studies of cultural phenomena have come to play in American marketing research.

Cultural Analysis in American Marketing

In approaching the study of the cultural environment of international market-ing, it is revealing to see how cultural analysis is being used in American marketing. If we scan textbooks in marketing, for instance, we are struck by

[1] Adamson Hoebel, *Man, Culture and Society* (New York: Oxford University Press, 1960), p. 168.

the fact that no self-respecting text of recent vintage is without one or more chapters on behavioral-science contributions to marketing. In addition to chapters on consumer behavior, there are numerous references to concepts from the behavioral sciences in the chapters on marketing research, promotion, pricing, and so on. Even the product is likely to be defined in terms of psychic as well as physical utility. For example, the modern marketing manager is supposed to be familiar with the following concepts and their importance in marketing:

1. Reference groups
2. Social class
3. Consumption systems
4. Family structure and decision making
5. Adoption-diffusion, or the spread of innovation
6. Market segmentation
7. Consumer behavior

All of the above concepts are as applicable in foreign markets as in the American market. However, they cannot be applied in any meaningful way outside the cultural context. Just as the traveler must translate his money and conversation into the currency and language of the country he is visiting, so the international marketing manager must make his market analysis on the basis of each country's market characteristics, freeing himself from any peculiar American bias. This is all the more difficult because the cultural bias is usually an unconscious one.

Another evidence of the role of cultural analysis in American marketing is the number of persons trained in anthropology or sociology who are working in marketing. Major marketing companies employ such people on their research staffs. Others are employed in advertising agencies or in consulting firms. University consultants to industry today come not only from schools of business and engineering but also from departments of anthropology and sociology. Considering that most American marketers are born and bred in the American culture, such attention to cultural analysis is notable indeed. How much more important is such analysis in foreign markets, where the marketer generally knows even less about the overall culture than he does about the language—that is, very little.

Elements of Culture

There are varying definitions of the elements of culture, including one that counts seventy-three "cultural universals." For our purpose here, we will use a simpler list covering seven major areas. One of these, the political aspect of culture, will be discussed separately in Chapter 5.

1. Material culture
2. Language
3. Esthetics

4. Education
5. Religion, beliefs, and attitudes
6. Social organization
7. Political life (see Chapter 5)

Our discussion of these areas will not be definitive and perhaps would not satisfy the anthropologist. However, it should contribute to an understanding of some dimensions of the cultural environment and how they may affect the foreign marketing of the international firm. It should be noted that a broad definition of culture would include economics as well. However, by convention this is often treated separately, as we have done here.

MATERIAL CULTURE

Material culture will be considered as the tools, artifacts, and technology of a society. It is concerned with techniques and with physical things, but only those made or fashioned by man, as opposed to those found in nature. For example, a tree per se is not a part of the culture but the Christmas tree is, and so is an orchard. Material culture includes economic considerations, that is, the way the society organizes its economic activities. When we speak of a "technology gap" between Europe and America, we are referring to differences in the material culture of the two areas.

Some other descriptive terms that refer to the material culture are industrialized nation, agricultural nation, less developed country, stone age, atomic age, space age, and so on. The interrelationships between the material culture and all other aspects of life are profound and not always recognized, because we are so much the products of our own culture. It is primarily as we travel abroad that we begin to perceive that there is no single pattern of relationship between the material culture and the rest of life. Such "travel" need not be an actual voyage to a foreign country but can be done through study of books, cinema, and the like.

Marx and Material Culture

In discussing the relationship of material culture to the rest of life, Karl Marx went so far as to say that the economic organization of a society determines its behavior. This is the essence of his materialistic interpretation of history. Very few today would take such a strong position, but we can all readily see many examples of the impact of our tools, techniques, and economic organization on our society's behavior patterns. Noteworthy too is the two-way relationship between material culture and the other aspects of life; not only does our material culture affect our way of life, but the nature and quality of our life determine our material culture.

We will look first at the impact of material culture on our way of life. For example, the Industrial Revolution and the factory system brought about major changes in people's living patterns. When industry was still of the home or cottage type, there was no need for large agglomerations of people.

Small groups made up the producing units, and village life was the pattern. The growth of factories and the consequent demand for large numbers of laborers led to the expansion of cities and numerous changes in living habits. Many of these changes were not for the better, as the writings of Charles Dickens remind us. Karl Marx put it more strongly than Dickens by predicting the continuing immiserization of the workers that must eventually result in the revolution of the proletariat.

Mahatma Gandhi was somewhat in sympathy with this negative view of factories and industrialization. In part, he objected on the basis of the Buddhist and Hindu ideal of Nirvana or "wantlessness," but he also considered indus- trialization a negation of human values. He said:

Then take the question of machinery. I think that machinery is not necessary for us at all. We should use khadi (home-spun cloth); and therefore, we do not require mills. We should produce all the necessary cloth in villages, and we need not be slaves of machines. I am afraid, by working with machines we have become machines ourselves, having lost all sense of art and handwork.[2]

The complaints about mass-produced items and the prestige accorded hand- made articles today are in line with Gandhi's observation. So too is labor's complaint about the dehumanizing aspects of assembly-line operation. It is interesting to reflect that if Gandhi's ideas are widely accepted in modern India, they can seriously hinder India's economic development, especially industrialization. Gunnar Myrdal has suggested as much in his lengthy study, *The Asian Drama.*

To balance somewhat these negative views of industrialization, we can cite a Chinese philosopher, Hu Shih, who prefers the material civilization of the West. He considers the idea of the "spiritual" East compared with the "materialistic" West to be a form of "sour grapes" thinking. He says:

Let all apologists for the spiritual civilization of the East reflect on this. What spirituality is there in a civilization which tolerates such a terrible form of human slavery as the ricksha coolie? Do we seriously believe that there can be any spiritual life left in those poor human beasts of burden who run and toil and sweat under the peculiar bondage of slavery which knows neither the minimum wage nor any limit of working hours? Do we really believe that the life of a ricksha coolie is more spiritual or more moral than that of the American worker who rides to and from his work in his own motorcar . . . ? Mechanical progress means the use of human intelligence to devise tools and machines to multiply the working ability and productivity of man so that he may be relieved from the fate of toiling incessantly with his unaided hands, feet, and back, without being able to earn a bare subsistence, and so that he

[2] D. P. Mukerji, "Mahatma Gandhi's Views on Machines and Technology," *International Social Science Bulletin*, vol. 6, no. 3, 1954.

may have enough time and energy left to seek and enjoy the higher values which civilization can offer him.[3]

There are more current examples of the impact of material culture on our lives than the Industrial Revolution. An obvious one is the automobile. One would be hard put to trace out all the ramifications of its impact, but there are a few outstanding points that can be mentioned. One is its effect on American courtship patterns. Another is the effect on worker mobility and the development of our cities and suburbs. Yet another is its effect on consumer mobility with resultant changes in both shopping and consumption patterns. The automobile really is an "escape machine," as one advertiser classified it. This prompts one to speculate on possible changes in the Russian economy as Ivan begins to enjoy automobiles from the large plant Fiat is building in the USSR.

Television is another recent development in our material culture that has already changed consumer behavior significantly. The "TV dinner" is one of its minor results. Less observable but more important are its impact on consumption patterns—including much more than just recreation—as well as on general citizen and voter education. Political elections, American attitudes toward the war in Vietnam, and campus demonstrations are just three of the phenomena that have been influenced and shaped by the presence of this new medium. Marshall McLuhan speaks of the way this medium massages or influences our culture (*The Medium is the Massage*). George Orwell, in *1984*, sees it as the sinister eye of Big Brother. India and some other less developed countries are considering television as a tool of mass education for culture change and economic development.

The Idea before the Thing

To understand the true role of the material part of our culture, we must now look at how the other aspects of our culture help to determine what the material culture will be. The causal relationships go both ways, and it is somewhat of a chicken and egg proposition to decide where to start. If necessity is the mother of invention, there is some evidence that the idea and a certain cultural environment preceded the tool or technology invented. The tool or technology can, of course, later influence the culture that gave it birth, as did the automobile and television.

Some developments in our material culture have arisen from problems within the material culture itself, as when synthetic rubber was developed after our supplies of natural rubber were threatened in World War II. This does *not* mean that this development was determined by the material culture itself, however. People all over the world have faced similar problems in

---

[3] Hu Shih, "A Chinese Philosopher Prefers the Material Civilization of the West," from *Whither Mankind*, ed. by Charles A. Beard (New York: Longmans, Green and Co., 1928), pp. 28, 29.

agriculture and other parts of their economic environment. Not all have come up with equally satisfying tools and technologies, even though all have had a similar "need" for invention. The kinds of solutions that are sought and obtained, therefore, are determined by the nonmaterial elements of the culture. As Churchill said, "We shape our buildings; thereafter they shape us."

The importance of nonmaterial culture as a determinant of the material culture has been noted by many observers. Perhaps most famous was the analysis by Weber of the relationship between religion and the rise of capitalism. Weber suggests that the religious Reformation of eighteenth-century Europe and the resulting "Protestant ethic" were major forces behind the rise of capitalism, a particular form of material culture. Although it is perhaps unfair to say that a society gets the material culture it deserves, it is fair to say that a society gets the material culture it can absorb and live with. Many non-Western societies are trying to achieve industrialization, also a particular form of material culture. They are coming to the knowledge that there are cultural preconditions to be realized if the transplant of industrialization is to be successful. As is the case with heart transplants, the success of the operation depends less on the material culture (heart) transferred than on the ability of the host body to receive it.

Material Culture as a Constraint

Managers in international companies typically have no training in anthropology. They need to gain insight, however, into how the material culture in their foreign markets affects the success of their operations there. In regard to manufacturing, foreign production by the firm may represent what was discussed in the preceding paragraph—an attempt to introduce a new material culture into the host economy. This will usually be the case when the firm builds a plant in a less developed country. The firm generally checks carefully on the necessary physical and economic prerequisites for such a plant, for example, raw material supply, power, transportation, financing, and so on. Frequently overlooked or given only cursory examination are the other cultural preconditions for the plant.

In its analysis prior to making foreign production decisions, the firm must evaluate several aspects of the material culture in the host country. One is the economic infrastructure, that is, transportation, power, communications. Another is the financial infrastructure, that is, what kinds of banking, credit, or financial institutions are available to support the operation. In implementing a decision to build a plant, the production manager must answer other questions based on his findings from the above analysis. Do we need to adapt our production processes to fit the local economy? Will our plant be more capital-intensive or more labor-intensive than our plants at home? The production manager in the international company realizes what the economist long overlooked, namely, that production of the same goods may require a different production function in different countries. A study of both the material and the nonmaterial culture is necessary to determine the appropriate plant and production organization.

For Marketing

As regards marketing, it is equally important for the manager to understand the relevant aspects of the material culture in foreign markets. For example, the industrial marketer will find it useful to obtain or construct input-output tables for these markets. Where tables can be even partially designed, the firm has a better idea of how its products relate to the material culture and industrial structure of the country. Such information helps to identify customers and usage patterns.

In the giant diversified industrial economy of the United States, almost any industrial good can find a market. Going down the scale of development country by country, however, industrial-goods marketers will find increasingly limited markets, where they can sell only part of their product line, or perhaps not any of it. The better the picture of the material culture and industrial structure in world markets the industrial marketer is able to get, the better able he will be to identify and evaluate those markets that are the best prospects for his company. Obviously, the marketing prospects in countries where the principal agricultural implement is the machete will differ from those in which it is the tractor.

Consumer-goods marketers are also concerned with the material culture in foreign markets; such simple considerations as electrical voltages and use of the metric system of measurement, for instance, must be taken into account. Product adaptations may also be necessitated by the material culture of the family or consuming unit. Does the family have a car to transport purchases? Does the family have a stove to prepare certain foods, or a refrigerator to store them? Even in affluent Europe, the consumption of frozen foods is greatly limited by lack of freezer capacity in the home. If electrical power is not widely available, electrical appliances will be nearly unmarketable unless they can be battery powered. To women who wash clothes by a stream or lake, detergents or packaged soaps are not useful; there will be a market only for bar soaps. Such examples show how the material culture affects the product policy of consumer-goods marketers.

Parts of the marketing program other than product policy are also influenced by the material culture. The promotional program, for example, will be constrained by the kinds of media available. The advertiser wants to know the relative availability of television, radio, magazines, and newspapers. Is color TV available? How good is the reproduction process in newspapers and magazines? Are there advertising and research agencies to support the advertising program? The size of retail outlets will affect the use of point-of-purchase displays. The nature of travel and the highway system will affect the use of outdoor advertising.

Modifications in the company's methods and channels of distribution may be necessary. These changes must be made on the basis of the alternatives offered by the host country's commercial infrastructure. What kind of wholesale and retail patterns exist in the country? What kinds of warehouse or storage facilities are available? Is refrigerated storage possible? What is the nature of the transport system—road, rail, river, or air—and what area does it cover? Firms that use quite direct channels in the United States, with large-scale retailers and chain-store operations, may have to use indirect channels where there is a multitude of very small independent retailers. In some countries, average sales per retail outlet are less than 3 percent of those in the United States. In addition, these small retailers may be relatively inaccessible if they are widely dispersed and the transportation system of the country is inadequate.

If local storage facilities are insufficient, the firm may have to supply its own facilities or provide special bulk packaging to offer extra protection. Whereas highways and railroads are most important in moving goods in America, river transport is a major means in some countries. And in others, air is the principal means, as in some African nations. Thus, in numerous ways, international business management is concerned with the material culture in foreign markets. Although the manager uses a different vocabulary from the anthropologist, they are both dealing with the same cultural phenomenon.

Conclusions

In studying the material culture of a foreign country, the international manager first needs to recognize these cultural dimensions as they relate to his own operations. He can achieve this in part through careful analysis, but experience is the best teacher. Managers generally learn most about the impact of material culture on their operations by concrete experiences. As the firm gains operating experience in many different countries, it should be able to develop a rather good model of the interaction between the material culture and its own operations.

Where the firm has integrated its global experiences into practical knowledge, it enjoys one of the important advantages of multinational operations. But experience is not enough; in order to benefit from it the firm needs systematic analysis of the relevant literature and secondary data. This is the academic or staff side of the picture. As an example of one useful data source, the *United Nations Statistical Yearbook* lists over 200 environmental variables for about 200 countries. Almost two-thirds of these variables concern different aspects of the material culture of the countries: agriculture, manufacturing, energy, transportation, and so on.

Imperialism?

Perhaps the most subtle aspect of the international marketer's job is his role as an agent of cultural change. When he seeks to introduce his new products or processes into the market, he is, in effect, seeking to change the country's material culture. The change may be fairly modest—new food product—or it may be more dramatic—a machine that revolutionizes agricultural or industrial technology in the host country. The product or process of the international firm is alien in the sense that it did not originate in the host country. The firm must consider carefully the legitimacy of its role as an agent of change. It must be sure that changes it introduces are in accordance with the interests of the host country. This is especially important where host nationals have a

Marxian or Gandhian view of the impact of material things on their way of life. They may resent the firm's market penetration as a form of "Americanization" or "imperialism"; along this line, someone coined the term "Coca-colanization" in regard to American business activities abroad.

LANGUAGE

Language is the most obvious difference between cultures. Inextricably linked with all other aspects of a culture, language reflects the nature and values of that culture. For example, the English language has a rich vocabulary for commercial and industrial activities, reflecting the nature of the English and American societies. Many less industrialized societies have only limited vocabularies for industrial and commercial activities but have richer vocabularies than the English language for matters important to their culture.

Dr. Das, an Indian economist and civil servant, commented on the important role of the English language in India. He said it would be a serious error for India to replace English with Hindi or other Indian languages because none of them gives adequate expression to the modern commercial or technical activities which are necessary for India's economic development.[4] On the other hand, these other languages are more than adequate, indeed rich, for describing the traditional culture. To use another example, Eskimo has many different terms to describe snow, whereas English has one general term. This is reasonable because the difference in forms of snow plays a vital role in the lives of Eskimos. The kinds of travel, work, recreation, and other activities they can engage in depend on the specific snow conditions. Of course, in America the subculture of skiers has a richer vocabulary for snow than the nonskiers.

Because language is such an obvious cultural difference, everyone recognizes that it must be dealt with in some way if one is going to engage in intercultural activities. It is said that anyone planning a career in international business should learn a foreign language. Learning a foreign language is not detrimental to such a career, but neither is it always a necessity. If one's career is going to be importantly or exclusively involved with a particular country, learning that language will be very useful. Learning German or Japanese, however, is not a great help if one's career does not involve Germany or Japan. Because one does not usually know in advance where he will go, it is best to choose to study a language with the greatest international coverage. Americans are fortunate in having English as their mother tongue, because English is the closest thing to a world language for most international activities, especially commercial dealings. French and Spanish follow English as the languages used most internationally.

A Cultural Mirror

A country's language is the key to its culture. Anyone, diplomat or businessman, concerned with people and cultural change needs this key. Thus, if one is to work extensively with any one culture or nation, it is almost imperative that he learn the language. Many times this language will not be one he

[4] Lecture at the University of Michigan, March 25, 1970.

studied in college but rather a new language he has to learn only after receiving a foreign assignment.

Learning a language well means learning the culture, because the words and phrases of the language are merely concepts and ideas reflecting and describing the culture from which it was formed. Language is not only a key to understanding the culture; it is the chief means of communication within it. Good understanding and good communication are even more critical to the firm in a foreign environment than in the domestic culture because the firm is an alien abroad. The firm must understand and communicate with political leaders, employees, suppliers, and customers. In this aspect of culture, more than any other, the firm must "go native."

Study of the language situation within foreign markets can yield useful information about them. The number of languages in a country is a case in point. In a real sense, a language defines a culture; thus, if a country has several spoken languages, it has several cultures. Belgium has two national languages, French in the South and Flemish in the North. This linguistic division goes back to the days of Julius Caesar, but even today there are political and social differences—and hostilities—between the two language groups.

Canada's situation is similar to Belgium's, with both French and English languages and cultural groups. Many African and Asian nations have a far greater number of spoken languages. According to an official linguistic survey, the number of language and dialects spoken in India is 203. To moderate this diversity, a limited number of lingua francas have been developed which are used in communication between different groups. The most widely used language, and until recently the only official one, is English, which thus serves as the principal lingua franca.

In the Republic of the Congo separate tribal languages are spoken by the numerous tribes living there. Four African lingua francas partially link four regions of Congo, but the only national language is again a European one— French. Such situations present real obstacles to learning the "language of the people." The usual approach in these situations is to rely on the European language and the lingua francas for business and marketing communications. Unfortunately, these aren't the first language for any nationals.

Diversity: Linguistic and Social

There are other problems connected with language diversity within a nation. Many tribal languages are not written; for some that are, there are very low literacy rates. All intertribal and business communications are in the lingua franca, which is a written language. However, because the lingua franca is usually no one's native tongue, but a second language for all parties, it does not communicate as well as the parties' native languages. The European languages used as lingua francas in former colonies—for example, French in Congo—have the virtue of covering a wide range of territory. However, they have the disadvantage of being quite foreign to the culture in which they are used.

The difficulties in understanding and communicating with such culturally diverse groups are obviously great. Language differences within a country may indicate social as well as communication problems. In both Canada and Belgium, the two linguistic groups have occasionally clashed to the point where there have been incidents of violence between them. Congo, Nigeria, and India are examples of less developed countries where linguistic groups have engaged in such hostilities, although the incidents have been more violent.

Many former colonial nations have some linguistic unity in the language of the former colonial power, but even this linguistic unity is threatened in some countries. For example, in India it is proposed to make Hindi a national language along with English. Hindi has the advantage of being an Indian language but the drawback of belonging to just one segment of India's population. Non-Hindi–speaking groups then want *their* language to be a national language. The result is greater diversity instead of unity.

In Guinea, a small West African state of 3.6 million people, there are seven African languages considered major. As part of President Sékou Touré's literacy campaign, he encouraged the major tribes to become literate in their own language. French, which had been the language of the schools and of business, would thus be accorded less importance. Except for the political drawback of being the language of the former colonial master, French has the advantages of being (1) neutral between tribes, (2) the most national of the languages of Guinea, (3) the most useful language internationally, and (4) the most effective language for modern education and development.

It has been said that a language defines a cultural group, that nothing distinguishes one culture from another more than language. But what does it mean when the same language is used in different countries? French, for example, is the mother tongue not only for the French but also for many Belgians and Swiss. Spanish plays a similar role in Latin America. The anthropologist, however, stresses the *spoken* language as the cultural distinction. The spoken language changes much more quickly than the written and thus reflects the culture more directly. Although England, the United States, and Ireland use the same written English, they speak somewhat different "dialects." These three cultures are separate yet related, just as are the Spanish-speaking cultures of Latin America.

Even where a common language is spoken, different words are occasionally used as well as different pronunciations and accents. In Latin America, for example, the word for tire is not the same in all the Spanish-speaking countries. In England, they say "lorry," "petrol," and "biscuits," but in America, we say "truck," "gasoline," and "cookies." It should be noted, incidentally, that even within one country, for example, the United States, where almost all speak "American"—there are different cultural groups, or subcultures, between which the spoken language varies. For instance, parents continually have problems understanding their teenage offspring.

Language as a Problem

Man communicates almost all his ideas through language. Thus business and marketing are highly dependent on communication for results. If management is not speaking the same language as its various audiences, it is not going to enjoy much success. In each of its foreign markets the international company must communicate with several audiences: its workers, managers, customers, suppliers, and government representatives. Each of these audiences has a distinctive communication style within the native language common to all. The number of language areas the firm operates in approximates the number of countries it is selling in. Any advantage gained by the fact that one language may be used in more than one country is partly offset by the fact that in many countries, more than one language is necessary.

This language diversity in world markets could be an insuperable problem if it meant that international managers had to master the language, and the culture, of all their markets. Fortunately, that is not the case. It is true that to be effective, any person assigned to a foreign operation for a period of a year or more should learn the local language. However, cultural bridges are available to the international firm in many markets. For example, in countries where the firm is operating through a distributor, he may act as the bridge between the firm and its local market. He may speak the language of the exporter and probably has a business-commercial orientation. Thus in more than one sense he speaks the "language" of the firm as well as his own.

In advertising to a market, the firm can rely on the communication skills of a local advertising agency. The international advertising manager must be able to communicate with the agency, but agency personnel, like the distributor, probably speak his language—especially if the international firm communicates principally in English. For example, the Dutch electronics firm Philips N.V. uses English as the official company language, in spite of the company's being domiciled in the Netherlands. Because of its widespread European and global operations, it finds that English is the most useful language for maintaining contact with all its markets.

In countries where the firm has subsidiaries and its own personnel, the language requirement becomes greater. The firm then has more extensive and intensive communication with its audiences and more direct management contact. Even here, however, the language burden is lessened because, among its national managers, the firm can usually count people of the "third culture." This expression is often used to describe nationals who, through their experience, have become so familiar with another culture that they become a bridge between the two. The international firm that has such people in its employ has one of the best solutions to both the language gap and the culture gap in its foreign operations. Indeed, to develop such people is a key task of international management, among both the firm's national and its expatriate staff.

We have suggested that there are ways to circumvent the language problem in international marketing. However, we hasten to add that language *is* a critical factor, because it is the key to understanding and communicating with the local market cultures around the world. The implication is that the international firm does need language capabilities, not only among its distributors and other collaborators, but also among its own personnel. Furthermore, the individual who expects to undertake international marketing and management responsibilities had better expect to get some foreign language facility himself.

Canada provides an illustration of a situation requiring linguistic sensitivity on the part of the international firm. In labor negotiations in the province of Quebec, General Motors helped underwrite the cost of an interpreter to provide documentation in both French and English. GM agreed to recognize the French language version of the contract as official.

Other guidelines recommended to alleviate tension between the two groups were (1) bilingual labeling and advertising; (2) bilingual annual reports and press releases (French in Quebec); (3) bilingual executives for operations in Quebec.[5]

ESTHETICS

Esthetics refers to a culture's ideas concerning beauty and good taste, as expressed in the fine arts—music, art, drama, and dancing—and the particular appreciation of color and form. There are important international differences in esthetics, but they tend to be regional rather than national. For example, Kabuki theater is exclusively Japanese, but Western theater includes at least all of Western Europe plus the United States and Canada in its audience.

Musical tastes too tend to be regional rather than national. In the West, a great number of countries enjoy the same classical and popular music. In fact, with modern communications and phenomena such as the Beatles, popular music may become truly international. Nevertheless, there are obvious differences between Western music and that of the Middle East, black Africa, or India. Likewise the dance styles of the African tribal groups or the Balinese are quite removed from Western dance styles. The beauty of India's Taj Mahal is different from that of Notre Dame in Paris or the Lever Building on Park Avenue in New York.

Design

The esthetics of a culture probably does not have a major impact on economic activity. However, in esthetics lie some significant implications for international business operations in different cultures. For example, in the design of its plant, product, or package, the firm should be sensitive to local esthetic preferences. So far as possible, design should be appropriate and pleasing to local tastes. Occasionally, this requirement may run counter to the firm's desire for international uniformity or standardization, but the firm at least must be aware of the positive and negative aspects of its designs.

A historical example of lack of cultural sensitivity is illustrated by the early Christian missionaries from Western nations who were often guilty of architectural "imperialism." The Christian churches built in many non-Western nations almost always reflected Western rather than indigenous architectural ideas. This was not usually done deliberately or with malicious intent but because the missionaries were culture bound in their esthetics; that is, they had their own ideas as to what a church should look like, ideas that reflected the esthetics of Western culture.

[5] *Business International*, January 15, 1971, p. 21.

The United States government faces a similar problem in designing its embassies in foreign countries. The new American Embassy in India received praise both for its beauty as a building and for the way it blended in with Indian architectural ideas. The new American Embassy in London, however, has received more than its share of criticism for various things, including the size of the sculptured American eagle on top of the building. Some Britons also took exception to the architecture of the London Hilton. For the firm, the best policy is to design and decorate its buildings and commercial vehicles to reflect local esthetic preferences.

Color

The appreciation and significance of different colors can vary from culture to culture. In America, for instance, we use colors to identify emotional reactions; for example, we "see red," we are "green with envy," or we "feel blue." Black signifies mourning in Western countries, whereas white is often the color of mourning in Eastern nations. Certain colors have particular meanings because of religious, patriotic, or esthetic reasons. The marketer needs to know these cultural patterns in color preference in planning his products, packages, and advertising. Effective advertising especially must be culturally sensitive. For any market, the right choice of colors, illustrations, and appeals will be related to the esthetic sense of the *buyer's* culture rather than that of the *marketer's* culture.

Music

As noted above, there are cultural differences in music. An understanding of these differences is critical to the firm, for example, in creating advertising messages that use music in some way. William Malm, the ethnomusicologist, notes that non-Western music uses musical materials to achieve effects generally unused and unlooked-for in Western countries. The music of non-literate cultures is generally *functional*, or has significance in their daily lives, whereas the music of literate cultures tends to be separate from the people's other concerns. For example, a Western student has to learn to "understand" a Beethoven symphony, but an aborigine assimilates his musical culture as an integral part of his existence. Malm says that to understand the symbolism in different kinds of music requires considerable cultural conditioning. Therefore, esthetic homogeneity in music throughout world cultures is not possible.[6] One implication for the firm is that wherever it can use music in its operations, it had best "go native."

Brand Names

The choice of brand names is affected by esthetics as well as by language and law. Frequently, the best brand name is one that is in the local language and pleasing to the local taste. This necessarily leads to a multiplicity of brand names. Some international firms try to avoid brand-name multiplicity by searching out a nonsense word that is pronounceable everywhere but has no

[6] Interview at the University of Michigan, summer 1970.

specific meaning anywhere; "Kodak" is a famous and successful example of this. In other cases, local identification is important enough that firms will seek local brand names in all their markets.

In general, we may conclude that the esthetics of a particular culture does have an impact on a firm's marketing there, and often in ways that the marketer is unaware of till he has made mistakes. In the area of esthetics, more than in most others, the firm needs sophisticated local inputs to avoid ineffective or damaging use of esthetics. These inputs may be some combination of local marketing research, local nationals working for the firm, and a local advertising agency or distributor.

EDUCATION

To an American, education usually means formal training received in school. A well-educated person, for example, is one who has had many years of such training. Often implicit in such a characterization is some judgment as to the quality of the schooling as well as the quantity. In this formal sense, the aborigines in Australia or the Pygmies in Africa are not educated; that is, they have never been to school. However, this formal definition of education is too restrictive. Education includes the process of transmitting skills, ideas, and attitudes, as well as training in particular disciplines. Even primitive peoples have been educated in this broader sense. For example, the Bushmen of South Africa are well educated in the restricted culture in which they live.

One function of education is the transmission of the existing culture and traditions to the new generation. This is as true among the people of America as among the aborigines of Australia. However, education can also be used for cultural change. Russia and Mainland China are notable examples, but this again is an aspect of education in most nations of the world. For example, in India educational campaigns are carried on to improve agriculture or to quell the population explosion. In Britain, business schools are established to improve the performance of the economy. In Western Europe, educational reform is undertaken to eliminate the technology gap.

International Differences

In looking at the educational system of foreign markets, the observer is limited primarily to information about the formal process, that is, education in schools. This is the only area where UNESCO (United Nations Educational and Social Council) and others have been able to gather data. Literacy rates are the principal single indicator used to describe educational achievement in different countries. This corresponds to the use of per capita income figures to describe the level of economic development.

In addition to literacy rates, the education information available on world markets refers primarily to national enrollments in the various levels of education—primary, secondary, and college or university. Table 4–2 gives a picture of some international differences on these measures of formal educational attainment. Analyzing this kind of information for relevant markets can give the international marketer an insight into the nature and sophistication

Table 4-2 Educational Participation—Selected Nations

NATION	POPULATION	LITERACY RATE	STUDENTS TOTAL	STUDENTS FEMALE	PERCENT FEMALE	PERCENT POP. ALL LEVELS	PERCENT ABOVE LEVEL 1
United States	201,152,000	97–98%				28.6%	10.4%
1st level			57,484,000	27,475,000	47 %		
2nd level			36,542,000	17,814,000	48.7		
3rd level			14,145,000	6,988,000	49.4		
			6,801,000	2,677,000	39.4		
Australia	12,031,000	98–99%				24.5%	9.6%
1st level			2,953,000	1,322,446	44.8%		
2nd level			1,798,500	873,285	48.6		
3rd level			1,001,420	404,160	40.4		
			153,000	45,000	29.4		
Mexico	34,923,000	65–70%				25.9%	3.7%
1st level			9,048,290	4,160,126	46 %		
2nd level			7,772,257	3,702,724	47.6		
3rd level			1,121,745	430,644	38.4		
			154,289	26,758	17.3		
Portugal	9,465,000	60–65%				13.3%	3.9%
1st level			1,260,494	586,716	46.5%		
2nd level			891,082	433,043	48.6		
3rd level			333,080	139,581	41.9		
			36,332	14,092	38.8		
Kenya	8,636,000	20–25%				15.3%	1.3%
1st level			1,324,514	513,089	38.7%		
2nd level			1,209,680	484,650	40.1		
3rd level			109,867	28,439	25.9		
			4,967	n.a.	—		
Nepal	9,413,000	1–5%				5.3%	0.8%
1st level			474,252	71,029	15 %		
2nd level			394,700	56,222	14.2		
3rd level			69,317	13,045	18.8		
			10,235	1,762	17.2		

Sources: *United Nations Statistical Yearbook*, 1969, pp. 57–71, 716–740; *Statistical Abstract of the United States*, 1969, p. 103; *Encyclopedia Americana*, 1969, vol. 15, p. 695.

of consumers in different countries. One can also observe a rather good correlation between educational attainment and economic development. Harbison and Myers noted this relationship in their study *Education, Manpower, and Economic Growth.*[7]

Because in general only quantitative data are available, there is a danger that the qualitative aspects of education might be overlooked. Furthermore, in addition to the usual limitations of international statistics, there is the problem of interpreting them in terms of international business needs. For example, the firm's needs for technicians, marketing personnel, managers, or distributors will have to be met largely from the educated manpower in the local economy. In looking for appropriate people, the firm is concerned not only with the level but also with the nature of their education. Table 4–2 does not give any indication as to the kind of education available at the different levels.

Training in law, literature, music, or political science is probably not the most suitable education for business needs. Yet in many nations such studies are emphasized almost to the exclusion of others more relevant to commercial and economic growth. Too often, primary education is preparation for secondary, secondary education is preparation for university, and university education is not designed to meet the needs of the economy. University education in many nations is largely preparation for the traditional prestige occupations or is based on the classical concept of the educated man. Although a nation needs lawyers and philosophers, it also needs agricultural experts, engineers, business managers, and technicians. The degree to which the educational system provides for these needs will be a critical determinant of the nation's ability to grow and develop economically.

Education and International Marketing

The international marketer has a role in cultural change. Therefore, he must be somewhat of an educator in his own right. The products and techniques the international firm brings into a local market are generally new to that market. The firm must educate consumers and workers as to their uses and benefits. Although the firm does not use the formal educational system to accomplish its own educational goals, its success will be constrained by that system. The firm's ability to communicate will depend in part on the educational level of its market.

The international marketer is further concerned about the educational situation in foreign markets because it is a key determinant of the nature of the consumer market and the kinds of marketing personnel available. Some implications are the following:

1. If consumers are largely illiterate, advertising programs and package labels will need to be adapted.
2. If girls and women are largely excluded from formal education, marketing programs will differ greatly from those aimed at the American housewife.

[7] F. E. Harbison and C. A. Myers, *Education, Manpower, and Economic Growth* (New York: McGraw-Hill Book Co., 1964).

3. Conducting marketing research can be difficult, both in communicating with consumers and in getting qualified researchers.

4. Products that are complex or need written instructions may need to be modified to meet the educational and skill levels of the market.

5. Relations with, and cooperation from, the distribution channel will depend partly on the educational attainments of members in the channel.

6. The nature and quality of marketing-support services, such as advertising agencies, will depend on how well the educational system prepares people for such occupations.

RELIGION

In this chapter we are concerned with the cultural or human environment of international business. We have already seen several aspects of this environment. The material culture, language, and esthetics are, in effect, outward manifestations or observable physical behavior of a culture. If we are to get a full understanding of a culture, however, we must gain a familiarity with the internal, psychic, or mental behavior that gives rise to the external manifestations. Generally, it is the religion, beliefs, and attitudes of a culture that provide the best insights into its behavior. Therefore, although the international company is primarily interested in knowing *how* people behave as consumers or workers, management's task will be aided by an understanding of *why* people behave as they do. Even in America, studies of worker and consumer motivation are used extensively.

There are numerous religions and religious groups in the world; here we will discuss briefly animism, Buddhism, Christianity, Hinduism, Islam, and Shinto. We selected these on the basis of their importance in terms of numbers of adherents and their impact on the economic behavior of their followers.[8]

Animism

Animism is the term used to describe the religion and philosophy of primitive peoples. It is often popularly defined as "spirit worship," as distinguished from the worship of God or gods. Animistic beliefs, or traces of them, have been found in all parts of the world. With the exception of revealed religion, some form of animism has preceded all historical religions. As Frazer put it in *The Golden Bough*, "An Age of Religion has everywhere been preceded by an Age of Magic."[9] In many less developed parts of the world today, animistic ideas affect the behavior of the people.

The idea of magic is a key element of animism. Magic is the attempt to achieve results through the aid and manipulation of the spirit world. It represents a nonscientific approach to the physical world. When cause and effect relationships are not known and understood, magic is given credit for results. The same attitude prevails toward many modern-day products and techniques.

[8] This section draws upon J. N. O. Anderson, ed., *The World's Religions* (London: Inter-varsity Fellowship, 1951), 204 p.

[9] James G. Frazer, *The Golden Bough* (London: Macmillan & Co., abridged ed., 1922), p. 56.

For example, during the author's years in Congo, he had an opportunity to see the persistence of animism alongside modern educational activity. First, traditional witchcraft and the casting of spells were occasionally practiced. Second, reactions to European products and practices were often based on a magical interpretation. As one instance, a number of Africans affected the wearing of glasses. Because many Europeans wore glasses, it was felt that the wearing of glasses enhanced the intelligence of the wearer. As another instance, dispensaries established by Europeans were quite successful in replacing the witchdoctor, because the white man's medicines, especially penicillin, were obviously better "magic" than the "dawa" of the witchdoctor. Some consumer-goods marketers in Africa have not hesitated to imply that possession of their products gives magical qualities to the owners. Of course, the same is occasionally true of marketers on American TV.

Other aspects of animism include ancestor worship, taboos, and fatalism. All of these tend to promote a traditionalist, status quo, backward-looking society. Because such societies are more interested in protecting their traditions than in accepting change or progress, marketers and development planners face difficult problems when working with them. Their success in bringing change will depend on how well they understand and relate to the culture and its animistic foundation.

Hinduism

There are perhaps 400,000,000 to 500,000,000 Hindus, almost all of them living in India. In a broad sense, about 90 percent of India's population is Hindu, but in the sense of strict adherence to the tenets of Hinduism, the number of followers would be considerably smaller. It is a common dictum that Hinduism is not a religion but a way of life. The origins of Hinduism go back to about 1500 B.C. Hinduism is an ethnic, noncreedal religion. A Hindu is born, not made, so an American cannot become a Hindu although he can become a Buddhist, for example. Modern-day Hinduism is a combination of ancient philosophies and customs, animistic beliefs, legends, and, more recently, Western influences, including Christianity. One of the strengths of Hinduism over the centuries has been its ability to absorb ideas from outside while remaining Hindu; Hinduism tends to assimilate rather than to exclude.

Because Hinduism is a racial or ethnic religion, many of its doctrines apply only to the Indian situation. However, they are key factors in understanding India. One ancient and important doctrine and practice is the caste system. Each member of a particular caste in Hindu society has a specific occupational and social role, which is hereditary. Marriage is forbidden outside of caste. Although efforts have been made to weaken this system in modern India, it still has a rather strong hold in practice. Discrimination based on caste is forbidden by the Indian constitution, but such deep-rooted customs do not disappear with the passage of a new law. The caste system is aimed at conserving the status quo in society at large.

Another element and one of the strengths of Hinduism is *baradari*, or the "joint family." After marriage, the bride goes to the groom's home. After a series of marriages, there is a large joint family where the father or grandfather is chief authority. In turn, the older women have power over the younger. The elders advise and consent in family council. The Indian grows up thinking and acting in terms of the joint family. If he goes abroad to a university, the joint family may raise the funds. In turn, he is expected to remember the family if he is successful. *Baradari* is aimed at preserving the family.

Veneration of the cow is perhaps the best known Hindu custom; Gandhi himself called this the distinguishing mark of the Hindu. Hindu worship of the cow involves not only protecting it; eating the products of the cow is also considered a means for purification. Another element of traditional Hinduism is the restriction of women, following the occasional belief that to be born a woman is a sign of sin in a former life. Marriages are arranged by relatives; although a man may remarry if widowed, a woman may not. This traditional attitude toward women makes it all the more remarkable that India has a woman in its highest office, Prime Minister Indira Gandhi.

Nirvana is another important concept, one that Hinduism shares with Buddhism. It will be discussed under Buddhism in the following section. The marketing implications of Hindu thought and practice will be considered under Religion and the Economy.

Buddhism

Buddhism springs from Hinduism and dates from about 600 B.C. Buddhism has approximately 350,000,000 followers, mostly in South and East Asia from India to Japan. There are, however, small Buddhist societies in Europe and America. Buddhism is, to some extent, a reformation of Hinduism. It did not abolish caste but declared that Buddhists were released from caste restrictions. This openness to all classes and both sexes was one reason for Buddhism's growth. While accepting the philosophical insights of Hinduism, Buddhism tried to avoid its dogma and ceremony, stressing tolerance and spiritual equality.

At the heart of Buddhism are the Four Truths:

1. The Noble Truth of Suffering states that suffering is omnipresent and part of the very nature of life.
2. The Noble Truth of the Cause of Suffering cites the cause to be desire, that is, desire for possession and selfish enjoyment of any kind.
3. The Noble Truth of the Cessation of Suffering states that suffering ceases when desire ceases.
4. The Noble Truth of the Eightfold Path which leads to the Cessation of Suffering offers the means to achieve cessation of desire. This is also known as the Middle Way because it avoids the two extremes of self-indulgence and self-mortification. The eightfold path includes (1) the right views, (2) the right desires, (3) the right speech, (4) the right conduct, (5) the right occupation, (6) the right effort, (7) the right awareness, and (8) the right contemplation. This path, though simple to state, is a complicated and demanding ethical and contemplative system. Nirvana is the reward for those who are able to stay on the path throughout their lifetime or, more probably, lifetimes.

Nirvana is the ultimate goal of the Hindu and Buddhist. It represents the extinction of all craving and the final release from suffering. To the extent that such an ideal reflects the thinking of the mass of the people, the society would have to be considered antithetical to such other goals as acquisition, achievement, or affluence. This is an obvious constraint on marketing.

Islam

Islam dates from the seventh century A.D. It has some 300,000,000 to 400,000,000 adherents, mostly in Africa and Asia. The bulk of the world of Islam is found from the Atlantic across the northern half of Africa, the Middle East, and across Asia to the Philippines. Although there are different schools of thought or sects in Islam, there is enough similarity among them to permit identification of the following elements of interest to us.

Muslim theology, *Tawhid*, defines all that a man should believe, whereas the law, *Shari'a* prescribes everything he should do. The Koran (*Qur'an*) is accepted as the ultimate guide. Anything not mentioned in the Koran is quite likely to be rejected by the faithful. Introducing new products and techniques can be difficult in such an environment. An important element of Muslim belief is that everything that happens, good or evil, proceeds directly from the Divine Will and is already irrevocably recorded on the Preserved Tablet. This fatalistic belief rather restricts any attempts to bring about change in Muslim countries; to attempt change may be a rejection of, or contrary to, what Allah has ordained. The name Islam is the infinitive of the Arabic verb to submit. Muslim is the present participle of the same verb, that is, a Muslim is one who is in submission to the will of Allah.

The Five Pillars of Islam, or the duties of a Muslim, include (1) the recital of the creed, (2) prayer, (3) fasting, (4) almsgiving, and (5) the pilgrimage. The creed is brief: There is no God but God, and Mohammed is the Prophet of God. The Muslim must pray five times daily at stated hours. During the month of Ramadan, Muslims are required to fast from dawn to sunset—no food, no drink, no smoking. As the Muslim year is lunar, Ramadan sometimes falls in midsummer when the long days and intense heat make abstinence a severe test. The fast is meant to develop both self-control and sympathy for the poor. During Ramadan work output falls off markedly, which is probably attributable as much to the Muslims' loss of sleep as to the rigors of fasting, because the average family spends much more on the food consumed at night during Ramadan than on the food consumed by day in the other months.

By almsgiving the Muslim shares with the poor. It is an individual responsibility, and generally in Muslim lands it is in lieu of any government program. The pilgrimage to Mecca is a well-known aspect of Islam. The thousands who gather in Mecca each year return home with a greater sense of the international solidarity of Islam. In light of the Arab-Israeli conflict, one other religious duty might be mentioned—the duty of *jihad*, or holy war. The Muslim must be ready to answer any call to war against the infidels. He who dies in a *jihad* is a martyr and assured of paradise. Thus there can be a very strong religious sanction, in addition to patriotism, in the wars of Muslim nations. The war with Israel was not declared a *jihad*, however.

In matters of consumption relevant to the firm, Muslims are not allowed to consume pork or alcohol. There is also a prohibition against usury, although this is often ignored in modern business practice. The role of women is quite restricted in Muslim nations. The marketing implications of Islam will be discussed under Religion and the Economy.

Shinto

Shinto, "the way of the gods," is a national religion that contains elements of ancestor and nature worship. It is the principal religion of Japan's 100,000,000 people, but this does not mean that Buddhism is not often practiced as a personal religion alongside Shinto. Among the more important aspects of modern Shinto are (1) reverence for the special or divine origin of the Japanese people and (2) reverence for the Japanese nation and the imperial family as the head of that nation. We use the term *modern* Shinto because when the imperial powers were restored in 1868 state Shinto became a patriotic cult, whereas sectarian Shinto was purely religious. Of course, sectarian Shinto, through ancestor worship, also affects Japanese attitudes. In many houses there is a god-shelf with a model of a shrine in which the spirits of the family ancestors are thought to dwell and watch over the affairs of the family. Reverence is paid to them and the sense of the ancestors' spirit is a bulwark of the family's authority over the individual.

The impact of modern Shinto on Japanese life is reflected in an aggressive patriotism. The Japanese mobilization for World War II and their behavior during it are striking examples of that patriotism. More recently, the economic performance of Japan is due, in part at least, to the patriotic attitude of all those working in the economic enterprise. The family spirit has largely carried over to the firm, which has meant limited conflict and greater cooperation and productivity. Taoism, a religion that has had some impact on Shinto, stresses seeking virtue through passivity, a concept which seems to characterize many oriental religions. Shinto, by contrast, stresses the search for progress through creative activity. Japan's economic performance seems clearly to follow the Shinto path. The aggressive Japanese attitude is reflected in the company song that begins and ends every workday at Matsushita.

For the building of a new Japan,
Let's put our strength and mind together,
Doing our best to promote production,
Sending our goods to the people of the world,
Endlessly and continuously,
Like water gushing from a fountain.
Grow, industry, grow, grow, grow!
Harmony and sincerity!
Matsushita Electric![10]

[10] *Wall Street Journal*, August 1, 1969, p. 6.

Christianity

Since most readers of this book will be from countries where Christianity is the dominant religion, little time need be spent describing it. What concerns us here is the impact of the different Christian religious groups (Roman Catholic and Protestant) on economic attitudes and behavior. Two well-known studies have dealt with this subject: Max Weber's *The Protestant Ethic and the Spirit of Capitalism* and R. H. Tawney's *Religion and the Rise of Capitalism*. The Eastern Orthodox churches are not discussed here, but in their impact on economic attitudes they would be similar to Catholicism.

Roman Catholic Christianity traditionally has emphasized the Church and the sacraments as the principal elements of religion and the way to God. The church and its priests are the intermediaries between God and man, and apart from the Church there is no salvation. Another element in Roman Catholicism is the strong distinction between the religious orders and the laity, with different standards of conduct applied to each. Along with this distinction there is an implicit difference between the secular and religious life.

The Protestant Reformation, and especially Calvinism, made some critical changes in emphasis but retained agreement with Catholicism on most of traditional Christian doctrine. The Protestants stressed that the church, its sacraments, and its priests were not essential to salvation: "Salvation is by faith alone." The result of this was a downgrading of the role of the church and a consequent upgrading of the role of the individual. Salvation became more of an individual matter.

Another change in emphasis by the reformers was the elimination of the distinction between secular and religious life. Luther said all of life was a *Beruf*, a "calling," and even the performance of tasks considered to be secular was a religious obligation. Calvin carried this further and emphasized the need to glorify God through one's calling. Whereas works were necessary to salvation in Catholicism, works were evidence and assurance of salvation in Calvinism.

Hard work was enjoined to glorify God; achievement was the evidence of hard work; and thrift was necessary because the produced wealth was not to be used selfishly. Through such a cycle came accumulation of wealth, capital formation, and the desire for greater production as one's Christian duty. The Protestant Reformation thus led to a greater emphasis on individualism and action (hard work) as contrasted with the more ritualistic and contemplative approach of Catholicism. Though Weber's emphasis was the impact of religion on work attitudes, there appears to have been a concomitant impact on attitudes toward consumption and acquisition.

Although it is useful to recognize the separate thrust of Roman Catholic and Protestant Christianity, it is also important to note the various roles Christianity in general plays in different nations. Some nations are varying mixtures of Catholic and Protestant, and the resulting ethic may be some combination of both doctrines. The impact of Catholicism in these countries will obviously be different from what it is in the overwhelmingly Catholic countries such as Italy, Spain, or Brazil.

Religion and the Economy

In our discussion of the various religions, we suggested some economic implications that we will elaborate on here. Religion has a major impact on attitudes toward economic matters. Under the section Attitudes and Values we discuss the different attitudes religion may inspire. Besides attitudes, however, religion may affect the economy more directly.

1. Religious holidays vary greatly among countries, not only from Christian to Muslim, but even from one Christian country to another. Italy, for example, has approximately thirteen religious holidays, depending on how Sundays fall. In general, Sundays are a type of religious holiday in all nations where Christianity is an important religion. But Sundays are not regarded as such in the Muslim world, where, however, the entire month of Ramadan is a religious holiday for all practical purposes. The international firm must see that local work schedules and marketing programs are related to local holidays, just as firms in America plan for the big consumer marketing season at Christmas.

2. Consumption patterns may be affected by religious requirements or taboos. Fish on Friday for Catholics used to be a classic example. Taboos against beef for the Hindus or pork for Muslims and Jews are other examples. The Muslim prohibition against alcohol has been a boon to companies like Coca Cola. On the other hand, dairy products find favor among Hindus, many of whom are also vegetarian.

3. The economic role of women varies from culture to culture and religious beliefs are an important cause. Women may be restricted in their capacity as consumers or consumption influencers, as workers, or as respondents in a marketing study. These differences can require major adjustments in the approach of a management or company conditioned in the American market. "Women's Liberation" has not yet taken root in all countries.

4. The caste system restricts the kind of participation its adherents have in the economy in a broad way. The company will feel the effects not only in its personnel and staffing practices but also in its distribution and promotional programs, because it must deal with the several market segments set up by the caste system.

5. The Hindu joint family has important economic effects. A particular form of nepotism is characteristic of the family business. Staffing will be based on considerations of family rank more than on other criteria. An American manager working in India needs to get a good cultural orientation before introducing American-style organization charts and staffing procedures. Otherwise, his "improvements" may reduce output rather than increase it. Furthermore, consumer decision making and consumption in the large joint family may well have patterns different from those in the American family, requiring an adapted marketing strategy.

6. Religious institutions themselves can play a role in economic matters. The church, or any organized religious group, can often block the introduction of new products or techniques if it sees the innovation as a threat. On the other hand, the same product or technique can be more effectively introduced

if the religious organization in question understands it and sees it as a real benefit to itself and its followers. Even Nasser, who was the Muslim ruler of a Muslim nation, had to get the support of Islamic leaders and theologians to further his program for modernizing and developing Egypt. The theologians had to be persuaded that Nasser's modern reforms were not contrary to the spirit of the Koran. In the political field, the action of Buddhist monks in Vietnam is a striking example of how religious belief can inspire its adherents to action beyond the purely religious sphere, even to the unfortunate extreme of self-immolation in this case.

7. Finally, religious divisions in a country can pose problems for management. If these divisions mean hostility among the various groups, the firm may find that it is in effect dealing with different markets. In Northern Ireland there has been strong Catholic-Protestant hostility. In India, the Muslim-Hindu clashes led to the formation of the separate Muslim state of Pakistan, but the problem is not completely settled yet. In the Netherlands there are major Catholic and Protestant groups that have their own political parties and newspapers. As with caste or other forms of discrimination, such religious divisions can cause difficulty in staffing an operation or in distributing and promoting a product. In other words, religious differences may indicate market segments that require separate marketing strategies and media.

The general tenor of these remarks is that the international firm must be aware of religious differences in its foreign markets. This means more than tolerance. It means a sensitivity to critical differences and a willingness to make adaptations where these are called for in operations or products. To cite one example, the firm that is building a plant abroad might plan the date and method of opening and dedicating the plant to reflect the local religious situation. In some countries this might entail religious officials and ceremonies, including, perhaps, a ritualistic sacrifice.

ATTITUDES AND VALUES

Much human behavior depends on attitudes and values. These values often have a religious foundation and usually imply approbation or a moral judgment. Some examples of differing values include piety in Buddhist countries; family responsibility among middle-class Indians; masculinity among males in Latin America; personal achievement among North Americans. Our values and attitudes help determine what we think is right or appropriate, what is important, and what is desirable. A number of attitudes relate to economic activities, such as attitudes toward work, achievement, scientific method, and private property. Some relate quite directly to marketing, and these are the ones we will look at here.

Attitudes toward Marketing Activities

Ever since Aristotle, activities related to selling have failed to gain high social approval. The degree of disapproval, however, varies from country to country. In countries where marketing is rated very low, marketing activities are likely to be neglected and underdeveloped. Capable, talented people will not be drawn into business. Often marketing activities will be left to a special class, or perhaps to expatriates. One is reminded of the role of medieval bankers played by the Jews, or the merchant role of the Chinese in Southeast Asia. In any case, the international firm can have problems with personnel, distribution channels, and other aspects of its marketing program, depending on a country's attitude toward business in general. There is a brighter side to this picture, however. Because marketing is well accepted and developed in the United States, the American firm abroad usually has a comparative advantage in marketing.

Attitudes toward Wealth, Material Gain, and Acquisition

The United States has been called the "affluent society," the "achieving society," and the "acquisitive society." These somewhat synonymous expressions reflect motivating values in our society. In America, wealth and acquisition are often considered the signs of success and achievement and are given social approval. In a Buddhist or Hindu society where nirvana or "wantlessness" is an ideal, people are not so motivated to produce and consume. Marketing men obviously prefer to operate in an acquisitive society. However, as a result of the revolution of rising expectations around the world, national differences in attitudes toward acquisition seem to be lessening.

Attitudes toward Change

When an international company enters a foreign market it invariably brings change by introducing new ways of doing things and new products. Americans in general accept and expect change. The word "new" usually has a very favorable connotation in America and even facilitates change when used to describe techniques and products. Many societies are more tradition oriented, revering their ancestors and their traditional ways of producing and consuming.

The marketing manager as an agent of change has a different task in such traditional societies. Rather than emphasizing what is new and different about his product, he might seek to relate it to traditional values, perhaps noting that it is similar but better. In seeking to gain acceptance of its new product, the firm might try to get at least a negative clearance—that is, no objection—from local religious leaders or other elite opinion leaders. It is important that any product meet a market need and fit in with the consumption system. Beyond that, however, the product must also fit in with the overall culture and value system if it is to be accepted.

Attitudes toward Risk Taking

Risk taking is usually associated with entrepreneurial activity. However, the consumer also takes risks when he tries a new product. Will it do what he expects it to do? Will it prejudice his standing or image with his peers? Middlemen handling the untried product may also face risks beyond those associated with their regular line. In a conservative society, there is a greater reluctance to take such risks. Therefore, the marketer must seek to reduce the risk as perceived by his customers or distributors. In part, he can accomplish this through education; in part, he must use guarantees, financial arrangements, or other marketing techniques.

Attitudes and Consumer Behavior

The various attitudes we have been discussing are all relevant to understanding consumer behavior in the markets of the world. The international marketing manager must have such an understanding if he is to develop effective marketing programs for these markets. Because of the impossibility of his gaining intimate knowledge of a great number of markets, he must rely on help from others in addition to his own research on consumer behavior. Those who may assist him in understanding local attitudes and behavior include personnel in the firm's subsidiary, the distributor, and the advertising agency.

SOCIAL ORGANIZATION

Social organization refers to the way man relates to his fellows. Man everywhere is a social creature, but the way he relates to his fellows differs somewhat from society to society. The primary kind of social organization is based on *kinship*. In America, the key unit is the family, which includes only the father and mother and the unmarried children in the household. The family unit elsewhere is often larger, including more relatives. The large joint family of Hinduism was discussed previously. In many other less developed nations there is also a large, very numerous *extended family*. Those who call themselves brothers in Congo, for example, include those whom we call cousins and uncles.

The extended family in many developing countries fulfills several important social and economic roles. It does not necessarily depend on a specific religious sanction, as does the *baradari* of Hinduism. The extended family provides mutual protection, psychological support, and a kind of economic insurance for its members. In a world of tribal warfare and primitive agriculture, this support was invaluable. Although the importance of the extended family is decreasing, it is still significant in many parts of the world. To the international marketer, the extended family means that consumption decision making takes place in a larger unit and in different ways. Pooled resources, for instance, may allow larger purchases. The marketer may find it difficult to determine the relevant consuming unit for some goods. Is it a household or family? How many members are there?

There may be other negative implications of extended-family relationships. For example, the brother who gets a position as retail salesclerk may feel it necessary to give his family special treatment, including free merchandise. He would not consider this theft, because he feels he is responding to a higher value than private property—his responsibility to his family. The family member who gets a good-paying job in the city, on the other hand, may be deterred from using his new-found consumption ability because an older brother or other relative may lay claim to the item on grounds of seniority.

Common territory provides the base for another kind of social grouping. In America, it can be the neighborhood, the suburb, or the city. In many countries of Asia and Africa, it is the tribal grouping. The tribe is often the largest effective unit in many countries, because the various tribes do not voluntarily recognize the central government. Gradually, diverse tribes are being formed into single nations, that is, nationalism is replacing tribalism. However, the transition is often slow and bloody, as Biafra testifies; and even in Europe, the Welsh are still not overly happy about being under British rule. For the marketing man, these groupings might be a clue to market segmentation in many countries.

A third kind of social grouping is the *special interest group* or association, which may be religious, occupational, recreational, or political. Special interest groups also can be useful in identifying different market segments for particular products or promotion. Apart from these three kinds of social organization, there are others that may cut across the three original categories. One is *caste or class groupings*. These may be rather detailed and rigid as in the Hindu caste system, or they may be more loose and flexible as in the American social classes. Americans have a democratic, relatively open society, but there is still much concern about social standing and status symbols. Nevertheless, social class is more important and more rigid in many other countries. The marketer must be aware of this in planning his strategy in different national markets.

Another kind of grouping based on *age* occurs especially in America and some of the other affluent industrialized nations. For example, we recognize both the "senior citizen" and the teen-age subcultures. Senior citizens usually live and act as separate economic units with their own needs and motivations. And although teen-agers commonly do not live apart from their families, they are nonetheless very much a separate economic force to be reckoned with in marketing. Indeed, in American marketing and advertising, the youth appeal often appears dominant. As noted in our discussion of the extended family, there is much less separation, social as well as economic, between age groups in Asia and other less developed areas. There is generally strong family integration at all age levels and a preponderant influence of age and seniority, in contrast to the youth motif in America.

A final aspect of social organization concerns the *role of women* in the economy and society. Women are seldom on a par with men as participants in the economy, and the degree of their participation declines as one goes down the scale of economic development country by country. The extent to which they participate affects their role as consumers, consumption influencers, and workers in the money economy, as well as their attainment of formal education. Even developed countries exhibit significant differences in attitude toward female employment. For example, the Germans are more critical of wive's employment than are the people of any other large Western country. And in France, rising affluence actually reduces female employment, which is just the opposite of the situation in the United States. In 1964, 55 percent of

American wives between forty and fifty years old were in the labor force, versus 35 percent of French wives in the same age group. These differences will be reflected in both household income levels and consumption patterns.

CONCLUSIONS

Our discussion of the cultural environment has been suggestive rather than comprehensive. Its primary purpose has been to alert the prospective marketer to the kinds of cultural parameters that can affect his international marketing programs. Identification of these parameters is important because many of them are assumed known or constant in the domestic environment but become critical variables in the international market. However, this brief survey is not sufficient to convey any expertise in this area. The practitioner needs to draw his expertise from a variety of sources: (1) the literature (such as the readings noted at the end of the chapter); (2) outside experts or consultants; (3) company experience in foreign markets; and (4) local nationals associated with the company—for example, employees, distributors, advertising agency personnel, and the like.

Table 4–3   Matrix Relating Cultural Variables to Marketing Functions

CULTURAL VARIABLES	MARKETING FUNCTIONS				
	PRODUCT	PRICE	PROMOTION	DISTRIBUTION	MARKET RESEARCH
Material culture Education Language Esthetics Political Attitudes, values Social organization					

Our point in this chapter is that international marketing management is a function of the cultural environment. One way of organizing a study of the cultural interrelationships would be to use a matrix as illustrated in Table 4–3. Of course, this table is merely indicative; it would have to be much more detailed to be operational. For example, one would need more than a general recognition that promotion is a function of certain environmental variables; he would need to analyze how the firm's advertising appeals and copy are related to literacy rates, media availability, color preferences, attitudes relevant to its product, and so on.[11]

[11] For a further discussion along this line, see Richard N. Farmer and Barry M. Richman, *Comparative Management and Economic Progress* (Homewood, Ill.: Richard D. Irwin, 1965), chaps. 2–4.

Questions

4.1   What is culture?

4.2   How can marketing be considered a cultural phenomenon?

4.3   Farm Equipment Company is seeking markets in black Africa. How would the material culture of that area affect the company's product policy?

4.4   What is the relationship between material culture and economic growth?

4.5   Discuss the role of the international marketer as an agent of cultural change. Is this role legitimate?

4.6   "Language is a mirror of the culture." Discuss.

4.7   How can the international marketer deal with the problem of linguistic diversity in world markets?

4.8   How does linguistic diversity within a foreign market pose problems for the international marketer?

4.9   Discuss the implications for the marketer of the international differences in esthetics, for example, music, color, form.

4.10 How is international marketing constrained by the educational level in foreign markets?

4.11 Discuss the marketing implications of the following religious phenomena: (a) religious holidays, (b) taboos, (c) religious institutions (church and clergy), (d) nirvana.

4.12 What particular constraints might arise in marketing to a traditional Muslim society?

4.13 Discuss the following attitudes in relation to their impact on marketing in a country: (a) attitude toward acquisition, (b) attitude toward change, (c) attitude toward risk taking.

4.14 Evaluate the marketing significance of these aspects of social organization: (a) the extended family, (b) tribalism, (c) the role of women in the economy.

4.15 The marketing research department of Convenience Foods Company has asked you to prepare a cultural analysis of a South American nation in which the company is considering operations. What would you do?

Further Readings

Books:

A Survey of Europe Today (London: Readers Digest Association, 1970).

Anderson, J. N. D., ed., *The World's Religions* (London: Inter-varsity Fellowship, 1951).

Arensberg, Conrad M., and Arthur H. Niehoff, *Introducing Social Change* (Chicago: Aldine, 1964).

Benedict, Ruth, *Patterns of Culture* (New York: Mentor Books, 1946).

Farmer, Richard N., and Barry M. Richman, *Comparative Management and Economic Progress* (Homewood, Ill.: Richard D. Irwin, 1965).

Goode, William J., *Religion among the Primitives* (New York: Free Press of Glencoe, 1951).

Harbison, F. E., and C. A. Myers, *Education, Manpower, and Economic Growth* (New York: McGraw-Hill Book Co., 1964).

Hoebel, Adamson, *Man, Culture and Society* (New York: Oxford University Press, 1960).

McCreary, Edward A., *The Americanization of Europe* (New York: Doubleday and Co., 1964).

Stephens, William N., *The Family in Cross-Cultural Perspective* (New York: Holt, Rinehart and Winston, 1963).

Tawney, R. H., *Religion and the Rise of Capitalism* (New York: Mentor Books, 1953).

Webber, Ross A., *Culture and Management* (Homewood, Ill.: Richard D. Irwin, 1969).

Weber, Max, *The Protestant Ethic and the Spirit of Capitalism*, trans. by Talcott Parsons (New York: Charles Scribner's Sons, 1930).

Yinger, J. Milton, *Religion, Society, and the Individual* (New York: Macmillan, 1957).

Articles:

Sherbini, A. A., "Marketing in the Industrialization of Underdeveloped Countries," *Journal of Marketing* (January 1965), pp. 28–32.

Data Sources:

Banks, Arthur S., and Robert B. Textor, *A Cross Polity Survey* (Cambridge: M.I.T. Press, 1964).

Russett, B. M., et al., *World Handbook of Political and Social Indicators* (New Haven, Conn.: Yale University Press, 1964).

Statistical Abstract of the United States (annual).

United Nations Demographic Yearbook (annual).

United Nations Statistical Yearbook.

5

THE POLITICAL-LEGAL
ENVIRONMENT

The politics and the laws of a nation are part of its culture. Both influence the practice of international marketing. This chapter will examine the nature of the political-legal environment and its impact as a constraint on international marketing management. We begin with the political environment.

THE POLITICAL ENVIRONMENT

The political environment of international marketing includes any national or international political factor that can affect its operations or its decision making. The elements of this environment that will concern us here are the role of the government in the economy, economic and political ideology, international relations, and business-government relations in general. The political scientist usually looks at different variables because he is interested in political behavior and organization per se and not in how these factors relate to business activity. Nevertheless, the political scientist can provide useful information to the international marketer, who is usually unqualified in this critical area.

The political environment has come to be recognized as the major factor in many international business decisions. One study has shown that nationalism and dealings with government were considered the major problems facing international management.[1] In spite of its importance, Franklin Root found that there is a lack of any *systematic* evaluation of political risks by American companies when appraising foreign investment opportunities.[2] The

[1] Michael Duerr and James Green, *The Problems Facing International Management* (New York: National Industrial Conference Board, 1968), p. 2.
[2] Franklin Root, "U.S. Business Abroad and the Political Risks," *Business Topics* (Winter 1968), p. 79.

purpose of our discussion here will be to introduce the international political environment to the international marketer in such a way that he becomes aware of its implications for his management task. The first element of that environment we consider is the role of government in the economy.

Role of Government in the Economy

The days of laissez faire are past, and today all governments play important roles in the economy of their countries. These roles are basically of two kinds: participatory and regulatory. Most governments play both, but in differing degrees. Looking first at the participatory role, we find that government participation or ownership is greatest in the communist countries, which is to be expected on the basis of their ideology. In some noncommunist less developed countries, government ownership of business is also high more because of the lack of a private sector than because of ideology. It is less prevalent though all-important, in some sectors of the Western industrialized countries. Italy, for example, has a very large public sector.

Participator

The international marketer has several reasons for concern about government ownership of economic activities. One is that government ownership may preclude operations by his firm in certain markets. In India, for example, certain sectors of the economy are reserved exclusively for government enterprise. Another is that government ownership may mean that the firm's only customer in a country is the government. This is clearly the case in selling to communist countries, where the firm can deal only with a state trading organization. It is also the case in countries where the government runs an industry that represents the firm's total market, such as a socialized medical program or the railroads. When the firm faces a government monopsony in a country, its market power is greatly reduced.

Government participation can also take the form of partnership with the firm if the firm establishes a subsidiary in the country. Where government requires joint ventures and the private sector is inadequate, the government may be the only available partner. Such a partnership poses strong constraints on marketing management in that country. The so-called controllable elements of the marketing mix will be less controllable. Nevertheless, the firm does well to consider governments as partners where there is no altrnative. It is unwise to rule them out merely because of a management ideology favoring private enterprise. Such doctrinaire approaches do not help solve problems.

Regulator

The marketer is familiar with the government's role as regulator of his economic environment. Governments plan and direct, tax and regulate the economy. The regulations imposed through monetary and fiscal policy will especially affect the marketer's use of the pricing and credit tools. But in general a country's laws affecting different elements of the marketing mix will most frequently influence the marketing manager's task. In most countries, there are laws and regulations concerning products, promotion, and pricing. The marketer is not so much concerned with the existence of such laws as he is with the international variation in them. He is also worried about the possible discriminatory use of such laws against the international ("foreign") firm. The extent and nature of these laws will be discussed under The Legal Environment of International Marketing.

Ideologies and Marketing

The marketing concept and marketing management were originally American phenomena. They have also found a home in countries that are closest ideologically to the United States. That is, the countries where marketing activity is strongest and most advanced are generally democratic and capitalistic, sharing a common Western tradition (Japan is a partial exception). These are also the home countries of most international firms. Does this mean that marketing is antithetical to societies that are nondemocratic, socialistic, and do not share the same Western tradition? It is true that marketing has no ideology of its own, except that marketers themselves tend to be motivated by profit and prefer the free market to a planned economy. However, marketing managers are products of their own culture and usually share its ideologies.

Because marketing is a cultural as well as an economic and technical activity, its ideological environment will affect its performance. All the functions of marketing must be carried on in any society that is above the subsistence level, but the way these functions are performed will vary according to the cultural and ideological environment. One implication of this for the international marketer is that he must be ready to free his marketing program from the ideological ties of his home country. After all, marketing means adapting to the market.

Capitalism, Socialism, or Democracy?

The American marketer will find that marketing can function effectively in ideological environments which differ from that of the United States. A firm can market effectively—both for itself and for the benefit of the people— in a nondemocratic society. A firm can market effectively also in a socialistic society if private enterprise is allowed there at all; India, for example, allows international marketing whereas East Germany does not. As individuals, marketing managers may have strong ideas about democracy, socialism, or a particular ideology, such as apartheid in South Africa. It is appropriate for him to have these ideas, but they should not determine his marketing program.

In deciding whether to operate in countries where ideologies conflict with those of management, or those of the international firm's home base, there will be both moral and practical considerations. Where there are moral issues, the decision must satisfy the conscience of the decision makers. Although ethical questions should affect business decisions, a danger lies in the too common tendency toward self-righteousness and a feeling that "our way is best." This attitude fosters a lack of understanding and sympathy for other viewpoints. After all, marketing is an economic function of the firm, not a means for spreading the American, British, or any other way of life. In regard to practical considerations, the firm will be interested primarily in the long-run profit potential; this in turn will depend on (1) the market potential of the country in question, (2) the possibility of adverse action by either the host or the home government, and (3) the reaction of customers in other markets. For example, American firms selling to communist countries have been threatened by boycotts at home in their major market. Firms dealing with Israel run the risk of an Arab boycott.

South Africa is one nation where international firms' operations have been questioned by critics in the firms' home countries. The following observation throws some light on the political implications of an international firm's operations there.

Social changes and industrial developments in South Africa are the most serious threat to the present system, which is based on the assumptions that racial groups can be mutually insulated from competitive and "contaminating" contacts and that the position of these groups can be fixed and enforced by legislative and administrative action. While this might have been possible in static rural societies, South Africa is no longer rural . . . . The labor demands of the mines and of a burgeoning industry constantly draw Africans into the vortex of urban and industrial life . . . . Both Europeans and Africans are being drawn into a complicated industrial order. Complete separation is obviously not possible, and restrictive regulations for industry based on rigid concepts of caste are extremely difficult to enforce. Industry has a vested interest in more flexible arrangements and, with the growing scarcity of skilled labor, does not look with favor upon government edicts which define skills and jobs in racial terms.[3]

Nationalism

A particular ideology common to all nations is nationalism. Nationalism means that *we* are different from and/or better than *they*. The respectable form of nationalism is called patriotism. The excessive form is called chauvinism. Nationalism in its original meaning as a unifying force in the formation of nation-states had a good image: *e pluribus unum*. Today it is considered a divisive force, hindering regional and international cooperation. The essence of nationalism is that the residents of one country see themselves as the "we" group and all other nations as the "they" group. Implicit in such a division is the idea that "they" are somewhat of a threat to us.[4]

The existence of nationalism has several implications for the international marketer. First, it means that he must not let his own nationalism color his marketing program. His task is selling products, not carrying the flag. Second, his firm, as a foreigner in all of its international markets, may be a victim

[3] W. O. Brown and H. Lewis, "Racial Situations and Issues in Africa," in *The United States and Africa*, ed. by Walter Goldschmidt (New York: American Assembly, Columbia University, 1958), p. 152.
[4] For a fuller discussion of the role of nationalism, see John Fayerweather, "19th Century Ideology and 20th Century Reality," *Columbia Journal of World Business* (Winter 1966), pp. 77–86.

of local nationalism, or xenophobia. A possible strategy to avoid this might be to develop as national an image as possible. As we will see later in detail, developing such an image will affect policies on branding, promotion, and distribution, as well as other elements of the marketing mix. Indeed, one of the challenges facing the international marketer is finding how best to adapt to the demands of local nationalism without diminishing the international strengths of the firm.

Stability

Stability of a country's political environment is a major concern of the international marketer. The country need not be stable in the sense that change is absent, but what change there is should be gradual and nonviolent. Many international marketing decisions have a fairly long time horizon. Abrupt or violent changes in the political-legal parameters can upset what otherwise would be a good medium- or long-range marketing program. What the firm really is looking for in its international markets is reasonable continuity of government policies and actions toward business, especially international business. Great uncertainty in this area leads to negative decisions, that is, no investment, or reduced activity or withdrawal from a market.

Indicators of Instability

Political instability has no precise definition but there are certain indicators the international marketer should evaluate. One is frequency of changes in regime. Changes in the ruling party or group usually mean changes in the political environment of business. These changes need not be radical to be significant for the firm's operations. Businesses, like individuals, can adjust to many different political-legal environments, but if the environment alters frequently, consequent uncertainty can prevent optimal adjustment. Discontinuities in government policies can occur even with peaceful changes of regime; they are apt to be much greater, however, with a violent overthrow, or a *coup d'état*. Castro's coming to power in Cuba is one striking example among many others. Action against foreign companies is a frequent result of these changes in regime, as the new leaders rally the people against the foreigner.

Another indicator of political instability is the incidence of violence, disruptions, and demonstrations in a country. Good statistics in this area are not yet available, but political scientists are developing some useful measurements including the number of deaths by violence, size and number of demonstrations, and man-days lost through strikes. Even in the absence of violence, potential instability can be discerned if serious inequities exist in a society. For example, several years before Castro came into power in Cuba, a marketing research team with an American firm was investigating investment opportunities in Latin America. They reported that Cuba should be avoided because the social problems and inequities made Cuba ripe for revolution. This was at a time when the Batista regime appeared very stable. Or, to cite another example, before the Biafran war Nigeria was the most stable country in black

Africa. The important conclusion is that countries which have had a record of stability may not have a stable future if underlying conditions are not sound.

Yet another indicator of political instability can be the various cultural divisions in the country. In Chapter 4 we saw how these factors operate. Here we will indicate their relation to political instability. Linguistic diversity, if not a cause of trouble, is usually associated with it. Ceylon has had a great deal of violence between the Tamil minority and the Sinhalese majority. India had riots when Hindi was made a national language alongside English. Developed countries too have their troubles in this area as evidenced by Belgium and Canada. Tribal differences can be another source of trouble. Congo, India, and Nigeria are three countries that have made headlines in recent years because of tribal conflicts.

A final source of political division and instability is religious. The example involving the most violence is the Hindu-Muslim conflict which led to the formation of Pakistan as a separate Muslim state. Another instance also involving violence is the Protestant-Catholic conflict in Northern Ireland. All these cultural divisions in a nation have marketing implications in their own right. They take on added significance when they indicate instability in the political environment of international marketing.

International Relations

The international firm usually is concerned primarily about its marketing *within* each of its markets. However, there are two reasons for the international marketer to be concerned about the host nation's international politics as well as its internal political environment. First, the international firm is seen as a foreigner, one of the "they" group, in each of its markets abroad. Therefore, it is automatically involved with the country's international relations, no matter how neutral it may try to be. Second, many national operations of the firm are related to operations in other countries on either the supply or demand side, or on both. The firm as international marketer is thus almost inevitably involved in and concerned about the international relations of its various host countries.

One important aspect of a host country's international relations is its relationship with the firm's home country. American firms abroad will be affected by the host nation's attitude toward American foreign policy, including the Vietnam war, foreign aid, attitude toward Israel, and so on. Where the host nation dislikes any aspect of American policy, it may be the American firm that is bombed or boycotted along with the United States Information Service office in the capital of the country. English or French firms operating in the former colonies of those countries will be affected by that relationship, sometimes favorably, sometimes otherwise.

A second critical element is the host country's relations with other nations. If a country is a member of a regional grouping, such as EEC or LAFTA, that fact will influence the firm's evaluation of the country as a market as well as the firm's marketing program and logistics there. If a nation has particular friends or enemies among other nations, the firm will have to modify its international marketing and logistics to comply with how that market is supplied and to whom it can sell. For example, the United States limits trade with communist countries and has an absolute embargo on all trade with five of them. Black African nations restrict trade with Rhodesia, Portugal, and South Africa. Arab nations may boycott and otherwise punish companies having any dealings with Israel.

"Egyptian authorities have frozen Ford Motor Co. bank accounts in Egypt while they press a customs claim against the company. They say Ford owes $1.7 million on imported parts used in its plant in Alexandria. The action came in the wake of last week's decision by the Arab Boycott Office to black-list Ford and Coca-Cola for dealing with Israel. Later, the Office added RCA to the list. RCA had licensed an Israeli company to press its phonograph records."[5]

Another clue to a nation's international relationships and behavior is its membership in international organizations. We have mentioned regional groupings already, but there are many other kinds of international organizations that affect a national member's behavior. One is military agreements such as NATO, SEATO, and so on, which affect the economies of the members and may restrict unilateral military or political action on their part. Membership in GATT reduces the likelihood that a country will impose new trade barriers. Membership in IMF, the World Bank, or a development bank aids a country's international financial situation and increases its resources for development, but it also puts constraints on the country's behavior. Many other international organizations or agreements impose certain behavioral rules on their membership. These agreements cover patents, communication, transportation, and other items of interest to the international marketer. As a rule, the more international organizations a country belongs to, the more general regulations it accepts, and the more dependable and predictable is its behavior. Some of these international agreements are discussed under The Legal Environment of International Marketing.

Conclusions on the Political Environment

We have looked at the various aspects of a nation's political environment as they affect business-government relations and as they constrain the task of international marketing management. The political environment is an important variable not only in the initial decision to invest in a country but also in the continuing marketing operation there. As we will see repeatedly in Part II of this text, decisions on product policy, pricing, promotion, and distribution all will be influenced by the host country's political environment. An adverse or hostile political environment can lead to governmental and popular reactions ranging from expropriation and bombing to strikes, boycotts, and discriminatory regulations and taxes.

[5] *Business Week*, December 3, 1966, p. 120.

How can management approach the problems posed by the political environment? The first step is to become fully informed of the situation and to analyze this information. The firm's intelligence operation must go beyond traditional market research to include the political environment. For example, a few of America's large international companies have their own equivalent of the State Department's country desks, the purpose of which is to provide political analysis of foreign markets on a continuing basis to help the firm anticipate and prepare for change. On a more modest scale, such ongoing analysis is necessary for any firm with important stakes in foreign markets.

There are several different kinds of information sources to meet the firm's political intelligence needs. Usually a great deal of published material is available for background on a country. Current periodicals, such as *Commerce Today* and *Foreign Affairs*, and specialized information services provide useful data and analysis. The firm's Washington representative (see Chapter 14) and the foreign embassies there are sources of up-to-date information. The Department of State has representatives all around the world who generally have a good picture of the situation in their country. Finally, the firm's own subsidiaries or representatives in its markets should be a primary resource. Local nationals working with the firm should be able to relate the local political environment to the situation of the firm.

For information on the political environment to be useful to the international marketer, he must know how it relates to his task. He develops this understanding by analyzing the experience of his own firm and that of other companies in his markets. We have suggested some key relationships in this chapter. Others will be noted in the chapters on management in Part II. The elements of company marketing strategy must be related to the political environment. As a method of approach, Richard Robinson notes several questions the firm might ask in evaluating the political vulnerability of its product policy, among which are the following:

1. Is the product ever subject to political debate regarding adequacy of supply (gasoline, transport facilities, public utilities, tires, and so on)?

2. Is the product a critical input for other industries (cement, steel, power, machine tools, and so on)?

3. Is the product socially or politically sensitive (drugs and medicines, foods)?

4. Does the product have national defense significance?[6]

In 1970, when Libya nationalized the service station outlets of the foreign oil companies, the government minister said: "This commodity is of extreme importance to the nation and shouldn't be left in the hands of foreigners."[7]

There are several other aspects of management response to the political

[6] Richard D. Robinson, *International Business Policy* (New York: Holt, Rinehart and Winston, 1964), pp. 141, 142.

[7] *Wall Street Journal*, July 6, 1970, p. 3.

environment. One is the advisability of maintaining neutrality. Regardless of management's attitudes, political involvement can only hurt the firm. Although the firm's operations may have a political impact (see the quotation about South Africa on page 117), this impact should result from its economic operations and not from its active political involvement. Contingency planning is another necessary part of management's response. The international marketer should plan how he will alter his marketing policies and level of involvement to meet any possible change in the political environment.

As the firm's political vulnerability in a country increases, it should lower its exposure and visibility. This usually means "going more native" in ownership, staffing, branding, promotion, and other company policies. A good public relations program, another important element of management response, keeps open communication channels from the firm's public and responds sensitively to its needs and desires. This is especially important for the international firm, which is a foreigner in all but one of its markets. We discuss thoroughly the nature of the public relations function and its relationship to international marketing in Chapter 14. Here it is sufficient to note that a sound public relations program is a key element in the firm's adjustment to its political environment. Finally, international managers must add diplomatic skills to their other abilities.

THE LEGAL ENVIRONMENT OF INTERNATIONAL MARKETING

The political environment in a nation includes the prevalent attitudes toward business enterprise, both domestic and foreign. From this political climate is generated the legal environment for business, that is, the nation's actual laws and regulations pertaining to business. It is important for a firm to know the legal environment in each of its foreign markets because these laws constitute the "rules of the game." At the same time, the firm must know the political environment because it determines how the laws are enforced and indicates the direction of new legislation or regulation. Marketing and the law is a subject covered in almost every marketing course and the law as a critical parameter in international marketing is no exception. However, the legal environment of international marketing is more complicated, having three dimensions. For an American firm these are (1) United States laws, (2) international law, and (3) domestic laws in each of the firm's foreign markets.

United States Law and International Marketing

Every American student of marketing has become familiar with such important laws affecting marketing as the Pure Food and Drug Act and the Robinson-Patman Act. Oddly enough, these are not the American laws that concern the international marketer; other areas of American law relate more specifically to his task. The international marketing considerations most affected by American law are exporting, antitrust, and organization and ownership arrangements.

Exporting

The United States has a variety of controls on export trade. First, there are general restrictions against *trading with communist countries*. In the case of Albania, Communist China, Cuba, North Korea, and North Vietnam, the restriction is a rigid ban on sales to these markets and even applies to sales of American subsidiaries abroad. The ban also prohibits the sale of components that go into a foreign firm's products which are destined for one of the prohibited markets. For example, the French government at one time wanted to sell jet planes to Communist China. However, the inertial guidance system for this aircraft was supplied by General Electric. General Electric was forbidden to sell this key component to the French for this purpose. This ban can be avoided only if the American company owns less than 50 percent of the foreign operation supplying the parts. In this case, the American company does not have responsibility for the decision. A changing political climate, for example, the Nixon overtures toward China, may modify these restrictions.

Another United States export control relates not to the target markets but to the *nature of the product* exported. The American government, through the Department of Commerce, controls exports through a licensing program. The department publishes a manual indicating the export requirements for different kinds of commodities. For the export of a wide range of goods, only a "general license," easily obtainable from the Department of Commerce, is needed. The goods covered by a "general license" are usually those obtainable from many other countries and those considered of no significance to national security. In order to export restricted goods, or those destined for certain countries, the firm needs a "validated license." This license is more difficult to obtain and more restrictive in nature. It specifies a shipment of specific goods within a given time period.

There is a general prohibition against exporting certain types of products considered strategic or sensitive. For example, United States law prohibits the export or sale of technical data or commodities related to nuclear weapons and closely controls the sale of explosive devices, armaments, various copper goods, and electrical, mechanical, or other devices primarily used for surveillance of communications. These controls are imposed on the grounds of national welfare and safety. Violation can mean severe punishment. In one incident, a manufacturer and his executive secretary were fined $10,000 and imprisoned for five years for illegal exportation of missile-firing devices. Even though the United States is considered to be a relatively free-trading nation, these export controls may add up to a fairly significant constraint on both the product-line and market-selection decisions of the international marketing manager.

Another restriction on the international marketer's freedom to export is in the *pricing* area. In Chapter 14 on pricing, we will analyze all the variables in export-pricing decisions. Here we will merely note one of them—the Internal Revenue Service (IRS). Although the international marketer would like to base his export prices on supply and demand and internal company considerations, the IRS can examine and have a voice in the price he sets on exports to foreign subsidiaries. In other words, the IRS has a say in international transfer prices on exports to foreign affiliates of American companies. On such exports the exporter might wish to charge a low transfer price as a way of aiding the subsidiary, of gaining income in a lower tax jurisdiction, or for some other reason. However, the IRS will not allow such transfer prices if they are unduly low because they would lower the firm's profits in America and therefore lower corporate income taxes paid by the firm in the United States. An "unduly" low transfer price on such exports, which account for one-fourth of all United States exports, would mean higher profits and taxes in the foreign jurisdiction at the expense of tax revenue in the United States.

Antitrust

It might seem strange that United States antitrust laws would affect the *foreign* business activities of American companies. However, that is a real and occasionally disturbing fact of life for international management. The opinion and practice of the United States Justice Department is that even if an act is committed abroad, it falls within the jurisdiction of American courts *if the act produces consequences within the United States*. In terms of the theory of general equilibrium in economics—that is, everything depends on everything else—many activities of American business abroad will have some repercussions on the American domestic market. That is the meaning of international interdependence. However, the question arises primarily in three kinds of situations: (1) when an American firm *acquires* a foreign firm; (2) when it engages in a *joint venture* abroad with an American or foreign firm; or (3) when it makes some overseas marketing *agreement* with another firm.

When an American firm expands abroad by acquiring a foreign company, the Justice Department will be concerned about the possible impact on competition in the United States. It may take action under Section 7 of the Clayton Act, which prohibits certain corporate amalgamations that could lessen competition. Action would be more probable if the acquisition were in the same product line as the company. Two examples show possible outcomes. It will be noted that although there may be uncertainty as to the outcome of a Justice Department inquiry, there is no uncertainty about the department's interest in foreign mergers and acquisitions of American companies.

The Gillette Company in 1967 acquired the German company Braun AG, one of Europe's largest manufacturers of electric razors. Braun razors are marketed in the United States under private brands by Ronson, which has an exclusive distributorship running until 1976. The Justice Department contended that the acquisition eliminated potential competition between Gillette and Braun and lessened competition between Gillette and Ronson. The Justice Department also claimed that the acquisition would further enlarge Gillette's already dominant position in the shaving market in the United States. While the antitrust suit was in process, Gillette signed an agreement to operate Braun as a separate concern.

In the 1960s, Chrysler acquired a majority interest in both Simca of France and Rootes of the United Kingdom. Since these companies were in the same product line, automobiles, the Justice Department naturally made an investigation. However, in this case the department proposed no objection to either acquisition. The department ruled that because Simca's and Rootes' sales had previously been very low in the United States, their acquisition by Chrysler had a negligible effect on commerce within the United States. Perhaps Chrysler's relatively smaller share in the American automobile market also weighed in their decision.

There are no sure guidelines to possible Justice Department actions regarding joint ventures or acquisitions of American firms abroad. However, any such moves by a large company certainly will be investigated and probably will be challenged if the two companies are in the same product area. Smaller companies have greater freedom to expand overseas by any route that seems best to them.

Webb-Pomerene Associations

Given the interest of the United States government in extending its antitrust enforcement to the foreign activities of American companies, it is all the more surprising to discover the Webb-Pomerene or Export Trade Act which deliberately permits the cooperation of competing firms in export trade. This 1918 act specifically excludes from antitrust prosecution the cooperation of competitive firms in the development of foreign markets; that is, firms that compete domestically can collaborate in exporting. The law was passed following study and recommendations by the Federal Trade Commission. The Commission report noted that "if Americans are to enter the markets of the world on more nearly equal terms with their organized competitors and their organized customers, and if small American producers and manufacturers are to engage in trade on profitable terms, they must be free to unite their efforts."[8]

The commission's intent was that American exporters be given countervailing power to enable them to compete against foreign oligopolies or cartels and to prevent foreign monopsonists from playing off one exporter against another. It was expected that this would be especially helpful to smaller firms that could combine and gain economies of scale in setting up export operations.

Although this cooperative export activity is specifically exempt from prosecution under American antitrust law, there are two qualifications. (1) The collaboration of domestic competitors for foreign business must not affect or tend to lessen competition *within* the United States. In other words, the exemption from antitrust is only to help American producers meet noncompetitive conditions abroad, not to encourage or permit any reduction of competition in the domestic market. (2) Exemption from antitrust prosecution does not extend to "unfair methods of competition." That is, in their

[8] FTC, *Report on Cooperation in American Export Trade*, part I (1916), p. 8.

business practices abroad, American firms must follow the same standard of behavior that is required in America. The dual standard which the act allows applies only to organizational questions, not to trade practices.

Webb-Pomerene associations provide one route for selling overseas and are discussed further in Chapter 11 on distribution. They are relevant here to illustrate the rather ambivalent attitude of the United States government toward antitrust in international business; however, it is generally true that antitrust prosecution is more likely to be undertaken against the large company, and Webb-Pomerene exemption is more likely to be granted the small company in international business. In each case, the United States government extends its legal jurisdiction to include the foreign activities of American companies. By so doing, it constitutes an important element in the legal environment of international marketing, constricting or expanding the alternatives offered American companies in foreign markets.

Taxes and Organization Form

TAX HAVENS   American tax law is another major legal influence on international marketing. We have already mentioned the role of the Internal Revenue Service in export transfer pricing. Tax laws themselves influence company decisions on how to organize for international marketing. Before 1962, American firms could set up foreign-base corporations where it was possible to accumulate income earned abroad. United States taxes were not payable on this income until it was remitted to the parent company in America; the amount of taxes payable was thus in effect an interest-free loan from the United States Treasury to these foreign operations. This provision aided the foreign expansion of American companies in the 1950s. Because of United States balance of payments deficits, the tax law was changed in 1962 to require payment of United States income taxes at the time the income was *earned* rather than when it was *remitted*. The effect of this change was greatly to diminish the use of the so-called "tax havens." Generally, however, the less developed countries are not covered by this change in the law because the American government wants to encourage investment expansion there.

WHTC   For their Latin American and Canadian marketing, American companies can gain tax savings by organizing a Western Hemisphere Trade Corporation (WHTC). By a rather complicated formula, a company's WHTC will pay a lower income tax rate in the United States than the parent company. Although the WHTC must be incorporated in the United States, 95 percent of its income must be derived from sources outside the country. The tax savings are an incentive to form a WHTC, but a company must compare the savings to the administrative costs and other problems of organizing such a separate subsidiary. Because of the lower income tax rate, there is a temptation for the producing division to give a low transfer price to the WHTC. However, the company may be charged by the IRS with giving too low a transfer price in order to earn the income in the WHTC and avoid the higher regular tax rate.

The Eli Lilly Company was charged with seeking to avoid United States taxes through low transfer prices to its WHTC. The IRS won the suit and Eli Lilly had to pay several million dollars in back taxes and penalties, although the company claimed the lower prices to its WHTC were accounted for by the services it performed for the parent company.

DISC AND ETC   Largely because of America's continuing balance of payments problems, a variety of export-promoting devices have been tried by the government. One dates from the 1962 Revenue Act and is called the Export Trade Corporation (ETC). The purpose of ETC is to encourage companies to increase exports by exempting from taxation some of the export-trade income, when it is earned through the medium of an ETC subsidiary. In practice, the qualifications for becoming an ETC were so strict that relatively few firms formed an ETC subsidiary. In 1970, a new plan of a similar but more liberal nature was proposed. It was initiated by the Treasury Department and called DISC (Domestic International Sales Corporation). Like WHTC and ETC, DISC would be a domestic subsidiary for foreign sales and would enjoy tax benefits.

The details of all these arrangements for gaining tax benefits in exporting are not important here. What is significant is the potential impact of United States tax law on the firm's method of organizing in order to export from America. America needs to expand exports, and tax incentives seem to offer the strongest motivation to firms. If the firm's goal is profits, management must consider American tax laws in organizing its international marketing activity; Tax law thus becomes another parameter along with the usual market and company factors. The firm's choice of a country to supply international markets will depend in part on the export incentives offered by different countries.

International Law and International Marketing

It is difficult to discuss international law, and even more difficult to find international laws. There is no international law-making body which corresponds to the legislatures of sovereign nations. By the same token, there is no international executive to enforce international law, and no real judiciary to try cases in international law. The World Court in The Hague offers only a partial and very limited exception to that statement. What then is international law? For our present discussion, we will define international law as the collection of treaties, conventions, and agreements between nations which have, more or less, the force of law. These treaties and conventions may be bilateral, between two nations, or multilateral, among many nations. International law in this sense is quite different from national laws which have international implications, such as the American antitrust laws. The international extension of the influence of American laws is done on a unilateral basis. International law involves some mutuality, with two or more countries participating in the drafting and execution.

What is the impact of international law on international marketing? There are many international treaties and conventions that have either a general or a specific impact on decisions made by the international marketing manager. We begin our discussion with those international agreements having a general effect on international business and go on to those dealing with more specific marketing questions. Then we look at the legal implications of regional groupings, one of the more significant growth areas of international law.

FCN and Tax Treaties

The United States has signed bilateral treaties of Friendship, Commerce, and Navigation (FCN) with many countries. FCN treaties cover several aspects of commercial relations between the two signing nations. They commonly protect and identify the nature of the right of American companies to do business in those nations with which the United States has such a treaty, and vice versa. FCN treaties, among other things, usually guarantee "national treatment" to the foreign subsidiary; that is, it will not be discriminated against by the nation's laws and judiciary. This nondiscrimination may not always be realized, but it is more likely in an FCN-treaty nation than elsewhere.

Of a similar type are the tax treaties which the United States has signed with a number of nations. The purpose of the tax treaty is to avoid double taxation; that is, if a company has paid income tax on its operations in a treaty nation, the United States will tax that income only to the extent that the foreign tax rate is less than the American rate. Thus, if the corporate income tax rates are equal in the two countries, there is no tax to pay in the United States on income earned in the other country. One effect of this policy has been to encourage foreign governments to raise their corporate income tax rate to the American level. They can thus increase their tax revenues without hurting the foreign subsidiary. The only loser is the Internal Revenue Service. Obviously, tax-treaty nations are, other things being equal, better places for a subsidiary than countries that do not have such a treaty.

IMF and GATT

The International Monetary Fund (IMF) and the General Agreement on Tariffs and Trade (GATT) were both discussed in Chapter 2. Here we want merely to note that both agreements are part of the limited body of effective international law. Both agreements identify acceptable and nonacceptable behavior for the member nations. Their effectiveness lies in their power to apply sanctions. The IMF can withhold its services from members who act "illegally," that is, contrary to the agreement. GATT allows injured nations to retaliate against members who have broken its rules. In IMF and GATT we come reasonably close to finding international bodies with legislative, executive, and judicial powers—prerequisites for true international law.

The international marketer is interested in the activities of both IMF and GATT because their major concern is akin to his own, namely, the maintenance of a stable environment conducive to expanding international trade. He is concerned about IMF's ability to expand liquidity for international finance and to reduce exchange controls in his markets. He is concerned about GATT's ability to reduce national barriers and restrictions on international trade. One specific aspect of GATT worth mentioning is its antidumping code, a code designed to set an internationally accepted procedure for dealing with dumping, that is, the practice of selling goods at a lower price in foreign markets than in the domestic market. Such a code limits the firm's ability to use marginal cost pricing on its exports. which will be discussed in Chapter 14.

The international legal implications of GATT and IMF provisions do not apply to the international marketer's behavior, but rather to the behavior of the nations within which he is marketing. The environment for international marketing is more dependable and less capricious because of the activities of these two organizations. The firm's selection of markets and its international logistics patterns will be affected by the continuing operations of GATT and IMF.

UNCITRAL—A Step Ahead

The United Nations (UN) is interested in the development of an international law consistent with its own goals. One step taken by the UN was the establishment in 1966 of the International Trade Law Commission (UNCITRAL). UNCITRAL's goal is to promote a uniform commercial code for the entire world, an important and very ambitious program. The first step is the analysis of national laws and the small body of international law. The second and a more difficult step is the formulation of new international conventions and model laws to standardize commercial codes. The commission's priority areas are international sales and payments, commercial arbitration, and shipping legislation. It is working with governmental and private groups, such as the International Chamber of Commerce. This is an area of great significance to the international marketer and also one where the interests of the multinational corporation coincide with those of the UN. A globally uniform commercial code would eliminate many irritations and frictions in international marketing management.

ISO

Numerous other international organizations and agreements have a semilegal influence on international trade and marketing. Several of these are also members of the United Nations' alphabetical family: UNESCO, ILO, WHO, and so on. Because they are less directly concerned with international trade, however, we will not discuss them here. We will identify only the organizations most pertinent to international marketing, to give a feeling for the kind of legal and regulatory environment the multinational firm will encounter. One group whose activities are of special interest to the international marketer is the International Standards Organization (ISO). Industry groups in most of the major industrial countries participate in the work of ISO, but the United States has been a laggard here. The ISO has no less than 114 technical committees through which it is working toward the development of uniform international standards in the technical and industrial fields.

Differing national standards and specifications are a major hindrance to international trade and specialization. But standardizing is a very slow and difficult task because the changing of national standards often hurts vested interests. In this area multinational companies and their subsidiaries can have a voice in determining what will be the legal standards for tomorrow. Each national subsidiary of the company can present its views, perhaps joining forces with its national trade association, to the relevant body in that country. Thus, when the international negotiations are held, the company can be sure that its viewpoint is presented and through the voice of each of its subsidiaries in the various nations. Perhaps because the export market is relatively small compared to the domestic market, American industry has been less active in ISO than other exporting nations. This lack of interest may be costly in the long run; they may find themselves closed out of many markets. For example, Western Hemisphere standards for television sets are different from those set by the International Telecommunications Union (ITU). This difference has cost some American manufacturers millions of dollars in lost sales to areas with other standards, namely, Africa, Asia, and Europe.

Patents

Patents are registered on an individual-nation basis but there is also an International Convention for the Protection of Industrial Property, called the Paris Union. Over eighty nations are members, and even the Soviet Union has joined. There are two major benefits to membership in the Paris Union. First, foreign holders of patents have the same patent rights and remedies for infringement as do domestic holders; that is, foreign holders enjoy national treatment. Second, any patent filing in a member nation carries with it a one-year protection period in the remaining countries. Thus application for a patent in America provides a one-year grace period in which to apply in any or all of the other member nations, without fear of another party being granted a valid license on the product or process.

The Paris Union provides some relief from the chaos of completely individual and arbitrary national appoaches to patenting. Major weaknesses of the union are that application must be made separately in each country and that each country has somewhat different rules and criteria for filing. This fragmentation makes the cost of filing very high (as much as $40,000) for companies, not to mention costly duplication of effort by national patent offices. For example, it is estimated that 10 percent of the development costs of the Hovercraft were spent on securing patents around the world.[9]

Because of the costs in time and effort of the Paris Union approach, efforts have been made to develop a more streamlined and efficient international patent system. Since 1967, discussions have been held in Western Europe with delegates from the United States, Japan, and the Soviet Union, as well as from the Western European countries. Participating nations account for over 80 percent of the world's patent applications. The reform is expected to lead to a new international agreement whereby an acceptable application filed by an inventor or company in one country will automatically be valid in other

[9] *Economist*, June 17, 1967, p. 468.

member countries. The patenter would still have to file and pay separate fees to each nation, but the overall time and search costs would be greatly reduced, both for the applicant and for the granting nation. After one member nation has validated an application, others will accept it without each one having to repeat the whole process to satisfy its particular requirements. This change in international law should expedite the international transfer of technology to the benefit of all.

Trademarks

Trademarks are another form of industrial or intellectual property of great significance to the international marketer. Like patents, trademarks or brands must go through a national registration process to be protected internationally. Costs may be as much as $200 per country, but trademark registration is nevertheless less time consuming and costly than patent registration. There are two major international trademark conventions which aid the international marketer. One is the International Convention for the Protection of Industrial Property discussed above. This ninety-year-old organization covers trademarks as well as patents. The Paris Union allows a six-month protection or priority period in the case of trademarks, as contrasted with a one-year period for patents. That is, registration of a trademark in one member country gives the firm six months in which to register in any other member countries before it loses its protection in those countries.

The second major convention is the Madrid Arrangement for International Registration of Trademarks. The Madrid Arrangement has only twenty-two members, mostly in Europe. The United States is not a member, although an American firm's subsidiary in a member country can qualify for its benefits. The principal advantage offered by the Madrid Arrangement is that it permits a registration in just one member country to qualify as registration in all twenty-one other member countries, with appropriate payments. This is the direction the new patent arrangements are taking, as we have seen. The convenience and economies of scale are evident—it might be called a form of international one-stop shopping.

The former French colonies have their own multinational arrangement. Members of the African and Malagasy Union allow a single registration to cover all members. The remaining French colonies are in an even better situation. A registration in France is automatically extended to them without separate application. And an Inter-American Convention for trademark protection gives coverage for the Western Hemisphere similar to that given by the Paris Union.

NATO Export Controls

Patents and trademarks are covered both by national laws and by international agreements. This dual coverage is a common phenomenon in international law. The subject matter is the same as in national law, but the jurisdiction is expanded to cover several nations. Another example is export controls.

We have already seen how the United States controls the export of certain goods, and there is an international agreement of similar intent. NATO (North Atlantic Treaty Organization) has a Coordinating Committee (CoCom) designed to prevent the sale of any strategic goods or technology to the communist nations, if such a sale would threaten the security of the West. The prohibited list has grown smaller over the years, and its administration depends partly on the temperature of the Cold War. Although the United States is a NATO member, its own controls are stricter. Therefore, CoCom regulations do not affect an American firm although they may affect that firm's affiliates in other NATO countries.

The International Air: ICAO, IATA, ITU, Intelsat

The area in which some of the most specific international laws and regulations are developing is the use of the air for international travel and communications. Two regulatory bodies concerned with international air travel and freight are the ICAO (International Civil Aviation Organization) and the IATA (International Air Transport Association). The ICAO is a United Nations organization with 112 country members. One of its principal functions is to set world-wide standards for aviation equipment and international air travel, covering not only aircraft but also ground facilities and the training of civil aviation personnel. Although nations may have their own domestic standards and regulatory agencies, ICAO is supreme at the international level. The ICAO assembly is the legislative body to which all members belong. Its elected council is the executive body, but the council also acts as arbiter between member states. ICAO thus includes the legislative, executive, and judicial functions in one organization.

IATA

IATA membership is composed of international airlines, about ninety of them, rather than nations. For these airlines, IATA is the most important factor in the international legal environment. ICAO regulations, being primarily technical, are not very controversial; but IATA regulations are commercial and, therefore, much more sensitive. IATA's principal activity is the regulation of international air fares and rates. These rates and fares are set through negotiations by the member airlines but must be approved by their governments. Thus IATA embodies a strange blend of private and governmental international regulation.

ITU and Intelsat

The International Telecommunication Union (ITU) is another United Nations organization. It has a membership of 135 countries, larger than the United Nations itself. ITU formulates regulations for international communications via radio, telephone, and telegraph. The International Telecommunications Satellite Consortium (Intelsat) is an offspring of ITU designed to deal with the new satellite communications technology. Only about half the ITU members belong to Intelsat. Intelsat is another example of an international agreement designed to regulate a specific field, in this case, global communications by satellite.

What are the implications of these four organizations for the international marketer? First of all, many large international companies are producing goods or services regulated by these four organizations. For these firms, the rulings of the international group are usually more important to product specifications than are domestic regulations. Furthermore, almost all international companies are suppliers or customers of the regulated companies. Customers of these internationally regulated companies will find that the quality, availability, and costs of their services will be influenced by the international agreements. Suppliers to these industries will find their product specifications and even potential demand affected by the international body. For example, IATA agreements will affect the speed of adoption of a new aircraft. Intelsat agreements will help to determine procurement patterns in that field, as each government tries for a piece of the action for its national industry.

A final reason for examining these organizations is the implications they hold for the international legal environment of tomorrow's global marketing. All these organizations were born out of the pressures of modern technology. By shrinking the globe, modern technology has created a need for an expanding jurisdiction over human activity. As each year the nations become less and less islands unto themselves, international laws and agreements become increasingly necessary. And as technology and international business continue to grow, so will this need for *international* law and regulation. This in turn will facilitate the expansion of international trade and business and minimize international conflict. International companies, through industry associations, conferences, and their governments, will have a voice in what the new international laws will be. Marketing inputs will be important in determining the position of the company on this matter.

Regional Groupings and International Law

As we saw in Chapter 2, many nations have felt the need for larger market groupings to accelerate their economic growth. Such multinational regional groupings have developed or are developing on all continents. The European Economic Community (EEC), the European Free Trade Association (EFTA), the Latin American Free Trade Association (LAFTA), and the Central American Common Market (CACM) are the most notable examples. What each regional grouping has found, however, is that economic integration alone is not sufficient, or even possible, without some international legal agreement. Initially, this takes the form of the treaty or convention that establishes the regional grouping. Inevitably, however, as integration proceeds, further international legal agreements or conventions are necessary. In this way, the body of international (regional) law grows. Because these groupings are primarily *economic* alliances, the international (regional) law that develops relates primarily to economic and business questions. Therefore, regional groupings provide a growing development of international law of great interest to multinational companies.

The EEC Example

The basic law of the EEC is the Rome Treaty. In many economic matters, the Rome Treaty is becoming the important law of the six-nation area. As the Treaty is implemented by the Council of Ministers and the Commission of the European Communities, the following agreements have or will become the law of the EEC:

1. The elimination of national tariffs between members
2. The establishment of a common outer tariff to nonmembers, replacing national tariff laws
3. A common agricultural policy
4. A common transport policy
5. The approximation of their respective municipal law to the extent necessary for the Common Market
6. Monetary union, including budget and fiscal harmonization.

There is continuing debate in Europe over how much supranational power the EEC should have and how much powers should remain in the hands of the individual national members. At the same time, a growing body of EEC law is slowly being formed, in part as a result of the "harmonizing" or standardizing of national laws. In one way or the other, the results are the same —one uniform law rather than six national laws, which were often in conflict with each other. Reinforcing the strength of international law in the EEC is the European Court of Justice. Though less famous than the World Court, it is really more active and effective in dealing with supranational legal questions.

The Latin American Experience

The Central American Common Market has had a rather successful career, something like that of the EEC. Achievements and goals include a customs union, a regional industrial policy, and coordinated regional policies and laws in public health, labor, education, transport, and agriculture. In other words, the CACM is moving toward a true common market, as is the EEC, with similar implications for the internationalizing of the business law of the region. On the other hand, the Latin American Free Trade Association has made only halting progress toward economic integration. National tariffs and other laws still impede the exchange of goods among LAFTA members. As a partial offset to the failure of the free-trade area, however, is a unique phenomenon called the complementation agreement.

Complementation agreements, usually initiated by industry, basically are agreements to free trade on a narrow, specific list of products for specific countries. Since the LAFTA-wide free-trade area is so slow in coming, manufacturers have proposed narrower agreements covering their product line in LAFTA countries where they have plants. The governments concerned often have been glad to accept and sign these, giving them the force of law, because they avoid the problems of a general free-trade area while conferring some of its benefits.

The problem of a free-trade area lies in each nation's fear that its industry will be hurt by imports from industries in other member countries. To avoid economic injury, a nation can choose to trade in those industries where it has some strength as well as select other member countries that do not pose a great competitive threat. The benefits of a free-trade area are economies of scale in a larger market and cheaper imports. It can be seen that a multi-national company with plants in several LAFTA countries could be the major element in such a complementation agreement. The firm could rationalize production among its LAFTA plants, gain economies of scale, and assure to its host nations the benefits of free trade in that product area and protection of their domestic industry at the same time.

Some of the complementation agreements and the firms and countries involved are shown in the following list. The flexibility as to extent of product coverage (electronic tubes versus chemicals) and number of countries (from two for glass to eight for chemicals) is evident.

1. *Data-processing equipment and punchcard stock—IBM—Argentina, Brazil, Chile, Uruguay*
2. *Electronic tubes—RCA, GE, Philips, others—Agentina, Brazil, Chile, Uruguay, Mexico*
3. *Glass—Corning, Pilkington—Argentina, Mexico*
4. *Chemicals—several companies—Argentina, Brazil, Chile, Colombia, Mexico, Peru, Uruguay, Venezuela.*[10]

The World of International Law
The body of international law is small compared to the very extensive development of domestic law within nations. Nevertheless, we have seen a number of examples of international law. Although our survey has been brief, it illustrates the diverse ways international law can impinge on the activities of the international marketing manager. Furthermore, international law, whether bilateral, regional, or global, is the growth area in the legal environment of international marketing, the area of greatest change and expansion.

Because agreement is easier to obtain the smaller the number of countries involved, regional international law will grow faster than international law on a broader scale. The international company will find that this expanded international law generally facilitates international trade and marketing. This is why the UN is seeking a global commercial code. But even if the firm considers a change unfavorable to its operations, it will want to be well informed of developments so as to optimize corporate performance within the new constraints.

[10] *Business Latin America*, April 16, 1970, pp. 121, 122.

Foreign Laws and International Marketing

American laws play a ubiquitous role in American business practice as well as in the study of business administration at American universities. The laws of foreign nations play a similar role in the activities of business within their boundaries. The importance of foreign laws to the international marketer lies not so much in his international marketing as in his domestic marketing in each of his foreign markets. The problem arises not from the fact that nations have laws affecting marketing, for the marketer is accustomed to that, but rather from the fact that the laws in each of his foreign markets tend to be somewhat different from those in every other market. The development of international and regional law is gradually lessening these national legal differences, but standardization of laws affecting marketing is still some distance in the future.

Common Law versus Code Law

Before considering national peculiarities in marketing law, we will look briefly at the two basic legal systems that underlie all individual national law. Each country derives its national legal system from either the common-law or the civil- or code-law traditions. Common law is tradition oriented; that is, the interpretation of what the law means on a given subject is heavily influenced by previous court decisions in that area, as well as by usage and customs. Common law depends less on detailed statutes and codes of law than on precedents and previous decisions. If there is no specific legal precedent or statute, common law requires a court decision. If the marketer wishes to understand the law in a common-law country, he must study the previous court decisions in matters of similar circumstance, as well as the statutes. Common law is English in origin and is found in the United States and other countries that have had a strong English influence on their development, usually a previous colonial tie.

Civil or code law is based on an extensive and, presumably, comprehensive set of laws organized by subject matter into a code. The intention in civil-law countries is to spell out the law on all possible legal questions, rather than to rely on precedent or court interpretation. The "letter of the law" is very important in code-law countries, but this need to be all-inclusive may lead to some rather general and elastic provisions, permitting an application to many facts and circumstances. Because code-law countries do not rely on previous court decisions, various applications of the same law may yield different interpretations. This can lead to some uncertainty for the marketer, even though the laws seem specific.

Code law is a direct legacy of Roman law. It is predominant in Europe and in all other nations of the world that have not had close ties with England. Thus code-law nations are more numerous than common-law nations. Many civil-code systems are greatly influenced by the French, German, or Spanish systems, because of previous colonial or other close relationships. For example, the German code has had a great influence on the Teutonic and Scandinavian countries.

The difference between common law and code law is significant for the international marketer. For one thing, business matters are treated separately in code-law countries because there is a specific code for business, the commercial code. (The other codes are the civil, the administrative, and the criminal.) On the one hand, such an individual code may mean a greater understanding of the problems of business; on the other, if the written code is antiquated, it may not fit current business practice and needs. In this situation, the common law is more flexible and adaptable. Some common-law countries, notably the United States and the United Kingdom, have also codified their commercial law, thereby lessening the difference between the two systems at least as far as commercial law is concerned. The United States has, for example, the Uniform Commercial Code.

In general, code-law countries practice a more strict and literal interpretation of the law than do common-law countries. One example of this different emphasis is trademark-registration regulations. In common-law countries, ownership of the trademark is determined by priority in *use*. The first user is the owner. In code-law countries, ownership is established by priority in *registration*. An American company moving into a code-law country with its established brands may find that some local citizen has registered these brand names. The firm then cannot use them, unless it can buy the rights back from the local owner, the one who registered them. In some countries, unscrupulous people can make a living registering foreign trademarks and selling them back to the international company when it wants to sell in that market. Though legal, this kind of trademark piracy is questionable behavior and is especially common in certain countries. We will discuss the question of administration of brands and trademarks in international marketing in Chapter 8 on product policy.

Foreign Laws and Foreign Marketing

One familiar with marketing law and regulation in the United States will not be surprised at the range of laws affecting marketing in foreign markets, although he may be surprised at the lack of such regulation in some less developed countries. We will not endeavor to catalog foreign laws but rather to show how they influence marketing—that is, product, price, place (distribution), and promotion. The treatment will be brief and suggestive of the problem areas. A more extensive study is in order only when considering a specific problem or market. Management implications will be considered again in Part II in relation to the international marketing task.

PRODUCT   If we consider product in the broad sense as everything the consumer receives when making his purchase, the international marketer will find many regulations affecting his product. The physical and chemical aspects of his product will be affected by laws seeking to protect national consumers as to its purity, safety, or performance. As the Thalidomide tragedy showed, nations differ as to the strictness of their controls in this area. The Food and Drug Administration had not cleared the drug for sale in America, but many deformed babies were born in Europe from its legal use there.

In a similar vein, foreign manufacturers were disturbed by the American safety requirements for automobiles, because this meant that they had to modify their products to meet the needs of one particular market. Because the American market is large, the necessary adaption was not so costly or serious a problem as meeting the peculiar requirements of a small market. Nevertheless, Jaguar Cars stopped selling Jaguar sedans in America in 1968 because of United States safety requirements. This highlights what frequently appears to be the protectionist use of these laws. Although consumers should be protected, different safety requirements are not necessary for the consumers of every country. By maintaining different national standards, nations seem to be saying that consumers in other countries are not being adequately protected. The real reason nations often persist in their particular legal requirements is that they provide a way to protect their own producers.

Foreign market laws also constrain the marketer's freedom as to other product features, such as package, label, and warranty. For example, in Belgium the containers in which pharmaceuticals for *external* application are put up for sale must be manufactured of yellow-brown glass and have a regular octagonal shape. In addition, the words "Usage Externe—Uitwendig Gebruik" must be molded in relief on the containers themselves. (Belgium is bilingual.) In spite of this example, it is true that the predominant packaging influence will be the distribution and market requirements for the product.

Labeling will generally be subject to more legal requirements than the package itself. Some of the usual labeling items covered include (1) name of product, (2) name of producer or distributor, (3) description of ingredients or use of product, (4) weight, either net or gross, and (5) country of origin. As to warranty, the marketer has relative freedom to formulate a warranty in all countries, whether under common or code law. Competitive and market factors would be the major determinants of his warranty. However, code-law countries generally place a stricter product liability on the producer than do common-law countries, which have had the tradition of *caveat emptor*—let the buyer beware. This difference would not be reflected in the written warranty but rather in the legal liability of the producer.

Brand names and trademarks are important product attributes that also face differing national legal requirements. In general, however, nations fall into one of the categories discussed earlier. Most of the larger nations are members of the Paris Union or some other trademark convention. Furthermore, the aforementioned distinction between code- and common-law countries is important in determining legal rights to the brand or mark. The actual law in each country is reviewed periodically in *Commerce Today*, the biweekly publication of the Department of Commerce. One important thing for the international marketer to know is the countries where brand piracy is a problem.

PRICING   There is no foreign counterpart to the American Robinson-Patman Act, but price controls are pervasive in the world economy. Resale-price maintenance (rpm) is the most common law relating to pricing. Many nations have some legal provisions for rpm, but the extent and meaning of rpm vary from country to country. In Norway and France, for example, rpm is allowed only by special government exemption. Greece, India, Peru, and others are more liberal in allowing rpm. Although many countries still allow it, the trend is away from rpm, either because of government restrictions on it or the difficulties of enforcement.

Surprising to the American marketer is the fact that some countries allow price agreements between competitors under certain conditions. Some form of governmental price-control authority is another pricing law that is on the books of a majority of nations. The price controls may be active or potential, and they may be economy-wide or limited to certain sectors. For example, in the mid–1960s, France had an economy-wide price freeze. At the other extreme, Japan controls the price of only one commodity—rice. Generally, price controls are limited to "essential" goods, such as foodstuffs. The pharmaceutical industry, particularly in Europe and Latin America, is one of the most frequently controlled as to price.

The pricing-control mechanism sometimes takes the form of controlling allowable margins. For example, Ghana sets the manufacturer's margin at between 25 and 40 percent, depending on the industry. Argentina allows a standard 11 percent "profit" on pharmaceuticals, whereas Belgium fixes maximum prices and both wholesale and retail margins on pharmaceuticals. In the 1960s these margins were 12.5 percent and 30 percent respectively. For new drugs *growing out of research in Belgium*, the manufacturer was allowed a higher markup for five years. Germany does not set margins, but has an obligatory price register that details both prices and margins for public knowledge. Although tax laws are not pricing laws, the excise or value-added tax systems of countries do have a significant impact on the firm's pricing. The management implications of all these pricing regulations will be discussed in Chapter 14.

DISTRIBUTION   Management of distribution is an area with relatively few laws to constrain the marketing manager. He has a high degree of freedom in choosing his distribution channels from among those available in the market. Of course, he cannot choose channels that might not be available in a market for economic, technological, or legal reasons. For example, France has a specific legal prohibition against door-to-door selling, but the Singer Company in France has received a special exemption from this law. One of the major legal questions in distribution management is the legality of exclusive distribution. Fortunately for the marketer, this option is allowed as an alternative in most markets of the world. In fact, the strongest legal constraint does not even apply to those firms managing their own distribution in foreign markets, but rather to exporters who are selling through distributors or agents there.

For firms that do not have their own marketing subsidiary in a country, careful selection of an agent or distributor is critical in two ways. First, the quality of the distributor will help to determine the firm's success in the market. Second, the contract with the distributor may commit the exporter to a marriage that is difficult and costly to terminate. Therefore, the chief legal problem for the exporter is to be aware of national laws concerning distributor contracts so that he may avoid the potential problems associated with them. It is much easier to enter an agency agreement than to end one.

PROMOTION   Advertising is one of the more controversial elements of the marketing mix and is subject to more legal control than some of the others. Most nations have some kind of law regulating advertising, and advertising groups in many nations have self-regulatory codes alongside the law. Advertising regulation takes several forms. One pertains to the message and its truthfulness. Much of the "puffery" in American advertising would be illegal in foreign markets. In Germany, for example, it is difficult to use comparative advertising and the words "better" or "best." In fact, Germany has rather extensive and complex regulation of advertising. In Argentina, advertising for pharmaceuticals must have the *prior* approval of the Ministry of Public Health.

Another form of restriction on advertising relates to control over the advertising of certain products. Governments consider some products more critical or sensitive than others and therefore restrict their promotion. For example, Britain allows no cigarette or liquor advertising on television. Finland is more restrictive and allows no newspaper or television advertising of political organizations, religious messages, alcohol, undertakers, slimming drugs, immoral literature, or intimate preparations. A more indirect restriction on advertising is the prohibition of all advertising in certain media. A number of nations allow no commercials on radio or TV. Another indirect restriction is the growing popularity of taxes on advertising. These taxes may apply to all advertising or discriminate among media. For example, Peru has an 8-percent tax on all outdoor advertising, whereas Spain taxes cinema advertising in particular.

Sales-promotion techniques tend to encounter much greater restriction in foreign markets than in America. In the United States, there is often no constraint on contests, deals, premiums, and other sales-promotion gimmicks. The situation is quite different elsewhere. For contests, it is a general rule that participation must not be predicated on purchase of the product. Premiums may be restricted as to size, value, and nature. For example, a premium may be limited to a certain fraction of the value of the purchase it accompanies, and its use might also have to relate to that product; that is, steak knives could not be used as a premium with soap, or nylon stockings with a food product. Free introductory samples may be restricted to one-time usage of the product, rather than a week's or month's supply. National variations are great in this area, but in almost all cases the American marketer will find himself severely limited in conparison to what he can practice at home.

Promotion through personal selling in foreign markets does not run into the kinds of legal problems encountered in sales promotion. The major legal constraint arises from the contractual relation with the sales force (as in the case of the distributor or agent). This is not only a marketing problem but a personnel problem.

The Enforcement of the Laws

The international marketer has a very practical interest in foreign laws. He wants to know how they will affect his operations in a particular market, and for this purpose it is not sufficient only to know the laws. He must also have some idea how the laws are enforced. Most nations have a number of laws on the books that have long since been forgotten and are not enforced. Others may be enforced haphazardly and halfheartedly, whereas still others may be very strictly enforced. Thus the international marketer must look beyond the laws themselves to the current and potential standing of the laws relating to marketing. An important aspect of enforcement, for instance, is the degree of impartiality of justice. Does a foreign subsidiary have as good a standing before the law as a strictly national company? Courts have been known to favor national firms over foreign subsidiaries. In such cases, the laws in themselves may be general but biased enforcement makes it a case of one law for the foreigner and one for the national in practice. Knowledge of this discrimination is helpful in evaluating the legal climate.

The Firm in the International Legal Environment

Whose Law? Whose Courts?

Domestic laws obviously govern marketing within a given country. Questions of the appropriate law and the appropriate courts may arise, however, if the transaction involves international marketing. We have seen that there is very little international law that can apply to international marketing disputes. Moreover, there is no international court in which to try them. The famous World Court in The Hague allows only nations to appear before it, and it has very little business anyway, as nations hesitate to put themselves in jeopardy outside their own boundaries. All of which leads to the question of jurisdiction in international marketing disputes.

When commercial disputes arise between principals of two different nations, each would probably prefer to have the matter judged in his own national courts under his own nation's laws. By the time the dispute has arisen, however, the question of jurisdiction has usually already been settled by one means or another. One way parties can decide the issue beforehand is by inserting a *jurisdictional clause* into the contract. Then when the contract is signed, each party agrees that the laws of a particular nation, or state of the United States, will govern.

If the parties did not have prior agreement as to jurisdiction, the courts where the appeal is brought will decide the issue. One alternative they have is to apply the laws of the nation or state *where the contract was entered into*. Another way the courts may settle the jurisdictional question is on the basis of *where contract performance occurs*. In one of these ways, then, the issue of which nation's laws shall govern is already out of the company's hands when a dispute arises. Most companies prefer to make that decision themselves and therefore insert a jurisdictional clause into the contract, reducing somewhat the uncertainty surrounding the transaction and making possible the choice of the more favorable jurisdiction. Of course, the choice of jurisdiction has to be acceptable to both parties.

The decision as to which nation's courts will try the case will depend on who is suing whom. The issue of which courts have jurisdiction is separate from the issue of which nation's laws are applied. Suits are brought in the courts of the country of the person being sued. For example, an American company might sue a French firm in France. This kind of event leads not infrequently to the interesting situation where a court in one country may try a case according to the laws of another country; that is, a French court may apply the laws of New York State. This could happen if the parties had included a jurisdictional clause stating that the laws of New York State would govern in case of a disagreement arising out of their contract; it could also happen if the French court decided that the laws of New York State were applicable for one of the other reasons mentioned in the preceding paragraph.

Arbitration or Litigation?

For his export sales and his dealings with agents and distributors, the international marketer is interested in laws and contracts. The laws and contracts provide for two things: (1) They spell out the responsibilities of each party; and (2) they provide for legal recourse to obtain satisfaction. Actually, however, international marketers consider litigation a last resort and prefer to settle disputes in some other way. For several reasons litigation is disliked as a way of settling disputes with foreign parties. Litigation usually involves long delays, during which inventories may be tied up and trade halted. Further, litigation is costly, not only in terms of money but also often in terms of customer good will and public relations. Firms also frequently fear discrimination in the judgments of the foreign court. Litigation is thus seen as an unattractive and abrasive alternative, to be used only if all else fails. Even if the court suit is won, it is often a hollow victory.

More peaceful ways to settle international commercial disputes are offered by conciliation, mediation, and arbitration. Conciliation and mediation are rather informal attempts to bring the parties to an agreement or settlement. The intermediary bringing the parties together may come from many different sources, for example, another firm, a trade association, the International Chamber of Commerce, a Foreign Service Officer, and so on. Conciliation and mediation are attractive, voluntary approaches to the settlement of disputes. If they fail, however, stronger measures such as arbitration or litigation are needed. Because of the drawbacks of litigation noted above, arbitration is used extensively in international commerce.

Arbitration generally overcomes the weak points of litigation. Decisions are made much more quickly. Arbitration is also less costly and less damaging to good will, because of the less hostile nature and the greater secrecy of the proceedings. Decisions are often more equitable and informed, because of the expertise of the arbiters, and therefore more acceptable to the disputants. The parties in dispute often have a voice in selection of the arbitration panel and the place of arbitration. Arbitration has the further advantage of minimizing the differences between common-law and code-law countries. In a growing number of countries, arbitration awards have the status and enforceability of court decisions.

The arbitration procedure is relatively simple and straightforward. If the firms wish to settle disputes by arbitration, they had best include an arbitration clause in the contract. A common form is the one suggested by the American Arbitration Association:

Any controversy or claim arising out of or relating to this contract, or the breach thereof, shall be settled by arbitration in accordance with the Rules of the American Arbitration Association, and judgment upon the award rendered by the Arbitrator(s) may be entered in any Court having jurisdiction thereof.

When signing a contract including such a clause, the parties have agreed that (1) arbitration will be the method of settling disputes, (2) they will abide by the award of the arbitrators, and (3) the rules and procedures of a particular arbitration tribunal will apply.

When a dispute has actually occurred, the first step in arbitration is the naming of the panel of arbitrators. In some cases, each party may appoint one member, with the third chosen by the first two or appointed by an arbitration organization. Alternatively, the parties may accept a panel provided by the organization. Three leading arbitration organizations are the International Chamber of Commerce, the American Arbitration Association, and the Inter-American Commercial Arbitration Commission. Once selected, the panel conducts its hearing and renders its decision. Because of its particular form of operation and the expertise available, the arbitration process is much more expeditious than bringing suit in court.

The Court of Arbitration of the International Chamber of Commerce in Paris handled 115 cases in 1969, and the number grows steadily. The court itself is not an arbitral body, but it sets the ground rules and appoints the arbitrators. One of its appeals is that claims are handled in strictest secrecy. One case involved a licensing agreement between an American and a West German company. The licensee wanted the fee reduced because manufacturing costs were exceeding estimates. Both sides agreed to let an ICC arbitrator settle the matter.[11]

The Marketer Is Not a Lawyer

What are the implications for the international marketer of all of the legal parameters discussed in this chapter? The marketing manager is not a lawyer. Even if he were a lawyer, he could not cover all the domestic, international, and foreign legal aspects involved. Although the international marketer cannot know all the relevant laws, he must know which of his marketing decisions are affected by the laws. He will depend on legal counsel for knowledge and advice on the laws themselves. If he knows which decisions are affected by the law, he can call on legal counsel when he needs special knowledge. Legal

[11] *Business Week*, March 28, 1970, pp. 63, 64.

counsel in this case includes not only the domestic legal staff or that of the international division, but also representation for the firm's foreign markets as well.

The firm's need for legal expertise will be related to its international business involvement. If the firm is involved only through exporting or licensing, its legal needs are fewer than if it has foreign subsidiaries and joint ventures. In countries where it operates through licensees or distributors, these parties relieve the firm of some of its legal burden. Where it has subsidiaries, it will need local legal counsel. The international marketer will also need a reporting arrangement or information system which keeps him up to date on legal developments affecting his task.

We have noted many trends and developments in the legal environment of international marketing. Two of the major trends are the growth of regional law in regional groupings and the growth of international law under the pressure of expanding technology and international business. The firm must keep abreast of these and other developments. Indeed, it should make its voice heard in the deliberations leading to the new international conventions and agreements. It must do this not only to protect its own interest but also to share its expertise in the questions being discussed. The firm should support the growth of international laws and standards, such as the work of UNCITRAL and ISO. By so doing, it will promote the expansion of international trade and specialization and also increase the efficiency of its own international marketing and logistics. The international marketer is certainly not a lawyer. Nevertheless, international marketers can have an impact on the development of international or multinational law even while being constrained by it in their work.

Questions

5.1   What is the political environment of international marketing?

5.2   Discuss the potential constraints on the international marketer in nations where the government participates heavily in the economy, that is, where it owns and operates businesses.

5.3   Socialistically inclined governments are found not only in communist countries, but also in Africa, Asia, and Latin America. Can the international marketer operate in the latter group of nations?

5.4   Identify the possible constraints of host-country nationalism on the local marketing of the international firm.

5.5   How can the international marketer get a picture of the outlook for political stability in a country?

5.6   What is the international marketer's interest in a country's international relations?

5.7   What might an international firm do to reduce its political vulnerability in a host country?

5.8   Give examples of products that may be politically vulnerable if marketed by foreigners.

5.9   What are the three dimensions of the legal environment of international marketing?

5.10 Discuss the ambivalent attitude of the United States government toward antitrust in international business.

5.11 Explain the advantages to the international marketer arising from the Paris Union.

5.12 "The continuing growth of technology and international business will mean an increasing need for *international* law and regulation." Discuss.

5.13 Discuss the relatively rapid growth of regional international law.

5.14 Distinguish between common law and code law. Do the differences have any marketing significance?

5.15 Why is the international marketer concerned about the nature of law enforcement in foreign markets?

5.16 What is the significance of the jurisdictional question in international marketing disputes?

5.17 Why is arbitration preferred to litigation?

5.18 Since the international marketer is not a lawyer, how should he deal with the problems posed by the legal environment?

Further Readings

Books:

Behrman, Jack N., *U.S. International Business and Governments* (New York: McGraw-Hill Book Co., 1971).

Blough, Roy, *International Business: Environment and Adaptation* (New York: McGraw-Hill Book Co., 1966).

Brewster, Kingman, Jr., *Antitrust and American Business Abroad* (New York: McGraw-Hill Book Co., 1958).

Fayerweather, John, *International Business Management* (New York: McGraw-Hill Book Co., 1969), chaps. 3, 4.

Kindleberger, Charles P., *American Business Abroad* (New Haven, Conn.: Yale University Press, 1969).

Robinson, Richard D., *International Business Policy* (New York: Holt, Rinehart and Winston, 1964), chaps. 2, 3.

Articles:

Fayerweather, John, "19th Century Ideology and 20th Century Reality," *Columbia Journal of World Business* (Winter 1966), pp. 77–86.

Root, Franklin, "U.S. Business Abroad and the Political Risks," *M.S.U. Business Topics* (Winter 1968), pp. 73–80.

Vagts, Detlev F., "The Multinational Enterprise: A New Challenge for Transnational Law," *Harvard Law Review* (February 1970), pp. 739–792.

Vernon, Raymond, "Antitrust and International Business," *Harvard Business Review* (September–October 1968), pp. 78–87.

PART II

INTERNATIONAL MARKETING MANAGEMENT

In Part I, we looked at the environmental variables that are critical for international marketing management. Our tour of the world economy was not an around-the-word cruise for the purpose of gathering souvenirs, anecdotes, or home movies. It was rather a study or training program to help marketers become sensitive and responsive to that world economy in order to perform their task effectively within it.

In Part II, our focus moves from the environment to the task of international marketing management. Familiarity with the environment is a necessary but not sufficient capability of the international marketer. He must also know how to manage marketing in that environment. Therefore, in Part II we will emphasize the management decisions and problems that arise in international marketing. Our format here follows that of the popular marketing texts, allowing us to highlight and analyze the peculiarly international problems facing marketing management. Thus individual chapters in Part II are organized according to the decisions the international marketer must make.

6

MARKETING TO THE WORLD

THE INTERNATIONAL MARKETING TASK

What is the task of the international marketing manager? One could say that marketing is marketing and, therefore, marketing internationally involves the same functions as marketing domestically. These functions include marketing research and demand analysis; the development of policies and programs on product, pricing, promotion, and distribution; and the planning and control of the overall marketing effort. Such a breakdown reflects the organization of most standard textbooks on marketing management. It also describes the chapters in Part II of this book. These functions cover the so-called "controllable" variables in marketing. A large part of the challenge of international marketing management arises from the fact that both the uncontrollable and the controllable variables differ in multinational operations.

Foreign Marketing

The functions of marketing are indeed the same whether performed domestically or internationally. This is not to say, however, that the marketing manager's task is the same at home and abroad. Conducting marketing research or preparing a promotional program can differ greatly from country to country. In fact, one of the great challenges facing the international marketing manager is to design an optimal marketing program for each of his world markets. He must research each market and plan his product, price, promotion, and distribution strategies for it.

Since the international marketer can only partially replicate his domestic program, he must practically design a unique marketing program for each foreign market to meet the constraints of that particular market environment. There is, of course, some carry over in programs and strategies from market to market. The secret of success, moreover, often lies in finding the degree to which a uniform international approach can be applied, as contrasted with

149

tailoring individual programs to each national market. This will be a recurring question in the chapters that follow. In any case, foreign marketing is an important part of the job of the international marketing manager.

Standardized International Marketing?

The task of the international marketing manager would be greatly simplified if he could use a uniform approach all over the world. If the firm's foreign marketing followed the same standardized program in each market, the manager would only need to coordinate the programs in the various countries, which would remove some of the challenge from his job. Unfortunately, or perhaps fortunately, the world economy is a very complex place. As we have seen, not only do nations differ from each other but so do groups within nations. Such differences necessitate diversity in the foreign marketing programs of the international company.

Reduction of diversity is usually a necessary goal of the international marketer. Achievement of standardized marketing programs in foreign markets, however, is not a realistic target. The remainder of the text will deal with this question in various ways. We note it here because it has been in the forefront of discussions of international marketing.[1] Table 6–1 gives a graphic overview of some of the obstacles to standardization.

International Marketing

Designing marketing programs for many different national markets is the first major task of the international marketing manager. His second, and perhaps most distinguishing, task is the coordination and integration of all these national programs into an effective, synergistic international marketing activity. Because the multinational firm is not just a collection of national companies, management cannot be satisfied merely with good marketing programs in each national market. International marketing requires the performance of some marketing functions across national lines. Management should seek the advantages of synergism and economies of scale through its international marketing. These advantages will increase the profitability of its operations and strengthen its competitive position in foreign markets.

These two tasks of the international marketing manager, foreign marketing and international marketing, are complementary, but they are quite different in nature. The first is a traditional marketing management job, although it is greatly complicated by having to be performed in many different national environments. The second task is primarily organizational. The successful firm requires good performances in both, but different skills are necessary in each.

In the late 1950s, an American food company decided to get into the European market. The executives felt uncertain and inexperienced in this kind of

---

[1] See, for example, Robert Bartels, "Are Domestic and International Marketing Dissimilar?" *Journal of Marketing* (July 1968), pp. 56–61.

venture, so they decided to buy some European companies to get instant market position and know-how. In the first years of its ownership, the only change in the European companies' operations was the addition of an American financial man or controller to the staff.

In this instance we do not *see the American firm as an international marketer.* No marketing functions were being performed internationally. *The only international transfers here were investment dollars to Europe, dividends to America, and perhaps some financial and accounting practices from American headquarters. After a few years the American parent company began to add its products to the European product lines and to transfer some of its marketing know-how to its subsidiaries. Only at this time did it become a true international marketer.*

As this example shows, there is a critical difference between carrying on foreign marketing (through such a subsidiary) and being an international marketer. The difference is critical to both the country where the investment is made and the company making the investment. The host country gains little if the contribution of the foreign firm is only an initial inflow of capital, which is gradually offset by an outflow of dividends. (Of course, if capital is scarce nationally when the investment is made, foreign money may be welcome just for itself.) In addition to capital, however, the host country generally desires managerial and operational contributions, not least of which are in the marketing area—for instance, new products, a marketing orientation leading to greater efficiency and consumer satisfaction, and the like. In short, the foreign "intruder" would do well to bring in something that is not available locally, and this contribution should be a continuing thing to justify the firm's continued presence as a foreigner. The host country or concerned groups within it are in effect, asking What have you done for me lately?

When in Rome—Be Different

This difference between foreign and international marketing is also critical to the firm residing in foreign markets. Although the foreign firm should behave as a proper guest in the host country, this does not mean it should be just like the national firm. On the contrary, it is permitted in precisely because it is different in certain significant ways. In this context, good international marketing is part of the defensive posture of the foreign firm.

Not only in public relations should the firm be concerned about international marketing. Another major consideration is profitable operations. A company going into a foreign market has certain handicaps that its national competitor companies do not—for instance, the fact that it is foreign, its lack of familiarity with the market, and so on. To overcome these disadvantages, the firm must have offsetting strengths in other areas, including marketing. Its superiority in marketing will obviously not come from copying the behavior of the national firm. It must be doing something more than, or different from, what that firm is doing. This difference may come from any or all parts of the marketing program: product or product line, service, pric-

Table 6–1 Obstacles to Standardization in International Marketing Strategies

FACTORS LIMITING STANDARDIZATION	ELEMENTS OF MARKETING PROGRAM				
	PRODUCT DESIGN	PRICING	DISTRIBUTION	SALES FORCE	ADVERTISING & PROMOTION; BRANDING & PACKAGING
Market characteristics					
Physical environment	Climate; Product use conditions		Customer mobility	Dispersion of customers	Access to media; Climate
Stage of economic and industrial development	Income levels; Labor costs in relation to capital costs	Income levels	Consumer shopping patterns	Wage levels, availability of manpower	Needs for convenience rather than economy; Purchase quantities
Cultural factors	"Custom and tradition"; Attitudes toward foreign goods	Attitudes toward bargaining	Consumer shopping patterns	Attitudes toward selling	Language, literacy; Symbolism
Industry conditions					
Stage of product life cycle in each market	Extent of product differentiation	Elasticity of demand	Availability of outlets; Desirability of private brands	Need for missionary sales effort	Awareness, experience with products
Competition	Quality levels	Local costs; Prices of substitutes	Competitors' control of outlets	Competitors' sales forces	Competitive expenditures, messages

Marketing institutions					
Distributive system	Availability of outlets	Prevailing margins	Number and variety of outlets available	Number, size, dispersion of outlets	Extent of self-service
Advertising media and agencies			Ability to "force" distribution	Effectiveness of advertising, need for substitutes	Media availability, costs, overlaps
Legal restrictions	Product standards Patent laws Tariffs & taxes	Tariffs & taxes Antitrust laws Resale price maintenance	Restrictions on product lines Resale-price maintenance	General employment restrictions Specific restrictions on selling	Specific restrictions on messages, costs Trademark laws

Source: Robert D. Buzzell, "Can You Standardize Multinational Marketing," *Harvard Business Review* (November–December 1968), pp. 108, 109. Reprinted by permission.

ing, distribution, or promotion effectiveness. Naturally, the broader the base of its marketing strength, the stronger its competitive position—and the greater its potential contribution to consumer welfare in the host country.

Synergism in the International Company

How does the international marketer gain the strength to compete in different foreign markets? One source of power may be the firm's experience in a large, competitive domestic market. If it has survived and grown in a tough home market, it has developed some marketing capability. After all, marketing skill can be defined as the ability to survive and grow in the marketplace. This is considered an advantage of some American companies in Europe, for example.

Another element of strength for the international marketer derives from the very fact of the firm's international operations. A truly multinational company is more than a collection of national companies. Its organization should produce a synergistic effect, where the whole becomes greater than the sum of its parts. This synergistic effect is something other than merely avoiding sub-optimization. However, it can be said that there is sub-optimization or less than peak efficiency in the international company when this synergism is not present.

Sources of Synergism

The sources of synergism in the international company can be several. We have already mentioned experience in a competitive buyers' market in the home country. *Multinational operations*, also mentioned, contribute in different ways. One derives from the fact that no country has a monopoly on brains, in spite of the "technology gap" or "management gap" we hear so much about. If a firm is operating in many countries, it is probable that its number of new product ideas and marketing innovations will be greater than those of a firm of similar size operating in only one country. We learn best from *experience,* and the multinational company has, in effect, more experience than the purely national operation. We assume, of course, some decentralization in the organization as well as an appropriate communications system.

An American manufacturer of consumer durables allowed its foreign subsidiaries wide latitude in choosing the products they would retail. Successful innovations by some of its subsidiaries led to major changes in the parent company's product line. Not all innovations by the subsidiaries were successful, but the example does show some of the potential contributions of multinational operations.

A large European consumer-goods company wanted to apply this principle of synergism to its advertising programs. It enlisted the aid of its advertising agencies in various countries by requiring from them an evaluation of each advertising campaign: How it was implemented; how it worked out; and the particular reasons for its relative success or failure. Such a detailed "reason why" evaluation means that experience in one country can be better related to experiences in other countries. To a certain degree, one country thus serves as a "test market" for advertising in other countries. This plan allows the firm to go beyond the old advice, "Repeat your successes and drop your failures." It enables the company to determine how success or failure in one market is related to the situation in another.

Another source of synergism lies in the division of labor possible in the international company. Just as Adam Smith found specialization, *the division of labor*, the source of the wealth of nations, so might a corporation find it the source of greater effectiveness and wealth. Such division of labor applies not only to production—that is, rationalization or product-by-plant operations—but also to many aspects of marketing. Finding the right allocation of marketing activities between parent company and subsidiaries and between the subsidiaries themselves can mean greater marketing effectiveness through a form of economies of scale.

A large consumer products firm had operations, including marketing research, in ten European countries. The company eventually found it was more efficient to have one large, well-qualified marketing research staff at European headquarters than ten small-scale activities. The central staff works on a service basis to all the subsidiaries.

When IBM took their "$5 billion gamble" in developing the System/360 computers, they followed the principle of division of labor by assigning parts of the product development task to their major subsidiaries, that is, the United Kingdom, France, and Germany. This presumably not only helped the development of the overall system but also generated enthusiasm in the participating subsidiaries because they had a real "piece of the action."

INTERNAL DETERMINANTS OF THE INTERNATIONAL MARKETING TASK

In Part I we looked at the external environmental constraints on international marketing. Here we will consider the constraints or determinants peculiar to the firm or industry. The international marketing manager will find help or hindrance within his own company and industry situation, quite apart from the external environment. The variables we will examine here are the following: (1) the role of top management; (2) company size; (3) the company's international business experience; (4) the product and the industry; (5) the firm's level of involvement in international business; (6) company organization for international business; and (7) company goals.

Support of Top Management

Crucial to any international business endeavor is the support of top management. If top management is really sold on international marketing, then the financial, personnel, and other resources will be forthcoming to facilitate the marketer's task. Where international business is a poor relative of domestic operations, the international marketer is almost sure to see mediocre results. In today's world where international business is so large, and more and more top executives have had international experience, it is increasingly probable that top management support will be available for the international marketing effort.

Top management support is necessary in both large and small companies. For example, many small companies have achieved export success and have received presidential "E" awards for their contributions to America's balance of payments. In almost every one of these cases, it was the owner or a chief executive of the company who was responsible for the export effort. Two of America's leading electrical equipment companies, General Electric and Westinghouse, provide examples on the big-company side. Both firms got new chief executives in the mid–1960s: Fred Borch at GE and Donald Burnham at Westinghouse. In each instance, the companies experienced a change and expansion of their international activities. The Watson brothers at IBM are another example of top management's contributing to international business growth.

Size

The story of David and Goliath is interesting precisely because the small does not usually triumph over the large. In international marketing, the options available to the manager will depend partly on the size of his firm. DuPont in 1958 had no production facilities outside of North America, but it did have an export business of several hundred million dollars. Less than a decade later, DuPont had over fifteen plants in several different countries of Europe. It established a regional headquarters in Switzerland, and a major part of its European sales came from European production.

Obviously, relatively few companies could follow DuPont's strategy for expanding their European markets. The small firms, which have proportionally as attractive foreign markets as DuPont, are limited in their market alternatives. Most commonly, they will operate internationally through exports or licensing. Their international marketing programs, in turn, will be predicated on and limited by that form of operation. We will see this in detail in the chapters dealing with the various marketing functions.

Not only the absolute size of the company is important. The actual or potential volume of a company's *international* business is a further constraint. Although a company is very large in its domestic market, competitive, legal, or other restrictions might keep its potential international business down to a very modest level. Two examples of companies in such a situation are United States Steel and American Telephone and Telegraph. Where a firm is thus restricted, the international marketer is seriously limited in the kinds of alternative programs and strategies he can realistically consider.

A further consideration having to do with size is the firm's actual or potential sales volume in individual foreign markets. A firm may have a large volume of international business derived from many markets, but the volume probably varies greatly from market to market. In those countries where the firm does a big business, the marketing manager may have a range of strategic alternatives as large as in domestic operations. In those countries where the actual or potential sales of the firm are small, the marketer will have limited resources and fewer alternatives. International differences in volume of business and market share are common in the international company. The international marketer cannot carry market share from country to country as he does his passport.

Company Experience

Company experience is another constraint on the international marketing manager. A firm that has been engaged in international business over a period of years develops a tremendously valuable store of experience, contacts, and market position. It may also develop some rigidities, of course. The firm new to international markets will face a somewhat different set of marketing alternatives. For one thing, the newer firm probably will not even be aware of just what all the alternatives are. It will lack experienced people who know both foreign markets and international marketing. Partially offsetting this limitation of the newer firm is its ability to start with a clean slate, not being bound by previous commitments.

Heinz and Campbell are competitors in the American market, but only Heinz was overseas during the first half of this century. Campbell entered the European market with direct investment in the 1950s. Largely because of their lack of foreign marketing experience, Campbell had great difficulty establishing a market position in Europe. Many years went by before any black ink appeared on the books.

Westinghouse conducted its international business almost entirely by exporting and licensing until the mid–1960s. General Electric had numerous foreign production facilities, in addition to exports. After Burnham became president of Westinghouse, the firm decided to add foreign production to its international marketing strategy. The company encountered great trouble implementing this decision. There were two major reasons: (1) The company had very few experienced executives to work in these foreign operations, since all company experience had been through exports and licensing; (2) When Westinghouse tried to buy plants in Europe, it encountered governmental opposition in some countries.

Another relevant aspect of experience is the firm's experience in its domestic market. If a company has had an extensive and successful marketing history in a competitive domestic market, it is in a stronger position to market internationally than a firm lacking such experience. For example, the Organization for Economic Cooperation and Development (OECD) gave this as a reason for the success of many American companies in Europe. The OECD study of scientific instrument manufacturers noted several advantages American firms derived from their American experience:

1. The size of the U.S. market and its associated research and development activities favored American firms over their European competitors.
2. American firms are strong believers in marketing research and market forecasting. They carried this over to Europe.
3. American firms maintained closer contact with customers and paid more attention to customer complaints and suggestions than did European competitors.
4. American firms were quick to exploit product innovations.

The study concluded that the Americans' advantage was primarily in marketing and management, as no general or deeply rooted technology gap was found to exist in scientific instruments.[2] Such experience is no substitute for foreign-market knowledge, but the implied marketing orientation and know-how make entry to foreign markets easier.

The Product and the Industry

Marketers find their programs for marketing consumer goods different from those for marketing industrial goods. The international marketer will also find differences in his marketing alternatives deriving from his product and industry. Bulky products or products that encounter high tariffs, for instance, will have special supply and logistics problems in international marketing. Products that are technically complex and require demonstration or installation also have limited-channel alternatives. Perishable products or those that need service will require international marketing programs that take into account these characteristics.

Some differences go beyond individual products and are industry-wide. For example, industries in which there is a great deal of government buying and a preference for national suppliers give the international marketer few alternatives. Defense industries are an example. Another industry variable will be the amount and kind of competition encountered in foreign markets. In those product categories where foreign competition is weak and fragmented, the international marketer will have greater flexibility in choosing strategies. Even in domestic marketing, we are aware of the impact of the nature of the product and industry on marketing programs. The same constraints apply to international marketing, with a few additional ones. We will discuss these international aspects more fully in our chapters on the various marketing functions.

The Level of International Involvement

In this day of international or multinational companies, international marketing tends to be associated with the giants in the upper part of the *Fortune* 500. Actually, the number of American firms engaged in some form of international marketing is several thousand rather than a few hundred. The roads to international markets are varied enough to allow most manufacturers to participate, almost regardless of size. This is true because international marketing is not an all-or-nothing affair; rather, there are several ways to

---

[2] Reported in *International Commerce*, February 3, 1969, p. 21.

participate in international markets, and they represent varying degrees of commitment or involvement. Some of the major avenues are noted below. Level of involvement will be a primary determinant of the strategies and alternatives available to the international marketer.

Export

The first and simplest way a firm can participate in international markets is through exports. Exporting can mean simply the sale of a firm's products in foreign markets, perhaps by an agent. As the export business becomes more interesting to the firm, it is likely to engage in more marketing. In addition to selling products, the firm may send promotional materials or a marketing or service representative to help the importer, or it may give advertising allowances. In this later stage, the firm has increased its international marketing but it is still at the export level of involvement.

Sales or Marketing Subsidiary Abroad

Establishing a subsidiary represents a greater commitment by the firm in that it is physically present in the foreign country. Instead of exporting to a foreign importer, it is exporting to itself. In general, the reason for such a step is that the firm wants to take charge of its foreign sales and marketing program for greater effectiveness and profits. The international marketing transfers in this case are likely to be more extensive than in ordinary exporting, especially in greater parent-company guidance on matters of promotion and distribution. The marketing subsidiary is probably in regular communication with the product divisions and/or the export division of the parent company.

Licensing

The licensing step involves foreign production of the firm's product. Whether or not much international marketing occurs depends on the circumstances. At the minimum, one could say that the firm's products are moving internationally. The licensing contract may also contain marketing requirements to be met by the licensee. Additionally, the licensor may provide sales materials and marketing assistance, perhaps even training the licensee's sales and service personnel.

Westinghouse, which works primarily through licensees rather than through its own plants abroad, provides much marketing assistance and know-how to them. At the other extreme, some licensors leave the whole marketing task to the licensee and are international marketers only in the sense of making their products available in other countries.

Joint Ventures (between an International and a Domestic Firm)

As in licensing, joint ventures also involve foreign production of the firm's product. Because of the shared equity, however, joint ventures are a greater commitment by the firm than licensing. In fact, licensing agreements often lead to joint-venture arrangements. The amount of international marketing going on in a joint venture is probably greater than under a licensing agreement. This is not necessarily true, however, and depends on what the respective partners have to contribute to the joint venture.

Scott Paper Company joined with a raw-materials supplier in a venture in Belgium. The Belgian partner obviously had little consumer marketing experience nor even established consumer distribution channels. In this instance, Scott had to carry on the marketing program as a true international marketer.

A contrary example in the same field is the case of Kimberly-Clark, also in the home paper-products area, which entered into a joint venture in Germany with a Unilever company. Since Unilever is a large, experienced consumer-goods marketer, Kimberly-Clark presumably had a relatively smaller international marketing contribution than did Scott in the former example.

Wholly Owned Foreign Production

The firm makes its greatest commitment to international involvement when it becomes the sole owner of foreign production. Along with its 100 percent equity goes complete responsibility for both production and marketing. Because this step, of all the steps considered, represents the greatest investment and interest by the firm, it usually carries with it the greatest amount of international marketing transfers. The company wants not only to protect its investment but also to maximize the return from it. To get this return, management will seek the appropriate degree of localized decision making. This will almost always be less than 100 percent, if the subsidiary is to realize any benefit from its parent. Furthermore, to avoid suboptimization, any national subsidiary must be integrated with the marketing activities of other subsidiaries. These undertakings require a great many international marketing transfers.

In one kind of transfer, the parent will help the subsidiary's marketing by drawing on its own fund of knowledge and experience; in another, the subsidiary will supply information to the parent, adding to the parent's marketing experience and know-how. Yet another form of international marketing transfer is the exchange of experiences among all members of the multinational company, which can be done through company headquarters, the product divisions, or on a regional basis—that is, for Europe, North America, Latin America, and so on. Thus, ideally, international marketing involves transfer in not one but several directions. Nor does such transfer occur haphazardly, but under the optimizing eye of the international company.

Organization

The task of the international marketing manager will also be determined by the way his company is organized for international business. If the company handles foreign sales on a product-line or *divisional basis*, the international marketer may be limited to that product line and to the countries in which it is selling. The international marketer will have broader responsibilities if the firm is organized on a *functional basis*, that is, if it has a vice-president in charge of marketing, who is concerned with global marketing. The international marketing manager will also have broad responsibilities if the firm handles all nondomestic business through an *international division*. In this case the firm might have both a domestic and an international marketing executive.

A geographic or *regional form of organization* could indicate yet a different interpretation of the international marketer's task. If the firm is organized into divisions for North America, Europe, Latin America, and so on, the marketing manager might have multinational responsibilities, but within a particular region rather than globally. Finally, the international marketer's job will be affected by his company's policies and practices concerning *decentralization* of responsibility and decision making. Where the firm considers most of its foreign subsidiaries as profit centers and gives them great authority over local marketing decision, the international marketer may have primarily an advisory capacity. On the other hand, where the firm has more centralized international decision making, the international marketing executive will have very broad responsibilities for all foreign markets. Chapter 16 probes organizational questions more thoroughly.

Goals for International Marketing

The kinds of activities, programs, and decisions appropriate for a corporation will depend on what its goals are. Businessmen and business students usually evaluate decisions in terms of corporate goals. Good business decisions are those that best help the corporation to achieve its goals. If we are to evaluate international marketing programs and decisions, we must relate them to company goals.

Profits

What are the goals of business firms? Although each firm may have some goals peculiar to itself, there are certain common denominators in the goals of business enterprises. The traditional economist would have said that the firm's major goal is profit maximization. Today there are social critics of business who say the same thing, but with a more negative connotation; that is, business is concerned only with profits and does not care about side effects of its activity, such as pollution, accidents, and the like. Unfortunately, that has been true in some cases.

Hopefully, business management is more responsible than the critics imply. If it is not, such responsibility will be forced upon it, not only domestically but in foreign markets as well. It should be noted, however, that a striving for profits is not bad in itself. Indeed, the unprofitable corporation is serving neither society nor itself well. Even the Russians recognize that. Profits are, and should be, one goal of the corporation, internationally as well as domestically. Profits are one indicator of the economic efficiency that society should demand of its business sector.

Survival and Growth

We have learned that self-preservation is the first law of nature. This applies to political and economic as well as to biological activity. The firm is concerned for its survival as a prerequisite for reaching its other goals. For many firms, especially American, growth is another major goal. Growth psychology seems part of the American way of life, and business firms often want greater sales and market share, even more than profit maximization. *Fortune*'s prestigious "500" rankings are based, after all, on sales volume, and executive salaries seem to relate more to the volume of a firm's sales than to its profits.

There is no particular virtue about growth as a corporate goal. However, some growth may be necessary to maintain or increase efficiency and to avoid technological obsolescence. In foreign markets especially, the international firm must grow to some minimum size to serve the markets effectively. Once the firm reaches some reasonable market position in a foreign economy, however, it may have to limit its growth goal in that market. National competitors or others in a spirit of nationalism may react against the international firm that grows "too big" in a particular country. Although many managers want their firm to be number one in its industry or product line, such a goal might be politically unwise in many foreign markets.

Good Citizen

Adam Smith said he was suspicious of any firm that claimed to be operating for the public welfare. He felt that a firm should be seeking profits and the "invisible hand" of the marketplace would assure that the public was being served. Many businessmen and business writers feel that way today. They say the public is best served when the firm makes and markets its products efficiently and profitably. However, there are many others, businessmen as well as critics of business, who feel that profits are not a sufficient criterion of business performance. A firm's behavior in relation to employment, pollution, and other social problems is not necessarily reflected in its profit figures. Therefore, many firms in their public-relations programs stress their social role.

Should the international firm have some standard of good citizenship or social responsibility as one of its goals in foreign markets? The answer would depend in part on what the firm does domestically. Even if the firm identifies growth and profits as its primary or only goals in world markets, it still must give due consideration to the social constraints noted in Part I. The achievement of growth and profits, as well as survival, in foreign markets will depend on how the host society evaluates the firm in its *overall* operations. This evaluation will include more than just economic efficiency. The firm can consider these constraints as necessary evils to be lived with or worked around; or it can take a more positive approach in its search for growth and profits by also seeking to make a maximum social contribution wherever its operations impinge on the host economy.

Synergy

One other goal is peculiar to international marketing. That is the search for synergism in international operations. Each national operation should receive special benefits from belonging to the multinational family, and the overall corporation should be stronger because of the interrelationships in its global marketing program. In preparing the marketing program for a particular national market, the international marketer will be more effective if he can utilize inputs from elsewhere in the multinational company. Likewise, the total international marketing program will be more efficient if there is appropriate coordination and division of labor among the various national members of the company. Achieving this synergism is an important goal of the international marketing manager, affecting his choice of marketing strategies.

The Relation of Goals to International Marketing

The international firm will have overall corporate goals governing its global operations. It may also have particular goals for particular markets, such as a given volume of sales or a given market share. The marketing manager, as the bridge between the firm and the market, should help the corporation determine which goals are appropriate in which markets. After establishing these goals, he will use them as decision criteria in preparing marketing strategies for each market. Although the marketer will inevitably be concerned with profitability, and probably with growth, he must also consider the overall market reception given to his firm. In discussing the task of the international marketing manager in the rest of this text, we will be concerned with some combination of the following goals or decision criteria: profits, growth, market satisfaction, and synergy. For example, the product or distribution strategy in a foreign market will be designed to satisfy all four of these goals.

A PHILOSOPHY FOR INTERNATIONAL MARKETING?

Businessmen are noted for their pragmatism and emphasis on results. An undoctrinaire approach is certainly more conducive to effective economic performance than are management practices constrained by tradition and ideology. Nevertheless, management cannot do without a philosophy, or at the very least some well-conceived and articulated goals, guidelines, and policies for its operations. In fact, even the critics of business are asking for this. One of the contributions of the professional approach to management in the post–World War II period is that many executives have asked themselves certain fundamental questions, such as, What kind of business are we in? or, What do we want to be doing? Firms no longer identify themselves merely as manufacturers of a particular product. They tend to see their economic and social role in much broader terms. This new insight helps them to remain more flexible and perform more effectively.

Firms that are international marketers have perhaps an even greater need for a guiding philosophy because of the greater dynamism and uncertainty in international operations. With the increasing challenges posed by host governments in foreign markets, the international firm needs to have a good idea of what it is trying to do. Business enterprises, unlike religious institutions, do not usually have their credo spelled out. If they have one, it is usually implicit and fragmentary. An interesting exercise for a student (or executive) would be to try to spell out the international marketing philosophy of a particular firm. Much of it would have to be deduced from company practices, but some could probably be obtained from company documents and executive speeches.

The following is a list of a number of company attitudes and policies towards international marketing. The list is suggestive rather than comprehensive and was derived from statements issued by different companies, or from interviews and speeches of executives.

1. *We go into a country for keeps.*
2. *We believe in staffing our overseas operations with nationals of that country as much as possible.*
3. *We consistently invest part of our profits in the country where they are earned.*
4. *We try to give the foreign market the product it wants, not what we think it should have.*
5. *We keep first-hand contact with our foreign markets.*
6. *We are careful to respect the customs, traditions, religions, and sensitivities of foreign people.*
7. *We desire to make contributions toward a nation's aspirations for growth.*
8. *We want to serve people everywhere with the best products at the lowest cost.*
9. *We have a policy of joint ventures with citizens of the host country.*
10. *We build facilities abroad to defend old markets threatened by new competition.*
11. *We want to participate in growing opportunities abroad.*
12. *We adopt our operating methods to the needs of the host country.*
13. *We seek to be a constructive part of the host-country environment.*
14. *We go abroad to spread our risks.*

The reader will note that the statements cover more than just international marketing. It is obviously impossible to separate marketing from the overall operation of the firm. Some of the items appear to be public-relations statementsc, and some of them probably were. Nevertheless, in this collection of attitudes and policy statements, one can see some elements of a philosophy for international marketing. Although such a philosophy would need to be tailored to the situation of each firm, there would undoubtedly be many common elements as well.

In closing our discussion of company goals and philosophy for international marketing, it is perhaps appropriate to recall the words of the great English philosopher, Alfred North Whitehead, on the potential role of business in society: "A great society is a society in which its men of business think greatly of their functions."

THE INTERNATIONAL MARKETING MANAGER

We have been discussing the international marketing manager's task. Now we want to look briefly at the man himself. What kind of person is needed for this work? This is difficult to answer. Companies have not often articulated their practices and policies. The question is further complicated because there is usually a discrepancy between the speeches of top executives on the subject and the actual practices of personnel managers and company recruiters. There is, however, general agreement on a few basic requirements.

1. The international marketing manager must know his company intimately so that his decisions are indeed company decisions.
2. The international marketer must be a skilled marketer so that he can perform with technical competence.
3. The international marketer needs to be sensitive to foreign cultures and acquire an understanding of them. This cultural empathy is necessary in his personal and business relationships as well as in his decision making concerning marketing to those foreign environments.

Beyond these broad requirements, job specifications would vary from company to company. Examples of actual advertisements seeking to recruit people for international marketing positions give some idea of these specifications. The examples, which are quoted only partially, are from the *Wall Street Journal* from various issues appearing in 1970.

1. *Food, Oils, Chemicals Company Seeks International Marketing Manager. Degreed person with international marketing management experience.*

   Duties and responsibilities will involve supervising the coordination of overseas marketing activities, the release of technical marketing services to overseas operations, and the maintenance of the marketing reporting system for all overseas operations. Will provide marketing liaison between overseas affiliates and the parent company, and coordinate sales training of overseas sales personnel.

2. *Agricultural and Construction Equipment Firm Seeks Sales Manager International.*
   Management opportunity in international marketing.

   Desire field experience with related products. Degree required. Marketing major preferred. Knowledge of Spanish language is desirable.

3. *Consumer Products Company Seeks Marketing Manager for Latin America.*

   Desire man with minimum of five years experience in marketing consumer products. Candidates must have Latin American experience and fluency in Spanish. New York location with extensive travel.

4. *Equipment Manufacturer Seeks Sales Engineer—International Operations.*

   Desire technically oriented individual with international business or export sales background. Degreed person with fluency in French, German, or Spanish. Some travel from Midwest location.

5. *Lawn Care Equipment Company Seeks Director, International Marketing.*

   Executive to be primarily responsible for the sale of company's products in foreign markets. Relocation to Europe required after several months at company headquarters.

6. *Industrial Engineering Products Company Seeks Export Sales Manager.*

   To direct established export operation. Will direct field sales and distributor personnel. Fluency in Spanish desired. Also experience in Latin America and Far East marketing.

7. *Consumer Packaged Goods Company Seeks International Marketing Manager—Europe.*

   Responsibilities include advising and assisting European affiliates on marketing and sales programs with emphasis on marketing strategy, new product introduction, creating sales promotion campaigns, training of sales personnel and trouble-shooting major markets.

   European experience with consumer goods company plus fluency in French or Spanish desired.

   Chicago based with travel abroad.

8. *Feed Supplements and Animal Health Company Seeks Market Development Coordinator.*

   To coordinate sales promotion/marketing work with European and Far East offices. Reporting to chief executive. Must have administrative ability, sales experience, and familiarity with market surveys and statistical programs. International business experience helpful. Chicago based with some international travel.

These advertisements show some of the range of responsibilities a person may encounter in international marketing. Numbers 1 and 7 indicate very broad responsibilities. The extent of the task is not clearly spelled out in the other advertisements. This listing is not a random sample of job descriptions in international marketing, but it is indicative of company requirements as they relate to our discussion above of the international marketing task. Noteworthy in these advertisements is the emphasis placed on experience and language facility, especially in one of the major European languages and in Spanish for Latin America.

We have now concluded our general discussion of the firm as world marketer. In the next chapters we turn to an examination of the various specific functions an international marketer must perform so that his firm may be an effective marketer to the world.

Questions

6.1 The international marketing manager can be said to have two tasks, foreign marketing and international marketing. Discuss.

6.2 Can the firm's marketing be standardized across different markets? Explain.

6.3 Why should a multinational firm be different from its national competitors in a market?

6.4 "A multinational firm should be more than a collection of national firms." Discuss.

6.5 What are the possibilities for synergism in the multinational company? Define and give examples.

6.6 A company's options in international marketing depend not only on the external environment but also on the internal company enviroment. Discuss the following internal constraints: (a) company size; (b) company experience.

6.7 What benefits from American experience may accrue to the international marketing of an American firm? What drawbacks might arise?

6.8 Contrast briefly the international marketing task of the exporter as compared with that of the firm with wholly owned foreign plants.

6.9 Select a firm and prepare a brief international marketing philosophy for it.

6.10 What do you feel are the requirements for an international marketing manager? Write a job description for such a position in a firm you are interested in.

Further Readings

Books:

Martyn, Howe, *International Business* (London: Collier-Macmillan Ltd., 1964), esp. chaps. 1, 16.

Miracle, Gordon E., and Gerald S. Albaum, *International Marketing Management* (Homewood, Ill.: Richard D. Irwin, 1970), chaps. 1, 4.

Patty, C. Robert, and Harvey Vrendenburg, eds., *Readings in Global Marketing Management* (New York: Appleton-Century-Crofts Meredith Corp., 1969).

Ryans, John K., Jr., and James C. Baher, *World Marketing—A Multinational Approach* (New York: John Wiley and Sons, 1967).

Stanley, Alexander O., *Handbook of International Marketing* (New York: McGraw-Hill Book Co., 1963).

Articles:

Bartels, Robert, "Are Domestic and International Marketing Dissimilar?" *Journal of Marketing* (July 1968), pp. 56–61.

Buzzell, Robert D., "Can You Standardize Multinational Marketing?" *Harvard Business Review* (November–December 1968), pp. 102–113.

Yoshino, Michael Y., "Marketing Orientation in International Business," *M.S.U. Business Topics* (Summer 1965), pp. 58–64.

7

INTERNATIONAL MARKETING INTELLIGENCE

When a firm initially considers marketing to the world, it finds world markets to be "foreign" in several senses of that word. They are located outside the firm's home country; they have different languages, currencies, and customs; and they are alien and unknown to the management of the firm. Lack of knowledge of world markets is thus the first barrier to be overcome in marketing internationally. Marketing decisions cannot be made intelligently without knowing the environment and parameters that bear on them. For this reason, our study of international marketing management will begin with the intelligence function. What we consider in this chapter is the nature and scope of international marketing intelligence.

BREADTH OF THE TASK

International marketing intelligence is broader and more comprehensive than traditional domestic marketing research. It is true that all the firm's domestic marketing-research studies are *potential* candidates for international application; areas in which useful information can be obtained are consumer behavior, product acceptance, distribution-channel decisions, and promotional appeals. However, international marketing research adds a new dimension that goes beyond these conventional marketing problems to larger questions of planning, evaluation, and control of international marketing; that is, the firm needs an *information system* for international marketing. The purpose of this intelligence operation is the gathering of whatever information is necessary to make sound international marketing decisions; identifying and measuring market potential in foreign markets is only one part of this broad task.

An aspect of the broader coverage is the importance in foreign markets of many cultural, political, and macroeconomic variables that are ignored, or assumed to be constant, in domestic studies. Another aspect is the attention paid to the international parameters. In general, it can be said that all the domestic and international variables discussed in Part I are important elements for international marketing. Although many of these are extraneous and irrelevant in domestic marketing research, they are nevertheless critical to international marketing intelligence.

We have suggested that international marketing intelligence involves the creation and maintenance of an information system, which should, of course, be part of the company's overall information system for international business. Viewed from this perspective, international marketing intelligence includes several different tasks, one of which is marketing research on individual foreign markets. In itself, this is a broad task and could include any kind of research project undertaken by the firm in its home market. But international marketing research must go beyond this to include a previous investigation of *whether* the firm should enter the market, and, if the answer is affirmative, suggestions as to *how* the firm should enter the market.

Another and unique aspect involves intelligence on the specifically international parameters affecting marketing decisions. One group of these parameters includes the international economic factors considered in Chapter 2, for example, balance of payments problems, financial and commercial policy considerations, and so on. A second group includes the political-legal aspects of international relations, as discussed in Chapter 5. A third element is the analysis of competition. Although the firm must analyze the competitive situation in each of its national markets, this kind of analysis alone is not sufficient for international marketing. Because competition in many industries is now international or global, the study of the competitive situation must also be multinational. For example, the automotive, chemical, and electronics industries are engaged in truly international competition. Analysis of competition in such industries cannot be limited to studies of individual markets.

Finally, international comparative studies are a further dimension of analysis for the firm that wishes to maximize its effectiveness abroad. As can be seen, the distinctiveness of international marketing intelligence arises from two factors. First, the firm is operating within a number of foreign (different) environments. Second, it is conducting business *between* these foreign markets. These differences necessitate not only the adaptation of domestic techniques but also the development of new methods of analysis. An example of the international researcher's task can be given through a 1969 *Wall Street Journal* advertisement of an international company seeking such a person.

The advertisement read as follows: "The International Division is seeking a research analyst to work on broad scope individual projects relating to international economic and marketing research. . . . The general subjects which will be researched are economic statistics, sales and marketing forecasts, distribution methodology, market planning on existing and new products, and related subjects which would have an impact on aggregate marketing plans for given geographical areas. . . . Because of the scope of the projects, it is necessary to have a much broader familiarity with economic and marketing subjects than may be normally required for a marketing research professional." [*Emphasis added*]

The smaller firm in international marketing will have information needs similar to those of the large firm. However, it will be less able to conduct the same kind of marketing intelligence operation. Therefore, it must rely more on others for its international information needs. For example, the firm may rely on its distributors, licensees, or joint-venture partners. Or it may choose to market through a combination export manager, depending on his knowledge of foreign markets.

WHAT INFORMATION?

An enormous amount of information is available on all the countries of the world, but there are also significant information gaps in certain matters of interest to business. The researcher, however, does not need *all* the facts or information about foreign markets. To economize on research funds and effort and to facilitate storage and retrieval of the data, the researcher wants only relevant information, that is, information necessary to international marketing decision making.

Few would disagree with the relevance criterion just cited. By itself, however, it is not an operational guideline. In order to be workable, it must be defined more completely, including identification of the international marketing decisions that will be made using the information gathered. In a broad sense, marketing involves all the decisions a firm makes in relating to its market. The initial decision, of course, is whether to enter a foreign market. Richard Holton, using game-theory language, suggests three questions that marketing intelligence should consider.

1. Who are the players? or, Who are the competitors, customers, suppliers, government officials, and others who can affect our operations?
2. What strategic alternatives or actions is each player likely to consider?
3. What are the probabilities attached to each strategic alternative?[1]

Once a decision has been made to market in a particular country, the conventional marketing questions will arise. For convenience, these are usually classified into functional areas, such as product decisions, pricing decisions, channel decisions, and so on. These decisions can be further broken down until eventually a very specific local issue is reached, for example, What kind of package and label should we use for our floor wax in the Philippines? Such a question gives relatively specific guidance to the researcher for his information gathering because it narrows down the investigation and focuses on a limited list of parameters.

[1] Richard H. Holton, "Marketing Policies in Multinational Corporations," *Journal of International Business Studies* (Summer 1970), pp. 1–20.

Each firm needs to understand its own marketing program and to identify the people making both general and very specific international marketing decisions. The next step is to find out what marketing decisions these people make, as suggested in the preceding paragraph. The final step is to determine the information necessary for these marketing decisions.

How does the researcher or the international marketing manager fulfill these requirements before doing the actual research? Who makes international marketing decisions? Where are they? What decisions do they make? These initial questions can presumably be answered by the man in charge of international marketing. He is responsible for international marketing performance. He, along with those in his chain of command, should be able to identify the decision makers and the kinds of decisions they make. It is, in fact, impossible to have an effective organization without knowing what its critical members (the decision makers) are doing.

The last and most difficult question is that of determining what information the decision makers use to make their decisions. As a starting point, each one would probably have a checklist of data necessary for his own decisions. For example, in planning the annual advertising campaign in country X, the subsidiary advertising manager would have a list including the following items: budget allowance; competitors' activity; distributors' promotion; media costs, availability, and coverage; and so on. As experience and sophistication increase, the checklist becomes a "model," which includes not only the data but shows their interrelationships.

For the firm new to international marketing or to a given foreign market, no tested model may be available to refer to. Then management must develop the appropriate checklist or model. The researcher is not without guidelines, however. He would start with the model or checklist of information needs that the firm has developed for domestic operations, examining it carefully to see how the new foreign context would affect it. Studying it with an awareness of possible differences should minimize the errors that result from unquestioning application of a domestic approach to a foreign situation. Insights to the foreign changes required could be obtained in part from potential foreign collaborators, for example, distributors, advertising or other service agencies, licensees, or joint-venture partners. If the firm already has foreign experience but is new to a particular foreign market, it can draw upon all its other foreign experience in approaching the new market. Comparative analysis (discussed under Comparative Analysis for International Marketing) can be very useful in reducing the firm's ignorance about the new market.

USE OF DOMESTIC TECHNIQUES

American companies are accustomed to employing a wide range of sophisticated marketing-research techniques in their domestic market. In their international operations they would like to draw upon the same tools and techniques. To what extent is this possible? Of course, this is putting the question the wrong way. The researcher should ask instead, What marketing intelligence do I need, and what is the best way of getting it? This approach focuses on the information problems to be solved, not on the techniques that happen to be available. Nevertheless, it is useful to consider the applicability of domestic marketing research techniques to foreign marketing situations. It should be noted that the question is only relevant to marketing research within foreign markets. Any international data or intelligence would require different methods from those used in domestic marketing research.

The questions the firm needs to ask in foreign markets are the same ones it asks in the domestic market; that is, What are consumer product preferences? What is our brand image? Which advertising copy is most effective? and the like. Whether the techniques used to elicit the information are also the same is quite another matter. Two of the basic methods of collecting data are questionnaires and observation, which would be important in foreign markets as well. (The use of secondary data or the purchase of marketing intelligence involve the same methods, but at one step removed from the firm.) However, the kinds of questionnaires and observation methods that can be used in foreign markets may be very different. In other words, the specific tools and techniques used at home may not be applicable in foreign markets.

The problem facing the researcher is similar to that facing the international marketing manager, that is, to what extent does he need to adapt his domestic approach to get the best results in foreign markets. An added complication is that the answer will probably vary from market to market. The marketing researcher will start with the information need in a particular market. He will then determine how to satisfy the information need. Because of his background, he will probably try some domestic technique that has worked well for him. This can be a good starting point because the technique has been proved, he is familiar with it, and he wants to use the best tools available in his task. However, because of differing conditions in the foreign market, the researcher must frequently modify his methods, or even look for another approach.

To use domestic marketing research techniques effectively in other countries, the international marketing researcher must have three special skills. First, he must be very well versed in the techniques themselves. He must know their assumptions and limitations. Second, he must know the degree to which their application is related to culture. If the application of a technique is affected by the social and cultural character of the market or is limited by the economic infrastructure, the researcher must recognize these relationships because they will change in a foreign environment. Third, the researcher must have reasonably good knowledge of the foreign environments in which these techniques are to be applied. To create a happy marriage between the techniques and the market, he must know and match the characteristics of both parties. Essentially, the researcher should separate the "pure" technique from its cultural trappings so that he can take it unencumbered into the new foreign environment where it will mesh with local conditions in an appropriate way.

To use a parallel, the problem is not unlike preparing astronauts to function in space or on the moon. We know the earth environment and the way our equipment and techniques function in it. These are the first two skills. To have a successful space or moon program, we must develop the third skill, that is, knowledge of the space or moon environment, so that we can adapt our equipment and techniques to function effectively out there. Our discussion of the impact of the foreign environment on the use of marketing research technique has been rather abstract. The relationship will be more evident in the specific examples given in the next section, Problems in Foreign Marketing Research.

We will not be discussing the variety of techniques available for domestic marketing research in foreign markets. These techniques are the same, basically, as those used in the firm's home market. It is assumed that the reader is already familiar with these from other sources.[2]

PROBLEMS IN FOREIGN MARKETING RESEARCH

A variety of problems arise in the conduct of foreign marketing research. To cope with them requires flexibility and imagination on the part of the researcher, in addition to the three skills mentioned above (knowledge of techniques, their relation to the domestic culture, and understanding of the foreign environments). The problems can be classified into four categories: (1) cultural problems; (2) technical problems; (3) data problems; (4) the economic problem.

Cultural Problems

Much of marketing research involves getting information from people about their attitudes and preferences concerning a company's products, brands, prices, or promotion. This reliance on human subjects as the primary source of inputs for marketing intelligence gives rise to what we might call "people problems" for the researcher. Whereas the production manager can usually count on his inputs to behave the same way in all countries, the contrary situation prevails in marketing. People think, feel, and generally behave differently from country to country. This is glorious diversity from many viewpoints, such as that of the tourist; however, it is a complication for the researcher, who might prefer a tidy uniformity which is more manageable and efficient—that is, which gives economies of scale.

Languages

Language is the initial cultural difference that comes to mind when one thinks of foreign markets. At the minimum, language difference poses problems of expense and communication. For the American firm, there is probably the expense of double translation. First, the research design and specifications (and perhaps even complete questionnaires) must be translated from English into the language of each of the countries where a particular study is to be

[2] See, for example, Paul E. Green and Donald S. Tull, *Research for Marketing Decisions* 2nd ed. (Englewood Cliffs, N.J.: Prentice-Hall, 1970).

conducted. Then, on completion of the study, the results must be translated back into English to be meaningful to the user of the research. Of course, that marketing research which is designed and used exclusively by a national subsidiary does not need to go through these steps. However, much of the benefit of multinational operations is lost to the company if *all* marketing research studies are done on an ad hoc, exclusively national basis.

More important than translation expense is the communication problem. Language is not merely a collection of words and sounds; it is a reflection of the culture itself. A person from one culture may have difficulty communicating in another even if he has learned the language. Knowing how to order a dinner or even how to carry on a social or business conversation does not mean that one can capture the significant but subtle differences in meaning that may be important in a marketing-research project. Thus the more translations that are made (or the more often the culture gap is passed), the more noise or static there will be in the communication, with consequent loss of message. There are ways of dealing with the problem, such as idiomatic translations or using nationals to prepare the research, but the static can never be completely eliminated. motivation and attitude studies present the greatest difficulties; objective data are more easily obtained. As a corollary, language and communication difficulties are generally greater in consumer market research than in industrial market research where technical factors are more important.

The communication problems are magnified when a country has several languages, a situation that arises especially in less developed countries.

In the Republic of Congo, for example, the official language is French, but only a small part of the population is fluent in French. Most Congolese can converse fairly well in one of the four lingua francas of the country. However, in speaking of matters of the heart, most Congolese will use their own tribal language. For many kinds of marketing intelligence, this "language of the heart" provides the most useful information. However, there are scores of such languages in Congo but very few people who could do an adequate translation into another language, especially into English or a European language. Compounding the problem is the fact that very few of the tribal languages have written alphabets. Only oral communication is possible.

Language diversity may be one of the few problems that will diminish with time. For one thing, English is increasingly important as a world language, which is helpful in two ways. First, for some kinds of research English can be used without translation, or at least as a common denominator tying national projects together. Second, collaborators in the research will often know both English and the national language well enough to bridge the communications gap satisfactorily.

For example, the Marketing Science Institute was conducting research in several foreign countries for a comparative marketing study. National research organizations were hired to do the actual interviewing and field work in each country. In Italy, an Italian organization was hired, in Japan, a Japanese group, and so on. In each case, the nationals knew English well enough to help prepare the questionnaires and conduct the research with a minimum of static in the communication.

Another factor tending to reduce the language problem is the spread of modern communications technology. With satellite communication spreading, and transistor radios present in almost every village of the world, people are tuning into fewer common languages while sharing more common concerns. Along with increasing travel and mobility, these developments will gradually bring more common denominators, both in language and other aspects of culture. As modernization continues around the world, this will be one of its inevitable results.

Social Organization

Much of marketing research is concerned with the buyer's behavior and gaining insights into his decision process. Such research is predicated on the assumption that the decision makers and the decision influencers have been fairly well identified. When the researcher moves into foreign markets, he will usually find that the social organization is different enough that he must identify anew the decision makers and influencers if he wishes to conduct effective research. This does not mean that each foreign market necessarily has a unique pattern, but it does mean that extra study is needed before preparing or adapting a research design in a foreign market. Such adaptation can affect adversely the efficiencies otherwise attainable in international marketing research; the more the research has to be adapted to each national market, the fewer the economies of scale realized.

A particular aspect of social organization is the family structure. In America, the family is an atomistic unit composed of father, mother, and the children living at home. In many countries, the family is extended to include grandparents, uncles, aunts, and cousins. Where this extended family is a critical factor, it is especially difficult to determine the decision makers and influencers for the purchase of particular goods and the relevant family unit for whom the purchase is made.

Differences in social organization affect the industrial market as well as the consumer market. The nature of the management and decision-making structure in foreign companies is likely to be quite different from that in American companies. One reason is the greater importance of family businesses in other countries. When family business is combined with an extended family structure, it means that the family relationships must be identified by anyone wanting to market to the firm. Organization charts or titles are much less meaningful than family ties.

Another reason for differences in decision making is the differing views on the nature and role of management. There are a variety of national attitudes toward professional management, scientific approaches to management, and centralization versus delegation of authority. For the researcher in foreign markets, these factors complicate his identification of the appropriate research respondents and his determination of the marketing efforts needed to reach them. The problem is not one of choosing techniques but one of identifying the socio-cultural environment in which the techniques will be applied.

The role of women in society and in the economy is far from uniform around the world. In America, the woman has perhaps the most power in the disposition of the consumer dollar. She is the purchaser as well as principal decision maker for many goods. In addition, she is an important worker, not only in the economy at large but also in marketing research activities. Generally, both these feminine roles tend to decrease and change in quality as one descends the scale of economic development or enters different cultures. Part of the researcher's problem is to determine just what the woman's role in consumption decisions is in each society.

Another problem may be that the woman is difficult to reach as a respondent in a marketing research project. In Moslem countries, for instance, she may not be permitted to talk with a strange man (the researcher), especially if her husband is not present. Furthermore, in many countries women would not be available to use as interviewers or in other market-research tasks. Both social and educational constraints are at work here. Socially, women may be consigned to a retiring, passive role; educationally, they may not be trained to qualify for participation in market-research kinds of activities.

Getting Responses

Marketing activities and the marketing profession are not held in high esteem in most countries. Manufacturers have a production orientation and little concern or interest in the market or in conducting or participating in marketing research. In such cases where the respondents are business people (producers or distributors), their reluctance to participate may stem from various motives. Where tax evasion is a common business practice, the businessman will suspect the questioner of being a government revenue representative rather than a legitimate market researcher, or he may be reluctant to respond for fear of giving up information to competitors. The idea of businessmen giving information to anyone, government or private person, is much less accepted abroad than in America. One of the researcher's greatest problems here is trying to demonstrate the value of the research to the respondent himself. Unless he can do this, he can accomplish little with business respondents.

Consumers too are reluctant to respond to marketing-research inquiries. This may be in part the result of a general unwillingness to talk to strangers, a reaction especially common from female respondents as noted above. Even male respondents, however, are more reluctant to discuss personal consumption habits and preferences than are American men. That marketing is more developed in America than anywhere else in the world is frequently remarked upon. Marketing research, both in companies' conduct of it and in citizens' response to it, reflects the general American marketing orientation. The reasons again are more cultural than technical.

In contrast to the reluctant respondent is the cooperative and willing respondent who feels obliged to give responses that will please the interviewer rather than to state his true opinions or feelings. In some cultures this is a form of politeness, but it obviously does not contribute to effective research.

Reluctant or polite responses are not the only barriers to effective marketing research. Occasionally, even if willing and objective, the respondent is not able to answer meaningfully. For example, illiteracy is a barrier when written material is used in consumer research. This problem can be avoided by using purely oral communications with respondents, although the responses must be written down by the interviewer. Even when the interview is oral, however, a communication problem that could be called "technical" illiteracy may arise. That is, the terms or concepts used in the study might be foreign to the respondent, even though in his own language. He may not understand the question and thus be unable to answer. Or he may answer according to his misunderstanding, giving a useless response.

Quite apart from the terms used, the respondent may be unable to cooperate effectively because he is being asked to think in a way foreign to his normal thought patterns. He is being asked to react analytically rather than intuitively. Because he does not reason or think in the same way the interviewer or research designer does, he may not be able to answer in a meaningful way. Even business respondents may have similar difficulty if they are asked in their own language about stock turnover or other business concepts which they have never used or thought about. Whatever the particular cause of the inability to respond, it is basically a translation problem. The research designer must be able to translate not only the words but also the *concepts* into the cultural pattern of the respondent. The cultural gap must be bridged by the research designer.

Technical Problems

In addition to the human and social difficulties just considered, the researcher in foreign marketing encounters technical problems that he is totally unaccustomed to at home. The problems we will consider here arise primarily in less developed countries. Good research is a function not only of proper design and preparation but also of implementation, which is often contingent upon external factors the researcher cannot control. The researcher usually depends on some economic and commercial infrastructure in conducting his research.

Mail surveys, for example, require both literacy and a reliable postal service. Many less developed countries are largely rural and postal service in these areas is not very dependable. Therefore, mail surveys may not be an available option. Data collection by telephone avoids the literacy problem but runs up against the greater difficulty that most families do not have phones. A telephone survey is almost impossible unless the researcher wants to sample a high-income segment of the market. Even for a survey of businessmen, telephones might not be available for contacting small producers or distributors.

If mail and telephone surveys are not practical, the researcher is left with personal interviewing as an alternative. With a largely rural or village population in the poorer countries, the problem then becomes, How does the interviewer reach the people? Probably he does not. Poor roads and lack of automobiles or regular public transportation mean that the rural population may not be economically reachable. Surveys may be limited primarily to urban areas where these technical problems are less important.[3]

The economic infrastructure (communications and transportation) has been discussed, but there is an aspect of the commercial infrastructure that also bears on the conduct of marketing research. Especially in foreign markets is the firm unlikely to be able to do 100 percent of the total marketing research task. Because of its smaller market and staff there, it depends on supporting services available in the local economy. Such resources include personnel qualified to do interviewing or other research tasks and firms that will handle all or part of the actual research. Because of the large American market and the strong demand for marketing research, a great number of specialized supporting services are available in the United States. A profitable market for these services exists in America, even though they are less necessary here than in many other countries.

Unfortunately, the smaller size of most foreign markets coupled with the lesser development of marketing activities there mean that research-support services usually are not available, especially where they are most needed. Organizations like A. C. Nielsen have moved into many industrialized countries but into few less developed areas. Consumer panels and other research techniques tend to be available in Western European markets but, again, absent from most other countries. Because such operations are too costly for any one firm to establish, these kinds of techniques and services are crossed off the list of available tools for the researcher in many foreign markets.

Data Problems

The difficulties facing the firm's marketing research also hinder data gathering by governments and other groups. Thus the secondary data sources so important in market analysis are generally less available in foreign markets. Again there is a correlation with the level of economic development: The lower the per capita income in a country, the weaker the statistical sources. The statistical data are also frequently inconsistent and unreliable with regard to their quality as well as their availability.

Although most governments take a census and gather other statistics in their administrative activities, these are of varying quality and usefulness. The use of probability sampling is necessarily limited where the nature of the relevant universe cannot be reliably determined from the data available. Quota sampling is limited for the same reason, so the most frequently employed technique is the convenience sample. This is defensible primarily because of a lack of alternatives. However, there is room to doubt if the results are worth the effort. Trade associations are often important data sources for particular industries. Unfortunately, trade associations do not even exist in some coun-

[3] For further detail, see Harper W. Boyd, Jr., Ronald E. Frank, William F. Massy, and Mostafa Zoheir, "On the Use of Marketing Research in the Emerging Economies," *Journal of Marketing Research* (November 1964), pp. 20–25.

tries, whereas in a number of others, their data are neither very complete nor reliable.

We have been considering the data problems in individual foreign markets, but another difficulty arises when comparing several foreign markets. When the researcher makes a list of the kinds of comparative data he needs from the several markets, he will find many gaps when he tries to compile the data. On some items, perhaps no country has data, and on others, only half the countries have them. This is not the extent of the difficulty, however. Even when the analyst has data from all the countries on certain items, he will often find that the data are hardly comparable. The lack of comparability may result from varied causes. Different base years may have been used in different countries, or the underlying definitions were not the same. What is called a "commercial vehicle," a "wholesaler," or a "family dwelling" may mean something a bit different in each country. Differing degrees of accuracy in data gathering can be another cause of lack of comparability.

Finally, the private data- and information-gathering agencies so valuable in American marketing research are often missing in foreign markets. Wards Automotive Reports, the Dodge reports on the construction industry, and the Audit Bureau of Circulation (ABC) are examples of widely used data services. In addition to these are the information services or studies available from magazines and newspapers, universities, banks, advertising agencies, and so on. No other country has the wealth of information services available to the American marketing researcher; and some countries have practically no services at all.

The Economic Problem

Marketing research entails very large expenditures in the American economy. These sums can be quite effectively used here, however, because of the size of the market and the kind of expertise available. In a relatively homogeneous and affluent market of 200 million people, marketing research can have a high pay-off. The skills available within producing firms and service organizations can assure rather efficient research. In foreign markets, the cost may be the same to design and implement a marketing study as it is in the United States, but the potential market is smaller, usually involving a much smaller population as well as a lower per capita income. For example, even though India has a population two and one-half times as large as the United States, its total GNP is much less than one-tenth the American GNP. In considering the smaller size of the foreign market added to the other problems noted above, the researcher must ask himself, How much research can I afford to do abroad? as well as, How can I do marketing research abroad?

It is not easy to do the necessary cost-benefit analysis to answer the economic question of how much research to carry on in foreign markets. Calculating the cost of research abroad involves less reliable figures than the researcher has for the American market, partly because the research methods may vary. Calculating the benefits is also difficult because less is known about the foreign market. Nevertheless, both costs and pay-offs have to be figured in the best way possible so that intelligent marketing-research decisions can be made. Comparative analysis of foreign markets is one useful approach (see under Preparing a Comparative Analysis for Marketing) to getting a feel for the cost-benefit parameters there.

Another approach to the problem of costly marketing research in small markets is to conduct no formal research there at all. Rather than conduct a market potential study, a firm might test a market by exporting there for a year or so. Exporting can be a low cost way of getting a feel for a market. In this sense, the export level of involvement can be a way of "buying information" on a market before making a heavier commitment there. This approach can be in lieu of, or in addition to, more formal market studies.

DEALING WITH INTERNATIONAL MARKETING RESEARCH PROBLEMS

Defining a problem is the first step toward its solution. A preliminary and general identification of problem areas in international marketing research has been sketched above. The individual researcher in a company will need a more specific analysis of the problems peculiar to his own situation. However, the problems would fall within the general outline given. Once the problems have been identified, what approaches are possible? A firm might, of course, forget about international marketing research since the problems are so great and the results so often uncertain. However, the costs of missed opportunities or marketing mistakes must be compared to the costs of improved marketing intelligence.

For example, an American tire producer built a plant in France without any special market research. The company felt it knew the market because of its experience in exporting there. However, driving habits were undergoing changes with resultant changes in the kind of tires wanted. Soon after the plant went on stream, costly production adjustments had to be made to match the new market demand. An initial result of this experience was the hiring of a skilled international marketing research executive by the company's international division. A few years later when another plant was to be built in Italy, the company conducted a detailed marketing analysis before giving the project the green light.[4]

None of the difficulties of international marketing research are easily solved. Perhaps it can be said that in general the international market researcher must exercise more ingenuity and be more skilled at improvisation than his domestic counterpart. Because the environment gives him less support, and because tested tools and techniques may not be available, he must depend more on his own insight and creativity. Beyond this basic requirement, however, there are some ways of minimizing the difficulties encountered.

In dealing with the cultural problems in marketing research, the analyst is

[4] Vern Terpstra, *American Marketing in the Common Market* (New York: Praeger, 1967), p. 120. Other similar examples can be found here.

trying essentially to bridge the cultural gap which separates him from the various national markets he is interested in. The gap is most obvious in the case of language but may be even more important in the case of social behavior and attitudes. One way the researcher can bridge the cultural gap is to become familiar with the relevant foreign cultures. However, this is a time-consuming and expensive approach, provided it is even possible. Although such exposure and experience are necessary in an international marketing research operation, they do not provide an adequate answer to the cultural gap, especially if a number of foreign markets are involved.

What the research activity requires is the enlistment of national participants, those who are actually members of the cultures and markets being studied. There are various ways of getting this national assistance. If the firm is new to a market, it can hire a national research agency to supply local knowledge (assuming such an agency is available) while it contributes its own marketing research expertise. The national agency's personnel should help the firm avoid the cultural blunders and communication failures that result from an approach entirely foreign to the market.

If the firm already has some experience in a foreign market, it is in a much stronger position—first, because experience is the best teacher and, second, because there are many more nationals it can call on. Its distributors and service agencies in the country have some interest in the firm's success and can supply local understanding. Its own national employees can be even more useful in this regard.

This enlistment of nationals is a necessary step in bridging the cultural gap in international marketing research. Unfortunately, it is not a step sufficient to resolve all the cultural problems noted above. For the rest, ingenuity and hard work are required, and even then some difficulties will still remain. The same is true of technical, data, and economic problems. The passage of time and the growth and development of foreign markets will improve their economic and commercial infrastructure. In the meantime, however, the researcher can only improvise around these limitations. The firm cannot afford to develop the necessary technical or data services all by itself. The multinational company does, however, have resources which can help the researcher to overcome, at least partially, the handicaps he faces. As the multinational company gathers information and experience in many foreign markets, it can use these to increase its understanding of all foreign markets through comparative analysis.

Comparative Analysis for International Marketing[5]

Comparative analysis is an attempt to organize information and experience to maximize their usefulness. In international marketing, this means that the company gathers and organizes its intelligence from all its global operations

[5] The discussion here draws on research conducted by the writer and Professor Yoshino of U.C.L.A. and reported in *Comparative Analysis for International Marketing*, Marketing Science Institute (Boston: Allyn & Bacon, 1967). (Co-authors: Bertil Liander and Aziz A. Sherbini.)

to see what new insights can be gained. When considering the markets of the world, one can make various assumptions. One extreme assumption is that all markets are like the United States market. Another extreme assumption is that each market is completely unique and unlike any other foreign market. If the first assumption were true, the firm's products and marketing strategies would be the same all over the world and international marketing would be the same as domestic marketing. (There would also be no need for textbooks like this.) If the second assumption were true, the firm would have to start from scratch in each foreign market without being able to draw on its experience elsewhere.

The experience of multinational companies as well as our own intuition tell us that neither of these extreme assumptions is true. Although many markets of the world have characteristics similar to those of the American market, it is often the differences that are important to the marketer. Conversely, although each national market has its peculiarities, it also has enough similarities to some other markets that the firm can draw upon its experience elsewhere in entering the new market. The task for the international marketer and researcher is to discover the critical characteristics of foreign markets in which differences or similarities are important for company decisions.

Preparing a Comparative Analysis for Marketing

The tourist traveling from country to country is on the lookout for things that are different from what he is used to at home. The marketing researcher going from market to market, literally or figuratively, is looking for both similarities and differences. The researcher, furthermore, is concerned only with certain kinds of similarities and differences, that is, those which affect marketing decisions. To guide himself, the researcher must have a model of market behavior for his own firm; that is, he must know how the firm relates to its market environment.

Such a model probably would be developed initially from the company's domestic experience and then tested and adapted according to its experience in foreign markets. From the model, the researcher can identify the parameters critical to marketing decisions. Such an approach is likely to yield a recognition that a single market model does not fit all the company's global operations but neither are 150 market models necessary for the firm's 150 foreign markets. The countries probably will fall into several categories or groups.

Grouping or classifying things, whether they be markets or information bits, is an important step in understanding them. It has even been said that classification is the beginning of science. Darwin and Linnaeus, for instance, became famous for their classifications that increased our understanding of the world of zoology and botany. The Standard Industrial Classification (SIC) system is a useful way to organize information about the industrial economy. Of course, there are inappropriate classifications too, which do injustice to the data and therefore make analysis incorrect.

The stereotype is an example of improper classification. Grouping countries by geographic region could be another, if the countries are not homogeneous in the characteristics important to the firm's marketing strategy. Geographic grouping of countries has been practiced in part because of the nature of communications in the international company. However, for purposes of marketing planning and strategy, it is often more meaningful to organize information independent of geography and according to commonality of important marketing characteristics.

Rostow classified the nations of the world in five categories according to level of economic development. Geographers, political scientists, and others have developed other classification systems which are useful for their work. Marketing researchers can do the same. First, it is necessary to identify the country characteristics important to international marketing decisions. Because these may vary depending on the product or function, no general model is available. Each company must develop its own, but it can benefit from studying the general approaches to classification developed by others. After the relevant country characteristics have been identified, countries can be grouped according to their similarity in these critical dimensions.

If meaningful market groupings can be developed by the firm, there are several potential advantages. One is the economy of preparing general marketing strategy for a small number of country groupings rather than a completely ad hoc strategy for each foreign market. Another advantage is in evaluating potential or performance in foreign markets. To evaluate a country operation by itself is difficult, and management often shies away from making comparisons with other foreign markets. If, however, countries are grouped according to similar market characteristics, such cross-country comparisons are more valid and useful. A further advantage to country groupings lies in overcoming some of the problems in international marketing research.

That country groupings are advantageous in regard to economies of scale is not just a theoretical possibility. Some major American companies are using such country groupings for analysis and planning in foreign marketing.

A large American electronics company was doing correlation studies on foreign markets, comparing company product sales with various data on the countries. What emerged very distinctly was a threefold grouping of all the firm's foreign markets. (In terms of a scatter diagram, there was not a single line to fit the data but three roughly parallel lines.) Further analysis corroborated the validity of the threefold grouping. As a result, the firm revised its method of planning marketing strategy in foreign markets. Instead of preparing annual marketing guidance on an individual-country basis, the company began preparing guidance for the three groups of countries, with a brief appendix for each market to cover whatever peculiarities it had.

An executive in a food company read a summary article about Rostow's stages-of-development theory. He was intrigued and wondered how this might apply to his company's extensive foreign operations. He collected data on market indicators and on performance of the firm's major products in foreign markets. The markets were grouped according to a level-of-development con-cept. From this analysis, he discovered a significant relationship between the volume *and the* types *of product sold and the level of economic development. The appropriate groupings were not geographic; they were based primarily on economic data. This approach contrasted with the company's traditional one of analyzing operations only within regional divisions (Europe, Latin America, and so on). The executive believed his approach would be helpful in developing a model of product mix appropriate to various levels of develop-ment. The model could be used as a guideline in changing the product mix in a given country as it moved from one stage of development to another.*[6]

Noteworthy here is that the executive could not get the data needed for his analysis from the firm's existing reporting system for foreign subsidiaries. As any review of a company's information system will reveal, some currently gathered data were not being used and other data potentially useful for decisions were not being gathered. In this case, the changes in the reporting system were not costly.

Comparative analysis of meaningful country groupings can help to over-come some of the problems in international marketing research. One such problem is the data gaps that appear when the researcher wants to investigate one or more foreign markets. If the firm has been able to analyze its foreign markets and group them in a way significant for its operations, it will be less hindered by the data gaps that appear in its analyses. If the country with missing data is part of a larger, relatively homogeneous group, the researcher can, with some justice, assume that the values for the missing data are similar to those he has for other countries in the same group. Although this assumption will not always be completely correct, the probabilities favoring it are much greater than if he were to consider the country in isolation or to compare it with other countries not similar in characteristics important to the company.

Comparative analysis is also useful in overcoming the economic problem of the expense involved in conducting marketing research in many small foreign markets. In many instances, the costs of a research study are relatively unrelated to the size of the market. This means that marketing research costs may be prohibitive in many of the firm's smaller markets. The firm can either act without market-research inputs or use country groupings to minimize the costs.

Assume that a firm has grouped its foreign markets into four categories, A, B, C, and D (as one pharmaceutical firm has). Categories C (thirty coun-tries) and D (forty-seven countries) are the poorer, smaller markets for the firm. To act appropriately in each market, it would be helpful to have market-research inputs from each, but costs are prohibitive compared to profit potential there. The firm might decide to conduct research in a sampling of countries in categories C and D—say, five C countries and seven D countries— and extrapolate the results to other countries in the respective categories.

[6] Liander et al., *Comparative Analysis for International Marketing*, p. 27.

This approach needs to be taken with care, but it seems better than the alternatives of doing no research at all or carrying out high-cost research in all seventy-seven countries. The arguments for and against such an approach would apply to any use of stratified sampling techniques.

A further justification of country groupings and comparative analysis in international marketing lies in the current practices of multinational companies. In interviews with international executives, a recurring theme was the emphasis on the importance of experienced personnel over formulas or techniques for problem solving. Of course, the value of experience is that the experienced person is carrying over to a new market or situation something learned in a previous market or situation; that is, the experienced person is making his own comparative analysis. We suggest that such comparisons can be made more general, formal, and explicit. This is in line with the trend toward more scientific decision making which is receiving such emphasis in domestic business management.

With companies as with individuals, the broader their experience, the more they can generalize and deal with new experiences. To achieve synergism, the international company needs to collect, analyze, and organize its own extensive experience so that it can capitalize on it in more sophisticated and effective marketing to existing and future national markets. Although many companies have this resource of extensive international experience, not all have been able to use it fully because individual experiences have not been gathered together and analyzed. If the firm's international experience resides only in individual managers and employees, it may not be effectively retrievable and usable.

INFORMATION SOURCES FOR INTERNATIONAL MARKETING

Because of the distance and "foreignness" of foreign markets, the beginning international marketer knows little about them. To market effectively abroad, he may feel a need to know at least as much about foreign markets as he does about the home market. Where and how can such knowledge be obtained? Fortunately, in spite of occasional data problems, there is a wealth of information on foreign markets. The discussion here will indicate the different kinds of information sources. Generally speaking, there are three basic sources of foreign market information: (1) secondary sources or published information; (2) experienced and knowledgeable individuals within the domestic market; and (3) travel to foreign markets for personal investigation. Most foreign market research should cover the first two sources before undertaking the third, relatively costly step. Our discussion will focus on the first two kinds of sources.

The United States Government

The Department of Commerce

No organization in the world gathers more information than the American government. Fortunately, some of its work is useful to the firm selling internationally. The Department of Commerce is the chief government source of foreign market information, and it actively seeks to aid American firms in selling abroad. This assistance is available through personal consultation at any one of the thirty-seven Department of Commerce field offices located in major cities around the United States, or in Washington, D.C. Although a trip to Washington may be more expensive than a visit to a field office, it may be more productive, because the country and the product experts are there. The field offices can relay only imperfectly the information available in Washington. Additionally, the department gathers and publishes information on many topics of interest to the international marketer. An overview of those publications will be given here.

Commerce Today, the department's biweekly magazine, is an excellent current source of trade leads and information on the latest developments in world trade. The *Overseas Business Reports* are a regular updated series of reports on most major markets of the world. Relevant information covered in these reports includes economic and marketing data on the country, guidelines on how to do business there, copyright and trademark laws, business and import regulations, and the like. In addition to these kinds of international market information, the Department of Commerce offers specific guidance in locating customers, agents, or licensees in foreign markets. (See Figure 7–1.)

For two notable reasons these Department of Commerce aids provide a good starting point for much foreign market research. First, they cover a wide range both as to subject matter and as to geography; and second, all this material and assistance is available at very modest cost. We indicate only a few of the department publications here. There is a comprehensive bibliography of all these publications called the *International Trade Check List*. It is published about twice a year and is available without charge.

Other Government Departments

Other government departments and agencies also provide assistance or information on international trade matters. Among these are the Agency for International Development, the Federal Trade Commission, and the Tariff Commission. The Department of Agriculture publishes such things as a sixty-page study on *The Agricultural Economy of Tanganyika* and the Department of Labor publishes a periodical entitled *Labor Developments Abroad*. These examples are merely to indicate the extent of the United States government's interest in foreign countries and the way its information services can benefit the international marketer. In a sense, the government is a subsidized information service. The international marketing researcher should be aware of what is available from the government and use whatever is relevant as a valuable and inexpensive input.

Foreign Governments

No foreign government can match the extensive international trade information of the American government. Nonetheless, many of them have a large amount of very good data on their own economies, much of which is available through the country's embassy or consulate general in America. In some

Keys to Export Profits:

MAKING TRADE CONNECTIONS ABROAD—Call, write or visit your Department of Commerce Field Office (see list of office addresses) or the Commercial Intelligence Division, Bureau of International Commerce, U.S. Department of Commerce, Washington, D.C. 20230. The practical aids described below are available to you.

TRADE LISTS help you find customers, distributors, agents, and licensees abroad.

Each list includes names and addresses of firms handling a specific commodity in one foreign country; basic trade and industry data with a brief analysis of international trade in the particular commodity; controlling government regulations, and related information. Lists of importers and dealers show relative size of each firm, products handled, territory covered, and size of sales force.

• *$1 per country for each commodity classification. See page 7 for lists of classifications and countries covered.*

AUTOMATED TRADE LISTS were first released in June 1967. Designed to eventually replace the Trade Lists described above, the new automated lists designate by 5-digit Standard Industrial Classification (SIC) number the products handled by each foreign firm. The entry for each firm includes its name, mailing address, name and title of chief executive, function, type of organization, date of establishment, size, whether the firm has a U.S. representative, language of correspondence, and date of the World Trade Directory Report from which the data were obtained. Included are the names of importers, distributors, agents and manufacturers. Automated Trade Lists have been published for the major U.S. trading areas. New and revised lists are regularly announced in **International Commerce.** Requests for automated lists should include a description of the product and/or SIC number, and the type of foreign organization desired. Examples are: importer of lumber; manufacturer of toys; distributor of fertilizers; exporter of electronic components; agent for drugs; producer of dairy products; and retailer of office machines.

• *$1 per country for each principal SIC product category.*

WORLD TRADE DIRECTORY REPORTS provide descriptive and background information on specific foreign firms. They are not credit reports, but they do contain names and addresses of sources of credit, financial, and commercial data.

WTD reports are prepared by the U.S. Foreign Service and the typical report includes information on type of organization, method of operation, lines handled, size of firm, sales territory, names of owners and officers, capital, sales volume, general reputation in trade and financial circles, and names of the firm's trading connections. The complete name, street and city address of the foreign firm must be given when asking for this service.

• *$2 each.*

FOREIGN MARKET REPORTS SERVICE makes available to the American business community unclassified reports prepared by the U.S. Foreign Service.

These reports on commodities, industries, and economic trends contain information helpful to American business in its foreign market research efforts.

The monthly accession list announcing current reports, classified by Standard Industrial Classification (SIC) code and country, can be obtained free.

TRADE CONTACT SURVEYS are specially designed to locate agents, distributors or licensees abroad. These surveys are made by the U.S. Foreign Service in a specified country to locate several firms which meet your requirements and which express an interest in your business proposal. A survey usually is completed in 60 days. The report of the survey includes pertinent marketing data in addition to names, addresses, and brief descriptions of the prospects recommended. Individual *World Trade Directory Reports* on the prospects are included in the survey. Applications should be submitted on form IA-963, and must be accompanied by sales literature and the fee. $50 per survey.

ABOUT ORDERING: When ordering Trade Lists, World Trade Directory Reports, and Trade Contact Surveys, checks and money orders to cover the fees should be made payable to the Department of Commerce and submitted with your order.

Figure 7–1   Department of Commerce Helps.

cases, further information can be obtained from the country itself, through either a distributor or a subsidiary there. If the country is seeking to attract foreign investment, its information services and assistance are likely to be especially good. They will probably have a development office in the United States, such as the Indian Investment Center in New York City. As do United States government information services, foreign governments' services tend to be inexpensive but valuable inputs to a foreign market study.

International Organizations

Chief among international organizations, of course, is the United Nations and its affiliated organizations. Although there are disagreements about the success of many UN activities, there is no doubt about its major role in gathering and disseminating information about all aspects of the world economy. Its economic commissions conduct numerous studies and issue regular publications such as the *Economic Survey of Europe* and the *Economic Survey of Latin America*. The *United Nations Statistical Yearbook* is an invaluable source of data on over 200 countries. The affiliated International Monetary Fund issues the monthly *International Financial Statistics*. The General Agreement on Tariffs and Trade (GATT) publishes world-trade data.

Many of the UN agencies are relatively unknown to the general public, but they are doing work that is important to international corporations. For example, manufacturers of pharmaceuticals, foodstuffs, and hospital and sanitary equipment must be up-to-date on the publications and activities of the World Health Organization (WHO). Personnel managers in international companies need to be informed about the publications and services of ILO (International Labour Organisation). Companies producing foodstuffs, fertilizers, or farm equipment are interested in the activities of the Food and Agriculture Organization (FAO). In fact, FAO has established the Industry Cooperation Program to promote closer relations with industry groups having interests similar to its own. Some of the international companies belonging to the program are General Foods, H. J. Heinz, Merck, Sharp and Dohme Int'l, Union Carbide, Nestle, Massey-Ferguson, Unilever, and Shell.[7]

There is an interesting illustration of the value of the UN information services. One of America's largest international companies, headquartered in New York, hired a UN statistician. The major reason for the hiring was not the man's capabilities in statistics, but rather his familiarity with the UN information operation.

Although no other organization covers the world as fully as does the UN, other international or regional organizations provide useful information. The Organization for Economic Cooperation and Development (OECD) is the

---

[7] Only an overview of United Nations activities and publications has been given here. For a useful comprehensive survey, see *The UN and the Business World* (New York: Business International, 1967), 140 pp.

most active. Its bimonthly *General Statistics* gives the major economic indicators for the member countries (the industrialized countries of the West). The OECD also conducts and publishes excellent special studies on many other topics of interest to the international marketer, for example, *Analysis and Evaluation of Distribution Structures and Distribution Channels in Selected Consumer Goods Industries.*

Other regional organizations supply information on their respective regions. Two of these groups, the European Free Trade Association (EFTA) and the European Economic Community (EEC), are especially useful for information on developments affecting the economic integration of their areas. A number of American companies have located their European headquarters in Brussels partly just to be near the power center of the EEC. The EEC also has an information center in Washington, D.C.

Business and Trade Associations

A great number of business associations are partially or exclusively concerned with international business matters. For industries that have international trade interests, the industry trade association will often provide useful information to its members. The chemical industry, for example, has such an association; and the office-machine industry has the Business Equipment Manufacturer's Association (BEMA).

One large producer of office machines was entering the Latin American market. In trying to evaluate the potential in the various countries, the firm found that the most useful and accurate guidelines were the export statistics and other information supplied by BEMA. At practically no cost to itself, the firm got a reading on all the Latin American markets, which helped it to establish appropriate quotas and marketing strategies.

Not all trade associations can be this helpful, but with the growing volume of international business, more of them will be offering services along this line. Trade associations in Europe are increasingly important information sources, too. For example, information pools have been established in the electronics and synthetic-fibers industries there.

Many *specialized associations* deal with specific aspects of international trade and are most knowledgeable in their own area of interest. These associations cover such topics as foreign credit, shipping, insurance, and arbitration. The International Advertising Association, for instance, deals with the facts of international advertising in the world today. It makes an annual survey of international advertising and acts as a clearinghouse for the interchange of knowledge and experience in the field of international advertising. Both users and practitioners can benefit from this specialized expertise.

Other business associations are of a more general nature, not limiting their interests to a particular industry or function. On a national level are the *Chamber of Commerce of the United States* and the National Foreign Trade Council. The former organization has a Foreign Commerce–Foreign Policy Department to serve its members interested in international affairs. Most

American chambers of commerce abroad are members of the Chamber of Commerce of the United States. These overseas members offer valuable foreign trade and investment services to both members and nonmembers. From the vantage point of their overseas position and experience, they can offer first-hand, up-to-date accounts of the situation in their national markets.

The Chamber of Commerce of the United States also publishes a comprehensive and useful *Foreign Commerce Handbook*, a 170-page guide to organizations and information sources. This handbook is an extensive treatment of the kinds of sources we cover only briefly in this section. Within the United States, over 100 local chambers of commerce maintain foreign trade bureaus or other facilities to serve the special interests of members engaged in foreign commerce. One advantage of these local bureaus is the freedom members feel to ask questions when they know each other personally.

The *National Foreign Trade Council* is the principal association of American companies concerned with doing business abroad. Major banks, transportation companies, insurance companies, manufacturers, and others are members of this "blue-chip" organization. It has area, country, and general committees made up of member-company executives who have wide working knowledge of international business activities and problems. Consultative and informational services are available to individual members. The *American Management Association* has regular seminars and workshops on international business topics. *The Conference Board* publishes various studies of interest to international marketing management.

On a local level, there are over fifty foreign trade associations or *world-trade clubs* in major cities around the United States. These are especially strong in the port cities and in such large centers as Detroit and Chicago. However, they are also located in other inland points, such as Louisville, Memphis, Salt Lake City, and Denver. In membership and interests, these groups are small-scale versions of the National Foreign Trade Council. Small firms participate to a greater degree and the businessmen members usually are at a lower level of management responsibility than their NFTC counterparts, but their international trade interests are quite similar.

The international trade clubs generally do no publishing, but they are extremely valuable for the personal exchange of information and experience among members. As the members get acquainted at their regular meetings, they feel free to call on other members whose experience can help solve their problems. If a member has just returned from a tour of Latin America, has been dealing with a foreign currency or credit problem, or has been involved with trade problems in a given country, he is generally willing to share his experiences and the lessons gained from them. This sharing of experiences is a valuable education and information resource to firms in the area.

Service Organizations

Many companies are in the business of selling services to firms engaged in international trade. To do their own job effectively, they must keep up with relevant international developments. The experience and information they gain are usually available free to their client companies. Some of the principal service organizations of interest here are banks, transportation companies, advertising agencies, and accounting firms.

The *major American banks* are doing an increasing amount of business with America's international companies. They have expanded overseas themselves, either through branches or through correspondents, and in doing so have developed a good intelligence system on the countries where they have interests. Both to encourage further client business with themselves and to keep the client from costly errors, the banks provide counsel and information on international business questions. In fact, this service is one of their major competitive tools vis-à-vis other banks. Trade leads, marketing reports, and country files are among the information the banks might supply, in addition to financial advice. Bank information services may be available to clients in letters and in printed-report form or through personal consultation with bank officers.

The Chase Manhattan Bank provides a guide for exporters, which is mailed to clients. The following kinds of information are included.
1. *A brochure on methods of export financing.*
2. *A brochure on how the Export-Import bank helps finance exports.*
3. *Annual and updated information on foreign import and exchange regulations.*
4. *Bulletins on collection experience, including foreign balance of payment data and comments.*
5. *A list of relevant officers in the bank's international department who may be consulted on other questions.*
6. *Additionally, it is noted that information can also be obtained from its economic research division. Telephone number given.*

Although the big New York banks are leaders in information services because of their size, location, and experience, large banks in many parts of America are getting more and more involved. For example, the National Bank of Detroit, an inland bank, makes available much of its international research material to customers, even though it does not publish a regular information service. The officers of its international division frequently assist customers personally on international business questions.

By *transportation companies* we mean principally the international airlines and the steamship companies. Pan American Airlines (PAA) and Trans World Airlines (TWA) want to see American companies expand their international business because then more businessmen and cargo will move by air. To promote this, they offer a variety of marketing and information services. PAA has an international marketing services division that helps customers and potential customers find overseas markets and distributors or agents. A firm can indicate the products and markets it is interested in and receive a free report on possibilities.

PAA also puts out a monthly magazine, *Horizons* (in six languages), which includes international trade opportunities. TWA and leading foreign airlines (BOAC, KLM, Air France, Japan Air Lines, for example) offer roughly similar services. The Committee of American Steamship Lines offers similar international marketing help, as do individual shipping lines. Farrell Lines, for instance, ships primarily to Africa and can offer useful information and advice on marketing problems and opportunities on that continent.

Advertising agencies with offices in foreign countries can provide useful market data and marketing intelligence in their respective markets. Agency clients can draw on the agency's general knowledge of the market and also get more specific guidance in marketing their own products. The *large accounting firms*, too, have expanded their international interests, becoming informed especially on financial, legal, and tax matters in international business. Besides offering client advisory services in this area, some of the firms have extensive published material. Price Waterhouse, for example, has a series of *Information Guides* "for those doing business outside the United States." The series is kept up-to-date through periodic revisions. The *Guide to Argentina* is a 140-page booklet. *International Tax and Business Service* is the Haskins and Sells service.

Information for Sale

In all of the previous information and intelligence sources discussed, the provision of information was either free or at nominal cost. In the case of governments, the information service is subsidized. In the other cases, the supply of information is incidental to the main business of the supplier. Now we will discuss those organizations whose principal *raison d'être* is the provision of information for a price. Domestic examples of such organizations are A. C. Nielsen, Ward's (automotive reports), and Dodge (construction reports). Many of these domestic information services have no counterpart in foreign countries because the market is often too small to support a profitable operation. There are, however, other organizations that have extensive international coverage.

One important information source on foreign business is found in the numerous directories of foreign firms in manufacturing, retailing, and other lines of business. Some cover just one country, but others are international or regional in coverage. There are even guides to these directories so that one can locate all those relevant to his particular need. An example is *Trade Directories of the World*, a loose-leaf volume by Croner Publications.

A number of companies gather, organize, and publish information about a variety of parameters affecting international trade and marketing. Their publications tend to emphasize economic, financial, and legal parameters, although occasionally they will discuss cultural and political factors as well. Dun and Bradstreet is one of the companies actively providing international financial and marketing information to those who buy its services, both banks and manufacturers. Among the most important of its dozen publications are the *International Market Guide—Continental Europe* and *International Market Guide—Latin America.*

Two rather widely used services have an entirely international focus. The *Economist Intelligence Unit* (EIU), which is associated with the *Economist* magazine is one. EIU services include quarterly reports on economic and political matters for most countries of the world, as well as regular reports on *Marketing in Europe* and other special topics. EIU also will conduct specialized market studies for individual firms, but in this capacity, of course, they compete with other consulting firms.

The other widely used international information service is *Business International* (BI), which has correspondents in seventy-five cities in all parts of the world, except the communist-bloc countries. BI publishes four weekly newsletters that report on political and economic developments affecting international business as well as on companies' international experiences and problems. The weekly letters specialize by area: Europe, Asia, and Latin America. Other major BI services include *Investing, Licensing and Trading Conditions* (in over fifty countries) and *Financing Foreign Operations*, both annual services with loose-leaf supplements.

Finally, major consulting and market-research groups have overseas offices and activities. As American business has expanded abroad, these groups have followed their clients. Many can offer intelligence services abroad that are as good as those they offer at home. Not only American groups are available for foreign market intelligence; more and more, local organizations in the major industrial countries compete with the American consulting and research groups. The "technology gap" in this area is being steadily eroded. Besides the general market-research groups, such specialized market information services as A. C. Nielsen are operating in major foreign markets. As international business expands in volume and competitiveness, the researcher can expect the quantity and quality of foreign market information services from both the major American organizations and their competitors to grow along with it.[8]

Other Companies

A notable feature of international business is that more information is exchanged among manufacturing firms on their international interests than on their domestic interests, perhaps because they feel their lack of knowledge about foreign markets requires greater reliance on all sources of assistance. The exchange does not concern competitive information, which might be illegal under antitrust, but rather general information on the business practices and the political and economic environment of foreign markets. A part of this information exchange occurs through the auspices of some of the organizations mentioned earlier, that is, trade associations, foreign trade clubs, the National Foreign Trade Council, and so on. In fact, the specific purpose of many of these groups is to promote such an exchange of experiences for the benefit of their numbers.

---

[8] See, for example, Robert C. Albrook, "Europe's Lush Market for Advice–American Preferred," *Fortune* (July 1969), pp. 128 ff.

Even apart from common membership in a group concerned with international trade, companies often seek information on international business problems from other firms. A company considering business opportunities in Latin America might well visit one or more other American companies that have Latin American experience to get a feel for the business environment there. When one of America's largest chemical companies was planning its initial investments in Europe, it held preliminary conversations with other American companies who had been operating in Western Europe for many years. This kind of information provides a useful supplement to that gained from secondary sources.

Company Experience

All the information sources considered until now have been outside the company. All are valuable either for the information or for the vicarious experience they provide. Nevertheless, the company's own experience is still the best teacher. When a firm first considers some form of international business involvement, it must rely entirely on outside sources and the experience of others; but as the firm gains experience on its own, it will find this the most valuable resource of all. Although foreign operations provide the most comprehensive kind of familiarity with foreign markets, even operating only through exports can be a very helpful educational experience.

If the firm's only international involvement is through exporting, it is not physically present in foreign markets. However, if the firm is aggressive in its export program, it can establish a good international intelligence system and gain valuable international experience. Although the firm itself is not present in foreign markets, it has representation there, either through agents or through distributors. Depending somewhat on the importance of its line to the foreign distributors, the exporting firm can make them a part of its international intelligence system. Even though the exporter cannot demand reports from distributors as a parent company can from its foreign subsidiaries, some useful market feedback should be obtained from them in the normal course of business.

Good distributor support by the exporter should increase the distributors' willingness to cooperate. Furthermore, travel to foreign markets by the export manager will give the company direct contact that will help management to better interpret information from distributors as well as from other sources. If the firm later decides to establish foreign subsidiaries, it is likely to have a good foundation of information and experience based on its export operations. Naturally, the firm that handles exports through outside firms or in a passive manner will not have this same experience to rely on. Thus the firm can gain very useful intelligence on individual foreign markets through a limited form of involvement, and from this experience it can make better (safer?) decisions about a heavier commitment to a market.

Multinational companies with many foreign subsidiaries are in the best position to benefit from local information sources and experience. They are not limited to requesting cooperation from independent distributors but can rely in large part on their own personnel. The only problem or limitation the firm faces in its subsidiary markets is the same one it faces at home: the development of an appropriate management or marketing information system.

In approaching this problem, the firm will find the small size of some of its foreign markets to be a disadvantage. Offsetting this, however, is the advantage of its experience in its American operations and its experience in all of its foreign markets. By carefully analyzing all of its multinational experience and using some kind of comparative analysis, as discussed earlier, the multinational firm should be able to develop a market intelligence system which is more effective than that of its national competitors. Many of the national competitors probably take a more intuitive approach to their operations, as compared with the relatively analytical or professional approach of the American multinational company. In any case, the development of an effective market information system could be a competitive advantage of the international firm.

EVALUATING INFORMATION

In the preceding section, we highlighted the wealth of information sources for international marketing research. Because source materials are relatively abundant, the researcher's problem is often not how to find materials but how to select and evaluate them. There are three criteria needed to evaluate international information sources: (1) the quality of the information; (2) its relevance to the decision maker's needs, and (3) its cost.

Quality of the Information

Timeliness

Everyone recognizes the need for "good data" but that expression needs more precise content. One quality of good data is *timeliness*—it should be up-to-date. All printed information is by nature historical, of course, but some data are older than other data. The researcher needs especially the most recent material, and he may also want that from earlier periods as a basis for comparison and for determining trends. The number of years since data were published is usually, but not necessarily, an indicator of their timeliness.

The researcher's primary objective is an accurate picture of the current situation. The timeliness of the data depends on what significant changes have occurred since their publication. For example, a public opinion poll in a political campaign may be out of date in a week. On the other hand, statistics on such items as per capita income, literacy rates, or the age distribution of a population might be reasonably valid five years or more after publication. Where the variables considered change rather slowly, the researcher can be less disturbed by having to work with the "old" data, as he must do frequently in international research.

Accuracy

Another aspect of the information's quality is its *accuracy*. Accuracy includes timeliness, but statistics published at the same time still may differ greatly in accuracy. If a census or a demographic study were undertaken in a given year in both the United Kingdom and the Republic of the Congo, it is highly probable that the latter study would be less accurate, because of the research problems sure to be encountered in sampling techniques, communications, and general administration.

Definitions are important to accuracy. In some instances, the statistical categories are too broad to be of value to the researcher. A category called "commercial vehicles" that includes taxis and all kinds of trucks is not very helpful to a firm supplying parts to a particular segment of that market. A category called "farm equipment imports" that groups parts, finished products, and units for assembly in one value figure is not very useful to a firm looking for a market for a particular kind of farm machine.

Objectivity of the information supplier can be another key to the accuracy and reliability of the information. If the supplier of information has an interest in presenting a certain image or in encouraging a certain kind of behavior based on the information, such a bias could be dangerous to the information user. Information that has these public relations or advertising aspects cannot be accepted on a par with more objective data. As a case in point, during a cholera epidemic in 1970 several countries did not report their cases because they feared such information would put a damper on their tourist trade as well as leave an unflattering image of their country in the minds of the public at large.

Comparability

Comparability is another important dimension of data quality. Although individual country or market studies are not uncommon, most international marketing research rightly involves country comparisons. To choose the best country in which to operate or to choose appropriate marketing strategies for different countries, the firm should compare alternatives. The company's internal information system facilitates comparability by standardized accounting and reporting procedures for foreign subsidiaries, but comparability is more difficult to obtain for information coming from outside the firm. Although the United Nations is doing much to improve data gathering around the world, much remains to be done.

In any multination study, the researcher will encounter several comparison problems. For some variables, only part of the countries will have statistics; for others, the statistics will have been gathered in different years or will include different things under a given definition. "Supermarket," "wholesaler," and many other economic and demographic terms often mean different things in different countries. A serious lack of comparability on critical items may influence the firm to conduct extra research of its own to supplement the data where they are weak. Skillful use of comparative analysis can help to minimize the problem.

Relevance of the Data

The international market researcher is not in the encyclopedia business; he is concerned only with decision making in his firm. Therefore, he is interested only in data that are useful for international marketing decisions. In courtroom language, he is not interested in the "whole truth," but only in that part of the "truth" that affects him. Much information that is otherwise of good quality will not interest him if it is not relevant. If the firm's internal information system is operating ideally, the subsidiaries are sending to the international headquarters only information that will be acted upon; the subsidiaries have no complaints about useless paper work, and headquarters is running an effective system.

Information available outside the firm usually is gathered for a large general audience, and much of it is not specific to the needs of the firm. Before buying or accumulating such outside information, the firm must evaluate its usefulness to whatever the business at hand. This relevance criterion points again to the importance of a marketing information model to help the firm set up an effective and efficient system. The model guides the establishment of the internal reporting system as well as the selection of outside information sources.

Cost of the Data

Eventually some cost-benefit analysis should be made of the whole international marketing information system. Unfortunately, such an analysis is not really feasible today, even domestically. Nevertheless, the firm will do well to have some criteria to follow in deciding whether to hire another international marketing researcher, to buy an information service, or to hire an outside research group to make a study. The benefits of improved decisions will be set against the costs incurred.

A food company executive wanted to change the reporting system for foreign subsidiaries in order to undertake some new comparative studies of foreign markets. A research assistant was hired, subsidiary reports were modified, and some new outside information sources were added. Traceable costs came to about $10,000 in the first year. The executive felt that this was modest in view of the better decisions he could make on marketing strategy and product policy in foreign markets. Once the adapted system was instituted, the extra costs went down greatly because the new approach was a modification of the old system rather than an addition to it.

Although some information comes to the company without a price tag or at a nominal cost, no information is really free. The firm always incurs expense in gathering, analyzing, organizing, and storing or discarding the data. Because these costs can be high, the researcher must be selective in his sources; in effect, he must look the gift horse in the mouth. *Redundancy* is a related issue. Some of the publications or information services the company receives cover the same ground. Although redundancy can never be completely eliminated if outside sources are used, it can be minimized with resultant savings in time and storage costs. Some redundancy may even be desirable if one source is a check on another. If both sources use the same inputs, however, there is no corroborative value.

Cost must also be related to the relevance of the information. Some information is low in cost but not very specific to the company's particular needs. A special market study by a consulting firm is apt to be quite expensive but also very specific to the company's needs. Part of the research manager's task is to get the right mix of general secondary sources along with the more expensive primary sources. Before he hires a market-research group or sends a researcher on a trip overseas, he should extract what he can from the less costly information inputs. When he gives an assignment to an outside research group, he should then be able to avoid duplicating what the company already has acquired.

A large chemical company was considering building a plant in a less developed country. It sent a young researcher there to investigate the market and the investment climate. After a one month stay abroad, he prepared a report. Much of the material in the report was available back in America. Some of the other material in the report was sketchy and of limited value because of lack of background preparation for the trip. Better planning and integration would have given the company a more useful report at a much lower cost.

ORGANIZING FOR INTERNATIONAL MARKETING INTELLIGENCE

How to find the best division of labor among the various parts of the international company—that is, between the national or regional headquarters and the national subsidiaries—is a major organizational problem. An aspect of the problem is the relation between domestic and international marketing research. Because the proper organizational arrangements for international marketing intelligence will depend somewhat on the particular circumstances of each firm, we will discuss only general guidelines here. Some of the determinants are the level of decision making in the firm, its degree of foreign involvement, and its overall organizational structure for international business.

Level of Decision Making

Marketing decisions can be made at several levels in the multinational company. Many are made at the national subsidiary level, some at regional headquarters, others at the international division or corporate headquarters.

Subsidiary

For decisions made within the foreign subsidiary, most information is gathered and stored locally, if storage is necessary. Such decentralization is probably most efficient. The market intelligence operation of a foreign subsidiary, however, is not likely to be the same as that of a purely national company doing business in that country. The subsidiary should receive valuable inputs from its multinational affiliation, among them techniques and guidelines from the parent company and copies of studies and findings from other country operations of the parent firm. Furthermore, specific decision makers such as the local advertising or product managers presumably would be receiving assistance and information from their counterparts at regional or international headquarters.

A further difference between the local affiliate and the purely national company lies in the use made of the data gathered. The subsidiary is likely to transmit some of its information on to its parent, perhaps because some of the decisions using this information are made at a higher level in the company, or perhaps because the regional or international headquarters want data from all subsidiaries in order to do comparative market studies. In addition, instant communication and computerized information systems make possible more centralized decision making. Nevertheless, much of the information gathered at the national level will stay within the country because it is not needed at other levels in the company. Indeed, a frequent complaint of subsidiary management is that much of the information they are transmitting is never used.

International Headquarters

At both the regional and the international headquarters level, the marketing information needed is broader and more general, corresponding to the types of decisions and studies made there. The two basic sources of information at international headquarters are the country subsidiaries and the data gathering done at headquarters itself. In order to guide and coordinate multinational operations, headquarters needs to know conditions in all of its markets, and it requests the relevant data from its country subsidiaries.

Data supplied by the subsidiaries serve two purposes. First, they provide a basis on which to make decisions for, or to give guidance to, the individual subsidiary. Second, they can be used for comparative studies of foreign markets. The understanding and marketing sophistication of the multinational company should be greater than that of a collection of national companies. Comparative studies are one means of achieving this increased international marketing sophistication, as we discussed earlier.

International headquarters itself will do some marketing intelligence work, in addition to that done at the subsidiary level. This division of labor is, in fact, one of the strengths of the multinational firm. If this activity is well organized, the company is doing more marketing intelligence work than its national competitors and doing it more effectively; such is the synergism possible in international operations.

International headquarters will gather information that is either not possible or not feasible to gather at the subsidiary level. Occasionally, even data on individual nations can be better obtained apart from the subsidiary. Whereas the subsidiary is concerned with daily operating problems, headquarters can take a broader view. Some international companies have regional or even country desks similar to those of the State Department where all kinds of information are gathered and analyzed. The political and economic pulse of the relevant nations is taken continually to keep the firm apprised of developments which may affect its operations there.

Data that come from international sources are probably best collected and analyzed at international headquarters to avoid duplication of effort by the subsidiaries. Some examples are reports and materials from the United Nations and its affiliated agencies, for example, the World Health Organization, the Food and Agricultural Organization, the International Monetary Fund, and so on. Information on international economic and competitive conditions also would be gathered at headquarters. If a corporation has several subsidiaries in an area such as Latin America or Europe, the research on regional developments such as the Latin America Free Trade Association or the European Economic Community should not be done at the subsidiary level where there would be great duplication. As can be seen, the international marketing intelligence operation involves a division of labor between different levels of the organization, both as to the kinds of data gathered and the kinds of analysis undertaken.

Regional Headquarters

Although the simplest division of labor in information gathering and analysis is between the national level—the subsidiary—and the international level—international headquarters, those companies with large regional operations and regional headquarters may divide the labor further, that is, between the international and regional levels. This division has little impact on intelligence operations in the national subsidiaries. Regional headquarters would do most of the intelligence work for its region, but international headquarters would still have to coordinate and analyze studies on a global scale. The addition of regional efforts is no substitute for global analyses in the international company. If international headquarters provides no overall coordination, suboptimization probably exists in the company's international marketing intelligence activity.

Regional headquarters may have a large or a small role in marketing research activity, depending on the size of subsidiary operations. If individual subsidiary operations are large, the subsidiaries may have strong marketing research activities of their own, including a direct correspondence link with the international headquarters marketing research department. These circumstances could lead to a small role for marketing research at regional headquarters, perhaps as coordinator. By the same token, small subsidiary operations may not be able to support a strong marketing research activity of their own. In the latter case, regional headquarters may play a big role in marketing research because the necessary expertise and economies of scale are possible only on a regional basis, as the following example shows.

One American consumer-goods company has ten European subsidiaries. Whereas it once had a small marketing research activity in each country operation, it centralized all of these in London when it established a European regional headquarters there. The vice-president said: "We're centralizing our 'MR' to have one good department rather than ten half-baked operations. It operates on a service basis to all our European subs."[9]

---

[9] Terpstra, *American Marketing in the Common Market*, p. 125.

A contrary example is that of a much larger industrial-goods company with sales in Europe of several hundred million dollars. This firm had marketing research groups in each of eight major European countries, as well as at European headquarters in Paris (over fifteen people), and at international headquarters in New York (over forty people).[10]

The Level of Involvement

In our comments thus far about marketing research activity we assumed that the firm had wholly or majority owned ventures in national markets. If the firm's presence in a market is through an importer-distributor, a licensee, or a minority joint venture, the amount and kind of marketing research it can do will be limited. It must then try to cooperate with its representative in the market and supplement this with whatever other efforts are desirable and feasible. The smaller firm is less able to conduct extensive research and must rely more on outside sources such as service organizations and distributors.

But no matter what its circumstances, if the firm is present or represented in a market, it has both a need and some capability for local marketing research. In the discussion of foreign operations as a source of information, we showed that even foreign distributors can be a part of the firm's international information system. One large American firm that operates primarily through licensing conducts marketing studies in the licensees' markets. It does this on its own because it feels the licensees do not have the capability. The licensee is given a copy of the study and receives the benefit without payment. The licensor benefits from the improved marketing of the licensee as well as from his good will.

Centralization or Decentralization?

Several factors contribute to a decentralization of marketing research activities. The larger the activity of a foreign subsidiary grows, the greater the possibility of national marketing research becomes. Some minimum market size must be reached for an indigenous activity to be practical. If foreign subsidiaries are profit centers, they are more likely to carry on their own marketing research. As marketing research capability grows in different countries, more can be done in these markets. Our discussion on levels of decision making reinforces these points. The more the marketing decisions made locally, the greater the need for generating local information. On the other side of the coin, the larger and the more complex the firm's international business becomes, the less able the firm is to centralize its marketing research activity effectively.

Decentralization does not mean that international headquarters' role decreases in importance. Each subsidiary will receive guidance and expertise from the center, which will coordinate activities among the subsidiaries and see that duplication is avoided. Headquarters is the clearing house for all foreign operations, assuring the transmission of successful approaches and avoiding the repetition of ineffective methods. It also serves as the liaison with

[10] Terpstra, *American Marketing in the Common Market*, p. 125.

domestic marketing research activities, which are usually the source of the latest developments. Thus decentralization is a new division of labor in the organization brought about primarily by the growing importance of international business, and it does not eliminate the important role of international headquarters.

In-House or Outside Experts?

After deciding upon the kinds of information desired and the nature of the marketing research needed, the marketing manager must decide where in the organization the research can best be done or whether it should be done within the company at all. In effect, the administration of international marketing research often involves a sort of make-or-buy decision in the firm. The manager wants honest and useful market intelligence at reasonable cost. Internal company research activity may not always be the best source; occasionally outside expertise is.

A number of factors might encourage or require the firm to call on outside agencies to conduct the market research it needs in a foreign market. If the firm is completely *new to a market*, it may require a certain amount of outside help from agencies located in that market. As the firm gains experience, it can assume these activities in-house. If the firm has a *small volume* of business in certain foreign markets, it may prefer hiring the studies to hiring the staff necessary to carry them out itself. Or it may take the alternative of setting up an in-house staff on a regional basis, as in the example cited earlier. For *specialized or one-time studies*, the firm may find that generating all the start-up costs does not pay if there is an outside agency specializing in the area and offering economies of scale. In some cases, the firm has no alternative to buying the intelligence outside. Consumer panel data or Nielsen retail audits are examples of information the firm could not generate on its own.

The firm's *level of involvement* in a foreign market can be a constraint. If the firm is represented in a country only by a distributor or licensee, it is limited in its marketing research possibilities. Because it can usually count on very limited market information from the distributor or licensee, it may have to hire national agencies to gather whatever intelligence it feels is necessary in such markets. *Peak load needs* may also suggest outside help. Because peak loads are infrequent, the firm cannot afford to hire full-time staff to deal with them and economizes by relying temporarily on outside agencies. *Company practice* in its domestic operations tends to carry over to its international operations. If the firm is not a major practitioner of marketing research in America, it will carry its casual approach with it abroad, perhaps maintaining a small in-house activity and hiring occasional studies by outside agencies. The firm may seek *objectivity* through the hiring of an outside agency. The report of an outside agency is often thought to have a greater impact on managements' decisions than the same findings presented by an in-house group.

Although the major portion of international marketing research is done within the marketing companies themselves, a number of situations arise that suggest the use of outside expertise. A company should rarely, if ever, decide to rely exclusively on one extreme or the other. Each firm should make the practical economic decision based on its evaluation of all these variables as they relate to its own situation.

Factors Favoring Do-It-Yourself

Since most foreign market research is done within the marketing companies, identification of the factors that encourage this practice is useful. A major reason for a firm to conduct its own marketing research in foreign markets is its *need to develop company expertise* in this area. If all marketing research is done by outsiders, the firm may get good research results but end by knowing less about its market than if it had done the studies itself. In-house conduct of foreign market research can be the best means of learning about the market.

One of the resources of the multinational company is its experience, and it gains more experience the more directly involved it is in all of its marketing program, including especially marketing research studies that are continuing or repeated. Hiring outside help for a specialized, one-time study may be a practical measure because the expertise the firm would gain by doing the study in-house probably would not be used again. In this case, the outside firm may have the economies of scale by virtue of its continuing work in the area.

The firm that has a steady volume of marketing research activities may find it *cheaper* to run its own shop. Spreading skills and expenses over a sufficient volume of activity can make in-house research truly more efficient than relying on outsiders, especially if marketing research know-how is carried over from domestic or other international operations. This kind of efficient organization is, or should be, part of the synergism of multinational operations. Some firms that are leaders in particular product areas find that the high costs of "educating" the outside researchers in the peculiarities of their industry make their use undesirable. Communication problems also may contribute to encouraging in-house activity. Communication of the research design to the outside agency and communication of the findings to the company may both involve static and loss of value. This problem is more likely in foreign markets than in the American market. Finally, in some foreign markets, the outside expertise simply may not be available, so the firm is forced to rely on its own resources.

CONCLUSION

This chapter has examined varied attributes of the task of international marketing intelligence. One may approach marketing management from the viewpoint of the four "P's" (product, place, price, and promotion) or from the viewpoint of analysis, planning, and control. In either case, good information is necessary for effective performance. We do not intend the chapter to be a how-to-do-it primer. Rather, in focusing on the particular aspects of *international* marketing intelligence, we intend that it should help the person already informed about marketing research to acclimate himself to the environment of world marketing. Assuming the availability of appropriate information, we will now turn to decisions required in other areas of marketing, where such information will be used. We begin with product policy.

Questions

7.1 "International marketing intelligence is broader and more comprehensive than domestic marketing research." Discuss.

7.2 What information is necessary in international marketing intelligence?

7.3 Can domestic marketing research techniques be used in researching foreign markets? Explain.

7.4 What problems does language diversity pose for multinational marketing research?

7.5 Why is it often more difficult to get responses to marketing research in foreign countries than it is in the United States?

7.6 Explain how the economic and commercial infrastructure in a country can affect the marketing research task there.

7.7 Define the "data problems" in international marketing research.

7.8 What factors must be considered in answering the question, How much market research can I afford to do abroad?

7.9 How can the international marketing researcher deal with the problems encountered in his task?

7.10 How can the international marketer prepare a comparative analysis of his foreign markets?

7.11 How might comparative analysis and groupings of foreign markets aid in solving international marketing research problems?

7.12 Discuss the United States government as an information source for foreign markets.

7.13 Identify several of the United Nations agencies and publications of interest to the international firm.

7.14 Name some of the business and trade associations that provide assistance to the international marketing researcher.

7.15 Identify firms in your own community and determine what kinds of foreign market assistance are available to them locally or within the state.

7.16 Suggest criteria for evaluating information in international marketing research.

7.17 "Because marketing is done in the local market, marketing research needs to be decentralized." Discuss.

7.18 What kind of division of labor is feasible in the marketing research of the multinational company, that is, between subsidiary and international headquarters?

7.19 How should the firm decide whether to gather its own intelligence or to buy it outside?

Further Readings

Books:

Alsegg, Robert J., *Researching the European Markets* (New York: American Marketing Association, 1969).

American Management Association, Inc., *Marketing Research in International Operations,* AMA Management Report no. 53 (New York: American Management Association, Inc., 1960).

Green, Paul E., and Donald S. Tull, *Research for Marketing Decisions,* 2nd ed. (Englewood Cliffs, N.J.: Prentice-Hall, 1970).

Kracmar, John Z., *Marketing Research in the Developing Countries* (New York: Praeger, 1971).

Liander, Bertil, Vern Terpstra, M. Y. Yoshino, and A. A. Sherbini, *Comparative Analysis for International Marketing* (Boston: Allyn & Bacon, 1967).

National Industrial Conference Board, *Researching Foreign Markets,* Studies in Business Policy no. 75, 1955.

Root, Franklin R., *Strategic Planning for Export Marketing* (Scranton, Penna.: International Textbook Company, 1966), chap. 2.

The U. N. and the Business World (New York: Business International, 1967).

Articles:

Albrook, Robert C., "Europe's Lush Market for Advice—American Preferred," *Fortune* (July 1969), pp. 128–131.

Boyd, Harper W., Jr., Ronald E. Frank, William F. Massy, and Mostafa Zoheir, "On the Use of Marketing Research in the Emerging Economies," *Journal of Marketing Research* (November 1964), pp. 20–25.

Hodgson, Raphael, and Hugo E. R. Uyterhoevens, "Analyzing Foreign Opportunities," *Harvard Business Review* (March–April 1962), pp. 60–79.

Holton, Richard H., "Marketing Policies in Multi-national Corporations," *Journal of International Business Studies* (Summer 1970), pp. 1–20.

Keegan, Warren J., "Acquisition of Global Business Information," *Columbia Journal of World Business* (March–April 1968), pp. 35–41.

Litvak, Isaiah A., and Raymond A. Young, "Marketing Research by U. S. Subsidiaries—Domestic or Imported?" *The Business Quarterly* (Summer 1965), pp. 62–69.

Stobaugh, Robert B., Jr., "How to Analyze Foreign Investment Climates," *Harvard Business Review* (September–October 1969), pp. 100–108.

8

INTERNATIONAL PRODUCT POLICY: THE BASIC PRODUCT AND ITS ATTRIBUTES

When a manufacturer considers entering international markets, usually he is concerned about his profit-making prospects there. This often resolves itself into a simple question: Can I sell my products in foreign markets? The manufacturer realizes that the primary reason his company is accepted abroad is the product or service it offers to the host country. As a result, international product policy is the cornerstone around which all other international marketing activities must be designed.

In these chapters on product policy, we will look at the following questions. The firm should ask itself, What should we be selling overseas? We consider how the firm may best compete and make money abroad and examine the possibility that the firm might be exploiting things other than its traditional products.

Another question concerns the actual products of the firm. Because much of international marketing consists of selling the firm's traditional products, the firm must ask, To what degree must we adapt our domestic products in order to sell them in foreign markets? We examine the various forces bearing on this question.

Yet other questions have to do with the various product attributes and features, such as packaging, labeling, brands and trademarks, and warranty and service policies. How are these product features affected as the product moves internationally? Is international uniformity possible or, if it is not, what modifications are necessary? In the last section of this chapter we consider the international marketing parameters of these questions.

In Chapter 9 we will deal with two other aspects of international product policy, (1) the selection and management of the international product line and (2) the organization of product planning and development in international business.

WHAT TO SELL

The product is the heart of the marketing endeavor; the product brings buyer and seller, the firm and its market, together. It is in the area of product that the interests of the firm and the interests of the customer overlap the most. Paraphrasing Hamlet, the manufacturer says, "The product's the thing wherein I'll catch the interest of the consumer."

The critical role of the product in international marketing is no different from what it is in domestic marketing. The difficulty lies in determining what that product should be. For the firm, the product is the thing that it sells. The question, What is the right product for international markets? can be rephrased as, What should the firm be selling in international markets? We will look at this question before turning to the more traditional product considerations.

The firm is an organized collection of varied resources which it will use in the most effective way to achieve its goals. These goals usually include profits and return to shareholders, and growth in size and influence of the firm. To achieve growth and profit in the domestic market, the firm often increases its sales of present and future products. In foreign markets, the means of achievement may not be the same.

The firm has many diverse resources that enable it to compete successfully in the marketplace; some of these, such as plant and equipment and financial resources, are indicated on the balance sheet. Of course, financial strength derives not only from cash on hand but also from the ability to get money, an asset not readily seen on the accounting record. Experience, talent, personnel, know how, and good will are other rather intangible strong points of the firm. When considering entry into foreign markets, the manufacturer must evaluate all these internal factors in relation to the relevant external factors in each foreign market.

Goods versus Services

As he enters foreign markets, the manufacturer can again ask himself, What kind of business should I be in? He will find a wider range of possible answers than he finds at home because the firm is less encumbered by previous commitments than it is domestically. Thus the firm may sell a different product in foreign markets from the one it sells domestically. The firm can capitalize on its resources in ways other than selling its traditional products—it may not sell a product per se at all, in fact. Instead it could sell rights or services in the foreign market to buyers interested in the competitive advantage to be gained by the purchase. Rights that can be sold include brands and trademarks, patents on products or processes, or secret know-how. Marketable services include skills in research, production, marketing, or general management.[1]

The franchising business is an example of the sale of rights; Howard Johnsons and Kentucky Fried Chicken, for instance, get income from the use of

---

[1] See Richard D. Robinson, *International Management* (New York: Holt, Rinehart and Winston, 1967), pp. 18–24.

their names. Coca-Cola has licensed bottlers and distributors around the world who pay for the right to use its famous name. In these cases, the rights sold are only part of the total product the owner is selling. Most commonly, in fact, the right to use the name is tied in with some product sale or management service. Because of the increasing international popularity of franchising among both sellers and buyers, a Uniworld Franchise Development Corporation has been formed to bring the two together.[2]

The growth and potential of franchising is illustrated further in the following examples of companies engaged in it on an international basis:

Manpower, Inc. (temporary personnel)
Sheraton Corp. and Holiday Inns (hotels)
Mary Quant (UK—fashion designs)
Skol Int'l. (UK—beer)
Paint-a-Car System, Ltd. (UK)
Revlon (Cosmetics)
Castor International (Italy—appliances)
Alfa Romeo (Italy—autos)[3]

There are many international examples of the license or sale of product or process patents. Such patent rights can be sold outright or licensed to foreign producers. Westinghouse has been a leading practitioner of the licensing approach to foreign markets. Another example is the Pilkington Company of Britain, which invented the "float glass" process. Pilkington makes its profit in foreign markets from the licensing of the process rather than from selling the glass itself.

Services

The sale or hire of services is a relatively recent phenomenon in international marketing. Actors, entertainers, and professional athletes have long hired management services—but not from manufacturers. Recently, however, the city of Los Angeles hired some of the aerospace companies for their systems know-how, not for their products; and the federal government has asked for more business assistance in managing urban problem solving.

Abroad, Litton Industries signed a contract with the Greek government for management services in connection with Greek development plans. Hilton and Intercontinental Hotels have management contracts for hotels abroad, under which arrangements they usually earn their return solely on the sale of consulting and management services with little or no equity involvement. To the American hotel firm, such arrangements have the distinct advantages of (1) minimal risk, because they have no capital investment to be destroyed or expropriated, and (2) a strong competitive position, because they are selling hotel marketing and management skills, the thing in which their com-

[2] *Business Abroad* (September 1969), p. 11.
[3] *Business International*, February 17, 1967, p. 52.

parative advantage is greatest, rather than dealing in foreign real estate. Might not similar advantages exist for many manufacturing firms who have strengths in management and marketing?

The service industries are by nature more adapted to the sale of skills versus the sale of products, but the manufacturing industries too can benefit from giving more attention to ways of operating internationally that capitalize on their greatest comparative advantages but at the same time minimize their exposure and risk. One possible approach is *the turn-key operation*, which involves constructing a plant to the point where it is a going operation and then turning it over to the owner. In this case, the firm is selling its technical and engineering skills and may also be training foreign nationals to run the plant. It gains not only from the immediate sale but also may profit further from supplying materials and equipment for the operation. Thus the firm might gain continuing business while minimizing its investment and risk. For example, Parsons & Whittemore has built turn-key paper mills all over the world—with a related company supplying much of the equipment.

Management contracts or the sale of management services are different from turn-key operations. They are concerned less with construction than with long-run management relations and often include the supply of goods and equipment as well as the sale of management know-how. Management services usually are an important part of franchising agreements. The sale of management services can take various forms. We will give a few examples to illustrate some of the possibilities.[4]

Some years ago, United Fruit sold its banana land holdings to nationals of several Latin American countries. The company continues to market the bananas raised by these associate producers, and sets standards and provides technical assistance. The company has thus left the capital-intensive production side but continues to sell its marketing services.

Kaiser Aluminum and Chemical Corporation is active in foreign processing and fabrication of raw materials. In 1969, the company established Kaiser Trading Company to deal in commodities internationally. The company expected that only one-fourth of the anticipated $200 million volume would be for the parent company's commodity needs. It planned to look for barter deals, too, which could give the firm access to new commodities—and help it operate in countries with balance of payments problems.

Kaiser Trading Company offers a full range of services including financial, shipping, terminal, and inbound freight and delivery service to clients at a fee.[5]

U.S. Steel formed a subsidiary, USS Engineers and Consultants, Inc. (UEC). The function of UEC was to negotiate and service management and technical

[4] For a detailed analysis of management contracts, see Peter P. Gabriel, *The International Transfer of Corporate Skills* (Boston: Harvard University, Division of Research, Graduate School of Business Administration, 1967).

[5] *Business Week*, August 2, 1969, p. 88.

assistance contracts, drawing on the management and technical expertise developed by USS during seventy years of steel making. One of the first contracts (for five years) was with a Brazilian steel company. The assistance program was planned to equal twenty man-years of UEC consultant time in Brazil and thirty man-years of training of Brazilian staff in the United States. The assistance covered production planning, quality control, cost accounting, marketing, personnel relations, and accident protection.[6]

THE PRODUCT ITSELF

What is a product? Manufacturers may define it as the thing they sell: a tire, a deodorant, a cake mix, a computer. As such, it can be defined in terms of its physical or chemical characteristics. A more market-oriented definition might be based on the task it performs or the role it plays in the buyer's consumption system. The economist calls the product a bundle of utilities, by which he means everything the buyer receives in the product, including psychological utility as well as physical and chemical dimensions. But when the adjective "foreign" or "international" is added to product, any one of these definitions will change in some significant way.

For example, the foreign or international products the firm sells are probably in some way physically or chemically different from its domestic products. Certainly the foreign customer's definition of the firm's product is different from that of its domestic customers, either in terms of the role it performs or in terms of the bundle of utilities it offers. On a more prosaic and practical level, the packaging, labeling, branding, and warranty aspects of the product are likely to be different.

The question important to the firm, of course, is not semantic but operational—What should our foreign or international product be? Any modern student of business would answer, The product that best meets the goals of the firm. Although this answer gives limited guidance to the producer, it is correct, and its virtue lies in that it does not focus automatically on the domestic products of the company. Many firms have run into trouble by assuming that the right product for foreign markets is the same one that made them rich and famous in America.

An American greeting-card producer entered the German market with U.S.-style greeting cards. The design, folding, and use of sentiment or verse were new to Germany but were based on the successful American example. The actual sentiment or greeting was translated from successful American verse. After several years, the company was still not showing satisfactory profits and was considering whether to sell or adapt its Germany operation. Although greeting-card sales were rising in Germany, what kind of cards should be offered by the American company remained unclear.

[6] *Business Latin America*, January 8, 1970, p. 14.

An American food company began foreign operations in the 1950s after modest success in exporting its products over a number of years. In establishing foreign production, the executives prided themselves on the fact that the soups produced in foreign plants were identical in quality and taste to those produced in its American plants. It developed, however, that most foreign consumers had somewhat different tastes and habits concerning soup, and the foreign operations were in deficit after several years. The international marketing manager was reviewing the firm's product policy.

Although the right product for international marketing is probably not identical to the product sold domestically, neither are these products completely different and unrelated. With the exception, noted above, that the firm might market skills or services instead of products, a rather close relation between the firm's foreign and domestic products is likely. Given the firm's resources and competitive strengths, it is improbable that the company could attack both a new foreign market and a completely different product line at the same time. Therefore, although the soups, greeting cards, or automobiles sold abroad generally are not identical to their American counterparts, they are nevertheless in the same product category and require similar kinds of know-how, both in production and in marketing.

Standardization versus Adaptation

As the above discussion indicates, the product problem for the international marketer is partly to decide how far he can go with his American product and how much he must modify it; that is, will he market one product, or will he market several products, individually adapted to the national markets. Product standardization offers the obvious attraction of economies of scale in production and marketing. Against this potential advantage must be weighed the probability of foreign market acceptance of the American product versus the likely sales and profits of the nationally adapted product. We assume that the "right" product is the one bringing greatest continued profits to the firm. A cost-benefits analysis is needed to find the right product on the standardization-adaptation continuum.

The benefits accruing to the firm from product adaptation (or international market segmentation) would be greater market acceptance and, therefore, greater sales than of the standard American product. Whether the increase in sales yields greater profits depends on the costs of adaptation. In addition to the higher product costs caused by shorter production runs will be extra research and development costs as well. New market research is necessary to find out what form the adaptation should take. To recognize that foreign markets are different is one thing; to identify the relevant differences and their implications for product design is quite another—and more expensive—thing. Although it is comforting to the marketer to know that modern management methods are available to deal with questions like standardization versus adaptation, still it is not always easy to identify all the costs and benefits and come up with the right answer. The method is useful, but the skill and experience of the marketer remain critical.

Factors Encouraging Standardized Products Internationally

Many factors influence the firm's decision to standardize its product; it must be able to identify these in order to make an informed decision. Among the factors that encourage uniformity of products in a firm's international markets are the following.

1. Economies of scale in production. If a product has only one production source, to standardize the product will gain the economies of long production runs, assuming that decreasing total costs per unit prevail over the entire range of output needed to satisfy world markets. As the company multiplies production facilities around the world, the validity of this argument will decrease. Similarly, as the optimum size of plant becomes a smaller proportion of world demand, pressure toward product uniformity will decrease.

2. Economies in product research and development. If the firm offers the identical product around the world, it gets more mileage out of its product research and development efforts. Less research need be directed toward the peculiar needs or desires of diverse national markets, leaving more to be directed toward the search for new products. Uniformity yields a similar advantage in product development expenses. If products are uniform around the world, product development activities can be more easily centralized at lower costs.

3. Economies in marketing. Even when marketing is done on a national basis, economies of scale are possible with uniform products. Although sales literature, sales force training, and advertising may vary somewhat from country to country, at least in language, they will be much more similar when the product is uniform than when the product must be adapted for each national market. Service requirements and parts inventories are easier with a standardized product. When a promotional carry over from one market to another occurs because of common language and media spillover, it is not a wasted carry over but an extra return on the advertising.

4. Consumer mobility. If the product is one the consumer might purchase when traveling, product standardization is probably necessary to retain his loyalty. Examples of such products are Gillette razor blades, Kodak film, and Hilton Hotel services.

5. The American image. Products considered typically or peculiarly American might advantageously retain their American character in foreign markets. Wrigley's chewing gum, various American cigarettes, and Levis are some products in this category. Furthermore, girls around the world have "dreamed" in their standard American Maidenform bra.

6. The impact of technology. Products in which technical specifications are of critical importance tend to be uniform internationally. Differences signifi-

cant in the international business environment are "people differences," that is, cultural differences; physical and chemical processes usually do not change when crossing national boundaries. In general, then, industrial goods are much more standardized than consumer goods. Even when industrial goods are modified, the changes are likely to be minor—an adaptation of the electrical voltage or the use of metric measures.

7. Operating via exports. If a firm reaches foreign markets only through exports, very likely it is selling uniform products around the world. Even in the improbable event that it is informed of foreign market peculiarities requiring adaptation, it will not be interested in undertaking the greater costs and difficulties of modifying products that face the firm relying exclusively on domestic production for world markets.

Factors Encouraging Product Adaptation

As a general rule, the greatest argument for adapting products is that by doing so the firm can realize greater profits. The economies referred to above in regard to product uniformity represent cost minimization, not necessarily profit maximization. Modifying products for national or regional markets may raise revenues by more than the costs of adaptation, which would mean greater profits in spite of increased costs. Apart from this general argument, there are several specific factors that encourage product adaptation.

1. Differing use conditions. Although a given product fulfills a similar functional need in various countries, the conditions under which the product is used may vary greatly from country to country. Climate, for instance, has an effect on products sensitive to major changes in temperature or humidity, making it necessary for the manufacturer to modify these products for tropical or arctic markets. Even within the United States, cars in northern markets tend to have heaters as standard equipment, whereas in southern markets they have air conditioners. Consider too the differences in oil drilling in the Sahara compared with offshore drilling or exploration in Alaska. Another factor that can make product adaptation necessary is differences in the skill level of users, especially between consumers in highly industrialized nations and those in less developed countries. In regard to cars, trucks, and tires, differing road and traffic conditions may require product changes to meet customer needs. Variations in national habits of wearing and washing of clothes may necessitate different kinds of washing machines or soaps and detergents.

In some countries, clothes are worn a longer time between washings than they are in America. Thus a different washing process is needed.

In some European countries, the women wish to use boiling water for washing, so the washing machine must have a special heater built in.

In many countries, washing is done by a stream and not within some closed machine or container. Bar soap is much preferred to packaged soaps in these markets.

2. Other market factors. The logic of the machine argues for mass production of standardized products, but the needs and desires of the market may demand product modifications. The *income per capita* of the world's nations ranges from over $3,000 to under $100. This affects not only the size and nature of consumer durables, but even the packaging of inexpensive consumer products. As recently as 1968, Italy passed a law forbidding the sale of cigarettes on an individual, one-at-a-time basis. *Consumer tastes* happily are not identical around the world. Therefore foods, fashions, and other items differ from market to market, even varying significantly in neighboring countries. For example, in cars, the French show a strong preference for four-door models, whereas the Germans select two-door models.

3. The influence of government. Nations may exert their sovereignty by forbidding certain goods produced by international companies to be imported or manufactured in their country. Conversely, they may require that the product be manufactured locally and not imported. National demands for *local production* or a high degree of "local content" in the product often lead the international firm to modify it. Governments' *taxation policies* can affect the nature of the products offered in their markets, a notable example being the European tax on car and engine size that has been a predominant influence on car design there.

Government regulations on products, packaging, and labeling are an important cause of product variation among countries, especially in the areas of foods and drugs. For example, the required amount of sugar in a jar of jam, or the number of units of penicillin in a bottle, may be legally different from country to country. Government specifications affect industrial goods, too, as important product variables. For example, trucks, tractors, and tires (oem) often must meet different government specifications in different markets. The rise of regional groupings and growing international trade provide a modifying influence, but the differences will not disappear rapidly as long as national producers find government regulations such an effective form of protection against foreign firms.

The Michelin Company has been the dominant tire supplier in the French market. It has expressed little interest in the development of European or international tire specifications, as such standardization most likely would help Goodyear or another foreign company get a stronger position in France.

4. Company history and operations. Some firms have foreign subsidiary operations that predate World War II. Because of the economic nationalism prevailing at that time, these subsidiaries were largely self-contained national operations. Many of them developed products for their markets without regard to international product uniformity within the company. Some carry over of this practice still exists even though markets are much more international today.

The firm that has production facilities in several countries will find product adaptation easier than will the firm that must rely on exports from domestic plants, even if the former has never produced national products for national markets. The very fact that the firm has plants in various nations makes economies of scale or costs of product adaptation problems much less difficult than those facing the exporting firm. National subsidiaries operating as profit centers also can exert pressure on the parent firm to localize products. Because they are interested in profits, they seek the product that will sell best in their market; and because they want to prevent having their functions taken over by a regional or headquarters office seeking to coordinate international marketing, they try to be as "national" as possible.

Deciding on Product Standardization

We have noted a variety of pressures and influences encouraging standard or modified products in international marketing. The marketing manager must first recognize and evaluate these factors and then make decisions about the degree of uniformity desirable in his products. As a preliminary step, he might eliminate the areas where he really is not free to decide, that is, where government regulations or technical requirements are of overriding importance. If the food or drug authorities in ten different countries have established ten different product specifications for a firm's product, the firm must simply adapt to the awkward situation. Similarly, if a country uses electrical power on a 200 volt–50 cycle system and the firm making electric products is used to a 110 volt–60 cycle system, the firm must unquestionably adapt to the technical requirements of the user country.

In the above situations, however, the firm is not entirely helpless. Although probably it can accomplish little by itself, especially since it is a foreigner trying to change regulations that favor national producers, it can work through its trade or industry association toward harmonization of government and technical requirements. Because of increased regionalism, international trade, and international business, support is growing for international standards to replace national regulations. The firm can also join forces in its trade or industry association to encourage its own government to raise the issue at trade negotiations when nontariff barriers are discussed.

We come now to the variables that the firm can control more directly, or that it at least can make decisions on. Companies generally prefer uniformity of product in international marketing, primarily because of economies of scale in production and marketing. Occasionally, too, executives get psychic satisfaction from selling the same product around the world, but here we will assume that the decision criterion is profits. That is, the degree of product uniformity sought is that which yields the most profits to the firm. Uniformity is not sought for its own sake.

If profits are the criterion, the marketing manager must evaluate the factors affecting product adaptation and seek the most profitable compromise. Although market factors such as income levels and consumer habits may suggest adaptation, the marketer must try to determine whether the increased sales and profits from adaptation are greater than the costs of adapting. The company history of relatively autonomous subsidiaries may have led to product diversity. Does the new situation, including regional grouping and perhaps rationalization of production, mean that uniformity is now more profitable and, therefore, necessary?

In most situations, the question cannot be answered in either-or terms. Instead, the marketing manager must search for the optimal degree of adaptation. He will face such questions as, How much should product A be modified for country B? or, How can I reduce the diversity of product A in our European operations? One approach he might take is to standardize those product attributes that can be standardized—that is, where existing differences are not really necessary—and to leave differences where these are important to the market or government.

An American producer of home-care products has subsidiaries in most Western European countries. Although its product lines were similar in all the countries, individual product attributes differed significantly from country to country. These differences had arisen in part because the national subsidiaries had originally operated exclusively for their own national market.

When the European Common Market began to integrate the national markets, the company decided to centralize production in one country to gain economies of scale. This required the elimination or minimizing of product differences. For one product, floor wax, for instance, the firm agreed on one container size and shape so that the filling machines could work efficiently and container inventories could be reduced. The labels for all markets had the same format, color, and design—even though the brand names and language differed. This provided the advantage of visual similarity for possible TV advertising. As a result of the different use conditions, the floor wax itself came in several different compounds; these were maintained because they were essential from the consumer point of view.

This example demonstrates the possibilities of increasing product uniformity for production and marketing economies while retaining product differences essential for market reasons.

PACKAGING AND LABELING

Many of the international considerations presented in the discussion of the basic product would apply with equal force to such auxiliary product features as the package, label, or warranty. Other special factors affect these product features, however, and we will note these separately in relation to their impact on each feature.

Packaging

Should a firm use the same packaging in foreign markets that it uses in its domestic market? Packaging is a large industry and many American companies have spent great sums finding the best packaging for the products they sell in the United States. Whether this same packaging can be used in foreign markets depends on whether the conditions affecting package choice are similar. Packages need to be analyzed in both their protectional and their promotional aspects.

The kind of product protection needed in one market may differ from that needed elsewhere. A hot, humid climate probably requires a package different from that needed in a cooler, drier area. The amount and kind of transportation and handling the product receives can also dictate packaging differences; stronger protection must be built into the package if it will be subjected to bad roads, long distances, and frequent or rough handling.

Long, slow distribution channels also increase the demands on the package. If one market has a three-month cycle of production to final consumption and another market has a six- or eight-month cycle, the latter market probably will require a more durable and expensive package. This is especially true if the market with a slow distribution cycle also has bad transportation and other conditions punishing to packages, as is frequently the case. For this reason the poorer, less developed countries may require more expensive packaging in spite of their lower purchasing power. In addition to these effects of conditions within the channel, the way the final buyer himself handles and uses the product will also affect the package. If the buyer has a slow usage rate and lacks appropriate storage or handling facilities, the demands on the package are increased correspondingly.

Promotional aspects of packaging, those package attributes which help persuade the distribution channel members to handle the product and the final consumers to buy it, will often vary among foreign markets too. Channel members want minimum breakage and theft, plus ease of handling. The retailer is concerned about shelf-storage and display aspects. A country with a large number of very small retail outlets may want a package different from the one desired by a country where self-service supermarkets are becoming popular.

The kind of package that will help persuade the consumer to buy the product will depend on a number of local cultural factors. (For industrial goods, the consideration would be more purely economic.) What colors and shapes do consumers prefer in the various markets? What kinds of packaging, styles, and materials do they like? Some products sold in aerosol or glass containers in America are sold in tubes in Europe. Countries exhibit similar differences in their preferences for metal over glass or plastic over paper, and so on.

Package size is one of the most important packaging variables in international marketing. The major determinant of appropriate package size for consumer goods is the income level in the particular market under consideration. Low incomes usually mean low usage rates and small purchase amounts. For example, items such as razor blades are sold by the single unit rather than by the package. Even in Italy, single cigarettes were retailed until 1968, and one British marketer noted that the smallest size of detergent available in American supermarkets was the largest size available in the United Kingdom.

Shopping habits often reinforce income constraints on package size. If daily rather than weekly shopping is the practice, the need for large packages is reduced. Furthermore, if the shopper has no car in which to carry the merchandise home, the desirability of large packages is lessened. At the level of the channel intermediaries, similar influences are at work. For example, one food processor, which sells in forty-eight–can cases to the channel members in America, sells in twelve- or twenty-four–can cases to different European markets. As incomes rise, these constraints may change correspondingly, of course.

Packaging Decisions

The first step in selecting a package for a market is to determine national preferences and requirements by examining cultural, distributional, and competitive aspects of the problem. Then the firm must find out how best to meet national preferences. Hopefully, it can take the most convenient and economical course, that is, select a package already in use in other markets. But if a modified or new package is necessary for the new market, the firm must set about evaluating the costs. What new costs are generated by development of a new package or by changes in filling or packing machines and procedures? If a new plant is being built for the new market, these problems are less important. They become critical, however, when one production source serves several national markets.

If markets all require different packaging, the production and packaging operations will be less efficient. From the production point of view, standardization of shapes, sizes, and packaging materials is desirable, but differences in colors and esthetics of the package can be maintained because they create relatively little expense and affect packaging inventories primarily. Even in esthetics, however, standardization is desirable if the goods are promoted in international campaigns or are "tourist goods." For example, Kodak's yellow film packages are familiar to all international travelers.

In its analysis of market needs and preferences in packaging, the firm should be alert to the possibilities of innovation. As consumer habits change, incomes rise, or retailing becomes more modern and large scale in a given market, the firm might find the appropriate package to be different from what currently exists in that market. The multinational firm, from its vantage point of operations in many different cultures and levels of economic development, should be able to identify such trends and lead in packaging innovations.

To complement this general discussion of packaging, we give the following two concrete examples, the first a case of an ethical drug company and the second that of an American food marketer operating in Europe.

The company found four variables that affect its package size in various markets. These are (1) government reimbursement practices (with socialized medicine in most markets), (2) doctors' preferences, (3) patients' needs, (4) competitive practices. These factors lead to different sizes in different markets.

The company had no less than three different sizes of packages in Europe for one of its leading products—about one ounce difference between them.

One was from its English plant, another from its French plant, and the other
from its Italian licensee. All three packages were developed at different times
in different markets, but came to compete in overlapping market areas. Non-
renewal of the licensing contract eliminated one. The other two were stand-
ardized.[7]

Labeling

Language

Labeling is closely related to packaging, but it has its own particular decision
parameters. The major elements are language, government regulations, and
consumer information. Even if labels were standardized in format and message content from country to country, still the language would probably vary
in each market. If the label contains an important verbal communication for
consumers, usually it must be in their language, which means different language labels in most foreign markets. The resulting economic loss is slight
because only printing diseconomies are involved, rather than the greater diseconomies associated with the higher production costs of package or product
modification. Occasionally, however, firms try to avoid even this cost. One
way is through the use of multilingual labels; for example, one label would
carry information in French, German, and Italian for a product serving all
three markets. Some national markets, such as Belgium, Canada, and Switzerland, are multilingual and thus require multilingual labels even within a single
market.

The use of multilingual labels to serve several national markets may or may
not be advisable, depending on consumer sentiment in the various countries.
If the multilingual label conveys an international or cosmopolitan image that
is favorably received by consumers, it is desirable. If it conveys a foreign or
non-national image, it is perhaps undesirable. As one consumer goods marketer
with wide international operations remarked, "Except in Belgium and Switzerland, which are multilingual anyway, it clutters up the package and makes it
look like a foreign product. We don't want to lose that local identity. It pays."[8]
Interestingly, such local identity may be more important to a multinational firm
than to a purely national company.

Another way of avoiding different language labels for each country is the
use of the same language everywhere. This is feasible and even desirable in
some circumstances. If the label has little or no important message or information to communicate to the consumer—as in the case of perfume, for example
—the language question becomes unimportant. An example of a situation
in which a single-language label is desirable is where a product has a particular national image; the language of that nation on the label would reinforce
the image.

For similar image reasons, such products as perfumes or cosmetics might be

---

[7] Vern Terpstra, *American Marketing in the Common Market* (New York: Praeger,
1967), pp. 75, 79.
[8] Terpstra, *American Marketing in the Common Market*, p. 77.

labeled in French in non-French–speaking countries. For other products, an an American or English image might be useful and the labels could be in English in all markets. Take, for example, the French producer of chewing gum. Since this is considered an American product, the French producer wanted it to look American. Thus he chose the brand name "Hollywood" and printed the label entirely in English, except for the word *Tirez* (pull) on the package opener. As another example, an American bra manufacturer uses his American package and label intact all over the world.

Fairly extensive information must be communicated to the customer about the use of some products. In this situation, the label may still have very brief, one-language copy but be supplemented by a detailed multilingual insert inside the package, as in done with photographic film and ethical and proprietary drugs.

Government

Differing government requirements are of major importance in labeling. Whereas the firm may have a choice regarding the language it uses on its labels, it must conform completely to national government requirements. Countries' labeling laws vary widely, those of the less developed countries making the fewest and simplest demands. Some of the aspects covered by government regulations include mark-of-origin, weight, description of contents and ingredients, name of producer, and special information as to additives, chemical or fat content, and so on. With all these variables, each country inevitably has a somewhat different configuration of requirements. Equally inevitably, these requirements serve to give some protection to national producers.

> *In keeping with a Europewide trend toward improving protection of private consumers, the Norwegian Parliament has passed a law giving the Family and Consumer Ministry discretionary powers to require more comprehensive labeling of consumer goods. As is usual with this type of measure, Norway may use the requirements to make the importation of certain foreign goods more difficult.*[9]

A final aspect of labeling is the manufacturer's own interest in using the package and label to promote the product. Because labeling is one of his avenues of communication with his customers, he is more interested in the marketing aspects than in the legal and linguistic questions. The producer wants the label to encourage purchase and facilitate use of his product in order to assure consumer satisfaction and repeat purchase. The message or copy that will accomplish these goals depends in part on the nature of the product and in part on the particular consumption system into which his product fits. These consumption systems are usually culturally determined and thus may vary from country to country. This fact may be a further source of lack of labeling standardization in international marketing.

[9] *Business Europe*, June 21, 1968, p. 198.

Making decisions on labeling for foreign markets is somewhat easier than making decisions on other marketing questions for two reasons. (1) Concerning government regulations, the firm has no decision—it must conform. (2) Concerning costs, the firm can afford nonstandardized labeling because it is much less expensive than nonstandardized products or packages. For the rest, the procedure is routine: Determine the needs and desires of the market (consumers and intermediaries) and design the label that best satisfies them while it also satisfies those of the producer. Although this procedure could lead to different labels in each market, the firm's demands for international uniformity should be recognized where they are important. As in some of the examples cited, international uniformity may be more important to the firm than national distinctiveness. Finally, the firm may work through the industry and trade associations in its various markets to try to attain greater uniformity in the relevant national regulations. The EEC, for instance, has this uniformity to some extent.

BRANDS AND TRADEMARKS

Selecting brands and establishing brand policy are important questions in international marketing. One problem is deciding how to protect the company's brands and trademarks. Another is deciding whether there should be one international brand or many different national brands for a given product. Some of the considerations in brand policy are the same as those already discussed under other product attributes. In this section we will not repeat those; instead we will emphasize factors peculiar to international branding problems. A further question is the role of private branding in international marketing.

Global Brands or National Brands

The major argument for a uniform global brand on a product is economies of scale. The argument is the same as that for product uniformity, except that the economies in brand uniformity are promotional as distinguished from the production economies of a standardized product. Whether a single international brand is indeed the best policy, or even a possible policy, depends on a number of considerations.

The Legal Dimension

There is a legal dimension to international branding that may limit the possibilities for a global brand. In the United States, brand ownership is established by priority in use. In many foreign markets that are under a code-law system, brand ownership is legally established by priority in registration. A firm that wishes to carry a brand name to foreign markets might find that in some of them, someone else has already registered that name. This person may be legitimately using the name himself, or he may have pirated it. As an example of the former, the Ford Motor Company chose the name Mustang for one of its cars. Later on it found that it could not use this brand in Germany because an established firm was making bicycles under that name. In this particular case, Ford was not greatly disturbed because it was already marketing a special European line of cars in Germany under the Taunus brand name. In some other situations, loss of rights to a brand name could be much more serious.

Brand piracy is quite another matter. The "pirate" is someone who deliberately registers brand names to profit from the situation by selling them back to the firms that originated them. In certain markets, such as in Mexico or Germany, where brand name registration is easy and inexpensive, individuals can make a living by this practice. When the manufacturer wishes to enter the product in one of these markets under his regular brand name and finds that someone has already registered that name, he must negotiate with the legal owner. If they can agree on a price, the producer has obtained legal ownership of his brand. If they cannot reach an agreement, the producer must find another brand name—or keep his product off the market.

The most notorious example of brand and trademark piracy occurred in the mid–1960s. Dr. Robert Aries, a chemist, registered 330 trademarks in Monaco under a new international trademark convention. Some of the names registered were Bendix, Boeing, BBC, DuPont, Chase, Morgan, Harpers, Mitsubishi, The New Yorker, Sears, and Texaco. Dr. Aries took advantage of loopholes in European laws and the fact that many companies missed filing deadlines. The affair was a cause célèbre *for a couple years and engaged many corporate lawyers for some time.*

PROTECTION: WHEN AND WHERE?   How does a company protect its brands and trademarks, which are often among its most valued possessions? The solution is primarily legal, and the first step is to have expert legal counsel. All we will do here is sketch some dimensions of the problem. The first decision a company must make is whether to seek protection for a brand or trademark and in what countries. Obviously, it is better to have registered a brand or mark in a foreign country than to have to buy it back. This might suggest a policy of immediate registration of all of the firm's brands and trademarks in all countries, which would be a good solution if registration were free or nominal in cost. But fees can run to over $100 per mark per country and thus some choices must be made following a cost-benefit analysis.

Although protection may come through use in common-law countries or through registration in code-law countries, frequently registration must follow use in the one group, and use must follow registration in the other. This usually means two kinds of costs involved in protecting the mark—registration costs and "use" costs. Registration involves a fee that can run to over $100; "use" is defined legally and varies from country to country. In order to meet the requirements of brand use, a product may have to be sold or even manufactured locally. But in some cases, the export sale of a few cases of a product has been sufficient to be defined as use of the brand for purposes of protection. In the latter situation, use costs are relatively modest.

Given the costs of protecting brands and trademarks, the marketing man must evaluate each market and each brand to determine whether to seek protection. Generally, the company name—IBM, Ford, and so on—and the major brands—Coca-Cola, Kodak, Gillette—would be protected in all foreign markets. More selective protective coverage would be given to secondary brands. Some brands might have no foreign market protection at all, if foreign sales of that brand were expected to be minimal.

A second decision on brand protection will be necessary in many countries that require the holder to renew his rights periodically and pay a renewal fee. As can be seen, the management of international brand protection can be a complex task, involving both legal and marketing expertise. Perhaps it is not surprising that a number of executives in a study of the subject felt that the expense of wide coverage was not always worthwhile. Their admonition was, "When in doubt, don't."[10]

Cost-benefit analysis was suggested in deciding whether to protect a given brand. The same kind of analysis would apply in deciding what price the firm could afford to pay to buy back rights to its brand from a brand pirate. The costs of purchasing the rights to the original brand and the sales with that brand would have to be compared with the costs of establishing a new brand name and the sales associated with it. Of course, a third alternative is not to enter the particular product in that market at all, which would mean no costs and no sales.

Sometimes the expression "brand piracy" may refer to a different situation. In some markets of the world, such as in a number of Far East countries, American marketers find many local imitations or copies of their brands. In fact, the product, package, and brand are all designed to be as close as possible to the American product, so that customers will think they are indeed getting the American product. Some examples are the following:

IMITATION	AMERICAN BRAND
Yalf locks	Yale
Coalgate, Goalgate, and so on	Colgate toothpaste
Del Mundo	Del Monte
Pang's Cold Cream	Pond's
Hotex, Potex, Katex, and so on	Kotex

One Formosan drug maker confessed: "If our product doesn't look like the U.S. original, we can't sell it."[11] Although such imitation may be the sincerest form of flattery, it means lost sales to the American firm whose well-established brand is being copied. The firm will have difficulty protecting itself against this form of brand piracy because legal action is of limited value in most of these countries. Consumer education through advertising, although a possibility, is an expensive way to attack the problem—and all too probably an ineffective way in these low-literacy markets. This burden is part of the cost of establishing a strong brand position in these markets.

[10] "Establishing a Worldwide Patent and Trademark Policy," *Management Monograph No. 25* (New York: Business International, 1965), p. 24.
[11] *Time*, June 15, 1967, p. 83.

Cultural Aspects

Even if a firm has no legal problems in securing rights to its brand name in foreign markets, it may encounter cultural barriers hindering the use of its established brand. One problem may be that the name is just not pronounceable in the local language. Names successfully developed for the American market simply may not be able to travel to many foreign countries. The longer the name and the more specifically American, the less likely its suitability in foreign languages. Consider the contrary example of some names that have traveled well abroad: Ford, Kodak, Coca-Cola, Esso.

Choice of the name Esso was influenced by the fact that it can be identically pronounced in most of the world's languages. In its Spanish operation, Sears has not introduced its American brand names, such as Kenmore or Allstate, but simply labels most of the goods "Sears." In Castillian Spanish, however, Sears sounds nearly the same as Seat, the name of Spain's leading automobile manufacturer. Because of the automobile producer's complaints, Sears agreed to add "Roebuck" to labels on goods having even a remote association with automobiles.

Another cultural problem is that a brand name may have an undesirable or obscene connotation in the foreign language. Pepsi Cola introduced a line of noncola drinks in America under the name Patio. Although the name was pronounceable in Spanish, its connotation was not very pleasant; the company switched to the name Mirinda as its foreign market brand on noncola drinks. A leather-care products manufacturer planned to market in the EEC under the brand name Dreck. He chose the name because it "sounded virile," but he changed his mind about using it when he discovered that in German it means "dirt."[12] For various reasons Maxwell House becomes Maxwell Kaffee in Germany, Legal in France, and Monky in Spain.

When faced with cultural and linguistic barriers to the use of one of its established brands, the firm must seek the best alternative. Occasionally, the firm is lucky and a small change in spelling is sufficient, as when Wrigley changed the spelling of Spearmint to Speermint in Germany to facilitate German pronunciation of the name. Esso markets its Engro fertilizer around the world, but in French-speaking countries the name could be associated with the French expression *en gros*. This association was distracting rather than obscene, but to avoid it Esso added one letter to the name, making it Enagros for French-speaking countries. More frequently, however, the firm will have to seek another brand name, as Pepsi did with Patio.

If a brand does have an undesirable connotation in the foreign market, it is unlikely to carry over good will from its use elsewhere. The question then becomes whether to develop a new brand for just one market, for a number of foreign markets, or for all international marketing. There are usually significant advantages to minimizing the number of brand names on a given product. If legal or cultural barriers exist in several markets, the firm might decide to create a new brand for international markets but maintain the

[12] *Printers' Ink*, April 14, 1967, p. 29.

original brand name in the domestic market. Pepsi still sells Patio beverages in the United States, but internationally all its noncola beverages are Mirinda. Some of the factors affecting such a decision are the number of markets needing a new brand, the good will attached to the established brand, and the advertising carry over from market to market.

Other Marketing Considerations

Several other general influences bear on the decision as to the number of international brands for the firm's products. First of all, there is a difference between the firm's *major brands* and its secondary or tertiary brands. On its leading products, the firm is likely to have the same brand all over the world; for instance, Coca-Cola and Pepsi Cola are global, even though these companies have multiple brands on secondary products. Firms maintain brands in part because a great amount of international good will has been built up for the company's leading products and the costs of switching in terms of this attitude would be great. If the items are tourist goods or benefit from multinational advertising, the advantages of uniformity are so much the greater. Secondary brands may not be known or recognized in foreign markets, so choosing a new and more suitable international brand is more feasible.

Another factor affecting the international branding decision is the *importance of brand to the product sale*. For many consumer products, the brand name is a critical factor in the consumer's decision to purchase. Because of this, firms invest heavily to establish and maintain a strong favorable brand image and consumer franchise. For other products, factors such as price, services, product performance, or quality are more important purchase determinants than the brand name. Where the brand is relatively unimportant, the firm does not spend heavily to promote it and therefore does not mind using different brands in foreign markets. The costs or disadvantages of multiple brands are low in this case because the firm is spending its marketing dollars in other areas.

As a generalization, one can say in regard to industrial goods that the international brand question is relatively unimportant, although the company name may be very important. Although the brand names on the individual products may be almost unknown, the company name and/or trademark may tie many diverse products together and play a significant role. The ethical drug industry provides an example of such international trademark variation. Following is one trademark pattern for a product of the Eli Lilly Company.

Cordran-N (Flurandrenolone with neomycin sulfate, Lilly)

DRENISON WITH NEOMYCIN	International English
DRENISON AVEC NEOMYCINE	French-speaking areas
SERMAKA-N	Germany
DRENISON COM NEOMICINA	Portuguese-speaking areas
DRENISON CON NEOMICINA	Spanish-speaking areas
ALONDRA-F CON NEOMICINA	Argentina
DRENISON-N	Venezuela
DROCORT MED NEOMYCIN	Sweden

The international branding question has a further aspect, that between *established products versus new products*. The company usually has too much investment in the good will associated with the brand on its established products to permit easy changing of the brand for foreign markets. If the firm has a stream of new products coming from its product development activity, however, it does not have the same kind of promotional investment to protect by brand uniformity. In fact, one could argue that as the multinational company develops new products, it should also search for brand names of international suitability as part of a truly international outlook. International brand uniformity, in addition to the possible advantages it offers, is easier to achieve on new products because brand names can be chosen for a world market in the first place.

The *legacy of established foreign operations* can lead to a confusing international branding situation. Some companies have subsidiaries established before the rise of regionalism and the postwar freeing and expansion of international trade. They operated these subsidiaries as purely national concerns for the most part, making little attempt to integrate branding or other marketing policies. This was a defensible practice at the time because trade barriers effectively separated most national markets from each other. In today's world these national markets tend to be open to regional and international trade, requiring much more integration and uniformity in consequence. An American food company illustrates the problem.

The company had several European subsidiaries formed in the 1930s. These subsidiaries took some of the leading brand names from the American operation—but put them on different products. In the internal free-trade area of the EEC these different products with the identical brand name began to appear in overlapping market areas. Obviously some changes and coordination were necessary. Regional headquarters had to modify the situation to assure regional integration of brand policy.

Dual brands for similar products, arising from acquisition or joint venture, can pose a serious barrier to brand standardization. Often the quickest way to enter a foreign market is to acquire a national company in the desired product area. Should the acquirer's brand then replace the existing brand, be added to the line, or be left out? If the acquiring firm is operating in many markets of a region like Europe, there are probably promotional economies of scale in having just one brand on a product. But if the firm chooses its own brand, it will lose the good will attached to the existing national brand. As one food marketer noted: "Our name and symbol aren't important. What counts is getting in the market with a product. You keep the name you acquired, as that is part of what you paid for."

In some product areas, dual brands are a way of making a two-pronged attack on the market, as exemplified domestically in the detergent industry. Goodyear makes both Goodyear and Kelly tires in America and bought a German tire company called Fulda also. In a new plant in Greece, Goodyear produces all three brands and probably gains much better distributor coverage thereby. A farm-equipment producer bought an Italian firm in the same line. The acquiring firm kept brands and identities completely separate and used the acquisition merely to expand its total share of the market. Private branding can be one way of implementing a dual-brand, two-pronged attack on a market.

Private Branding in International Marketing

The considerations involved in private branding in international marketing are generally similar to those in domestic marketing. The manufacturer usually is opposed to private branding (making and labeling his products with the distributor's brands) abroad as well as at home. However, the same pressures that lead to private branding in the United States are also at work in foreign markets. Large-scale retailing, mail-order retailing, and discounting are increasing in many important foreign markets, especially in Western Europe and Japan. Where these distribution developments are strong, manufacturers may have to use distributor's brands, in addition to their own, in order to get adequate distribution coverage or to meet price competition. For example, this was the case for General Electric's television sets in West Germany.

Another kind of situation may confront the smaller firm in international marketing if it wishes to market abroad through a combination export manager (see Chapter 10) rather than through its own export department. The combination export manager may want his own brand on the goods to give himself greater control and protection in his market development work. If the producer accedes, he gives up developing a market for himself, which may hurt him later if he wants to go more directly into foreign markets.

International Brand Management: Conclusions

A problem in international brand management is whether to protect or register a brand and in which markets. As already discussed, the marketer and a lawyer consult on this question. Another problem is whether to have uniform global brands or several different national brands for the firm's products. We suggested that a firm may gain promotional economies of scale with standardized brands, although it may nevertheless decide to individualize brands in its international marketing for several good reasons. The trend in the multinational company, however, is toward greater brand uniformity, and part of the marketing manager's task is to manage the transition. Just as regional markets in the United States blended into a national market, so national markets of the world are moving toward a regional or global market.

Reducing brand diversity involves phasing out one brand while minimizing the loss of good will associated with it. One way the company might do this is to emphasize the company name and trademark or symbol as a link between the old and new brand names. Even in the contrary situation where a firm wants separate brands in different countries, it can use the company name, trademark, and package design for maximum visual similarity in spite of the difference in brand.

S. C. Johnson Company markets home-care products in many European countries and prefers nationalized brand names for greater local consumer identification. However, to maximize visual similarity for promotion, the package shape, label design, and color are identical, including the company symbol. Thus the products appear very much alike in different markets, even though the brand name and the copy on the label differ from country to country.

A *family brand approach* is another way a firm can reduce brand diversity. Sears simply uses the Sears label in Spain rather than all of its American brand names. Esso uses the Atlas brand for its tire, battery, and accessory business in the United States as well as in some foreign markets, but used the Esso brand exclusively when it introduced these items into Germany. Such an approach gives the promotional strength of the Esso name to all the products retailed and economies of scale in promotion.

A further problem of international brand management is the development of brand names for new products. Increasingly in the multinational company, these brand names should be designed for global markets. As a caution, we note that brand uniformity is not a goal in itself; the goal is finding effective brand names that promote sales. As one international marketer commented: "We don't want a weak brand name just because it's registrable everywhere." The more specific a brand name is to the product, such as Hotpoint for stoves, the less likely it will be able to travel. For this reason some companies search for meaningless short words that have no specific language affiliation. One of the most successful examples is Kodak.

The computer can be programmed to print out 44,900 four-letter combinations or about 500,000 five-letter combinations. Brand-name candidates then need to be checked out for potential legal complications and for possible objectionable meanings in the various languages. Standard dictionaries, incidentally, are not sufficient for this check because the foreign equivalents of the English "four-letter words" must be avoided.[13] Although this approach could lead to global brand names, they might lack the individualized touch that some products benefit from. In this case, an individualized national approach could still be preferable.

WARRANTY AND SERVICE POLICIES

The buyer of a product usually is seeking not its physical or chemical attributes but rather what the product will do for him. He is buying utility and performance, not physical characteristics. Thus when he considers buying technical or mechanical products, such as consumer durables or industrial equipment, his decision will be influenced favorably by warranty and service policies offered as part of the total product. The manufacturer may consider warranty and service to be something apart from the product, but he is more

---

[13] "Avoiding Brand Name Bloopers Overseas," *Business Abroad*, July 24, 1967, pp. 17, 18.

attuned to his market if he sees them as integral parts thereof. This point of view is as necessary to international marketing success as it is to domestic, but its implementation is more difficult internationally.

Warranties

A warranty is a promise by the seller that his product will do what it is supposed to do. An express warranty can give the buyer the reassurance he often needs before purchase. This reassurance can be especially important to multinational companies selling in foreign markets. Any uneasiness on the part of the buyer about purchasing from a foreign—that is, unreachable— company can be largely offset by strong warranty and service programs. A very good example of this is the success of Volkswagen in the United States. In international marketing the warranty questions are quite simple: (1) Should the firm have the same warranty internationally that it has domestically? (2) Should the firm keep the same warranty for all foreign markets or adapt on a country-by-country basis? (3) Should the firm use the warranty as a competitive weapon? Or perhaps these questions can be reduced to one major one: What is the best warranty policy for the multinational company?

From the manufacturer's point of view, warranties have both protective and promotional aspects. They help to protect the manufacturer against unreasonable claims by limiting his liability concerning the product and its performance. If the warranty also offers sufficient reassurance to the buyer as to the product and its performance, it can be one of the promotional factors persuading him to buy, especially if one producer's warranty promises more than another's. The promotional aspect of warranties is the one most likely to change in international marketing.

Standardization?

A number of parameters affect the decision to have a standardized international warranty policy or not. First, warranty standardization does not offer the kind of economies of scale in production and promotion that standardization in product, packaging, or branding offers. Because the firm has little to gain from international warranty standardization, except, perhaps, administrative convenience, we might not expect to see serious efforts in this direction; however, some external pressures may encourage standardization.

1. If the market the firm is serving is truly international, having different warranties in different countries may be an impossible policy. For example, the customers of the firm may themselves be international companies—in construction, mining, petroleum, or manufacturing. Such customers would probably be unwilling to accept a warranty on a product delivered to a Latin American operation if it were different from that on the same product delivered to a European operation.

2. Another pressure toward warranty standardization is the travel of the product itself from market to market, for instance, tourist goods. If the product is purchased in one market but may need service in another market, it is highly desirable that the warranty be the same in both markets. This is why warranties are uniform throughout the American market. On automobiles, for example,

it will probably be necessary to have uniform warranties in a regional market like Western Europe. The growth of regional economic groupings around the world, in both social and legal aspects, is a further encouragement to standardized warranties.

3. The nature of the product itself may encourage warranty standardization. On products where saftey is a critical factor and human life can be endangered, warranties are more likely to be uniform because the basic need of the consumer or user is the same all over the world. Products in this category include drugs, airplanes, and elevators.

4. A final pressure toward uniformity is internal to the company. If the company has just one production source for world markets, uniform warranties are more likely; but if the firm serves markets from plants located in many different countries and having different quality-control standards, uniform warranties are less feasible. Related to this point is another factor concerning the firm's international organization. One study concluded that universal warranties are offered primarily by firms having the world-wide service programs to support them.[14] This highlights the fact that a warranty is only meaningful to the extent that it has a service program backing it.

Although standardization in warranties is less rewarding to the firm than other kinds of standardization, we can see from the above discussion why some international firms are nevertheless standardizing their warranties. Some firms with standard international warranties are Allis Chalmers, Bell & Howell, Brunswick (bowling equipment), Caterpillar, A. B. Dick, Parker Pen, Sunbeam, and Volkswagen.[15]

Or Localization?

Although a few strong pressures encourage uniform international warranties, several advantages and inducements influence the firm to tailor its warranties to the conditions of individual national markets.

1. Firms lack the incentive to standardize their warranties because they receive no significant economic gains by doing so.

2. Having many production sources, each with a different quality-control standard, can make it difficult and costly for the firm to give a uniform guarantee to customers of the different plants because there is not a uniform production capability behind the guarantee.

3. Differing use conditions in various foreign markets can make a universal warranty too expensive a proposition. Operating equipment in extreme heat, cold, humidity, dust, or salty sea air can cause breakdowns that arise not from product defects but from the particular adverse use conditions. Driving a car or truck on primitive African roads causes greater wear than does driving the same mileage on an expressway. American Motors, for example, does not give a universal warranty expressly because of the differences climate, terrain, and road conditions make to the operation of its products. Of course, an alternative is to design specialized products for each particular use condition.

4. Warranties are especially useful as competitive promotional tools. Because the competitive situation of the firm varies from country to country, it often finds

[14] *Business International*, June 16, 1967, p. 187.
[15] *Business International*, p. 187.

it desirable to vary its warranties to meet promotional requirements in differing national markets.

5. If a firm does not have an international service network of fairly even quality, it will find it difficult to offer a uniform warranty in all of its markets. If the warranty is to be more than mere words, the firm must be capable of fulfilling its service requirements everywhere; that is, uniform warranty implies uniform service capability. This is extremely difficult to achieve in global marketing.

We have not provided a clear answer to the marketing manager's question about warranty standardization, either between American and foreign markets or among foreign markets themselves. The particular situation of the firm and the industry need to be examined before any decision can be made. Generally, however, it appears that warranty standardization is a less critical factor in the firm's international operations than standardization of other product attributes.

Warranties as a Competitive Tool

Because the promotional aspect of warranties is important, the possibility of using them as a means of competition arises. We see examples of this in the American market, ranging from the automobile industry to the blanket guarantee of satisfaction offered by the Sears Roebuck Company. Although this competitive tool is also available in international marketing, whether it is used depends on the firm's circumstances in its various markets. First, the kind of competitive weapons a firm uses depends on its own strengths as well as on the strengths and practices of competitiors. If foreign market competitors compete on warranty, the multinational firm usually needs to be competitive; that is, the firm must offer a warranty as good as that offered by the others, unless the firm has offsetting competitive advantages in other areas.

Second, the firm's position in the particular national market can determine whether it competes on warranty. Someone has observed that it is the weaker firm in an industry which offers the most spectacular warranties. This may be because the warranty is a competitive weapon that can be quickly prepared as compared with product line or distribution advantages.

The Simca Company was one of the smaller members of the French and European automobile industry. It is now owned largely by the Chrysler Corporation. Not long after Chrysler became the majority stockholder, it became the first European manufacturer to guarantee certain essential parts of its new Simca autos for two years or 60,000 kilometers. This significant expansion of warranty coverage in the European automobile industry was meant to give a boost to Simca's market penetration similar to the boost Chrysler had received earlier in the American market when it introduced the five-year–50,000-mile warranty.

Note also that Chrysler had warranties in Europe different from those in America. When it began selling Simcas in the United States, Chrysler did apply the five-year–50,000-mile warranty to the imported cars but maintained the two-year warranty in Europe.

Third, the firm's production and technological skill may determine whether it uses a warranty competitively. A warranty can be stronger, longer, or better for the buyer if the producer's quality-control and production skills are such that the product is indeed more reliable than competitors' products. If this increased quality and reliability are realized, warranty can be increased without a corresponding increase in service and repair costs. In a study conducted by the author, several American marketers claimed this kind of technological edge. Said one: "In our field, American products have the edge. We're the Cadillacs of the field and the consumer will often pay a premium. We've always led in warranties and the Europeans must come up to ours."[16]

Fourth, competitive use of warranty depends on the service facilities that support it. No lasting gain can be achieved by offering a warranty that cannot be fulfilled by product reliability and service support. Whether the firm uses warranty competitively will depend further on the total competitive arsenal it has available. Although warranty can be a useful tool, it is more easily imitated than some other competitive weapons. Therefore the appropriate strategy is related to a number of other variables. As one marketer noted, "If we can be first in warranty, we tell the story and get the benefit of leadership. Elsewhere we try not to disturb the market."[17]

Service

This section concerns postsale service. We consider presale service under Personal Selling in Chapter 14. Warranty and service policies are quite intimately related in principle but differ in practice. Designing a warranty is largely a legal and verbal exercise, although with marketing implications. Creating an international service capability can involve investment in facilities, personnel staffing and training, and setting up a qualified distribution network serving all the firm's markets. The management question here is not one of standardization; it is rather the practical question, How can I offer the best service to all my customers around the world? Because customers buying a product from a foreign (non-national) firm tend to worry more about service than they do when buying from a national firm, the multinational company needs to be especially concerned about its service capability.

The issue of standardization of service does not arise because it is impossible of fulfillment. Even in the American market where the automobile companies have uniform warranties, they do not offer uniform service. As any car owner knows, the service will vary from dealer to dealer, even in the same city. Nevertheless, most companies try to offer the best service possible in all markets because consumer satisfaction and repeat purchases will relate to the service received, especially as compared with similar service offered by the competition. Providing adequate service, a continuing problem for manufacturers in domestic marketing, is an even more complicated problem in international marketing. The customer's *need for service* is a function of

[16] Terpstra, *American Marketing in the Common Market*, p. 80.
[17] Terpstra, *American Marketing in the Common Market*, p. 81.

his use and maintenance conditions, and these may vary greatly from market to market.

Japanese machine-tool producers found that their American customers used (punished) the machines more than their Japanese customers. Because of their higher labor costs, American firms used the machines more intensively and could not afford down time for maintenance. The Japanese producers had to modify both their product and their service program in selling to the American market.

On the other hand, the manufacturer's *ability to supply service* is a function of his international involvement and distribution network. Most of the companies selling internationally do not have subsidiaries in all their foreign markets. They must rely on their distributors to provide service where they have no facilities of their own. Finding good foreign distributors is always a key step to success, but finding ones that can also service the product is even more critical. Often the distributors' service programs must be aided or supplemented by efforts of the producer.

Handling Service Problems

International service problems can be attacked in several different ways. One method is to establish a good international distributor network with adequate service capabilities. Even before that, however, the product should be designed with both service and user in mind. If the product is designed with service in mind, repairs will be easier and cheaper and can be carried out conveniently by the foreign distributor, whose capabilities may well be less than those of the servicer in the domestic market. If the product is designed with the user in mind, his use conditions and maintenance abilities (or lack of them) are foreseen and accounted for. This suggests that a simple, sturdy, though primitive, product may be more suitable for some markets than the latest automatic device, which is really more efficient but also more fragile and in greater need of maintenance.

Because of the difficulties in finding ready-made international distributor networks with adequate service capability, many firms supplement their distributors' efforts. They establish service training programs, for instance, which they may accomplish in one of three different ways.

1. One possibility is to invite distributor service personnel to America for training. The feasibility of this depends on the number of people involved and the length and complexity of the training program. Generally, the fewer the people and the more complex the training, the more desirable it is to bring them to America to get some economies of scale in the program. Overseas distributor personnel might be able to participate in programs given for American service trainees if the language problem can be overcome.

2. When it is not economic to bring distributor service personnel to America for training, the training must go to them. A traveling training program is one

way to accomplish this. A team or teams of trainers can be sent to cover the firm's foreign distributor network, either on an individual-country or on a regional basis. The Armstrong Company, which sells flooring and ceiling materials, had a mobile van training unit traveling around Europe in addition to fixed training centers in Germany and in Paris.

3. As the Armstrong example shows, training of foreign distributor personnel can also be conducted by fixed-location training centers, which would be necessary when the nature of the equipment and training program do not lend themselves to travel. Many multinational companies are setting up training centers around the world, usually on a regional basis. Caterpillar has established such training centers in São Paulo, Melbourne, Geneva, and at its home office in Peoria, Illinois.

One of the service difficulties in multinational marketing is the parts problem, which involves either expensive parts inventories in each market or shipping and importation delays (not to mention customer irritation) in receiving the part from some central storage. No one has found an easy answer to this problem, but General Electric tried a novel approach.

With each group of appliances sent to a distributor, GE sent along a spare-parts kit, compiled on the basis of a statistical analysis of failure rates of various parts in various countries. It was expected to contain at least enough parts to cover the warranty period. This was sent out prepaid, supplanting the cumbersome system of giving distributors credit for each part replaced on the warranty (the distributor kept the parts, whether he used them all or not). For GE the advantages were savings in freight and customs costs (because of bulk rates), elimination of wasteful accounting, and—most important—elimination of shipping delays.[18]

Much of our discussion to this point applies to any product needing servicing. It is worthwhile, however, to note some of the special factors bearing on the service of industrial products. The industrial customer requires uninterrupted production, therefore minimum down time for repairs. One way to satisfy him is through preventive maintenance, perhaps selling a service contract with the equipment, but this is easier to carry through in concentrated markets than in markets where customers are spread out. For example, Otis Elevator visits its distant customers about every three months to check for signs of machine wear or stress. In the concentrated markets where Otis has trained personnel, its visits are on a weekly basis.[19]

Another way to supply fast service is to send either the part or a repairman by air. In some instances, the part can be flown to a service center (or even to America), repaired, and flown back more quickly than it can be repaired under alternative service methods. General Electric, for example,

---

[18] *Business International*, July 14, 1967, p. 219.
[19] *Business International*, p. 245.

requires that many mobile items be sent to the factory, but to make the process as rapid as possible, it has franchised independent service shops overseas to do the repairs. By having these shops in enough markets, GE expects to accomplish reasonably prompt service. GE's goal is to have a global chain of about 125 franchised service outlets.[20]

If the part or equipment cannot be flown, the repairman can fly to the customer, an approach unlikely except with very expensive, large, and highly technical products. For the manufacturer-seller of such equipment, however, this centralized method offers some economies of scale in his service operation. American Machine and Foundry (AMF) uses this approach, sending specialists from the United States or from overseas subsidiaries.

The nature of the firm's international business involvement is another important determinant of its service program. Firms operating exclusively via exporting must rely on the service capabilities of their foreign distributors. As the firm establishes operations abroad by joint ventures and by acquiring marketing or manufacturing subsidiaries, it gains a physical presence in foreign markets that adds greatly to its service capabilities. It still has problems of training service personnel, but it is now dealing with its own employees rather than with independent outsiders. Although operating through licensees is akin to exporting in that the licensor must rely on an outside firm (the licensee) to do the servicing, it has an advantage over exporting in that the licensee should have greater expertise because he is manufacturing the product.

The producer can supplement the efforts of both distributors and licensees with special training programs or regional service centers. Westinghouse, a major American licensor and exporter, conducts training courses for service personnel of its distributors and licensees. In Europe, it has a sales-service center in Geneva with a skilled technical staff to back up the firms associated with it. Naturally, the larger and more widespread a firm's international business, the more its international service program can resemble its domestic activity.

From this discussion we can see that administration of a multinational service program involves many dimensions and possible trade-offs. The goal is maximum consumer satisfaction and good will at the lowest cost to the seller. Elements that can contribute to this optimum result include (1) product design, (2) service training programs, (3) parts inventories, (4) quality control, and (5) decisions as to kind of international business involvement, that is, exports, licensing, or foreign operations. Getting the right balance of these elements is part of the international marketing manager's task when he prepares his marketing mix.

Service as a Competitive Promotional Tool

As a minimum, the international marketer of technical products needs service capability to accredit himself with foreign buyers. They will hesitate to purchase his product, however good, unless they are assured of service backup.

---

[20] *Business International*, p. 245.

Service can be used in more aggressive ways, however. The firm with a strong service program can gain a competitive edge over its rivals. The multinational firm often has such an edge because of its size and experience. Volkswagen in America is one example. In the author's study of American marketing in Europe, he found that many American firms claimed that their quality control and service programs were important factors giving them a strong market position in Europe. For example, when the French subsidiary of the Singer Company was considering adding extra consumer durables to its line, it first investigated consumer reaction. It found that most of the survey respondents would be quite willing to buy an appliance from Singer. The reason? "Good service." The company's service reputation had given it an advantage very hard to duplicate.

Company-conducted service operations provide close, continuing contact with customers, which can yield insights into customer needs, ideas for new products, and opportunities for future sales. These advantages are realized most fully when a service contract is sold with the product. An American chemical company, while servicing a major customer in Europe, found new uses and applications for some of its chemicals that it was able to market to its American customers. So important is this need for service that many companies set up service facilities for a foreign market as soon as they begin manufacturing or selling there. In keeping with this practice, some companies will not accept a sales order from an area that they cannot service. When a program and budget for international marketing are being prepared, service needs to receive attention equal to that given to such items as product development and promotion.

Questions

8.1   Identify ways in which the firm can make profits in foreign markets in addition to, or apart from, selling its traditional products. What rights or services can it capitalize on?

8.2   Distinguish between a turn-key operation and a management contract. What are the benefits of using these approaches?

8.3   What factors favor global product uniformity?

8.4   What factors work against global product uniformity?

8.5   How can a firm decide what degree of international uniformity is desirable in its products?

8.6   Discuss the protectional and promotional aspects of packaging for international markets.

8.7   Evaluate the international labeling situation facing (a) a pharmaceutical firm and (b) a razor-blade manufacturer.

8.8   Explain the problems of brand and trademark protection in international marketing.

8.9   Should a firm have one brand world-wide? Would your answer differ among products, for example, deodorants, photographic film, computers?

8.10 Soft Drink Corporation has the well-known brands "Red Pop" and "1 Up" as well as lesser known brands. The firm recently acquired soft-drink companies in Europe and Latin America with established local brands. Advise the company on its international brand policy.

8.11 What are the considerations involved in establishing a warranty policy for international markets?

8.12 "International standardization of service is impossible to realize." Discuss.

8.13 Industrial Control Corporation began exporting to major European and Latin American markets two years ago. Now service problems are beginning to threaten future sales. What elements or approaches might the company undertake to improve service? What is involved in creating an international service capability?

Further Readings

Books:

"Establishing a Worldwide Patent and Trademark Policy," *Management Monograph No. 25* (New York: Business International, 1965).

Fayerweather, John, *International Marketing,* 2nd ed. (Englewood Cliffs, N.J.: Prentice-Hall, 1970), chap. 5.

Gabriel, Peter P., *The International Transfer of Corporate Skills* (Boston: Harvard University, Division of Research, Graduate School of Business Administration, 1967).

Miracle, Gordon E., and Gerald S. Albaum, *International Marketing Management* (Homewood, Ill.: Richard D. Irwin, 1970), chap. 13.

Robinson, Richard D., *International Management* (New York: Holt, Rinehart and Winston, 1967), pp. 18–24.

Root, Franklin R., *Strategic Planning for Export Marketing* (Scranton, Penna.: International Textbook Company, 1966), chap. 3.

Terpstra, Vern, *American Marketing in the Common Market* (New York: Praeger, 1967), chap. 3.

Articles:

"Avoiding Brand Name Bloopers Overseas," *Business Abroad,* July 24, 1967, pp. 17, 18.

Keegan, Warren J., "Multinational Product Planning: Strategic Alternatives," *Journal of Marketing* (January 1969), pp. 58–62.

Nagashima, Akira, "A Comparison of Japanese and U. S. Attitudes toward Foreign Products," *Journal of Marketing* (January 1970), pp. 68–74.

Schooler, Robert D., "Product Bias in the Central American Market," *Journal of Marketing Research* (November 1956), pp. 394–397.

Sommers, Montrose, and Jerome Kernan, "Why Products Flourish Here, Fizzle There," *Columbia Journal of World Business* (March–April 1967), pp. 89–97.

9

INTERNATIONAL PRODUCT POLICY: PRODUCT LINE AND PRODUCT PLANNING

In Chapter 8, we discussed the management questions concerning the basic product appropriate for international marketing. We also considered the various product features, such as the package, label, and brand name, and the problems these encounter in world markets. In this chapter, we will treat two further aspects of international product policy. The first of these will be the selection and management of the international product line. The problems and opportunities the firm encounters in its various foreign markets often combine to generate an international product line that is not identical to the firm's domestic line.

The second management challenge we will take up is the task of product planning and development in the multinational company. Can foreign markets piggyback on the American new-product activity, or is some kind of international division of labor necessary or desirable within the multinational company? No absolute answers are available to this question, but the approach taken by the firm will be an indicator of how international it really is.

INTERNATIONAL PRODUCT LINE

Deciding on the right individual products for the firm's international marketing is only one aspect of product policy. The next step is to determine what family of products should be offered, that is, the firm's international product line. The general guideline again is that the best product line is the one which best meets the firm's goals in international marketing, or, usually, the line offering the greatest potential for growth and profits.

As a starting point, the firm might examine its domestic product line. Most of the firm's experience, know-how, and competitive advantage is related to its domestic line. The move to foreign markets should be based on these strengths. Other elements in the analysis are the needs and opportunities in foreign markets. The ultimate international product line is the result of some synthesis and compromise among the domestic strengths of the firm and the differing market opportunities in the various foreign countries. Here we will identify some of the factors affecting this synthesis so that better informed decisions can be made as to how to reach it.

Domestic versus International

If a firm has a diversified product line, its international product line is quite unlikely to be identical to its domestic line. The history and rationale for each are different. The domestic line of a firm is a function of many and diverse influences, some of which are tradition, inertia, lack of good cost-profit analysis, and vested interest; others, more defensible, are common raw materials, excess capacity in production or marketing operations, acquisitions or mergers, the competitive situation, and the requirements of the market or channel.

Although the domestic product line is less than the ideal in many companies, the firm has a good opportunity to start with a clean slate internationally. As the vice-president of a pharmaceutical company noted: "We were fortunate in our international product line in being able to start from scratch. We didn't have to carry anybody's favorite products or any weak sisters." In international markets the firm may be able to field an "all-star team" with no weak sisters on it. The strongest products can be selected, making use of the firm's greatest competitive advantage. The firm is, in effect, better able to choose its players and its game abroad than it is at home.

The foreign product line frequently is shorter than the domestic for several reasons. Because of financial, market, or information limitations, the firm usually is not able to carry its full domestic line when it first moves abroad, even if it wants to. However, the firm probably will not want its full line abroad, but only its strongest products where it is best able to compete successfully. By entering a limited product line into foreign markets, the firm also can test the market before taking a bigger plunge. As a few strong products prove themselves, they pave the way for other products that might not be able to make it alone. The initial foreign product line cannot be too narrow, however, because it would spread the entry cost burden over too few products and prejudice the profit prospects. Marketing and administrative costs of foreign sales bear less heavily as they are spread over more products.

We have been considering the management interests of the firm as they affect its international product line, but the external parameters are equally important. Although the international product line can be considered the sum of all the products the firm sells outside its home market, probably the line is composed of many different national product lines; thus the international product line is, in effect, the summation of the firm's national lines. We must look at the factors affecting these national lines in order to understand the complete international line.

National Product Lines

What are the determinants of the firm's product line in a given foreign market? We have mentioned the internal considerations, so let us look at the external factors in particular markets. Differences in the *competitive situation* will cause differences in product lines. If established competition in the foreign market is particularly strong in one of the firm's products, the costs of market penetration might be prohibitive for the newcomer. A product both suitable and desirable on other counts could be ruled out because of this competitive hurdle. As an example, an American firm does not sell margarine in Europe, although that is one of its main products in the United States. The reason is the strongly entrenched position of Unilever in margarine sales throughout Europe.

A different kind of competition is faced by the oil companies in Mexico. Pemex, the government company, has a monopoly on the sale of gasoline, the major companies' principal product. The only items left to them, if they wish to sell in Mexico, are the oil and lubricating products. The reverse situation can also occur. Whereas strong competition in the American market may have kept a company from entering certain product areas, the absence of such competition in foreign markets might make entry of these same products in the foreign line very attractive, even though they are not sold by the company domestically. This is especially true if there is a reasonable carry over of production or marketing know-how on these products.

The *market situation*—that is, consumer tastes, desires, and habits—is another determinant of the national product line. In consumer goods, local tastes might not be receptive to certain models, styles, or flavors. The cost of changing this resistance through promotion might be too great to undertake in terms of the probable sales of the product. Consumer habits also may hinder acceptance of certain products. For example, frozen foods in Europe find consumer acceptance in taste tests but have only limited sales because of lack of freezer capacity in homes.

Similar situations may prevail in the industrial market. The production function is more labor-intensive in some countries than in others, and the kinds of office or plant equipment required would vary accordingly. On another level, if a chemical firm has a line of products for the paper industry, it cannot sell these in those foreign markets that have no paper industry. Thus both the industrial structure and the state of technology in each country cause the industrial-goods marketer to vary his product line from country to country.

Impact of Method of Entry

The nature of the firm's involvement in foreign markets is another product-line determinant. If the firm enters a market through *exports* only, it theoretically has freedom to choose as many or as few products as it wants in each market. Although subject to the market and competitive constraints discussed, the firm still enjoys wide choice beyond these. Once it establishes an export operation, it will feel some pressure to expand the product line to gain economies of scale; but if it uses an export middleman, this pressure becomes less urgent because he can spread his cost over other products he carries, just as the manufacturer's agent does domestically. National preferences, tariffs, and transport costs are other restraints on the export line.

The *licensing* approach offers less freedom in product selection. Appropriate licensees may not be available for all the products a firm wants to enter in a given market; licensees may not have a satisfactory level of technology, or the likely candidates may be licensed already to competitors. Even if the firm finds suitable licensees, possibly they are producing somewhat related products that compete with those of the licensor. The existing product line of the licensee can thus limit the product line of the licensor in that market.

For example, Pepsi Cola pulled a coup on entering the French market when it obtained Perrier as licensee. Perrier gave Pepsi instant widespread distribution in France. However, Perrier also had a line of soft drinks in the noncola areas, which restricted Pepsi's ability to sell its own noncola line in France. Occasionally the firm can overcome such limitations by using different licensees in a country. The feasibility of this course of action depends on such factors as the availability of licensees and the divisibility of the licensor's product line. If the licensor's products are somewhat competitive, the licensee would not want another firm in his country to be involved.

The positive side of licensing's impact on the national product line is that it can avoid tariff and transport cost restrictions which can eliminate items from the export line. Also, preference for national suppliers favors licensing over exporting.

The *joint-venture* approach can restrict the firm's foreign product-line flexibility, too. Most joint ventures of international firms bring together two companies, each with a particular experience and product line, just as does the licensing approach. If the national partner has complementary products in its line, this will confine the product-line expansion possibilities of the international partner. In a "marriage" with a national partner, either via licensing or joint-venture arrangement, the international firm must examine carefully the product dowry of the "bride-to-be." The dowry sought by the international firm is not usually one made up of products but rather one comprised of production and distribution facilities and local knowledge. Joint ventures have a general product-line impact similar to that of licensing.

Wholly owned foreign operations appear to offer the greatest product-line flexibility. Although the usual market and competitive restrictions exist, no national partner limits the product line. The firm can produce any or all of its products in its own plants abroad. This freedom of choice in product line may be more apparent than real, however, because the firm will want to produce only those products that will be profitable in terms of costs and sales. If some products require short production runs, the cost constraint could cause them to be omitted from the line even though no other restrictions exist. Of course, if these products could be imported, that cost constraint would no longer apply.

We have discussed the impact of the nature of foreign involvement on international product-line decisions as if the firm were entering a foreign market by one method exclusively. Actually, many firms enter some foreign markets using two or more approaches in combination. Such combinations increase the product-line options open to the international company in different national or regional markets. The limitations inherent in any one approach no longer apply when different approaches are combined.

The Westinghouse Company has chosen the licensing approach for several of its products in the European market. In spite of the product-line limitations in licensing, Westinghouse overcame these, at least partially, by two methods. First, it expanded its European line with a wide range of complementary licensees in different member countries of the Common Market. Its EEC product line could thus be rather broad even though limited in any one country.

Second, by integrating its licensee suppliers with components from the United States, Westinghouse landed some large complex equipment orders that would normally be impossible to obtain by a licensing approach, or even by export, because of national preferences. As this example indicates, product-line strategies abroad cannot be determined merely by considering the advantages and disadvantages of different approaches. It is rather a question of the overall integrated strategy of management in foreign markets.

Management of the International Product Line

When the firm becomes an international marketer, it has to make an initial selection of its international product line. Even if the initial selection were optimal, internal and external factors may change, requiring corresponding adaptation of the product line. Part of the marketing management task is the development and maintenance of the optimal international product line in the face of changing conditions and pressures.

Some of the pressures for change arise within the company itself. For example, company goals for world markets may expand. If foreign growth potential in the company's industry looks more dynamic than domestic potential, the firm may decide to expand its foreign commitment, entering more products in more markets. As a company's international involvement changes from exclusive reliance on exports to a combined approach, including foreign production, the right mix of products also will change. Usually the greater foreign commitment (represented by the firm's foreign production and investment) means an expanding international product line.

The company's domestic product line changes with time as a result of many pressures, including acquisitions, mergers, or new product development. With a greater variety of product resources to draw upon, the international marketer is apt to expand his foreign offerings. In fact, often these newer products are the ones most attractive abroad as well as at home.

External pressures for product-line change are more numerous. To analyze these, the firm might review all the external parameters that bore on the initial product-line selection, note how these have changed, and evaluate the implications of the changes for its current product line. Some of the parameters to consider are consumer income, tastes, and habits; the state of technology and the industrial structure in different markets; government restrictions and taxes, including tariffs; and competition. All these are dynamic factors affecting the firm's sales and profits. Adaptation in the international product line is a major tool of the marketing manager in maintaining a strong company share in a changing market.

Drop-Add Changes

Although recognizing the pressures on the international product line is important, identifying and evaluating them is only part of the manager's task. He must make the appropriate responses to these pressures; that is, he must manage the product line. A key to product-line management is knowing when to drop and add products. Some question arises concerning the firm's approach to dropping and adding products: Can it be done on a global or even international level, or is it best kept at the national level?

DROPPING PRODUCTS In theory, a product should be dropped when it is unprofitable—or even when it is profitable, if the resources allocated to it could earn a higher return elsewhere. Some of the parameters involved are the costs of maintaining the product; its importance to consumers and retailers; costs and rewards of product rejuvenation; and costs and returns of other alternatives. The value of these parameters is likely to vary from market to market, so there is probably no single international solution.

If we assume one production source for a particular product, the multinational marketer should evaluate all the costs and benefits, not only in its domestic market but throughout its global market area, before making a decision to drop the product. Although the product may not be profitable in the firm's important domestic market, it could be in the growth phase of its life cycle in several foreign markets with different income levels and habits. The firm might drop the product domestically but accelerate marketing in the product's growth markets abroad. At first, the situation would involve domestic production but exclusively foreign marketing of the product, but eventually foreign production too would be likely.

If the product has several production sources as well as several markets, the firm must evaluate a greater range of possible source and market combinations before making a decision to drop the product. Such a situation could lead to different product lines for different markets and away from a uniform international line. Some diversity of product line should not displease the company, however, as its goal, presumably, is to have the most profitable—not the most uniform—line.

ADDING PRODUCTS Experience shows that companies' product lines tend to grow, both internationally and domestically. Thus adding products is an important concern of the international marketing manager. As new products come from product development activity, market opportunities, mergers and acquisitions, and so on, decisions must be made as to their addition to the existing line. The standard decision rule is simple to state: Add the product if this represents the most profitable use of company resources.

In the international company the necessary cost-benefit analysis would need to be done on either a national-market or a regional-grouping basis. Not only does the number of markets make the problem complex; also the variations in both company situation and external environment among its foreign markets make evaluating the cost-benefit factors there difficult and uncertain.

Procter and Gamble (P&G) has added many products to its original soaps and detergents line in the United States. In Europe, the company has stayed with soaps and detergents. However, Mr. Morgens, president, said, "We want to build an organization and business in Europe as strong as we have in the U.S. When we decide the organization in Europe is ready, we will add other products just as we have here."[1]

On the *cost* side, an international company may have several possible production sources for the new product. Production costs (including labor and raw materials) will vary from nation to nation as will other cost factors such as tariffs, special taxes, and regulations. Marketing costs also differ for the same firm in its different markets. Wholesale and retail margins vary even among European Common Market countries. The firms own product line and marketing mix might not be the same in neighboring countries.

On the *benefit* side, the benefits to the firm of adding the new product are dissimilar in its various markets around the world. In each country, sales of the product will depend on local tastes and income levels, the nature of competitive offerings, as well as other market factors. The quality of the company's intelligence on foreign markets is usually lower than in the domestic market, and also the decision maker is further removed from the market, unless the decision is decentralized to a national manager. These latter two factors make the analysis even more uncertain than domestic projections. The marketing manager must make skillful use of the best decision techniques, including subjective probabilities. Comparative analysis of international markets (discussed in Chapter 7) is one useful technique to increase his understanding of individual foreign markets.

The drop-add practices of the international marketer involve a number of national decisions. For two reasons these decisions are different from those facing national firms in the same markets: (1) The multinational firm wants to optimize its global profits, not just those in certain national markets; (2) an international decision must take into account more variables both on the supply and demand side and on the cost and benefit side. As a result, the international firm may not add a product even though it would be profitable to do so in a particular country, or, on the other hand, it may add a product that is not at all profitable in a particular country.

[1] *Wall Street Journal*, September 2, 1969, p. 26.

The government of a less developed country, Paratina, approaches a large international food marketer operating within its borders. It requests the firm to market a high-protein–low-cost food product. In addition to the normal profitability study of the Paratina market, the firm would ask some further questions. Does this product have possibilities in other low-income markets? Could Paratina serve as a test market on this product for our international division? What would be the government or public relations pay-offs in such a venture—in Paratina and elsewhere? What kind of social responsibility does a foreign food company have in less developed countries, and how does this product relate to that? It is unlikely that the decision would be made only in terms of the Paratina market.

A similar situation would face an agricultural-equipment manufacturer asked to market a special tractor suitable for small-scale farming. The question could arise in different ways in other product lines and markets. For example, a European marketing subsidiary of a diversified electronics company wants to add a small electric organ to its product line. The subsidiary says it can purchase the product private-branded from another European producer, if the parent company does not wish to manufacture it. Marketing management at European headquarters and the international division would try to relate this request to their desire for the optimum international product line.

Conclusion

Thus we see that the task of managing the product line internationally is similar to the domestic challenge, that is, maintaining the optimum product line. The technique of cost-benefit analysis is also the same. Despite these surface similarities, however, the problems of product-line management facing the multinational firm are much more complex than those encountered in a purely national operation.

Some of these complexities have been noted and need merely be reviewed here in closing our product-line discussion. The multinational company must consider the product line in relation to many national markets (over 100 for some firms). There are probably different national production sources with individual costs and production possibilities. (The economist might say they have different comparative cost structures.) The decision maker also has problems because of the diversity and quality of his information inputs. The number of options is further affected by the firm's level of involvement in different national markets. Finally, different competitive situations and governmental constraints must be factored into the decision model.

INTERNATIONAL PRODUCT PLANNING AND DEVELOPMENT

Our last topic under international product policy should perhaps be the first. Placing it in this order, however, reflects more the real world than a theoretical approach would. Although product planning and development is in some sense an initial or beginning marketing activity, in reality, every company engaging in international marketing has an existing product or line of products. Product planning and development, therefore, is concerned with the future products and product line of the company.

Under this subject we will consider three primary activities: (1) the search for new product ideas; (2) the evaluation of these ideas and selection of candidates for development; and (3) the actual development of the new products. These are the steps undertaken by a purely domestic company as well as by a multinational company. We will be concerned with the impact of international operations on the management of this product development activity.

The rationale of new product development is not hard to find. It has become a cliché to say that we live in a rapidly changing world, but this cliché cannot be ignored by marketing management. Consumer tastes and habits change about as fast as technology. Competition is ever quicker with its imitations and substitutes. These forces combine to shorten the life cycles of the firm's products. To maintain company growth and profit requires a constant introduction of new products. A firm that does a better job than its competitors in this regard can gain an added advantage: an image as a progressive, innovative company. In international marketing, this image can be an important promotional asset. For example, companies associated with the American space program have gained easier foreign market sales because of this image.

Strategy of Product Development

Underlying the process of product planning and development must be a well-conceived statement of company strategy and philosophy concerning this activity. This statement should be developed at the highest level in the firm, because the statement determines what kind of business the firm will be in tomorrow.

Product development involves many technical and practical problems, but success in product development demands more than just the resolution of these problems. *Success also demands the formulation of a sound framework relating corporate goals, resources, and opportunities to the product-planning process.* From the company's viewpoint, new product ideas have no intrinsic goodness (or badness). New products are good for the company only insofar as they aid in achieving company goals through the best use of company resources. The company's strategy statement on product development gives the guidance necessary for success.

Generation of Product Ideas

Within the guidelines of the corporate strategy statement, the first step in product planning is to generate a list of new product ideas from which the most attractive ones can be selected for development. Some of the many possible sources of new product ideas are (1) company employees, (2) company research and development activity, (3) customers, (4) distributors, (5) salesmen, (6) inventors, and (7) competitors. All of these are available to the international company as well as to the domestic firm. An added dimension to the international firm's situation, however, is whether it makes use of these idea sources in all its foreign markets. In other words, is the firm an international marketer with a purely domestic product-planning activity? Such a position is possible. Later we will examine whether it is desirable.

Organizations and publications that report internationally on new inventions, products, and processes—including new patents—represent a source of product ideas especially interesting to the international firm. As this kind of service becomes more comprehensive and more readily available, the firm's need for in-house research along the same lines will decrease correspondingly. For example, a major American chemical company maintains an office in its Swiss headquarters which has as its only task the perusal and noting of new product ideas in European trade, company, government, and patent office publications. Visits to the international trade fairs, especially in Europe, are important even for domestic companies. Some of the fairs are general industrial expositions, but others are formed around a specific industry or product, for example, photo, automotive, or aircraft and space equipment (Paris Air Show).

The planning programs of governments and international agencies are another source of ideas for international marketers. In particular, these planning reports yield sales leads, so they are publicized by the Commerce Department and other international business organizations. In addition to sales leads, companies can get new product ideas from studying the plans, needs, and desires of the world's nations and groups of nations. Because these plans cover all phases of economic activity, most firms can benefit from studying them. Projects in agriculture, infrastructure development, health, education, housing, and so on, can mean new product opportunities to equipment and chemical manufacturers, food and pharmaceutical firms, publishing houses, and school-supply companies. It is important to note that these product ideas would not generally arise in conducting normal operations in America because special foreign market needs must be met by special products.

When Turkey decided to create its own truck-building industry, it wanted maximum local content in its vehicles. Chrysler designed a completely new truck that was simpler to put together than the imported models. The Chrysler subsidiary in Turkey turned out over 4,000 trucks a year and saved Turkey between $5 million and $10 million in foreign exchange.

Sweden's Tetra Pak has been one of Europe's leading manufacturers of packaging machinery. For over a decade it has had a close association with two United Nations agencies—the Food and Agriculture Organization (FAO) and the United Nations Children's Fund (UNICEF). As a result, Tetra Pak has supplied machinery for over 100 projects throughout the developing countries and is usually in on the planning stage.

A number of American companies are working on low-cost–high-protein foods for less developed countries. Six companies have even received research grants from AID to help them develop such products. Among the companies are Pillsbury, Monsanto, and Swift & Company.

A rather surprising example comes from the Ling-Temco-Vought aerospace division. In 1965, LTV made a proposal to officials of ECAFE (the UN's Economic Commission on Asia and the Far East). The result in 1968 was the "Kid," a completely amphibious, half-ton capacity, all-purpose vehicle. It was the first step toward replacement of the water buffalo in agriculture and transportation in the Far East. In demonstrations, the "Kid" moved steadily through a flooded rice paddy, but a water buffalo bogged down. The "Kid" moved up to twenty miles per hour on land. The vehicle was developed to be in economic reach of Asian governments and individuals. The price was estimated to be about $1,500.[2]

This kind of new product idea source has several advantages. First, because the idea is generated by a market need, its realization is less speculative than that of an idea based only on technological possibilities. Second, these market needs are high-priority national or international items, thus quite assured of financing. For example, the United Nations Development Program submitted ninety-five new projects in 1968 and the approved financing for these was $232 million. Part of this was United Nations money, but the rest was from the recipient governments. Third, responding to market needs represents a healthy market-oriented way to get new product ideas. Besides the possible market pay-offs, the firm can acquire a more favorable company image by identifying itself seriously with the problems of its market in this way. Fourth, the firm may reap rewards in other markets by selling there the product originally developed for one particular country.

Goodyear developed a tire for the tough driving conditions on Peru's roads. These tires contained a higher percentage of natural rubber than those manufactured elsewhere, and they had better tread. As a result, Peruvians preferred them to imported tires. The performance reputation spread to other countries with similar problems.[3]

A novel but important source of product ideas for international business is a look back into American technological history. Firms accustomed to operating only in America or other advanced industrialized economies sometimes forget that the whole world does not operate in the same technological age. The Vietnam war handicapped the United States because it was, in many ways, a war fought with old-fashioned technology, neutralizing America's technical edge over the enemy. The Navy developed a "new" plane for

---

[2] *International Commerce*, May 6, 1968, p. 6.
[3] *Business Latin America*, July 3, 1969, p. 216.

Vietnam. Although it was jet powered, its speed was under 600 miles per hour and its chief virtues were slowness, cheapness, and simple gadgetry.[4] Similar kinds of "backward" product development can be profitable in many foreign markets. According to good marketing logic, the best product for a market is one that best fits its use-conditions and buyer-consumption systems, not necessarily the one that uses the most advanced technology of the producer.

An exporter of agricultural machinery designed a new hand-operated *grain thresher for his export markets. The machine received its inspiration from century-old models on display at the Smithsonian Institution.*

National Cash Register developed the NCR 80, a crank-operated *cash register. It is selling thousands of the models in the Philippines, the Orient, Latin America, and Spain. With only half the parts of more advanced registers, the machine sells for about half the price of the cheapest models available in America.*[5]

A related source of new product ideas is to visualize products in terms of the foreign buyer's consumption system. This concept is not new in America[6] but needs greater application in international marketing. Although, as we remarked, the marketer must first visualize the firm's product or potential product as part of the foreign user's overall consumption system, as a second and critical aspect of this activity he must eliminate cultural bias in interpreting that consumption system. Many products have status as well as functional aspects, and these will often vary from market to market. Unless the marketer is careful to remove his culturally tinted glasses, he is likely to misinterpret the relative role of function and status and make errors in product design and promotion. The same holds true in analyzing the functions or activities of the buyer in connection with a product. All over the world people engage in the same activities: eating, sleeping, playing, working, engaging in agriculture or other kinds of production. Although the activities are the same, the way they are done and their cultural significance can vary, and the differences are important for product development. The following example illustrates this.

Colgate Palmolive Company sells soaps and detergents all over the world. Detergent sales are very low in many less developed countries although clothes are washed there with reasonable frequency. A major deterrent to detergent sales is the fact that women wash their clothes by streams where detergents would be wasted. Colgate asked an inventor to develop a simple manually operated washer. The device resembles an old-fashioned butter churn and is

[4] *Time,* November 17, 1967, p. 32.
[5] *Wall Street Journal,* May 27, 1969, p. 1.
[6] See Boyd and Levy, "New Dimensions in Consumer Analysis," *Harvard Business Review* (November–December 1963), pp. 129–32.

operated by a pumping action. It gets clothes clean and eliminates some of the drudgery of the earlier method—and detergents work well in it. The product's price was set at about $10 and was successfully test-marketed in Mexico. Colgate also planned to introduce a domestic model for summer campers.

Product Ideas in the International Company

Probably the international company will do best to take its product ideas from all its international sources. A possible exception is in areas of the most advanced technology where *only* technological considerations are important, such as computers, jet aircraft, or space-exploration equipment. Even in these areas, however, domestic orientation in product ideas is unlikely to be wise, first because use conditions or possible applications can be expected to vary in different parts of the world, even on high-technology items, and second because it is not only arrogant but also dangerous to assume that planners or researchers in one country will come up with all the best product possibilities.

Much is made today of the economies of scale in large research and development centers. But although their output has indeed been respectable, still the engineers, scientists, and thinkers working in these centers are all subject to the same environmental conditions and influences; their newspapers, recreation, and social-civic-economic concerns are similar. Such a homogeneous situation can lead to a certain conformity in thinking, or a form of "tunnel vision." More idea centers spread out among many different countries are likely to provide a more complete range of new product ideas.[7] In regard to all these products where market conditions are more important than technological conditions, the argument for international inputs on new product ideas is much stronger. Even for IBM, a company strong in technology, product specifications include inputs from at least twenty countries around the world.[8]

If international input is desired for new product planning, how can it be achieved in the company's organization? Much will depend on the volume of the firm's international business and the nature of its involvement in foreign markets. The firm with a small volume of foreign sales has fewer resources and facilities for getting new product ideas from abroad. It can subscribe to published services or hire a research organization on a retainer basis, but it probably cannot do much within its own organization. As foreign sales grow, the options available to the firm also increase.

EXPORTER   The firm involved only via exporting is concerned about ideas from its present and potential markets but it is not physically present in these markets. It does, however, have some kind of distributor representative in its present markets. If the company's line is important enough to the distributor,

---

[7] See Jewkes et al., *The Sources of Invention* (New York: St. Martin's Press, 1959).
[8] *Business Week*, December 19, 1970, p. 140.

he can be counted as part of the company's intelligence network. (See Chapter 7.) As his sales force contacts the market, the ideas and insights they gain relative to the firm's product line should be available to the firm. Obtaining this kind of cooperation from foreign distributors requires skilled management of a sort we discuss in Chapter 11.

The exporting firm need not rely only on distributor cooperation, however; depending on its product, it may receive some feedback from customers. More importantly, the export manager and perhaps marketing or technical specialists from the firm can visit foreign distributors and markets personally. This kind of specialized observation of differing competitive environments and use conditions can be highly rewarding in terms of ideas for new products or applications. The extent of such visits will be determined partly by the sales volume supporting them and partly by the aggressiveness of management in international business. Firms in generally similar situations vary widely in the amount of attention and support they give to foreign markets.

LICENSOR   International business involvement through foreign licensees poses particular problems as well as opportunities for the licensor. In the strict sense, the licensee is an independent party, much like the foreign distributor. He is bound to pay royalties on what he produces and sells in his market, but usually he is not bound to cooperate in other ways. Nevertheless, licensors have gained profitable new product ideas from their licensees.

By the very nature of the arrangement, the licensee has some technical expertise relating to the licensor's product. Because of this expertise and his experience in marketing the product in his country, he might well come up with new applications or product ideas. This happens often enough that many licensors make contract provision to benefit from it. Cross-licensing clauses can be included in contracts, too, whereby new product developments connected with the licensed product are made available to the other party, whether developed by the licensee or the licensor.

JOINT VENTURE   The joint-venture approach to foreign markets gives the international firm a management voice in the local company. Whether this is an advantage for new product ideas depends on several factors. Generally speaking, the greater the equity and management role of the international company, and the more passive or neutral the national partner, the more the local venture can be considered an integral part of the international operation. If the national partner has a significant equity (this can be less than 50 percent) in the venture and a producing-marketing interest of his own, he will have a great interest in claiming, or at least sharing, new product ideas and developments.

The national partner may be relatively passive in the management of the venture if it has no marketing interests of its own, as, for example, when it is a government agency or a party with a purely financial interest in the venture. In the latter situation, the international firm would probably have more complete access to and control of new product developments. In any joint venture, the rights of the national partner must be safeguarded but conflict is less likely when the national partner has no marketing interests of its own.

WHOLLY OWNED SUBSIDIARIES   Wholly owned foreign subsidiaries are without the constraints found in other kinds of involvement. The problems of encouraging cooperation or sharing results no longer exist. The only limitations to using foreign subsidiaries as part of international product planning lie in the size of the foreign subsidiary and in the company's international organization setup.

Where the subsidiary is a small operation, it is able to do less in all aspects of product planning. However, it should be involved in some aspects so that its market is represented. Foreign subsidiary participation in product planning and development will depend further on whether corporate management feels it necessary to involve the subsidiary. We suggested that, for optimal results, foreign subsidiaries and markets should be participants in the product-planning process. The new products will best fit international markets if these markets have been consulted in their planning.

The minimum role for the subsidiary is the assignment of responsibility to one person for new product ideas. The other extreme is for the subsidiary to duplicate the product-planning organization of the domestic operation. Although a number of companies do make new product ideas a responsibility of subsidiary managers, hardly any go to the aforementioned extreme because the duplication of effort would be wasteful. The synergism of multinational operations comes from elimination of such duplication and the establishment of an appropriate international division of labor. Thus, although all foreign subsidiaries are represented, they do not all have to have a complete activity, as would purely national concerns in these markets. Further and more extensive discussion of organizational aspects will follow the sections on Screening Product Ideas and Product Development.

Until now we have mentioned only the international side of the company's operations. For many multinational companies, especially American, domestic operations are the principal source of new product ideas. This must be counted as part of their strength in multinational operations. The international new product activity should be part of the total corporate new product program. General discussions of product development in a domestic company are available in regular marketing texts and we will not repeat them here. Our emphasis is on the complications and contributions of international operations to the firm's new product activity. It bears repeating that there must be appropriate collaboration or integration of the domestic and international sides of the new product activity. Otherwise, the firm will have duplication of effort and suboptimization in its total operations.

Screening Product Ideas

An effective search for new product ideas will turn up candidates from all the firm's markets. The next step is to evaluate these and select the ones most promising for further research and development. The relevant questions are, Where is the screening done? and, How is the screening done?

Where?

An initial screening of a new product idea should be conducted in the market where the idea originates. If the firm has no subsidiaries but only agent or distributor representation, however, the screening would have to be done in a neighboring country with a subsidary or at regional or international head-quarters. There are two advantages to doing the initial screening at the national level: (1) It helps to assure that the ideas in the organization are not merely thought up to meet a quota or some other arbitrary standard but rather have met at least a preliminary feasibility test; and (2) it educates subsidiary management in a useful kind of product-market analysis. The contribution of national subsidiaries would, of course, vary according to their size and sophistication.

The initial national screening, although useful, should not be too rigorous. Subsidiary personnel in general would not be able to conduct a rigorous screening, they would lack inputs from the rest of the international operation, and several subsidiaries might come up with similar product ideas. For all to do a comprehensive screening job on the same idea would be wasteful. Furthermore, each of several subsidiaries might reject an idea on the basis of its own national market situation, whereas in a multinational context the idea might be extremely viable. A modest market in many countries could add up to a very profitable volume internationally.

After a preliminary evaluation at the national level, a more comprehensive review can be conducted at either the regional or the international level. Although the regional organization can play a useful role in coordinating new product activity in the region, its review is no substitute for the global view of international headquarters. Giving the region too much autonomy on this question can lead to suboptimization because new product feasibility generally must be evaluated in broader, if not in global, terms. Although the regional organization might conduct the initial or intermediate screening, it should never be responsible for the final evaluation of new product ideas.

Not only in the initial screening can national or regional organizations participate. Once the international or corporate new product group has collected ideas from all foreign and domestic sources, it will again pass by the subsidiaries. Each idea has had a preliminary evaluation at the national level and perhaps a further review at the parent-company level, but not all the ideas have been seen by all national members of the company. The national com-panies must market these new products, if adopted, and their specialized knowledge of their own markets can add very useful second-level evaluations to ideas originating in other country's operations. In this way, each new product idea gets a comprehensive global evaluation so that the firm can make more optimal new product decisions.

The top management of the Singer Company made a decision to market white goods (appliances) in Europe. When the idea was presented in Europe, the Germany subsidiary disagreed and suggested they market TV sets instead of white goods. The subsidiary's position was supported by market research

*and local experience. Shortly after, the white goods cartel in Germany col-
lapsed and prices declined severely. TV prices, however, remained stable. In
short, the subsidiary's viewpoint saved management from a serious error.*[9]

*When an IBM World Trade company has an idea for a new product, it
draws up a documented study known as a market requirement procedure that
goes to IBM World Trade headquarters for review. The case study includes
factual and intuitive data and covers such items as specifications for the
machine, functions of the machine, and sales estimates. The details are then
disseminated to all local and foreign offices, which in turn document their
need for such a machine. If enough demand for the product is assured, the
original request is sent to IBM's systems development division for a feasibility
study, a look at the proposed equipment from the point of view of development
and production costs and other factors.*[10]

The Screening Process

The purpose of generating new product ideas is to have a wide list of alternatives from which to choose. The goal of the screening process is to assure that
the best products are chosen from this list. As usual in our discussions, we
define the best products as those with the greatest probability of increasing
overall company growth and profits. Occasionally other corporate goals will
affect product choices, and we will note these as they arise. Although the
screening process itself can be rather complicated—many companies have
developed checklists or grids to aid in it—our discussion will be rather
simple and straightforward, emphasizing the international dimensions.

ORGANIZATIONAL IMPLICATIONS   An effective new product activity must have
continuing support in the organization: Funds must be allocated to it and
personnel made responsible for it. One organizational method used by some
companies is to establish a corporate "new product" or "product planning"
group or committee, perhaps headed by a high-level executive such as a vice-
president for research and development, as is the case with a large manufacturer of farm equipment. This corporate group can either have total
international responsibility or else coordinate various subgroups in the international and domestic divisions.

At the regional or national-subsidiary level is a product planning person
or group that reports to the corporate group. As noted earlier, each national
organization in the company should devote some effort to product planning,
even though the amount of time and the number of people involved will vary
according to the size of the firm's operations in the country. Although each
national organization must be represented in product planning, their separate
efforts must be coordinated centrally to avoid duplication. We gave some
indication of an appropriate division of labor within the company in the

[9] "Introducing a New Product in a Foreign Market," *Management Monograph No. 33*
(New York: Business International, 1966), p. 12.
[10] "Introducing a New Product in a Foreign Market," p. 15.

preceding section on where the screening process should be done. We described a three-step process: (1) initial screening of an idea in the national organization where it originates; (2) total international screening by a corporate group; and (3) the major ideas circulated to all national organizations so that all ideas receive a screening in terms of national market suitability.

Screening Criteria

Because of the many ramifications in developing a new product, product ideas are best screened on the basis of several criteria, rather than on only one. Expected profit might be one such suitable criterion, but it is itself a function of many other variables. In the screening process, these variables should be specifically identified to show how the expected profit figure is derived. When a number of variables or criteria are used for screening, generally the product ideas scoring highest on the greatest number of criteria are those selected for development. We will use a twofold classification of criteria to simplify discussion: (1) productions factors and (2) marketing factors.[11]

PRODUCTION CRITERIA   A product is more likely to be profitable if it relates favorably to the existing production capabilities of the firm. The more the new product utilizes the existing plant capacity and equipment, technical know-how and labor skills, the less the product will cost in terms of both money and learning time. If the product uses the same raw materials or by-products of materials already used by the firm, so much the better. The diversified company obviously has a wider range of product choices because of its diversified production skills and facilities. Perhaps not so obviously, the multinational company also has a wider range of product choice. First, the company is probably more diversified than it would be if it were not international (see our discussion of product line, showing the diversifying effects of international operations); and second, if the firm is producing in many countries, probably it has a somewhat different production function—that is, a different mix of the factors of production—in each. This fact of international economic life the economists call comparative advantage.

As regards product choice, these international differences mean that the product which is not suited to an American plant might nevertheless fit in well at the company's French or Brazilian plant. Conversely, although a product idea from a foreign subsidiary might not match local production capability, it may be well suited to the production facilities in a more advanced country or in the firm's American facilities. The various production variables add up to some kind of cost figure for the product. If labor costs are important for some new product, for example, it could be that a foreign production source gives a much more favorable new product evaluation than does the American plant. In this way, the multinational company applies the principle of comparative advantage to its own benefit. Thus, the international-

---

[11] See Rewoldt et al., *Introduction to Marketing Management* (Homewood, Ill.: Richard D. Irwin, 1969), pp. 157–166.

ization and diversification of production facilities in the multinational company give it a wider range of alternatives when evaluating new product ideas on the production criteria.

MARKETING CRITERIA   The checklist of production variables helps the evaluator to envision the supply side of the new product picture. For the demand side of the picture, marketing criteria are needed. Again the firm would benefit if the new product were to fit in with the marketing skills and facilities it is currently using. As with the production match, this piggybacking possibility means easier introduction and economies of scale. Some of the marketing criteria considered by the firm are its marketing skills, the distribution channels it is using, good will attached to the company name or brands, life cycles of existing and proposed products, and relation of new product sales to existing product sales; that is, Does the new product enhance or replace the old? Also affecting the marketing evaluation are the competitive situation, and, perhaps most important of all considerations, market demand for the new product.

Obviously these marketing considerations for new product evaluation can vary considerably in the firm's foreign markets. The firm's marketing know-how should be a common denominator running through its international operations, but such uniformity is usually more a goal than an accomplished fact. The distribution channels available and used by the firm are seldom identical in all markets. Except for a few such names as IBM, Coca-Cola, and Singer, the consumer image and good will attached to the company name and brands will probably vary widely from market to market.

The life cycles of present and proposed products, too, will tend to vary in different world markets. This can be an advantage for the firm in that it can count on a longer overall product life in its international operations than in any of its national operations. As we demonstrated in our discussion of product line, the competitive opportunities and challenges for new products will vary from country to country. Market demand for the new product will be partly a function of factors peculiar to each country, such as tastes, habits, and income levels.

In an evaluation of new product ideas according to these marketing variables, each potential new product will probably have a somewhat different score in each country. Common denominators may appear, however, that indicate an international market for the product, but this is more likely among products such as industrial goods where purely technical considerations predominate. For other products, the firm will seek the largest possible market area with a reasonable degree of commonality.

If the most desirable market, a global market, is not feasible for the product, the international firm can next consider groups of countries as constituting an interesting market. These groups can be regions, such as Latin America or Europe, or groups of industrialized nations or less developed countries. Finally, the firm can occasionally find single national markets that are large enough to warrant a particular new product development, as is, of course, the United States market. Although development of a new product for a single national market can sometimes be sound strategy, more frequently, realization of the synergistic effects possible from carrying a product to several or all of its international markets is the firm's best course.

In the screening of new product ideas from both the production and marketing sides, the fact of international operations adds a new dimension to the analysis. The review becomes more complex but, at the same time, more interesting to the firm because its options increase—alternatives are open to it that are closed to domestic firms. For example, the common yes-or-no answers to product screening in the domestic market are replaced in the international market by, "Yes, this is O.K. for Europe," "Yes, this is good for our less developed country markets," or "Yes, that looks good for Latin America. Later we'll see where we can move it next."

In this discussion on product screening we have not used detailed checklists or grids, both of which can be developed and can be very useful to a company. In the same way and for the same reason, we have kept our discussion of organization for new product evaluation rudimentary. Our focus is not on the technical aspects of the question, which, although important, must usually be tailored to the particular needs of an individual company (the case approach). We have emphasized, therefore, the international dimensions and implications of the question. In the same vein we will now look at two further aspects of the screening process.

LEGAL AND OTHER INFLUENCES   Thus far we have considered the beneficial impact of international operations on the new product process. As we turn now to legal and other factors that bear on new products, we will see some of the more negative aspects of international operations. These can be called constraints in the most restrictive sense of the word. The legal part of new product screening is very technical and must be done by corporate legal staff or outside experts, but we will list some of the questions they must answer in their legal investigation.

1. Does the product fall within the legal scope of the company's charter? Is the idea already patented?
2. Can we patent it in the relevant markets? What conflicts are possible on the product claim? (The same questions would apply to brand and trademark production).
3. What import or export regulations might apply to this product?
4. What packaging, labeling, or other product requirements affect this product in our foreign markets?

To the extent that the answers to these questions differ from country to country, the advantages of international operations are compromised. On this matter, the international marketing manager finds himself in the same camp with the free-trading economist. From his macroeconomic viewpoint, the free trader says that the international division of labor is advanced and the wealth of nations is augmented by unfettered trade. From his microeconomic viewpoint, the manager favors free trade because the multinational company can operate most efficiently when freed from barriers. The two are really talking about the same thing, that is, how to achieve efficiency and greater mobility of resources in the world economy.

Two other factors that may be important in the new product evaluation process are (1) the existence of special company goals in addition to profits and growth and (2) the global logistics situation of the firm. In the former situation, the product selection process may lead to different results; that is, some products may be accepted even if they do not score highest on the profit and growth indicators. For example, a firm might make such a decision on the basis of certain social or economic problems in its markets or because it wishes to create a particular image for itself, say, good citizen, progressive, concerned.

Products selected to meet these goals might not be immediately related to profit maximization. This is not to say, however, that the company should not have these other goals; long-run profit and growth are probably increasingly related to overall corporate behavior and image. Food companies asked to develop high-protein–low cost-foods in less developed countries where they are operating might find it difficult to refuse, even if they want to. Although they will try to seek the most profitable solution to the problem, they will also be concerned about government relations, company image, and the international repercussions of any decision.

The international distribution or logistics situation of the firm can be another major constraint on product selection. We have been considering the advantages to the firm of multinational markets for its new products, but the availability of these markets cannot be automatically assumed. Not only may the aforementioned legal barriers limit access to some countries, but also the costs and burdens of international distribution can restrict market accessibility. In theory, international operations give the firm an attractive variety of production sources and market combinations. In practice, the number of combinations is limited by legal restrictions, distribution costs, and other barriers.

Perishable products or those with high transport costs may be limited to serving national or regional markets from a given production source. The firm should keep in mind, however, that transportation barriers tend to diminish steadily with time as technical progress enables movement of more and more goods internationally each year. Developments in transportation, such as pipelines, containerization, and giant jets; and in processing, such as freezing, dehydrating, and liquefying, mean that yesterday's domestic product becomes tomorrow's international product. Tariff barriers, although still effectively adding to the costs of distribution, were also greatly reduced in the twenty-five years following World War II. The future course of tariffs, however, is less predictable than that of transportation.

Product Development

Hopefully some of the new product ideas have survived the screening process to emerge as candidates for development. The screening process is necessarily rigorous because the costs of preparing a product for the market are so great that not many errors can be permitted. Once selected, the product candidates must go through what is often a long, expensive, and complicated process before actually reaching the marketplace. Engineering, production, and marketing are involved in this development process, as well as other factors from inside and outside the organization. To coordinate the complex endeavor, the firm may use some form of critical-path scheduling.

We will not go into the engineering or technical aspects of product development here; our concern is the management of product development in the multinational company. The question the company faces is simple: Where should we conduct our product development activity? Is everything to be done in our American (domestic) operations, or should some or all of it be done in our foreign operations? The same questions apply to product testing and market testing. *How* product development or testing is done is a subject for another course; management of the process is the aspect with international import.

Domestic Product Development for Global Markets

Among the strong arguments for the firm's conducting all product development in its domestic operations are the following: In its domestic market the firm usually has the greatest experience and expertise, as well as the largest technical staff and the best facilities; and centralizing all product development, domestic and international, may give significant economies of scale as compared with those obtainable through a fragmented effort. To those who say that foreign market needs must be considered, it might be answered that, with a proper screening process and good international communications, the needs of foreign markets can be fed into the domestic development activity. Furthermore, to the extent that engineering and technical factors predominate, little difference may exist between foreign markets and the domestic market.

The aerospace division of Ling-Temco-Vought (LTV) developed a mechanical substitute for the water buffalo in South East Asia (see p. 248). This product with little or no domestic market was completely developed in the United States. Some of the reasons are the following: (1) LTV had no foreign production or development facilities and limited foreign business. (2) The local product requirements were fed into the American development activity. (3) Although the product met specific Asian needs, technical considerations were considered uppermost. However, later results in the field showed that more field testing would have eliminated several serious problems.

The nature of the company's involvement in international business also determines where its product development will take place. For example, firms operating internationally only through exporting or licensing cannot realistically consider developing products abroad. The shared-control problems of joint ventures hinder the firm's product development in markets where it has such ventures. The agreement might specify areas in which the joint venture will engage in product development activity and exclude other areas in which the partners might come into conflict. Even the firm that completely controls its foreign operations may have difficulty getting qualified personnel for product development. The problems of control and protecting the secrecy of new product activities may be greater in foreign markets. Finally, if a firm has relatively small international operations, it might be able to support only one development activity, which would be the one it already has domestically.

In addition to these strong arguments for centralizing product development in the domestic operation are others that may be less defensible. Because the firm's domestic activity is already set up, it can be argued that expanding it is more efficient than setting up new product development activities overseas. This argument may have much validity in the short run, but not so much over the long term. Chauvinism, or excessive national pride, which is often accompanied by a certain feeling of mistrust of foreigners, may be another factor affecting this decision as well as many others in international business. Such emotional considerations are the more troublesome because they are unstated and often unconscious.

International Product Development

Because of all the strong arguments and pressures for a centralized product development activity, that many firms which market internationally develop all their products domestically is not surprising. Indeed, most international marketers probably do so, although not the largest ones which are the most visible and the most reported on in the news media. Today, however, numerous and growing countervailing pressures are forcing the international company (*with foreign operations*) at least to consider seriously the establishment of one or more product development activities abroad. We will examine these pressures, some of which can be considered as arising from within the organization, others from the environments in which it operates.

PRESSURES FROM WITHIN THE ORGANIZATION 1. Companies with well-established foreign subsidiaries usually encounter *demands for more local autonomy*. The subsidiary likes to run its own show as much as possible, especially when it is already operating as a profit center. This natural human desire may be reinforced by the nationalistic feelings of foreign subsidiary personnel, most of whom are probably citizens of the local country. Participation in such a fundamental corporate activity as development of new products is one of the most forceful ways of showing that one has "a piece of the action." In this situation, the firm must weigh the pay-off in improved morale against any loss of efficiency in product development.

2. Multinational companies may have "inherited" or acquired foreign operations with *existing product development activities*. Firms with a long history of foreign operations find that the nature of international business has changed since about 1950. Before that time, their subsidiaries were operating mostly on a national market basis. Because high tariffs and other forms of economic nationalism prevented them from exporting or importing many goods, it was natural for each subsidiary to be a rather self-contained operation, even engaging in local product development. With the liberalizing of

trade in recent decades, these subsidiaries have been integrated into a regional or international operation. Nevertheless, for the parent company to eliminate their product development activity is not easy, even if it wants to. Perhaps the best alternative in these cases is to assure that product development is coordinated internationally.

3. Many companies, in particular some large American firms that began their foreign operations rather recently, have expanded internationally partly through *acquisition* of existing foreign businesses. Acquisition proved the quickest way to get in on expanding markets, such as the EEC. But whatever the reason for the acquisition, an acquired firm usually comes with its own product development activity. The acquiring firm may find it difficult to eliminate this activity and may seek instead to integrate it with the rest of its operation. There may be strong local pressures in this regard. For example, before Chrysler was permitted to take over majority control of Rootes Motors in England, the government required a guarantee that substantial research and development be continued in the English operation. They feared a brain drain, with the possibility of product development being carried on entirely in Detroit.

4. The increasing importance and complexity of product development in the firm may lead to a *need for expansion*, with foreign operations getting a part of it. The work on very large-scale projects may be too much for any one group to handle, and decentralization may be a better approach. Similar pressures would be present if the company were working under a time constraint. Both of these factors can perhaps be illustrated by IBM's development of the System/360 computers, a very large-scale and lengthy activity that has been called their "$5 billion gamble." By giving their major European subsidiaries significant parts of the overall project, IBM probably realized a quicker and more efficient solution than it would have had it tried to conduct the entire development in the United States. The international division of labor paid off.

5. Although a major argument for a centralized product development activity involves efficiency and economies of scale, sometimes *efficiency may be greater* with an international division of labor. We know that in production the largest plant is not always the optimum size, and the same is probably true of development activities. After a certain point, economies of scale may turn into diseconomies. The fact that engineering and scientific personnel are less expensive abroad can mean more development for the dollar internationally. If additional pay-offs can be gained in training and morale in the subsidiaries as well as in local public relations, the arguments grow in favor of some foreign product development.

Unilever is one international company that deliberately seeks the advantages of international research and development. The company has development activities in four European countries as well as close liaison with its associated companies in the United States and India. As a vice-chairman stated, "By locating research and development activities in a number of countries, an international company can take advantage of its unique ability to do research in a variety of national environments, . . . The probability of success is increased if there is good liaison between the laboratories . . . . There is a greater chance of sparking off new ideas."[12]

PRESSURES FROM THE ENVIRONMENT   1. The *governments* of countries where subsidiaries are operating often exert strong pressure for local research and development activity by the international company. The government wants the international company to be as much like a national company as possible, or, perhaps more accurately, the government wants the company to operate locally as it does in its home country. The government does not want its country to be a disfavored member of the international company.

If the firm exports to the country, the government would prefer local production. If it gets local production, it then wants local product development. Eventually, it may desire that even basic research be done locally. Because the firm must depend so much on a government's favor, it does well to consider these wishes even if it does not always yield to them. Beyond relations with the government itself, the firm needs to consider relations with the general public. Benefits in public relations could balance the costs of establishing some local activity. Furthermore, sometimes the firm can gain advertising benefits if it can say that certain products were developed nationally for national tastes.

Canada wants more development work done locally. As an official put it, "We want to encourage American subsidiaries to develop product specialization in Canada, starting right at the laboratory stage." The authorities point with approval to such examples as RCA Victor in Montreal which has worldwide responsibility from its parent company for engineering and manufacturing wide-band microwave equipment. One key difference in the Canadian situation is that, in addition to the pressure, there will be incentives in the form of greater government support of industrial R&D.[13]

2. *Local market needs* can be another encouragement to decentralized product development. Some products require continuous local testing during the development process if they are being designed primarily to meet market specifications (tastes, use conditions, and so on) rather than technological standards. Development close to the market is practical because these use conditions usually cannot be simulated in the firm's domestic laboratories. According to this reasoning, one would expect to find consumer goods developed locally more often than industrial goods.

American tire technology cannot be adapted easily to European roads and weather, so Goodyear and Goodrich have European R&D facilities. Firestone

---

[12] *Progress, the Unilever Quarterly*, vol. 52, no. 296 (1968), p. 186.
[13] *Business Week*, December 28, 1968, p. 84.

was behind on this score but began a $7-million facility near Rome in 1968. While awaiting completion, the company worked jointly with Ferrari to design and produce a new racing tire. A by-product of this effort was a new passenger-car tire, the Cavallino, designed especially for Europe.[14]

Beacham's Brazilian subsidiary felt there was a local demand for a deodorant with a strictly feminine image. The Brazilian staff developed the product and made extensive local tests of the deodorant and perfume element. From these tests, the Brazilian company developed and introduced the product. Within one year it was already vying for number one position in the market.[15]

Research versus Development

Until now, we have made no distinction between research and development in our discussion of decentralized product development. Actually, the process loosely called R&D has several different degrees or stages. Distinguishing between them is important in making decisions about internationalizing them. Basic research is, almost by definition, something in which purely technical considerations of physics or chemistry predominate. Usually the company has no great need and feels no great pressure to internationalize its basic research. As the process moves through applied research, development of products, and adaptation of products, the need for decentralizing the activity increases. Thus many foreign subsidiaries will have facilities for making product adaptations for local markets, far fewer will have a real product development activity, and fewer still will be doing basic research.

Problems in Decentralizing Product Development

We have noted pressures encouraging the firm to undertake foreign product development activities as well as some of the possible advantages in its doing so. Now we will examine some of the problems in managing an international product development operation. One problem is the start-up costs of learning time in the foreign operations. Because product development is a rather advanced kind of industrial activity, foreign subsidiaries, even those good at handling production problems, will not necessarily have ready-made product development capabilities. Several years' learning time may be required before the foreign development operation becomes as efficient as the domestic.

Another administrative problem is coordination and avoidance of duplication among subsidiaries and the related question of communications. In fact, good communications are the necessary tool to assure coordination and integration of development activities in the international company. Various subsidiaries working in the same product areas will tend to come up with similar development projects if left to themselves, with resultant competition and duplication. Proper organizational control and good communications

[14] *Business Week*, June 15, 1968, p. 132.
[15] *Business Latin America*, March 20, 1969, p. 94.

can prevent this from happening. Someone at the parent company or corporate level must know what every subsidiary is doing and be responsible for co-ordination of the various national efforts. The subsidiaries, too, need a picture of the total corporate effort to avoid overlap and to facilitate fruitful exchange of ideas.

Among the various control and communication techniques available to help achieve international coordination, one of the most important is the budget. By specifying budget allowances and the development projects they cover, the firm can avoid duplication of effort quite effectively. The control should not be so tight as to stifle local initiative, however. One producer of farm equipment allows subsidiaries to spend up to $5,000 on any development project that interests them. If the amount is greater than $5,000, formal budget approval is necessary. IBM also allows subsidiary competition up to a certain point at which the competition is stopped and only one lab is allowed to continue the project. This limited competition can lead to better product development. Another control technique is to have each product development activity report back to the responsible executive using formal procedures. Regular, well-designed reports can keep the executive *au courant* between the annual budget meetings.

Budgets and reports are a necessary but not a sufficient means of managing international product development. Other kinds of communication are necessary—written, oral, and face-to-face. The manager of international product development should make the rounds of subsidiaries at least once a year. A yearly meeting of all key development people is another necessity. In some companies, informal meetings on a regional basis too are common.

To solve its communications problem, IBM rented transatlantic telephone lines for several hours a day and intensified the exchange of scientists and technicians between its European and U.S. laboratories. In addition, each European laboratory had a full-time communications officer to maintain close contacts with other labs in Europe and in the United States.[16]

Another problem the company faces is in trying to satisfy the development desires of local subsidiaries and governments in all of its markets. Although some internationalization of product development is probably necessary and desirable in the firm, for the firm to have such an activity in each country where it has a subsidiary is not called for. For the sake of efficiency, only a few subsidiaries will be so favored. For example, an American manufacturer of home-care products has more than ten European subsidiaries but a product development activity only at European headquarters. It has more than sixty people on its development staff in Europe, but this group is a complement to the basic research and development group in America which numbers over 300.

Many less developed countries lack both the qualified personnel and the

[16] *Business Europe*, March 22, 1967, p. 91.

infrastructure to support such an activity, but many of them have a strong desire for local R&D and intend to encourage (or force) international companies to be contributors. In order to satisfy these countries' desires, management will have to come up with creative solutions. In some of these countries, local R&D operations are being established either by government or by private parties. As these operations gain a reputation for competence, they will be a useful support for local subsidiary activity.

The Instituto Nacional de Tecnologia Industrial in Argentina has aided companies in a wide variety of product areas: paint, shock absorbers, auto headlights, cement, paper, cheese, and so on. There are several such organizations in Mexico also. One of them has worked with Corn Products in developing a vegetable-base milk substitute. A number of other subsidiaries of international companies have used their service, such as Geigy, General Foods, and Gillette.[17]

Product Testing

As part of the development process, the product must be tested under realistic final-use conditions. The testing can be separate from the rest of the development process, so the question arises as to the best place for the international company to test its products. The firm would be happy to find itself in the simple but rare situation in which its product is subject to similar technical requirements and use conditions throughout the world. The more common situation, however, requires that the number of testing areas be greater than the number of product development locations.

Although LTV's development of the "Kid" to substitute for the water buffalo in Asia was carried out entirely in the United States, the actual testing was done in Asia. This led to refinements in the product. If products are very sensitive to local tastes and use conditions, testing in each market may be necessary. The success of Beacham's Brazilian subsidiary in developing a new deodorant product was due in part to their being able both to conduct and respond to extensive local testing of the product.

A further reason for product testing in a number of markets is to meet national requirements as to product specifications and performance. For example, in the case of food products, drugs, and electrical or transportation equipment, some local testing may be necessary for government authorization to sell. In the case of pharmaceuticals, there is often a special factor. The American Food and Drug Administration (FDA) approval of new drugs is a very careful but time-consuming process. Drug manufacturers can often test and certify their drugs in foreign markets and begin marketing there before getting final approval in America, thus expediting international introduction of the product. The firm should be virtually certain of FDA approval, however, or it will be in an awkward position in its foreign markets if its product is deemed unfit for American users.

[17] *Business Latin America,* April 24, 1969.

Finally, local product testing may be advisable for promotional reasons. Although the firm must test its own products vigorously to guarantee quality and performance, there may be promotional or other advantages in having local testing done outside the firm. In some cases, the firm may improve its local public relations by using a national organization such as the Argentinian and Mexican R&D companies mentioned above. These national organizations can assist both in development and in testing of products, and this collaboration can also help to further the growth of the R&D infrastructure in the host countries. In Europe, which has many testing organizations, the firm may use one or more because of the promotional value to be gained from its seal or certification. Such certification may be more valuable to an international firm than to a local firm if it is advantageous for the international firm to appear more native. Organizations providing certification are foreign counterparts to such American organizations as Good Housekeeping, Underwriters' Laboratories, and United States Testing Company.

Although Abbott Laboratories develops its new drug products in the United States, it then sends them to universities and hospitals around the world for testing. Findings are reported in various national medical journals. This has the dual advantages of extensive international testing under different conditions, plus the publicity value when findings are reported.

Market Testing

In a sense, a product is tested in a market whenever it is introduced there; but our major consideration here is preliminary market testing before full-scale introduction of the product. How extensive must preliminary market testing be in the international company? Does the domestic experience suffice, or must testing be done in every market? Even for very technical products, a domestic market test is unlikely to be sufficient. Because of differing use conditions and the overall consumption system into which the product fits, some foreign market testing will be necessary. Fortunately for the international firm, although no one country is exactly like any other, there are enough similarities that full-scale market testing is probably not necessary in every country.

If the firm conducts a comparative analysis of its foreign markets (see Chapter 7), it should be able to form country groupings based on criteria relevant to the particular product at hand. From these groupings, then, the firm can select certain countries as test markets for their groups. Just as American firms use test market cities that acceptably represent the United States market for them, so the international firm can choose test market countries to get economies of scale in international new product introduction.

Unilever wanted to introduce a new deodorant in nine European countries where it had strong subsidiaries in this general product area (toiletries). However, it did not wish to have to conduct nine individual market tests. After a discussion of several company delegates, a region in France was selected as representative of the average overall development of the deodorant market in Europe, halfway between the more developed northern countries and the less developed southern countries. This region was to be the test market for all nine countries.

After a market test in France showed very strong sales performance, the product, Rexona deodorant, was launched successfully in the eight remaining subsidiary countries. To get this success, of course, required cooperation among the nine subsidiaries, as well as overall coordination from head-quarters.[18]

CONCLUSION

We have seen that the *process* of product planning and development in the international company is similar to that in domestic firms. However, this does not mean that the process is duplicated in each foreign subsidiary of the firm. Neither can it be successfully confined to the firm's domestic operations. Rather, it must be a multinational and international activity, involving a division of labor and various exchanges between the parts of the multinational firm. Only by so doing can the firm adequately meet its own needs as well as those of host countries.

Questions

9.1   Why is the firm's international product line unlikely to be identical to the domestic? What are the determinants of the firm's product line in a given foreign market?

9.2   How is the nature of the firm's involvement in foreign markets a product-line determinant? Answer this by contrasting the international product line alternatives open to the exporter as compared to those open to the licensor.

9.3   Discuss the decision to drop or add products from or to the line of the international firm. What decision criteria should be used and how does it differ from the same decision in a domestic firm?

9.4   Convenience Foods Corporation has just acquired the leading French manufacturer of snack foods. Should the company add these products to its line in other markets? What considerations are relevant?

9.5   What elements would most likely be contained in a new product development strategy statement in the multinational company?

9.6   "The multinational firm has an advantage over the domestic firm in the generation of new product ideas." Comment.

9.7   Identify some of the special "new product idea" sources for the international firm. Does any source have particular advantages?

9.8   How can international input for new product planning be achieved in the international firm? Contrast the new product idea possibilities available to American Drug, Inc., which only exports, with those available to Pharmaceutical International, Inc., which has several wholly owned foreign plants.

9.9   Where and how should new product screening be done in the international firm? What should be the role of the foreign subsidiary in this process?

[18] *International Advertiser*, vol. 12, no. 1 (1970), pp. 10–19.

9.10 What *marketing* criteria are relevant for evaluating and screening new products in the international firm? Which of these differ from those in the domestic firm?

9.11 Where should the international firm conduct its product development activity? What considerations are relevant?

9.12 Discuss the forces and pressures within the multinational company both for centralized and for decentralized product development.

9.13 The media and government of Latinia (a less developed country) are pressuring General Computers, Inc., to engage in research and development at the firm's local plant. What factors should be considered by the company in responding to these pressures?

9.14 "Product testing must be done locally, even if product development is centralized." Discuss.

9.15 Is a full-scale market test necessary in every country the firm wishes to sell a product?

Further Readings

Books:

"Introducing a New Product in a Foreign Market," *Management Monograph No. 33* (New York: Business International, 1966).

Jewkes, John, et al., *The Source of Invention* (New York: St. Martin's Press, 1959).

Rewoldt, Stewart H., et al., *Introduction to Marketing Management* (Homewood, Ill.: Richard D. Irwin, 1969), chaps. 5, 6.

Terpstra, Vern, *American Marketing in the Common Market* (New York: Praeger, 1967), chap. 3.

Articles:

Boyd, Harper W. and Sidney J. Levy, "New Dimensions in Consumer Analysis," *Harvard Business Review* (November–December 1963), pp. 129–132.

Rijkens, Rein, et al., "An International Advertising Success," *The International Advertiser,* vol. 12, no. 1 (1971), pp. 10–19.

10

DISTRIBUTION: ENTERING FOREIGN MARKETS

The distribution question facing the international marketer is very simple to state: How can I most profitably get my products to foreign customers? In order to determine an appropriate international distribution system, the marketer must deal with this question in two stages: (1) the firm's method of *entry* into foreign markets and (2) the selection of distribution channels *within* each of the firm's foreign markets. A subsequent important management task is the integration and coordination of global distribution, or global logistics. Thus we will discuss these three major problems of distribution: (1) how to enter foreign markets; (2) selecting channels within foreign markets; and (3) managing global logistics. This chapter will deal with the first of these questions. Chapter 11 will discuss the last two questions.

HOW TO ENTER FOREIGN MARKETS

We will assume that the firm has made a decision to sell internationally and that it has selected the markets it wishes to sell to. The firm then faces the question of how to reach these markets. The range of alternative means is wide enough that almost any company in any product area can find an appropriate way to reach foreign markets. The nature of entry and commitment ranges from indirect exporting to wholly owned production facilities in foreign markets. Figure 10–1 shows graphically alternative methods of market entry from a base of either domestic production or foreign production.

Before exploring these alternatives, the firm will find it useful to determine what it wants or requires from its channel to foreign markets. Specifying the nature and performance required of the channel is an important guide to choosing the one that best meets the needs of the firm.

269

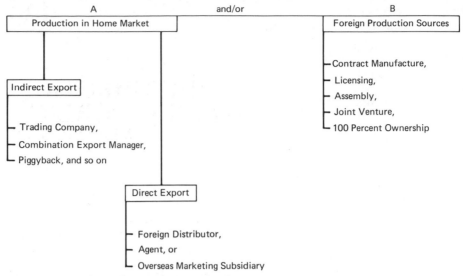

Figure 10-1   Alternative Methods of Foreign Market Entry

Decision Criteria for Entry Method

The selection of a company's best method of entry to foreign markets depends on several factors, some of which are peculiar to the firm and its industry. A few of these major variables are the following: (1) *company goals* regarding the volume of international business desired, expected geographic coverage, and the time span of foreign involvement; (2) the *size* of the company in sales and assets; (3) the company's *product line* and the nature of its products (industrial or consumer, high or low price, technological content); and (4) *competition* abroad. The firm must evaluate these factors for itself; we merely note them here because our decision model will not help in evaluating them —that is, a case by case approach is necessary.

Beyond the factors peculiar to the firm and its industry are other decision criteria that relate more generally to the method of entry to foreign markets. This second group includes factors relatively independent of the firm and its industry.

Number of Markets Covered

Different entry methods offer different coverage of international markets. For example, wholly owned foreign operations are not permitted in some countries; the licensing approach may be impossible in some markets because the firm cannot find qualified licensees; or a trading company might cover some markets very well, but have no representation at all in other markets wanted by the producer. To get the kind of international market coverage it wants, the firm will probably have to combine different kinds of market-entry methods. In some markets, it may have wholly owned operations; in others, marketing subsidiaries; in yet others, local distributors.

Penetration within Markets Covered

Related to the number of markets covered is the quality of that coverage. A combination export manager, for example, might claim to give the producer access to sixty countries. The producer must probe further to find out if this "access" is to the whole national market or if it is limited to the capital or a few large cities. Having a small catalog sales office in the capital city is very different from having a sales force to cover the whole national market.

Market Feedback Available

If it is important or desirable that the firm know what is going on in its foreign markets, it must choose an entry method that will provide this feedback. Although in general the more direct methods of entry offer better possibilities of market information, feedback opportunities will depend in part on how the firm prepares and manages a particular form of market entry. Our discussion of the various entry alternatives will illustrate this further.

Control Available

Management control over foreign marketing ranges from none at all—for example, selling through a trading company—to complete control coupled with complete responsibility. The firm may want a strong voice in several aspects of its foreign marketing, for instance, pricing and credit terms, promotion, product quality, and servicing of its products. The extent to which such control is critical to the firm will bear heavily on its choice of entry method.

Sales Volume Possible

The sales volume available to the firm in a foreign market depends not only on the size of the market but also on the nature of the firm's representation there.

Operating Costs

Sales volume is not a particularly meaningful figure by itself. It must be related to the costs involved in making the sales. Therefore, the firm must investigate the initial and continuing costs of different entry methods as well as whether the costs are fixed or variable in relation to sales.

Profit Possibilities

Presumably, profit is a major goal of the company. In evaluating the profit potential of different entry methods, the long-run sales volume and costs associated with each entry method must be estimated. Costs and profit margins are less important than total profit possibilities. For example, one entry method may offer a 25-percent profit margin on a sales volume of $2 million, but another may offer a 17-percent profit margin on a sales volume of $10 million. The latter entry method probably would be more attractive, even though it has lower profit margins and higher cost margins, because the total profit available is greater ($1.7 million as opposed to $500,000).

Investment Required

Investment requirements are obviously highest in wholly owned foreign operations. Plant investment, however, is not the only consideration; capital also may be required to finance inventories and to extend credit. Since the amount of capital required varies greatly by method of market entry, this investment need will be an important determinant for most firms.

Flexibility

If the firm expects to be in foreign markets for the long run, some flexibility in its method of entry is important. Any entry method optimal at one point in time may be less than optimal five years later. Not only do the environment and the market change, so too do the company situation and goals. The firm therefore wants flexibility, the ability to change its involvement to meet new conditions. It may wish either to expand its involvement to take advantage of rapidly growing markets, or to contract its operations because of adverse political or market developments.

Although not easy to achieve under any circumstances, this flexibility will be much greater where the firm planned for it in choosing its method of entry. For this reason, firms sometimes gain experience with limited forms of involvement before committing themselves heavily to a market. As we will see later, however, using distributors and licensees may not always offer the desired flexibility even though they are limited forms of foreign market involvement.

Personnel Requirements

Not only capital requirements vary by method of entry; so do personnel needs. Generally, the more direct and more complicated kinds of involvement require a larger number of skilled international business personnel. If the firm is short of "internationalists," it will be constrained in its alternatives.

Risk

Foreign markets are usually perceived as riskier than the domestic market. The amount of risk the firm faces is not only a function of the market itself but also of its method of involvement there. In addition to its investment, the firm risks inventories, receivables, and—perhaps—even the market itself. When planning its method of market entry, the firm must do a risk analysis both of the market itself and of its method of entry.

The aforementioned risks are not only commercial and traditional; in foreign markets the firm is also faced with political risks. The firm's political vulnerability may differ from market to market for various reasons, but the firm's level of involvement will be a factor. Generally, the heavier, the more direct, and the more visible the entry of the international firm in the foreign market, the more vulnerable it is politically.

A Simple Decision Model

The various criteria for evaluating foreign market-entry methods can be combined in a matrix, as is done in Table 10–1. The firm will find that each of the entry methods will have a somewhat different "score" on the different criteria or dimensions. By relating these scores to the firm's own situation and needs, management can choose the most appropriate entry strategy.

The approach illustrated by Table 10–1 seeks to answer two questions: (1) How well can the firm market through any particular entry strategy? and (2) What are the costs and benefits of different entry strategies? De-

Table 10–1 Matrix for Comparing Alternative Methods of Market Entry

ROUTE	MARKETS	MARKET PENE-TRATION	MARKET FEEDBACK	CONTROL	SALES	COSTS	PROFITS	INVEST-MENT-	FLEXI-BILITY	PER-SONNEL	RISK
1. Indirect export											
2. Direct export											
3. Marketing subsidiary											
4. Marketing subsidiary with contract manufacturing											
5. Marketing subsidiary local assembly											
6. Licensing											
7. Joint ventures											
8. 100-percent ventures											

pending on its size and needs, the firm can use the matrix to select entry strategy for individual markets, for regions, or for the whole international market. The large firm could even apply this approach by product line or division. We will now turn to a consideration of the entry methods themselves.

INDIRECT EXPORTING

The firm is an indirect exporter when its products are sold in foreign markets but no special activity or organization for this purpose is carried on within the firm. In fact, the firm is not engaging in international marketing, in any real sense, with indirect exporting. Its products are carried abroad by others, and its distribution problems are similar to those related to domestic sales. Although by exporting products in this indirect way the firm can open up entirely new markets without special expertise or investment on its part, its control over market selection and marketing strategy is apt to be very limited. There are several different methods of indirect exporting.

Foreign Sales through Domestic Sales Organization

A marketer likes nothing better than to have a buyer come to him, and occasionally even a foreign buyer will do this. Products are sold in the domestic market but used or resold abroad in several ways.

1. Foreign department stores or wholesale or retail operations that have buying offices in America may come across a producer's good and find it desirable for their market, or the producer may try to persuade them that his product is good for their market. In fact, if the potential volume is adequate, the producer may even modify his product to assure that it meets the foreign buyer's desires.

2. American and foreign manufacturers and firms in extractive industries often have American offices to procure equipment and supplies for their foreign operations. In selling to the American firms in this category, a company would have the advantage if it is already supplying their domestic operations. Reaching the foreign firms in this group would require special market information on buyer needs and behavior and creation of a suitable marketing approach to satisfy them. Again, if the potential volume is sufficient, the producer can consider product modification to satisfy this market segment. A peculiar but similar example would be selling to the United States government for post exchanges or embassies abroad.

3. A slightly different situation arises when companies with multinational operations do not have a separate procurement office for foreign subsidiaries but buy certain equipment and supplies for them through their regular domestic purchasing mechanism. In this case, a regular domestic supplier of the multinational company would have an advantage. Many small and medium-sized industrial marketers can trace their international involvement to such a beginning.

An American company builds a plant in a foreign market. It buys a machine from its regular domestic supplier through the normal domestic procedure. The machine is shipped and installed in the new foreign plant. A foreign producer visits the plant and takes note of the machine. Sometime later the American supplier receives his first foreign order. Such a sequence of events has often led to an active export involvement by the supplying firm. It has benefited from the demonstration effect and received a free introduction to the foreign market. Although such experiences can lead to profitable exporting, they are too random to be part of a firm's strategy.

4. International trading companies with offices in the United States are very important for some markets of the world. If these markets are on the firm's select list, it should consider using one of these companies. Most of the large international trading companies are of European or Japanese origin. In Japan, for example, some of the largest enterprises in the country are these trading companies, such as Mitsui and Mitsubishi. They handle over 80 percent of all Japanese imports. The trading companies of European origin are important primarily in trade with those nations that are former European colonies, particularly Africa and South East Asia. The United Africa Company, which is part of Unilever, is the largest trader in Africa and would give the best market coverage, especially in West Africa.

The size, stability, and market coverage of these trading companies make them attractive potential distributors, especially when coupled with their credit reliability. Not only do they cover their markets well but also they can service the products they sell. There are some potential drawbacks to the use of trading companies, however. They are likely to carry competing lines, and the latest product added might not receive the attention its producer desires. In addition, some of the developing countries resent trading companies associated with the former colonial master, and this resentment restrains some trading company operations. A few countries have even nationalized their foreign trade, for example, Burma and Egypt, in part to get rid of foreign influence.

The sales derived from these kinds of indirect exporting are as good as domestic sales, but they may be less stable and reliable. Because it is so far removed from the ultimate market, the firm can do very little to control these sales. In contrast to domestic sales, there is not only a distance gap, but also an information gap and a control gap. Although the firm welcomes any new sales, those arising from the sources mentioned here may prove too uncertain to be included in long-run planning. This fact might move the firm in the direction of more control over its foreign sales.

Combination Export Managers (CEMs)

Combination export managers represent another form of indirect exporting, but one important and different enough to warrant special discussion. Traditionally, the CEM has been considered as acting as the export department of the producer; that is, the producer gets the performance of an export department without establishing one within the firm. The term "combination" in his title derives from the fact that the CEM performs this export management function for several firms at the same time, just as a manufacturer's agent represents several manufacturers.

As compared with other indirect approaches, working with a CEM generally means the firm has closer cooperation and more control. The CEM often uses the letterhead of the manufacturer, negotiates on his behalf, and gets his approval on orders and quotations. Theoretically at least, the CEM approach to indirect exporting seems ideal for the medium-sized or smaller firm contemplating an export program.

The following list enumerates the advantages of using a CEM.

1. The producer gains instant foreign market knowledge and contacts through the existing operations and experience of the CEM.
2. The commission method of payment commonly used means that costs are variable and the CEM is motivated to expand sales.
3. The manufacturer is spared the burden of developing in-house expertise in the technical aspects of exporting, which is not only a saving in time and administration but also a significant cost saving because all the CEM's export management costs are spread over the sales of several manufacturers.
4. Consolidated shipments offer freight savings to the CEM's client.
5. A line of complementary products can get better foreign representation than the products of just one manufacturer, and perhaps better foreign market feedback also.

Evaluating the CEM

In practice, a relation with a CEM may not produce all the desired results. Some CEMs are too new or too small to have sufficient foreign market knowledge and contacts. In addition, the ideal of the CEM with a limited number of related lines is not always realized; paid on a commission basis, the CEM needs volume to survive and may take on too many lines from unrelated product areas. In such a case, the manufacturer is probably getting neither the expertise nor the promotion he requires. The CEM may want a worldwide exclusive contract but not have world-wide coverage. His market coverage has to be matched against the market targets of the producer.

One advantage cited for the CEM is that he gives the manufacturer access to instant foreign market knowledge and exporting know-how. This can be a potential disadvantage if the producer never develops such capabilities himself because he continually relies on the CEM. As foreign sales grow, it may become important that the producer be able to do his own exporting. Although initially the CEM may offer great economies, at some volume-of-sales point it is more profitable for the manufacturer to set up his own export department. If and when the manufacturer reaches this point, he will want his own foreign market knowledge and exporting know-how.

Looking at the relationship from the CEM's viewpoint is revealing. He is often vulnerable to the extent he does a good job. He builds up foreign markets in the manufacturer's name and with his brands. When the market is well secured, the manufacturer may decide to do his own exporting to this now-large foreign market. The CEM, of course, loses a major source of revenue. Through mergers, too, the CEM can lose clients.

To protect themselves, many CEMs have changed the nature of their operations, using their own letterhead to establish their own identification. Instead of selling on commission, they buy for resale to control the prices and terms more effectively, and they may even use their own brand on some products. They try for a larger list of clients so that the loss of one or two is not so damaging. The manufacturer does not have as close relations with or as much control over the new type of CEM, but he is not necessarily a less effective CEM than the more traditional type.

Many smaller firms should consider the CEM alternative when evaluating export possibilities. Although the potential advantages and limitations need to be kept in mind, the decision will not be based on an abstract listing of pros and cons. The exporter-to-be needs first to develop his own list of export requirements and targets and then to match these against the capabilities and market coverage of various CEM candidates. Even if no CEM scores as high as desired on this evaluation, the potential exporter still might find the CEM better than the alternatives.

As of 1969, the United States had the following nine *associations* of combination export managers.

Overseas Sales & Marketing Association of America, Inc., One East Wacker Dr., Suite 300, United of America Bldg., Chicago, Ill. 60601.
National Association of Export Management Companies (NEXCO), Inc., 99 Church Street, New York, N.Y. 10007.
Florida World Trade Association, P.O. Box 171, Miami International Airport, Miami, Fla. 33148.
Export Managers Association, c/o Pan Commercial International, Inc., 108 Grove Street, Worcester, Mass. 01605.
Council of Ohio Combination Export Managers, 690 Union Commerce Bldg., Cleveland, Ohio 44115.
Michigan Association of Export Management Companies, 1616 Ford Bldg., Griswold St., Detroit, Mich. 48226.
Export Managers Association of Southern California, 612 South Flower St., Suite 742, Los Angeles, Calif. 90017.
Combination Export Managers Association of Connecticut, 222 Rimmon Rd., North Haven, Conn. 06473.
Southwest Association of Exporters, Inc., Box 2514, Dallas, Tex. 75222.[1]

Cooperation in Exporting

In addition to the combination export manager approach just discussed are other special possibilities in export marketing that fall short of full involvement and commitment by the firm. Cooperation in exporting is another such way to enter foreign markets without bearing the full costs and burdens of

[1] *International Commerce*, August 25, 1969, p. 7.

an in-house export department or foreign investment. Among the various forms of cooperation in exporting are Webb-Pomerene associations, joint export associations, piggybacking, and other ad hoc arrangements.

Webb-Pomerene Associations

We discussed the legal aspects of Webb-Pomerene associations in Chapter 5. These associations are notable in that they permit otherwise competing firms to collaborate for export marketing, thus offering to the firm a unique alternative in cooperative exporting. We will examine the management considerations in evaluating this alternative and briefly review current practice.

Firms joining in a Webb-Pomerene association can gain many potential benefits. Together they can research foreign markets more effectively and obtain better representation in them. They may find that by establishing one organization to replace several sellers, they can realize more stable prices. Selling costs can be reduced just as in the CEM approach. Through consolidating shipments and avoiding duplicated effort in all the export details, they can realize transportation savings. A larger group can achieve standardization of product grading and create a stronger brand name, just as the California Fruit Growers Exchange has done with Sunkist products. As the legislators intended, most of the benefits derive from economies of scale and the countervailing power made available through joint efforts. Flexibility is a final advantage that should be noted. Many degrees of cooperation and product and market coverage are possible, so joining a Webb-Pomerene association is not an all-or-nothing affair.

With the many attractions of Webb-Pomerene associations, it is surprising that not more of them are operating. Over 200 associations were established under the Webb-Pomerene or Export Trade Act, but many of these were formed soon after the act was passed and were never actually operated. The number in 1966 was thirty-one, as seen in Table 10–2. Such associations accounted for 17.5 percent of United States trade in 1930, but generally the total has been much lower—between 4 and 5 percent since World War II. Table 10–2 shows that agricultural and primary commodity groups predominate. Although 252 of the 321 companies belonging to associations had annual sales of less than $10 million, some very large firms also belong. For example, the Rubber Export Association includes Goodyear and Firestone; the Potash Export Association includes International Minerals and Chemicals; the Textile Export Association includes Burlington Industries and J. P. Stevens.

A survey conducted in 1967 showed the following major functions being performed by Webb-Pomerene associations:[2]

1. Centralized export distribution
2. Selection of foreign sales agents
3. Price setting and division of markets
4. Product standardization

[2] Robert L. Curry, "Webb-Pomerene Export Associations," *Oregon Business Review* (July 1967), pp. 1–5.

5. Stabilization of credit conditions
6. Joint storage and surplus disposal
7. Bargaining with shipping conferences or governments for more favorable treatment.

Table 10–2   Registered Webb-Pomerene Associations

NAME	LOCATION	PRODUCTS	MEMBERS
Agricultural Products, Inc.	Danville, Ill.	Soy beans, meal, oil and by-products	3
American Film Export Association	New York	Motion picture films	2
American Motion Picture Export Co. (Africa), Inc.	New York	Motion picture films	7
American Railway Car Export Association	New York	Railroad cars	5
Amertool Services, Inc.	Cincinnati	Machine tools	15
Anthracite Export Association	Harrisburg	Anthracite coal	6
California Dried Fruit Export Association	Santa Clara	Dried fruit	22
California Rice Export Association	San Francisco	Rice and by-products	4
Carbon Black Export, Inc.	New York	Carbon black	5
Concentrated Phosphate Export Association, Inc.	New York	Concentrated phosphatic materials	5
Export Foods, Inc.	Rochester, N. Y.	Packaged and canned fruits and vegetables	17
Flour Mills Export Association	Minneapolis	Flour	19
General Milk Sales, Inc.	Los Angeles	Canned milk	2
Kaolin Clay Export, Inc.	New York	Kaolin clay and other products	4
Machine Affiliates, Inc.	New York	Machine tools	13
Motion Picture Export Association of America, Inc.	New York	Motion picture films	8
Northwest Dried Fruit Export Association	Salem, Ore.	Dried fruit	4
Pacific Alfalfa Export Corporation	Los Angeles	Alfalfa	10
Pacific Coast Agricultural Export Association	San Francisco	Dried fruit	12
Pencil Industry Export Association	New York	Pencils and pens	3
Plywood International	Seattle	Plywood	26
Potash Export Association, Inc.	Ho-Ho-Kus, N. J.	Potash	3
Pulp, Paper & Paperboard Export Association of the United States	New York	Paper and tall oil	12
The Rubber Export Association	Akron	Rubber products, tires and tubes	7
Sulphur Export Corporation	New York	Crude sulphur	4
Television Program Export Association	New York	Television tapes	7
Textile Export Association of the United States	New York	Textiles	33
United States Alfalfa Export Corporation	Leawood, Kan.	Dehydrated alfalfa and and other alfalfa products	9
Vegetable Oil Export Corporation	Washington, D. C.	Soy-bean oil	6
Walnut Export Sales Company	Indianapolis	Oak and walnut lumber, logs and veneer	2

Source: Federal Trade Commission.

In the 1960s, the American government was actively promoting exports to help eliminate the deficit in the balance of payments, but surprisingly, at the same time the Justice Department was attacking Webb-Pomerene associations, in spite of their helpfulness in expanding exports. It is probable that legal uncertainty has prevented the formation of a number of new associations.[3] The position taken by the Justice Department is that these associations do have some unfavorable impacts on the domestic economy through their "cartel" activities. Specific criticisms include (1) the price-setting function, as opposed to accepted cost-reducing activities, and (2) the membership of giant companies that presumably could operate alone.

All things considered, the Webb-Pomerene approach is a good way for small and medium-sized firms to enter foreign markets. The legal and other problems are likely to affect big-company associations but leave room for profitable export cooperation among smaller companies.

Joint Export Associations (JEAs)

Because of America's balance of payments deficits, the government began a new export promotion drive in 1968. Firms willing to cooperate in JEAs would receive financial aid from the government. The exact nature of the program was not clearly spelled out, but the initial contract winners illustrate the *modus vivendi*.[4] The first five contract winners were combination export management firms which had demonstrated that they had a potential market which they could not develop without financial assistance. The five CEMs represented seventy-eight companies in fifteen states with a product coverage including electronic equipment, rubber products, machine tools, industrial instruments, and packaging technology. The government was to put up about 40 percent of the $1.4 million cost of the first projects. The five firms estimated that exports would be increased by $34 million in the first two years of the program.

The advantages to manufacturers would be those economies and efficiencies in any cooperative effort. The JEAs are, in effect, a strengthening of the CEM approach, allowing them to enter new markets and expand their programs. The considerations for the manufacturer would be the same as those in our CEM discussion, but with a somewhat more positive emphasis because of the favorable government attitude and financial assistance. The JEA, in principle, is not limited to CEM firms, however, and other kinds of association are possible. More experience with the program is necessary before adequate evaluation is possible. Nevertheless, it is another potentially valuable alternative for smaller and medium-sized firms wanting to expand foreign sales.

Piggyback Exporting

In piggyback exporting, one manufacturer uses its overseas distribution facilities to sell another company's products along with its own. Although not new—General Electric was doing it some fifty years ago—this method is

---

[3] See "Antitrust Suits Focus New Attention on Webb-Pomerene," *Business Abroad,* March 7, 1966, p. 24.
[4] "JEA Contract Winners," *Business Abroad* (March 1969), p. 7.

becoming more important today.[5] Two parties with somewhat different interests make up the piggyback operation—the carrier and the rider.

The *carrier*, the firm actually doing the exporting, is usually the larger firm with established export facilities and foreign market distribution channels. It may have several reasons for wanting to carry noncompetitive products of one or more other manufacturers. A manufacturer already experienced in exporting may find it profitable to piggyback to broaden or round out its product line. This can mean economies of scale in the export operation and may please overseas distributors by giving them more to sell. One big piggybacker, Borg-Warner, has gained as much as 15 percent of its export sales and profits from this operation.[6] A firm can offer extra customer convenience by selling related products; for example, Singer sells fabrics, patterns, and other sewing accessories in addition to its sewing machines. Companies faced with seasonal or cyclical declines in sales may piggyback to keep the export operation and distribution channels working at full capacity throughout the year.

Schick Safety Razor tried to enter the German market using an independent distributor. Although the distributor was aggressive, his sales force was too small to make the necessary retail calls for Schick. Because penetration was slow, Schick canceled its contract with the distributor.

Next, Schick signed on with the German sales subsidiary of a Swedish company with excellent coverage of the retail outlets that were important to Schick. Initially, sales went up rapidly, but then the Swedish company launched a very successful new product of its own. Schick sales dropped off again.

Finally, Schick established its own sales subsidiary in Germany (hiring an executive from Gillette). A large company sales force (fifty men) was hired to give the desired retail coverage. The costs of this direct approach would have been very high if only Schick products were sold, but fortunately American Cyanamid wanted a distributor for its Breck hair products. Although Cyanamid had its own sales force in Germany, the salesmen were selling different products to market that did not overlap with Breck markets. The outcome was that Schick became the distributor for Breck products in Germany.

Schick was so satisfied with its piggyback operation that it later signed to distribute in Germany the cosmetic products of another American company. Perhaps most important, Schick's own market share in Germany rose from 3 to 7 percent in one year. The large sales force made possible by piggybacking was probably a major factor in this result.[7]

PIGGYBACK DECISIONS   The potential *carrier* must consider piggybacking as just one among its alternative strategies if an existing export operation or distribution setup is not being used effectively. Weaknesses in the existing system, however, may be the result of marketing policies other than distribu-

[5] "Piggyback Sales Gain Momentum," *Business Week*, December 18, 1965, p. 70.

[6] "Piggyback Sales Gain Momentum," p. 70.

[7] Adapted from *Business International*, September 6, 1968, p. 282.

tion, or the weaknesses may be amenable to correction within the system. If the firm decides to maintain the existing distribution system and to increase volume or product-line coverage, then it must make a make-or-buy decision. Should it produce the extra products itself or get them outside? It might be noted that, for the carrier firm, piggybacking represents a sale of its know-how and services rather than a sale of its products.

Thus we can see that the carrier must make the piggyback decision in the larger context of its overall marketing program. Excess capacity in export distribution is not a sufficient reason for piggybacking. The firm must decide what its international or foreign product line should be, what its optimum international or foreign market distribution approach is, and, finally, how it can best supply the products it wants to sell.

A further question is where in the firm the piggyback decision should be made—at the top international level or at the divisional or foreign-subsidiary level? The answer will depend on (1) the uniformity of conditions facing the firm internationally, (2) the uniformity of the international product line as discussed in Chapter 9, and (3) the company's international organization as well as the degree of autonomy and profit-center approach in the foreign subsidiaries. Actual practice varies, as the following examples show.

Borg-Warner handles piggyback arrangements through the international arm of the company. This is the most common approach.

Honeywell gives the decision to the national affiliate but requires compatibility of the piggybacked product with the company's existing line and sales force.

Combustion Engineering does no piggybacking at the parent-company level but encourages its foreign affiliates to do so to offset the cyclical nature of their business.[8]

Some difficulties can arise for the carrier in piggybacking as well as the advantages cited earlier. Because the piggybacked products are not made by the carrier, its sales and service force must be trained to handle them. With technical products, quality control, warranty, and servicing can pose problems that the marketing firm will have to settle with the manufacturing concern.

For the *rider*, piggybacking is one alternative route to foreign markets. Like the CEM route, it offers established export and distribution facilities and shared expenses. The cost advantages to the rider are similar to those offered by the CEM approach or a Webb-Pomerene association, namely, only its sales commissions and advertising. The drawbacks are also similar, the primary one being lack of control over the promotion given the carrier's products. In the Schick example we cited before, Schick's dissatisfaction as a piggyback rider with the Swedish firm led it to form its own piggyback operation. The two critical factors in success are finding the right carrier partner and making an appropriate agreement meeting the needs of both.

[8] *Business International*, June 7, 1968, p. 182.

For firms interested in piggyback operations, the Department of Commerce offers a "marriage broker" service, bringing appropriate carriers and riders together. The Department of Commerce feels that this approach could significantly increase the number of firms exporting and also improve the balance of payments situation. The prospective carrier or rider can write to the department noting the products and countries it is interested in.

METHOD OF OPERATION   Although piggyback agreements tend to be more loose and flexible than agreements with combination export managers or Webb-Pomerene associations, the same points must be considered for the protection of carrier and rider. Among these are terms of sale, promotional arrangements, market coverage, and provisions for termination of the agreement. The Schick-Cyanamid agreement can again be used as an example.

The Schick-Cyanamid contract provided that Schick sell Breck domestics in its own name, but for the account of Cyanamid; that is, the products remained Cyanamid property until sold. Schick agreed not to sell its own similar products or similar products of a third company. Should any question arise concerning "similarity" of a new product, Cyanamid had to be consulted before a marketing decision was made.

The contract stipulated that Schick was to receive a higher commission during the launching period. Cyanamid was authorized to check Schick's accounts with an independent auditor and to withdraw Breck cosmetics from the market if sales were disappointing. Should Schick be taken over by a third company, Cyanamid had the right to cancel the contract immediately.

In selling, piggybacking offers the following two types of arrangements: (1) the carrier sells the rider's products on a commission basis, as an agent or CEM might do; (2) the carrier buys the products outright from the manufacturing company, acting more in the manner of an independent distributor. The latter alternative is more common, but the appropriate choice depends on the particular situation and desires of the two firms.

Branding and promotional policy can be variable in piggybacking. In some instances, the carrier may buy the products, put its own brand on them, and market them as its own products. In this case, the company does the total marketing job, as Borg-Warner does with auto replacement parts it buys from other manufacturers. More commonly, the carrier retains the brand name of the producer and the two work out promotional arrangements between them. The choice of branding and promotional strategy is a function of the importance of brand to the product being exported and of the degree to which the brand is well established.

Borg-Warner kept the producer's name on the small appliances it bought from Hamilton Beach. It had similar agreements for the Toastmaster products of McGraw-Edison and the garbage disposers of In-Sink-Erator-Company.[9]

[9] *Business Week*, p. 72.

As we have seen, the piggyback approach offers attractions to the marketing firm (carrier) as well as to the manufacturer (rider). It can be flexible as to product and market coverage. For the manufacturer, it can offer quick entry into foreign markets and economies of scale in exporting. It is an approach favored by the government, as evidenced by the role played by the Department of Commerce in bringing carriers and riders together. With these favorable aspects, it is a method of entry to foreign markets well deserving of investigation by the firm wanting to initiate or expand foreign sales.

DIRECT EXPORTING

In our discussion of indirect exporting we have examined the many ways of reaching foreign markets without really working very hard. Indeed, in some of the indirect approaches, foreign sales are handled in essentially the same way as domestic sales; the manufacturer engages in international marketing only by proxy, that is, through the firm that carries its products overseas. Both the international marketing know-how and the sales achieved by these indirect approaches, however, are probably limited.

The combination export manager approach or cooperative exporting (via a Webb-Pomerene association or piggybacking) requires a greater involvement by the firm than indirect exporting but should also result in greater experience and sales. The firm can choose to commit itself still further to foreign involvement, however, by going beyond indirect exporting approaches to direct exporting.

The difference between indirect and direct exporting is that in the latter the manufacturer himself performs the export task rather than delegating it entirely or largely to others. In direct exporting, the tasks of market contact, market research, physical distribution, export documentation, pricing, and so on, all fall on the shoulders of the export department or export manager of the firm. Direct exporting usually results in greater sales for the firm than does indirect exporting. Whether it also yields greater profits will depend on whether the sales increase is greater than the increase in costs from running an in-house export operation.

The choice between indirect exporting and direct exporting is analogous to the choice between selling through a manufacturer's representative and using the firm's own sales force in domestic marketing. The advantages of directness are not only greater sales, but also greater control, better market information, and development of in-house expertise in international marketing. The costs of going direct are high because the direct exporter bears them alone, whereas they are shared in the indirect or cooperative approaches. Although we are contrasting direct and indirect exporting, they are not mutually exclusive. A firm might choose to export directly to certain large markets but export indirectly to reach a number of smaller markets.

The Task of Export Management

To gain the potential benefits of direct exporting, the firm must pay the costs of performing the export management task in-house. Depending on the size of foreign sales, export management may range from a part-time activity for one person to a large export department with a specialized staff and a full-time export manager. As a further variation, the export department could be a part of the international division, or there could be separate export departments in the product divisions of multidivisional companies. Regardless of the volume of export sales or the organizational structure set up to deal with them, however, export management has certain tasks to perform.

Choosing Foreign Markets

In indirect exporting, foreign market coverage is usually dictated by the company that takes the product abroad, that is, it is already selling in certain markets and these are the ones it can offer the manufacturer. Of course, the manufacturer can occasionally add other markets by using other intermediaries that cover the additional markets wanted. To avoid legal and administrative problems, however, the manufacturer must take care to avoid an overlap of national territories of two intermediaries. By direct exporting, management can make its own selection of markets to be cultivated.

In theory, the firm could have the whole world as its market. In practice, it is usually limited to a part of the world's markets. For an American company, United States restrictions on trading with communist countries might eliminate those countries from management's consideration. It must be remembered, however, that East–West trade is expanding and many good market opportunities will be found there, all in accord with government policy. On economic grounds, the firm may eliminate other markets in order to concentrate on those offering the greatest potential. Some markets may be too small or poor; others may have too much competition; yet others may have high tariff barriers or trade restrictions on the firm's products.

To choose the best export markets, the firm needs some analytical approach to help it evaluate and rank markets according to potential. Among the variables the firm must consider are demand factors, competition, and government. The kinds of approaches and information sources needed for such an analysis were discussed in Chapter 7.

Choosing Representatives in the Target Markets

Once the firm has selected its markets, it must have representation there. If both the markets and the firm are large enough, the firm can establish its own sale subsidiary, thereby exporting to itself in the foreign market and controlling its marketing program there. The more frequent approach, especially in smaller markets, is to select a local representative to distribute the firm's products. The representative can be a distributor or manufacturer, but his title is less important than his ability to do the job.

The firm would do well to have several distributor candidates in each target market, names of whom can be obtained from many different sources: Department of Commerce trade lists, foreign business directories, commercial banks, steamship companies, airlines, and so on. After the firm obtains a list of candidates, it must secure information about each candidate in order to select the best one. The firm will want to know the method of operation of the candidate (Does he buy for his own account? Does he carry inventory? How many salesmen does he have? What product lines does he carry?) and his effectiveness and reliability in marketing—and in paying his bills.

A Dun & Bradstreet report or a Department of Commerce World Trade Directory report (see Figure 10–2) can give useful information on these questions. Follow-ups through banks, other American clients of the candidate, and his other references can help to round out the picture of each candidate. All this can be done in the home country of the exporter.

Even with all this information gathered, however, the export manager is prudent to plan a visit to the target markets before choosing distributors there. From such a visit not only will he get a feeling for the markets that written reports cannot convey, but also, and more important, he will gain further impressions and information on the distributor. The distributor is perhaps the most critical single factor in the exporter's success. Also, once the exporter has signed a contract with a distributor, the laws of the country may make it very difficult and costly to break the contract and get another distributor. For these reasons, the initial selection must be made very carefully.

Paying a personal visit to the better candidates and viewing their operations will help the export manager to make the best choice, and establishing personal familiarity will make future written communication more meaningful. In some markets, the firm will not be able to develop a list of acceptable distributor candidates, in which case it might be happy even to find one that is being used by a competitor.

Controlling Distributors

The export manager, responsible for getting his products to foreign customers, is both helped and hindered by the use of foreign distributors. Although these distributors take care of foreign distribution, their interests do not always coincide with the exporter's, especially if the exporter's products represent a small part of the distributor's business. The exporter cannot really control the distributor, but he can try to assure that he works effectively.

The first step in control is proper selection of the distributor. The next is drawing up a strong agreement (contract). Rather than depending on the contract, however, the export manager should see to it that good performance is in the self-interest of the distributor. Some of the ways of getting distributor cooperation include appropriate margins, marketing helps, cooperative advertising, and good communications. One important part of this communication is the occasional visit of the export manager. Having the distributor visit the exporter's offices and plant also can be good for his morale and performance. If product service by distributors is necessary, some training of distributor personnel can be done, either abroad or at the domestic plant.

Toro Manufacturing Company held its first international sales conference in Switzerland. The three-day conference was attended by Toro distributors from thirteen Western European countries. These distributors had previously attended the firm's annual meetings in the United States but felt these meetings were not oriented to their particular marketing needs. The face-to-face contact between Toro personnel and the European agents helped Toro to gain better insights into the marketing problems of each of the countries represented. The language problem was solved by the use of simultaneous translations by personnel borrowed from United Nations operations.

Physical Distribution and Export Documentation

Once the firm has made agreements with foreign distributors, it must get the product to them. This task of physical distribution differs in several respects from the way it is done in the domestic market. Different shipping companies and modes of transportation will be necessary; for example, the use of ships and airplanes is more common in exporting than in domestic selling. Export packing and packaging usually are more costly because the greater distances and numerous changes in modes of transportation require that the product be handled more frequently. Of course, air shipments can avoid some of these problems.

A further complication of shipping to foreign markets is export documentation. Although the Department of Commerce in 1970 reduced the paperwork required for exports, it is still greater than that required for domestic shipments, and then the importing nation usually has documentation requirements of its own. Finally, insuring shipments to foreign markets also is somewhat more complicated than insuring domestic shipments.

The complications we are discussing here, combined with firms' lack of familiarity with foreign markets, have deterred many firms from giving adequate consideration to foreign market opportunities. A number of studies of exporters compared with nonexporters have shown this to be true. Therefore, the Department of Commerce export expansion programs have stressed how these two problem areas can be met and overcome, and we have cited useful information sources in Chapter 7. The Department of Commerce itself is the leading one, of course.

Although paperwork and other complications do involve some extra work and cost, they should not be considered insurmountable barriers. Many sources of expertise outside the firm are ready to help the exporter. Overseas freight forwarders are skilled and efficient in handling physical distribution and some of the documentation; banks will take care of the international financial complications; insurance companies can handle the insurance of foreign shipments and even cover credit extended to foreign customers through the Foreign Credit Insurance Association (FCIA). There are even companies that will do the firm's export packaging.

Most exporters use some outside expertise, the amount often depending on the volume of export sales. The exporter has, in effect, a make-or-buy decision. Can he do these tasks more efficiently in-house, or should he purchase them outside? As export volume increases, the exporter will tend to do more and more in-house.

May ------- Revised ----- X
File Number -------

WORLD TRADE DIRECTORY REPORT

U. S. DEPARTMENT OF COMMERCE
Bureau of Foreign Commerce
Form 841—(3-5-54)

1. Name ___Ets. Doe___

2. Address ___65 Ave. d'Eylau___   ___Paris___   ___France___
   (Number)   (Street)   (City)   (Country)

3. (a) Importer of ___all kinds of hard and soft___ (e) Wholesaler of ___ - - -___
   ___wood, timber and lumber___

   (b) Retailer of ___ - - -___   (f) Manufacturer of ___ - - -___

   (c) Exporter of ___same as (a)___   (g) Commission merchant handling ___ - - -___

   (d) Jobber or factor handling ___ - - -___   (h) Sales or indent agent selling ___same as (a)___
                                                       (State qualifications on reverse)

4. Preferred language of correspondence ___French & English___ { Cable address ___KLEINWD___

   { Codes used ___Bentley's___

5. Buys from following countries ___U.S.A., Sweden, Denmark, Norway, Germany___
                                   (State proportions. If domestic, so state)

6. Organization ___Corporation___   ___1941___ ___(reorganized 1946-1952)___
   (Corporation, partnership, etc.)   (Year established)   (Country where organized)

7. Head office ___Paris___   Branch houses ___Le Havre, Bordeaux___
                (Location)   (Location)

8. Sales territory ___France and European___ Number of traveling salesmen employed ___2___
                   ___countries___

INFORMATION HEREIN IS FURNISHED U. S. TRADERS IN STRICT CONFIDENCE; SECONDARY DISTRIBUTION PROHIBITED

9. Representatives in United States ___Grove Trading Co., 2150 West 57th St., New York, N. Y.___
                                     (Name)   (Address)   (If purchasing agent, so state)

10. Financial references ___Banque Francaise du Commerce Exterieur, Paris, France; Sixth___
    ___National Bank of New York, New York City___

    Trade references ___See reverse___
                     (Give references in U. S. whenever possible and American references abroad)

11. Capital { Authorized ___14,000,000___ Volume of business ___250,000,000___ No. of employees ___12___
            { Paid in ___Frs. 8,500,000___   (Annual sales, state currency)
            (State currency; U. S. preferred) Frs. 420 equal to U.S. $1.00

12. Indicate relative size of concern (check): Very large _____ Large _____ Medium _X_ Small _____
                                                              (Consider relative volume of business done by firm in its community)

13. Managers or partners (name, title, age, nationality) ___Jean Doe, President, 59 (French),___

    ___Harry Ferrand, Vice President, 50 (Belgian), Francois Meuble, General Manager,___
    ___56 (French)___

14. Capital stock controlled by ___the above___
                                (Name of persons most interested financially)

15. Selling agents for ___see reverse___
                       (State names of all firms; if exclusive, so state; use reverse side if necessary)

16. Indicate general reputation of concern ___Very good___
                                            (See reverse side for additional comments)

17. Date of report ___March 1, 19--.___ Source of information ___John N. Brown, Second___
                                        ___Secretary of Embassy___ (Name and post of preparing officer)
    Use other side or separate sheet, if necessary, to give additional information

COMM-DC 38517

Figure 10-2

Source: U.S. Department of Commerce.

8 (h) State the sales ability and experience of agent, based on local and American references, lines handled and how long, types of trade called upon, and the specific channels of distribution observed:

The firm is a commission and indent sales agent for manufacturers and exporters abroad. It has about twenty years experience in this market. It operates from a well-equipped office in a centrally located commercial building in Paris, with modern warehousing facilities in Surret, a suburb of Paris. Ets. Doe appears to have good connections with a number of large and medium-sized local import houses. It is a member of the French Federation of Importers of Woods and of the Seine Syndicate of Lumber and Timber Importers.

REPRESENTATIONS OF ETS. DOE, PARIS, FRANCE

Name of firm	Products	Year Agency Obtained
Ross Timber Co., 37 Washington Ave., Vernon, Oregon	Softwoods	1943
Stafford & Fox Co., 319 Adams St., Seattle, Washington	Millwood	1951
James Moore, Inc., 1609 Jefferson Ave., Augusta, Maine	Plywood	1947
Everett & Morris Corp., 19 Madison St., New York, N. Y.	Hardwoods	1957
Lehman Chemical Co., 65 E. Monroe St., New York, N. Y.	Wood Preservatives	1955
Grady Cummings & Hunt, 1235 Clay St., Philadelphia, Pa.	Railroad Crossties	1941
Otto Ehrlich, 6 Kraemerstrasse, Augsburg, Germany	Lumber	1958

16 (continued). Provide a digest of the firm's trading experiences including information obtained from banks, showing the highlights in the firm's history including changes in lines handled, variations in annual turnover and capital; this should be a performance record of this firm:

The firm was established in 1941 by Jean Doe as an individual enterprise, which was changed to a partnership with Harry Ferrand in 1946. By public record dated July 15, 1952, the firm was reorganized as a corporation. Although the firm has undergone three reorganizations in its structure, the management and its activities have not experienced any substantial change.

The balance sheet of July 31, 1964, shows a capital of Frs. 8,500,000; liabilities Frs. 3,724,536, and assets Frs. 11,263,471. The several local trade sources consulted stated that the firm is generally considered by the trade to be reliable, competently managed, and of good general repute.

The officers are energetic and experienced businessmen with good connections in local financial and social circles, and the firm can be recommended as a representative for United States firms.

COMM- DC 36517

Other Marketing Tasks

Additional marketing responsibilities of export management include market intelligence, pricing, and promotion. In indirect or cooperative exporting, the gathering of marketing information is done by the firm selling abroad, if it is done at all. The firm supplying the goods may get little market feedback. To perform effectively, the export manager must get continuing market information. Some market information is available from domestic sources. Foreign distributors are another important source, and we have discussed ways of securing their cooperation. When actual or potential export volume is large enough, the export manager himself should visit foreign markets to keep informed. We have described the market intelligence function more fully in Chapter 7.

Pricing for foreign markets involves several new dimensions. First the manager must decide whether to quote in United States dollars or foreign currencies. Then he must decide whether the quote should be f.o.b. (free on board—plant or port of exit), or c.i.f. (cost, insurance, freight) to foreign port, or one of several other possible quotes. Should exports be at full cost or marginal cost pricing? How should the firm handle tariffs and the other add-ons to the plant price? If promotion is needed for exported products, the export manager must take the responsibility for it. He may work with an export advertising agency and/or with national distributors in cooperative advertising programs. The questions of export pricing and promotion are discussed in detail in Chapters 12, 13, and 14.

In concluding this section on export management, we must note that many of these export tasks will be modified and eased where the firm exports to its own sales subsidiaries in foreign markets rather than to independent distributors. The export manager and the subsidiary can divide the labor between them, the subsidiary doing most of the local market research, pricing, and promotion.

FOREIGN MANUFACTURING AS FOREIGN MARKET ENTRY

So far we have assumed that the international marketer entering foreign markets by any method was supplying world markets from domestic plants. This is implicit in any form of exporting—indirect, cooperative, or direct. However, under certain conditions the firm may find it either impossible or undesirable to supply all foreign markets from domestic production sources.

Several different factors may encourage, or indeed force, the firm to produce in foreign markets if it wishes to sell in them. For example, transportation costs may render heavy or bulky products noncompetitive by the time they are shipped from the domestic plant to the foreign buyer. Foreign tariffs or quotas on imports can prevent entry of an exporter's products, and in many countries, the government's preference for national suppliers can also shut the door to goods produced outside the country. In foreign markets where governments practice such preferences, a firm that is a heavy seller to governments must produce there. Any of these conditions could force the firm to manufacture in foreign markets in order to sell there.

More positive factors also encourage a firm to produce abroad. Some foreign markets are large enough to warrant an efficient plant size, especially regional groupings such as the European Common Market. In addition, local production allows better interaction with foreign market needs concerning product design, delivery, and service. Sometimes foreign production costs are lower, allowing the firm to be more competitive abroad, especially when transportation and tariff savings are added in. For many firms that were late in entering foreign markets, acquiring an existing foreign producer, or cooperating with one, is the quickest, and perhaps the only, way to get into a market. The firm might be induced to undertake foreign production to gain any of these advantages even though it has the option of serving the market, at least partly, by exports.

Varied Approaches to Foreign Manufacture: Assembly
Once the firm has decided to enter certain of its foreign markets by manufacturing within them, it has several different alternatives to choose from. Foreign production operations may range from assembly plants, contract manufacturing, licensing, or joint ventures, to wholly owned foreign plants. In each approach, foreign manufacturing is the source of the firm's product in the market, but the extent of the firm's involvement in the production and the marketing processes varies with the approach it chooses.

In foreign assembly, the firm produces domestically all or most of the components or ingredients of its product and ships them to foreign markets to be put together as a finished product. Assembly operations abroad involve less than full-scale manufacturing but still require that a significant portion of final product value be added in the foreign market. Notable examples of foreign assembly are the automobile and farm equipment industries. Where transportation costs on a fully assembled vehicle or piece of equipment are very high, the firm might be more competitive by shipping CKD (completely knocked down) and putting the product together within the target market. Another reason for foreign assembly is the tariff barrier; many countries have much lower tariffs on unassembled equipment than on assembled. By forcing local assembly, governments feel that they increase local employment and other economic benefits from the enterprise.

The pharmaceutical industry is another example of extensive assembly operations, although in this case they should perhaps be called "mixing" operations. Again because of transportation or tariff barriers, a firm will ship key ingredients to foreign markets and add bulky liquids or other ingredients locally, plus the capsule and packaging. In similar fashion, Coca-Cola ships its syrup to foreign markets, where local bottles add the water and the container. These assembly or "mixing" plants abroad represent partial local manufacturing by the firm; they are a compromise between exports and local production, having elements of both.

If an assembly plant involves foreign investment by the firm, which often happens, the firm must make an investment decision as well as a decision on how to enter the market. However, the investment commitment is not necessarily included in a decision to assemble abroad. The firm can assemble its products in foreign markets through licensing arrangements without making a capital outlay. For example, American Motors licensed Renault to assemble its cars in Belgium.

Company-owned assembly operations usually are combined with a company marketing subsidiary in the same market. When the assembling or "mixing" operations are run by a licensee, he may handle the local distribution as well. For example, Renault distributed Ramblers in some parts of Europe, whereas American Motors handled the distribution in other European countries through its Swiss sales subsidiary. Coca-Cola is usually distributed by national organizations licensed by the company.

Contract Manufacturing

Contract manufacturing abroad is foreign manufacturing by proxy; that is, the firm's product is produced in the foreign market by another producer under contract with the firm. Because the contract covers only manufacturing, marketing is handled by a sales subsidiary of the firm. Contract manufacturing is feasible when the firm can locate foreign producers with the capability of manufacturing the firm's product in satisfactory quantity and quality. Although the foregoing is an obvious statement, in many markets such capability cannot be found and contract manufacturing is not an alternative open to the firm. One enterprising manufacturer in Honduras was producing under contract for three American firms: American Home Products, Colgate, and Procter and Gamble.

Contract manufacturing may be an attractive alternative if the firm's competitive advantage lies in the areas of engineering, marketing, and service rather than in production. For example, Procter and Gamble in Italy had several of its products manufactured under contract. P&G concentrated its own efforts on the marketing of the products. Contract manufacturing obviates the need for plant investment, something the firm may wish to avoid if the market is politically uncertain or if the firm is short of capital.

Contract manufacturing enables the firm to avoid labor and other problems that may arise from its lack of familiarity with the economy and culture of the country, but at the same time the firm gets the advantage of advertising its product as locally made. This may be useful in public relations or for government procurement purposes. If a market proves too small or risky, it is easier and less costly to terminate a manufacturing contract than to shut down the firm's own plant. Other advantages include transportation savings (compared to exports), occasionally lower production costs abroad, and possible exports of components or supplies to the contract manufacturer.

A few drawbacks to the contract manufacturing approach may limit its application. For one, the manufacturing profit goes to the local firm rather than to the international firm, but this is not too serious if sufficient profit remains on the marketing activities. For another, finding a satisfactory manufacturer in the foreign market is often difficult, and if one is found, the firm runs the risk of training a future competitor. This danger is lessened where brand names and trademarks are important to the product. Quality control, too, will usually be a greater problem when production is done by another firm.

From our discussion, the advantages of contract manufacturing appear to outweigh the drawbacks. To underestimate the practical problems of locating and working with a contract manufacturer, however, is dangerous; nevertheless, this avenue should be given serious attention in a world where foreign investment is increasingly criticized and threatened.

Del Monte chose contract manufacturing as a low-risk way to produce in the Central American Common Market (CACM). Del Monte had been exporting to Central America since the 1930s but felt that the time had come for local production by the mid-1960s. The first step was straight contract production by Del Campo, a Costa Rican firm in the canned foods industry. Del Campo put out twenty of the Del Monte product lines, using Del Monte recipes. The agreement was on a straight price per item basis, with Del Monte handling its own distribution.

After two years, Del Monte concluded that it had found a competent local partner, so a closer relationship was worked out. Del Monte began to supply assistance in production, packing, and marketing to Del Campo. Del Campo began to produce Del Monte products for all the CACM countries and also to market *them in Costa Rica. Del Monte also negotiated an option for up to 67 percent of Del Campo's equity, which could be exercised after 1970.*[10]

Licensing

Licensing is another way the firm can get local production in foreign markets without a capital investment on its part. It differs from contract manufacturing in that it is usually for a longer term and involves much greater responsibilities for the national party. A licensing agreement is an arrangement wherein the licensor gives something of value to the licensee in exchange for certain performance and payments from the licensee. The licensor (the international company) may give the licensee (the national firm) one or more of the following things: (1) patent rights; (2) trademark rights; (3) copyrights; (4) know-how on products or processes. Any of these may be given for use in a particular foreign market, or the licensee may have rights in several countries or for a whole continent.

In return for the use of the know-how or rights received, the licensee usually promises (1) to produce the licensor's products covered by the rights; (2) to market these products in his assigned territory; and (3) to pay the licensor some amount related to the sales volume of such products. Note that the licensee takes on a much greater role than the foreign manufacturer who produces under contract from the international firm. The licensee takes over the marketing task in his market in addition to production and is thus the complete foreign market presence of the international firm for the products covered.

[10] *Business Latin America*, March 6, 1969, pp. 78, 79.

Evaluating Licensing

Several features of the licensing method of entry to foreign markets are attractive. First, it requires no capital outlay and thus need not deter even small companies. Second, it is often the quickest and easiest way to enter a foreign market. Even the firm that has capital may have to go through a slow and difficult process to establish local production and to get distribution facilities. Third, the firm gains access to local market knowledge, thus avoiding the problems of adjusting to the foreign economic and cultural environment which come with establishing its own foreign operations.

A fourth advantage is that many foreign governments favor licensing over direct investment because licensing brings technology into the country with fewer strings and costs attached to it. Thus licensing may gain government approval more quickly than, or even in place of, direct investment. And from the licensor's viewpoint, there is no investment to be expropriated. Finally, the general advantages of foreign production also apply to licensing, that is, savings in tariff and transport costs, local production where national suppliers are favored, and so on.

The disadvantages of licensing are less numerous than the advantages, but they may carry greater weight. One of the chief fears about the licensing approach to foreign markets is that the licensor may establish his own competitor. During the five or ten years of the licensing agreement, the licensor may transfer enough expertise that the licensee can get along without him, and thus he may lose that market, and perhaps neighboring markets, to his former licensee. Of course, this is less likely where strong brands or trademarks are involved.

Another reason for hesitancy about licensing is the limited returns it provides. Although no capital outlay is necessary, the royalties and fees from licensing are not "gravy" to the licensor, who must invest management and engineering time. A direct investment approach to the foreign market requires greater effort and resources from the firm, but it may also yield much greater profits. Licensing returns are limited primarily to a percent of the licensee's sales, commonly 3 to 5 percent.

Yet another possible drawback to licensing is the problem of controlling the licensee, or administering the agreement. Although the contract should spell out all dimensions of the agreement and the responsibilities of each party, misunderstandings and conflicts can arise in its implementation. Frequent areas of conflict are quality control, the marketing effort of the licensee, and interpretation of the exclusiveness and extent of the licensee's territorial coverage. These problems arise partly because an agreement that met both parties' interests at the time of signing can become unsuitable to one or both as the years go by and conditions change.

One American equipment producer had a French licensee for over thirty years. The licensee was very capable and aggressive in developing the French market, and the licensor was very satisfied. However, when the European Com-

mon Market eliminated territorial restrictions between member nations, the American licensor found the French licensee competing with its own subsidiaries in other member countries. The American firm was unhappy about this but was afraid to terminate the agreement for fear the licensee would go off on his own and be an even more dangerous competitor, taking the French market with him.

Managing the Licensing Agreement

Firms that use licensing as their entry into foreign markets and welcome its profit contribution have developed certain techniques for minimizing the dangers inherent in it. We note some of these techniques below.

1. Selection of the licensee is critical because it is a question of a long-run relationship. The firm should select a number of candidates and evaluate each carefully. Many American companies have chosen licensees by responding to an initiative from a foreign producer, without considering alternatives. An optimal result is less likely with this kind of selection.

2. The licensing agreement needs to be carefully drafted to recognize and protect the interests of both parties. The licensor must assure that it retains some effective control over the life of the agreement, even after the initial transmission of rights and know-how. Some important elements of the agreement include territorial coverage, duration, royalty rate, protection of trade secrets, a minimum performance clause, and provision for quality control.

3. The licensor can maintain some control by shipping a few key parts or ingredients rather than giving the licensee rights and know-how for a complete package; in this way the licensor can keep the licensee somewhat dependent.

4. The licensor can increase control by obtaining an equity interest in the licensee, either by sending capital abroad or by accepting equity in lieu of royalty payments. Many joint ventures have grown out of licensing arrangements in just this way. The equity interest makes it more difficult for the licensee to go his own way after the agreement has expired.

5. Greater control can be retained by the licensor if it limits the product and territorial coverage of the agreement. In the same vein, it might provide for separate licensing agreements to cover new products and improvements it develops. However, if there is a probability that new products and improvements may come from both parties, the agreement should provide for such a two-way flow.

6. The licensor can retain greater control if the foreign market registration of patents and trademarks is in *its* name rather than in the licensee's name.

7. The greatest means of encouraging effective licensee performance is to make the agreement continually attractive to it. The licensor does this by helping the licensee with production and marketing problems as well as by maintaining a technological, product, and marketing edge so that the licensee always has something to gain from the agreement.

Growth of Licensing

Various studies have shown that the number of licensing agreements of American companies is growing every year. Not only are receipts from foreign licensing increasing, but a majority of companies stated that licensing revenues constituted a higher *percent* of their foreign income in 1967 than in 1962.[11] It should be noted that licensing income is not limited to royalties but includes such items as the following:

1. Technical assistance fees
2. Sale of components or materials to licensee
3. Lump-sum payments for transfer of rights or technology
4. Technology feedback
5. Royalty-free reciprocal license rights
6. Fees for engineering services
7. Sales of machinery or equipment to licensee
8. Management fees.

The typical company receives over five different types of return on its licensing agreements.[12]

Some American companies are heavily involved in foreign licensing, as the following examples illustrate: (1) A leading American producer of building materials had fifty-eight foreign licensees providing an annual net contribution of $2 million after taxes. (2) An automotive equipment manufacturer had close to 500 different licensing agreements abroad, bringing in millions of dollars in royalties. Additionally, the company said it was receiving valuable new technical developments from its licensees.[13] In recent years, European and Japanese companies are also becoming more active in foreign licensing as their technologies improve. With the increasing criticism of foreign investment, companies must continue to consider licensing as an alternative route to foreign markets.

A brief case study of an American company's licensing experience will conclude our discussion of licensing.

The Manhattan Shirt Company had licensees in over thirty countries, many of them in the developing nation category. These were administered by the company's International Licensing Division, whose manager spent 40 percent of his time traveling abroad. Though Manhattan shirts are a nonpatentable product, the company felt that its brand name and know-how were very licensable.

The company's method of operation is instructive. Manhattan began with

---

[11] National Industrial Conference Board, "Appraising Foreign Licensing Performance," Studies in Business Policy, no. 128 (1968), pp. 5, 6.
[12] NICB, "Appraising Foreign Licensing Performance," pp. 52, 53.
[13] *International Commerce*, April 22, 1968, p. 20.

a market survey. This was followed up by a search for licensee candidates in the more attractive markets. The licensing manager visited each prospective licensee on his home grounds before making a selection. One criterion was that Manhattan shirts be an important part of the licensee's business, so that they be given proper attention. The licensee's production people were required to come to the United States for training. Sales training was given in the licensee's country.

The licensee was required to advertise. Whereas sales and production training were included in the royalty fee, advertising had to be at the expense of the licensee, although the size of the commitment varied by country. Often the company took a part of the first year royalties and rebated a portion to be used by the licensee for advertising, above his regular commitment.

Manhattan set up an exchange of information between members of its licensing "family." This was good for morale and also for the exchange of experiences. Most of the important technical information came from Manhattan's domestic operations. The data was supplied to licensees at the same time it became available in the United States. The manager felt that his periodic visits to licensees not only helped their performance, but helped Manhattan to control the agreement.

For quality control, the company required random samples of every licensee's production. Revenue control was maintained by traveling auditors who checked licensee's production and sales reports. The company liked to limit the territory of a licensee. If he was given more than one country, Manhattan liked separate minimum performance clauses for each market.[14]

Joint Ventures in Foreign Markets

Foreign joint ventures in manufacturing have much in common with foreign licensing arrangements. Both usually involve foreign manufacturing and distribution by a foreign firm. The major difference is that in the joint venture, the international firm has an equity position and a management voice in the foreign firm. The equity share of the international company can range between 10 and 90 percent, but generally it is between 25 and 75 percent. Instead of seeking an acceptable technical or legal definition of a joint venture, however, we will use the following practical one: A joint venture is a foreign operation in which the international company has enough equity to have a voice in management but not enough to completely dominate or control the venture. Note also that we consider only joint ventures between an American firm (or other international firm) and a firm that is native to the country where the venture is located.

Contract manufacturing and licensing are joint ventures of a sort, and so is the exporter working with his foreign distributor, but in none of these relationships are the ties so strong as in the joint venture. As in the progression from going steady to being engaged to being married, each step represents a stronger tie. With the expansion of international operations since World

[14] Adapted from *Business Abroad*, October 16, 1967, pp. 25, 26.

War II, joint ventures have become increasingly important. Whereas three-quarters of all foreign manufacturing subsidiaries established before 1946 were wholly owned, the percentage had dropped to just over half by 1968.

To Join or Not To Join

In evaluating the joint-venture approach to foreign manufacturing, its advantages and disadvantages must be compared with both the lesser commitment of contract manufacturing and licensing and the greater commitment of wholly owned foreign production. Whatever cost and market benefits derive from foreign manufacture will, of course, be obtained in the joint venture approach as well as in any other. As compared with a lesser commitment, joint ventures have the following advantages: (1) potentially greater returns from equity participation as opposed to royalties; (2) greater control over production and marketing; (3) better market feedback; and (4) more experience in international marketing. Disadvantages include a need for greater investment of capital and management resources and a potentially greater risk than with a nonequity approach.

When the partial ownership in joint ventures is compared with wholly owned foreign production, a different picture emerges: (1) A joint venture requires fewer capital and management resources and thus is more open to smaller companies; (2) a given amount of capital can be spread out among more countries; (3) the danger of expropriation is less when a firm has a national partner than when the international firm is sole owner.

Many foreign governments prefer or even demand joint ventures because they feel that their nations get more of the profits and technological benefit if nationals have a share. India, Japan, and Mexico have been especially restrictive about foreigners owning over 50 percent of any venture in their countries. Also, finding a national partner may be the only way to invest in some markets that are too competitive or crowded to admit a completely new foreign operation.

Joint ventures compare unfavorably with wholly owned operations on only a few points, but often the points are critical. Each of the partners that share control of the joint venture has his own goals, needs, and interests, which will often conflict with those of his partner. The national partner has his personal interests, and they relate primarily to the operation in his own country. The international firm's interests, on the other hand, relate to the totality of its international operations; actions it takes to further global operations may appear detrimental from the viewpoint of the national partner. Some points over which conflicts arise are (1) transfer pricing, (2) earnings —pay out or plow back? and (3) product line and market coverage of the joint venture.

Although shared equity means also shared control and conflict of interest, it may involve in addition an unequal sharing of the burden. Occasionally, international companies with 50–50 joint ventures feel that they are giving more than 50 percent of the technology, management skill, and other factors that contribute to the success of the operation but receiving only half the profits. Of course, the national partner contributes local knowledge and other intangibles that may be underestimated. Nevertheless, some international companies that are leaders in their industries feel that the joint venture partner gets too much of a "free ride."

The major weakness or complaint about joint ventures compared with 100-percent ownership is that it is difficult to integrate them into a synergistic international operation. When the international firm wishes to standardize product design, quality standards, or other activities, it may encounter disagreement from a number of its national joint-venture partners. Thus, where standardization, international exchange, and integration are important to the effectiveness of the international company, the joint-venture approach can be a hindrance. The American automobile companies and IBM prefer 100-percent ownership for this reason. Conversely, where the national operations have differing product lines and localized marketing, joint ventures pose much less of a problem.

Two case histories will illustrate widely contrasting aspects of company philosophy and practice in joint ventures. One is a statement of the Scott Paper Company, a firm believer in joint ventures. The other recounts the sad and costly experience of Xerox.

Our foreign policy: Get there early and get married.

Scott was an early arrival in fifteen countries. And our growth overseas is as spectacular as the opportunities there. Only five years ago, our affiliates outside the United States were doing some $80 million a year. Last year, our affiliates achieved $176 million.

Across the world in Japan, we've been established for nine years. Last year alone, our facial tissue business grew 50%. But that's not really so surprising. The facial tissue business is growing three to five times faster overseas than it is here.

We have an even vaster new market opening up to us in the developing countries of Latin America. In one of the largest of these, our bathroom tissue sales have doubled every five years. Even so, in that country, less than a quarter of the people use bathroom tissue.

In Europe, in addition to our traditional business we have another growing enterprise. Scott Graphics/Europe is a special manufacturing and marketing group that includes electrostatic office copy systems, microcopy systems, and other photographic and graphic arts specialities that utilize a whole different kind of expertise.

All in all, there are some 500 million people in Scott's markets outside the United States. Which means our manufacturing and marketing facilities now can serve at least 80% of the Free World purchasing power. The potential is there. And so is Scott.

We're there in an unusual relationship, too, as the 50-50 partner in most of our overseas affiliates. Not 51-49. 50-50. That 1% we don't have has yielded substantial dividends. In mutual trust. In the high caliber of the corporate partners it has brought us in each country. In the knowledgeable people they bring us. It's a successful marriage if ever we heard of one. And the honeymoon has only just begun.[15]

In 1956, Xerox Corp. faced tremendous growth in the United States market. Faced with the great difficulty in meeting rapidly growing American demand, the company felt it could not begin to tackle the rest of the world. Xerox therefore joined with the Rank Organization in the United Kingdom to form a 50%-50% joint venture Rank–Xerox (RX). Xerox gave the venture an exclusive license in perpetuity to manufacture and sell all xerographic machines outside North America.

During the intervening years the basic agreement has changed little, although it has been repeatedly adjusted both as regards the equity and profit splits as well as the markets in which RX has exclusive sales rights. RX's share capital by 1968 was $53.8 million, of which the Xerox contribution was $32.6 million (although the voting split was still 50:50). By 1968 the earnings split was 50:50 up to $16.5 million: and Xerox two thirds, Rank one third after that figure was reached.

The more important adjustments concerned the marketing arrangements. In 1963 RX sold marketing rights for Latin America to Xerox in return for a 5% royalty on all subsequent net sales and rentals earned in Latin America, plus a payment to Rank of 7,500 shares of Xerox stock, worth approximately $3.3 million at that time. In 1966 a similar agreement was made for marketing rights in the British West Indies, again with a 5% royalty to RX but no stock payment to Rank.

Although Xerox has consolidated Latin American sales since 1964, industry sources put the figure at between 2% and 5% of total. If this is accurate, Xerox has paid RX a royalty of between $2.6 million and $6.6 million for the privilege of marketing its own products in the western hemisphere since 1964, even though Rank acknowledged in 1963 that it had been able to do little to increase sales in the area. Xerox has had to invest about $20 million in Latin America to make the sales and rentals, out of which the 5% was taken.

The original agreement has just been amended again in an apparent further effort to correct the original mistake. The key points of the latest agreement:

Xerox paid Rank $7.5 million in stock for the right to stop paying the Latin American royalties. In other words, beside the investment Xerox has had to make on its own to market its own products successfully in Latin America, it has had to pay Rank a total of between $10 million and $14 million over a five-year period for the privilege of doing so.

Xerox paid Rank $12.5 million in Xerox shares for the right to name 13 directors of RX to Rank's 12.

Xerox agreed to pay Rank $5 million over the next five years for marketing advice for Xerox Data Systems (Rank has no EDP product lines).

[15] Advertisement in the *Wall Street Journal*, January 20, 1970, p. 13.

What the Rank Joint Venture Seems To Have Cost Xerox
(in $ millions)

Stock payments in 1969	*20.0*
in 1963	*3.3*
Half of RX accumulated profits	*54.0*
Half Fuji-Xerox profits	*1.8*
5% royalty payment for Latin American sales	*4.6*
	83.7
Advisory fee, 1970–74	*5.0*
	88.7

Burnham and Co. of New York estimates that RX will earn
$339 million during 1969–72, which would swell the Xerox
losses by $169 million more.

Xerox licensed RX to manufacture and sell all of its other products in the eastern hemisphere, including such new ventures as EDP hardware and services and library and education systems. These products are all developed and produced by Xerox in the US, where Xerox's development and research costs are estimated at between $50 million and $80 million annually. Since the earnings and equity splits of RX will remain the same, RX will pay Xerox an 8% royalty on the sale of any of these new products. But two thirds of any costs related to RX's distribution of these new lines will be picked up by Xerox; only one third by Rank.

Although Rank is not committed to put up its one third share, its equity in RX will be reduced if it does not. If Xerox acquires or diversifies into new product businesses Rank may veto any such expansion that will cost it more than $60 million.

While the latest agreement clears up some of the inequities of the 1956, 1963, and 1966 agreements at a very high price, it creates some new ones. Xerox's freedom to expand in the lush European (and Japanese) markets is sharply constrained by having to work through RX. Even with control at the director level, RX is a UK firm that must work through some of the world's toughest capital outflow controls. Even the Rank chairman was quoted as being surprised at the Xerox decision to license all its products to RX.

In toto, the 1956 agreement and the subsequent efforts to correct it have cost Xerox shareholders something over $80 million, and may cost over $200 million by 1971 (see above table).[16]

Wholly Owned Foreign Production

Wholly owned foreign production represents the greatest commitment to foreign markets by the international firm. In principle, "wholly owned" means 100-percent ownership by the international firm. In practice, the international firm usually achieves the same results by owning 95 percent or even less. The

[16] Reprinted from Jan. 2, 1970 issue of *Business International* with the permission of the publisher, Business International Corp. (N.Y.).

chief practical criterion for wholly owned ventures is not the completeness of ownership but the completeness of control by the international company. Complete management control is often achieved with something less than 100-percent ownership.

Make or Buy?

The international firm can obtain wholly owned foreign production facilities in two primary ways: (1) It can buy out an existing foreign producer—the acquisition route—or (2) it can develop its own facilities from the ground up. As a variation on the acquisition route, the firm can buy out the equity of a joint-venture partner. The acquisition route was especially popular in the 1960s in Europe, but it offers certain advantages in other times and places too.

Acquisition is generally a much quicker way for a firm to get into a market than building up its own facilities. Acquiring a going concern usually means acquiring a qualified labor force along with it. Getting workers, let alone qualified ones, is difficult in many markets, so this feature by itself could lead a firm toward acquisition. By acquiring an existing concern, a firm also gains national management personnel, local knowledge, and contacts with local markets and government. And in some markets, acquisition may be the only way to enter if the industry has no room for a completely new competitor.

The alternative to acquisition is the establishment of a new facility, a method that may be desirable or necessary in certain circumstances. For example, in some markets, the international firm will not be able to find a national producer willing to sell out or else the local government will not allow the firm to sell to the international company. This was the case in France with de Gaulle's worry about the "American challenge." In other markets, producers may be willing to sell but lack the caliber of facilities needed by the technology of the international firm.

For its part, the international firm may prefer a new facility to an acquisition. If the target market has no personnel or management shortages, the firm feels less pressure toward the acquisition route. Furthermore, if the firm builds a new plant it can not only incorporate the latest technology and equipment, but it can also avoid the problems of trying to change the traditional practices of an established concern. A new facility means a fresh start and an opportunity for the international company to shape the local firm into its own image and requirements.

Deciding on Solo Operations

Evaluation of the attractions and limitations of the sole-ownership approach to foreign markets is easier now that we have considered all the other alternatives. The advantages of wholly owned ventures are few but powerful. One hundred percent ownership means 100 percent of the profits go to the international firm, eliminating the possibility of a national partner's getting a "free ride" and sharing in profits beyond its real contribution. Complete ownership also permits the international firm to acquire greater experience in international operations and better market contact. These benefits would tend to accrue to the national partner if the firm had a lesser degree of involvement.

With no national partner, no inefficiences arise from conflicts of interest. Perhaps the overriding argument for complete control, however, is the possibility of integrating various national operations into a synergistic international system. Lesser degrees of involvement are likely to lead to international sub-optimization, as national partners have goals that conflict with those of the international firm.

The limitations to the 100-percent ownership approach are several. For one thing, it is costly in terms of capital and management resources. The capital requirements prevent many firms from practicing a complete ownership strategy, and although very large firms do not often find capital availability a constraint, they may face a shortage of management personnel.

One of America's largest companies (in Fortune's *top twenty) conducted all of its international business via exports and licensing for many years. In the mid–1960s, management decided that an equity approach would mean greater long-run profits. The company began to implement this decision, but progress was very slow. The impediment was not a lack of capital but a shortage of company managers with the necessary international experience. The company also had problems locating desirable firms to acquire. It had begun the equity approach a bit late in the game.*

Another drawback to 100-percent ownership is the probable negative host-government and public-relations effects. Most nationals feel their participation in the venture should not be limited to supplying just labor or raw materials. Some governments go so far as to prohibit 100-percent ownership by the international firm and demand licensing or joint ventures instead. A further risk deriving from these national feelings is expropriation, which is much more likely and more costly with wholly owned operations. The firm has more to lose because it has more eggs in one basket.

Finally, 100-percent ownership may deprive the firm of the local knowledge and contacts of a national partner. The local collaborator often would serve as a buffer between the international firm and its various national audiences. This role of the national partner as a cultural bridge can be its major contribution, helping the firm to avoid mistakes and frictions in its diverse encounters with nationals in business or government. By taking the acquisition route, the firm has more chance of retaining such nationals than it does in setting up a new operation. The same applies to a wholly owned operation developed from a joint venture. With wholly owned foreign operations, the firm can gradually develop nationals who can be a culture bridge, but the process is slow compared with such opportunities offered by other kinds of involvement.

CONCLUSIONS

Just as there are many different kinds of foreign market opportunities, so there are several different ways for a firm to get its products into foreign markets. In this chapter, we have discussed many methods of foreign market entry, noting some of the advantages and disadvantages of each. In concluding, we *cannot* say that there is one best way to enter a foreign market. The way best for the firm depends not only on its own size, capabilities, and needs, but also on the opportunities and conditions in the target markets; the firm must analyze its own situation, considering how the variables discussed here apply. A careful analysis of alternatives should lead to more optimal results than merely responding to initiatives coming from outside the firm, which is the way many firms have carried on their international business.

Earlier in this chapter, we presented a matrix relating the various entry methods to some of the principal decision variables (see Table 10–1). Now that we have discussed briefly the nature of the different approaches, another matrix may be helpful. Table 10–3 distinguishes among the entry methods according to the various flows involved (goods, money, equipment, and so on). This matrix of Luostarinen is a useful way of summarizing many of the operational differences between the levels of involvement.

Flexibility is an important aspect of the firm's choice of entry strategy. Rather than rigidly following a single approach, the firm may want variation, depending on conditions within its different markets. Larger markets may permit more direct approaches, whereas smaller markets may be better served by less direct entry. In some firms, it may be appropriate to use different entry strategies for different product lines or divisions. Flexibility over time is also a major consideration. As conditions change, the optimal strategy may change; the firm can only gain by anticipating developments and adapting to them, rather than getting out-of-date or fighting against them. An example of one such development is the desire of most nations for licensing or joint ventures rather than 100-percent ownership by the international firm. Finding creative answers to such developments is the key to the viability and success of the international corporation. We cite the following two examples to show how companies' strategies change over time.

Weyerhaeuser Company, Tacoma, Washington, set up its own corporate sales offices in South America, Europe, Australia, and several countries in the Far East. The move was a significant departure from the traditional policy of most U.S. forest products companies to sell overseas only when an excess supply was on hand, or when overseas prices were higher than domestic ones. Weyerhaeuser made its decision to go into foreign markets permanently when exports topped 8 percent of the company's total sales volume.

A large European chemical company had a five stage strategy in its approach to foreign markets.

Stage 1. Limited sales, a form of market testing, through trading companies or independent distributors who bought for their own account.

Stage 2. Where markets looked promising, the company sent field representatives to aid the distributor. This was done in Nigeria and East Africa, for example.

Table 10-3 International Flows by Level of Involvement

TYPE OF FOREIGN OPERATION	FLOW OF GOODS AND MATERIALS					FLOW OF FINANCIAL CAPITAL							FLOW OF PHYSICAL CAPITAL		FLOW OF HUMAN CAPITAL		
	FINISHED PRODUCTS	SEMIFINISHED PRODUCTS	PARTS	SPARE PARTS	RAW MATERIALS	PAYMENTS	FEES	ROYALTIES	INTERESTS	EQUITY CAPITAL	LOAN CAPITAL	PROFITS, DIVIDENDS (REPATRIATIONS)	MACHINERY	EQUIPMENT, TOOLS	KNOW-HOW	INDUSTRIAL RIGHTS	PERSONNEL
Indirect export	x*			x*		x*											
Direct export	x			x		x											
Own export (Marketing subsidiary)	x		x**	x		x			x	x	x	x			x		
Licensing								x					x††	x††	x		x
Contract manufacturing							x						x††	x††	x††	x	x††
Co-production							x						x	x	x		x
Own assembling	x†	x	x			x		x†	x	x	x	x	x	x	x		x
Own manufacturing	x†	x	x	x	x	x	x		x	x	x	x	x	x	x	x†	x

* If the middleman in the home country is a buying middleman the different flows in the first stage of operation take place in the home country.

† May be included as a suboperation or as a supplementary operation.

** Easily assembled parts may be assembled in a sales outlet.

†† May be included in the contract.

Source: Reijo Luostarinen, *Foreign Operations of the Firm* (Helsinki, Finland: Helsinki School of Economics, 1970, mimeographed), p. 10.

Stage 3. Where the field representatives reported strong sales possibilities in a sizable market, the company moved to establish its own sales organization.

Stage 4. If the company sales subsidiary developed the market to a highly profitable degree, the company considered plant investment. The first step was a compounding or assembly plant to mix and package ingredients imported from Europe. Two examples of this are Brazil and Mexico.

Stage 5. The final step is a complete manufacturing plant. Such a plant might produce only a few of the many products of the firm depending on local raw material supply and markets. The company has such a plant in India.[17]

Questions

10.1 Using Table 10–1, rate the various entry methods on each dimension. Score from 1 to 8 on each dimension, the lowest score being the most desirable—for example, the one giving the *most* markets scoring 1, the least markets scoring 8, and so on. For some dimensions, the most desirable score would go to the lowest value; that is, the lower the costs, investment, personnel, and risk, the better the score. Compare results and evaluate the uses and limitations of this approach.

10.2 Why does the international firm often have to combine different levels of market entry to reach world markets effectively?

10.3 "For some markets international trading companies offer the best entry." Discuss.

10.4 Explain the several attractions of the CEM approach to foreign markets. What kinds of firms would not generally be interested in the CEM approach?

10.5 Identify the marketing functions that may be performed by a Webb-Pomerene Association.

10.6 How can the carrier and the rider both benefit from a piggyback exporting arrangement? What decisions must be made by the carrier in such an arrangement? By the rider?

10.7 In moving into direct exporting, what tasks must the firm undertake?

10.8 Why is great care necessary in choosing the firm's representatives in foreign markets? What procedure might be followed in selecting foreign distributors?

10.9 Identify the various sources of assistance available to an *exporter* in your community or state. Locate specific company names if possible. The Yellow Pages might help.

10.10 What are the attractions to foreign production as a form of market entry? the deterrents?

10.11 When is contract manufacturing feasible? When is it desirable?

10.12 "Foreign assembly represents a compromise between exports and local production." Discuss.

10.13 Discuss the attractions and the dangers of the licensing form of entry into foreign markets. How can the multinational firm minimize the dangers?

10.14 Identify the various kinds of income available through licensing.

10.15 What are the advantages and disadvantages of joint ventures as compared with wholly owned operations?

10.16 Why do firms often prefer the acquisition route for obtaining wholly owned foreign operations?

[17] *Business Europe*, September 5, 1969, pp. 286, 287.

10.17 In view of the frequent local opposition to wholly owned foreign subsidiaries, what arguments, if any, can be made in their favor?

10.18 "Deciding on the method of entry into a foreign market is a critical decision because it will largely determine what marketing alternatives are open to the firm." Discuss.

Further Readings

Books:

Friedman, W. G., and George Kalmanoff, *Joint International Business Ventures* (New York: Columbia University Press, 1961).

International Marketing Institute (Boston), *Export Marketing for Smaller Firms,* 2nd ed. (Washington, D.C.: Small Business Administration, 1966).

Kramer, Roland L., *International Marketing,* 3rd ed. (Cincinnati, Ohio: South-Western Publishing Co., 1970), chaps. 21–29.

Lovell, Enid Baird, *Appraising Foreign Licensing Performance,* Studies in Business Policy No. 128 (New York: National Industrial Conference Board, 1969).

Luostarinen, Reijo, *Foreign Operations of the Firm* (Helsinki, Finland: Helsinki School of Economics, 1970).

National Industrial Conference Board, *Foreign Licensing Agreements, I: Evaluation and Planning* (1958), *II: Contract Negotiations and Administration* (1959), New York.

National Industrial Conference Board, *Joint Ventures with Foreign Partners* (New York, 1966).

Root, Franklin R., *Strategic Planning for Export Marketing* (Scranton, Penna.: International Textbook Company, 1966), chap. 5.

Stuart, Robert D., *Penetrating the International Market,* Management Report No. 84 (New York: American Management Association, 1965), chaps. 6–8.

Articles:

Curry, Robert L., "Webb-Pomerene Export Associations," *Oregon Business Review* (July 1967), pp. 1–5.

11

DISTRIBUTION: FOREIGN MARKET CHANNELS AND GLOBAL LOGISTICS

The preceding chapter on distribution considered only one question facing the international marketer: How do I get my products into foreign markets? We saw that there are many alternative answers—and combinations of answers—to that question. Once the firm has chosen an appropriate strategy to get its products *into* foreign markets, its next challenge is distribution of the product *within* foreign markets. Our first major topic in this chapter, therefore, will be a discussion of how the international firm manages foreign distribution; our second major topic will be the management of international logistics.

MANAGING FOREIGN DISTRIBUTION

Some firms whose products sell in foreign markets do not have to face the task of managing distribution within those markets. For them, this question was resolved, for better or for worse, when they decided on their method of entry into foreign markets. Firms that sell through trading companies, combination export managers, or other indirect methods usually must accept as given the foreign distribution offered by these intermediaries. The same is true but to a lesser degree for those that sell through licensing or direct exporting. Although the licensor is usually limited to the foreign market distribution offered by its licensee, the licensor can have some influence on distribution through its selection of the licensee as well as through their mutual contract arrangement. Furthermore, the licensor may be able to complement and assist the licensee's efforts. The export manager working with his foreign distributor is in about the same position as the licensor.

The firms that have direct responsibility for their foreign market distribution are those having sales or marketing subsidiaries in foreign markets or complete manufacturing and marketing operations there. The marketing subsidiary might receive its products as exports of some American or foreign plant of the international company or from a local contract manufacturer. Whatever the product source, the subsidiary marketing manager is responsible for local distribution.

The international company also has complete responsibility for distribution in those markets where it has jointly or wholly owned production operations. Having complete responsibility is different, of course, from having complete freedom or control. For example, the marketing manager in a joint venture will be constrained by the desires and practices of the national partner. The wholly owned foreign venture that resulted from an acquisition will also find its foreign market distribution options affected by the practices and personnel inherited from the acquired firm.

UNCONTROLLABLE ELEMENTS

The marketing manager in the foreign market must be aware of the environmental parameters that constrain his distribution strategy there. If the marketing manager is an expatriate, he will be familiar with distribution channels and practices of his home country, but this knowledge will be of limited value in the foreign market. Before choosing his distribution strategy, he must identify and evaluate the local environment of distribution. Some of the important elements to consider are the existing structure and nature of wholesaling and retailing, laws and regulations affecting distribution, and the country's infrastructure as it pertains to warehousing and transportation possibilities.

Wholesaling in Foreign Markets

The wholesaling functions (gathering assortments, breaking bulk, distribution to retailers, and so on) are performed in all countries, but with varying degrees of efficiency. Although occasionally in the American market, a manufacturer will perform some of the wholesaling functions himself, in foreign markets he is less likely to do so because of the smaller volume, even though he may feel it is more necessary because of the inefficiencies of wholesaling in some markets.

Size

In moving from one market to another, the marketer will observe various kinds of differences in wholesaling. One difference will be in the size and number of wholesalers. For example, Finland has one of the most concentrated, large-scale wholesaling operations among the countries of the world. Four large wholesaling groups account for most of the wholesale trade. One of these, Kesko (the Wholesale Company of Finnish Retailers) has a market share of over 20 percent and services more that 11,000 retailers. At the other extreme is Japan with its multiplicity of small wholesalers, and even levels of wholesalers, one selling to another before goods reach the retailer. Where the number of wholesalers is large relative to the size of the market, the contact and transaction costs of the manufacturer may be as great as in larger markets. This raises the consumer price, too, further limiting market penetration.

Since specialization is limited by the size of the market, wholesalers in smaller markets often carry broader, more diverse product lines than do their counterparts in larger countries. Even with the broader line, however, their staff and facilities are apt to be smaller. As a result, the manufacturer gets thinner and less effective market coverage and service. This weakness affects industrial goods even more than it does consumer goods because industrial markets are smaller and their service requirements greater.

Service

For the international marketer, another critical difference in wholesaling abroad is the quality of the services wholesalers offer the manufacturer. This difference is often related to the size of wholesaler operations. In some countries, wholesaling is made up of small, fragmented businesses offering inefficient service; but in some other countries, wholesaling operations offer service equaling or surpassing that found in the United States. The author visited facilities of Kesko in Finland and saw a truly impressive, sophisticated operation.

Even in some less developed countries rather good wholesaling is available through the big trading companies. For example, in many African nations, the United Africa Company has large wholesale operations to offer the manufacturer. However, in many nonindustrialized countries wholesaling is oriented to imports that have traditionally supplied most of the goods to the monetized part of the economy. As local production is established, a different kind of wholesaling, oriented to domestic supply and larger volume, is needed.

The marketing manager is concerned about the wholesaling structure in his foreign markets because he must see how wholesalers fit into his marketing program for each country. Do they cover the market? What functions do they perform? Can he reach the market without them? Consumer goods distribution outside the United States is generally carried on by a relatively large number of small retail establishments. Often the only way to reach them and cover the market is by the use of wholesalers, even though these may be relatively small and inefficient. For example, because of the multiplicity and dispersion of retailers selling soaps and detergents in Italy, Procter and Gamble was forced to use a very indirect channel there, that is, selling agent to wholesalers to retailers. Because the number of wholesalers was also large, the company had to use an intermediary even to reach the wholesaler level!

In some markets, the manufacturer is tempted to by-pass the wholesaler because of his costs or inefficiencies. Although this might lead to more efficient distribution, its feasibility needs to be carefully evaluated. Various factors, such as the power of the wholesaler or the critical functions he performs, may preclude the manufacturer from by-passing him. For example, in Germany, Kraft Foods found it would be more efficient to ship directly to the retailer. However, the wholesalers' control over the channel was strong enough to force Kraft to give them a payment, even though their services were not being used.

In Japan, international firms have encountered problems that encouraged some of them to ship directly to the larger retailers. This policy did not work because then the wholesalers would not cover the other outlets. Thus the firm usually has but two alternatives: 100 percent direct sales or no direct sales. Some firms, such as Coca-Cola or Nestle, have gone completely to direct sales, but the financial burden is high. Because many small dealers are financially weak, Japanese wholesalers often extend them liberal credit, sometimes as long as ten months. If the manufacturer wishes to go direct, he may have to carry the financial burden instead of letting the wholesaler carry it for him.[1]

Wholesaling and Economic Development

In concluding our discussion on wholesaling around the world, we can note as a generalization that the nature of wholesaling in a country tends to vary with that country's level of economic development. We have noted the kinds of variations found, so in summary we will indicate the findings of a study on the relationship of distribution to the level of economic development.[2]

1. The influence of the foreign import agent declines with economic development. Local production requires a different kind of wholesale operation.
2. Manufacturer-wholesaler-retailer functions become more distinct and separate with economic development. In Turkey, for example, the wholesaler plays a strong role in organizing production as well as distribution.
3. Wholesaler functions approximate those in North America with increasing economic development.
4. The financing function of the wholesaler declines, but wholesale markups increase with increasing development.

A word of caution is necessary here. Although there is a relationship between a country's economic development and its marketing institutions, this relationship is not always consistent or easy to identify. Work by Susan P. Douglas of Temple University indicates that individual firms may respond in different ways to environmental influences, leading to inconsistent patterns at the national level.[3]

Many of the considerations discussed above will apply also to the distribution of industrial goods. International differences are smaller with industrial goods because the markets are more concentrated and the technological requirements more universal. Yet still the industrial marketer will face adjust-

---

[1] See Herbert Glazer, "Japan Unbars a Door," *Columbia Journal of World Business,* (July–August 1967), pp. 43–49.
[2] George Wadinambiaratchi, "Channels of Distribution in Developing Economies," *The Business Quarterly* (Winter 1965), pp. 74–82.
[3] Susan P. Douglas, "Patterns and Parallels of Marketing Structure in Several Countries," *MSU Business Topics* (Spring 1971), pp. 38–48.

ments in his foreign market channels. An example illustrates how some very large American electronics companies adapted their distribution by going indirect in one of the largest foreign markets.

Semiconductor Specialists, Inc., Chicago, formed a sales and stocking facility in London. The organization distributed the products of several U.S. manufacturers in the solid-state circuit and integrated circuit fields to buyers in the British market. Among U.S. firms represented in England by Semiconductor Specialists were Fairchild, Motorola, RCA, Westinghouse, Signetics, ITT, Siliconix, General Electric, Clevite, Augat, and others.

Retailing in Foreign Markets

International differences in retailing are even greater than in wholesaling. The reason is that retailing more closely reflects the economic, social, and cultural life of different nations. The international marketer must be aware of these retailing patterns insofar as they impinge upon his marketing program in different countries.

Greater Numbers, Smaller Size

An American marketer looking at retailing in the markets of the world would be struck first of all by the differences in the numbers and size of retail businesses. The differences in the scale of retail operation can be measured in several ways. One method is to ascertain the *number of employees per retail establishment.* In 1967, Belgium had 1.9 employees per retail outlet; the Netherlands had 3.4; Swede had 5.5; and the United States had 6.4. The average *number of consumers per retail outlet* is another indicator of relative size. In 1967 Belgium and Italy had approximately 54 consumers per retail business; France and the Netherlands about 75; Finland 135; and the United States had 196.[4]

These figures show that even among the developed countries of Western Europe, the range of retailer size and performance is wide. Furthermore, retailing in the United States is a much larger scale operation than it is elsewhere. The comparison for food retailing alone is perhaps even more striking. Western Europe in 1967 counted an average of 145 inhabitants per food outlet, compared with 525 for the United States. Sales volume per retail outlet varies accordingly, with smaller and smaller sales recorded as one goes down the scale of development. The less developed countries, of course, generally have much smaller retail businesses than Western Europe. A firm accustomed to distributing in the American market faces adjustments when entering foreign markets with such different retail patterns.

We would like to note here that anyone who visits only the capitals or largest cities of most nations of the world will not get a true picture of the retailing structure of the country. The capital cities even of poorer nations

---

[4] Figures from James B. Jefferys of the International Association of Department Stores in conversation with author, November, 1968.

may well have a few department stores and supermarkets such as the tourist has seen at home. Such evidences in the small, modernizing sector of the economy, however, are not typical of the nation as a whole. Rather, they reflect the "dual economy" phenomenon; that is, the same country has two different economies, one of which includes the majority of the population in the villages and rural areas, and the other, the few large cities where some industrialization and commercial development have taken place.

Retailing Services

Another variable in retailing in world markets is the nature of the operation and services provided by the retailer to the manufacturer. Some of the services a producer might desire from his retailers include the following: stocking the manufacturer's product; displaying the product; selling the product; promoting the product (orally, by display, or by advertising); extending credit to customers; servicing the product; and gathering market information.

CARRYING INVENTORY   Stocking products would seem to be a minimum function of retailing anywhere in the world. Except perhaps for some mail-order business, such stocking is done by retailers in every country. The service they offer, however, is not identical. Small retailers in many countries carry very limited inventories and may be frequently out of stock in certain items. This is lost business for the manufacturer. The same space and financial constraints that cause the small retailer to handle limited inventory cause him to carry a limited line of products, and usually only one brand of a product type. New entrants to the market can have difficulty getting their products or brands accepted by retailers.

Because they are financially weak, small retailers may be able to carry certain products only if they do not have to invest in them; that is, the retailer carries the inventory physically, but the wholesaler or manufacturer carries it financially. We have already seen how this is a problem even in Japan, where small dealers may get up to 10 months' credit extension from their suppliers. Consignment sales are another possible answer to the retailer's inventory problem. An American firm selling prepared foods dealt with the problem partially by changing its case size from forty-eight–can cases in the United States to twenty-four–can cases and twelve-can cases in various foreign markets.

PRODUCT DISPLAY   Where the package plays a role in persuading or reminding the consumer to purchase, display is important. The kind of display a product gets in a retail outlet depends on the physical facilities (space, shelves, lighting, and so on), the manufacturer, and the product. The producer will find great international variation in all these display determinants. At one extreme, an African *duka* may have only 200 square feet of store space, no electric lighting, one door and one window, a few shelves running around two or three walls, and one or two tables. The itinerant vendor or the seller in the open market or bazaar would have equally limited facilities. Retail facilities range from these examples all the way up to the 20,000-square-foot supermarket or large department store familiar to Americans.

Retailer merchandising skills will correlate somewhat with the level of economic development, although many retailers in poorer countries have shown a flair for product display. Many firms distributing through supermarkets in America do not rely on the retailer for display of their product, except for shelf space. Representatives of the manufacturer will arrange the shelf display themselves, with the concurrence of the retailer. This kind of support for retail display will not be possible in many foreign markets because of the large number, small size, and dispersion of retail businesses and because the American firm may have a narrower line in foreign markets, offering too small a base over which to spread these promotional costs.

The retailer's attitude toward the manufacturer and his product may be determined by his previous experience with the manufacturer or by political considerations. If the retailer has had success with a firm's product or some favorable experience with the firm itself, he is more likely to favor the product in display and promotion. Unfavorable experience with the firm or product might cause him to ignore or even drop the product.

Kimberly-Clark in France was distributing Kotex through the pharmacie, which is not very much like an American drug store but is limited to dispensing medicines and selling related items. The company wanted to add supermarket-type outlets for Kotex, as in the United States. The supermarkets were willing to handle the product, but the pharmaciens were angry about the competition. As a result, they put all Kimberly-Clark products under the counter and refused to display them.

Occasionally products of international firms will suffer because of an unpopular action taken by their governments. As an example, one official of a Middle-Eastern nation was drinking a bottle of Coca-Cola when he heard the radio news mentioning an American transaction with Israel. He immediately took his bottle of Coke and poured it on the ground, associating the company with the actions of its home government. Where such problems arise with distributors or consumers, the firm can stress localized brand names and identity. Working against this, however, is the fact that often the American image or association is favorable to product sales. The firm cannot have it both ways.

PROMOTION OF THE PRODUCT   Product display is a part of retailer promotion. Although frequently it is all that a manufacturer can expect, occasionally the retailer might make some personal selling or advertising effort. This effort is more likely if the retailer has a favorable attitude toward the product and it is an important part of his sales and profits. Retailer use of the manufacturer's point-of-purchase materials is another form of retailer promotion. Use of in-store promotional materials is not easily available in many world markets, because the great numbers and small size of retail outlets make most point-of-purchase displays by the manufacturer either impossible or impractical. Retailer product advertising is a form of promotion that also tends to be limited in most markets because of the small size and resources of retailers and, in some countries, because of the high rates of illiteracy and lack of media. Because of the limitations of retailer promotion of the manufacturer's product, the firm must rely on its own advertising efforts in most markets.

OTHER RETAILING SERVICES   Credit extension, product service, and market information are other services a manufacturer might desire from his retailers. After our repeated mention of the limited resources available to retailers in most countries, it is obvious that the manufacturer is more likely to be involved in extending credit to the channel than in finding retailers who can ease the financial flow. Where product service is necessary, the retailer's ability to perform it will depend on his resources and his technical skills. Usually, the smaller the retailer, the less able he is to give service, so wherever the market is thin, service is difficult to provide. The burden of training service personnel and assuring product service will fall on the producer. Although this is true in most markets of the world, it is a greater problem in small markets. In fact, where the manufacturer is unable to assure adequate service, he may have to refuse to sell through certain retailers or even refuse to enter some national markets.

In Turkey in 1955, about 60 percent of all farm tractors were estimated to be incapacitated. International Harvester could find only about fifty qualified repairmen in its own Turkish organization and in the government equipment centers. To maintain its franchise with the consumers and the government, International Harvester undertook an extensive training program at several levels.[5]

Market feedback for the manufacturer is not something the retailer considers as his job. It is only to the extent that the manufacturer has contacts with the retailer that he can get market information from him. In relatively large markets and in selling through department stores, the producer often has contact with retailers or retail organizations. Furthermore, retail audit services are available in some large markets where A. C. Nielsen is operating. In small markets and in rural areas, very little retailer contact is practical.

Another problem may arise when the producer wants retailer cooperation for marketing or advertising testing. Retailers of a certain size and sophistication are necessary to make cooperation worthwhile. Even when these conditions are met, retailers may be very reluctant to cooperate, either because they do not understand the test and how it can benefit them, or because they are suspicious of any outsider's looking at some aspect of their business. Business-

[5] John Fayerweather, *Management of International Operations* (New York: McGraw-Hill Book Co., 1960), p. 142.

men in many countries are secretive about their operations and are afraid of tax investigators. This secretiveness also affects their relations with the producer. For example, one American cosmetics firm wanted to do "before" and "after" retail product audits to test an advertising campaign in a Latin American country. Only after great difficulty did it finally secure the participation of enough retailers to conduct the test.

Retailing and Economic Development

Wholesaling and retailing, as economic activities, are both related to the level of economic development. The following generalizations on retailing and development were reached in the Wadinambiaratchi study:[6]

1. The more developed countries have more specialty stores and supermarkets, more department stores, and more stores in rural areas.
2. The number of small stores declines and the size of the average store increases with increasing development.
3. The role of the peddlar and itinerant trader and the importance of the open-air market decline with rising development.
4. Retail margins get larger with economic development.

Distribution Trends in World Markets

Because most of the countries of the world are experiencing economic development and social change, to observe the wholesale or retail structure at just one point in time is not sufficient. Channel decisions must be based on what the structures will be like tomorrow, as well as what they are today. Statistics on distribution are nonexistent or very limited for most of the less developed nations. Fortunately, the marketing manager even so can get an idea of distribution trends there as well as in those countries that do have some statistics on distribution. Since the nature of wholesaling and retailing is related to economic development, the marketer can follow economic growth in world markets as a rough guide to predict distribution changes. Two of the most important variables here are per capita income and urbanization.

For the international marketer with an American firm, a review of the historical development of wholesaling and retailing in the United States is also instructive. Developments elsewhere often parallel those in the United States in earlier periods. Another aid to the marketer is the comparative study approach (see Chapter 7). Studies of a sample of markets where the firm is already selling should give insights not only to those markets but also to others with similar characteristics. A practical predictive model could be prepared for analyzing distribution developments.

Larger Scale

In the more affluent nations, the pattern of distribution developments is very similar to the United States pattern of recent decades. The major trend is toward fewer and larger units. Such countries as the Netherlands, Sweden,

[6] Wadinambiaratchi, "Channels of Distribution in Foreign Economies," pp. 77, 78.

and the United Kingdom have steadily decreasing numbers of retail units. Unilever, the British-Dutch giant, studied food retailing trends in the United Kingdom and concluded that the number of retail food outlets in 1977 would be only 135,000, down from 285,000 in 1950. Combined with this is the trend toward broader lines in each outlet—scrambled merchandising replacing small limited line stores. European department stores are expanding and strengthening their operations through mergers.

These trends mean stronger retailing and greater countervailing power vis-à-vis the manufacturer. The power of channel members is further reinforced by the growth of large-scale cooperative wholesaling, often on an international basis. For example, Spar International is a voluntary chain of over 200 wholesalers and 36,000 retailers in twelve Western European countries. As a result of larger operations and greater power, European retailers are demanding more private (distributor) brands. This poses a problem already faced by manufacturers in the United States.

The International Storekeepers

The globetrotting of American retailers is another significant development. Growing affluence and modernization abroad have attracted many firms. Although Woolworth's is an old hand at retailing in foreign markets, more recent arrivals include a blue-chip listing: Sears in Mexico, South America, and Spain; J. C. Penney in Belgium and Italy; Safeway in Great Britain, Germany, and Australia; Walgreen in Mexico; Jewel in Belgium, Italy, and Spain; Federated Department Stores in Madrid; Kresge in Australia; Avon in twelve countries; plus Tupperware, Singer, Fuller Brush, Stanley Home Products, and others.

The internationalizing of retailing is not limited to United States firms, however. They are merely joining the growing ranks of Canadian, British, Dutch, French, and others in international mergers and joint ventures. Manufacturers with international operations are beginning to encounter international distributor organizations—with important implications for marketing management.[7]

Other distribution trends include the growth of new kinds of retail operations. One of the fastest growth areas is mail-order retailing. In Great Britain, mail order doubled its share of retail volume in the 1960s to over 5 percent of the total. France and West Germany also have large and growing mail-order businesses. The Singer Company too is in mail order retailing in Europe. With the gradual demise of resale price maintenance in Europe, discount houses are growing in popularity. As more and larger discount stores and mail order operations are established, pressure will be brought to bear on the manufacturer's pricing and distribution policies.

Changes occurring in the more affluent economies have brought two other retailing developments. One is the rise of self-service supermarket operations.

[7] See Stanley C. Hollander, "The International Store-Keepers," *MSU Business Topics* (Spring 1969), pp. 13–22.

A Tokyo suburb has six supermarkets within 100 yards of each other. Unilever's study predicted over 30,000 self-service food stores in the United Kingdom by 1977 as compared with only 3,700 in 1957. Underlying this development are rising wages, labor shortages, and consumer acceptance of one-stop shopping. As more wives work or have other desirable things to do, shopping for convenience goods becomes a less attractive way to spend time. The second development in the more affluent economies is the appearance of shopping centers in or near the cities because of congestion in the cities, growing automobile ownership, and increasing leisure time for shopping outings.

MARKETING THROUGH FOREIGN DISTRIBUTION CHANNELS

Having considered some of the principal constraints on distribution in foreign markets, we will now look at the strategic decisions facing the international marketer. The questions we will consider are the following:

1. Should the firm extend its domestic distribution approach uniformly to foreign markets or adapt its distribution strategy to each national market?
2. Should the firm use direct or indirect channels in foreign markets?
3. Should the firm use selective or widespread distribution?
4. How can the firm manage the channel?
5. How can the firm keep its distribution strategy up-to-date?

International or National Patterns

The important question facing the international marketer is not whether his firm should have uniform distribution patterns in foreign markets. It is rather to determine the most profitable channels in each market. The goal is profits, not uniformity. A few factors may favor a standardized international approach, the major one of which is the realization of economies of scale. Although these are not as easily attainable in distribution as they are in production, there may be some. For example, the international marketing manager may be able to work more efficiently, the more similar his task is in the different markets. Also, the more similar the conditions, the more easily successful experiences in one country can be transferred to another.

Occasionally executive desire for uniformity is also a factor, but not one that should weigh heavily on the channel decision. It can be argued that channels used in one market should be tried in another because they have been tested. Although success in one market does give a presumption in favor of trying the same thing elsewhere, it is not a sufficient reason. Market analysis should be done before deciding on local channels.

Numerous pressures deter the firm from a completely standardized distribution approach. Some of these pressures are from the environment, others are internal to the firm. One external determinant of a firm's distribution channels is the existing distribution structure in a country, that is, the number, size, and nature of wholesale and retail operations. Because the distribution structure varies from country to country, the firm's alternatives also vary. Storage and transportation possibilities, plus the dispersion or concentration of the market, also help to determine channel alternatives. For example, Pepsi Cola uses quite similar channels all over the world, that is, local bottler to truckdriver-salesman to retailer. However, in sparse market areas, the company truck-driver-salesman is too expensive and the company has to find another method of contact and delivery to retailer.

Another channel determinant is the market. Consumer income and buying habits, which vary by country, are important considerations in deciding on the degree of directness and selectivity of distribution. Another variable is the strength and behavior of competitors. On the one hand, competitors may force a firm to use the same channel they are using because they have educated the market to that channel; on the other, competitors' strength in a given channel may effectively pre-empt that channel and force the newcomer to find some other way to the market, if he can. One American producer of prepared foods complained to the author about the actions of a cartel in Germany, which he said kept wholesalers from handling his products. He said they would let him in only if he agreed to join the cartel and to share the market. The firm new to a market always faces different alternatives from those established national firms face.

Finally, differences in the manufacturer's own situation might suggest channel differences from market to market. An important determinant is the firm's level of involvement in a market. Where the firm supplies a market through an importer-distributor, it has less decision freedom than where it supplies through a local plant. Similarly, working through a licensee or joint venture is more restrictive of channel selection than is working through a wholly owned operation. Even where the level of involvement is the same in two markets, the firm's product line and sales volume may differ. The smaller the line and the volume of sales, the less direct the firm can afford to go.

The international firm generally tries to use the same distribution channels from market to market. Although frequently adaptations are necessary, a firm's channels will be largely similar around the world, especially in industrial goods where the market is more concentrated and technical requirements more important than in consumer goods. However, even in consumer goods, there can be a strong carry over from country to country.

One of the more surprising examples is Tupperware in Japan. Tupperware Home Products, Inc., entered Japan in the mid–1960s. The only channel the firm ever used in America was selling by parties in the home with a housewife as hostess. The same channel was used in Japan, and in two years time, sales reached $15 million a year there. In spite of all the cultural and economic differences, the channel used in America was successful also in Japan.

Direct versus Indirect Channels

Because direct channels are almost always more effective than indirect channels, firms like to go as direct as they can. The factors affecting the decision are the same in foreign markets as they are in the firm's domestic market.

The major determinant is the volume of sales attainable. Where volume is large and concentrated, the firm can afford to go directly to the market. When the American firm considers foreign markets, it usually finds less possibility of going direct than in the United States. Many elements combine to make most foreign markets smaller and less concentrated, for example, lower incomes, narrower product line of the firm, smaller company sales, fewer large-scale buying organizations, and so on.

Most firms accept indirect distribution as the only feasible alternative in foreign markets. For example, Procter and Gamble in Italy uses a very indirect channel (see p. 310) and relies on advertising to pull products through the channel. Some firms, however, are trying for more direct distribution as the best way to attain a strong market position. Goodyear is working toward the establishment of its own franchised dealers in Europe, just as it has in America. Thinking along the same lines, the marketing vice-president of a large farm equipment firm said, "The first to have a controlled system of outlets will be the winner in Europe. That is the reason for Singer's success. You have to have your own outlets with people you can control."[8] These cases illustrate the attitude that the greater control, better market contact, and increased volume offset the greater costs of going direct. These cases also reflect the influence of experience. As the company's foreign experience increases along with sales volume, it often develops a desire for more direct channels.

An interesting example of different evaluations of a similar situation is provided by two American firms in the consumer paper products field. The companies are competing against each other in America and in Europe. In Europe, one firm follows a policy of direct selling to larger retail outlets, with call frequency a function of sales volume. It calls this "fishing where the fish are." The competitor began by using its own sales force but later switched to wholesalers. It felt that wider distribution was necessary for adequate volume, but it could not cover all the retailers with its own sales force.

Selective versus Intensive Distribution

Intensive or widespread distribution refers to the policy of selling through any wholesaler or retailer that wishes to handle the product. Selective distribution means choosing a limited number of resellers in a market area. Although a manufacturer usually wants to make his product as widely available as possible, he may find it necessary to select a limited number of distributors to make it worth their while to carry the necessary inventory, to provide service, and to give some time to promotion. On shopping or specialty goods, retailers may demand selective distribution, which protects their market by limiting competition. On mechanical industrial goods or consumer durables, a policy

[8] Vern Terpstra, *American Marketing in the Common Market* (New York: Praeger, 1967), p. 98.

of selective distribution may be the only way the manufacturer can get the cooperation of intermediaries in providing service.

In foreign markets, the decision factors are the same as in the United States, but the environment is different. Marketing abroad, manufacturers usually give exclusive franchises to importers or wholesalers at the *national* level. However, selectivity at the retail level depends on local market conditions. With a multiplicity of small retailers, the firm might have difficulty locating those that can handle its product effectively. Low consumer mobility also limits the value of selective distribution.

In countries with very uneven income distribution, the firm might well use selective distribution to reach its limited market target effectively, assuming it sells only to a group above a certain income level. For consumer durables or technical industrial products, the distribution in foreign markets might be much more selective than in the United States because of the thinness of the market and its relative concentration. As noted earlier, because of local retail structure and consumption patterns, a consumer paper-products firm practiced selective distribution even in European markets, "fishing where the fish are." Although these are not normally products for selective distribution in America, the channel follows the market.

Working with the Channel

Managing the channel to get effective performance is easiest, of course, when the firm sells directly to the retailer or to the ultimate consumer. The costs of direct distribution bring the benefits of control over market coverage, promotion, pricing, and service, as well as the flexibility to respond to market conditions and better market feedback. When the firm cannot afford to go direct, it must deal with independent intermediaries that are not on its payroll. The problem then becomes one of getting cooperation rather than one of maintaining control. Although this problem is not peculiar to the foreign markets of the firm, the firm's own situation and market conditions will vary from country to country, making channel management a somewhat different task in each market.

Manufacturers have developed many different techniques and approaches for encouraging cooperation from members of the channel. Some of these are attractive margins, exclusive territories, a valuable franchise, advertising support and cooperative advertising, financing, sales force or service training, business advisory service, market research assistance, and missionary selling. All of these are known to students of marketing and need no elaboration here. We will discuss just the international marketing application of some of them.

A firm needs to be competitive on *distributor margins* and will need to adapt to the level customary in each of its markets. Sometimes in trying to break into a market and gain distribution, the firm is tempted to beat competitors' margins, a form of price cutting and the easiest form of competition to imitate. Usually the weak firm that has no other advantages to offer will try this approach, but once the firm has made its entry it may have difficulty adjusting its margins.

We have discussed exclusive franchises and selective distribution. As to the *consumer franchise*, the international firm may or may not have a valuable franchise to offer its channel members. When the firm enters a new market, its brand is usually unknown. Middlemen may be reluctant to carry the product, unless the firm gives strong advertising support to create a consumer franchise. Some of the larger international companies, such as Philips, Unilever, IBM, or Westinghouse, are in a different position. Because of their size and reputation, they are usually considered as desirable suppliers in any market they enter. For example, many of the firms associated with America's space program have achieved an enviable market position with foreign market distributors and customers because of the favorable image.

Channel Support

Strong *advertising support* of a product makes the intermediaries more cooperative in handling it. International firms and especially American companies have an advantage over national firms in this respect. First, they have the financial resources to advertise extensively; second, they have more experience and expertise in advertising than most of their national competitors. A German competitor of Procter and Gamble noted that P&G was able to enter any Western European country and "buy" a 15-percent market share just on the strength of their advertising. The resources and experience of the international company also help in developing programs of cooperative advertising with channel members. The same financial resources make the international company more than competitive in extending credit for *financing the channel*.

Training

The size and experience of the multinational companies give them a competitive advantage in other avenues of obtaining distributor cooperation, such as *training of sales or service personnel*, business advisory service, and market-research assistance. A firm with operations in several countries can draw on this experience in helping distributors in any one market. It can gain economies of scale in developing qualified training personnel, and perhaps in operating a centralized training center for distributor personnel from several countries. Most national firms cannot match these advantages. Furthermore, the international firm can give additional prestige and incentive to distributors or to their personnel by holding regional meetings with distributor representatives from several countries. For example, European and Latin American regional meetings are increasingly popular. To a more limited degree, American firms bring distributor personnel to the United States.

Ford Motor Company (Overseas Tractor Operations) conducts training programs in Latin America for its own and dealers' employees. The training is in repair, maintenance, and utilization of tractors and equipment. The program has paid good returns in dealer relations. Prestige has been associated with training at a large Ford facility as well as with the foreign travel often required to attend. The instructors are drawn mainly from the United Kingdom, where one of Ford's three major tractor plants is located.[9]

Chrysler found a new way to train its far-flung network of dealers. It leased a DC-6 and outfitted it as a classroom with cutaway training units of rear axles, engines, transmissions, and so on, plus movies, slides, and other visual aids. The first trip was an eighteen-stop swing through Central and Latin America, with four days at each stop. The six-man training team gave sessions (in Spanish) on technical and product training, as well as sales and management methods. The dealers plus their sales and service personnel are included.

Attendance was 20 percent above expectations. There were also public relations benefits as favorable press and TV coverage was given at every stop. In Peru, the welcoming party included the President. The alternative of sending dealer personnel to the large Detroit facility is not really feasible. Latin American dealers estimate it would cost them $6,000 to do this. They cannot afford the cost, nor can they spare the men for the time required. Since many do not speak English, they would not get full benefit from the Detroit training program anyway.[10]

Another unique way in which the international firm can increase intermediaries' confidence and cooperation is by increasing its commitment to the distributors' national market. When the firm changes its supply source for a market from imports to *local production*, it increases its involvement in the market and reassures distributors. Not only is its reliability and image enhanced in the dealers' eyes, but also it can give better delivery and service to the channel members. Transportation, customs, inventory, and communications problems are all lessened once the international firm establishes local production.

Missionary selling is a way for the manufacturer to maintain contact with channel members and to help them to sell his product. In foreign markets with many small retailers, missionary selling is more difficult although still feasible because of lower wages there. Small retailers also may require more assistance and personal contact than large retailers. Where the foreign market is neither too small nor too thin, missionary selling can play the same role it does in the United States. The Wrigley Company in Europe provides an illustration. As chewing gum caught on in Europe during the 1950s, European competitors arose and used primarily a low price strategy to attack Wrigley's position. Rather than responding with price cuts, Wrigley used missionary selling to convince the retailer of the greater profits he could obtain with Wrigley's well-established, strongly advertised brand. The strategy was successful in maintaining the company's position.

Finally, we reiterate a key element in effective channel performance, that is, the need to select carefully the channel and its major members in the first

[9] *Business Latin America*, March 14, 1968, p. 82.
[10] *Business International*, August 23, 1968, p. 272.

place. When the product is well matched to the channel in each national market, the battle is half won. The following study of British and French practices is relevant here.

It was found that British firms tended to accumulate a large number of agents. Because the export departments were undermanned, visits to agents were infrequent and performance fell. Therefore, more agents were hired, who were visited less frequently, and so on. The French had fewer agents and often invited them to France (usually to Paris), thus improving relations. However, the French were more severe in getting rid of unsatisfactory agents, having a higher turnover than the British. In both countries, many firms were very casual about choosing agents, often doing it through chance encounters in restaurants and night clubs. However, the most successful French companies spent up to a year in consideration before selecting their foreign market representatives.[11]

Keeping Channels Up-to-date

The challenge of management is to keep on top of the changes occurring both inside and outside the firm. The management of distribution channels poses the same challenge. In international marketing the problem is compounded because the changes in the environment and in the firm are occurring at different rates in different foreign markets. Even if we assume that the international firm had an appropriate distribution strategy when it entered each of its foreign markets, this initial strategy is unlikely to remain the most desirable over time.

The variables affecting distribution channels are numerous. In any given national market, the situation of the firm evolves. Generally, the volume of sales increases, the product line expands, and the level of involvement undergoes a change, that is, from importer-distributor to marketing subsidiary, or from licensee to joint venture, and so on. Environmental changes are broader in scope. Developments in wholesaling and retailing institutions are taking place in all markets but are more critical in some than in others. Technological change in distribution and transportation as well as evolution in the purchasing behavior of buyers in both the industrial and the consumer markets exert pressure on the firm's channels. Laws affecting distribution are being initiated in some markets and changed in others. Finally, political developments such as regional groupings are changing the horizons of the firm.

Growth of the Firm in a Market

The international firm in most of its foreign markets is expanding. As the firm gets established in a market, its sales volume should increase and this success will lead to expansion of the product line offered in that market. At some level of sales, the firm will find it profitable to increase its involvement in that

[11] *Business Europe,* July 26, 1967, p. 240.

market, allocating greater financial and personnel resources to it. Where this growth occurs, the firm is able to take stronger control of its distribution, that is, to go more direct. In fact, this is the plan and strategy of many international companies. Indeed, as the firm gains operating experience in a number of nations, it should be able to design its own "model of market development" to aid in its strategic planning. Multinational marketing experience aids the marketing manager to plan in each individual market.

Environmental Change: Large-Scale Retailing

Although expansion of the firm in a market leads primarily to more direct distribution, changes in the environment have a more complex impact on the firm's marketing. The trends toward retail concentration and buying co-ops in Europe, for example, have a twofold impact. The concentration of the market in larger units means not only a greater possibility of direct distribution but also increased demand for private brands. The growth of large mail-order operations has the same result. La Redoute, a mail-order house, is the largest user of the French postal system. The bargaining power of these large groups, which prefer to buy directly, also affects the pricing policy of the manufacturer. The demise of resale price maintenance and the rise of discounting further affect pricing to the channel.

The strategic response of the firm to large-scale retailing may be either direct channels or dual chanels, that is, selling directly to large retail groups and indirectly to small retailers. Even though the firm may dislike the private brand approach, it might become necessary. In other cases, private branding may be the way to open up new markets. For example, some American firms had been unable to enter the German market because German wholesalers were unwilling to carry their products. The wholesalers' associations in Germany often have been strong enough to prevent the manufacturer from by-passing them, as they prevented Kraft Foods (see page 310). German manufacturers have agreed to this restriction on the condition that the wholesalers in turn act as a sort of buffer against foreign firms' coming into the market. The rise of large retail groups buying directly opens the way for non-German firms to break into the market, although perhaps with private branding required.

Large-scale retailing and buying organizations have caused manufacturers to make still other adaptations to the new power structure in the channel. The situation in the United Kingdom, which is a leader in European distribution trends, can be taken as an example. Manufacturers have increased their promotional activities to the large retailers, using missionary selling with them and supplying promotional materials, but at the same time they have reduced their efforts with smaller retailers. Even as they sell more directly to large retailers, they leave small independent retailers to be serviced by wholesalers; in effect, they adopt a dual-channel strategy. Not only is this strategy used by a food company like Heinz, but also by a consumer durables firm like Philips.

Other Changes

The firm must monitor other developments affecting distribution to be able to react effectively to them. In some markets, rising wages and labor shortages are drawing people out of low-wage retailing. More self-service retailing is one result. Such a situation caused the Nissan Motor Company in Japan to change its distribution channel. The company was sending salesmen door to door to sell cars, but the diminishing availability of labor for this kind of retailing caused the company to consider switching to American-style automobile showrooms.[12]

Technological developments, such as the "cold chain" emerging in Europe, will enlarge product-line possibilities. The "cold chain" refers to the availability of refrigeration in warehouses, trucks, and retail outlets. Unilever, which has a frozen-food line, found the major deterrent to growth to be the retail link of the cold chain. Many retailers could not afford the unit. Unilever helped retailers of a certain minimum size to finance the purchase of a frozen-food unit in the expectation that the growth in the company's frozen-food sales would be enough to cover financing costs and leave a satisfactory profit.

The multinational company has an advantage in studying and reacting to distribution developments. Experiences in some of its markets should prepare the marketing manager to anticipate developments in others. The American firm has a further advantage in that most distribution trends abroad follow the American pattern of development. For example, one American food company was dealing with European retailers worried about the disappearance of resale price maintenance. Because the company had gone through a similar experience in the United States, it was better able to handle the situation than were its European competitors. One task of the international marketing manager is to see that the relevant international experience and expertise of the firm are available when and where they are needed in the firm's global operations.

Managing distribution often requires changing the channel when conditions change; for example, the firm may go from indirect to direct distribution or add a new channel or type of outlet. After World War II, the leading American producer of ice cream faced a dilemma. Its traditional outlets were drug stores, but the new supermarkets as well were beginning to sell ice cream. Because adding supermarket outlets would irritate the members of the existing channel, the company decided to stay with its traditional channel. Eventually, of course, supermarkets became the overwhelming favorite outlet for ice cream. This is the kind of challenge facing firms in many markets, as the experience of Kimberly-Clark with Kotex illustrates (see page 314). Multinational operating experience helps answer such questions in individual markets. Although the firm may reap ill will from existing channels, it also may gain good will and a strong place in the new outlets by being the first to change. The firm would need to do an enlightened, though subjective, cost-benefit analysis in making making such decisions.

[12] *Business Week*, January 31, 1970, p. 71.

Internationalizing Distribution

The international firm may sell in more than 100 markets around the world, but its distribution channels generally are strictly national. This situation will change gradually with the development of regional groupings. As the groupings become close knit, the need for a channel structure identified and limited by political boundaries will be obviated. Instead manufacturers and wholesalers will be able to begin to think of natural (not national) market areas. The erosion of national boundaries to distribution is furthered by the growth of international voluntary chains and retail buying groups. These economic pressures work toward the realization of a true common market. International firms have already provided for this by rationalizing and centralizing production for market groupings. Distribution management also must prepare for the new market environment resulting from regional groupings.

Regional divisions within the organizational structure of the company may be the way to implement international or regional distribution. Many firms already have European divisions, Latin American divisions, and so on. Because transportation and geographic proximity are important in distribution to natural market areas, the marketing manager in the regional organization may gradually take greater charge of regional distribution strategy, leaving a different but lesser role for country subsidiary marketing managers.

The multicountry marketing operation needs some coordination or centralization of distribution at the regional level, such as took place as the United States became a unified national market. The director of European operations for an American chemical company observed a similarity between Western Europe and the United States. "Perhaps we'll have real international (European) distribution in ten or twenty years. Then the national companies would become regional sales offices like Chicago or San Francisco in the United States."[13]

In this section on the management of distribution, we have tried to restrict ourselves to channel structure and strategy. Since distribution is just one function of marketing, and marketing is just one aspect of the firm's operations, we have not been able to ignore other factors. Obviously, good distribution strategy is related to what the firm does in the rest of its marketing program. Thus we have seen that distribution strategy is related to questions of pricing, branding, product line, promotion, and even the firm's level of involvement in a market.

LOGISTICS FOR INTERNATIONAL MARKETING

Up to this point, we have been discussing distribution from the viewpoint of the financial and ownership flows of goods in international marketing. These generally fall under the heading of "distribution channels" or "distribution strategies." We have touched only incidentally on the physical movement

[13] Terpstra, *American Marketing in the Common Market*, p. 96.

of goods in international marketing, which is usually called "physical distribution." A somewhat broader term—"logistics"—has become popular in business usage. Robert McGarrah defines logistics as "embracing any activity concerned with choosing the quantity, time, or location of facilities to be used, or materials and products to be stocked or moved through the organization, from suppliers to customers in every market served."[14]

The important point to note about international physical distribution or logistics is that it is concerned with much more than transportation or the mere physical movement of goods. As the definition suggests, international logistics decisions affect the number and location or production and storage facilities, production schedules, inventory management, and even the firm's level of involvement in foreign markets. We will not give much space to a general discussion of physical distribution, as it is covered in most basic marketing texts. Specialized texts dealing exclusively with this subject are also available for anyone who wants to study the general principles.[15]

LOGISTICS WITHIN THE FOREIGN MARKET

Within each of its foreign markets, the firm must seek to optimize the performance of its physical distribution system. Although its approach will be essentially the same one it uses in its domestic market, a few differences will affect the physical distribution function in foreign markets. The following market variables require consideration: size and distribution of each nation's market for the firm's products, the supply situation in each market, the degree of urbanization, the nation's topography, and the transportation and storage facilities offered.

We discussed in Chapter 3 how nations differ in their transportation and communications infrastructure. They also vary in their favoritism and support of particular modes of transport, for example, rail versus truck versus inland waterway. Preference may be shown in taxes, subsidies, and/or regulation of different kinds of carriers. Such differences among EEC nations, for example, are hindering the rationalization of physical distribution in the Common Market.

We also saw in Chapter 3 that topography is one aspect of a nation's physical endowment. The existence of rivers, deserts, mountains, or tropical forests poses opportunities or challenges to management of physical distribution. Some Latin American countries, for example, are divided into almost mutually inaccessible regions by the Andes Mountains. Because these countries are not affluent markets, some firms do not even try to cover the whole country but content themselves with reaching one or two major urban areas. Bata Shoe Company in Peru is one of the rare firms that does more

---

[14] Robert E. McGarrah, "Logistics for the International Manufacturer," *Harvard Business Review* (March–April 1966).
[15] See, for example, Donald J. Bowersox et al., *Physical Distribution Management*, rev. ed. (New York: Macmillan, 1968), or J. L. Heskett et al., *Business Logistics* (New York: Ronald Press, 1964).

business in the rural areas than in the major cities. To cover these areas, Bata uses air, truck, rail, plus occasionally mule or launch to reach distant outlets.[16] In Europe, inland waterways can have the opposite effect, tying several nations together for the physical movement of goods.

The Congo provides an illustration of physical distribution problems within a national market. The author lived in the eastern part of Congo for a number of years. Imported goods destined for that region took the following path: (1) Ocean shipping arrived inland on the Congo River at Matadi, where it was unloaded and put on a train. (2) The train went to Kinshasa, the capital, by-passing the falls and rapids between Matadi and the capital. (3) At Kinshasa, the goods were put on a boat for a 1,000-mile river trip to Kisangani, where the river again was non-navigable. (4) There, the goods were put on a train for Kindu. (5) At Kindu, goods were trans-shipped by truck. It is not hard to imagine, therefore, that for many goods, physical distribution costs constituted the biggest element in the price. This was reinforced by the inadequate storage facilities and adverse climatic conditions causing damage and loss en route.

The above examples show that physical distribution problems are as important in limiting market opportunities on the supply side as are low incomes on the demand side. By the same token, however, improvements in logistics can open up new markets, even apart from increases in per capita income. Therefore, logistics management can offer the international marketer two ways for increasing profits: through cost reduction, the more traditional approach, and through market expansion.

INTERNATIONAL MARKETING LOGISTICS

If there were one world market, the problems of international marketing logistics would be basically the same as those in the domestic market. Differences in topography and demography do not change the principles of efficient physical distribution management. The problems in international logistics do not arise from geography but from politics. The world is not one market but a collection of individual national markets, each under the control of a sovereign government. Some of the ways governments separate their markets from others are the following:

1. Tariff barriers
2. Import quotas and licenses
3. Local content laws
4. National currencies and monetary systems, exchange control
5. Differing tax systems and rates
6. Differing transportation policies
7. Differing laws on products (food, drug, labeling, safety)

[16] *Business Latin America*, February 29, 1968, p. 66.

Because the world is made up of national markets, logistics management must try to adapt to, or overcome, the various barriers in order to achieve, as nearly as possible, an integrated world market in its own physical distribution system. The planner would start with a study of markets, comparative advantage (as discussed in Chapter 2), and location theory. He would then modify the preliminary design of the firm's physical distribution system to fit the political barriers noted above. The differing market situation in each country would dictate further modification. The different market situation results from the varying competitive environments and differing customer service needs and expectations.

The goal of marketing logistics is not merely reduction of costs but also the increase of profits through greater sales. Sales will increase if logistics improvements lead to amelioration of the system's customer service level. The appropriate customer service level for the firm varies among countries because of competition and customer expectations. ("Customer service level" here refers to delivery times, availability of parts and service, and other elements in the firm's ability to meet customer needs and desires.)

The firm's ability to develop its own globally integrated logistics system is affected by its levels of involvement in various foreign markets. In markets where it has wholly owned subsidiaries, the firm is best able to control the customer service level obtained from the system; joint ventures offer less control, and licensee and distribution markets offer the least control because they are the least integrated into the system. This is one reason why many firms prefer wholly owned ventures.

Probably the favored logistics arrangement would be for the firm to concentrate all its production in its home market and export to the world, gaining economies of scale and eliminating many international business problems. Three factors work against this arrangement: (1) transportation costs, (2) trade barriers, and (3) customer service needs. All these factors lead the international firm to choose a particular kind of involvement in each of its markets; it should make this choice, however, not only in terms of *local* market needs but also in terms of the firm's *international* logistics needs.

The Dynamic Environment

Designing an optimal logistics system for a firm's international markets is a difficult and continuing task, difficult because of the complexity of the variables, and continuing because of the dynamic nature of the variables. Almost every parameter of the system is subject to change. Not only are markets and competition dynamic, but transportation possibilities also have undergone a continuing revolution in the past few decades. In 1972 a sea route offers supertankers and containerization—and a closed Suez Canal; an air route offers the 707, the 747, the C5A, and the SST. We cannot assume that these represent the end of technological change. Rather, continuing improvements and economies are probable, opening new logistics possibilities.

Governmental barriers also change, not always for the worse. Tariff barriers have been greatly reduced in recent decades through GATT negotiations. Other trade restrictions have been lessened bcause of GATT, IMF, and similar international activities noted in Part I. The formation of regional groupings has had a favorable effect, allowing greater rationalization of the firm's international logistics, at least on a regional basis. Negative governmental changes from the firm's viewpoint are decreasing import allowances and demands for greater local content in the firm's products. Furthermore, many host nations, quite naturally putting their own interests ahead of the firm's needs, demand increases in exports from the international firms in their country. Changing international relations—for example, East–West or Arab–Israeli—also influence physical distribution patterns.

The Flexible Response

Considering the dynamic nature of the international logistics environment, the international marketer might reach one major conclusion: There is no definitive solution. This is a useful guideline if it helps the firm to avoid a costly search and large investments aimed at a definitive answer to its international logistics needs. The firm might better seek ad hoc, temporizing solutions that meet present needs and constraints. These can then be changed as the situation changes, without major new investment. Although perhaps representing second-best answers at any given time, in the long run they may add up to the best feasible solution.

Although an international firm can make major investments in plants and facilities on the basis of a currently ideal international logistics system, as changes occur in technology, the political situation (national or international), or its own international goals, the firm may find it necessary to make costly adjustments. Therefore, the firm should make major investments in such a way that they can be adjusted to a variety of possible future environments—technological, political, and strategic. The colloquial expression, "staying loose," is good advice for the manager of international logistics. He must keep his options open insofar as possible. Contingency planning is an inherent part of his *modus operandi*.

MANAGEMENT OF INTERNATIONAL LOGISTICS

Because physical distribution is one of the major cost elements in international marketing, profits often can be increased through cost reductions in the international movement of goods. Profits can be increased further if sales volume rises because logistics changes lead to an improvement in customer services. For these reasons, logistics deserves careful management attention in the international company. We will consider the principal elements in the management of international logistics, including the facilities and technology available to the manager as well as the need for international coordination.

Facilities and Technology

The facilities available to the manager of international logistics include (1) service organizations such as transportation companies and freight forwarders, (2) institutions such as free-trade zones and public warehouses, and (3) modern hardware such as computers, the telex, and containerization and jumbo jet planes.

The Freight Forwarder

The foreign freight forwarder is a specialist in both transportation and documentation for international shipments. Because of his expertise in this technical area, he is employed by a majority of companies to arrange the actual overseas shipment of their goods. Although the services he offers can be invaluable, he is only one part of the logistics system. Although the costs and customer service level offered by the system will depend on several things in addition to the efficient overseas shipment and documentation that the freight forwarder provides, use of such a specialist can facilitate the management of international logistics.[17]

Free-Trade Zones

Aware of the complications caused by some of the man-made barriers to international trade, some forty nations have established free-trade zones, free ports, public warehouses, and similar devices to overcome some of the problems. These facilities are generally government-owned, supervised by customs officials. They allow the firm to bring goods into the nation without having to pay customs duties, as long as the goods remain in the free-trade zone or warehouse, and many also allow some processing, assembly, sorting, repacking, and the like within the zone. The firm can gain several advantages from the use of such free-trade zones. A country provides these zones, of course, because it gains an increase in business activity within its borders, activity that would normally be driven away by its trade barriers.[18]

POTENTIAL ADVANTAGES   Among the potential advantages offered by free-trade zones are the following.

1. They permit the firm to realize the economies of *bulk shipping* to a country without having to bear the burden of custom duties. Duties need to be paid only when the goods are released on a *small lot* basis from the zone or bonded warehouse.
2. They permit the manufacturer to carry a local inventory at less cost than in his own facilities, because in his own facilities he must pay the duty as soon as the goods enter the country. If duties are high, the financial burden of covering the duty on goods in inventory is significant.

Bausch & Lomb, Inc., leased 500 square meters in the public bonded warehouses at the Netherland's Schiphol Airport. They shipped merchandise there at bulk rates from the United States. Bausch & Lomb used Schiphol as its European distribution center. It realized big savings by concentrating Euro-

---

[17] For a complete listing of freight forwarders' services, see Alexander O. Stanley, *Handbook of International Marketing* (New York: McGraw-Hill Book Co., 1963), pp. 240–242.

[18] For a general discussion of free-trade zones, based on the United States zones, see William A. Dymsza, *Foreign Trade Zones and International Business* (Trenton, N.J.: Research Section, Bureau of Commerce, 1964.

*pean inventories at one spot, yet it provided two-day delivery in Europe. This
system also permitted their distributors and agents to reduce their own
inventories, which improved distributor relations.*[19]

3. American exporters can use United States free-trade zones to bring in
low-cost foreign ingredients and avoid duty payments on products re-exported.
Ormont Drug & Chemical Company makes antibiotics in the New York
Foreign Trade Zone. Its raw materials, especially isoniazid, are purchased
from overseas suppliers at prices 25 percent or more below domestic rates.
They are imported duty free, but the completed products are exported immediately. There are extra savings from not having to ship through customs.[20]

4. The ability to engage in local processing, assembly, repacking, and
similar operations can mean savings to the international firm. It can ship to
the market in bulk or CKD, for advantageous freight rates. Then it can process,
assemble, or repack locally for local or regional distribution. For many
American and European firms, the local labor costs will be less than those at
home. For example, the free zones in Panama and Colombia have been popular
with many European and American firms, for example, Ronson, Goodyear,
Eastman Kodak, Ericson, Celanese, and so on.

An interesting variation on free zones allows a company to have a part of
its own plant declared a bonded warehouse. The advantages are the same as
those above, but it is even more convenient to the firm's regular operations in
the country. Belgium offers such facilities and they are used by many international firms. In a similar manner, the Brazilian government gave permission
to Caterpillar for an on-site free zone. Duties on Caterpillar imports are about
50 percent, so the savings are significant, especially since goods have to be
financed for about one year.[21] This may be a growing development in international trade.

EVALUATION OF FREE ZONES   The international firm should consider the
use of foreign trade zones and similar arrangements to see if any of their
potential advantages apply to its own situation. Their usefulness depends on
duty rates and the extent and nature of the firm's international operations.
Since free zones are primarily aimed at overcoming the inconvenience of tariff
barriers, they are less important for products with low duties. Furthermore,
the economies of bulk shipments and the use of low-cost local labor for
assembly are benefits that can be obtained *apart* from the use of free zones.

The international marketer and logistics planner must decide in which
markets free zones can play a useful role in the firm's overall logistics and in
which markets the firm is better off with its own or distributor facilities. The
free zone must be considered as just one part of the overall system; it cannot

[19] *Business Europe*, November 17, 1967, p. 366.
[20] *Business Abroad*, December 11, 1967, p. 27.
[21] *Business Latin America*, March 7, 1968, p. 76.

be evaluated in isolation. Furthermore, each zone or warehouse must be individually evaluated because some have not delivered the promised advantages. A review of Latin American free zones found some that were excellent and some that were unsatisfactory.[22] Other factors favoring the use of free zones are that they minimize the investment needs of the firm and have built-in flexibility. If they do not work out well, other alternatives can be tried and the firm has lost little.

Modern Technology

Supertankers, containerization, jumbo jets, refrigeration, and freeze drying all have at least two things in common: They are the result of modern technology and they affect the costs and ability of the firm in moving goods in international marketing. Physical distribution is very dependent on the state of the art in transportation and storage. Therefore, the international logistics planner must assure that his system reflects the economies possible with modern technology but at the same time is flexible enough to adapt to the new technological developments of tomorrow, without the firm's having to write off major investments in facilities.

The computer and developments in international communication are other results of modern technology that facilitate international logistics. They permit the speedy information flow and analysis necessary for the prompt response of an efficient system. With almost instant communication, the firm's distant markets and supply sources around the world can effectively be made part of the same physical distribution network. Establishing effective, rapid communications is as much a part of international logistics as the efficient movement of goods. They are interdependent, of course. The varied roles of modern technology can be illustrated best by an actual example.

The Australian office of an American maker of electronic components received an inquiry from a local manufacturer of electronic equipment. Three days later, detailed specifications, delivery dates, and prices had been agreed upon for a substantial order. The international sales manager said, "If we had used airmail along with the occasional trans-Pacific call, this order may or may not have been consummated in a couple month's time. It was our ability to be on-the-spot and to move quickly that clinched the deal." The elements involved included the telex, the computer, air cargo, and a local sales engineer. The steps were as follows:

1. *Inquiry received from prospective Australian customer.*
2. *Visit by sales engineer from Sydney office.*
3. *Three days of telex conversation between Sydney and California. The local salesman was the go-between with the customer. Contract terms settled.*
4. *The American firm did a computer analysis of its global producing and distribution facilities for this component.*

22 *Business International*, February 16, 1968, p. 52.

5. *The analysis led to a decision to manufacture in Europe and ship by air to Australia.*[23]

Not only does the example show the role of modern technology; it also shows how logistics is a total system, integrating production, distribution, and personal selling as complementary parts of international marketing.

Coordination of International Logistics

For One Market

Within each of the firm's markets, physical distribution will be handled primarily by the subsidiary or distributor there. However, corporate headquarters can and should provide assistance in the analysis, planning, and control of local physical distribution. It can contribute ideas and analytical techniques, such as distribution cost analysis, so that the best technology is available in each of its markets. Logistics is an area where quantitative methods and operations research approaches usually are very helpful. Furthermore, some governments, for example, Mexico, may require that the firm balance each dollar of imported components with a dollar of export. Obviously, the local subsidiary cannot solve this problem on its own. It must be integrated with operations elsewhere.

For Regional Markets

Operations within regional groupings will also need coordination, at least on a regional basis. As these groups achieve economic integration, a subsidiary or distributor in one member country cannot be considered merely a national operation. It becomes part of the larger regional market. For example, as the EEC reaches a common transport policy within the already attained customs union, physical distribution will have to be organized on an EEC-wide basis. Even in LAFTA, which has not achieved much integration overall, individual firms and industries are obtaining integration on a multinational basis through complementation agreements. We examined these in Chapter 5.

Internationally

Firms that have many markets and many supply sources for world marketing need overall coordination for an optimum global integration of supply and demand. Coordination is necessary to achieve the synergism possible in multinational operations. The firm will want to keep each plant operating at an efficient level as well as to maintain adequate inventories and customer service in each market. Such coordination is possible only on a centralized basis.

Centralized control of exports is one way to achieve international logistics coordination. One office, not necessarily at company headquarters, coordinates all export orders and assigns production sources for the order.

---

[23] Drawn from Richard G. Lurie, "Technology Spurs Pace of International Trade," *Clipper Cargo Horizons*, Pan American Airways publication (March 1967), pp. 3, 4.

Eaton Yale & Towne produces in forty-three countries in addition to the United States. All products are exported to more than 100 countries through a world-wide marketing organization based in Switzerland.

Centralized control of exports is often tied in with regional distribution centers where inventories are held for faster local delivery. For example, Caterpillar has an $8 million Far East parts depot from which it ships inventory and provides services to dealers and customers in nineteen Asian countries. Texas Instruments (TI) stocks materials in sixteen of the world's major market areas. TI also uses a computer-teletype-telephone hook-up with this global system.[24] We saw an example earlier (see page 334) of another electronics company using a variety of modern technologies to integrate its global supply and demand: European supply to fill Australian demand, arranged via California. With appropriate planning, distributors and licensees as well as the firm's own subsidiaries can be included in the integrated logistics program. Automatic Radio International has accomplished this successfully with 160 distributors and licensees in eighty countries.[25]

The firm can assure integrated international logistics under various organizational arrangements. The particular setup must be designed to fit the situation of the individual firm, but in any case, some centralized planning and control will be necessary if the *overall* corporate interests are to be satisfied in the international marketplace. In review, the benefits of efficient international logistics planning should be increased corporate profits produced by (1) more efficient and stable production levels at company plants in different countries, (2) lower cost distribution, resulting in part from the possibility of combining small orders into carload or planeload lots—for example, Squibb does this by using five major exporting points with intermediate break-bulk points around the globe[26]—and (3) better customer service levels in international markets.

In concluding our discussion on physical distribution, we present the following extended example to show the problems and opportunities in international logistics management.

In 1965, Dow Chemical Company processed 25,000 foreign orders and made 12,000 export shipments. Ocean freight costs came to $12 million. Dow handled these shipments from its Midland, Michigan, headquarters through its International Distribution and Traffic Department which had fifty-five employees. Dow had overseas manufacturing in twenty locations and bulk terminals or package storage facilities in more than thirty-five locations.

One of the projects of the department was the preparation of price lists enabling salesmen to quote a price on any chemical in more than 100 markets. Information necessary for these lists included insurance and freight costs,

24 *Business Week*, November 4, 1967, p. 67.
25 *Business International*, January 23, 1970, p. 27.
26 *Traffic Management* (October 1966), p. 68.

consular fees, and duties. Since some of these are constantly changing, maintaining a currently valid list was difficult. Computerizing helped here, and updated computer print-outs were sent to salesmen in each country as changes occurred.

One reason freight rates were changing was that the department was bargaining with over thirty steamship conferences on rates and classifications on its chemicals. By getting one chemical, Dowpon, *reclassified Dow cut its freight rate from $64 to $42 per long ton. This opened new markets by making it competitive with a similar German product.*

Because of the importance of volume shipping of bulky chemicals, the firm operated three vessels under long-term contract for bulk shipments. This was in addition to its regular-spot and medium-term charter arrangements. Dow's engineers also collaborated' with marine engineers on the design of specialized vessels. The great majority of company shipments were made in bulk to overseas bulk terminals.

Although Dow did all of its own logistics planning, it did use the services of freight forwarders—two on the Gulf Coast, one each on the East Coast, West Coast, and Great Lakes. The company also arranged to have the government establish a free-trade zone at Bay City, Michigan. One exception to the centralized physical distribution management at Dow was the European market. As its manufacturing and marketing operations grew in Europe, Dow found that decentralization was appropriate for control of shipments within Europe.[27]

Questions

11.1 Distinguish between the foreign market distribution task of the exporter and that of the firm with local subsidiaries.

11.2 Identify the major uncontrollable elements facing the marketer in planning his foreign market distribution.

11.3 In the *United Nations Statistical Yearbook,* look at the table entitled "Basic Data on Wholesale and Retail Trade." Evaluate the usefulness of these figures for the international marketer.

11.4 Discuss the relationship of wholesaling and retailing to economic development.

11.5 Many foreign markets have relatively large numbers of small retailers. How does this constrain the local distribution and promotion of the international marketer?

11.6 Consumer Products Company (in nondurables) is selling in Paragona, a country with a "dual economy." How might the firm's distribution vary between the two sectors of this economy?

11.7 What are the implications for the international marketer of the trend toward larger scale retailing?

11.8 Why do American firms often use less direct channels abroad than they use at home?

11.9 Why does the international firm often have an advantage over local firms in advertising support of the channel?

[27] Adapted from *Traffic Management* (October 1966), pp. 58–67.

11.10 Discuss the use of distributor training programs as a means of channel support in local markets.

11.11 How can the growth of the firm in a foreign market cause changes in its distribution there?

11.12 What are the current prospects for international channels of distribution? What factors would have to be evaluated?

11.13 Explain how international logistics involves more than transportation.

11.14 Identify some of the factors causing variation in the firm's logistics *within* foreign markets.

11.15 Discuss the political-governmental barriers in international logistics.

11.16 What are the implications of the dynamic environment for the international logistics planner? What factors must he consider?

11.17 What are some of the potential benefits a free-trade zone offers to the international marketer?

11.18 How can the international marketer aid logistics *within* a foreign market?

11.19 Is it necessary to have central coordination of logistics in the multinational firm?

Further Readings

Books:

Bowersox, Donald J., Edward W. Smykay, and Bernard J. La Londe, *Physical Distribution Management,* rev. ed. (New York: Macmillan, 1968).

Business International, *Developing Distribution in Europe,* A Business International European Research Report, August, 1969.

Dymsza, William A., *Foreign Trade Zones and International Business* (Trenton, N.J.: Research Section, Bureau of Commerce, 1964).

Fayerweather, John, ed., *International Marketing,* 2nd ed. (Englewood Cliffs, N.J.: Prentice-Hall, 1970), chap. 6.

Heskett, J. L., Robert M. Ivie, and Nicholas A. Glaskowsky, Jr., *Business Logistics* (New York: Ronald Press, 1964).

Hollander, Stanley C., *Multinational Retailing,* MSU International Business and Economic Studies (East Lansing, Mich.: Institute for International Business and Economic Development Studies, Division of Research, Graduate School of Business Administration, 1970).

Jefferys, James B., and Derek Knee, *Retailing in Europe* (London: Macmillan and Co., 1962).

Miracle, Gordon E., and Gerald S. Albaum, *International Marketing Management* (Homewood, Ill.: Richard D. Irwin, 1970), chaps. 17, 18.

Stacey, Nicholas A. H., and Audrey Wilson, *The Changing Pattern of Distribution* (London: Business Publications, 1958).

Terpstra, Vern, *American Marketing in the Common Market* (New York: Praeger, 1967), chap. 5.

Articles:

Douglas, Susan P., "Patterns and Parallels of Marketing Structures in Several Countries," *MSU Business Topics* (Spring 1971), pp. 38–48.

Goldstucker, Joe, "The Influence of Culture on the Channels of Distribution," *Marketing and the New Science of Planning,* ed. by Robert L. King (Chi-

cago: American Marketing Association, Fall Conference Proceedings, 1968),
p. 470.

Litvak, Isaiah A. and Peter M. Banting, "A Conceptual Framework for International Business Arrangements," *Marketing and the New Science of Planning,* ed. by Robert L. King (Chicago: American Marketing Association, Fall Conference Proceedings, 1968), pp. 460–467.

McGarrah, Robert E., "Logistics for the International Manufacturer," *Harvard Business Review* (March–April 1966), pp. 154–166.

Samli, A. Coskun, "Wholesaling in an Economy of Scarcity: Turkey," *Journal of Marketing* (July 1964), pp. 55–58.

Wadinambiaratchi, George, "Channels of Distribution in Developing Economies," *The Business Quarterly* (Winter 1965), pp. 74–82.

12

INTERNATIONAL
PROMOTION: ADVERTISING

Promotion is one of the most visible and controversial as well as the most culture bound of the firm's marketing functions. Marketing includes the whole collection of activities the firm performs in relating to its market, but in the functions of marketing research, product development, pricing, and distribution, the firm relates to the market in a quieter, more passive way. If firm and market communicate in the course of these activities, it is usually from the market to the firm. With the promotional function, however, the situation is quite different. The firm is standing up and speaking out, wanting to be seen and heard. For purposes of this book, we will define promotion as the communication by the firm with its various audiences, with a view to informing them and influencing their attitudes and behavior in a way favorable to the firm.

The subject matter of both Chapters 12 and 13 is not really "international promotion," but rather promotion in the multinational company. Since relatively little promotion is truly international, we are concerned primarily with the management of promotion in a number of separate nations. The international aspect is in the coordination of the various national promotional activities to make up the firm's integrated international promotional program. Promotion in international marketing plays the same role it does in domestic operations, that is, communication with the firm's audiences to achieve certain goals. Variations from country to country will occur, however, in all three dimensions of promotion: means of communication; audience; and even company goals and needs.

Promotion is usually aimed at enhancing the image and position of the company, its products, and its brands. We have seen, however, that the situation of the company, its product line, and its brand names often are not the same from one country to another. Therefore, the promotional task will not be exactly the same in every market either. Another dimension promotion frequently takes on in the international company is nationality; that is, the firm must decide whether to present itself as a local, foreign, or multinational company. Many of its other marketing decisions will be affected by its choice in this matter.

Our approach in these chapters will be to examine the various elements of promotion in the multinational company. We will discuss the following major topics: advertising, sales promotion, personal selling, special forms of promotion for international marketing, and public relations. We will try to give a picture of the state of the art in these areas and also highlight the kinds of problems and decisions facing the international marketing manager. Our examination of the promotional task in international marketing begins here in Chapter 12 with advertising; in Chapter 13 we will discuss the other elements of international promotion.

ADVERTISING

Advertising is the paid communication of company messages through impersonal media. The messages may be audio, as in radio advertising, visual, as in billboards or magazines, or audio-visual, as in television or cinema advertising. Although the management of advertising in the international company encounters special problems, advertising itself plays basically the same marketing role internationally as it does domestically. Everywhere it is used to achieve various marketing goals of the firm. Some of these goals or objectives include paving the way or getting leads for salesmen, gaining distribution for the firm's products, sale of the firm's products, improving brand image and increasing brand recognition, and so on. In every country, too, advertising is just one element of the marketing mix. Its role will depend on decisions made about the other elements of the mix in that country.

Because the principles of advertising do not vary internationally, but only the practice, we will not discuss principles. We assume that the reader is familiar with general advertising principles from other sources or from experience. Good general discussions can be found in the following texts: S. Watson Dunn, *Advertising: Its Role in Modern Marketing*, 2nd ed. (New York: Holt, Rinehart and Winston, 1969); James F. Engel, Hugh G. Wales, and Martin R. Warshaw, *Promotional Strategy*, rev. ed. (Homewood, Ill.: Richard D. Irwin, 1967).

We will begin our discussion of advertising in the international company with a review of the environmental constraints that influence it. Then we will consider the kinds of advertising decisions facing the international marketing manager.

CONSTRAINTS ON THE INTERNATIONAL
ADVERTISING PROGRAM

The international advertising program of a particular company is determined by two broad sets of constraints, one posed by the internal situation and character of the company, and the other by the international environment of advertising. The internal situation of the company will be considered when we discuss decision making in international advertising. We look first at the important elements of the international environment.

Languages: The Tower of Babel

We discussed the nature of the language problem in international business in Chapter 4; here we will examine its significance for international advertising. Construction of the Tower of Babel stopped when the workers could no longer communicate with each other. The manager of international advertising may feel that he is in a similar situation when he faces the diversity of languages in his world markets. Although some languages are used in more than one country, the fact remains that there are many more languages than countries. The international advertiser himself does not have to know all the languages of all his markets, but the firm's advertising messages must communicate in these languages. Even in the few cases where the product and its advertising appeals are universal, the language of the message will not be.

The practical implication of language diversity for the international advertiser is that he needs help in communicating with his markets. There is no communication unless a message has been received and understood. To achieve this understanding, the international advertiser needs local help in each of his markets. Technical accuracy or "perfect" translations are not sufficient; persuasive messages must speak the "language of the heart," and for this, intimate local knowledge is required. The local help available to the international advertiser is usually of two kinds: national personnel of its own in countries where it has subsidiaries and the advertising agency located in the market. In either case, the company gets the benefit of employees whose native language the company wants to advertise in. In bilingual Belgium, for example, the firm will have access to people who speak both French and Flemish. In other markets, the firm may rely on its national distributor to take care of the advertising. In a very real sense, the language problem in foreign markets is beyond the capabilities of the international advertiser; he can solve it only with the help of local expertise in one of these forms.

Role of Advertising in the Society

The Statistics

Another constraint on the advertising program of the firm in its world markets is the different role advertising plays in each nation. In some nations, advertising is very prominent and important, whereas in others it is almost nonexistent. Twenty billion dollars, or over 60 percent of the 1969 world-total advertising budget, was spent in the United States. Germany, Japan, and the United Kingdom also had over $1 billion expenditures each. Some further aspects of these international differences in advertising are shown statistically in Tables 12–1 and 12–2. In 1968, for example, the international average of per capita expenditures on advertising was about $17, but the variation around that average figure was fantastic. The United States per capita expenditure was almost $90, followed rather closely by West Germany and Switzerland.

Table 12–1 Per Capita Advertising Expenditures—1968

COUNTRY	(IN U.S. $)
United States	$89.56
Switzerland	67.76
West Germany	65.45
Sweden	50.87
Denmark	44.78
Canada	37.01
Australia	32.03
Netherlands	26.84
Norway	24.19
New Zealand	23.77
Finland	22.87
United Kingdom	21.31
Austria	19.72
Puerto Rico	18.36
Belgium	17.35
France	17.17
. . .	. . .
India	.16
Pakistan	.14
Nepal	.05

Source: *Advertising Age*, May 4, 1970, p. 26.

Table 12–2 Advertising Expenditures—1968

COUNTRY	AS % OF GNP
West Germany	2.87%
Switzerland	2.42
Jamaica	2.11
United States	2.05
Ireland	1.96
Denmark	1.76
Argentina	1.68
Sweden	1.58
New Zealand	1.49
Australia	1.45
Canada	1.35
Puerto Rico	1.35
Netherlands	1.35
Austria	1.27
Finland	1.27
Brazil	1.21
Mexico	1.19
United Kingdom	1.16
Bolivia	1.09
Japan	1.04
Norway	1.03

Source: *Advertising Age*, May 4, 1970, p. 26.

At the other extreme, some Southeast Asian nations had truly negligible amounts, for example, from 5¢ to 16¢ per capita, or less than 1 percent of the world average.

Another way of noting the role of advertising in a nation is to relate advertising expenditures to the size of the economy. Table 12–2, which lists those nations spending more than 1 percent of their national income on advertising, illustrates this procedure. On this measure, the United States is in fourth place. Not surprisingly, the list includes mainly Western European and other industrialized countries. What is notable is the presence of six Latin American nations on the list, including Bolivia, which is one of the poorest. This suggests that in spite of their lack of affluence, these Latin American countries are very receptive to the practice of advertising. A contributing factor, of course, is that it is these countries in the region that also have commercial radio and television.

Table 12–2 is also significant in its omissions. Germany and the Netherlands are there, but none of their Common Market partners. From Table 12–1 it appears that advertising is three to four times as important in Germany as in neighboring France, another example of a case in which the Common Market isn't "common." In a broader comparison, one can note the presence in the tables of all the Northern European countries and the absence of all the Mediterranean or Southern European countries.

The Cultural Factors

The statistics give us some picture of the economic role of advertising in various economies, but it is equally important to know why the statistics are as they are. In other words, What determines the role of advertising in a nation? Some of the determinants are economic and relate to the level of economic development of the country. Poorer nations whose inhabitants live near the subsistence level have little need for advertising. They have no surplus to sell and no distance or communications gap exists between the producers and the consumers. The situation changes steadily with increasing industrialization and affluence, which helps to explain why the rich industrialized nations predominate in Tables 12–1 and 12–2. Furthermore, richer nations have both better distribution of the various media to convey and receive advertising messages and more discretionary income to be enticed by advertisers.

Karl Marx to the contrary, however, economic factors are not a sufficient explanation of the role of advertising in a country. Economic reasons do not explain the differences between neighboring European countries, or why Bolivia spends relatively more on advertising than do dozens of countries more affluent. The explanation must be found rather in the area of culture. The cultural environment of advertising is composed of three elements: (1) the attitudes of consumers—hostile or receptive to advertising; (2) the attitudes of managers—aggressive or passive marketers; and (3) the attitudes of governments —restrictive or permissive toward advertising. The governments' attitudes, of course, will be reflected in the legal environment.

As an example of cultural influence, we can compare France and Germany. Advertising plays a lesser role in France than it does in Germany, not because France is poorer but because the cultural environment in France is less favorable to advertising. French managers are less aggressive in marketing than are German managers. French consumers are less receptive to advertising than are German consumers. The high volume of advertising in Germany is all the more significant because it occurs in spite of a strict regulatory environment.

The government must be considered part of the cultural environment. Although often its attitudes and actions on advertising may reflect those of the population as a whole, not infrequently, a certain government's actions will reflect the attitudes of various government officials who for personal or ideological reasons are hostile to advertising. Government attitudes lead to regulations limiting the nature and amount of the advertising appearing in a nation. For example, the Indian government once attacked the advertising volume of the foreign tire companies there. The United Kingdom made a similar attack on the advertising of soaps and detergents. Overall, government regulations —and taxes—can have a very restrictive effect on advertising, particularly those that pertain to media. For example, many nations allow no commercials on radio or television, eliminating two of the most popular advertising media. In the advertiser's favor is the trend toward minimization of these differences through the growth of international business, increasing affluence, and improved communications. Perhaps less welcome to the advertiser is another trend—the growing attention of governments to the practice of advertising.

Media Availability

The international environment of advertising has other noteworthy differences. Although some of these are related to the role of advertising in the economy, they have aspects worthy of mention here. One of these is the availability of media. We have noted that in many countries, some media are not available for advertising purposes because of legal restrictions. Quite apart from the law, however, other factors often limit media availability. In Chapter 3, we noted the great disparities in the communications infrastructure of nations. In newspapers, for example, India had thirteen copies per 1,000 population, whereas another Asian country, Japan, had 465 copies per 1,000 population. A company's advertising manager for Asia would face strikingly different situations in these two markets. Nigeria has five times the population of Peru, but Peru had more radios than Nigeria. In markets where cinema is an advertising medium, the advertiser may find per capita annual attendance ranges from one (Philippines, Tanzania) to twelve or more visits per year (Spain, Sweden).

Competition

The competitive situation is another variable in international advertising. In some markets, an American international company will compete against other American or international companies. In other markets, the competition will be purely national in character. Not only do the number and nature of competitors vary from market to market, but so do their advertising programs and strategies. Sound advertising strategy and tactics in one market will not necessarily be sound in another market with a different competitive situation. Furthermore, the approach of the international company will provoke different kinds of national reactions. In some countries, the international company provokes national competitors to follow its course of action; for example, Procter and Gamble's entry into Western European countries caused national competitors to increase their advertising. In other countries, an aggressive entry may cause nationals to demand that their government restrict the "intruder" to protect national producers.

Agency Availability

Other national variables facing the international advertiser are the advertising agency situation and the market demand for his product. The number and quality of advertising agencies in national markets runs a range about as broad as that for GNP figures. As a general guide, the quality of agency service in a country will correspond roughly to its level of economic development and the size of its economy. Thus India, a poor nation in per capita income, offered several rather good advertising agencies because its total market is so large. On the other hand, Ecuador, Iran, and Morocco had only one major agency each, even though their per capita income was higher than that of India. Consumer demand is another influence on advertising. As we noted throughout Part I, nations differ in income levels, tastes, and living styles, which are primary determinants of the demand for the firm's products. Since advertising is meant to stimulate this demand, the advertising manager must be familiar with and adapt to these local market characteristics.

Many international variables complicate the programs and strategies of the international advertiser, who must be familiar with them in order to design effective campaigns in his foreign markets. In addition to other complications, these constraints tend to cause diseconomies of scale in international advertising. One of the manager's major challenges is to overcome or minimize this limitation through effective coordination of his international advertising program.

ADVERTISING DECISIONS FACING THE INTERNATIONAL MARKETER

Whereas the domestic advertising manager's concern is with programs and campaigns prepared uniquely for the home market, his international counterpart has a more complex task. He must assure the development of appropriate campaigns for each of the firm's foreign markets and also try to get the right degree of coordination among the various national programs. Some of the questions he encounters in his task are common to the management of any advertising program. Others are unique to international advertising. We will examine seven decision areas in international advertising: (1) selecting the agency (or agencies); (2) choosing the message; (3) selecting the media;

(4) determining the budget; (5) evaluating advertising effectiveness; (6) organizing for advertising; and (7) whether to engage in cooperative advertising abroad.

Selecting the Agency

Many marketing functions are performed entirely within the company by company personnel. With advertising, the firm almost always relies heavily on outside expertise in the form of the advertising agency. Agency selection will usually be the first advertising decision the marketer has to make. Because the international advertising management task is twofold, the international marketer has special alternatives and specifications to deal with in selecting an agency. Two major alternatives are open to him: (1) a domestic agency with offices abroad or (2) foreign agencies in each national market. Various modifications of these basic alternatives are often available also, such as a domestic agency with foreign affiliates rather than branches, or independent foreign agencies grouped together in a loose organization to provide multinational coverage.

Selection Criteria

Naturally, the international marketing manager should choose the agency or agencies he feels would best help the company achieve profits as well as its other goals. Because this selection criterion is not easy to determine directly, it is helpful to identify subsidiary criteria that can aid in the choice. First, the international marketing manager should identify the specific agency alternatives that are available to his company and situation. For example, What agencies are located in his foreign markets? Which are pre-empted by competitors? Second, he might evaluate each agency, using the following criteria:

1. *Market coverage.* Does the particular agency or package of agencies cover all the markets he is interested in?

2. *Quality of coverage.* How good a job does this package of agencies do in preparing advertising in each of the firm's markets? Performance may frequently vary from market to market, but some agency or group of agencies will still be better than others.

3. *Market research, public relations, and other marketing services.* If the firm needs these kinds of services in its world markets, in addition to straight advertising work, how do the different agencies compare on their offerings of these facilities?

4. *Relative roles of company advertising department and agency.* Some firms have a large advertising staff that does much of the creative and strategic work of preparing advertising campaigns. These firms require much less of an agency than do companies and subsidiaries that rely on the agency for almost everything relating to advertising, except perhaps the budget. Thus a weak company advertising department needs a strong agency, and vice versa.

5. *Communication and control.* If the international marketer wants the possibility of frequent, convenient communication with the agencies in foreign markets and wishes to oversee and control their efforts, he will be inclined to tie up with the domestic agency that has overseas offices. The internal communications system of this agency network would facilitate communica-

tion for the international marketer. This point is somewhat related to the following criterion, because international communications become more important when there is international coordination of the firm's advertising.

6. *International coordination.* Does the firm wish to have advertising tailor-made to each national market? Or does it desire coordination of national advertising with that done in other foreign markets, and/or with the domestic program? One of the major differences between agency groups will be their ability to aid the advertiser in getting international advertising coordination.

7. *Size of company international business.* The smaller the initial volume of a firm's international advertising expenditures, the less its ability to divide it up among many different agencies. Volume may determine agency choice to assure some minimum level of attention and service. A small volume multiplied by a number of markets could be of interest to an international agency even if it is of no interest to an agency in any one market.

8. *Image.* Does the firm want a national or international image? Desire for local identification and good local citizenship might indicate that the firm should choose national agencies rather than an international one. This is the practice of IBM, for example.

9. *Company organization.* Companies that are very decentralized, with national profit centers, might wish to leave the question of agency selection to the local subsidiary.

10. *Level of involvement.* In *joint-venture* arrangements, the international firm shares decision making. The national partner may have strong preferences and/or long experience with a national agency, which could be the decisive factor. In *licensing* agreements, the whole question of advertising and promotion is largely in the hands of the licensee rather than in those of the international licensor. Selling through *distributors* also reduces the control of the international company. Sometimes the firm may have a cooperative advertising program with distributors, but generally the international marketer can choose only the agencies for the advertising paid for by his firm. Of course, where the firm has a 50-50 cooperative program with the distributor, it would probably have some voice in agency selection.

Trend to International Agencies

Increasingly the choice of an agency for international advertising is being made in favor of the domestic agency with offices abroad, especially for American companies. Several advantages and situations lead American firms to choose such an American international agency. Many companies feel that this approach yields cost savings, partly because it avoids some duplication of the research and creative activity in preparing advertising campaigns. The ease of communication with the agency's foreign branches is itself both a convenience and a cost saving to the firm. Where centralized control of advertising is desired, it is facilitated by dealing with one familiar agency with a similar international organization.

When companies want to present a united front to the world, following a policy of standardized or internationally coordinated advertising, the task is easier if the firm has the same agency all over. For example, when the Kodak Instamatic was introduced globally at the same time it was introduced in the United States, some of Eastman Kodak's foreign subsidiaries switched to the local office of J. Walter Thompson. Thompson's American account executive for Kodak was coordinating global advertising for the introduction. The choice of an American international agency is especially common in industrial-goods marketing where the appeals are more common from country to country and the advertising budgets are generally smaller. Some consumer-goods marketers too find that the same basic appeals can be used all over, and therefore an American international agency can be chosen. Examples are Maidenform ("I dreamed . . ."), Coca-Cola, and Pepsi Cola.

The internationalization of American advertising agencies is another evidence of international companies' preference for dealing with one agency in world markets. Some of the several different evidences of this trend are shown by Tables 12–3 and 12–4. Of the top fifty agencies in the world, only thirteen are non-American. Table 12–3 shows the top twelve in 1970, and only the fourth and the twelfth were foreign. Since that time, one-half of Lintas (the twelfth) was purchached by SSC&B, an American agency. Lintas itself was

Table 12–3 World's Biggest Agencies (estimated total billings, in millions)

RANK	AGENCY	1969
1	J. Walter Thompson Co.	$736.0
2	Young & Rubicam	522.9
3	McCann-Erickson	511.1
4	Dentsu Advertising (Japan)	440.5
5	Ted Bates & Company	375.1
6	Batten, Barton, Durstine & Osborn	356.2
7	Leo Burnett Company	355.9
8	Doyle Dane Bernbach	269.9
9	Foote, Cone & Belding	265.5
10	Ogilvy & Mather International	229.8
11	Grey Advertising	228.1
12	Lintas International (U.K.)	180.7

Source: *Advertising Age*, March 23, 1970, p. 36.

Table 12–4 Top Ten International Billing (U.S. agencies: billings in millions)

RANK	AGENCY	1969
1	J. Walter Thompson Co.	$292.0
2	McCann-Erickson	257.8
3	Young & Rubicam	151.6
4	Ted Bates & Company	145.2
5	Ogilvy & Mather International	77.0
6	Norman, Craig & Kummel	71.0
7	Leo Burnett Company	67.7
8	Foote, Cone & Belding	62.8
9	Compton Advertising	60.0
10	Kenyon & Eckhardt	45.0

Source: *Advertising Age*, March 23, 1970, p. 43.

the international advertising service of Unilever, a one-company effort to get effective international advertising service (Lintas equals *Lever International Advertising Service*). The foreign billings alone of J. Walter Thompson make it the world's eighth largest agency. Table 12–4 indicates that several American agencies are large businesses merely on the strength of their international billings.

American advertising agencies have gone international especially since the 1960s, motivated primarily by keeping up with their large American clients. In 1937, there were just four American agencies with a total of twenty-one offices abroad. By 1969, however, there were thirty-six American international agencies with 281 foreign offices. Over fifty American agencies do some overseas business. As one example of client pressure on agencies, no less than thirteen international companies in Canada switched from Canadian to American international agencies in the first five months of 1966.[1] This American expansion has not gone unnoticed by agencies in other countries. They, too, especially the English, have expanded their international ties and services to correspond more closely to the international business of their client companies.

The following are a few dramatic examples of the threat to a domestic agency that does not have international ties.

The Volkswagen advertising in America was handled very successfully by Doyle Dane Bernbach. When this American agency opened an office in Germany, the Volkswagen company dropped its national agency there and gave the Volkswagen account in Germany to the German office of Doyle Dane Bernbach.

A case well-remembered on Madison Avenue is that of the giant Coca-Cola account. Once held by the D'Arcy agency, the account was lost to McCann-Erickson in the United States after McCann got its foot in the door abroad. Since then D'Arcy has also moved into foreign markets.

In many other instances an international agency that covers foreign markets for a firm eventually has gotten its domestic advertising as well. This reflects the firm's desire for coordination, convenience, and economy in its total advertising program.

The situation of the domestic agency with foreign affiliates (rather than its own offices abroad) and the case of international groupings of independent agencies are somewhat different from the international agency group we have been discussing. Although in principle they are all the same, offering multi-market coverage and coordination, in practice some doubt exists as to whether the same degree of coordination can be obtained when independent agencies are collaborating. Further, some conflict may arise about fee-splitting with affiliates. Quality variation between countries might also be greater in these cases. It is easier, cheaper, and quicker for an agency to expand abroad

[1] *Business International*, May 5, 1967, p. 139.

through affiliates than through opening its own offices. However, once the better agencies in a country have been purchased or have signed an affiliation, the agencies left may prove to be the weak links of an international chain. If many links are weak, of course, the chain is not very useful.

As to continuing developments in this area, the words of one leading practitioner are thought-provoking. Tom Sutton, Executive Vice-President—International, J. Walter Thompson Company, said:

"In the last ten years, more than 150 fully-controlled foreign offices have been opened by U.S. and U.K. agencies alone. But rather than do what many international agencies do today, that is, provide full service in all major markets —and often many minor ones too, they may in the future have a small number of key offices concentrating on the guts of our business—concentrating on the creative side.

"In ten, twenty years' time an international agency might be able to concentrate its creative resources into, say, ten centers—let us say, New York, London, Paris, São Paulo, Buenos Aires, Sydney, one to cover the important area from Japan to the Indian subcontinent, one in Black Africa, one in Moscow and, perhaps, hopefully, one in Peking. Some of these may be the wrong centers and others may more usefully take their places. But I can foresee such concentration of main offices, with smaller service stations in other countries completing the agency networks.

"Such a development will be dictated by the shortage of qualified, experienced advertising professionals. We all employ some brilliant creative people, but we know that however brilliant they may be and however many we may be blessed to have, there is still a shortage.

"For agencies it is impossible, and will prove more so in the future, to have the same level of creative professionals in smaller capitals or market centers of the world as can be mustered in such developed advertising metropolises as New York, London, or Chicago.[2]

The Local Agency Survives

In spite of the trend of multinational companies toward using international agencies, the national agencies often show a strong survival capability. Several reason make them a continuing and viable alternative for the international marketer. Although international agencies offer multimarket coverage, their networks are not always of even quality. Their offices in some markets might be very strong, whereas in others they might be only average or even mediocre. If the firm needs a high quality of advertising in all of its markets, it might decide to use the best local agency in each market even if that agency does not belong to an international family.

Another promise of the international agency is coordination of the firm's advertising programs in different national markets. If the firm does not desire or require such coordination, it has less need to employ an international

[2] *The International Advertiser*, vol. 10, no. 2 (1968), p. 7. Emphasis added.

agency. The coordination provided by international agencies is not always effective, either. Some do a much better job than others. One international marketing executive, in referring to his own experience with such an agency, told the author, "They don't coordinate anything!" Performance is improving on this score, however.

Other company reasons for choosing local agencies include the desire for local image and the need or desire to give national subsidiaries responsibility for their own promotion. As one vice-president for European operations told the author: "Our gains from improved morale and performance from giving them this responsibility far outweigh any loss of efficiency from not requiring international coordination."

Of the several reasons for choosing national agencies instead of the international agency's office in the same market, most of those we have discussed have been negative, in the sense that they are based on weaknesses in, or a lack of need for, the international agency approach. A more positive reason for choosing a national agency is the special services or quality it has to offer. Although it is not uncommon for some of the best agencies in a market to be offices of an international group, in some cases the best agency for a firm will be an independent national agency. Just as in the United States, some relatively small but very creative shops can exist and compete with the giants of the industry. Sometimes their very independence and lack of size give them a flair and flexibility that may be just what the firm needs in that market. Some of the most successful campaigns are carried out by such agencies, and that is a major reason why the firm must consider them as one alternative when it selects an agency for a market.

Having made an appropriate bow to the independent national agencies, we again note the persistent trend toward the selection of international agencies by international companies. As the supermarket chains became predominant in food retailing, so the international agencies are growing in international advertising. Although there will always be room for a certain number of quality independent agencies in each market, their relative importance will decline. A Lintas executive even foresees a series of mergers, leaving perhaps only ten or fifteen big agencies handling large international clients.[3]

PepsiCo is an example of a company that uses American international agencies in many markets. When it moved into Japan in the 1960s, however, PepsiCo chose a Japanese agency rather than an American office or affiliate. The executive explained: "We were moving into a very complex market. We wanted a large Japanese agency that knew its way around the key media. The American affiliates just weren't big enough, at that time, to do the job." The same person also noted that "politics plays a role. If the parent corporation in the states uses J. Walter Thompson, the local sub will generally use the Thompson office in Tokyo."[4]

[3] *Business Week*, September 12, 1970, p. 58.
[4] *Business Abroad*, October 30, 1967, p. 37. Emphasis added.

The above discussion has highlighted the basic alternatives and considerations for the international marketer in selecting agencies for his international advertising. In concluding, we can reflect on the prediction of an experienced practitioner in this field. He said, "The old established middle-sized agencies are in the most trouble. The ones that will prosper are the international full-service agencies and the small nimble ones that can generate excitement."[5] Perhaps the problem of the latter will be to remain small and nimble.

Choosing the Advertising Message

A major advertising decision area for the international marketer is the determination of appropriate advertising appeals and messages for each of his foreign markets. In one sense, each national market is unique. This might suggest the need to develop special appeals and campaigns peculiar to each market, an awesome task if the firm is selling in a hundred markets or more. It can be even more complex if national markets are divided into different market segments insofar as the firm's products and advertising are concerned, as is often true for the United States market, for example. This brings up one of the important debates in international advertising circles; that is, Should the firm use national or international advertising appeals? Should it take a fragmented or standardized approach to its international advertising?[6]

The international marketer's basic problem, however, is not the one just noted, but rather how to develop the most effective international advertising appeals and campaigns, be they national, international, or something in between. The message obviously must fit the market if it is to communicate successfully. Fortunately, the principles and methods of creating effective advertising are the same in Italy and Peru as they are in Indiana and Pennsylvania. These principles and methods do not change in an international framework. Therefore we will not discuss these basic principles, which can be found in any good advertising textbook.[7] We will concern ourselves only with questions relating to the international aspects of advertising, which involve the local research on the particular national relationship of the product to the market and the designing of appeals that relate the two. Although people's basic needs and desires are the same around the world, the way these desires are satisfied may vary from country to country. Advertising appeals must meet local realities.

The design of national advertising is another area where the international marketer requires local help. Because he cannot know each national market intimately, he must get help from those who do. The sources of this assistance are the local subsidiary, partner, or distributor, and the local advertising agency. He may, in fact, completely decentralize advertising responsibility so that each national operation prepares its own advertising.

[5] *Time*, March 16, 1970, p. 90.

[6] See Erik Elinder, "How International Can European Advertising Be?" *Journal of Marketing* (April 1965), pp. 7–11; and John Ryans, "A Tiger in Every Tank?" *Columbia Journal of World Business* (March–April 1969), pp. 69–75.

[7] See references, page 381.

Complete decentralization would mean localized advertising in each of the firm's markets. The international marketing manager who is concerned about optimizing marketing operations on a global basis, however, might be dissatisfied with such complete decentralization, an approach that can lead to suboptimization. He will therefore wonder what he can contribute to local operations. This brings him back to the question of the international input into national advertising, or how international his advertising should be. Is it possible that good advertising in one nation can be effective in another? Can any economies of scale or synergism be achieved in international advertising? The problem of choosing advertising appeals and messages thus becomes related to the debate about the national versus the international advertising approach.

Localized or Standardized?

In the preparation of advertising campaigns in the international company, there are usually arguments for both an individualized national approach and a standardized international approach. The arguments reflect the subjective self-interested evaluations of the parties involved as well as the objective factors in the situation. In general, two groups tend to be biased in favor of a separate national approach: the management of the local subsidiary and the independent local agency. In each case, the weight of the argument depends in large part on the special local knowledge they contribute. The more practical it is for the international firm to treat their market as it does its other markets, the less important and necessary they are. Because of this vulnerability, both tend to be defensive about the uniqueness of their national market and the need for special approaches there. They will argue in terms of objective factors in the national environment, but their position is greatly influenced by their perceived vulnerability.

Human and subjective factors influence the other side of the argument also. The international agency and the international marketing or advertising manager tend to favor an international approach partly because of their own position and interests. For example, assume the situation where the international agency makes its bid for the international company's business in competition with an independent national agency. The international agency's competitive advantage may well lie in its internationalism and its ability to coordinate and integrate advertising on that basis. On the other hand, it may be less well established in the particular market than the independent agency there. Therefore, it will argue on the basis of its strong points and their appropriateness to the company's need, suggesting the international approach as the best solution for the company as well as the solution it is best equipped to provide.

The international advertising manager also would tend to have some bias toward an international approach. If each of the firm's foreign markets were indeed unique, thus requiring a national approach by those located in the market, the task and importance of the international manager would be diminished. If he wants to see himself as something more than an occasional advisor to a collection of national companies, he will likely press for the international approach and work for the coordination and integration of the firm's advertising in foreign markets. Another human element that sometimes enters here is the desire of top management to have "one name, one image, world-wide." When executives travel abroad, many of them like to see the same company image and advertising as they go from market to market. This desire may not be a decisive element, but it does play some role in the degree of internationalization realized.

The decision on the degree of international uniformity in advertising appeals will be affected by the human and organizational elements discussed above. As we pointed out in our discussion of agency selection, gains in subsidiary morale and performance can at least partially offset the potential losses in efficiency from taking a fragmented national approach. However, the decision should also rest heavily on objective data from the environment outside the firm. Ultimately, it should be the needs of the market and the communications possibilities that determine the approach used. The international marketer should choose the approach that is the most profitable in terms of sales achieved and costs incurred. Because measuring the sales results of advertising is difficult, however, he will also have to look at other variables affecting his choice of approach. The two kinds of advertising variables relevant here are those on the market side, having to do with the reception and understanding of the message, and those on the production side, having to do with both personnel and technology.

Market Considerations

Several factors influence the ability of the firm to use similar appeals from market to market. One element is the role the firm's product plays in the buyers' consumption system. If the product is used in the same way and meets the same consumer needs from country to country, similar appeals are more feasible. The international success of Coca-Cola, which takes an international approach in its advertising appeals, suggests that the product meets similar consumer needs or desires everywhere. This is probably true for some other low-priced consumer goods, a famous example of which is Esso gasoline as promoted by Esso's "tiger" campaign:

"Put a tiger in your tank." With small modifications and language changes, this campaign has traveled all around the world. Some examples of how the slogan came out:

Putt en tiger pa tanken
Ponga un tigre en su tanque
Kom en tiger i tanken
Metti um tigre nel motore
Tu den tiger in den tank
Pankaa tiikeri tankum
Mettez un tigre dans votre moteur[8]

---

[8] Ryans, "A Tiger in Every Tank?" p. 71.

Another market consideration is the similarity of buying motives from country to country. The same product may be purchased for a mixture of functional, convenience, and status reasons, but with a somewhat different combination of motivations in each country. The more alike buying motives are, the more desirable the use of common appeals. This is often the case with industrial goods but is less common with consumer durables.

General Electric used an international approach with its industrial goods but took a national approach with its consumer durables. The automobile market offers conflicting examples. Volvo emphasized economy, durability, and safety in both Sweden and the United States, whereas its advertisements stressed status and leisure in France, performance in Germany, and safety in Switzerland (scene of many fatal accidents).[9] On the other hand, BMW, selling in thirty countries, tried to maintain a uniform international image.[10]

LANGUAGE   Another market factor is language overlap and similarity from market to market. One world language would obviously facilitate uniform international advertising. Fortunately for those of us who use the English language, English is gradually coming to fill that global role. Eric Webster notes that "250 million people, one-tenth of the world's population, use English as their primary language, and nearly one in four—600 million—can in some degree be reached in English. More than 70 percent of the world's mail is written in English. Fifty-four percent of the world's business community use English as their main business language. Another 25 percent use English as their second business language, and only one in one hundred of the world's businessmen has no English at all."[11]

A surprising reinforcement for the increasing importance of English came from the French government. The French proposed eliminating the requirement for a second foreign language in secondary school. Eighty percent of French students choose English as their first foreign language. A French newspaper argued that "If we are satisfied with just knowing English, why shouldn't other countries be too?"[12] Such a move, especially by the French, can only increase the world role of the English language. Of course, the present role of English in the world does not yet permit international campaigns in English, except for some industrial or capital goods, or goods that appeal to some international jet set.

Although language overlap between countries is not sufficient to permit global advertising campaigns, a few multinational language areas do facilitate multinational advertising on a less-than-global basis. Minor examples are found in Europe where the German language covers Austria and most of Switzerland in addition to Germany, and where the French language covers

[9] *International Management* (March 1968), pp. 55, 56.
[10] *The International Advertiser*, vol. 10, no. 2 (1968), pp. 18, 19.
[11] *The Advertising Quarterly* (Winter 1967–1968), p. 34.
[12] *Time*, May 18, 1970, p. 63.

parts of Belgium, Switzerland, Luxembourg, and Monaco as well as France. More important examples are the following: (1) the English-speaking world, covering from 250 million to 600 million people in dozens of nations; (2) the French-speaking world, including all the former French colonies in addition to the European countries mentioned above; and (3) the Spanish-speaking world, including most of the Americas south of the United States. Even though not all residents of these language areas are fluent in the dominant language, its role is large enough to facilitate the internationalizing of advertising campaigns there.

A NOTE ON TRANSLATIONS   Although global language uniformity would certainly facilitate international and even global advertising campaigns, the existence of language diversity in the world does not, by itself, prevent the use of international appeals. If a language translation is the only adaptation needed in an advertising message, it does not modify the similarity of the appeal. Translation or even paraphrasing does not change the nature of the appeal; it is more a technical exercise. In spite of the many, usually humorous, examples of advertising copy translation errors—for example, "body" becoming "corpse"—the translation problem is much less difficult and serious than these examples suggest. These anecdotes are recounted frequently because they make interesting copy, or good jokes in a speech, but statistically they are not significant.

Concerning translation, a practitioner, David Kerr, vice president of Kenyon & Eckhardt, gives some interesting guidelines. He suggests that for English language advertising that is to be used in international campaigns, the English should be of the 5th- or 6th-grade vocabulary level and contain no slang or idioms. Furthermore, copy should be relatively short because other languages invariably take more space to say the same thing the English copy says.[13] It should also be mentioned that the growing use of visual presentation—pictures and illustrations—minimizes the need for copy and translation. Thus more and more European advertisements are purely visual, showing something, evoking a mood, and citing the company name. Emphasis on such simple illustrations also avoids part of the communication problem resulting from high rates of illiteracy in the poorer nations.

INTERNATIONAL MARKET SEGMENTS   Another market factor influencing the possibility of internationalizing advertising campaigns is the existence of international market segments; that is, market segments within an individual nation often have counterparts in a number of other nations. In many ways important to marketing and advertising, these market segments resemble their counterparts in other countries more than they do other segments in their own country. The international jet set has been mentioned as one example. The youth market is another, and probably includes two segments within itself: the adolescent group and the college-age group. The concerns of college students on all continents seem remarkably similar. International similarities

---

[13] Lecture at University of Michigan, Graduate School of Business, April 2, 1970.

among groups at that age level and even younger can provide a truly international market and appeal.

There are numerous examples of successful appeals to these national market segments which together constitute an international market for a product. One is the international success of the Beatles. Another is Levi Strauss & Company which has found a similar international market for its Levis. The company prepares its international advertising by beginning with its United States ads. One purpose of the advertising campaigns abroad is to achieve a similarity of appearance and image from country to country.[14] Company sales seem to attest to the correctness of this approach. Overseas sales rose 500 percent in five years. As someone has said, these groups do speak a common language—the language of youth.

A final market consideration is the gradual development of the world or regional consumer. What we already see in certain market segments will gradually expand to broader segments of the world's population. Technological advances in communications, transportation, and production lead to an international democratizing of consumption, just as has happened in the United States. Economic growth and increasing affluence reinforce this. We do not mean to say that everyone will be alike, but rather that market segments will become more international in scope, making possible greater use of internationally similar appeals in advertising. Supporting the growth of the regional, if not of the global, consumer is the development of regional groupings. The success of the European Common Market is certainly accelerating the emergence of the European consumer. As other regional groupings become strong and successful, they too will help to internationalize (on a regional basis) the consumers of the member nations. In the United States, for example, marketers speak of market segments on an interstate or national basis. They usually do not separate Michigan consumers from Maine or Missouri consumers. The United States, in a sense, is merely the first and most successful of the regional groupings.

Technical and Nonmarket Considerations

If the international marketing manager is to find an effective international approach to his advertising, the national markets must be receptive to such an approach. We have seen some of the market factors that bear on their receptiveness. If market conditions do permit a standard international message, then the manager must evaluate the more technical questions that will affect its feasibility and desirability. One important aspect is economic. Are there any economies or gains in efficiency in taking an international approach to advertising?

ECONOMICS   As long as agencies are paid on the commission basis, there would seem to be no chance for savings with a uniform international message,

[14] *Marketing Insights*, April 1, 1968, pp. 20, 21.

because the payment would be the same whether an international agency group or separate national agencies were used. Although this is true insofar as commission payments are concerned, gains could come in other areas. If the company uses a strictly national approach to advertising in each country, the creative work will probably vary greatly in quality. Small markets have small agencies and small budgets for doing creative work, not to mention a shortage of skilled personnel.

An international approach would permit larger amounts to be spent on developing a quality campaign with the best personnel available. The best agencies in the larger markets could create the campaign and that expenditure could then be "amortized" over many countries, large and small. The better campaign that results should more than pay for itself in increased revenues. In fact, the international campaign need be no more costly than the separate national campaigns if the work is covered by the normal commission payment to the agencies, but it can be more effective.

AGENCY RELATIONS   A uniform approach is also facilitated by the use of the same international agency in all or most of the company's markets. By using an international agency for this campaign, the company gains further economies and efficiencies because communication and coordination are easier, fewer contacts and less managerial time are needed. Additionally, the preparation of the international campaign, including inputs and testing in various markets, is much easier if the same agency is working in all the markets. Someone has already noted how the use of international closed-circuit TV will aid even further in the preparation and coordination of international campaigns, enabling agency people of several countries to get together conveniently and inexpensively on their in-house TV.

Another factor affecting the feasibility of internationally similar campaigns is the internal organization of the company. If the firm's international operations are very decentralized, with a high degree of local autonomy, international coordination and campaigns will be more difficult. Conversely, if the firm is centralized and has an international marketing or advertising manager with global responsibility and authority, international campaigns are easier.

MEDIA DEVELOPMENTS   Yet another factor influencing the feasibility of international campaigns is the availability of media. If the same media were available everywhere, international campaigns would benefit greatly. The fact that this situation does not exist somewhat hampers an internationally similar approach. The media do "massage the message" to some degree, and a campaign prepared for TV probably would not be identical to one prepared for radio or print media. This lack of media uniformity does not, in itself, prevent international campaigns, although it is something of a handicap. That it does not prevent the use of similar appeals is evidenced by domestic campaigns using the same appeals in several different kinds of media simultaneously.

In spite of the present differences in media availability, similarity in international media conditions is increasing steadily. Commercial TV and radio are coming to more and more countries. Satellite TV is becoming a truly international medium, bringing to the whole world such common messages as the Olympic Games or a voyage to the moon. Print media are less international, but the *Reader's Digest*, for example, reaches about forty countries in their own languages with its own kind of international appeal—and a great deal of advertising for international campaigns as well.

Several other American magazines have extensive international sales in their English-language editions and are expanding their coverage. There is also a Japanese version of *Fortune* based on the American editorial content. The French magazine *Paris Match* is the largest selling consumer magazine in Belgium. Looking toward media availability in the future, we see an increase both in international media and in the similarity of media conditions among countries as a result of (1) technological advances, (2) increasing affluence and economic growth in all nations, and (3) the continuing internationalization of world business. These developments will further encourage and facilitate international campaigns.

GLOBAL PRODUCT INTRODUCTIONS   Companies are leaning toward using more uniform international advertising campaigns because they are beginning to develop products for a global market and to introduce them simultaneously (or sequentially) in all their markets. One of the first examples of this was the around-the-world send-off given the Instamatic camera by Eastman Kodak in 1963. A second global spectacular was done by NCR (National Cash Register) in introducing its Century computer on all five continents, with simultaneous showings in 120 cities around the world.[15] As product development becomes more truly international and products are introduced in many countries within a short span of time, greater pressure is exerted on the firm to prepare an advertising program that is as international in scope as the rest of its marketing program.

MAKING A CHOICE   When the international marketing manager is faced with deciding what kinds of advertising appeals to use, he must weigh all the variables we have discussed. He will relate them to his own situation and choose the approach that promises to be the most effective for his firm. Although agencies and subsidiaries in each country must contribute input to determine the best appeals for their market, it is unlikely that a purely national approach will be taken in many of the firm's markets. There will probably be some internationalizing of the advertising.

The marketer's task is not to find global uniformity but to determine what degree of internationalization will make his overall advertising most effective. He may find that multimarket advertising on a regional basis is possible and desirable because of regional groupings, regional tourism, and media overlap. Or he may find that common language areas can profitably use common appeals. In any case, by seeking consumer similarities and common denominators, and by playing down national differences, similar appeals can probably be made effective in many countries. We have considered many firms that use basically the same appeals all over the world. A few others are

15 *Business Abroad*, March 18, 1968, p. 19.

Playtex and Maidenform, Revlon and Helena Rubenstein. Although the products associated with these names are of a personal nature, they succeed internationally with universal appeals.

The Prototype Approach

The best way to illustrate one method of internationalizing advertising in the international company is to cite the example of a large firm with long experience in many foreign markets. The company is Goodyear. Its experience included three different approaches tried over a period of several years.

The first approach, used for many years, was for each subsidiary to handle its advertising on an autonomous basis and to send copies of ads to Akron. It wasn't until 1960, however, that all these efforts were lined up side by side for management evaluation. The results showed uneven quality and a lack of consistency.

A second approach was instituted to bring some order into this diversity. Corporate requirements were established governing the use of the company name and logo. Also, more common elements were required to appear in all advertising. Because each subsidiary continued its own national approach, however, the result was continued diversity, with a few common pieces tacked on almost as afterthoughts. The result was "patchy and disorganized."

Finally management decided on a third approach, guiding international advertising from Akron, using prototype campaigns. These were to be based on common denominators drawn from consumer research in representative markets around the world. The international advertising department in Akron acted as the research coordinator. The finished ads were not prepared completely in the United States, but the prototype campaign pointed the way to more effective national efforts. The advertising manager of Goodyear International, Dean Peebles, and men from McCann-Erickson (Goodyear's advertising agency) made presentations of the program in each subsidiary market.

The Goodyear International Company has been very satisfied with the results of this internationally researched prototype program. What emerged were localized ads based on a worldwide theme, approach, and format. In general, the subsidiaries reacted favorably. This response was attributed partly to the careful research behind the prototype campaigns, and partly to the personal presentation made to each subsidiary.

In a few cases, the reaction was negative. Some used the prototype with no local inputs, and a few challenged the suitability of the prototype for their market. These cases were limited, however, and sales results over several years have convinced the company of the soundness of its approach.[16]

Selecting the Media

A third decision area in international advertising management is the selection of media for each national market. As Colin McIver notes, the principles of media selection are universal but their application can vary from country to

[16] *Printers' Ink*, May 13, 1966, pp. 56, 59.

country.[17] The desirable media in every country are those that reach the target market (the buying decision influencers) effectively and efficiently, that is, with a favorable cost-benefit result. One international difference, however, may arise immediately here: Those who have major influence on the purchase decision will not always be the same individual or group. The relative decision roles of husband versus wife, parents versus children, purchasing agent versus president will vary from country to country.

Those most familiar with the local scene—that is, the advertising agency and the subsidiary or company representative within the country—will do much of the local media selection. To the extent that they do the job, the international marketer or advertising manager need not get involved. For two or three reasons, however, the international manager might wish to have some voice in local media selection. Through his experience with the firm's operations in many countries, he may have useful insights to contribute to local operations. (This is another use of comparative analysis.)

Or the manager may wish to use international media alongside of, or in place of, strictly national media. Since international media cover a number of national markets, this decision would require some centralization. Then again, he may be able to contribute sophisticated techniques of media selection. Because more money is spent on advertising in the United States than in all the rest of the world, the technology is generally more advanced here. The American international manager can assure that these techniques are made available to company operations everywhere.[18]

Media Diversity

The role of the international manager in media selection is complicated and limited by the great international differences in media availability and use. The manager cannot take a successful media configuration from domestic operations and apply it in his international advertising because the same facilities generally will not be available. In Chapter 3, we saw how countries differ in their communications infrastructure, that is, in their availability of newspapers, radio, TV, and so on. In addition to that disparity, there is a great international difference in how existing media are used. Table 12–5 illustrates the differences in media usage in a number of countries.

DIVERSITY MEANS ADAPTATION   When media availability differs greatly from market to market, the international marketer will have to decentralize media selection somewhat and adapt to local possibilities. Since the local manager cannot follow exactly the media patterns used elsewhere, he must be creative in finding the local media that can reach his market effectively and efficiently. He will need to experiment with different media and promotional mixes.

---

[17] In S. Watson Dunn, *International Handbook of Advertising* (New York: McGraw-Hill Book Co., 1964), p. 133.

[18] For a discussion of media selection techniques see Philip Kotler, *Marketing Management* (Englewood Cliffs, N.J.: Prentice-Hall, 1967), pp. 475–482.

Table 12–5 Advertising Allocations by Medium for Selected Countries (for 1966, in percent)

	NEWSPAPER	MAGAZINES	OUTDOOR & TRANSPORTATION	CINEMA	RADIO	TELEVISION	DIRECT ADVERTISING	EXHIBITIONS	DISPLAY & OTHER
United States	34	8	1	Other	6	17	15	Other	19
Latin America									
Argentina	22	10	11	2	11	18	7	5	13
Colombia	33	2	2	2	26	14	Other	Other	22
Mexico	25	5	5	5	20	35	3	Not avail.	2
Venezuela	38	6	Not avail.	5	22	29	Not avail.	Not avail.	Not avail.
Europe									
Belgium	25	15	15	2	3	0.03	19	6	15
Germany	29	23	5	0.9	2	7	31	Not avail.	1
Italy	21	17	6	3	5	8	6	18	16
Netherlands	41	13	5	0.7	1.6	0.3	39	Not avail.	Not avail.
Sweden	37	13	3	Other	Other	Other	22	4	20
Switzerland	22	16	7	1		3	15	7	29
United Kingdom	31	17	5	1	0.5	18	8	3	16
Asia									
Iran	22	7	14	7	18	26	0.3	2	4
Israel	61	5	5	6	7	None	6	6	5
Japan	36	← 40 →	9	1	4	33	5	2	5
Philippines	36	9	20	5	23	13	Other	Other	Negl.
Turkey	36	9	18	4	5	None	15	4	9

Source: "Advertising Investment around the World," *The International Advertiser* (December 1967), pp. 18–19.

In Peru, Orange Crush used a wide range of media ranging from newspapers, TV, and radio, to cinema and point-of-purchase materials. Outside the capital, Lima, the company used billboards more heavily because taxes were lower in the provinces. On the other hand, the use of cinema slides was reduced in the provinces because it was not found very effective.[19]

Whom Does the Medium Massage?

Another factor hampering media decisions in many countries is the lack of reliable information on circulation and audience characteristics. The advertiser in the United States is accustomed to having audited and guaranteed data on the size of audience reached by the various media. In addition, he will often have a good breakdown on important audience characteristics, such as occupation, education, and income level. No other country has the same amount of information available, and the supply decreases rapidly as one goes down the scale of economic development. In many countries, the only circulation or audience figures are those supplied by the media themselves. Such unaudited figures are better than nothing, but they are bound to be somewhat suspect. In such cases, the advertiser might take on the role of detective, ferreting out clues as to the true situation and using his ingenuity to derive more accurate figures.

Another consideration complicating media evaluation, in addition to the difficulty of obtaining circulation or audience figures, is that whatever figures can be obtained or derived for the circulation of a medium do not necessarily indicate its true coverage. In countries where data can be obtained as to the number of TV or radio sets, the true audience may be much larger than the figures suggest. For example, in countries with low literacy rates, the average number of viewers per TV set is apt to be at least twice as large as in the United States. This principle also applies to the number of radio listeners, especially in less developed countries where a few receivers may reach a whole village.

Even with print media, the average readership varies from country to country. In less developed countries, one literate villager will read a newspaper or magazine for his illiterate neighbors. Even in more developed countries, one issue may pass from the initial purchaser or subscriber through several other readers. A French magazine with a circulation of 1.5 million estimated its total readership at 8.3 million.[20]

This lack of accurate media information introduces extra uncertainty and challenge in media selection in many countries. The answer to the problem in the long run is the expansion of media auditing and reporting services. In the short run, the advertiser must depend on his own ingenuity and experience. As the firm gains advertising experience in a market, it will learn about

---

[19] *Business Latin America*, February 29, 1968, p. 66.
[20] C. Laury Botthof, "One Common Market or Six Markets?" *Journal of Marketing* (April 1966), p. 16.

the relative effectiveness of different media there. Furthermore, comparative analysis of the firm's experiences in other similar markets can again be useful for the manager in the international company.

International or Local Media?

In his international marketing, the manager will sometimes have the alternative of using either national media or media that cover several national markets; both print and broadcast media, for example, have multimarket coverage. The print media with international market coverage include such American general-interest magazines as the *Reader's Digest* and *Time*, which reach most of the world's major markets, and *Paris Match* or *Vision*, which reach several European and Latin American markets respectively. Numerous technical and trade publications (usually American), in engineering, chemistry, electronics, the automotive industry, and so on, have an extensive and influential circulation around the world. One major use of international print media is for corporate-image advertising.

MAGAZINES, THE FIRST INTERNATIONALISTS   International magazines can offer a number of advantages to the international marketer where they correspond to his target markets. Among these advantages are audited circulation and audience data; quality reproduction of advertisements that reach an influential and quality audience; regional or national market circulation coverage for marketing to specific areas; and the lending of the magazines' prestige to companies and products advertised. An additional boon to the marketing manager is that he can place and pay for advertisements from one source, rather than having to deal with many separate national organizations.

The drawbacks of international magazines are that they usually have only English or Spanish editions (except for the *Reader's Digest*) and give only partial coverage of any particular national market. These advantages and limitations have to be evaluated in terms of the individual products and markets of the firm. For mass consumption items, the international magazines are less likely to be used because of their limited language coverage and low market penetration. However, for certain industrial goods, and for consumer goods and services that appeal to an affluent or sophisticated market, the international magazines may give just the selective or quality coverage the advertiser wants.

The potential role of international magazines is best seen by examples of their use.

A study of the chairmen and managing directors of the 500 largest companies in Western Europe showed their regular reading to include the following: More than two out of three read The Financial Times *(London), and almost the same number read* The Economist *(London). Fortune and* Time *were read by over half of this important audience.*[21]

---

[21] *Wall Street Journal*, January 29, 1964, p. 24.

A 1970 report on the 100 leading advertisers in international magazines showed the companies and products using this medium.[22] The largest category of users (twenty-one firms) was travel and tourism, mostly airlines. Pan American Airways was number one with about $1.5 million of advertising in this medium. The second largest category was the automotive industry (eleven firms), including cars, tires, and spark plugs. The next categories were alcoholic beverages (six firms) and smoking materials (five firms). All told, $100 million was spent in this medium in 1969. The nationality of the leading advertisers is also revealing. Thirty-six of the top 100 were American, seventeen were British, sixteen were Japanese, and eight were Swiss. Half the ads in American international magazines were placed by non-American companies.

Another kind of international package is offered by *national* print media. The growth of regionalism and regional trade is forcing national media to find some way to regionalize their coverage. For instance, collaborating with media in other member nations to offer some kind of common coverage and scale economies would strengthen their competitive position vis-à-vis the truly international media. The TOP 5 in the Common Market, a group including a leading newspaper in each of the major member countries, uses this strategy. It charges a standard rate, with a discount for using all five papers, and also provides free translation. The TOP 5 claims to offer the best of both the international and national media approaches by this method.[23]

RADIO   Although the broadcast media traditionally have played a smaller international role than the print media, advances in technology and the growing commercialization of these media are increasing their importance. International commercial radio is most important in Western Europe where at least four stations reach several nations. Because they have transmitting power up to 275,000 watts (United States limit is 50,000 watts), these stations truly can cover most of Western Europe. The leading station is Radio Luxembourg, which works three frequencies—long wave, medium, and short wave—and broadcasts in five languages. It counts over 40 million listeners from the British Isles to southern France and eastward into both Germanies, Austria, and Switzerland.[24]

Many of the top advertisers on this European radio station are American firms: Procter & Gamble, Colgate-Palmolive, Gillette, Nabisco, John Deere, 3M, and Coca-Cola. Radio Luxembourg's coverage corresponds to their market and marketing needs. If the national radio networks in the major European nations ever go commercial, it would threaten these "international" stations, all of which are located in tiny principalities. Until that time, however, they are the only commercial radio available in Europe; Latin America, by contrast, has many commercial radio stations *within* the various nations.

---

[22] *The International Advertiser*, vol. 11, no. 2 (1970), pp. 5–7.
[23] *The International Advertiser* (April–May 1968), p. 7.
[24] *Advertising Age*, April 25, 1966, p. 1.

Commercial radio is especially useful for reaching nonliterate populations, obviously.

TELEVISION   Commercial TV for international advertising is an area of potential growth. A modest amount of such advertising presently occurs almost accidentally as United States broadcasts reach into Canada (and vice versa) or German television commercials overlap into German-speaking Austria and Switzerland. However, there is practically no internationally organized approach to TV advertising. One exception worth mentioning is the Worldvision organization of ABC International. This American company has pioneered a network of TV stations in Canada, Latin America, the Caribbean, Spain, Africa, the Middle East, the Far East, and Australia, an area of twenty-five nations with over 25 million television homes. An advertiser working from his home base can buy various packages of nations in this network for an international campaign. For example, Pan American Life Insurance sponsored the Academy Aawards program, on a delayed basis, in fourteen Latin American countries. Other firms using parts of this international network for a single program include Ford, Sterling Drug, Nestle, Goodyear, Kellogg, Quaker Oats, and Pepsi Cola.[25]

Advancing television technology, increasing set ownership, and the needs of international business all suggest an expansion of international commercial television capability. In 1969, more than 110 nations had TV service, and over three-fourths of these nations had some form of commercial TV. These numbers increase each year. Also a potentially large number of hours can be devoted to the same broadcasting material all over the world; for example, programs on the Olympic Games, space shots, royal or presidential accessions (or funerals), important political events or acts of God, and sporting or theatrical events of general interest. The wide international popularity of some of America's television series is an indicator of the potential here.

The primary obstacles to the expansion of commercial TV are political. However, as nations see their neighbors expanding commercial time on TV and recognize the revenue potential for their own nation, increasing availability of commercial television is very likely. Alliances or networks such as the TOP 5 or Worldvision could arise to meet the need. The problem of language diversity can be handled through devices that can broadcast many language tracks simultaneously from a single satellite. Although dubbing language is the traditional approach, IBM and Hughes Aircraft are working on devices that will translate languages instantly and automatically.

Local Media

We have discussed international media at some length because they are an option peculiar to international marketing and because they may be a more significant alternative tomorrow than they are today. Nevertheless, the amount of advertising in national media is vastly greater than that done in international media, even allowing for the fact that much advertising in local

---

[25] *The International Advertiser*, vol. 10, no. 3 (1969), pp. 5–8.

media is done by national firms with very limited markets. National media predominate, even for the international advertiser (except, perhaps, for corporate-image advertising), because they offer certain marketing advantages. Local media allow a broader choice, ranging from newspapers, magazines, direct mail, cinema, and billboards to the broadcast media (where available commercially). They permit the use of the local language or languages and offer greater flexibility for market segmentation and test marketing. In general, local media do a better job of reaching and adapting to the local market, especially in promoting consumer goods.

Disadvantages, however, occasionally arise in using local media. Although the industrialized countries frequently offer the same kind of media quality that the firm finds in the United States, in many other countries print reproduction may be poor, rates may not be fixed, and audited circulation and audience data may not be available. The need to place the advertising as well as pay for it locally can be a further drawback if the firm has centralized control. Nevertheless, these disadvantages, where they exist, are not sufficient to seriously limit the use of local media by most international advertisers who need to reach a wide local market.

Most companies will make their media selection largely from local media. Where a real choice between local and international media is possible, the decision will be affected not only by the considerations we have discussed but also by the degree of centralized control the company has over international advertising, which presumably reflects some balance between the wishes of the subsidiary and those of the international manager. It will be affected further by whether the firm uses international or local campaigns, and whether it employs local or international agencies. Generally, decentralized decision making and the use of local campaigns and local agencies would result in a greater employment of local media than would the reverse situation. Furthermore, the drawbacks of local media are gradually being remedied, and efforts at cooperation, such as the TOP 5 example, enable them to remain local operations while taking on somewhat of an international flair.

Determining the International Advertising Budget

Among the many controversial aspects of advertising is the question of the proper method of determining the advertising budget. This is as much a problem domestically as it is internationally. However, the international advertiser must try to find an optimum advertising outlay for a large number of national markets, so his problem is somewhat more complex. In theory, it is not difficult to state the amount of money the firm should put into advertising abroad. In each of its markets, the firm should continue putting more money into advertising as long as an advertising dollar returns more than a dollar spent on anything else. In practice, this equimarginal principle is difficult to apply because of the impossibility of measuring accurately the returns, not only from advertising but also from other company outlays.

Because of the difficulty in determining the theoretically optimum advertising budget, companies have developed other more practical guidelines and rules-of-thumb to aid their decision making in this area. We will examine the relevance of these guidelines for the international advertiser and then consider some special factors present in multinational operations. Although the equimarginal principle noted above is difficult to apply with precision, it must nevertheless serve an an initial rough guide in setting the advertising budget. In other words, the marketing manager must remember that the advertising budget is not set in a vacuum, but that it is just one element of his overall marketing mix. Indeed, it is also just one element of his promotional mix. Therefore, he must have some idea as to whether a certain discretionary sum of money should go into advertising, or personal selling, or consumer price reductions, or product or package improvements, or something else. He must decide which effort or outlay will have the best effect on his short-run and long-run profits and goals.

Percentage of Sales

An easy method of setting the advertising appropriation in a country is to use a specified percentage of sales. Besides its convenience, this method has the advantage of relating advertising to the volume of sales and profits in a country and thus keeping advertising from "getting out of hand." This approach, perhaps the easiest to justify in the budget meeting, appeals to financially oriented members of management who like to think in terms of ratios and costs per unit. When the firm is selling in many markets, this approach has the further advantage of appearing to guarantee equality among them. Each market seems to get the advertising it earns and deserves.

For the firm that centralizes control over its international advertising, the percentage-of-sales approach has great appeal. Indeed, an international advertising manager located at company headquarters would have great difficulty employing any other budgeting method for fifty or 100 different country markets. Another argument favoring this method is the fact that many companies use it and it seems to have worked rather well for them. This proven acceptance and success makes the manager feel more secure in choosing the percentage-of-sales technique.

DANGERS   Despite its attractions, the percentage-of-sales approach to advertising budgeting has logical and practical limitations in international marketing. The major purpose of advertising is to cause sales, but this method perversely makes the volume of sales determine the amount of advertising. When sales are low or declining, advertising will decline, although long-range considerations might suggest that advertising should be stepped up. When a firm is entering a foreign market, for example, it may need a disproportionate amount of advertising to break in. Limiting the advertising expense to the same percentage-of-sales figure used elsewhere would be undesirable during the firm's first years in the market. Even Hershey, the famous nonadvertiser in the American market, began advertising when it entered the Canadian market.

The same argument applies to the introduction of new products into a market. As firms expand their international marketing, they introduce more and more new products into their various national markets. The advertising budget for these introductions should relate to the introductory needs rather than to some percentage of sales applied to existing products—or to the same products already being sold in other countries. Many firms want to expand their presence in world markets. Whatever way they do it will usually require significant advertising outlays.

The major weakness in applying a standard percentage-of-sales figure for advertising expenses in the firm's foreign markets is that this method does not relate to the firm's situation and needs in each market. The examples given —entering a market and introducing new products—are just two illustrations of the need for special treatment for special situations. In some countries, the firm may be well established with no strong competitors, whereas in others, it may be having difficulty getting and maintaining a franchise with distributors and consumers. Obviously, advertising needs are different in these two groups of countries. The second group might need twice the percentage of sales in advertising needed by the first.

Other factors differentiating the firm's situation from country to country are variations in media availability and coverage and the firm's level of involvement. Differences in media possibilities might mean that the firm will spend more on personal selling or other promotional tools in certain markets and less on advertising. In countries where the firm has its own subsidiaries, the advertising appropriation usually will be determined differently from the way it is in countries where the firm is represented by a licensee or importer-distributor. We will discuss the influence of the level of involvement further later on.

Our discussion has highlighted the limitations of using a standard percentage-of-sales figure for advertising budgets in international marketing. However, until more sophisticated techniques are made operational, many companies will continue to use some percentage-of-sales method. This will not necessarily be bad if the percentage is shown from company experience to be reasonably successful and if the method is somewhat flexible in application. Such flexibility would allow different percentages to be applied in different markets according to need, and would permit exceptions to the percentage for special occasions, such as entering a new market or introducing a new product.

Competitive Parity

Matching competitors' advertising outlays is a budgeting approach used by some companies. Although this approach may offer the firm some benefit of collective wisdom and assure that it does not lose ground to its competitors this way, the merit of the approach is dubious in domestic operations, and it is especially to be challenged in international marketing. As a practical matter, in most foreign markets the firm would not be able to determine competitive practice at all satisfactorily. Both sales and advertising figures of national competitors are much harder to obtain than in the United States, for example.

Another danger in following competitors' practice in local markets is that they are not necessarily right. In fact, the international firm is almost always a heavier advertiser than national firms in the same industry, probably due to its greater sophistication and more aggressive marketing posture. If anything, the international firm sets the standard for national competitors to follow rather than the reverse. This was very evident in Procter & Gamble's experience in Europe, for example. The fact that different competitors may employ different promotional mixes also hampers the use of this approach. In the United States, for instance, Revlon is a heavy advertiser, whereas Avon, a successful competitor, relies almost entirely on personal selling. Who should follow whom?

A final limitation to the competitive-parity approach in foreign markets is the difference in the situation of the international firm. It is a foreigner in the market, and this can be a handicap where nationalism is a factor. The international firm may have a different relationship to consumers and distributors which would be reflected in its promotion. Its product line and marketing program are also likely to differ from those of national competitors. Because of all these differences in the situation, needs, and strategy of the international company, it is improbable that the matching of competitors' advertising outlays would prove to be a sound strategy for the firm in foreign markets.

Objective-and-Task Method

Because of the recognized weaknesses of the above approaches, a majority of American advertisers use the objective-and-task method. This approach begins by determining the advertising objectives, expressed in terms of sales, brand awareness, or something else; next ascertaining the tasks needed to reach these objectives; and finally estimating the costs of performing these tasks. If this approach includes a cost-benefit analysis, relating the objectives to the cost of reaching them, it is a logical and desirable way to approach the problem.

The objective-and-task method is as relevant for markets abroad as it is for the United States. It logically seeks to relate the advertising budget in a country to the firm's situation and objectives there. The limitations to its use internationally are essentially practical. To use it satisfactorily, the firm must have good knowledge of the local market situation so as to be able to set specific and appropriate objectives. Except where it has strong local subsidiaries, the international firm will not have the intimate knowledge of the market that it has domestically. Thus for some of his markets, the international marketing manager will find it difficult to set appropriate specific objectives.

The international marketer's lack of familiarity with some of his foreign markets will also make him less able to define the role or task of advertising in those markets. For those countries where the international marketer lacks the familiarity to determine accurately both the objectives and the tasks of advertising, this approach has obvious limitations. In such cases, he might find a percentage-of-sales method more feasible and convenient. This is one instance where it is more important to be operational than to be "scientifically correct."

Quality versus Quantity

Discussions of advertising budgeting primarily revolve around the amounts to be spent on the various media. It is generally assumed that a given amount of advertising will produce a certain result. Sometimes ignored is the fact that some advertising is more effective than other advertising. The right advertising budget might well include some portion to be spent on improving the quality of the advertising, instead of merely increasing its quantity.

The creative work of the agencies usually is covered by their commission. In large markets for large accounts, this is ample payment incentive for good work. In the smaller markets of the international company, its limited advertising budget, and perhaps the caliber of agency personnel available, will not lead to quality advertising. Even in large markets, spending an amount beyond the agency commission for generating and testing alternative campaigns to increase the effectiveness of the advertising dollar is sometimes profitable. For the international marketer, the need for quality as well as quantity in his advertising might be an argument for multinational campaigns, at least in his smaller markets. The large subsidiary markets might be able to generate quality advertising on their own. However, the smaller markets, which are usually in the majority, might benefit from an international approach such as the Goodyear prototype cited earlier.

Some Special Considerations

Several special factors affect the amount of advertising the firm will do in foreign markets. These may affect either the way the budget is set or its level.

MEDIA RESTRICTIONS   In markets where certain major media do not exist or cannot be used commercially, the firm's advertising budget is apt to be relatively low. For example, many firms that advertise heavily on TV in the United States have smaller relative advertising outlays in markets where that medium is not available. Conversely, many firms greatly increase their advertising budgets when commercial TV becomes available in a market. When media regulations are very restrictive in a market, the firm may place greater reliance on other promotional tools.

LOW-INCOME MARKETS   At least two-thirds of the world's countries are less developed, or low-income, markets. Generally a limited amount of advertising is done in these economies and the consumers have limited discretionary income. Although these factors usually combine to lower the level of advertising of the international firm in such markets, there can be exceptions. Some firms selling low-priced consumer goods have successfully used rather heavy advertising outlays in low-income countries, for example, Colgate-Palmolive and Pepsi Cola.

COMPANY ORGANIZATION   The degree to which the firm centralizes its international operations will affect advertising budgeting. The more centralized the advertising control, the more uniform the budget process is likely to be from country to country. The percentage-of-sales approach is probable in this case. If the firm has highly autonomous subsidiaries, however, each one is likely to determine its own advertising appropriation, resulting in greater probable variability from country to country.

LEVEL OF INVOLVEMENT   A firm's involvement in foreign markets often ranges from an importer-distributor arrangement in some markets to wholly owned production-marketing subsidiaries in others. As the firm's market position, knowledge, and control vary greatly from one situation to another, so will its approach to budgeting advertising outlays. Subsidiaries were discussed in the preceding paragraph. Advertising budgeting of joint ventures will be constrained by the practices and desires of the other partner. Licensees may be entirely on their own, or a clause in the agreement may require them to make some advertising outlay. Distributors also may be on their own, or they may have a cooperative advertising program with the international firm.

The Culligan Company provides a fairly typical example. Culligan adds 2 percent to the basic purchase price paid by the distributor and matches this with an additional 2 percent from the corporation. This is a percentage-of-sales method of administering local advertising on a cooperative basis. In this case 4 percent of local sales is applied for local advertising.

COMPARATIVE ANALYSIS   Between the standardizing method of applying a uniform percentage to all markets and the laissez-faire method of letting each national market go its own way lies a middle ground. The international marketer might group his markets in two or more categories according to characteristics relevant to advertising. This method would yield more flexibility than the uniform approach and less chaos and more control than the laissez-faire approach. Categories might be based on size (markets with over $1 million sales and those with under $1 million), media situation (markets with commercial TV and those with no commercial TV), or other pertinent characteristics. Different budgeting methods or percentages could be tried and applied for each group, or within a group. An experiment in one country could serve as a test-marketing experience for the other countries of that group. This analytical technique can be useful for the international advertiser who has a large number of foreign markets.

Evaluating International Advertising Effectiveness

In the United States, where very great sums are spent on advertising, there is much concern about the usefulness of these expenditures. Since a firm is interested in profits, it wants to know how effective and profitable its advertising is. In spite of this concern, however, only a relatively small amount of the advertising budget is spent on measuring its effectiveness. In discussing the advertising budget, we suggested that firms should spend relatively more on quality aspects than they currently do. The firm's international advertising outlays are often smaller than those in domestic operations, especially for American companies. In spite of his lower budget, however, the international marketing manager needs to be equally concerned about his advertising's effectiveness if he is to maintain profitable operations. In fact, because criticism of advertising is apt to be greater in some foreign markets than at home, the manager may need a more sophisticated understanding of advertising's function than he would at home. This was a problem faced by Procter & Gamble and Unilever in Britain. The Monopoly Commission challenged their advertising outlays, asked the firms to reduce them, and also requested that they introduce some nonadvertised brands.

The pretest and the post-test are two approaches to measuring advertising effectiveness. The former, testing the advertising appeals and presentation before the campaign is run, is done primarily to choose the most effective among alternative campaigns. The latter is an evaluation after the advertising has appeared in the media. Post-testing can be of two kinds, testing either communications effectiveness or sales results. Ideally, the manager would like to know the sales results of his advertising, but because this effect is so difficult to measure, he must often rely on measurements of how well his advertising reached his audience.[26]

Testing advertising effectiveness is even more difficult in international markets than in the United States. One reason is that the markets are smaller and therefore budgets are smaller, but a more important reason is that few markets have the same facilities or experience in this work the United States and a few other industrialized nations have. Consequently, in most markets the international marketer has to rely on his own capabilities, plus whatever help his local agency might give. Because the international marketer has less than intimate contact with all his foreign markets, his ability to conduct an investigation of advertising effectiveness is limited. Thus three factors restrict the measurement of advertising's effectiveness in a majority of the world's markets: (1) smallness of the market, (2) lack of necessary facilities, and (3) the distance and communications gap between the market and the international marketer.

In this area the international marketer must again exercise his ingenuity. He does need some evidence of effectiveness if he is to develop sound advertising budgets. Once more comparative analysis may be useful to him. If the firm's foreign markets can be grouped according to similar characteristics, he can perform experiments with the advertising program using one or two markets in a group as test markets. Variables to be tested might include the amount of advertising, the media mix, the appeals, frequency of placement, and so on. Experience needs to be built up on a cross-sectional basis—that is, between countries—as well as on a historical basis, that is, over the years in

[26] For a discussion of measurement techniques and limitations, see Kotler, *Marketing Management*, pp. 486–492.

each market. Such experience, developed on a comparative basis, can help the firm to overcome some of its handicaps in measuring advertising effectiveness in foreign markets.

Organizing for International Advertising

Another decision area closely related to those already discussed is how to organize for international advertising. The decision both affects and is affected by the others; for example, the selection of advertising agencies and the type of campaign will be related to the way the company organizes for international advertising.

The firm has basically three organizational alternatives. (1) It can centralize all decision making for international advertising at corporate or international division headquarters. (2) It can completely decentralize the decision making to foreign markets. (3) It can use some blend of these two alternatives. A related issue is the personnel requirements at headquarters and in the markets abroad. Of course, the question of organizing for international advertising cannot be separated from the company's overall organization for international business. The firm is unlikely to be highly centralized for one function and completely decentralized for another. We will discuss overall organization for international marketing in Chapter 16, but it is useful here to consider the special factors affecting organization for international advertising.

Centralization

Complete centralization of international advertising implies that campaign preparation, media and agency selection, and budgeting are all done in the headquarters country. This might be necessary if the firm's international business is small or if it is confined to dealing with independent distributors or licensees. Complete centralization is possible, but less likely, where the firm operates through foreign subsidiaries that are able and desirous of having a voice in management decisions affecting "their" market.

Centralized control of advertising is more feasible if the firm works with one international agency that has branches or affiliates covering all of its markets. Thus the firm gains the local knowledge and contacts needed from outside but keeps its decision making centralized. Centralized control is also more feasible when the firm can have standardized international advertising and when the market and media conditions are similar from market to market. Examples are Pan American's running a campaign in *Time International* and Champion Spark Plugs' doing the same in all the foreign editions of *Reader's Digest*.

On the personnel side, centralized control implies that a person (or staff) at headquarters knows the foreign markets and media well enough to make the appropriate decisions. His communications network must be adequate for controlling the actual placement of the advertising in each market. Although in some cases he might be able to rely heavily on his international agency for help on these points, where he is dealing with subsidiaries abroad he cannot rely only on the agency. He must have some line authority over the subsidiary personnel dealing with advertising, just as the agency works with its own people in the same market.

The centralized approach creates rather strong demands for advertising personnel at headquarters but rather minimal demands for them at the subsidiary level. Economies of scale in staffing and in advertising administration are arguments for centralization. The potential dangers of centralization are rigidity, failure to adapt to meet local market needs, and stifling of local initiative, leading to morale problems in the subsidiary.

Decentralization

With complete decentralization of international advertising, each national market would make all its own advertising decisions. This approach could apply to any level of involvement from distributor or licensee to joint venture or wholly owned subsidiaries. Where this laissez-faire method is a deliberate company policy, it may result from several different considerations. (1) The volume of international business and advertising is too small to warrant headquarters' executive attention. (2) The communications problems between home and field render a centralized approach impossible. (3) The firm feels it can allow local decision making in this area to gain a more national image for itself. (4) The firm feels that the nationals know the local scene best and will be more highly motivated if given this responsibility.

Decentralized control is likely to be associated with national rather than international advertising campaigns and with the employment of independent local agencies in each market rather than members of an international agency network. Decentralization requires more expertise and personnel at the subsidiary level. In markets where the firm does not have its own subsidiaries, performance would depend entirely on the advertising skills and interest of the firm's licensee or distributor. The potential advantages of decentralization are the motivation given to the national operation and the possibility of getting more effective tailor-made advertising programs. The dangers are duplication and fragmentation of effort and inefficiencies in performance, especially in smaller markets.

A Compromise Approach

Between the extremes of complete centralization and complete decentralization can be found a majority of international companies that use elements of both approaches. Sometimes this compromise results from historical accident. Ideally, it should be planned in order to get the best of both and minimize their respective drawbacks. A compromise approach should entail finding the appropriate division of labor between headquarters and the country operations, each making its peculiar contribution according to its comparative advantage. One expert has called this "coordinated decentralization."[27] However, he emphasizes the "coordination" more than the "decentralization."

In a compromise approach, headquarters usually will play the more impor-

[27] Jere Patterson, *The International Advertiser* (December 1967), p. 35.

tant role, being "more equal" than the national operations. The central advertising manager will be responsible for international advertising policy and guidelines. The basic creative work and selection of overall themes and appeals generally will be centralized. The man at headquarters will also work with the coordinator from the international agency, if such an agency is used.

When the Kodak Instamatic was introduced around the world, the Kodak vice-president for marketing and the Instamatic account executive of J. Walter Thompson not only planned strategy together. They also traveled around the world together, visiting local subsidiaries and agencies. Rank-Xerox had a similar collaboration with Young and Rubicam in its European operations.[28]

The advertising or marketing manager at headquarters will establish standard operating procedures and probably prepare a manual for subsidiary advertising management, including budget and reporting forms. Common categories and formats make budgets and programs comparable from country to country so that they can be better analyzed and evaluated. The manager will act as a clearinghouse for international advertising, transferring relevant experience between countries and from domestic operations. He will organize meetings of advertising personnel to improve understanding and communications.

CPC International (Corn Products Company) has held annual world-wide marketing conferences to help advertising coordination. These meetings took place sometimes in the United States, sometimes abroad. In addition, meetings were held on a regional basis where marketing personnel discussed advertising programs and agency operations. The company used more than one agency in many markets because of the number of different brands it sold. In Europe, the company's largest region, the firm had a consumer-goods policy council, whose duties included selection of agencies and coordination of advertising programs.[29]

In this compromise approach, the role of subsidiary personnel will be strongest in media selection and in the adaptation of advertising appeals to local market needs. Although they will not have major creative and administrative responsibilities, they will have a voice in the decisions related most closely to their own market. As compared with a decentralized approach, this compromise requires a smaller staff and less expertise within the subsidiary.

"Coordinated decentralization" can be implemented in various ways. The prototype approach mentioned earlier is one way to have a high degree of international uniformity and still allow for critical local inputs. This involves local market research to find common themes and appeals, centralized design

[28] *International Advertiser* (December 1967), p. 26.
[29] *Advertising Age,* March 30, 1970, p. 4.

of the advertising, and some local adaptation of the advertisements. The Goodyear example has been cited. Esso also has used this approach in a global campaign for its Engro fertilizers.[30] A looser form of coordination is for headquarters to establish overall guidelines within which subsidiaries can create their own advertising (rules as to use of brand name, logo, white space, and so on). Headquarters then generally follows up with a review of local efforts, either before or after they have appeared in the media.

The firm can even use partial decentralization with distributors and licensees if it has appropriate agreements with them. It can either follow one of the methods above or modify these to suit its needs.

The Culligan Company prepared three different advertising approaches with its domestic agency. Then it met with its European licensees jointly to review them. A majority vote by the licensees decided which approach should be used. The licensee's agency placed the ads.

The MEM Company (maker of "English Leather" products) distributed United States ad copy to licensees. It allowed them discretion as to the use of the American advertisements, but many did use them, finding them well done and convenient for their own market. If the licensee used his own ad material, he had to have it approved by MEM. Of course, to have this kind of control over licensee or distributor advertising, the firm must pay for at least part of the local advertising. For example, Culligan and MEM paid one-half of the expense, sharing equally with the licensee.

Cooperative Advertising

A special decision area in international advertising arises when the firm sells through licensees or distributors. If it wishes to advertise in its foreign markets, it can choose one of three ways: (1) It can handle such advertising itself; (2) it can cooperate with the local distributor; or (3) it can try to encourage the distributor or licensee to do such advertising by itself. The last alternative is not really very feasible, so the choice is primarily between going it alone or cooperating.

Advertising Made in U.S.A.

When the firm chooses to handle its own advertising for distributor markets, it must arrange for the complete advertising program at home with few inputs from the markets concerned. Going it alone poses some difficulty because the international firm is not very familiar with those markets where its only contact is an independent distributor. This problem is lessened but not eliminated when the firm's agency has offices in those markets. However, the agency's network is unlikely to mesh very closely with the company's foreign markets. The agency tends to have offices in the larger markets, whereas many of the firm's distributors are likely to be in smaller markets. The company may have its own subsidiaries in the larger markets.

---

[30] *The International Advertiser*, vol. 10, no. 2 (1968), pp. 20–22.

In spite of the communications and control problems involved in centralized management of advertising for distributor markets, many firms do choose this approach, implementing it through an international or export advertising agency. Their feeling is that even with its limitations, this way offers more control and greater effectiveness than the alternatives. Working on a centralized basis with its agency gives the firm a strong voice in the management of the advertising, which is actually placed in markets far from company headquarters. The firm has general control over the quality and placement of these advertisements.

Cooperative Local Advertising

Many other firms that choose the alternative of developing their foreign market advertising programs in cooperation with their local distributors do so in an attempt to get the advantages claimed for the "coordinated decentralization" approach; that is, to get the appropriate division of labor and a contribution from each party according to its comparative advantage. However, cooperative advertising requires relatively more decentralization than does working with subsidiaries, which are controlled from headquarters.

Several potential advantages are claimed for the cooperative approach. For one, the exporter hopes to get more advertising for his money, either through a greater amount of advertising overall or through the same amount done on a shared basis rather than solely by the exporter. Furthermore, the cooperative program itself may be a motivation to the distributor to do more promotion. In markets where the distributor is better known, the exporter can trade on his distributor's reputation. The distributor through his knowledge of the local market and media can help choose the advertising that best fits the local situation. His local knowledge complements the advertising, product, and marketing expertise of the international company. He may also get better media rates as a national.

Partially offsetting the attractions of the cooperative approach are some limitations that occasionally arise and that keep cooperative international advertising from being used by all firms. Difficulties in control are major, breaking down into two kinds of control problems. The first relates to the quality of advertising done in the local market. If left largely to the discretion of distributors, the advertising quality will be very uneven from country to country. If the advertising is very poor, it could be a waste rather than a saving to the exporter. A related difficulty is that the distributor may emphasize *his* business and his interests rather than the exporter's. The second control problem concerns assuring that the distributors actually spent their advertising allowance on advertising. Occasionally the money is taken but no advertising placed. Bogus invoices might be sent.

Although the problems of cooperative advertising can be serious, they do not need to prevent its being used. Rather than choosing a centralized approach because of these problems, the manager might decide to eliminate or minimize the problems. If he takes the latter approach, he will find that working with an international agency with good foreign market coverage can help to control distributor placement of ads. Development of prototype or other advertising on a centralized basis will help standardize the quality of work from market to market. Because the exporter is paying part of the cost, he has the right to exercise some control along these lines. A further way to combat the problem of distributors' failing to cooperate is to establish sound but equitable guidelines that are clearly communicated and agreed upon. If the firm can implement these steps and manage its program effectively, it has a good chance of success with a cooperative international advertising program.

CONCLUSIONS

We have examined the environment and major decisions areas of international advertising management. The problems and uncertainties of advertising in domestic operations are magnified internationally by the number of markets involved and by the communications and information gaps between the markets and the international marketer. However, two factors offer the international marketer encouragement in his difficult task: (1) A good agency—or group of agencies—can be of inestimable help in solving some of the problems; and (2) the principles of sound advertising and advertising management are universal. The challenge to the manager is in applying these principles to the varied market environments he faces.

We will now turn to the other promotional tools available to the international marketer. Although we discuss these subjects here in separate chapters, the manager must evaluate them together because they are complementary and alternative tools in his promotional mix.

Questions

12.1   Identify the environmental constraints facing the international advertising manager.

12.2   Explain some of the reasons for the great international differences in advertising expenditures per capita. What is the significance of these differences for the international advertiser?

12.3   Home Care Products Company has just opened a marketing subsidiary in Spain. The company has been selling in twelve other Western European countries since World War II. The advertising manager at European headquarters must decide between the Madrid office of a large American advertising agency and a leading Spanish agency. What questions would you ask in advising him?

12.4   Explain the reasons for the dramatic growth of the international advertising agencies. Will this trend continue?

12.5   In view of this growth, why have local agencies survived?

12.6   Discuss the *subjective* bias of differing agencies and company personnel in the decision to choose a local or international advertising approach.

12.7   Identify the *objective* market and the technical or nonmarket factors affecting the decision on an international as opposed to a local advertising approach.

12.8   "To kill a message, translate it." Discuss.

12.9   What is the "prototype" approach to international advertising?

12.10 Why is it difficult for the international advertising manager to use the same media configuration in all his foreign markets?

12.11 When might the use of international print media be feasible and desirable? for which products and companies?

12.12 Evaluate the percentage-of-sales approach to setting the advertising appropriation in the multinational firm.

12.13 Discuss the potential use of comparative analysis in setting advertising budgets for foreign markets.

12.14 Discuss the influence of a firm's level of involvement in a market on its advertising budget there.

12.15 Why is the measurement of advertising effectiveness even more difficult in foreign markets than it is in the United States?

12.16 "Advertising management should be centralized in the exporting firm but decentralized to the foreign subsidiaries in the multinational firm." Discuss.

12.17 Explain the "coordinated decentralization" approach to the management of international advertising.

12.18 Discuss the benefits and problems in a program of cooperative advertising with local distributors in a firm's export markets.

Further Readings

Books:

American Association of Advertising Agencies, *Advertising Agency Business around the World* (New York, 1964).

Dunn, S. Watson, ed., *International Handbook of Advertising* (New York: McGraw-Hill Book Co., 1964).

Miracle, Gordon E., *Management of International Advertising,* Michigan International Business Studies No. 5 (Ann Arbor, Mich.: Bureau of Business Research, Graduate School of Business Administration, University of Michigan, 1966).

Root, Franklin R., *Strategic Planning for Export Marketing* (Scranton, Penna.: International Textbook Company), chap. 6.

Articles:

Donnelly, James H., Jr., "Attitudes toward Culture and Approach to International Advertising," *Journal of Marketing* (July 1970), pp. 60–63.

Elinder, Erik, "How International Can European Advertising Be?" *Journal of Marketing* (April 1965), pp. 7–11.

Fatt, Arthur C., "The Danger of Local International Advertising, *Journal of Marketing* (January 1967), pp. 60–62.

Patterson, Jere, "Coordinating International Advertising," *The International Advertiser* (December 1967), pp. 35–39.

Roostal, Ilmar, "Standardization of Advertising for Western Europe," *Journal of Marketing* (October 1963), pp. 15–20.

Ryans, John K., "Is It Too Soon To Put a Tiger in Every Tank?" *Columbia Journal of World Business,* vol. 4, no. 2 (March–April 1969), pp. 69–75.

Data Sources:

The following represent continuing sources (articles and data) on international advertising and promotion:

Advertising Age (weekly).

The International Advertiser (quarterly).

13

INTERNATIONAL
PROMOTION:
OTHER FACTORS

Although advertising is often the most prominent and costly element in the promotional mix of the international marketer, for some firms, especially those in industrial marketing, advertising is minor among the promotional factors. In either case, however, a sound promotional program almost inevitably involves other things in addition to advertising. In this chapter we will examine some of these "other things" the international marketer must consider, namely, (1) personal selling, (2) sales promotion, (3) the marketing mix as promotion, (4) special forms of promotion in international marketing, and (5) public relations.

PERSONAL SELLING

Besides advertising, personal selling is the major promotional tool available to the marketer. Often it is more important in international marketing than in the United States; that is, personal selling often takes a greater percentage of the promotional budget outside the United States. For at least two reasons personal selling has relatively greater importance in international marketing: (1) Restrictions on advertising and lack of media availability frequently limit the amount of advertising the firm can do profitably, and (2) the low wages in many countries—compared to those in the United States—allow the company to hire a much larger sales force. This second reason is especially applicable in less developed nations. A factor working in the opposite direction is the low status and prestige associated with sales work in most countries of the world.

The experience of Philip Morris in Venezuela illustrates the particular role personal selling can have in a market. The relatively low wages permitted the

382

company's sales department to employ 300 men. However, only one-third of these were salesmen. The rest were assistants who helped them with deliveries, distribution of sales materials, and so on. The salesmen were backed up with company advertising. Interestingly, this advertising was also economical as compared with the company's United States experience. In Venezuela, advertising was only about 2 percent of sales versus about 6 percent here.[1]

Another example is Sunbeam, which has had success with its appliances in Peru with a heavy emphasis on personal selling. Sunbeam had a dual brand policy. The distributor's sales force and the Sunbeam subsidiary's sales force overlapped in their market coverage—with different brands. This double coverage meant increased sales and market penetration.[2]

National, Not International

The subject we are considering, is essentially personal selling in the firm's foreign markets; it cannot really be called international personal selling. In discussing advertising, we could speak of having international campaigns and of using international media, but personal selling involves personal contact and is much more culture bound than the impersonal communication of advertising. As a result, even though international business and marketing have expanded tremendously in recent decades, personal selling activities are still primarily on a national basis. In fact, many national markets are divided into sales territories served by saleman recruited *only* from their respective territories. They do not even cover a national market.

A limited amount of personal selling does cross over national boundaries, most commonly that of industrial goods and especially big-ticket items. However, as international as IBM is in its operations, it still uses national salesmen exclusively in each of its markets. Some personal selling of consumer goods may also be international. This is done to some extent, for example, in selling exported goods to large wholesale or retail organizations that handle their own import arrangements. Although the growth of regionalism should encourage more international personal selling, economic integration is not the same as cultural integration. Experience in the EEC shows that personal selling activities are very slow to cross cultural-political boundaries.[3]

Personal Selling in Foreign Markets

One task of the international marketer is to determine the role personal selling should play in each of his foreign markets. In determining his promotional mix and strategy, he will rely on assistance from his subsidiaries and, hopefully, from his distributors. Comparative analysis of his markets will also be helpful. Once the role of personal selling has been decided, the actual admin-

---

[1] *Business Latin America*, October 30, 1969, p. 352.
[2] *Business Latin America*, p. 360.
[3] See Vern Terpstra, *American Marketing in the Common Market* (New York: Praeger, 1967), pp. 83–88.

istration of the sales force in a market will be similar to that in the firm's home market. That is, the same general functions must be performed: recruitment, selection, training, motivation, supervision, and compensation. These topics are covered extensively in texts on sales management,[4] so we will touch on them here only as they take on special international dimensions that relate to the marketing manager's sales management task.

Since personal selling essentially takes place on a national rather than an international basis, sales management must be largely decentralized to the national market. The international marketing manager will not have a sales force to manage. He will generally be an advisor to national operations, contributing whatever help and guidance he can because of his special position and authority. We will see that the international marketer has contributions to make to most tasks of sales force management.

Recruitment and Selection of Salesmen

Recruiting and selecting salesmen will be done within the local market by those who know the situation best. Two problems which may arise in trying to find salesmen in certain markets are that selling is a low-status occupation in most countries of the world, which causes the most attractive candidates to seek other kinds of employment, and that finding people with the educational and other characteristics desired by the company is often difficult. Problems and shortcomings encountered in the recruitment and selection process may have to be overcome or compensated for in the later steps of training and managing the sales force.

As an aid in recruitment and selection of salesmen, many companies develop job descriptions and personal specification lists to screen candidates. If these were uniform from country to country, international marketing management would be made easier. However, both may vary internationally. In the firm's foreign markets, the salesman's job will be a function of the firm's product line, its distribution channels, and its overall marketing mix, as well as of other variables in the firm's environment. Thus his job will not be exactly the same in all markets. Although each market has to develop job specifications to fit its needs, the greater the carry over from country to country, the more the international direction possible. The international marketer will search for similarities and common denominators to aid his supervision.

A question also arises as to whether there is a universal "salesman type," or profile, even for one industry. As job descriptions and market situations vary from country to country, so do other cultural influences and, probably, the "ideal salesman" profile. In many markets, a variety of religious, educational, and racial or tribal characteristics must be considered. Where markets are segmented in these dimensions, the sales force may have to be segmented also. Just as German salesmen generally are not used in France, so salesmen from one tribal or religious group often cannot be employed to sell to another

---

[4] See, for example, Kenneth R. Davis and Frederick E. Webster, Jr., *Sales Force Management* (New York: Ronald Press, 1968).

group in their own country. The world is full of examples of group conflicts that can be reflected in sales force requirements: English versus Irish, black versus white, French-speaking versus English-speaking Canadians, Hindu versus Muslim, Sinhalese versus Tamil, Ibo versus Hausa, and so on.

In some parts of the world, a particular group will be the major supplier of business people and salesmen, as were the Jews throughout Europe. The Chinese are the merchants and salesmen in many Asian nations today. Within the nation itself, a particular group or tribe may play this role. For example, the Parsees are a chief supplier of business enterprise in India; in Nigeria, the Ibos responded most eagerly to the training offered by the British, eventually occupying a majority of positions in government and business. The Biafran war, of course, significantly changed the role of the Ibos in Nigeria. Nevertheless, these examples indicate some of the particular considerations in recruiting and selecting a sales force in international marketing.

Although recruitment and selection of salesmen is done within the country itself, the international marketer can make some contributions to the local subsidiary. For example, he may introduce tests or techniques that have proved successful in domestic operations or in some other subsidiary country. Each country is not completely different from all others, and some degree of carry over and applicability of these techniques will be possible. By comparative analysis of company experience in many markets, and by collaborating with subsidiary personnel responsible for sales management, the international marketer should try to optimize the use of this international experience in his contributions to local operations.

Training Salesmen

The training of salesmen is another task done primarily in the national market. The content and nature of the training program will be determined by the demands of the salesman's job and the preparation he had upon joining the firm. These things will vary somewhat from country to country. Nevertheless, the international marketer also will have a voice in determining the nature and goals of the local training program. Because of the similarity in company products and policies from market to market, the national training programs will have many common denominators.

Drawing on the firm's domestic and multinational experience, the international marketer will seek to improve the effectiveness of each national training program. He can do this in part through supplying training materials, program formats, and ideas to each country operation. Annual or occasional international meetings of subsidiary personnel responsible for salesmen training can also promote the exchange of experience and the improvement of performance.

For some high-priced and/or high-technology products, training of salesmen may be at the international or regional level. Because selling to the industrial market has more similarities internationally, and because the selling task is more complicated, having centralized training of salesmen from several countries is more feasible. For example, a company's European or Latin

American headquarters could conduct a training center in conjunction with its other operations. This would allow better facilities, more highly skilled trainers, and perhaps economies of scale in training of salesmen (and other company personnel). IBM has such a center at Blaricum in the Netherlands. Some other American companies have them at their Brussels, London, or Swiss offices.

Another form of international training is the traveling team of experts from regional or international division headquarters. This may be part of a continuing training program in a firm. As the company finds new product applications, adds new products or product lines, or enters new market segments, the salesman's task might be changed, an especially likely event with a new generation of computers or industrial equipment or chemicals. The new selling task usually requires some additional special training, which can be accomplished either at a regional training center or by a traveling team of experts. Either way, the extra training should offer the advantages of specialization. It would be especially useful when the industrial marketer plans introduction of a new product or line into several countries simultaneously. We have already seen examples of this in Kodak's Instamatic camera and the NCR Century computer.

We have been discussing the training of salesmen in the firm's marketing subsidiaries in foreign markets. Where the firm sells through independent distributors or licensees, it has little control over the sales force, except to some extent in the initial selection and agreement with the distributor. Nevertheless, it is not unusual for firms selling industrial goods to give some specialized training to the salesmen of their distributors or licensees. This is generally done at no charge to the licensee or distributor. The international firm may consider it a profitable expenditure, however, because of its contribution to sales as well as to relations with the licensee or distributor. We discussed this more fully, with several examples, in Chapter 11.

A special phenomenon worth mentioning is the six-week training program offered for a while by the United States Trade Center in Bangkok, Thailand. Over twenty salesmanship courses were offered by the center to Thai salesman handling American products. After over 400 men had graduated, the center planned closing the course, but local demands led to a continuation. The costs of the program were covered by student fees, paid by their companies. Such a cooperative program can be a boon to an international company in less affluent markets where it sells through distributors.[5]

A particular sales force problem faces international companies in many markets. Because they are usually better marketers, and therefore have better trained salesmen, they tend to be "raided" by national companies. This means that they must either train more salesmen than they need (to cover the raiding losses) or find some way of keeping the salesmen with them, usually higher compensation.

[5] *International Commerce* (April 1970), p. 1.

Motivating and Compensating

Motivation and compensation of the sales force are very similar so we will discuss them together. Indeed, attractive compensation is often the chief motivator. Motivation can be more of a challenge abroad than in the United States for two reasons: (1) the low esteem in which selling as a profession is held, and (2) the cultural reluctance of prospective salesmen to talk to strangers, especially to try to persuade them—two essential elements of the salesman's job.

Although compensation is a prime motivator, there are other ways to motivate the sales force. Since much of it will depend on cultural as well as personal factors, the motivation must be designed locally to meet local needs. In countries where selling has an especially low status, the firm must make efforts to overcome this handicap. Training, titles, and perquisites are all helpful, as well as good financial rewards. In addition, special kinds of recognition can help the salesman's self image. For example, Philip Morris in Venezuela publicizes the achievements of its best salesmen and also gives them financial and other awards; periodically it gives a special party and banquet for the top four performers.[6]

Foreign travel is one kind of reward and motivation frequently employed by international companies. Salesmen from many markets would seldom be able to afford a trip to the United States or Europe. Their ability to earn such a trip through a good sales performance is a very strong incentive. In addition to providing access to tourist attractions, the company will usually entertain the visitors at headquarters, thereby adding to their knowledge and appreciation of the company. International companies are often better able to do this than national companies, both because of their size and because their internal logistics operations facilitate such efforts. They also gain economies of scale by entertaining salesmen from a number of different countries at the same time.

Firestone International sponsored a "Holiday USA" sales contest for three months in 1968. The salesmen of each organization who exceeded their quota by the greatest percentage won a one-week trip to the United States, all expenses paid. Forty-six winners spent three days sight-seeing in New York. They then spent one day at headquarters in Akron and had a banquet with executives. The next stop was to watch the Indianapolis 500 race. After this, they spent three days in Miami before flying home.[7]

A rather small company, Chesterton Packing & Seal Company, tried a similar effort but worked through its Japanese distributor, Nitta. It offered one-week vacation trips to Nitta salesmen who topped their quotas. The trips were to such Far East holiday spots as Hong Kong, Taiwan, and Manila. The first year of the contest, sales of Chesterton products jumped 212 percent. The distributor, Nitta, was so impressed that it adopted an incentive program for its other products.[8]

[6] *Business Latin America*, p. 352.
[7] *Firestone Worldwide* (November 1968), p. 1.
[8] *Business Abroad*, November 27, 1967, pp. 33, 34.

In the task of motivating and compensating the sales force, one of the challenges is to find the mix of monetary and nonmonetary rewards appropriate for each market. Among the nonmonetary factors are such things as training, counseling, supervision, and the use of quotas and contests. In monetary compensation, the question usually arises as to whether the form of payment should be a salary or a commission. This decision involves an international dimension as well as the usual considerations.

In many countries, salesmen are reluctant to accept an incentive form of payment such as a commission. They feel that this reinforces the cultural conflict and the negative image of personal selling. In such markets the firm will rely more on a salary form of payment rather than a commission. Some American companies, however, have been able to introduce incentive elements into their salesmen's remuneration even in these biased markets. In addition to the examples already cited is that of NCR in Japan.

> *NCR pioneered in the use of commission selling in Japan, a country where incentive payments were felt to be against the cultural pattern. However, a decade of experience in which NCR sales quadrupled and salesmen were increasingly satisfied seemed to argue to the contrary. In fact, the evidence convinced others to follow. Not only foreign firms, such as IBM, but even a number of Japanese firms began to model commission systems on the NCR example.*[9]

Controlling the Sales Force

With a commission form of remuneration, close control over the salesman is less necessary than with a straight salary payment system. However, regardless of the mode of payment, some control over salesmen's activities is necessary for optimal performance—both from the viewpoint of the company and from that of the salesman. Some of the control techniques are establishment of sales territories, setting of itineraries and call frequencies, use of quotas, and use of reporting arrangements. Because all these must reflect local conditions, they must be determined at least in part at the local level. For example, when some territories are less attractive than others, the firm may offer some extra reward to salesmen in the former to assure equal coverage of the market. Philip Morris did this in Venezuela, offering higher commissions for salesmen in the rural provinces.

Even though this activity is decentralized, the international marketing manager should participate to some extent in establishing the control techniques for the national sales force. For one reason, he has contact with domestic operations, which are probably the most sophisticated in these techniques, and this domestic experience can be a source of know-how for foreign markets. He can make the latest techniques available to all markets, to be applied where relevant and feasible. Furthermore, he can advise individual markets

[9] *Business Abroad*, pp. 33, 34.

on establishing sales territories, norms for sales calls, reporting arrangements, and so on.

The intimate local knowledge of national management is complemented by the international knowledge of the international marketer. Through a comparative analysis of similar markets, he has a better idea of what range of performance is possible and desirable in a specific market. Thus he can aid the local manager in setting appropriate norms for his national market. Especially when introducing a new product or line into its market, local management can benefit from relevant experience in the firm's other markets. In America, firms make various kinds of comparisons between sales territories. With appropriate modifications, the same kind of comparative analysis should be conducted for the firm's foreign markets; that is, the comparisons should be among groups of similar countries.[10] This is one way in which the international marketing manager can realize the benefits of the firm's multinational experience in sales forcé management.

Evaluating Sales Force Performance

Although he is far removed from day-to-day selling activities in foreign markets, the international marketer has a twofold interest in evaluating them. His first interest is in the performance of the individual salesman because the collective performances help to determine the firm's success in a market. He will not be personally involved with their evaluation, of course, but he will want to be sure that local sales force management is getting good performance, especially where personal selling is a major promotional tool. To this purpose he will help local management in applying the best techniques and methods of evaluation. He can assist them with ideas, reporting forms, ratios, and other criteria used elsewhere in the company's operations.

The international marketer's second interest in evaluating sales force performance is in making international comparisons. He wants to know not only how each country operation is performing in its local context—that is, relative to last year or to quota—but also how it compares with other markets. Such comparisons identify the countries needing the most help. They can also be used to motivate below-average markets to improve their performance. Some criteria for comparing countries can be personal selling cost as a percent of sales, number of salesmen per $1 million sales (to eliminate differences in wage costs), or units sold per salesman (to eliminate tax differences), and so on.

There are obviously many international differences that hinder such comparisons. In fact, the differences are so evident that some international firms deliberately try to avoid comparing countries. We say "try to" because every international executive inevitably makes such comparisons subjectively. It is better that they be made explicitly, on the basis of stated, defensible criteria which take account of relevant differences. For example, the European divi-

---

[10] Bertil Liander et al., *Comparative Analysis for International Marketing,* Marketing Science Institute (Boston: Allyn and Bacon, 1967), pp. 34–39.

sion of the Singer Company developed such a comparative framework for its sixteen European subsidiaries, including such economically diverse countries as Sweden and Spain. This framework became operational in the sense that it was understood and accepted by management in the sixteen subsidiaries.[11]

Level of Involvement and Personal Selling

Our discussion until now has been concerned primarily with markets where the firm has wholly owned subsidiaries and, therefore, company sales forces. Where the firm sells through independent distributors or licensees, the international marketer has no line authority to exercise. Because of this, it is all the more important that he exercise great care in the initial selection of such a representative. One of the main things a distributor has to offer the international firm is his sales force, which makes quality of sales force a major criterion in choosing a distributor. As noted earlier, the international firm usually can aid the licensee's or distributor's sales force by giving sales aids and materials and even special training. This can be very useful, but it is only a partial and limited form of control.

The licensee's or distributor's sales force is of critical importance for another reason. When an international firm wishes to expand its involvement in a market where it has a licensee or distributor, the most common method is to take over that licensee or distributor. In such a case, the sales force becomes the company's own. Although it is theoretically possible to dismiss the acquired sales force, there are many strong political and marketing (and often legal) arguments against this.

In joint venture operations, the international marketer may have a small voice or a big voice in the selling activities, depending on the capabilities and interests of both partners and on the terms of their agreement. The greater the control given to the international marketer in the marketing activities of the joint venture, the more the situation resembles that of a wholly owned subsidiary. The less the control, the more the situation resembles that in a licensing or distributor agreement.

Conclusions on Personal Selling

We have seen that personal selling is closely related to the cultural and other peculiarities of its local market. Sales force management is thus largely decentralized to the local operation. Nevertheless, the international marketer can and should play some role in most aspects of this task. We have seen how he can contribute special expertise and advice in every aspect of sales force management: recruitment, selection, training, motivating, compensating, and evaluating. He serves as the bridge and clearinghouse between domestic and foreign operations, and between the various foreign markets themselves.

American companies probably have some advantage in international sales force management because, as is the case with some other marketing functions, American experience is often an indicator of what is coming in other

---

[11] Liander, *Comparative Analysis for International Marketing*, pp. 38, 39.

markets of the world. Therefore, the American firm often can lead the way in sales force development abroad. As firms upgrade and improve personal selling activities in their American operations, they can draw on this experience for application elsewhere. Doing this effectively, however, depends on the international and comparative knowledge and skills of international marketing management.

SALES PROMOTION

Sales promotion here is loosely defined as a collection of selling activities that do not fall directly into the advertising or personal selling category, such as the use of contests, coupons, sampling, premiums, cents-off deals, point-of-purchase materials, and the like. It may be organizationally separated, but frequently it is part of either the advertising or the personal selling department. Nevertheless, sales promotion has some peculiar characteristics that warrant separate attention.

The sales manager is interested in any device or approach that will help persuade customers to buy his products. In addition to regular advertising and personal selling efforts, a variety of sales promotion activities have proved effective in selling merchandise in foreign markets as well as in the United States. This implies that international decisions on promotional budgets should include a consideration of sales promotion expenditures alongside of, or in place of, expenditures for advertising and personal selling. The firms that use sales promotion devices in the American market generally will find them as effective in other markets, if not more effective. Where incomes are lower, people are usually even more interested in "something for nothing," such as free samples, premiums, or contests.

Apart from economics, various other kinds of constraints affect the international use of sales promotion materials and approaches, one of which is legal. The laws affecting sales promotion are generally more restrictive elsewhere than they are in the United States. They may restrict both the size and the nature of the sample, premium, or prize. The value of the item received free must often be limited to a percent (say, 5 percent, as in France) of the value of the product purchased. In other cases, the nature of the item received free must be related to the nature of the product purchased, such as cups with coffee—but not steak knives with laundry detergent. Such legal restrictions may be a bother to one accustomed to the market situation in the United States. However, they are not crippling regulations, as evidenced by the amount of sales promotion activity going on around the world's markets. The laws are less of a barrier than a challenge to the ingenuity of the sales manager.

Another constraint is cultural. The premiums or other devices or methods used must be meaningful and attractive to the local consumer. Even though products themselves usually must be adapted to national markets, premiums will require greater local adaptation than do products. Meeting local consumer desires is thus one element of the cultural constraint. Another is the desires and capabilities of retailers and other intermediaries.

Many sales promotion activities require some retail involvement, that is, processing coupons, handling odd-shaped combination or premium packages, posting display materials, and so on. Getting retailer cooperation may be difficult, not so much because he has a negative attitude but because he lacks appropriate facilities and capabilities. Among the several problems that arise where there are large numbers of small retailers are the following: The retailers are difficult to contact; they have limited space and facilities; and they will often handle the materials in a way that the producer did not intend or expect.

A further constraint on the use of sales promotion is the local competitive situation. On the one hand, a firm can feel itself "forced" to use a particular sales promotion approach in a country because competitors are using it. The firm may see no advantage to the particular "gimmick" but nevertheless feel that it will lose sales and market position without it. A case in point is the United States experience with trading stamps in supermarkets and contests by gasoline retailers. A different situation can occur when the aggressive international company makes significant gains in a market with a strong use of advertising and sales promotion. National competitors might react to restrain such methods, either through trade-association action or political-legal channels.

A General Electric 50-percent joint venture in Japan had noticeable success in breaking into the air-conditioning market there. Two factors behind the successful entry were (1) overseas trips as prizes to outstanding dealers and (2) offering a free color TV set to purchasers of models priced above 300,000 yen (about $1,000).

The result was that the trade association drew up rules banning overseas trips as prizes for sales of air conditioners and setting a limit on the size of premium that could be offered. These rules were approved by the Japanese Fair Trade Commission. Company complaints led to a modification of the rules—no overseas trips as prizes for any home electric appliance dealers.[12]

Conclusions on Sales Promotion

We have noted some of the legal, cultural, and competitive constraints on the use of sales promotion in different national markets. Generally, however, these constraints do not prevent the use of sales promotion by the international marketer. They do require him to get good local market information before designing a sales promotion program for a country. Once these constraints have been satisfied, the major question is, How much of the promotional budget should be allocated to sales promotion? The marketing manager must evaluate the relative pay-off of advertising, personal selling, and sales promotion expenditures. These may differ by market as well as in the short run versus the long run.

The international firm should have some advantages over its national competitors in sales promotion. For example, there may be economies of scale

[12] *Business International,* August 29, 1969, p. 277.

in generating ideas for sales promotion and in buying or preparing materials to be used. Ideas and materials may be suitable for several different markets. One country can be used as a test market for others which are similar. Comparative analysis of company experience in many different markets will be helpful in evaluating sales promotion ideas and materials and in determining the appropriate budget percentage that should be allocated to it.

THE MARKETING MIX AS PERSUADER

We have discussed the three principal elements of the promotional mix: advertising, personal selling, and sales promotion. The purpose of all these promotional activities is to induce consumers or industrial buyers to purchase the company's products. As marketers know well, however, other factors also help persuade customers to buy—or not to buy—the firm's products. All the elements of the marketing mix have an influence on the sales and salability of goods and services. Because the elements of the mix have a somewhat different influence from country to country, the appropriate mix for a given market will have some degree of individuality.

The idea of the complementarity and substitutability of the various elements of the mix is familiar to all students of marketing. What we will note here are some of the international applications of the mix concept as related to promotion. Since we have already examined product policy and distribution, as well as the other elements of promotion, our treatment will be brief.

Product

Although the nature and quality of the product are presumably the major reasons a consumer buys it, consumer needs and desires for a given type of product often differ from country to country. By modifying his product for national markets, the international marketer can persuade more customers to buy it. Affluent markets may demand more style and power, larger size or capacity. Poorer markets may require smaller sizes, durability, and simplicity. Food products will vary internationally in the degree of sweetness or spiciness desired. Further differences will be found in the form, color, and texture of products. Revlon, in all of its world markets, uses frequent product innovation as a major promotional tool. Although this practice is not product modification for foreign markets, it does illustrate the use of product policy for promotional purposes.

Package

For many goods, the package is an important element of what the consumer perceives as the product. Adapting packaging to the individual national market may be effective promotion. In some markets, dual-use packages attract the consumer, who keeps the empty package or container for some other use in the home. Plastic squeeze containers are popular in some markets, whereas aerosol or perhaps traditional metal or glass are preferred elsewhere. Form and color are important here too. The label on the package should also serve a promotional role in its design, color, the language used, and the copy or text printed on it.

Brand

Brand policy can affect the attractiveness of the product. For some goods and services an international brand name will be more prestigious and trusted than a national brand. On the other hand, for many products, such as food and household items, individualized national brands are favored by international companies. Johnson's Wax and CPC International (Corn Products Company) are examples of firms pursuing such an individualized national brand policy. As we have noted elsewhere, other forces work against such a policy.

Warranty and Service

Many companies use warranties defensively; that is, they meet national competitors' warranties. Warranties, however, also can be used aggressively to promote sales. If the international company has a stronger quality control program and a more reliable product than national competitors, it may gain a promotional edge through using a more liberal warranty coverage. An American slide rule producer successfully entered Europe, original home of the slide rule, by promoting a lifetime guarantee. This proved very attractive to consumers.

Americans are not alone in their concern for product service, which includes such things as delivery, installation, repair and maintenance facilities, and spare parts inventories. Occasionally international firms are handicapped in some markets because they are not represented well enough to offer service as good as that offered by national firms. The international marketer must be especially concerned with this problem because a weakness in this area can offset strengths in other areas of marketing, including a strong promotional program. By the same token, a strong product service capability can be a most effective promotional device. For example, this has been a strength of Singer and IBM in many markets. Volkswagen in America is another example of a successful service capability, tying in with an effective advertising campaign. The firm's international logistics and level of involvement must be designed with service requirements in mind. Otherwise, its representation will be ineffective in certain markets.

Distribution, or Level of Involvement

Domestic marketers are aware of the promotional implications of different distribution strategies. Where convenience is important to the buyer, the firm must have widespread distribution. Where dealer "push" is important, more selective distribution is necessary. The same considerations apply in the firm's foreign markets. Even where international firms sell through an importer-distributor in a given market, they invariably give him an exclusive franchise for his market to encourage his support of the product. Generally, the firm would sign no other distributors in that market unless they were to distribute a different product line. This exclusive franchise is almost always necessary to get effective dealer promotion—or any dealer support for the firm's products.

For a firm to go from an indirect channel to a direct channel means that the distribution system is bearing a greater part of the promotional burden. The more direct the channel, the greater the push. In addition to the normal use and understanding of this strategy, going direct can have a special significance for the international firm in reference to its level of involvement in a market. An indirect channel means many links or intermediaries between the producer and the ultimate consumer. In international marketing, an indirect channel would be indirect or direct exporting (see Chapter 11).

The way the international firm can go more direct in distributor markets is to establish its own presence there with a marketing subsidiary. As with any more direct method, the firm's costs will increase. Many marketing benefits are associated with such a move, however, one of which commonly is a very favorable promotional effect on the firm's sales. A way of illustrating the benefits gained is to note the disadvantages of the exporting approach, which are usually overcome with a local subsidiary.

A study of the German market for American automotive parts showed the following complaints and drawbacks expressed by German buyers in dealing with American exporters.[13]

1. American exporters do not familiarize themselves with the market.
2. Management gives less attention to foreign business. Foreign inquiries are sometimes ignored.
3. There is a lack of reliability in delivery dates. Promises are not honored.
4. Price quotations are f.o.b.—United States plant. These are not very meaningful to German buyers.
5. Little or no German language material is available describing the firm's products. Some of what is available is poor.
6. Domestic customers get open account terms. Foreign buyers receive harsher terms, such as letter of credit.

The establishment of a foreign subsidiary is almost certain to eliminate all of these problems. Not only does it do much for the understanding, performance, reliability, and image of the international company, but also it can be one of the most powerful promotional tools the firm can use. Of course, the potential market must warrant the costs involved.

Price and Terms

The idea behind the demand curve and the elasticity concept is that buyers are sensitive to price. By changing the price, the marketer affects the attractiveness of his product. In other words, pricing has promotional aspects. If consumers in different countries have differing degrees of price sensitivity— that is, different demand curves—the international marketer should try to adjust his prices accordingly, if his costs permit this flexibility.

Quite apart from the elasticity concept, price may be able to be used promotionally in other ways. On products where there is a price-quality asso-

[13] Seminar of the Institute for International Commerce, University of Michigan, October, 1968.

ciation, the firm might wish to price above competitors to gain the quality image. Of course, this is most meaningful if the firm's product indeed has a quality advantage. In countries where consumer purchasing power is low, prices might be effectively reduced by modifying the product, for example, giving it fewer features and greater simplicity, or using smaller sizes or packages.

Export Pricing

On export sales, prices and terms can be used to promotional advantage in several ways. One is in choosing the currency for the price quote. Although the exporter usually prefers to quote in his own currency, the importer desires price quotes in his currency. This aids his purchasing and may protect him against variations in the exchange rate.

Another promotional aspect of export pricing is the specific quotation used. As noted in our chapter on pricing, f.o.b. plant prices are favored by the exporter. However, he can gain a promotional advantage by using a c.i.f. quote, which is preferred by the importer. Use of f.o.b. prices by American exporters was a specific cause of complaint by German buyers in the study quoted above.

A third promotional aspect of export pricing is in the terms extended to the buyer. Exporters often discriminate against foreign buyers in the terms given. For example, domestic buyers may be given open account terms, whereas foreign importers have to pay by letter of credit. This was also a complaint of the German importers. Foreign buyers would generally like to have the same terms as domestic buyers. Although this may not always be feasible, the exporter who wants to use pricing as a promotional tool will respond to market desires as far as he can. Thus he would move toward local currency price quotes, c.i.f. pricing, and more liberal credit terms to foreign buyers.

Credit

A final and very important promotional aspect of payment terms is the use of credit, in the sale of both consumer goods and industrial goods. However, the credit needs of industrial and consumer buyers vary from country to country. Sellers of industrial equipment abroad often find that the factor determining the choice of supplier is the liberality of credit terms. For American exporters this has meant increasing demands on the Export-Import Bank to extend export credit. For operations in some foreign countries it has meant a need for greater working capital to cover the more liberal credit terms required in their market.

For consumer-goods marketers, credit extension also can be a promotional weapon directed at both the channel members and the consumers. In many countries, wholesalers and retailers are small and financially weak. The international firm has to cover their credit needs in what seems to be an extremely liberal fashion, as compared with the firm's domestic experience. At the consumer level, the producer may find that very liberal credit is needed to sell durable goods. For example, credit extension has been one reason Singer has been able to maintain a reasonable market position in sewing machines in spite of lower priced competition.

Automobile dealers in Brazil found an ingenious way to sell cars in a money tight economy without credit, through a consorcio *or lottery. About eighty buyers got together enough money to buy two cars a month. Each month there was a drawing, and two lucky members got a car. They continued their monthly payments, however, until all members received their own car. It was akin to an installment sale, except that most* consorcio *buyers received a car earlier than they would have under an installment plan. The plan also eliminated the large down payments normally required and the heavy credit charges of Brazil's inflationary economy. The result was an expanding automobile market in Brazil.[14] This example cannot be generalized to many other products. However, it is significant in showing how ingenuity in managing prices and credit terms can be a most effective form of promotion.*

The Total Mix at Work: Timex in Germany

We have discussed the promotional aspects of the different elements of the marketing mix taken in isolation. In practice, of course, these elements are interacting and synergistic. We give the following example showing how one international company used the total mix in one foreign market. The company is U.S. Time Corporation, maker of Timex watches. The event is the company's entry into West Germany.

PRODUCT STRATEGY   *The company studied the competitive situation and found existing producers selling primarily high- and medium-priced watches— selling watches for status purposes. There were also sales of low-priced, low-quality watches, sold without guarantee and with the initial repair costing more than the price of the watch. The company felt that its products filled a gap between these two segments, both as to price and quality.*

SERVICE   *To beat the low-priced competition and to meet the high-priced competition, Timex provided service arrangements at moderate cost. Service was free during the guarantee period. After that, a new movement could be purchased for one-half to one-fourth the price of the new watch. This helped to upgrade the image of the inexpensive or "cheap" watch.*

GUARANTEE   *The company offered the first inexpensive watch with a guarantee. In fact, the guarantee was as liberal as those on high-priced watches, with free service or repairs during the first year. This was important in persuading a skeptical public about the quality of the inexpensive watch.*

PRICE   *Timex stressed its low prices but at the same time emphasized the quality and the guarantee. The company's prices were generally a step above the low-priced competition, but well below most of the higher priced com-*

[14] *Time,* July 21, 1967, p. 71.

petition. Other pricing decisions were to use resale price maintenance and to give retailers the same margins as on high-priced watches (33⅓ percent).

DISTRIBUTION   *Distribution strategy was one of the major elements in the Timex program in Germany. Since jewelers sold 75 percent of the watches, Timex needed that channel. However, the company also felt it necessary to add the large department stores and mail-order houses. Others who had tried this earlier had been boycotted by the jewelers. Timex was successful in persuading jewelers that its business was too profitable to ignore. The elements of persuasion were (1) giving the same margin as on expensive watches, (2) saving repair work by having the watches sent to the Timex factory in France, while giving the dealer 25-percent commission on the charges to the customer, (3) using resale price maintenance to protect them against discounters, and (4) a heavy publicity and advertising campaign (more than twice what all German competition spent). This made Timex the best known watch in Germany.*

PROMOTION   *A heavy advertising campaign, double the total competitive outlays, initiated the "hard sell" approach. Dramatic "torture tests" were used in the ads. Competitors called these undignified, but later on some began to imitate them. Eighty percent of the company ad budget went for television because of its coverage and dramatic effect. In a separate promotional effort, a missionary selling force toured Germany, explaining to retailers the advantages of handling Timex.*[15]

SPECIAL FORMS OF INTERNATIONAL PROMOTION

Several forms of international promotion are really part of the marketing and promotional mix and could have been discussed in the preceding section. However, because they are not normally considered with the promotional mix, and because they have special international features, we will examine them separately. These special forms of promotion in international marketing include the activities of governments, international trade fairs, and the Washington representative.

Governmental Assistance in Promotion

Many national governments assist their domestic industry in export marketing. This assistance usually takes three forms: informational, financial, and promotional. It is only the latter form that will concern us here. In Chapters 7 and 14, we can see the other forms of governmental assistance. Since most of the readers of this book will be in the United States, we will take that country as our example. Most developed nations will have programs similar to those described here, and some less developed countries also engage in activities along this line. In addition, the joint GATT-UNCTAD International Trade Centre in Geneva serves the less developed countries collectively for export promotion.

[15] Drawn from *Business Europe*, May 24, 1967, pp. 162, 163, and *Business Abroad*, February 5, 1968, pp. 27, 28.

The United States Example: The National Level

In looking at the situation in the United States, one must distinguish between the national government and the state governments. Promotional assistance for the international firm is often available at each level, especially for firms located in the industrial states. We will first look at the efforts of the federal government, which carries on numerous activities that can directly help the promotional needs of American exporters and international firms. The Department of State and the Department of Commerce are the principal sources of this help.

Department of State

The international commercial success of American business is one of the many concerns of the United States Department of State. Its Foreign Service Officers have as one of their responsibilities the promotion and protection of American business in the particular country of their location.[16] In addition to their informational activities, they maintain a commercial reading room with trade journals and catalogs of American companies. They report on trade opportunities and arrange contacts for American businessmen making a commercial visit to that country.

The extent and nature of their promotional assistance can be seen best through a specific example. This account reports the services of the United States Embassy in Nairobi, Kenya, to the Kennecott Copper Company.

1. *The Embassy's Sample Display Service put Kennecott's Koride 101 (a fungicide) on display for two and one-half months.*
2. *The Embassy mailed an agent search announcement to 950 East African businessmen, by way of its* Commercial Newsletter.
3. *It sent special letters to thirteen Kenya firms dealing particularly in agricultural chemicals.*
4. *It gave direct assistance to the Kennecott representative when he came to Nairobi to conclude negotiations.*

Results: Kennecott got its distributor for East Africa.[17]

Such services are all the more attractive because they are free to the firm, or have a very nominal cost at most.

For some major projects, the Department of State may play an even greater role. For example, the Indian government was considering a crash program for a great expansion of fertilizer production. The United States Embassy in India and the AID mission there worked with the Indian government and several large American companies to promote the project. The American companies involved included Bechtel Corporation, Lehman Brothers, Texaco,

---

[16] For a detailed description of their activities in this regard, see Roland L. Kramer, *International Marketing*, 3rd ed. (Cincinnati, Ohio: South-Western Publishing Co., 1970), pp. 64–71.

[17] *International Commerce*, April 6, 1970, p. 1.

Mobil Oil Company, Allied Chemical, and Food Machinery Corporation (FMC). The American government involvement included not only the AID mission in India but also Ambassador Bowles. According to some Indian officials, even "the hand of the White House" was obvious.[18]

In this particular instance, the project did not come to a successful conclusion. Nevertheless, it is useful in demonstrating the degree of promotional involvement that can occasionally come from the United States government on major international business undertakings.

Department of Commerce

Not surprisingly, the Department of Commerce, "the businessman's department," is most active in promoting the international business of American firms. We have seen how it is a major supplier of information on the markets of the world (Chapter 7). On the promotional side of international business, the Department of Commerce is equally active in a variety of programs. The principal promotional programs it offers to American firms are trade missions, the operation of permanent trade centers abroad, a commercial exhibitions program, and a sample display service.

TRADE MISSIONS   The department's Bureau of International Commerce sends ten or more trade missions abroad each year. Each mission takes from 200 to 500 or more business proposals from large, medium, and small American firms that either are engaged in international business or desire to be. A "business proposal" is a sales offer submitted by an American company, taken abroad by the trade mission, and discussed with potential customers. Summaries of business proposals are published in booklets written in the language of the country to be visited and widely distributed to the business community there before the trade mission arrives.

A trade mission composed of a few officials from the Department of Commerce plus several experienced American businessmen spends an average of thirty days overseas in addition to two or three weeks of preparation for the trip. Each business proposal is assigned to the mission member having the greatest competence in that product category. Mission members, who are volunteers screened by the department, are not allowed to conduct business on their own behalf, but only for the proposals they are given. Their travel and living expenses abroad are paid by the department. The missions are working groups as evidenced by the following example.

A trade and machinery equipment mission spent four weeks in the Netherlands. It stopped in fourteen cities, visited thirty-six plants, and held 503 interviews with Dutch businessmen. It presented 1,050 business proposals and developed 279 new export opportunities for American firms. Other trade contacts were brought back, and catalogs and directories were left with local businessmen.

[18] Ashok Kapoor, "The Consortium That Never Was," *Columbia Journal of World Business* (September–October 1969), pp. 63–70.

A variation on this program is the industry-organized government-approved trade mission. The department provides personnel and assistance for these, but since they conduct business for themselves, they pay their own expenses. In both cases, the results are the same: sales of the firm's products and/or signing of distributors or licensees in the target markets.

TRADE CENTERS   In 1961, the Commerce Department began its trade center program. The first four centers—in Bangkok, Frankfurt, London, and Tokyo —were a success, leading the department to add six more—in Milan, Stockholm, Paris, Sydney, Mexico City, and Buenos Aires. More may be established later.

Trade centers are attractive, permanent display facilities in key market areas. Each one is accessible to a majority of the national market in the country of its location. Exhibits in a trade center are limited to one line of products, for example, commercial laundry and dry cleaning equipment. Exhibits run from one to three weeks and represent the products of about thirty manufacturers, on the average. The department is especially interested in helping small firms but allows many large companies (General Electric, Eastman Kodak, and the like) to participate, partly as an inducement to smaller firms, which feel more secure with such an association.

Before an exhibit is run, extensive market research is done to assure that there is a demand for the line of products under consideration. This research is usually carried out by local consultants or technical firms familiar with the product category. The results are then made available to exhibitors. In addition, the center's staff will supply information on particular potential customers or agents of the exhibitor.

Besides providing well-located facilities, the center not only aids the exhibitor in preparing appropriate displays but also carries on an active advertising and direct-mail campaign to the relevant market. Invitations are sent to the trade, that is, to those interested in the products at the exhibit. Exhibitor response has been quite enthusiastic because of the results obtained. A Black & Decker participant noted, "I cannot emphasize too highly the value of the selective procedure. Our experience has shown that we were engaged 100 percent of the time talking to interested people directly concerned with buying our products." In the first seven years of the program, through June 1968, 7,673 American companies, exhibiting in 233 shows, sold almost $200 million worth of products and signed over 2,500 overseas agents. Of the exhibitors, over one-fourth were new to the market where the exhibit was held and 235 had never exported at all previously.[19]

The costs to the exhibitor are modest. The participation fee is less than $500 in addition to which the firm must pay the shipping costs for its products to the exhibit. The Department of Commerce guarantees the return freight but seldom has to pay because the products are usually sold. The firm must also supply a qualified person to man its booth. This could be the local dis-

[19] All figures from the Department of Commerce.

tributor, but frequently it is an executive from the United States, who is empowered to make contracts as well as terms.

The evident benefits of the trade center program in getting sales and distribution have accounted for its continued expansion and the growing involvement by the United States business community. The electronics industry has been the leading user of the program with over twenty-five exhibitions. Other leading industries with more than ten exhibitions each have included auto service equipment, medical equipment, heating and air-conditioning equipment, sanitation equipment, and packaging equipment.

Obviously, the industries that continue to use the trade centers have found them effective and valuable promotion. Although in some instances exhibitions at a trade center have not paid off, in spite of the market research done, the program has been one of the department's most successful trade expansion efforts. For many American companies, it has also been very helpful and inexpensive promotion in international markets.

COMMERCIAL EXHIBITIONS PROGRAM—TRADE FAIRS   Over 1,000 general and specialized international trade fairs take place each year. For some of the major fairs, the department's Bureau of International Commerce organizes American industry participation and offers a full range of promotional and display assistance. Except that these exhibits are held under the auspices of an international fair, the commercial exhibitions program (CEP) for trade fairs is run much like the trade center program. Market research is done before the fair and promotional display assistance from CEP is available before and during the fair.

Although the CEP trade fair program has been generally successful, again not all efforts have met with that fate. Furthermore, some larger American firms have felt that the government has sometimes leaned too heavily on them to assure successful participation in a particular fair, such as the Paris Air Show, in which an aerospace display can be quite costly. Where the program works well, it has the same pay-off as the trade center program, that is, immediate sales and the establishment of distribution abroad.

SAMPLE DISPLAY SERVICE   The Bureau of International Commerce runs a sample display service in connection with five American embassies abroad: Beirut, Addis Ababa, Nairobi, Bangkok, and Hong Kong. Others are planned. These are primarily places for American firms seeking representation abroad to show samples of their products, with descriptive and promotional litternature. A commercial officer at the embassy manages the display so the firm is not required to send its own representative. This sample display service ties in with other embassy services, as shown in the Kennecott Copper Company example cited above.

The States Promote International Business
Almost all the fifty states in the United States have some type of international business promotion program. The amount of support offered varies widely, but the programs share a common purpose, namely, to help firms within their

jurisdiction to increase their volume of business. The states' programs some-times overlap and sometimes complement those of the federal government. Table 13–1 shows the activities of state governments in aiding the *promotional* efforts of firms. The other kinds of assistance they offer have been omitted from this listing.[20]

Table 13–1   International Promotional Aid by State Governments

TYPE OF AID	NUMBER OF STATES
Organize trade missions to foreign markets	29
State exhibits at international trade fairs	25
Publish a directory of state firms in international business	24
Advertising in overseas market media	14
Direct mail advertising	8
Operate promotional offices in foreign countries	6

Source: Gerald Albaum, *State Government Promotion of International Business* (Tucson, Ariz.: University of Arizona, Division of Economic and Business Research, 1968), p. 9.

Relevance of Federal and State Programs for International Marketing

Table 13–1 shows the similarity between the efforts of individual states and those of the federal government. Not many of the state programs are well financed, however, thus their services are limited. A notable exception is New York. Where states do have reasonably effective programs, it is up to the firm to determine how state efforts can be incorporated into the firm's overall international promotion program. This applies to federal efforts also.

As a citizen and taxpayer, the firm is entitled to use both federal and state assistance. Because both are cooperative and subsidized efforts, the marginal cost to the firm is usually low. Therefore, if there are benefits to be derived, the firm should try to make federal and state promotional support a part of its own promotional mix for international marketing. It should be aware of those programs available to it and evaluate their potential contribution as part of the promotional mix.

International Trade Fairs[21]

Well over 1,000 international trade fairs take place in over seventy different nations of the world. Although trade fairs and shows are not uncommon in the United States, they play a much greater role in other countries. In the United States they tend to be shows or exhibitions, whereas abroad the emphasis is on "show and sell." American fairs often draw many visitors from

[20] For another aspect of state programs, see James D. Goodnow, "American Overseas Business Promotion Offices," *Michigan Business Review* (January 1970), pp. 6–11.
[21] For a fuller description of trade fairs, see Franklin R. Root, "International Marketplace: International Trade Fairs," *The American-German Review* (April 1965), pp. 20–25.

the general public. Abroad, the majority of fairgoers are other businessmen —managers, purchasing agents, salesmen, and engineers.

We have seen that the Department of Commerce organizes and assists American firms' participation at some of the major fairs. Because of the potential strategic value of these fairs, the international firm might wish to participate on its own in other international fairs covering its product lines. This can be done directly or by the foreign subsidiaries or representatives of the firm.[22]

International trade fairs are either general, covering many product categories, or specialized, displaying the products of a single industry. The annual Hanover Fair in Germany is the largest of the general fairs with over 5,000 exhibitors in twenty major categories.[23] Because so many buyers and sellers from different nations gather at a big general fair, contacts can often be made that might take years otherwise. Said one international marketer: "We had been trying to crack the European market for three years. After we came to the Hanover Fair last year, we soon had a complete network of European distributors lined up."[24]

Fair time can also be test market time. A firm can test sales and potential distributor reactions in a market before committing itself to any particular level of involvement there. If sales potential is proved, the fair will also help the firm contact candidates for distributorships or licensing agreements. The potential distributor or licensee favors the fair for the same reasons. He can personally see the manufacturer and his products and observe the market reaction to them. The fair provides a test market situation for both parties.

The specialized fair fulfills basically the same role but for a single product category. Two of the more famous specialized fairs are the Paris Air Show and the "Fotokina," or photo products fair, in Cologne. The "Fotokina," for example, is the major international showplace-and-battleground of German, Japanese, American, and other leading producers of photo products. The fair itself and the attendant publicity must be a major promotional concern of any firm in this industry. Although few specialized fairs are so critical to an industry as the "Fotokina," their importance is increasing with the growing internationalization of competition.

The East European Fairs

For firms trading, or wishing to trade, with the East European countries, both general and one-industry fairs are available. In principle, these fairs are the same as those described above. A major advantage for Western firms is the opportunity to meet the end users of their products and other important contacts whom they do not meet when negotiating with the foreign trade organizations of these countries. Drawbacks of these fairs are that they are relatively expensive and include many nonbusiness visitors. Selling displayed products for hard currency is also more difficult than in the trade fairs of Western countries.

[22] Root, "International Marketplace: International Trade Fairs," pp. 20–25.
[23] *Business Week*, May 4, 1968, pp. 56–58.
[24] *Business Week*, p. 58.

The Use of Trade Fairs

International trade fairs can offer many advantages, and even economies, to the international firm. Because of their strategic value, the international marketer must consider them when planning his promotional program. If he decides to use fairs, his first step is to identify those relevant to his products and markets. The biweekly publication of the Department of Commerce, *Commerce Today*, has a semiannual listing of the international trade fairs. Next, he must incorporate the firm's participation in the selected fairs into the planning of the annual promotional mix. Merely adding it on will result in inefficiencies and wasted effort.

In the fair planning stage, the firm must include its subsidiaries, distributors, and licensees to assure their effective participation so that maximum value can be obtained by all parts of the firm's operations. Naturally, an annual review of the role of the international fairs will indicate some that might be added and others that might be dropped, according to the evaluation of their contribution and cost.

The Washington Representative

Many American firms have an office or representative in Washington, D.C. When the firm is large enough to have several people in this office, one of them may have as his primary responsibility looking after the firm's interests in exports and overseas operations. This task will include an intelligence function, of course, but "basically the Washington specialist is a marketing man, whose beat includes the embassies and their supply missions, the international financing agencies, and the continuing round of high-level foreign visitors."[25] In other words, he is a very high-level salesman who does personal selling in a very strategic market.

The task of promoting and selling involves reaching the purchase influencers with informative and persuasive messages. This is the marketing part of the Washington representative's job. He has a critical market to cultivate among the international agencies, the embassies, and important foreign visitors. After he has made a sale, he may even help his customers arrange financing with the Export-Import Bank. Some of the contact work is long-range market development and may not result in immediate sales. The ultimate goal is the same, however: to increase the company's international business.

A firm with significant international business should consider a Washington representative for both the intelligence and promotional contributions he can make. It is hard to include him as a part of the international promotional mix, but he can often be a valuable addition to the firm's overall promotional effectiveness. Because of the critical nature of the market he contacts, great care must be exercised in selecting the man for this position. He must have diplomatic as well as marketing skills. One survey of Washington international representatives showed two common characteristics: (1) All had been heavily involved in marketing operations previously; (2) most had spent a number of years with the same corporation before moving to Washington.[26]

[25] *Business Abroad* (April 1970), p. 17.
[26] *Business Abroad*, p. 18.

Miscellaneous Efforts

Because each foreign market is to some degree unique, the varieties of promotional efforts possible are limited only by the ingenuity of the marketer. Special programs can be designed to meet particular situations and opportunities in different markets. The international marketer is interested in these particular national promotions not only for their success in one country but also in terms of their potential application in other markets. One country or region may serve as a test market for such promotions.

A novel approach that has been used by several firms is the "flying showcase," which involves outfitting an aircraft as a mobile exhibition for a company's products. The exhibit itself is similar to that in a trade center or international fair, but its mobility allows it to travel to many countries, thus providing the firm with economies of scale from the costs and efforts put into the exhibit program. As can be seen from the example below, such an effort can be helpful either for entering a region or for expanding the firm's involvement there. Although the total cost is much higher than for an exhibit in a trade center or fair, this can be more than offset by the number of countries covered and the more dramatic impact of a one-company flying showcase.

In 1968, Automatic Radio International (ARI) organized a ten-week flying-showcase promotion for twenty-two Western Hemisphere nations from Canada through Latin America. The purpose was to expand ARI's involvement and business in this area, which was lagging behind the rest of ARI's international sales. The 37,000-mile trip stopped in twenty-seven cities and received more than 6,000 visitors, including presidents and prime ministers as well as business prospects. All of these visitors saw and heard demonstrations of ARI's full line of radio, stereo, air-conditioning, and refrigeration equipment—thirty-two different products in operation.

Preparation involved several steps: (1) outfitting the aircraft as an exhibit; (2) advance mailing of invitations to target audience—names were gathered from local affiliates; (3) local United States embassies helping with press and television publicity and recruiting flying-showcase hostesses at each stop; (4) recruiting of a multilingual crew (Spanish and Portuguese); (5) preparing multilingual sales literature. ARI's president accompanied the trip for the full period.

The results were in line with ARI's goals. Eleven new distributors and licensees were added, additional dealers were added in existing markets, and several agreements were expanded. The firm considered the publicity received a valuable extra benefit for its continuing operations there.[27]

PUBLIC RELATIONS

Although public relations is concerned with images, it has not had a very good image of its own. Too often it is associated with telling the world how good the company is or with explaining away the company's mistakes. For our

[27] *Business Abroad*, May 27, 1968, pp. 22, 23.

purposes here, we will define public relations as the efforts of the company to be a good citizen in all of its markets. We are primarily concerned with corporate *behavior*, although we recognize that the corporate image and corporate communication with its various publics are essential elements of a public relations program. Christian Herter, Jr., gave another useful definition of public relations. He called it "corporate diplomacy."[28] Someone else has called the public relations function "the conscience of management." Public relations is especially important in international marketing because the foreign firm is often a victim of xenophobia.

Public relations is not exactly marketing, but good relations with the public are essential to marketing success. A firm that is seen as a bad or undesirable citizen may also find itself *persona non grata* in the marketplace. The extreme reaction could be a boycott of the firm's products. In another sense, public relations can be considered as the marketing of a product, the product being the firm itself. The firm's products can enjoy continued success in the market only because of their performance and intrinsic merit, as well as their image. However, the image of the product cannot be maintained if product performance is not consistent with it. The same reasoning applies to the image and behavior of the firm.

The various publics of the firm are broader than its market. They include all those with whom the firm comes in contact. The most critical audiences, of course, are those that can affect the health and success of the firm. The firm's publics in a given foreign market can include any or all of the following: stockholders, employees, customers, suppliers, distributors, competitors, and government, as well as the general public. The importance of any particular group will vary from country to country. The firm's level of involvement in a market will also affect the publics it must deal with.

The Nature of the Public Relations Task

Research

It is useful to return to our analogy of public relations as the marketing of a product, the firm itself. Just as the first job in marketing is to become familiar with the market, so the first task of international public relations is to become familiar with the various publics of the firm in each of its markets. This involves two aspects: (1) seeing others as they see themselves, rather than using a foreign viewpoint or stereotype, and (2) seeing the company as they see it. Thus public relations should begin with market intelligence. It follows logically that the initial communications in public relations are from the publics to the firm rather than the other way around, as is too common.

Gaining market intelligence about the firm's publics is not only the initial task of public relations; it is a continuing need, just as in marketing. The firm must keep open the communications channels from its publics. By being continually informed, the firm can practice preventive medicine rather than

28 *Vital Speeches*, April 15, 1966, p. 409.

finding itself forced into drastic surgery after serious trouble has developed. Too often, public relations has been used to fight fires rather than to prevent them.

Response to the Public

The purpose of intelligence gathering, of course, is to serve as a basis for action. The kind of action which is appropriate depends on the nature of the intelligence gathered. Occasionally the appropriate action in a foreign market will involve a statement or press release by the firm, as for instance, when misunderstandings or false statements are circulating. In many other instances, however, the appropriate response may be to modify the product, that is, to change the behavior of the firm. Where change is inevitable, it is far preferable to initiate the change voluntarily rather than to be forced into it by public or government action. In yet other circumstances, the correct response may be to do nothing. This would be true if the firm were unable or unwilling to change its behavior in a given situation and if a public response would exacerbate the problem. Maintaining a low profile is the answer in such a case.

Noting some host-country complaints about the international ("foreign") company is a helpful way to see a few of the problems the firm's public relations activity must deal with. In addition to problems peculiar to individual foreign markets, certain complaints tend to appear in most of the foreign markets of a firm. They arise primarily because the international firm is a foreigner in the market. The common thread running through them is that the foreign firm takes unfair advantage of the host country and otherwise abuses its position as a guest. These complaints often are expressed in emotional language, for example, "imperialistic exploitation." Table 13–2, which is a listing of Canadian rules for the behavior of foreign corporations shows them in their most rational form.

Good marketing means adapting to the market; good public relations means adapting to the firm's publics. In both cases, however, the firm is concerned about the costs and benefits involved. Although good public relations will eliminate or minimize many problems in foreign markets, some problems will persist in spite of the best corporate diplomacy. These problems provide the real challenge for management. It cannot always give in to government or public demands. There are times when management must stand firm.

Here as elsewhere, the best defense probably is a good offense. An active, imaginative public relations program as defined here is the best way to reduce the probability of extreme adverse reaction against the company. Many American companies have won praise and even awards from host governments for their corporate behavior and their imaginative and beneficial programs. Thomas Watson, chairman of IBM, has been decorated by no less than nine foreign governments. Esso, although expropriated in Peru, has a better image in Colombia. Esso organized a comprehensive collection of Colombian art and sponsored its presentation in the United States. The public acclaim led to new respect for Latin America. Esso received the Colombian government's highest decoration.[29]

[29] *Public Relations Journal* (August 1966), p. 34.

Table 13–2 Some Guiding Principles of Good Corporate Behavior for Subsidiaries in Canada of Foreign Companies

1. Pursuit of sound growth and full realization of the company's productive potential, thereby sharing the national objective of full and effective use of the nation's resources.

2. Realization of maximum competitiveness through the most effective use of the company's own resources, recognizing the desirability of progressively achieving appropriate specialization of productive operations within the internationally affiliated group of companies.

3. Maximum development of market opportunities in other countries as well as in Canada.

4. Where applicable, to extend processing of natural resource products to the extent practicable on an economic basis.

5. Pursuit of a pricing policy designed to assure a fair and reasonable return to the company and to Canada for all goods and services sold abroad, including sales to the parent company and other foreign affiliates.

6. In matters of procurement, to search out and develop economic sources of supply in Canada.

7. To develop as an integral part of the Canadian operation wherever practicable, the technological, research and design capability neces-sary to enable the company to pursue appropriate product development programs so as to take full advantage of market opportunities domestically and abroad.

8. Retention of a sufficient share of earnings to give appropriate financial support to the growth requirements of the Canadian operation, having in mind a fair return to shareholders on capital invested.

9. To work toward a Canadian outlook within management, through purposeful training programs, promotion of qualified Canadian personnel and inclusion of a major proportion of Canadian citizens on its board of directors.

10. To have the objective of a financial structure which provides opportunity for equity participation in the Canadian enterprise by the Canadian public.

11. Periodically to publish information on the financial position and operations of the company.

12. To give appropriate attention and support to recognized national objectives and established Government programs designed to further Canada's economic development and to encourage and support Canadian institutions directed toward the intellectual, social and cultural advancement of the community.

Source: Department of Trade and Commerce, *Foreign-Owned Subsidiaries in Canada*, Queen's Printer, Ottawa, 1967, pp. 40–41.

Obviously, the foreign marketing task is easier for a company that enjoys an attractive image based on positive achievements.

Organizational Aspects

Because of its need to be sensitive to local publics in each of its markets, the firm must rely heavily on local staff. The firm can centralize policy making and general administration, but day-to-day operations will be up to people within the market. The firm will have nationals on its staff in each country and may wish to use a local public relations agency where one is available. The international public relations manager will assure consistency in the firm's program and image from country to country. He also will act as a clearinghouse of ideas and experience, much in the fashion of the international marketing manager. The size of staff will be a function of the volume of the firm's business in a market. Even where there is no separate person responsible for public relations in a country, management must be aware of its role. Guidelines from central administration can help local management in this respect.

Regardless of the titles given to persons working on the firm's public relations program, these people should have sufficient prestige and influence to affect company decision making. This is essential, given the importance of good corporate behavior and image in foreign markets. Serious errors in public relations can more than offset a strong marketing program. There are some embarrassing examples of American firms that were good marketers abroad but that lost out in a market because of public relations failures.

Public relations is important to effective marketing, but the two functions can well be organizationally separate. Although public relations is a profitable activity for the company, its purpose is not immediate sales. By lumping the public relations and marketing functions together, the firm runs the risk that marketing management might take a short-run view, focusing on the annual profit and loss statement. Public relations should be sufficiently independent of functional management to be able to consider the interest of the public as well as the long-run interest of the firm in the particular market.

CONCLUSION

Gone forever are the days when business could concentrate exclusively on profits and efficiency. In world markets today, the multinational firm must be concerned about its several publics also. Indeed, it must be very careful in relating to these publics because its profits and efficiency will be affected by them as well as by the purely technical aspects of its operations. For this reason, corporate diplomacy has become an important element of international business management, and one in which future managers must develop expertise.

Questions

13.1 Why does personal selling often play a relatively larger promotional role in foreign markets?

13.2 Why is personal selling done largely within national boundaries rather than internationally?

13.3 Since most of the task of sales force management must be done within the national market, what contributions can the international marketing manager make?

13.4 How can comparative analysis of the firm's foreign markets help the international marketer with local sales force management?

13.5 Explain how the multinational firm may have an advantage over local firms in training the sales force and evaluating their performance.

13.6 Discuss the influence of the firm's level of involvement on the personal selling function in foreign markets.

13.7 Discuss the potential competitive advantage of the multinational firm in sales promotion activities in foreign markets.

13.8 Explain the use of the elements of the marketing mix as part of the firm's international promotion.

13.9 How does the establishment of local operations aid the firm's promotion in foreign markets?

13.10 Review the promotional services of the U.S. Department of Commerce, that is, trade missions, trade centers, and the commercial exhibits program. Who might use these, and how?

13.11 How might the firm use the international trade fairs?

13.12 Discuss the role of the Washington representative in international marketing.

13.13 Identify the various publics of the firm in foreign markets.

13.14 What would be the elements of a sound public relations program?

13.15 "Public relations is corporate diplomacy." "Public relations is selling the company to the public." Are these views consistent?

13.16 What is the relationship of public relations to marketing?

13.17 Federated Motors, a large American manufacturer of automobiles, has plants in several Latin American countries. Recently, the firm (along with several others) has been attacked in the newspapers of some of these countries. The general tenor of the attacks is anticapitalist, anti-Yankee, and anti-imperialist, although some more specific charges are listed also. Advise the firm on its public relations program.

Further Readings

Books:

Albaum, Gerald, *State Government Promotion of International Business* (Tucson, Ariz.: University of Arizona, Division of Economic and Business Research, 1968).

Davis, Kenneth R., and Frederick E. Webster, Jr., *Sales Force Management* (New York: Ronald Press, 1968).

Jefkins, Frank, *Public Relations in World Marketing* (London: Crosby Lockwood and Son, Ltd., 1966).

Kean, Geoffrey, *The Public Relations Man Abroad* (New York: Praeger, 1968).

Kramer, Roland L., *International Marketing,* 3rd ed. (Cincinnati, Ohio: South-Western Publishing Co., 1970), chaps. 4, 5.

Liander, Bertil, Vern Terpstra, Michael Yoshino, and A. A. Sherbini, *Comparative Analysis for International Marketing,* Marketing Science Institute (Boston: Allyn and Bacon, 1967, chap. 3.

Articles:

Barovick, Richard, "Washington's Elite Corps of International Reps for Corporate Business Abroad," *Business Abroad* (April 1970), pp. 17–19, 37.

Goodnow, James D., "American Overseas Business Promotion Offices," *Michigan Business Review* (January 1970), pp. 6–11.

Murray, Thomas J., "The Overseas Boom in Door to Door Selling, *Dun's Review* (November 1964), pp. 35–37.

Root, Franklin R., "International Marketplace, International Trade Fairs," *The American-Germany Review* (April 1965), pp. 20–25.

Sawyer, Howard G., "International Public Relations and Marketing: How To Make Them Work Together," *Business Abroad* (March 1970), pp. 30–31.

14

PRICING IN
INTERNATIONAL
MARKETING

Pricing is a critical and difficult marketing management function; critical because the firm's attainment of its profit goal is intimately related to the soundness of its pricing practices, and difficult because it depends on a complex web of cost, competitive, and demand factors. The diagrams of the economist in price theory show that the correct price is indicated by the intersection of the marginal revenue curve with the marginal cost curve. It is because these curves are impossible to construct in real life that pricing is so complicated.

If the firm could define its marginal revenue and marginal cost curves, pricing would be a simple exercise in mathematics. Or if the firm merely accepted the price of a purely competitive market, there would be no pricing function at all; the market, rather than the marketer, would set the price. But because these situations do not exist, consideration of the pricing function and pricing policies is necessary. The firm does have to make pricing decisions.

Several extra complexities are involved in pricing in international marketing in addition to the usual pricing problems faced by the national firm in its domestic market. Perhaps the best way to examine the pricing problems in the multinational company is to identify the kinds of pricing decisions the firm has to make. We will use the following classification of international pricing problems: (1) export prices and terms, (2) transfer pricing in international marketing, (3) foreign market pricing, and (4) coordinating pricing in international marketing.

EXPORT PRICES AND TERMS

Since the firm's first international involvement is usually through exporting, it is appropriate to begin our discussion with the question, How should the firm price for exports? Obviously, it should price to achieve its goal in export

413

markets. This goal may be long-run profits or short-run profits, or something else, perhaps a certain market penetration. In this discussion, we will assume that the firm is committing itself to exporting on a continuing basis and thus is concerned with long-run profits and market position. A short-run viewpoint, although not necessarily bad or shortsighted, does call for different pricing policies. The firm that sees export markets as dumping places for temporary surpluses or as a chance to make a one-time killing will have prices appropriate to these goals. This situation does not characterize most exporters, however, and we will consider the more common case of long-run export involvement.

The firm committed to export marketing on a continuing basis will encounter a number of questions not faced in domestic pricing. Some of these questions are, What is the relation between export prices and domestic prices? What about tariffs? transport costs? export packaging? insurance? foreign taxes?

Export Prices versus Domestic Prices

One starting point for the firm is to compare export prices with domestic prices. Should f.o.b. plant export prices be greater than, equal to, or less than domestic prices? There are arguments for each position. If costs associated with export sales are greater than those associated with domestic sales, perhaps prices should be higher also. A variety of costs may be peculiar to exporting; others may simply be higher for various reasons. For example, exports may require special packaging and handling. Extra costs may arise in translating and processing export orders, especially if extra government documents are needed both at home and abroad. Credit and collection costs may be greater. If the company has an export department, its operating costs may be higher as a percent of sales.

A careful cost accounting is needed, however, before concluding that costs are higher for exports. Some of the costs allocated to domestic sales would *not* apply to export sales, for example, domestic promotion or marketing research. Exports should have to bear only those costs for which they are directly responsible plus, perhaps, a share of general overhead expenses. Management should beware of the subjective attitude that foreign sales are less reliable or more risky; no buyer should be penalized just because he is foreign. The actual costs and risks of selling to the foreign buyer have to be carefully evaluated on an objective basis.

Even if export sales are found to have higher costs, it does not follow necessarily that the right export price should be higher than the domestic price. The best export price is the one that maximizes both the company's export profits and total profits. If foreign markets have lower income levels or more elastic demand curves, the most profitable export price may be less than the domestic price. The firm even may find it necessary to modify the package or to simplify the product to get the lower price needed for foreign markets.

What about making the export price the same as the domestic price? Setting the f.o.b. plant price the same for both export and domestic sales appears to be a nondiscriminatory way to price, making all sales equally attractive. Althought there is no a priori reason for export prices to be different from domestic prices, the proper pricing strategy is not a function of some abstract statement of equality or nondiscrimination. The best price for export markets and for the company is a compromise between market and company factors. The resultant compromise price is not necessarily the same as the domestic price; in fact, it is quite unlikely to be, because the internal and external price determinants are different in the export and domestic situations.

Export Price Less than Domestic

Setting the f.o.b. plant price lower on exports favors export sales. Some good reasons for such an approach are the following:

1. The lower income levels in foreign markets may require the firm to set a lower price to achieve sales in any volume.
2. Foreign competition may dictate a lower price.
3. The firm realizes that even with a lower f.o.b. plant price, the product still can be more expensive in the foreign market because of the transport and tariff costs and other add-ons. All these add-ons could price the product out of the market if the f.o.b. plant price were high.
4. The firm may consider that costs of exports are actually less because research and development, overhead, and some other costs are already covered by domestic sales.

Thomas Edison is said to have employed this marginal cost strategy in export pricing. He figured out that total profits from light-bulb sales would be much greater if he could just cover his marginal costs with some contribution to overhead from export sales. Of course, this strategy makes sense only if the foreign market has a more elastic demand curve and "needs" a lower price. If the foreign demand curve is the same as the American, the profit-maximizing price will be the same.

In evaluating this third approach, a new element enters. The firm that sells abroad at less than domestic prices may be accused of dumping. Dumping is the technical term to describe sales of goods in foreign markets at prices lower than those in the producer's home market. One might wonder why recipient nations complain of such favored treatment. The reason is that their producers claim that such low-price competition is unfair to them. Because of such producer resentment the industrialized countries tend to penalize imports sold at "dumping" prices. The less developed countries, on the other hand, favor the lower priced imports, unless they have a competing industry.

At a given point in time, marginal cost pricing may be the profit-maximizing strategy for the firm, given the cost and market situation. The firm is, in some sense, subsidizing export sales by not pricing on a full cost basis. When the time comes for a new investment decision, however, the firm must reconsider its export price base. Marginal cost pricing for exports may be appropriate when there is excess capacity; when new investment and/or new capacity are needed, company profit goals would probably indicate full cost pricing for exports. The excess capacity justification for lower export prices would no longer exist.

Another problem in lower f.o.b. plant prices for exports is that the producing division has less interest in export sales. In fact, they would have a bias against export sales as long as they can sell at higher prices domestically. Only when no domestic alternative presents itself are export sales interesting.

One of America's largest electrical equipment manufacturers noted that its producing divisions used incremental pricing (marginal cost pricing) when domestic demand was down. The export department thus found itself in a stronger market position when domestic sales were weak. Unfortunately, its position would reverse itself when domestic sales were strong. Even in this large company, export sales had only a residual, second-class position. As this pricing practice was based on domestic *supply and demand conditions, it is not surprising that the firm was having trouble maintaining a consistent position in* foreign *markets.*

Market-Oriented Export Pricing

Although the domestic price is a logical starting point in considering proper export prices, the firm runs a risk in beginning the export price analysis with an emphasis on domestic supply considerations. The proper question is not whether the export price is more or less than the domestic. The marketing manager or export manager instead should ask, What export price will maximize return on export investment? And the return on export activities should be compared with domestic alternatives.

A good starting point for export price analysis is the determination of conditions in foreign markets.[1] What are the demand and competitive situations in the target markets? At what price or within what price range could the firm's product sell? By determining the relevant demand schedules in foreign markets, the export manager can get a base price for evaluating export profit opportunities. Having figured out what the market will pay, the firm must see if it can sell at that price, a determination it makes by working back from the market price (base price) to the cost structure of the firm. The varioius intermediary margins, taxes, duties, transport costs, and handling costs must be subtracted from the consumer price. The resulting figure will help determine the firm's f.o.b. plant price for exports.

A numerical example will illustrate this approach. Assume the firm is selling a consumer product to an EEC country and market research shows that the target price in the market should be about 28 DM (Deutschemarks), 35 NF (new French francs), or $7.00 United States equivalent.[2] The analysis must begin with the $7.00 market price.

---

[1] See Franklin R. Root, *Strategic Planning for Export Marketing* (Scranton, Penna.: International Textbook Company, 1966), pp. 55–70.
[2] Assuming 4 DM to the dollar and 5 NF to the dollar.

1. Market price		$7.00
2. Less 40% retail margin on selling price		2.80
	Retailer cost =	4.20
3. Less 11% wholesale markup on his cost		.42
	Wholesaler cost =	3.78
4. Less 5% importer markup on his cost		.18
	Importer cost =	3.60
5. Less 10% value added tax on landed value plus duty		.33
	c.i.f. value plus duty =	3.27
6. Less 9% duty on landed value (c.i.f.)		.27
	Landed or c.i.f. value =	3.00
7. Less insurance and shipping costs to market		.40
		$2.60

This example indicates that $2.60 is the f.o.b. plant price which will allow the firm to meet the target foreign market price of $7.00. Obviously, the $2.60 price is the result of assumptions about channels, margins, and tax and duty rates, all of which vary by product and by country. Nevertheless, the illustration shows the kinds of add-ons that inflate export prices and complicate export price calculation. We have not considered market research, promotion, or export overhead costs here, but similar expenses are incurred domestically also. This example shows the kind of analysis necessary for the exporter to determine his competitiveness in foreign markets. Freight forwarders, distributors, and other service organizations would be information sources for such an analysis.

If this $2.60 f.o.b. plant price for exports compares favorably with the price for domestic sales, the firm is in a strong pricing position for exports. "Compares favorably" means that the f.o.b. plant price for exports is the same as, or greater than, the f.o.b. plant price for domestic sales. Exports, however, usually will not be found in this enviable pricing situation. The greater number of intermediaries and taxes involved in exporting tend to put exports at a pricing disadvantage.

If the $2.60 price is less than the f.o.b. plant price on domestic sales, the firm must consider several alternatives.

1. It can forget about exporting, which may be a wise decision *if* it has plentiful opportunity for profitable growth in the domestic market. If serious constraints threaten domestic growth, the firm may need to keep the foreign market option open.

2. The firm can consider marginal cost pricing for exports if it has excess capacity that is expected to continue for some reasonable time in the future. This would allow exports to increase the firm's profits for so long as no more attractive domestic opportunities arose. In this situation, it would not be accurate to say that export sales are less profitable than domestic sales, since there is no domestic market for this output.

3. The firm can try to shorten the distribution channel, for example, by selling direct to wholesalers or large retailers. Each step in the channel costs the firm

something extra. Whether elimination of certain steps lowers costs for the exporter depends on how well he can perform or shift the functions eliminated.

4. The firm can modify or simplify the product to make it cheaper or more competitive. A stripped-down model and smaller sizes or packaging are ways to achieve this. The company may also try to change the product to make it fit the requirements for a different, and lower, duty or tax classification.

5. The firm can consider foreign manufacturing or assembly or licensing as ways to tap foreign markets while avoiding many of the steps that inflate export prices. Although foreign manufacturing involves greater commitment, it could be the most profitable method if the foreign markets are large enough.

In the example given, duty rates were only 9 percent. In cases where duty rates are much higher, say, 30 percent or more, goods are often smuggled in to avoid the duty. This is not part of the firm's strategy, but it may happen where its goods enjoy a strong consumer franchise in the high-duty country. The firm might suspect that smuggling is going on if it observes unusually high exports to a neighboring country with a low duty on the product.

Export Price Quotes

Finding the right foreign market prices and f.o.b. plant prices is one important task of export marketing. In addition to proper pricing, however, the export marketer must be market oriented in his price quotations and conditions of sale. Although also true in domestic marketing, it has particular significance in foreign sales. The base foreign market price calculated above was a consumer price. Here we will consider the price and terms to the importer-buyer, who is usually the final buyer insofar as the exporter is concerned.

Currency of Quotation

A first question here concerns the currency used for the price quotation. The American firm quotes in United States dollars domestically and would like to do the same on exports. Quoting dollar prices is easier than figuring the price in a number of foreign currencies, especially if these change in value from time to time. The arithmetic is the least important aspect, however. Two other aspects have more influence on the choice of currency for quotation. First, the importer would prefer all quotes in his own currency for easier comparison of the offers of various foreign and national suppliers. Second, both exporter and importer may have strong worries about the foreign exchange risk. If the importer's currency is susceptible to devaluation, he would prefer the price quote in his own currency so that on the due date of his invoice he will not have to pay a larger number of francs or cruzeiros for a given dollar amount. Similar reasoning lies behind the American exporter's preference for a dollar quote: the exporter does not want to receive fewer dollars when payment is finally made.

Assume, for example, the American exporter has a shipment for France worth $5,000, or 25,000 NF, with payment due in sixty days in French francs. If the French franc is devalued by 15 percent between quotation and payment date, the importer will still pay 25,000 NF but this now translates into only $4,250. In this case, the exporter suffers heavy losses. Conversely, if the quote had been in dollars, the French importer would still pay only $5,000 but this would cost him 28,750 NF instead of 25,000, and he would be the loser. Although either party could hedge his position in the forward exchange market, the cost of hedging tends to be high precisely when it is most necessary, that is, when devalation is most likely. Hedging is often used as a precaution when imminent devaluation is not a threat.

How is the conflict resolved? The choice of currency for the price quotation depends partly on trade practice in the country and industry in question, but also partly on the bargaining position of the parties. In a buyer's market, the exporter will be anxious for sales and will tend to yield to the importer's desires. In a seller's market, the situation will be reversed.

In France in 1968–1969, serious concern arose about possible devaluation of the franc. Companies selling into France faced the threat with different strategies. Some firms refused to bill in French francs and demanded United States dollars or Deutschemarks. Although they changed their currency quotation, they continued normal credit terms. Other firms, for varying reasons, continued to quote prices in French francs but demanded payment in a much shorter time than they had before the currency crisis. Exporters that still had an open position in French francs, that is, an account receivable, could hedge in the forward exchange market. Because of the uncertainty concerning the franc, however, the costs of forward cover were very high. In May 1969, the ninety-day forward rate of the French franc against the dollar was at a discount of 29 percent per annum.

British sterling provides a somewhat different example. Because of its role as the world's second leading trading and financing currency, sterling quotes were used for trade not only with the United Kingdom but also for the pricing of many shipping services and much of the commodity trading originating in the Afro-Asian countries. Many of those involved in all these kinds of trade suffered losses in the 1967 devaluation of sterling. As a result, many countries and companies changed their pricing quotes out of sterling. The above examples showed currencies devaluing against the United States dollar. As American tourists and businessmen learned to their chagrin in August 1971, the American dollar can also depreciate relative to other currencies.

Export Price Quotations

Export price quotations are different from those used in domestic selling and generally more complex. The practices of many nations have to be considered. To lessen the confusion, two widely used lists of relevant definitions have been drawn up: the "Revised American Foreign Trade Definitions—1941" and another by the International Chamber of Commerce. Although these definitions are helpful in clarifying what is meant by the price quote, it is still useful to the exporter to assure agreement on the exact meaning of the terms he is using, so that he and the importer both know their respective duties and liabilities. See Table 14–1 for a listing of terms.

Table 14–1   Export Price Quotations*

I. ex (point of origin)
ex factory, ex mine, ex warehouse, and so on
II. f.o.b. (free on board)
1. f.o.b. (named inland carrier)
2. f.o.b. freight allowed to (named point of exportation)
3. f.o.b. vessel (named port of shipment)
4. f.o.b. (named inland point in country of importation)
III. f.a.s. (free along side)
f.a.s. vessel (named port of shipment)
IV. C&F (cost and freight)
C&F (named point of destination)
V. c.i.f. (cost, insurance, freight)
c.i.f. (named point of destination) ex c.i.f. Hamburg
VI. ex dock
ex dock (named port of importation)

* These quotes are defined in detail in the "Revised American Foreign Trade Definitions —1941."

The price quotations are important partly because they spell out the legal responsibilities of each party. The particular quotation to be used on a transaction is naturally open to conflict. The seller favors a quote that gives him the least liability and responsibility, such as f.o.b. (free on board) his plant. In this case, the exporter's responsibility and liability both end when the goods are put on a carrier at his plant. The importer-buyer, on the other hand, favors a c.i.f. price (cost, insurance, and freight to port of discharge) or an ex dock (port of importation) price,[3] either of which means his worries and responsibilities begin only when the goods are in his own country. The importer favors c.i.f. pricing also because it makes it easier for him to compare the prices of different exporting nations and those of national suppliers.

Generally, a market orientation would indicate c.i.f. (port of importation) pricing by the exporter. Note that the price quotation does *not* affect the total amount paid or received but merely indicates the division of labor in providing for various transportation, handling, and insurance arrangements. It may be that the total burden of these arrangements is lessened when each party does what he is most qualified to do. For example, the exporter would deal with his fellow nationals in arranging transport to the port, insurance, and overseas shipping, whereas the importer would deal through his own countrymen with the unloading and transportation in his country. Occasionally, the importer

[3] The ex dock (port of importation) price is greater than the c.i.f. price for the same destination because it includes unloading costs and duty.

is a large international organization—one of the Japanese trading companies, for example—that is better qualified to handle insurance and transportation than is the exporter. If the importer has such an operation, he can gain economies of scale by taking these tasks out of the exporter's hands.

Although the list of export price quotations goes far beyond those mentioned above, a lengthy technical discussion is not necessary here.[4] Our concern is to emphasize the strategic, rather than the legal, aspects of export price quotations. Once the export marketer has defined his goals and identified the relevant parameters, he can choose the export price quotation that best fits these constraints.

Export Credit and Terms

Export credit and terms is another area of technical and legal complexity, but our concern is to identify the marketing implications of credit and terms rather than the technical details. For the latter, banks, credit institutions, and manuals are available to aid the exporter.[5] What the export marketer needs to know is how the use of export credit and terms can help to achieve not just maximum sales but especially maximum profits in exports.

The task facing the export marketer is to choose payment terms that satisfy importers yet safeguard the interests of the exporter. On purely financial considerations, the exporter would favor very hard terms, that is, cash in advance of shipment—or even in advance of production for custom items. The competitive situation seldom allows such hard terms, but they may be used if political conditions are very unstable or if foreign exchange allocations for imports are uncertain in the country of destination. Of course, the foreign government may forbid cash-in-advance payments by its importers. Because importers dislike bearing the financial burden implied in cash-in-advance terms, the exporter normally can demand prepayment only when producing merchandise to an importer's specifications.

In lieu of cash in advance, the export marketer can consider a range of terms that generally increase the payment convenience and lessen the burden to the buyer while increasing the risks and financial burdens of the exporter. The common payment methods in order of increasing attractiveness to the *importer* are the following:

1. Cash in advance
2. Letters of credit
3. Time or sight drafts (bills of exchange)
4. Open account
5. Consignment

[4] For a good detailed discussion of export price quotations, see Roland L. Kramer, *International Marketing*, 3rd ed. (Cincinnati, Ohio: South-Western Publishing Co., 1970), pp. 131–148.
[5] See Kramer, *International Marketing*, pp. 262–319.

Letters of Credit

Letters of credit and drafts are the most common forms of export financing. They are relatively hard terms favoring the exporter in that they spell out specific responsibilities and payment times for the importer, although they do not preclude credit extension. For example, time drafts are customarily drawn for periods ranging from thirty to 180 days after sight or after date. The exporter usually feels more secure with a letter of credit than with a draft.

A *draft* is drawn by the exporter on the importer, who makes it into a trade acceptance by writing on it the word "accepted," followed by his signature. His signature makes payment his legal obligation. The *letter of credit* is similar, except that it is drawn on a bank and becomes a bank acceptance rather than a trade acceptance. The bank's entrance into the payment process means greater assurance of payment for the exporter.

Open Account

Open account sales are made on terms agreed to between buyer and seller but without documents specifying clearly the importer's payment obligations. Open account terms involve less paper work and give more flexibility to both parties. The legal recourse of the exporter in case of default is more complicated, and less satisfactory, than under the terms discussed previously. Open account sales are most attractive to the importer but, because of the risks to the exporter, they tend to be limited to foreign subsidiaries, other companies related to the exporter—that is, joint ventures or licensees—or certain foreign customers with whom the exporter has had a long and favorable experience.

As a further precaution in open account sales, the exporter must consider the availability of foreign exchange in the importing country. In countries with tight foreign exchange positions, imports covered by documentary drafts for collection generally receive priority in foreign exchange allocation over imports on open account.

Consignment

Consignment sales are not really sales because the exporter retains title until the importer sells the goods to final customers or third parties. Because the exporter owns the goods longer in this method than in any other, his financial burdens and risks are greatest. In addition, his legal recourse is more difficult in case of misbehavior by the importer. Foreign exchange allocations are also more difficult to obtain when the consignee has finally sold the goods. These problems tend to limit consignment arrangements to the exporter's branches or subsidiaries abroad.

Some points favoring the use of consignment contracts should be noted, however. The importer likes them because they reduce his risk and require no additional working capital. Of course, his working capital needs could also be covered by the exporter's extending credit to cover his sales period. However, when the exporter wants to introduce goods to a foreign market, something like a consignment arrangement might be necessary to encourage the importer to handle the new merchandise. Furthermore, if the exporter wishes to retain some control over the foreign market price of his product, this is most feasible under a consignment contract. He can set the price when he owns the goods, as he does under a consignment contract.

Managing Export Credit

In the decade following World War II, American firms had world markets almost to themselves alone. It was a seller's market, and American firms were the principal sellers. They could afford to be rather strict in the terms they extended to foreign importers. As European and Japanese companies began to enter world markets in the late 1950s and 1960s, they used credit as one way of breaking into markets where Americans had dominated. Their governments generally supported them with export credit loans and insurance. American firms began to lose sales as other nations established strong export positions. In many cases, the American companies' loss of market position was due to noncompetitiveness on credit rather than on price.

FCIA

American companies and their government were not very quick to react to the aggressive export selling by other nations. In late 1961, the Export-Import Bank of the United States (Eximbank) worked with the private American insurance industry to establish the Foreign Credit Insurance Association (FCIA). Over fifty leading stock and mutual insurance companies joined FCIA. Through the Eximbank, the government supports FCIA. It underwrites all the political risks and, on request, part of the commercial risks of the policies issued by FCIA.

FCIA has thus become a partnership between the Eximbank and private insurance companies to provide protection to American exporters when they are obliged to sell on extended terms. For various reasons, export credit insurance got off to a slow start, but improvements and expansion of the program led to greater use of FCIA facilities. In fiscal 1969, FCIA issued or renewed policies aggregating over $824 million.

FCIA credit insurance programs are of two types, short term and long term. Short-term coverage is up to 180 days and can be comprehensive or simply political. Comprehensive coverage includes both political risks—that is, currency inconvertibility, cancellation of import license, expropriation, loss due to war, and so on—and commercial risks—that is, insolvency and protracted default. Medium-term insurance is from 181 days to five years and includes the same choice of comprehensive or political coverage short-term insurance does.[6]

Credit as Marketing

Because credit extension to foreign buyers is often a competitive necessity for the exporter, he must seek to use it effectively rather than bemoan using it. To hear export credit managers boast that their credit losses are lower than

[6] Detailed information on FCIA is available free from their office at 250 Broadway, New York, N.Y., 10007.

those of the firm's domestic operations is not unusual. But actually their achievement is less than laudable because it reflects discrimination against foreign buyers by maintaining more rigid standards for them. Such a policy probably does not lead to an optimal level of export sales, and it weakens the firm's competitive position as well. The firm should accept credit extension as one of its competitive weapons to gain customer satisfaction and continuing relations.

The exporter can count on outside help for his credit task. In extending credit, the firm can use export credit insurance where this is deemed desirable. The American program through FCIA has counterparts in most major exporting nations. The credit manager can also count on help in getting credit information on foreign customers. The American firm has four possible sources. (The situation is similar in other exporting countries.)

1. Dun and Bradstreet has an international credit-rating service which parallels their domestic operation.
2. Banks can help through their foreign branch or correspondent relations.
3. The Department of Commerce's *World Trade Directory Reports* usually give names of other suppliers of the foreign firm, and these provide a valuable follow up to other sources. See Figure 10–2.
4. The Foreign Credit Interchange Bureau (FCIB) is the International Department of the National Association of Credit Management and is composed of active practitioners in the field. FCIB provides not only credit information but also offers a world-wide collection service.

Barter, An Old-New Method

Although the word "barter" conjures up images of primitive premonetary economies, it is also becoming an important method in modern export selling. It becomes, in effect, a way of pricing and putting terms on a company's exports. No company likes to exchange its exports for goods offered by the buyer; it prefers to sell for hard currencies that are a much more convenient medium of exchange. Nevertheless, barter deals are increasing because they open some markets that would otherwise be unreachable.

Many countries have chronic balance of payments deficits and consequent shortages of foreign exchange. To allocate this scarce foreign exchange, they set priorities on the imports they will allow into their countries. Firms whose products are not on the favored list of permitted imports face a difficult marketing task. The alternatives open to the exporting firm include giving up the market, manufacturing within the market, or possibly, bartering for some goods the country has in excess supply. If the nation can sell the goods itself for hard currencies, it prefers to do so. If it cannot sell the excess goods, however, it considers itself to have a relatively low opportunity cost for any imports it "buys" with them. The international firm can trade its products for these surplus goods of the country. It must then find some way to sell or use these goods to profit from the "sale," that is, the barter transaction.

Communist countries have been leading practitioners of the barter approach, but it is not limited to them, or even to the less developed countries with balance of payments deficits. For example, Ford of Britain has bartered cars for coffee (Colombia), cranes (Norway), toilet seats (Finland), potatoes (Spain), and cotton (Sudan).[7] Companies are not accustomed to the complexities of bartering and therefore often rely on specialized intermediaries to sell the goods they receive in exchange for their exports.

Because bartering is different, complex, and may well be less profitable than regular export sales, most firms would consider it a necessary evil or a third-best solution. In company planning, however, it is possible to consider a more positive approach. If a firm has unlimited opportunities in nonbarter transactions, it should probably pursue them to the exclusion of barter deals. However, if the firm has more production capacity than market opportunities, and if the future trading system will have numerous countries with balance of payments deficits and exchange restrictions, then the firm should consider how to optimize its profits in this real, albeit unhappy, situation.

In reacting positively to barter opportunities, the firm should evaluate the costs and benefits of the operation and set up the appropriate organization. Some of the costs are (1) the possibility of a lower return on some barter deals, (2) the risks in handling unfamiliar goods, (3) possibly longer time before payment is received, (4) the possibility of conflict with its hard-currency export markets, and (5) long and complex negotiations with buying countries, many of which lack expertise.

Some of the benefits of barter can be (1) the use of excess capacity to cover variable costs and to make a contribution toward fixed costs and total profit, (2) maintenance of exports and employment when these are important to the firm and the exporting country (this was a consideration for Ford of Britain), (3) entry into otherwise closed markets and gain of those governments' good will (possibly leading to a privileged position in the future, if these countries became hard-currency buyers), and (4) possible development of new economical supply sources. The country whose goods the firm is accepting may be able to be developed into a new supplier of components or raw materials for the firm.

In organizing for barter deals, a first requirement would be to have a market intelligence system to identify and evaluate opportunities. Special negotiating expertise also would have to be developed. Instead of relying entirely on intermediaries for selling the goods received, the firm might wish to increase its own capabilities in this direction as barter business becomes more important. Top management, of course, would have to actively accept barter dealings. Ford of Britain, for example, appointed one executive as "Special Transactions Manager."

Chrysler has been involved in barter deals on numerous occasions. The following are two examples of successful barter by the company's export department.

[7] *Business Abroad* (December 1968), p. 27.

A Middle-Eastern country had no foreign exchange but a surplus of hazelnuts. The government wanted to exchange trucks for hazelnuts. Chrysler finally located an import house that would buy 100 tons at a discount. The nuts were shipped to the import house. On receipt, the importer paid the money into an account against which several trucks were sold.

One year when coffee prices were low, Colombia had a serious foreign exchange shortage. A farm group had a surplus potato crop and wanted to buy trucks. Chrysler made contact with several American brokers. Then it was learned that the existence of a potato disease in Latin America meant that the United States Department of Agriculture would not allow the potatoes to be imported. Turning to Europe, Chrysler finally located a buyer in France. He in turn sold the potatoes to a manufacturer of industrial alcohol.[8]

Switch Trading

Switch trading is a more complex phenomenon for accomplishing similar results. Many countries have bilateral trade and payments agreements. Because the bilateral trade seldom balances exactly, these accounts usually contain a supply of nonconvertible currencies. The nation with these balances does not need them to buy more goods from the bilateral trading partner and it cannot use them elsewhere because they are inconvertible. Thus the nation is quite willing to transfer them to a third country, even at a discount, to obtain useful goods. The international firm may be able to sell its exports to such a third country through a specialist in switch trading. These specialists are located primarily in Austria and Switzerland. As Figure 14–1 shows, more than seventy countries have bilateral payments agreements. The communist countries are most heavily involved.

The practice of switch trading is not sufficiently widespread to be explained in detail here. Furthermore, it usually requires outside expertise. However, the international marketer should be aware of it as another way of entering otherwise closed markets. The evaluation of switch trading as an alternative method of selling involves very nearly the same considerations that were discussed above for barter.

Leasing in International Markets

Leasing is an important pricing-financing-marketing device for expensive equipment. Although more prevalent in the United States than abroad, leasing is rapidly growing in foreign markets. For example, Clark Equipment Company has a leasing subsidiary called Clark Rental Corporation. It leases forklift trucks. The vice-president expects that by the early 1970s, leasing will be more popular abroad than in this country.[9]

Although the principles and advantages of leasing are the same internationally and domestically, the advantages may be more important in foreign

[8] Henry F. Stevens, Credit Manager, Chrysler Export Division, in a lecture at the University of Michigan, March 1968.
[9] *Business Abroad*, May 13, 1968, p. 15.

markets than in the United States. For example, one advantage of leasing (to the lessee) is the ability to get expensive equipment at a low annual cost. In foreign markets, which are more short of capital than the United States, this is a very significant pricing-marketing argument. Another advantage to the lessee is the better service and maintenance available under the lease con-

Any countries that maintain bilateral trading agreements are potential candidates for switch trading as well. The table below indicates the bilateral payments agreements in force between major trading nations. Countries that are not included but do maintain bilateral payments agreements: Afghanistan, Burundi, Cameroon, Central African Republic, Congo (Brazzaville), Congo (Kinshasa), Cyprus, Dahomey, Indonesia, Iraq, North Korea, Laos, Mauritania, Mongolia, Nepal, Netherlands, Niger, Rwanda, Senegal, Sierra Leone, Somalia, Sweden, Taiwan, Upper Volta, Uruguay, North and South Vietnam. In addition to the agreements shown, certain countries that are non-IMF members have agreements with other non-IMF members that are not depicted.

Figure 14–1 is a matrix ("BI's Road Map to Major Bilateral Payments Agreements") whose rows and columns are the following countries, in the same order on both axes: Albania, Algeria, Argentina, Austria, Belgium, Brazil, Bulgaria, Cambodia, Ceylon, Chile, Mainland China, Columbia, Cuba, Czechoslovakia, Denmark, Finland, East Germany, Ghana, Greece, Guinea, Hungary, Iceland, India, Iran, Israel, Lebanon, Mali, Mexico, Morocco, Norway, Pakistan, Paraguay, Peru, Poland, Portugal, Rumania, Spain, Sudan, Switzerland, Syria, Tunisia, Turkey, UAR, USSR, Yugoslavia. An "X" in a cell indicates a bilateral payments agreement between the row country and the column country; the diagonal (self) cells are shaded.

The approximate agreements indicated for each country (reading across its row) are:

- **Albania:** Algeria, Austria, Ghana, Greece, Lebanon, USSR, Yugoslavia
- **Algeria:** Albania, Austria, Cuba, Czechoslovakia, Hungary, Iceland, Mali, Poland, Rumania, UAR, USSR, Yugoslavia
- **Argentina:** Mainland China, Mexico, Pakistan
- **Austria:** Brazil, Greece, Hungary, Poland, Rumania, USSR
- **Belgium:** Yugoslavia
- **Brazil:** Austria, Ceylon, Czechoslovakia, Denmark, Finland, Greece, Guinea, Hungary, Poland, Portugal, Rumania, USSR, Yugoslavia
- **Bulgaria:** Albania, Algeria, Austria, Brazil, Cambodia, Ceylon, Chile, Cuba, Ghana, Greece, Guinea, Hungary, India, Israel, Mali, Morocco, Pakistan, Rumania, Spain, Syria, Tunisia, Turkey, UAR, USSR, Yugoslavia
- **Cambodia:** Bulgaria, Ceylon, Cuba, Ghana, Poland, USSR, Yugoslavia
- **Ceylon:** Brazil, Bulgaria, Cuba, Ghana, Guinea, Poland, Rumania, Spain, USSR, Yugoslavia
- **Chile:** Argentina, Cuba, Peru, Poland
- **Mainland China:** Albania, Cuba, Czechoslovakia, Denmark, Ghana, Hungary, Poland, Rumania, Rumania, Spain, Tunisia, USSR, Yugoslavia
- **Columbia:** Cuba, Czechoslovakia, Ghana, Greece, Guinea, Hungary, Poland, Rumania, Spain, USSR, Yugoslavia
- **Cuba:** Albania, Cambodia, Chile, Ghana, Guinea, Mali, Mexico, Morocco, Poland, Spain, USSR
- **Czechoslovakia:** Algeria, Austria, Brazil, Denmark, Finland, Ghana, Greece, Guinea, India, Israel, Lebanon, Mali, Morocco, Pakistan, Rumania, Spain, Sudan, Syria, Tunisia, Turkey, UAR, USSR, Yugoslavia
- **Denmark:** Brazil, Ghana, Guinea, Hungary
- **Finland:** Brazil, Czechoslovakia, Denmark, East Germany, Hungary, Poland, Rumania, USSR
- **East Germany:** Algeria, Austria, Brazil, Ghana, Guinea, Hungary, India, Israel, Mali, Morocco, Pakistan, Rumania, Spain, Sudan, Syria, Tunisia, Turkey, UAR, USSR, Yugoslavia
- **Ghana:** Albania, Bulgaria, Ghana, Guinea, Hungary, Mali, Morocco, Poland, Rumania, UAR, USSR, Yugoslavia
- **Greece:** Bulgaria, Guinea, Hungary, Poland, Rumania, UAR, USSR, Yugoslavia
- **Guinea:** Albania, Algeria, Bulgaria, Ghana, Greece, Hungary, Mali, Morocco, Poland, UAR, USSR, Yugoslavia
- **Hungary:** Algeria, Austria, Brazil, Ceylon, Cuba, Ghana, Greece, Guinea, India, Iran, Israel, Lebanon, Mali, Morocco, Pakistan, Poland, Rumania, Spain, Sudan, Switzerland, Syria, Tunisia, Turkey, UAR, USSR
- **Iceland:** Brazil, Ghana, Greece, Poland, Rumania, USSR
- **India:** Brazil, Ghana, Greece, Poland, Rumania, Spain, UAR, USSR, Yugoslavia
- **Iran:** Ghana, Poland, Rumania
- **Israel:** Brazil, Bulgaria, Hungary, India, Poland, Rumania, Spain, Turkey, UAR, USSR
- **Lebanon:** Ghana, Greece, Poland, Rumania
- **Mali:** Albania, Algeria, Ghana, Greece, Guinea, Mali, Morocco, Poland, Rumania, Switzerland, UAR, USSR, Yugoslavia
- **Mexico:** Argentina, Cuba, Mexico, Spain
- **Morocco:** Ghana, Greece, Guinea, Hungary, Pakistan, Poland, Rumania, UAR
- **Norway:** Greece, Guinea
- **Pakistan:** Ghana, Greece, Hungary, Paraguay, Poland, Rumania, Yugoslavia
- **Paraguay:** Argentina, Cuba, Pakistan, Peru, Poland
- **Peru:** Chile, Paraguay
- **Poland:** Albania, Austria, Brazil, Ceylon, Cuba, Ghana, Hungary, India, Iran, Israel, Lebanon, Mali, Morocco, Norway, Pakistan, Rumania, Spain, Sudan, Switzerland, Syria, Tunisia, Turkey, UAR, USSR, Yugoslavia
- **Portugal:** Brazil, Hungary, Greece, Rumania, Poland, UAR
- **Rumania:** Algeria, Austria, Brazil, Cuba, Ghana, Greece, Guinea, Hungary, India, Iran, Israel, Lebanon, Mali, Morocco, Pakistan, Poland, Spain, Sudan, Switzerland, Syria, Tunisia, Turkey, UAR, USSR, Yugoslavia
- **Spain:** Brazil, Cuba, Czechoslovakia, Ghana, Guinea, Hungary, Rumania, Switzerland, Syria, Tunisia, Turkey, UAR, USSR, Yugoslavia
- **Sudan:** Czechoslovakia, Ghana, Guinea, Hungary, Israel, Poland, UAR
- **Switzerland:** Ghana, Greece, Guinea, Hungary, Poland, Rumania, Syria, UAR, Yugoslavia
- **Syria:** Czechoslovakia, Cuba, Ghana, Hungary, Poland, Rumania, Spain, UAR, USSR
- **Tunisia:** Czechoslovakia, Cuba, Ghana, Hungary, Mexico, Poland, Rumania, UAR, USSR, Yugoslavia
- **Turkey:** Czechoslovakia, Ghana, Greece, Iran, Poland, Rumania, Spain, UAR, USSR, Yugoslavia
- **UAR:** Albania, Algeria, Ghana, Guinea, Hungary, India, Israel, Mali, Morocco, Poland, Rumania, Spain, Sudan, Switzerland, Syria, Tunisia, Turkey, USSR, Yugoslavia
- **USSR:** Algeria, Belgium, Cambodia, Ceylon, Mainland China, Czechoslovakia, Finland, Ghana, Greece, Guinea, Hungary, India, Israel, Mali, Pakistan, Poland, Rumania, Spain, Syria, Tunisia, Turkey, UAR, Yugoslavia
- **Yugoslavia:** Albania, Algeria, Austria, Brazil, Cambodia, Ceylon, Czechoslovakia, Cuba, Finland, Ghana, Greece, Guinea, Hungary, India, Mali, Pakistan, Rumania, Spain, Turkey, UAR, USSR

Figure 14–1   BI's Road Map to Major Bilateral Payments Agreements

Source: Reprinted from *Solving International Business Problems*, with the permisson of the publisher, Business International Corp. (N.Y.), 1969, p. 29.

tract. In countries with shortages of trained mechanics and technicians, this maintenance service is another strong marketing argument for leasing.

Leasing in international marketing can be supported by other special arguments. In several countries, *capital incentives* (investment grants) are offered to promote capital expenditures on new plant and machinery. In addition, numerous *tax incentives* are applicable to firms investing in capital equipment. Of course, both benefits apply to outright purchase as well as to leasing. In many situations abroad, however, the lessor can absorb the tax advantages in ways not available to the lessee, thus enabling him to pass a portion of the savings on to the lessee.[10]

Leasing in international marketing is not limited to the export form of involvement but may be used in other forms as well; for example, the firm's foreign subsidiaries may well use leasing. However, unique support is given to the exporter-lessor by the Export-Import Bank of the United States. Eximbank will provide comprehensive guarantee coverage either to American companies engaged in leasing to foreign markets, or to foreign companies that import American equipment for leasing to their customers. This extra support and protection makes leasing a more attractive pricing-marketing alternative for exporters of expensive equipment.

TRANSFER PRICING IN INTERNATIONAL MARKETING

The management of export prices and terms is the first, and often the only, international pricing task facing firms. Once the firm expands its involvement beyond exporting, however, it will encounter the other international pricing problems noted at the beginning of this chapter. When a company begins to establish foreign subsidiaries, joint ventures, or licensing agreements, its international pricing becomes more complex. Transfer pricing (intracorporate pricing) is one area that has special implications for international marketing. We will consider these implications in this section on transfer pricing in international marketing.

Transfer pricing refers to prices placed on goods sold within the corporate family, that is, from division to division or to a foreign subsidiary. Transfer pricing is a problem for the large international corporation on at least two levels. The firm must search for appropriate prices on goods moving (1) from the product division(s) to the international division, and (2) from the international division to foreign subsidiaries. Where the producing division itself sells directly overseas, the first transfer-pricing situation is eliminated. Since the international division structure is common to many companies, however, it is worthwhile to examine this particular problem that can arise in selling abroad.[11] We are assuming that both the product division and the international division are profit centers.

---

[10] See George C. Parker and Henry S. Miller, "International Leasing," *Columbia Journal of World Business* (September–October, 1970), pp. 77–82.

[11] For a good and more extensive discussion of transfer pricing, see Business International, *Solving International Pricing Problems* (New York, 1965). This section is indebted to that report.

Product Division to International Division

Many firms are organized into producing divisions and an international division. The first step of goods financially, although not necessarily physically, on their way to foreign markets is from the former to the latter. The transfer price paid by the international group to the producing division should have certain characteristics if it is to optimize corporate, rather than divisional, profit. In relation to the producing division, the price should be high enough to encourage a flow of products for export. Where service or follow up is needed, the price should make the producing division willing to provide it. The transfer price will do this if sales to the international division are as attractive to the producing division as sales to other parties. The price to the international division may be even lower than to other parties if the services the international division renders (market research, promotion, and so on) warrant this.

From the viewpoint of the international division, the transfer price should be low enough to enable it to be competitive in the foreign market, to encourage promotion of the product, and to cover its costs and leave a satisfactory margin. Obviously, there is room for divisional conflict here. The producing division wants a high price, and the international division wants a low price to show profitable divisional performance. The transfer-pricing mechanism must be such that the overall corporate profit interest does not get ignored in the divisional conflict. Quite possibly a profit margin that is unattractive to one or the other division, or to both, might be worthwhile from the overall corporate viewpoint..

Assume that the producing division makes a product at a full cost of $50. It sells this to outside buyers for $60, but the transfer price to the international division is $58. The producing division may be unhappy because the markup is 20 percent lower to the international division ($8 versus $10). The international division adds its various export marketing expenses of $10 for an export cost of $68. For competitive reasons, the international division cannot sell the product for more than $72, or a $4 return. Since this is less than 6 percent of sales, the international division is also unhappy. However, the return to the corporation is $12 on $72, or almost 17 percent ($8 from the producing division plus $4 from the international division). The corporation may find this very attractive, even though both divisions are unhappy with it.

Many different approaches can be taken to solve this transfer-pricing problem. One solution is to eliminate one or the other division as a profit center. The producing division can be judged on the basis of costs and other performance criteria instead of profit. Then it can sell to the international division at a price enabling the latter to be competitive in foreign markets. Market pricing will not be handicapped by the internal markups of the transfer-pricing process, and the total corporate profit will be given greater attention.

On the other hand, the international division can operate as a service center rather than as a profit center, thus eliminating one source of conflict.

Some question arises, however, as to whether a *selling* organization will be as efficient and as motivated when it is not operating under a profit constraint. A related possibility is to have the international division act as commission agent for the producing divisions. Where the international division is not a profit center, its expenses can be allocated back to the product divisions.

Transfer at Manufacturing Cost

Where the profit centers and transfer price are maintained, several pricing alternatives are possible. At one extreme, and favoring the international division, is the transfer at direct manufacturing cost. This would be the lowest cost, probably well under what the producing division could obtain from other customers. The producing division dislikes selling at manufacturing cost because it feels it is subsidizing the international division and thereby losing out when compared with other profit centers. The firm may offset this by an accounting or memorandum profit to the producing division on their sales for export, but such memorandum profits, unfortunately, are never as satisfactory as the real thing. When the product division is unhappy, the international division may get sluggish delivery and product service because the product division satisfies more attractive domestic opportunities first.

Transfer at Arm's Length

The other extreme in transfer pricing is to charge the international division the same price any buyer outside the firm pays. This price favors the producing division because it does as well on internal as on external sales, or even better. The services rendered by the international division in addition to the elimination of the credit problem can make export sales especially profitable to the product division selling at an arm's length or outside buyer's price.

If the product has no external buyers, however, a problem arises in trying to determine an arm's length price. An artificial price has to be constructed. Further difficulties arise not only because such a price fails to take into account the services performed by the international division, but also because the international division may be noncompetitive with such a price. Finally, there is no necessary reason that the price to foreign buyers should be determined by the domestic market, since supply and demand conditions differ in foreign markets.

Transfer at Cost Plus

Between the transfer-pricing extremes just discussed is a range of prices that involve a profit split between the producing and international divisions. Starting from the cost floor, cost-plus pricing attempts to add on some amount or percentage that will make the resulting compromise price acceptable to both divisions. The "plus" may be a percentage negotiated between the divisions, a percentage of product division overhead, or a percentage return on product division investment. Transfer prices may vary from a low of cost plus 5 percent to as much as cost plus 20 percent. Further important variation can be caused by using different definitions of cost. In any case, the pricing formula is less important than the results obtained. A good transfer-pricing formula should consider total corporate profit and encourage divisional co-operation. It should also minimize executive time spent on transfer-price disagreements and keep the accounting burden to a minimum.

International Division to Foreign Subsidiary

When the international division sells goods to a foreign subsidiary of the company, the transfer-pricing problems are somewhat different. The same general criteria apply; that is, total corporate profit must be considered, inter-divisional cooperation is necessary, and management must be able to control and evaluate the contributions of different divisions. In crossing national boundaries, however, several new factors come into play, namely, the require-ments of domestic and foreign tax authorities and foreign customs officials. The firm's level of involvement is another complication because the company may want to charge a different price to each kind of buyer—wholly owned subsidiary, joint venture, licensee, and distributor. This is especially trouble-some if the firm has more than one kind of involvement in a given market.

Domestic Tax Authority's Interest

Where countries have different levels of taxation on corporate profits, it is not a matter of indifference to the company where it accumulates its profit. The firm would like to use the transfer price to get more profits in low-tax coun-tries; that is, it would like to use a low transfer price to subsidiaries in low-tax countries and a high transfer price to subsidiaries in high-tax countries. ("High" or "low" is used in reference to the tax level in the domestic country.)

American companies, for example, would be tempted to sell at low transfer prices to all countries that have lower corporate tax rates than the United States. The American Internal Revenue Service (IRS), however, is on guard against this because IRS does not want to lose taxable income to other coun-tries. Therefore, IRS carefully scrutinizes the transfer prices of international companies to assure that they are not too low. One specific demand of IRS is that export prices bear a share of domestic R&D expenses. The IRS is against marginal cost pricing and wants to be sure that an equitable portion of the income remains under United States tax jurisdiction. Another reason a firm might wish to use low transfer prices is as a method of financing new subsidiaries abroad. Regardless of the firm's motive, however, the IRS looks askance at low transfer prices.

Foreign Tax and Customs Authorities

Foreign *tax* authorities, like the IRS, wish to maximize taxable income in their jurisdiction. They watch for "unreasonably" high transfer prices. Motivations behind high transfer prices to a country could be several, based on conditions in that country. One is a high tax rate on corporate profits. Another is restric-tions on profit repatriation. Even if a country has a low corporate profit tax rate, it makes no sense to accumulate profits there if they cannot be remitted to the parent company. Fear of devaluation could be still another reason for a high transfer price to a foreign subsidiary. Profits, even if remittable, are eaten away by a devaluation.

Foreign *customs* authorities have interests that conflict with those of their colleagues in the tax office. Whereas foreign tax officials watch for high transfer prices, customs authorities watch for low transfer prices. Customs officials in many countries refuse to accept intercorporate transfer prices that are lower than arm's length distributor prices as a basis for duty valuation. They may raise the duty base by from 10 to 50 percent of the invoiced price.

For two reasons the customs authorities may have an interest in the base price on which duty is charged. On the one hand, they are concerned with the amount of revenue collected—a higher duty base means more revenue—and on the other, they are interested in the protection effect of the duty—an ad valorem tariff gives greater protection, the higher the duty base. Whatever their motivation, customs authorities are on guard against duty avoidance through low transfer prices. The firm wishing to aid a subsidiary by low transfer prices may be hindered by the customs authorities.

The Level of Involvement

We have been discussing international transfer pricing between a domestic division and a wholly owned foreign subsidiary. A new factor enters in when the firm sells to other foreign companies with which it has some association. Other things being equal, a firm would want to sell at a higher price to a joint venture than to one it fully owned. It would desire an even higher price from licensees or distributors. A low price to joint ventures or licensees means, in effect, that some of the profit is being given away outside the firm rather than merely being transferred to another part of the company.

If the firm has only one kind of involvement in each of its foreign markets, it will have some flexibility in pricing differently to each level because different tax and customs authorities are involved. Where the firm has two or more kinds of buyers in a market, the authorities will challenge different prices based merely on the fact of ownership. They will probably accept some difference based on services performed for the seller. Even with just one kind of involvement per country, the firm's pricing flexibility is constrained by its domestic tax authorities (the IRS in the United States, for example). These authorities also can challenge differences in export prices that are based only on ownership differences. Strictly speaking, transfer pricing is not involved when the firm sells to companies in which it has no equity. However, the pricing problems become related because of the surveillance of the tax and customs authorities.

Managing International Transfer Pricing

We have seen many variables that affect international transfer prices. Further sources of variation that have not been discussed include differences among the firm's product lines and between components and finished goods. Yet another constraint is the network of intercorporate relationships that often exists in international operations. Although we have considered only sales from a domestic division to a foreign subsidiary, in reality, foreign subsidiaries may sell to each other, to licensees and joint ventures, or to the domestic divisions. Joint ventures and licensees may sell to wholly owned subsidiaries. All this suggests that many different pricing arrangements are possible. Probably an optimal pricing formula exists for each of the permutations. However, developing, administering, and defending all these pricing formulas could be a monumental management task. Some simplification is probably desirable.

The need for simplification of international transfer pricing arises partly from efficiency considerations but also partly from developments outside the firm. Foreign customs officials and foreign and domestic tax authorities limit the firm's flexibility in pricing between national markets and between levels of involvement. The IRS, for example, can observe and compare an American firm's export prices to all markets and all types of buyers. It can demand justification for those differences it considers unwarranted.

Another pressure for simplification is exerted by communication among buyers. It is becoming common for subsidiary managers, licensees, or distributors to have regional meetings during which they inevitably compare notes about the prices they are paying. Discovery of price differences can cause some of them to be dissatisfied and lead to reduced performance. Yet another pressure for simplification results from the web of intercorporate relations mentioned above, for example, sales between foreign subsidiaries, joint ventures, and licensees.

The pricing alternatives for selling abroad are similar to those in domestic transfer pricing: cost, cost plus, or arm's length pricing. An export price based on direct cost is probably not acceptable to the domestic tax authorities, however, so the alternatives are really cost plus or arm's length. Some form of cost plus usually can be worked out that satisfies both domestic and foreign tax authorities as well as foreign customs authorities. The more uniform the cost-plus formula is, the better it can be defended. It might not be the most profitable formula, however.

Where an arm's length price can be determined, it has the advantages of simplicity, uniformity, and maximizing profit in the domestic operations of the company. Unfortunately, it might not achieve the firm's goals abroad. The result is that the firm will probably need a variety of international transfer-pricing formulas that meet internal goals while satisfying the external constraints. A limit on the number of formulas used will be set by the costs of developing and administering them.

Conclusions

In concluding our discussion of transfer pricing in international marketing, we can give no simple solutions. We have touched only briefly on a complex and intricate problem. In approaching this problem, the expertise of many different people is needed. The accountant, legal counsel, tax adviser, and division managers are all suppliers of input to the solution. The international marketing manager's' contribution will be primarily concerned with two aspects of the problem: the supply of goods to world markets and the foreign market impact of the transfer-pricing process. Tax considerations are important but should not outweight sound business practice and corporate pricing goals, that is, motivation, control, and evaluation of divisional or subsidiary performance as well as market penetration.

FOREIGN MARKET PRICING

Management's concern in both export pricing and international transfer pricing is with the problem of getting goods *into* foreign markets at some price that is appropriate to company goals. In both cases, the problem is one of *international* pricing. Foreign market pricing is concerned with pricing policy *within* foreign markets; as such it is a matter of *domestic* pricing rather than international pricing. However, it is a major concern of the international marketer for two reasons: (1) The firm's prices in any given foreign market are usually related to supply and demand factors beyond that nation's boundaries, and (2) an important part of the international marketing manager's task is the coordination of domestic marketing programs in each of the firm's foreign markets, which includes pricing policy.

Because foreign market pricing is pricing for a national market, all the factors and strategies in pricing that are discussed in domestic marketing texts would be relevant to any foreign market. A regular marketing text may have as many as five chapters devoted to pricing questions. We will not duplicate that coverage but merely try to indicate its relevance to foreign marketing situations. Although we will not discuss all these pricing topics, we list them in Table 14–2 so that they are in our mind as we look at foreign market pricing.

Table 14–2   Topics in Pricing Policy

A. Variables Affecting Pricing
1. Costs
2. Demand
3. Competition
4. Government (laws, such as resale price maintenance, Robinson-Patman, and so on)
5. Company goals
6. Distribution structure and channels

B. Pricing Problems
1. New products versus established products (or product life cycle pricing)
2. Product-line pricing
3. Fixed price versus variable price
4. Original equipment (OEM) versus replacement sales
5. Geographic pricing
6. Channel pricing versus pricing to consumers

C. Other Topics in Pricing
1. Price in relation to the rest of the marketing mix
2. Break-even analysis
3. The Bayesian approach to pricing decisions
4. Skimming policy versus penetration pricing

The problem of finding the "right" price in a foreign market is quite similar to the task in the domestic market. The pricing problems and other topics noted in Table 14–2 (B and C) are relevant for any foreign market as well as for the domestic market. This carry over from domestic to foreign market pricing will facilitate and abbreviate our discussion here. We will note only the problems peculiar to the task facing the international marketing manager, one of which arises, of course, from the very number of markets for which "right" prices must be found. This is a difficulty because each market has a different pricing situation, that is, the variables affecting pricing (see Table 14–2 A) change from market to market.

Before proceeding further, we should note that the international marketer has a foreign market pricing problem especially in those markets where the firm has a sales or marketing subsidiary. In markets where it is represented by a distributor, licensee, or other intermediary, the firm practically gives up much of the local pricing authority to that intermediary. A second point of clarification concerns the price we are discussing. The firm's margin is determined by the price it receives when it sells the product to a buyer outside the firm. However, the volume of sales and, ultimately, profits are determined primarily by the price paid by the final consumer. It is the ultimate consumer price that we are considering, although the two are inextricably related.

Foreign Market Variables: Costs

Costs always play a role in pricing, if only to set some kind of floor under the price. The costs relevant to foreign market pricing include everything necessary to get the product to the ultimate buyer. When a firm operates in just one market, the relevant costs are easy to determine although often difficult to allocate among different product lines. In the international firm, it is not easy to determine the relevant costs for a particular market. A subsidiary in one country is usually part of an international network on both the supply and the demand sides. Allocating indirect costs *among countries* is similar to the problem of allocating them among different product lines. In addition, the international firm has a different cost structure in each of its markets, as we will see.

Manufacturing Costs

Of the various kinds of costs that must be covered by the foreign market price, one, of course, is manufacturing costs. When the products sold in a market are produced in that market, determination of manufacturing costs is no problem. Complications arise when a market is served by other production sources in the international company. Some of the questions are the following: If the firm has several plants, which plant's costs should be used? Should variable or full costs be used? What does "full costs" mean for a product coming from a plant in another country, that is, what R&D, overhead, and so on? Obviously, some costs, such as local advertising or marketing research, do not apply to products sold in another country.

The general guideline is that a market price should cover those production and related costs *for which it is responsible*. This then becomes a problem of cost accounting, but one of great interest to the marketer in the subsidiary receiving the goods.

Marketing Costs

Distribution and marketing costs also must be covered in the foreign market price. Physical distribution costs include two elements when the products come from outside the country: transportation *to* the country and transportation *within* the country. Subsidiary management wants the lowest landed cost in its market. It would like to choose not only the lowest cost production source but also the one closest to its market. These goals may conflict, so the choice would go to the source with the lowest total delivered cost.

Because tariffs can be an important part of delivered cost, the subsidiary would tend to prefer a source from a country having favorable tariff relations with its own. Thus a subsidiary in the EEC would choose another EEC subsidiary because no tariff barriers exist to add to its costs. For the same reason, American firms have often supplied Australia or India from Canadian or British subsidiaries rather than from the United States. Because all these countries are in the British Commonwealth, they had lower tariffs for each other than for nonmember countries like the United States. Transportation, storage, and inventory costs within the country should follow the normal rules for efficient logistics.

Marketing costs in the foreign market price are primarily those generated within that market by the national subsidiary. Occasionally, however, the firm incurs costs for marketing research or other marketing services rendered by a regional division (or international division) on behalf of the national subsidiary. The amount and nature of the local marketing costs will vary from one foreign market to another. This variation derives in part from differing product lines and company goals in each market.

Other variation results from the difference in marketing mix from country to country. Even though a firm might wish to use the same mix in all markets, the situation with regard to competition, distribution, media, and so on, would probably not allow it this uniformity. The concept of the marketing mix includes, of course, an evaluation of the degree to which the firm competes on a price basis. With all this variability in costs for individual markets, it is obvious why the firm has a different cost basis for pricing in each of its national markets.

Inflation

In many foreign markets, one cannot discuss costs without considering a special determinant of costs, that is, inflation. Almost all countries face some gradual increase in prices over time. However, continuing strong inflation characterizes a limited number of countries. In those markets where price levels rise by as much as 10 percent or more every year, pricing is a different problem. With the major exception of oil-rich Venezuela, the South American nations are notorious for inflation. Some Asian nations are in the same league. Table 14–3 gives an indication of the amount of currency depreciation for selected countries over a ten-year period.

At first glance, selling in an inflationary market might appear to be a marketer's dream. People are anxious to exchange their money for something that does not deteriorate so fast. Indeed it would be a good situation for sellers, if it were not for other factors that usually accompany high rates of inflation. First, rising costs may go up faster than prices. Second, governments have a propensity to resort to price control to restrain inflation. The countries with high inflation are usually those with strong price controls, as noted below. Third, countries with rampant inflation usually have strict controls over foreign exchange. Profits earned in that country might not be remittable to the parent company, at least not until they have been eroded by the devaluations that usually accompany inflation.

Pricing for inflationary markets requires accounting for changing values over time. Material and other costs of a product must be recovered (plus a margin for profit) at the time of sale—or at the time of payment, if credit is extended. If prices are stable, pricing can be a simple process of addition. If prices are rising rapidly, addition of the various cost elements at the time they were incurred will not assure that the *current* value of these costs is recovered.

Table 14–3   Inflation Rates—Selected Countries

	ANNUAL RATES OF CURRENCY DEPRECIATION, 1958–1968	INDEX OF VALUE OF MONEY, 1968 (1958 = 100)
Guatemala	0.2%	98
El Salvador	0.3	97
Venezuela	0.9	92
Thailand	1.2	89
United States	1.9	83
Philippines	3.8	68
Finland	4.7	62
Japan	4.7	62
Israel	4.9	61
Denmark	4.9	60
Turkey	7.3	47
Colombia	9.6	37
Peru	9.6	37
Yugoslavia	10.2	34
Korea	10.8	32
South Vietnam	13.5	23
Chile	20.1	11
Argentina	23.8	7
Brazil	32.1	2
Indonesia	58.9	less than 1

Source: First National City Bank.

The following examples illustrate these contrasting situations. The currency unit is the Brazilian cruzeiro, a currency that has experienced rapid inflation for many years, as seen in Table 14–3.

Stable currency situation.

Raw materials	250	cruzeiros
Overhead	100	"
Labor	100	"
Packaging	50	"
Total costs	500	cruzeiros
Gross profit (10%)	50	"
Selling price (cash sale)	550	cruzeiros

Inflation rate of 36 percent a year.

Assume that raw materials were purchased four months before being used in the product; labor costs were incurred one month before product sale; overhead was charged for a two-month period; and packaging materials were purchased three months before sale.

Raw materials	250 + 30 (12% inflation for 4 months) 280	cruzeiros
Labor	100 + 3 (3% inflation for 1 month) 103	"
Overhead	100 + 6 (6% inflation for 2 months) 106	"
Packaging	50 + 4.5 (9% inflation for 3 months) 55	"
Total costs		544 cruzeiros
Gross profit 10%		54 "
Selling price (cash sale)		598 cruzeiros

Although both examples illustrate the problem simply, the second example is a gross oversimplification. In reality, many more cost elements go into a product than the four general headings given here; for example, marketing costs are not mentioned. In addition, each of the cost elements will have a rate of inflation different from the average given by some general price index (here 36 percent a year increase in the *general* price level). Finally, time may elapse between production and sale—as well as between sale and payment. This additional time is a further inflation cost to be considered in the price.

Another problem arises if the firm encounters government price controls that prevent any raising of the price beyond 550 cruzeiros. This was the situation facing foreign-owned public utilities in Latin America. As a result, almost no foreign owned public utilities remain there. Drug firms are in another sensitive product area. Where the firm does have freedom to raise prices, it often does better to make frequent small price increases than occasional large increases that jolt the consumer. Such was the experience of many companies in Brazil. At one time when inflation was particularly high, companies raised their prices 7 percent on the first of every month.[12]

---

[12] *Business Week*, March 13, 1965, p. 108.

Foreign Market Variables: Demand

As every student of economics has learned, price is determined by supply and demand. Ideally, price should be set at the point of intersection of the marginal revenue and marginal cost curves. The supply or cost side we have looked at briefly in preceding paragraphs. A market-oriented manager knows, however, that the "right" price is one that suits the market or demand side.

Theoretically, and probably practically also, the international firm faces a different demand curve in each of its markets. Demand for the firm's products is a function of the number of potential consumers, their income or ability to pay, their tastes, habits, and attitudes relating to the product, and the existence of competing products. It is most improbable that these will be identical in any two markets. An American firm will find another variable to be the local attitude toward America and American products, which can either boost or limit local demand. The task of demand analysis in a foreign market is similar to that in domestic marketing.

Foreign Market Variables: Competition

In a purely competitive market, all producers would sell at identical prices. In the imperfectly competitive real world, the firm must also be competitive; that is, it must take note of competitors' prices. However, it has some freedom to sell above or below competitors' prices. Many American firms abroad generally do not try to undercut the competition but prefer to compete on a nonprice basis. For example, the Singer Company was facing strong price competition in sewing machines in a Far Eastern market. Singer was able to maintain a strong market position even though its prices were significantly higher than prices of the Japanese machines. The company emphasized product quality, liberal credit terms, and sewing classes for buyers in its successful attempt to maintain market position.

The *nature of competition* is a variable in foreign market pricing. The number of the firm's competitors and the way they compete will differ between Belgium and Brazil, or between Italy and India. Even in neighboring countries the competitive situation differs. For example, a drug firm charged 25 percent more for an identical prescription dosage in Belgium than in neighboring France. The firm had a strong position in the Belgian market, where it also had a plant. It was relatively weak in the French market, and the government health service was threatening to buy from Italian drug "pirates." (These "pirates" made the drugs without royalty payments to the originating firm and thus had no R&D expense to cover.) At that time, Italy was not a member of the International Patent Convention on drugs.

Another example of differing *competitive behavior* comes from the automobile industry. An executive with an American automobile producer complained about Renault "dumping" cars outside the French market, that is, selling them at less than full cost. He said that Renault (owned by the French government) was more interested in maintaining employment in France than in making profits. Therefore it was willing to sell cars at a loss for the political benefits of more stable employment. He said that it was much easier to compete against more "rational" profit-oriented companies than against a government-owned firm.[13]

Competition in a foreign market depends further on *business and government attitudes.* In America, both business and government are quite strongly in favor of competition; in fact, no other country puts such emphasis on competition as a regulator of the market. The Rome Treaty contains a competition policy for the EEC in Articles 85 and 86 of the treaty. The competition policy or practice varies greatly among EEC member countries, however. Germany has the strongest antitrust policy in the EEC, yet cartel-like agreements in Germany have an important effect on pricing. Industry-wide price contracts are common in France.

The American firm often will find its chief competitor in a foreign market to be another American firm. This is somewhat of an advantage to the manager, in that he can understand the way the American firm competes. A little twist often occurs in the situation, however, because American competitive positions are sometimes reversed overseas, with the number-one stateside firm being number two abroad. For example, Campbell leads in the United States, whereas Heinz leads in foreign markets. In other cases, leadership may depend on which firm was first to enter a particular market.

Foreign Market Variables: Government and Pricing
Resale Price Maintenance

The role of government in pricing has several aspects. One is government's competition policy, as just discussed; another is legislation on pricing, such as the American Robinson-Patman Act. Although actual legislation on pricing is not very frequent in foreign markets, except in the area of resale price maintenance (rpm), the government plays no small role in pricing, as we will see. Rpm, or "fair trade" pricing, has become rather unimportant in the United States, being found on only a limited line of products. It still plays a more important role in foreign markets, but the trend is everywhere away from rpm rather than toward expansion of it.

The United Kingdom abolished resale price maintenance in 1965, except for goods whose manufacturers had filed application for exemption. The results were a drop in prices at the retail level, a change in retail margins, and a reduction in the number of small retail outlets. Only a few lines of goods are still covered by rpm in the United Kingdom. Kodak, Ltd., ended rpm on its color film and published a list of "recommended" prices that averaged about 20 percent below previous rpm prices. The company expected its pretax profit would decline by $2.8 million as a result of the change.

Resale price maintenance is on the way out in most other European countries, as well as in Britain. Germany, France, and the Scandinavian countries have generally prohibited rpm, although in Germany goods with narrow

[13] Interview with the author.

distribution and moderate margins occasionally can still use it. Kodak and other camera and film makers were forced to drop rpm in Germany in 1970, however, because of their inability to enforce 100-percent compliance. If just one wholesaler or retailer evaded rpm, the system was ruled not "complete" and therefore had to be abandoned.

General Electric's German subsidiary found that the end of rpm led to retailer price wars and damaged its channel relations and sales. Since the company could no longer maintain distribution control through rpm, it had to use nonpricing measures. The higher priced products were given a new brand name and sold direct to a restricted list of retailers. The middle-of-the-line products retained the traditional brand name and were sold through wholesalers. The major price cutters, that is, discounters and mail-order houses, were supplied private brand products through a new distribution company.

Some European countries are resisting the trend away from rpm. Among these are Belgium, Spain, and Italy. Here the manufacturer can continue to use rpm, but he must be aware of changing market conditions. It is not wise to fight for a system that is dying, especially if it is against the best interests of the consumer. In Japan, rpm is allowed to manufacturers of consumer goods who get specific permission of the Japanese Fair Trade Commission. The major difficulty for the manufacturer is to enforce rpm in the long indirect channels that are common in Japan. Smith, Kline and French, by using selective distribution, was relatively successful using rpm with its Contac cold remedy. The firm had only nine wholesalers for all of Japan and signed rpm contracts with each. They, in turn, signed contracts with about 7,000 retailers.[14]

Government Price Control

In World War II, the United States government instituted price controls throughout the economy, setting up an Office of Price Administration to oversee the price freeze. This was discontinued after the war, and since then American firms, apart from public utilities, have had little price control by their government—the only notable exceptions being some moral suasion or "jawboning" aimed at a few of the major industries and some not very effective wage-price guidelines. Of course, in 1971, President Nixon made a major effort toward an economy-wide price freeze. The situation in other countries is quite different. In many markets of the world, the governments play a much stronger role in controlling prices. The way governments control prices can be shown best by examples.

ECONOMY-WIDE CONTROL   Sometimes governments try to control all prices in the economy. For example, Brazil in 1969 revised its price control operation and set up an Interministerial Council on Prices (CIP). If a manufacturer wished to raise prices, he had to fill out a questionnaire and apply to

[14] Robert E. Weigand, "Retail Pricing in Japan," *Business Topics* (Winter 1970), p. 25.

the CIP. The CIP analyzed the cost picture and profit margins before rendering a decision. In its anti-inflation battle, Chile had a listing of controlled prices on agricultural and industrial goods. Price increases on industrial goods were limited to specific percentages, regardless of wage or other cost increases.

The same kind of broad controls are also found in Europe. France instituted an economy-wide price freeze in 1963 and maintained it rather strictly until 1967. Then, following devaluation of the franc in 1969, a new price freeze was imposed on manufacturers as an anti-inflationary measure. Both the Netherlands and Norway had broad price freeze programs in 1969 to hold down the increase in cost of living associated with the change to a value-added tax system. Value-added taxes have been adopted by most Western European countries, following the French system. Because the changeover often resulted in price increases, governments attempted to counteract the inflationary pressures by price controls. Fear of inflation prompted Belgium to postpone adoption of the value-added tax system. In late 1970, Denmark adopted an almost complete price freeze because of its unfavorable balance of trade situation. The price freeze was part of the solution urged upon the country by the IMF and the OECD.

SELECTIVE CONTROLS   Governments often show a concern for particular product prices as well as for overall price levels in their economy. For example, in the United States, public utility rates are regulated and official concern is sometimes expressed about the prices of critical or sensitive products, such as drugs, steel, or automobiles. Other governments also have special concern for certain products, especially if they are produced by foreign firms. The German Federal Cartel Authority (FCA) once called in the managers of four foreign-owned subsidiaries in the petroleum field: Esso, Shell, BP, and Texaco were charged with "unjustified" price increases. FCA was concerned about the firms' transfer prices into Germany.[15]

A government study committee in Britain recommended that drug prices be negotiated between the companies and the Ministry of Health. Argentina froze drug prices from 1963 to 1967, then passed a law limiting margins on drugs. In the area of raw materials, the British Gas Council set the selling price for natural gas drawn from its sector of the North Sea fields by private companies. Chile pressed Anaconda and Kennecott to raise the price on Chilean copper sold abroad. (This was before Chile took over these firms.) In these cases, management pricing flexibility is reduced, if not eliminated. The problem then becomes working with costs and other elements to try to find a profitable combination within the government price constraint.

Foreign Market Variables: Company Goals

Company goals may differ not only between domestic and international operations but also between individual foreign markets. In some countries, the firm will want a strong penetration and a growing share of the market, whereas, in others, it might be satisfied with a holding action, maintaining a presence

[15] *Business Europe*, November 24, 1967, p. 374.

there until conditions look better or until it is able to take a more aggressive stance.

The pricing policy appropriate for any given market will be determined partly by the firm's goals in that market. Thus a penetration pricing strategy could be followed in one market, a pre-emptive pricing strategy in another, and a skimming pricing strategy in yet another. The company goals in a market are probably related to its level of involvement. Where the firm has a production and marketing subsidiary, for example, it may need a penetration pricing strategy. In markets where it has only a distributor, the firm can better afford a skimming or higher price strategy. A joint venture puts a special constraint on pricing because the international firm must consider the goals and desires of its national partner as well as its own.

Foreign Market Variables: Distribution Structure and Channels

A final determinant of the firm's price to consumers in a foreign market is its distribution channels there. Because the structure of distribution varies from market to market, so do the firm's channel alternatives. We discussed this in the chapters on distribution, but here we are especially concerned with the pricing implications. Although different channels obviously may have different costs, using the same channel in two countries does not necessarily indicate costs will be similar. The costs, services, and margins of a given channel are not the same from country to country. This suggests that a channel decision may be also a pricing decision. The firm may be forced to choose a particular channel in a market to get the consumer price it needs. Table 14–4 illustrates the intercountry variability of channel costs; the figures are for a packaged food product shipped into France and Germany.

Table 14–4   Cost Variability of the Same Channel in Different Countries

	TRANSMISSION			WHOLESALE MARGIN	RETAIL MARGIN
	DUTY	TAX	IMPORTER		
France	3%	25%	12%	15 %	31%
Germany	12%	6%	23%	12.5%	20%

Source: Vern Terpstra, *American Marketing in the Common Market* (New York: Praeger, 1967), p. 116.

The Common Market tends to moderate such differences, but as long as the differences exist, they are a major determinant of the firm's final consumer price in each market. Where such costs make a firm noncompetitive in a market, it may have to change its source of supply—for example, to local manufacturing—as well as its distribution channel and pricing.

Conclusions on Foreign Market Pricing

In concluding our discussion of foreign market pricing, we will review some management pricing strategies that might be used to deal with the variables discussed above. Of course, any pricing formulas or techniques the firm uses in its domestic market should be evaluated for use in foreign markets, including the break-even approach and Bayesian analysis.

In dealing with *costs* in a foreign market, the marketing manager needs good cost accounting and control techniques, but also he often has other options not available to national firms. The international marketer may control costs through a choice of supply sources with differing production costs, tariffs, and transportation charges. He may further affect costs by changing the firm's level of involvement in a market. For example, Chrysler's Rootes subsidiary found that with a plant in Iran, it could sell a Hillman automobile at an Iranian price of $2,520. The price of the same car imported from Britain was $4,200.

This is not always a two-way street, however; it is easier to expand the firm's involvement than to reduce it. For example, to go from a production and marketing subsidiary back to a distributor arrangement requires selling the plant, which can be difficult. In dealing with inflation, a replacement cost formula was suggested. Other approaches to the problems stemming from inflation include sourcing from, and selling to, other markets of the company and using transfer pricing to control costs or to get profits out.

In facing *demand* in a market, the firm has less flexibility than it has in facing costs. Demand is usually considered an uncontrollable factor. The marketer must adapt his price, and perhaps product and distribution as well, to the local demand. Of course, demand occasionally can be influenced in the manufacturer's favor through promotional activities or where consumers make a price-quality association concerning the firm's product, thus enabling it to sell above competitors' prices yet find good demand. A German cosmetics manufacturer found this out by accident. He was exporting into France and paying high duties, so his prices were high in France. After the Common Market was formed, duties between France and Germany were gradually eliminated. He then found it more profitable to retain the same consumer price as when the high duties were in effect because the quality prestige image associated with his product maintained a strong demand at the high price, thus giving him a higher profit margin.

In regard to *competition*, the marketer must determine the appropriate relation between his and competitors' prices. He may have some flexibility in meeting national competitors' pricing through the logistics arrangements possible in the international company. He should be able to gain economies of scale through multinational production sources and markets. Using nonprice competition may offer further pricing flexibility.

Government is often a powerful constraint on pricing, but the firm does have some freedom. At one extreme, the firm can avoid those markets where government price controls are too rigid or unreasonable. If the firm is already in such markets, the extreme alternative is to withdraw, as the foreign-owned public utilities effectively did in South America. A more common and generally more desirable alternative is to cooperate with the government, presenting the company's arguments when price increases are needed and working toward an effective compromise.

Canada tried an unusual tack in controlling prices. The government in 1970 gathered 300 of the nation's top business leaders for two days of discussion and debate. Eventually, they all agreed to hold the line on prices for the year 1970. Of course, the government had policing powers and sanctions available in its Prices and Incomes Commission. Where governments allow resale price maintenance (rpm), the firm may wish to use it to control and protect its distribution channels. However, given the trend away from rpm in world markets as well as consumer interest in lower prices, the firm should be ready to take other nonprice measures to assure its distribution. We have seen that in dropping rpm in Germany, General Electric used a combination of branding strategies, pricing, and channel changes to assure continued market coverage in the different outlets.

Pricing and the Marketing Mix

Although we have discussed pricing in partial isolation from the rest of the marketing mix, obviously the kind of price a firm can have in any market will be intimately connected with the rest of its marketing program, that is, product policy, distribution, promotion, and so on. To supplement the several examples we already cited to show some aspects of these interrelationships, we provide the following more complete and realistic illustration.

In the early and mid–1960s, the major oil companies in Britain saw discounters come in and take 10 percent of the market by emphasizing lower prices. The major companies were slow to react till Esso finally took the lead. In 1967, Esso cut prices by as much as 6½ cents on an imperial gallon to meet the discounters head on. The visible and necessary price cut, however, was combined with, and made possible by, a complex series of moves. The following steps were among those which permitted a significant pricing change.

1. *Reduction in number of gasoline grades from four to three*
2. *A shuffling of octane ratings*
3. *Pulling out of marginal stations.*
4. *Reduction of dealer margins by ½ cent a gallon*
5. *Dredging to allow supertankers to reach the Esso refinery at Frawley*
6. *Building of Britain's longest pipeline*
7. *Bargaining hard for new, lower freight rates*

Items 5 through 7 served to reduce costs of physical distribution. *Items 1 and 2 represented* product changes. *Items 3 and 4 were changes in* distribution strategy. *All were necessary to permit a price cut that would not mean an equivalent loss of profits.*[16]

COORDINATING PRICING IN INTERNATIONAL MARKETING

The final pricing question to consider is the degree to which the international marketer must integrate and coordinate prices in different national markets. For most marketing functions, the international marketer faces the issue of

[16] *Time*, March 17, 1967, pp. 98, 99.

international standardization of practice versus local adaptation. For example, how much product or promotional uniformity is desirable or profitable internationally? The same issue arises in pricing.

Final Consumer Prices

We have noted that the international firm faces a different supply and demand situation in each of its national markets. This indicates different optimum prices for each market, or, in more technical terms, different marginal revenue and marginal cost curves lead to different profit-maximizing prices. Given the unique situation in each national market, the firm would be unwise to try for uniform consumer prices from country to country. Again, the important goal is profits, not uniformity. If the firm has national subsidiaries operating as profit centers, this situation indicates the use of national rather than international prices. Profit center operation implies decision-making authority over factors affecting profits, which would certainly include pricing and would lead to different subsidiaries having different prices.

Even apart from the supply and demand situation of the individual firm or industry are external factors causing price differences from market to market. The EEC is called a common market, but a 1967 study by the EEC Statistical Office showed that indeed there is no common market in pricing. Even with tariffs removed, the differences in taxes, price supports or controls, efficiency, and tastes from country to country led to the great disparities shown in Table 14–5.

The table shows only the highest and lowest prices on each product with the lowest price underlined. Prices for the other countries fall in between. Of the fifteen products listed, in only five of the cases is the difference between

Table 14–5 High–Low Prices in EEC Countries (on selected commodities)

PRODUCTS (PRICES IN $ U.S.)	BELGIUM	FRANCE	GERMANY	ITALY	NETHER-LANDS
Canned peas			.09	.14	
White bread		.17	.41		
Coffee (250 g)		.50		1.07	
Man's wool suit		76.10		51.10	
Women's stockings				.81	.64
Spring mattress		56.97			30.82
Refrigerator		175.46	126.57		
Electric razor	18.71	23.46			
Table TV		326.10	198.05		
Ball-point pen	.11	.06			
Type 1 car			1354.65		1605.00
Gasoline		.41		.41	.33
Toilet soap			.30		.15
Aspirin		.24	.38		
Color film	2.56	5.15			

Source: EEC Statistical Office.

the lowest price and the highest price less than 50 percent. Thus, even between neighboring countries of a "common market," there are striking price differences on similar or identical products.

The difficulty of maintaining uniform consumer prices in different markets does not mean that pricing *strategies* cannot be consistent from market to market. A company can maintain a uniform policy of pricing at the market, above it, or below it in each country. Even though final consumer prices differ, the firm can be consistent in being at the same particular part of the price spectrum in each country. For example, Lovable Company, a manufacturer of feminine underwear, concentrates on the low- to medium-priced segment of the market, aiming at penetrating the mass market with its pricing. It not only prices below other American firms in foreign markets but also frequently beats local competition as well, both in price and in quality.[17]

Where the international firm wishes to implement a uniform and consistent pricing strategy in all of its markets, it has a real need for central coordination and control. The diversities in different markets and levels of involvement must not be allowed to nullify the firm's pricing strategy.

Pricing to Intermediaries or Large Buyers

Pricing to intermediaries or large buyers involves some considerations not arising in pricing to final consumers. A seller can have different prices for different buyers successfully if the buyers are in separate and distinct markets. Table 14–5 showed great price disparities that persist in part because consumers do not or cannot travel to another market where the product costs less. Where markets do overlap or are related in some way, it becomes difficult to have nonuniform prices. Some factors in international marketing are exerting increasing pressure toward uniform pricing among markets, especially for intermediaries.

One pressure for international price uniformity comes from *regional groupings*. As tariffs are removed, markets gradually merge. In the EEC, this tying of markets is reinforced by antitrust law. Wholesalers in one country can sell to buyers in another member country. A kind of pricing arbitrage can take place to equalize prices in the different countries. For example, one reason resale price maintenance on photo film broke down in Germany was that a German wholesaler bought film from Belgium, which has no rpm on film. He sold the film in Germany at less than rpm prices and won the case brought against him. Under the Rome Treaty the German manufacturer could not restrain legally the export trade of the Belgian seller. Thus in the EEC where wholesalers in different countries are charged different prices by a manufacturer, they may make their own price adjustments by buying and selling to each other.

The *increase in international business* activity is itself a pressure for price uniformity. When a firm sells to another international firm in several different markets, it usually cannot charge different prices, except where transportation costs and duties cause the variation. The same pricing situation may apply

[17] *Business International*, August 15, 1969, p. 263.

when the firm sells to *governments*, which may demand a price as favorable as that received by anyone else. *Competition* is often very international today. When a firm faces the same American, European, or Japanese competitors on all continents, prices tend to become more uniform in all markets.

Multinational distribution is another factor. A firm may have distributors in several markets, each receiving different discounts. But when these distributors gather at a regional meeting of European or Latin American distributors and compare notes, the markets, which used to be separate, become related. More uniform distributor prices result. All these situations indicate that increasing internationalization of business and better communications direct the international company toward more uniform pricing.

Finally, *government tax and customs authorities* influence the reduction of price differences between countries. The Internal Revenue Service checks on the export prices of American companies and challenges price differences it finds out of line. Tax and customs authorities elsewhere also look at the international firm's prices on goods entering or leaving their countries. The easiest way to justify such prices is to show that they are the same all over, and that no country is being discriminated against. Although such government surveillance does not eliminate all price differences in international marketing, it does limit them.

Control Techniques

Apart from various external pressures toward or away from uniform international prices, the firm itself must play a conscious role. To obtain optimum performance in the international company, some central coordination and control of pricing is necessary. Various methods are available to control pricing in international operations. Consumer prices are least susceptible to control, except where the firm has *direct distribution* to consumers. Singer, Avon, and Tupperware are examples in this category, as well as many firms selling to the industrial market. Similarly, the firm has greater control over pricing where it has its own *sales subsidiary* in a market than where it sells through distributors.

As noted, a few countries allow *resale price maintenance* as a form of control. Where this is not available, the firm is concerned both about distributors that price too high—and limit the market—and those that price too low—and cause an erosion of prices and margins. Use of *recommended, listed, or advertised prices* may help to restrain distributors' pricing independence. Use of *consignment selling* is an effective, though costly, way to control prices. Extension of *credit* to the buyer may be another way of maintaining greater control over prices. In general, anything that ties the seller to the producer gives the producer some degree of control.

Subsidiary Pricing of Exports

Controlling subsidiaries' pricing is another task of the international marketer. Where subsidiaries are profit centers, they need reasonable pricing freedom on *sales within their own market*. In this case, the annual budget and product margin agreed upon by parent and subsidiary may provide sufficient control. Where several subsidiaries *export* the same product, central control over export prices is needed to avoid suboptimization. If each subsidiary were to try to maximize its own sales and profits, the total company might suffer.

Coordination of export prices can be approved in two ways when the firm has several different national production sources for a product. In the absence of coordination, each subsidiary producing the good would set its own f.o.b. plant price, and buyers in other markets would choose the plant offering the lowest delivered cost. The resultant situation would be that the buyers determine the logistics of the producing company, that is, which plant is the supplier. Even if satisfactory to the supplying subsidiary, and perhaps to the buyer, to the overall firm this practice may result in suboptimization. To avoid this, firms sometimes set *uniform f.o.b. plant prices on exports* for each producing subsidiary. The customer still chooses the source offering the lowest delivered cost, but the firm has greater control over subsidiary export pricing. The subsidiary also has an incentive to reduce costs because with a fixed export price, any cost reduction is added entirely to its profits.

Another way of controlling export prices is to require all exports to be handled through *one export organization*, regardless of source or destination. This is occasionally applied to licensee and joint-venture exports, as well as to those of wholly owned operations. Such an organization may be located in Switzerland or Panama, but also in New York City or Midland, Michigan (in the case of the Dow Chemical Company). The centralized export operation can set the prices to customers and direct the logistics of the operation to get the most efficient production source, lowest landed cost, and greatest total company profit. Such a centralized operation can offer economies of scale in logistics administration and optimization of global supply and demand for the company.

CONCLUSIONS

In this chapter we have looked at the four principal pricing decision areas facing the international marketing manager: export pricing, international transfer pricing, foreign market pricing, and international coordination of pricing. Under these general headings, we examined the many particular considerations involved in international pricing decisions. Simple conclusions are not forthcoming from such complexity.

One general, though not very meaningful, conclusion is that pricing decisions depend on many other elements in the firm's approach to foreign markets. Therefore, although pricing can be separated for discussion purposes on a *ceteris paribus* basis, the pricing decision seldom can be made in isolation. For this reason, the pricing decision usually is made after decisions on the other international marketing variables. Of course, there is a great deal of interaction among all these variables.

Questions

14.1 "Export prices should be higher than domestic prices because of the headaches involved." Discuss.

14.2   Why should the consumer price in the foreign market be the starting point for export price calculations?

14.3   What are some of the extra costs that may arise in export sales as compared with domestic?

14.4   Why does the American exporter usually prefer a dollar quotation? Why does the foreign importer prefer a price quoted in his currency?

14.5   What is the importance of the various export price quotes, for example, f.o.b., c.i.f., and so on.

14.6   What does it mean to have "market-oriented" export prices and terms?

14.7   When the "market-oriented" export price (f.o.b. plant) turns out to be less than the f.o.b. plant price on domestic sales, what can the firm do?

14.8   "We are proud of the fact that our export credit losses are a much lower percentage than the percentage lost on domestic sales." Discuss.

11.9   Should an exporter or international firm ever consider barter sales? How can the firm prepare to handle such transactions?

14.10 Discuss leasing in international marketing.

14.11 Explain the potential conflicts in transfer pricing between the producing division and the international division.

14.12 Identify the particular international constraints in transfer pricing between the international division and the foreign subsidiary.

14.13 Suggest some general guidelines that might be used by a firm for its international transfer pricing.

14.14 Discuss the various cost differences the firm encounters in pricing within foreign markets.

14.15 How can a firm deal with inflation in its foreign market pricing?

14.16 "The firm faces a different demand curve in each of its national markets." Discuss.

14.17 Discuss governments as a constraint on foreign market pricing of the multinational company.

14.18 Is it possible or desirable to have identical consumer prices in foreign markets?

14.19 Can the international marketing manager have any control over prices in foreign markets?

Further Readings

Books:

Business International, *Solving International Pricing Problems* (New York: 1965).

Kramer, Roland L., *International Marketing*, 3rd ed. Cincinnati: South-Western Publishing Co., 1970), chaps. 8, 15–18.

Root, Franklin R., *Strategic Planning for Export Marketing* (Scranton, Penna.: International Textbook Co., 1966), chap. 4.

Terpstra, Vern, *American Marketing in the Common Market* (New York: Praeger, 1967), chap. 6.

Articles:

Keegan, Warren J., "How Far Is Arm's Length?" *Columbia Journal of World Business* (May–June 1969), pp. 57–66.

Parker, George C., and Henry S. Miller, "International Leasing," *Columbia Journal of World Business* (September–October 1970), pp. 77–82.

Ross-Skinner, Jean, and Rory Gotley, "Barter Deals Boost Export Sales," *Business Abroad* (December 1968), pp. 27–28.

Shulman, James, "When the Price Is Wrong—By Design," *Columbia Journal of World Business* (May–June 1967), pp. 69–76.

PART III

COORDINATING INTERNATIONAL MARKETING

Our study of international marketing to this point has focused on two principal aspects: (1) the environment of international marketing and (2) the management of marketing within that environment. In Part I we saw many of the environmental parameters, both national and international, that cause international marketing to be something other than a mere extension of the firm's domestic marketing practice. In Part II, we looked at the various functional tasks that comprise international marketing management, that is, marketing intelligence, product policy, pricing, and so on.

Although analytically it is possible and desirable to speak of international promotion, international distribution, and the like, as separate functions, here we are concerned with the overall task of international marketing management and how the separate functional tasks are blended together into an effective international marketing mix. In Chapter 6, we spoke of the need for synergism in multinational marketing. Synergism is also needed in blending the various elements of the marketing mix. In both cases, effective results are achieved through careful analysis, planning, and coordination of the relevant variables.

In Part II, we discussed planning and control as they relate to the management of specific marketing functions. Here in Part III, however, we will deal with the comprehensive and integrative aspects of international marketing management. Through planning, organization, and control, the various functions or elements of the marketing mix are blended and managed to achieve a total and effective international marketing program. Chapter 15 begins by discussing international marketing planning. Chapter 16 follows with an examination of the organizational framework in which international marketing is managed. A discussion of the control process concludes the chapter.

15

INTERNATIONAL
MARKETING PLANNING

INTRODUCTION

Some Definitions

Planning is preparing for tomorrow. It involves decisions on *where* one wants to be tomorrow and *how* one is going to get there; that is, it includes goals and strategies. Planning must be done on a company-wide level for all management functions. The marketing plan is just one part, although an important one, of the overall company plan. The comprehensive international marketing plan, in turn, is composed of several subsidiary elements. These subsidiary elements may be some combination of individual foreign market plans, product or divisional plans, or functional plans. Thus one could find company examples of international marketing plans for the French or Mexican market, for the small-appliance or data-processing division, or for the international advertising program for next year.

A further distinction in planning concerns the time dimension. There can be short-range and long-range plans. Short-range plans cover in great detail the targets and programs for the immediate future, usually for a fiscal or calendar year. Long-range plans are concerned with the situation five, seven, ten, or more years away and address themselves to broader issues in much more general terms. The people working on long-range plans probably are not the same ones working on short-range plans. Another distinction must be made between planning and the plan. Planning is the continuing process of looking ahead and preparing for the future. The plan is a concrete document resulting from the planning process.

Analysis

Analysis involves the study and evaluation of the various parameters and functions of international marketing management. On a general level, that is what we did in Parts I and II. Such an analysis is designed to give an accurate and meaningful picture of the current situation. Of course, the purpose of clarifying the present situation is to help identify the best means for progressing to some desired future situation. In this way, analysis is the prelude to planning or, more accurately, the first step in planning.

Importance of Planning

Planning activities represent an expenditure or investment of company resources. Such an expenditure can be justified only if the benefits attained sufficiently outweigh the costs incurred. Although some of the benefits of planning are hard to quantify, they are nonetheless real. For one thing, the costs of sound planning are small relative to operating costs in foreign markets, which means that a small improvement in effectiveness or a new opportunity uncovered can easily offset the costs of planning. Furthermore, the costs of planning can be compared to the costs of insuring against serious strategic errors or missed opportunities in the marketplace. Being first down the road is of little advantage if one is on the wrong road. Planning helps to choose the right roads to achieving company goals. The need for planning is thus twofold: first, to avoid errors in the market, and, second, to recognize opportunities and challenges in order to meet them effectively.

Other "fringe benefits" of planning are the following:

1. It encourages systematic forward-thinking by management.
2. It results in a better international coordination of company efforts.
3. It leads to better preparation for emergencies and obviates the likelihood of costly improvisation.
4. It provides for continuity of effort and direction.
5. It gives participating executives a stronger sense of their integration with the rest of the company activities, that is, between subsidiary and parent, or between the different marketing functions.
6. It provides for a continuing review of operations and a continuing education for participating management.

Domestic versus International Planning

The planning *process* is similar in both domestic and international operations. Our discussion therefore will merely highlight the ways in which planning is modified in the multinational company. One practitioner's view of the differences is given in Table 15–1.

Short-Range Planning

Short-range planning for international marketing we will define as the establishment of marketing targets and the preparation of operating programs to meet those targets. The time span will usually be one operating year, whether a fiscal or a calendar year. IBM World Trade Corporation uses a two-year operating plan but revises it annually. Although the international marketing plan is just part of the firm's overall plan for international business, it is the only part that concerns us here. The overall short-range plan for international

Table 15–1 Domestic versus International Planning

A number of external elements affect plans and planning. They may also differ between domestic and international operations:

DOMESTIC PLANNING	INTERNATIONAL PLANNING
1. Single language and nationality	1. Multilingual/multinational/multicultural factors
2. Relatively homogeneous market	2. Fragmented and diverse markets
3. Data available, usually accurate and collection easy	3. Data collection a formidable task, requiring significantly higher budgets and personnel allocation
4. Political factors relatively unimportant	4. Political factors frequently vital
5. Relative freedom from government interference	5. Involvement in national economic plans; government influences business decisions
6. Individual corporation has little effect on environment	6. "Gravitational" distortion by large companies
7. Chauvinism helps	7. Chauvinism hinders
8. Relatively stable business environment	8. Multiple environments, many of which are highly unstable (but may be highly profitable)
9. Uniform financial climate	9. Variety of financial climates ranging from over-conservative to wildly inflationary
10. Single currency	10. Currencies differing in stability and real value
11. Business "rules of the game" mature and understood	11. Rules diverse, changeable and unclear
12. Management generally accustomed to sharing responsibilities and using financial controls	12. Management frequently autonomous and unfamiliar with budgets and controls

Source: William W. Cain, "International Planning: Mission Impossible?" *Columbia Journal of World Business* (July–August 1970), p. 58.

marketing can be composed of several elements, including, for example, a marketing plan for each foreign market, plans for individual product lines, and a plan for international product development. The amount of planning and the complexity of the plan will depend on the size and complexity of the firm's international business.

Elements of the Marketing Plan

Situation Analysis: Where Are We Now?

The company must analyze its current situation as to the controllable and uncontrollable variables in each of its markets. What are the important characteristics of demand, competition, distribution, law, and so on? What problems and opportunities are evident in the current situation?

Objectives: Where Do We Want To Be?

Given a good understanding of where the firm is in its different markets around the world, management can propose realistic objectives that are appropriate for each market. These objectives should be challenging, but they should also be reachable in terms of the analysis of the firm's position in the market. The objectives must also be specific and spelled out in meaningful terms if they are to be operational.

Strategy and Tactics: How Can We Best Reach Our Goals?

Once the international marketing manager has identified concrete objectives for his foreign markets, he must prepare a plan of action to reach these objectives. His approach will include arranging the various elements of the marketing mix and assigning specific responsibilities to marketing personnel and to the marketing functions.

The marketing plan could be broken down in more detail, but these three basic elements are sufficient for our purpose. They provide an adequate framework for discussing the planning problems of the international marketing manager.

The short-range planning task of the international marketer has two basic parts: (1) developing the plan for each foreign market and (2) integrating the national plans into a coherent international plan.

Developing Plans for Individual Markets

Although some planning must be done for each of the firm's foreign markets, the amount and nature of the planning will depend on the firm's volume of business and level of involvement in each market. In markets where the firm does a small volume of business, the amount of planning it can afford to do will be small also, unless, of course, the firm has a goal of greatly expanding its business in such a market. Thus the amount of planning may be related to the potential volume of business in a country as well as to the present volume. The second major constraint on national market planning is the nature of the firm's commitment to the market. We will examine this constraint before discussing the planning process itself.

Level of Involvement

EXPORTING   When the firm sells to an importer or distributor in a market, it is not physically present to do a situation analysis or to design an appropriate strategy for the market. Although the firm can compensate partially for this limitation by visiting export markets, the planning process is seriously hindered if the firm does not have a continuing personal company presence in the market. In its export markets, the firm must rely on its local representative for most of the data for all three parts of the plan. The representative's interest in cooperating as well as his ability to do so may leave much to be desired. A good reporting and information system will help to make the best of a weak situation, especially when the distributor can be induced to cooperate. We noted some methods for encouraging distributor cooperation in Chapter 10, and in Chapter 7 we discussed methods of getting foreign market information for planning. Further on in this chapter we will examine the benefits of comparative analysis for overcoming some of these limitations of the international planning process.

LICENSING   In markets where its only representation is through licensees, the firm is in about the same position as with exporting: It has no personal company presence in the market, and its licensee will cooperate in the planning process only to the degree that it is to his own interest. One factor, however, probably places the licensor in a stronger planning position than the exporter. The licensor's business is usually more important to the licensee than the exporter's is to the importer. This may be reflected in a stronger contract as well as more rigid information reporting requirements in a licensing agreement. Furthermore, the sales of a particular licensee may be related to the sales of other products of the company, making him more dependent on the licensor.

JOINT VENTURES   Joint ventures offer more favorable circumstances for planning; the firm does have its own personal representation in the foreign market, enabling it to make a better situation analysis. The joint venture arrangement can present serious difficulties for the planner, however. The local partner may have objectives and strategies different from those of the international firm. He also will want the situation analysis conducted from the viewpoint of the joint venture rather than from that of the international corporation. Therefore, even the joint venture operation cannot be integrated easily into the international planning process. Joint ventures tend to take on a separate life of their own. The problem diminishes as the percent of the international firm's ownership increases, which is a partial explanation for many international firms' preference for wholly owned ventures.

WHOLLY OWNED SUBSIDIARIES   A wholly owned subsidiary, whether for marketing alone or for both production and marketing, eliminates the problems encountered in the other kinds of involvement. The international marketing planner can count on company personnel to participate in the planning process. The international planner and those working in the various national subsidiaries will probably have a line relationship.

   The focus of our discussion here will be the planning process when wholly owned subsidiaries are involved; the treatment will not be complete, of course, because the international company must plan also for those markets where it has a lesser degree of involvement. However, a discussion of planning with wholly owned operations will gives an adequate picture of the planning process. Then the appropriate limitations and modifications can be noted for those countries where the firm has a lesser involvement. Besides degree of involvement, another variable to consider in the international planning process is that the firm's product line also may vary from market to market requiring the planning to be modified accordingly.

The Plan for the National Market

SITUATION ANALYSIS   The firm inevitably will find itself in a different situation in each of its national markets. It will use one basic method to examine these situations, however, and by doing so, the firm may well give its subsidiaries an advantage over their national competitors. As the international firm develops planning expertise, it can make this expertise available to all its subsidiaries, thereby enabling the subsidiaries to save the time and money involved in developing the expertise on their own. In each of its markets the firm examines the same variables—for example, demand, competition, law, and so on—and uses a standard analytical and reporting format. Then when the international planner receives the national plans he is better able to interpret and evaluate them.

In addition to the relevant variables in the local situation, the national analysis should identify the problems and opportunities expected to arise during the period of the plan. These problems and opportunities will trigger and guide the strategic planning. The actual conduct of the situation analysis is primarily a marketing research job. The format used is derived from that employed in the firm's domestic market. Undoubtedly international and local market modifications of the domestic approach would be necessary, but it provides a useful starting point. The more carry over from the domestic to the foreign planning approach, the better comparisons the firm can make of opportunities in the two areas. Such comparisons are necessary for a firm that wants to optimize its performance on an international basis.

The techniques used for national planning also probably will derive from domestic practice. These techniques usually are most highly developed in the firm's domestic operations. The firm should assure that the best planning tools and models are used in each of its markets. There is nothing peculiarly international about most planning *techniques*, so they will not be discussed here.

SETTING OBJECTIVES   Having determined its current situation, each national subsidiary must set objectives to be attained during the period of the plan. Traditionally, objectives have been set by extrapolation or by some manager's rule-of-thumb or whim. The purpose of the situation analysis is to enable objectives to be set more realistically. The objectives should relate the resources of the firm to the problems and opportunities in the local market; in addition, they should be spelled out specifically for the various products of the firm and for the different marketing functions. The national subsidiary should play a major role in setting its own market targets. Its participation will help to keep the targets related to the market and assure the firm of the subsidiary's cooperation in reaching them.

The actual objectives in the national plan should be quite detailed and specific. Some items that could be included are the following:

1. Target sales of each product, in units and dollars
2. Target market share by product
3. Target number of new distribution outlets

4. Target percent of brand awareness
5. A new product introduction with a specified sales or distribution level
6. Local market test of new product by target date
7. Export target of some dollar or percent-of-sales level
8. Specific marketing research activities to be completed

STRATEGY AND TACTICS   The analysis of the company's situation in a particular foreign market leads to the formulation of specific objectives or performance targets. The role of strategy is to determine the firm's general
approach to reaching its goals. Tactics indicate the specific tools and programs
that will be used to implement the strategy. For example, a firm might have
an objective of reaching a certain sales volume or market share in a country.
Its strategy might be to compete on a nonprice basis by emphasizing product
quality, by introducing new and improved products, and by making a strong
promotional effort. Its operating plan would then spell out in detail the particular tools and techniques to implement the strategy, including an appropriate budget. For instance, the plan would identify the product development
activities for the year; the specific new product to be introduced, its timing
and marketing program; the advertising program, including appeals, amount
and timing, and media schedules; and so on.

The operating plan that spells out the firm's tactics is usually the most
comprehensive and lengthy part of the short-range plan. It includes a calendar of events; the assignment of responsibility to the marketing people in
the firm and to those working with the firm, such as distributors, advertising
agencies, and marketing research groups; and the budget allocations to facilitate the fulfillment of these responsibilities. Large companies may even use
PERT or some other critical-path scheduling technique as part of their operating plan. The international marketing manager's responsibility is to oversee
the development of such short-range operating plans for each of his foreign
markets. To keep his task manageable and to operate efficiently, however,
he must realize some synergism or economies of scale in his planning effort.
His efficiency can be improved by the proper division of labor in the organization and by the use of comparative analysis.

Division of Labor in International Planning

The firm's overall organization for planning is a topic best pursued elsewhere.
Our interest here is in the organizational relationships in international marketing planning. *Who* contributes *what* to national operating plans? What are the
respective roles of corporate headquarters and the national subsidiaries?

We are assuming that neither completely centralized nor completely decentralized planning is desirable. Instead, some kind of interactive planning is
most effective, drawing on the best capabilities of each part of the company.
From the center, the international marketing manager and corporate headquarters should contribute planning know-how. Based on its domestic and
international experience, the firm should have developed planning expertise
which it can pass on to all its foreign operations so *their* planning effec-

tiveness is improved. This transfer includes planning guidelines and outlines, a planning schedule, and perhaps the training of subsidiary personnel in planning.

If the national subsidiary is not a self-contained operation, corporate head-quarters can provide information inputs for the situation analysis as to how the subsidiary's operations are related on the supply and/or demand side to the rest of the firm's international operations. The international marketer will, of course, also have his own ideas as to appropriate objectives for each market. Because of his international experience, he will have valuable ideas about effective strategies and tactics too.

Thus the international marketer contributes to all three aspects of the national operating plan: (1) He gives guidance and information to the situation analysis; (2) he gives a corporate viewpoint as to the desirability and appropriateness of various subsidiary objectives; and (3) he transfers corporate international know-how about strategies and tactics.

The national subsidiary obviously must do the major part of the actual planning, but in this planning, it has an advantage over its strictly national competitors. Because of help and know-how received from its corporate parent, the subsidiary of the multinational firm should be a more effective, sophisticated planner. The major contributions of the local subsidiary are (1) the actual work of preparing the plan and (2) local knowledge. Whereas the international parent has planning expertise, only the subsidiary has the intimate local knowledge needed for a realistic plan. Most of the hard data for the plan, therefore, must be supplied locally. The plan resulting from the data is more effective because of the complementary contributions of the two parts of the multinational firm.

The actual planning process will often work as follows:

1. The subsidiary receives planning guidelines and schedules from the parent.
2. The subsidiary prepares an operating plan and submits it to the parent.
3. Parents and subsidiary negotiate to reconcile differences about the plan.
4. A compromise results in an agreed upon plan and budget which become the operating program for the next year.

International Coordination of National Plans

Then final role of the international planner is to coordinate the national plans into an effective international plan for all the firm's markets. This coordination is not done *after* all of the national plans have been completed; rather, *it must start at the beginning* of the planning process and continue with it. Otherwise, the national plans will come up with conflicting claims on company resources and require expensive and time-consuming revision. Therefore the coordination begins with guidelines sent to each national operation at the beginning of the planning period. National plans may be modified during the planning process, but the communications between subsidiary and parent must be such that these changes can be coordinated within the overall international plan.

Comparative Analysis for International Planning

Comparative analysis is not a new topic but rather a continuation of our discussion of the role of corporate headquarters in the international planning process. The ability of the international marketing manager to contribute to the subsidiary's planning derives from two sources, the firm's domestic experience and its international experience. If the manager has analyzed carefully the company's operations in all of its markets, certain patterns, groupings, and observations probably have emerged. He will begin to understand in what ways these markets are alike and in what ways they are different. At the simplest level, he might note a difference between industrialized and nonindustrialized countries. At a more sophisticated level, he might find that his foreign markets fall into three, four, or five categories or groupings according to their behavior on the sale and use of his firm's products. He can begin to classify countries on the basis of characteristics that are relevant for his marketing activities. Comparative analysis is an attempt by the firm to maximize the value of its multinational experience.

Comparative analysis in international marketing involves three steps. First, the relevant variables or dimensions of national markets must be identified. Here these variables are those that affect the firm's marketing program. Second, the variables must be measured in each of the firm's markets and the similarities, differences, and patterns or groupings that emerge must be noted. Third, the collected data must be classified and analyzed.

The first step, identifying the relevant variables, is a form of model building whereby the firm gains an understanding of its interactions with the market. Although such a model need not be, and probably is not, a complex mathematical formulation, still every firm has some model or picture of how it relates to its markets. This model may be implicit, but it is more useful if made explicit. The second step, measuring markets on these dimensions, is part of the marketing research and information system activity of the firm. The third step, analysis and classification, is the task of the international marketing manager and his staff, requiring both experience and analytical skill.

The contribution of comparative analysis to international planning lies in setting objectives and determining strategies. The tendency and temptation in setting objectives is to consider each national market as unique. The national subsidiary likes to see itself that way because its power is enhanced vis-à-vis the parent. If the subsidiary is indeed one of a kind, it plays a bigger role in setting its own objectives and evaluating its own performance. If instead the international manager, through careful analysis of the firm's multinational experience, can determine that a particular subsidiary or market bears similarities to others, he can then play a greater role in setting objectives.

He can perhaps raise subsidiary objectives and ask for greater performance if his comparative analysis has shown that this is reasonable for subsidiaries and markets with similar characteristics. International comparisons are often unpopular with subsidiary management precisely because it claims its situation is different from that in countries with which it is being unfavorably compared. A well-done comparative analysis and classification, however, assures that the subsidiary is being compared with others in a similar situation.

In determining strategies and tactics for particular markets, comparative analysis is also useful. If markets have been identified and grouped according to their similarity on the straegic and tactical variables, the international marketer can help to plan strategy for a particular market based on his firm's experience in these other similar markets.

A pharmaceutical firm used an A, B, C, D rating or classification system to guide its detail men in scheduling call frequencies for doctors. The doctors who had the greatest influence on adoption and use of an ethical drug had an A rating, and so on. This system was used in the firm's domestic operations. The international division of the company adopted a similar rating or classification system for foreign markets. It was used to prepare the promotional strategies and budgets for these markets.

An electronics company was studying sales and performance data of one of its major product lines in foreign markets. The various analyses showed clearly three distinct market groupings for this product line. This led to a change in the firm's international planning. Instead of preparing individual planning guidance for each of the foreign markets, planners began preparing guidance for three groups of countries. They added just one page of individual material for each country to handle anything that was peculiar to it.

COMPARATIVE ANALYSIS FOR EXPORT MARKET PLANNING   We have been looking at planning especially in terms of countries where the firm has subsidiaries. Comparative analysis can help the exporter too. The exporter's planning is handicapped by his lack of continuing first-hand contact with his markets. As he accumulates experience in a large number of markets over a period of years, however, he can partially overcome this handicap. An analogy might be useful here. The parent of a ten-year-old child has some understanding of ten-year-olds and can make some predictions about their behavior; but a person who has taught ten-year-old children for a number of years should have a better understanding and be able to make better predictions. The company that has only domestic operations is like the parent; its understanding of other country markets is limited. The experienced exporter is like the teacher; and if he has organized and analyzed his multinational experience, he should overcome, at least partially, the handicap of a lack of personal presence in his export markets.

LONG-RANGE PLANNING
Some Distinctions
Time

For present purposes, we will define international long-range planning as the analysis of the future international environment of company operations, the establishment of company goals for that environment, and the determination of overall strategy to reach those goals. As in short-range planning, the firm is concerned with expected change and what it means for the firm. However, several distinctions separate short-range and long-range planning. One is the *time span*: Short-range plans usually are for one year, which means a one-year horizon and planning cycle; long-range plans more commonly encompass five or more years.

The long-range planning process is more an ongoing than a recurring activity, and it is often relatively independent of the annual short-range planning cycle. Actual company practice varies as to the time horizon of the various plans. For example, CPC International plans on a one-, five-, and ten-year basis. The five-year plan is considered an extension of the one-year plan and is therefore more operational than long range. The ten-year plan for them is the true long-range plan where new environments and markets are considered.

Environment

A more important distinction between the short-range and long-range plans is in the *environmental assumptions* each makes. Parameters considered fixed in the short run become variables in the long run. In fact, one of the major purposes of long-range planning is to identify and evaluate the potential, but distant, changes in the environment so as to prepare to respond to them effectively. The following items are among those that are probably constant for the short-run but not for the long-run plan: the level of technology, or state of the art; the nature of the demand for the firm's products; the company's product line; the number of countries in which the firm is operating; the firm's level of involvement in foreign markets.

For example, the traditional concern of long-range planning was merely to determine what facilities and financing might be needed to meet future demand for the firm's *existing* products. Today, long-range planning is more concerned about what the firm's *future* products and markets should be. On the international side, these additional questions might arise: Should we be selling products or services abroad? (See Chapter 8.) What new markets should we be in? What should we be doing in East–West trade? What kind of involvement should we have in foreign markets?

As one specific example, Table 15–2 shows the chapter headings for an actual long-range planning study conducted by one of America's largest manufacturing concerns. This particular study involved only the consumer side of the firm's business and was limited to its European market involvement. Each chapter had numerous subheadings, of course.

Detail

Another difference in long-range planning is the amount of *detail* or specificity required. As noted above, the short-range plan must be very specific, as it is a sort of job description by which individuals and subsidiaries will be evaluated. By contrast, the long-range plan gives no marching orders but merely alerts the company to approaching change and gives general guidelines as to further investigation. Long-range planning is a kind of early warn-

Table 15–2   A Long-Range Planning Outline for One Firm Considering the European Market

CHAPTER
1. Environment
2. Industry Evaluation
3. Future Competitive Environment
4. Company Goals for Europe
5. Market Requirements
6. Consumer Developments—Socio-Economic
7. Technical Rationalization
8. Distribution Developments
9. Taxes and Legal
10. Organization Structure and Intra-Company Relations
11. Conclusion

Source: Material given to the author. Name withheld by request.

ing system for possibilities of approaching change. However, until the exact nature of the change can be identified—that is, until it comes closer in time —no specific directions can be given. In contrast to the detailed operating plan and budget resulting from short-range planning, the result of long-range planning is usually general memoranda given to key individuals or committees for their further consideration. Of course, the shorter the plan's time span, more specific its coverage must be.

Personnel

The *personnel* needs in long-range planning are also different from those in short-range planning. Operating personnel in the subsidiaries and in the international division are involved in short-range planning, but long-range planning concerns staff people removed from day-to-day operations. For instance, long-range planning requires a higher level of executive involvement; a special long-range planning committee or similar arrangement is likely to include key executives on a regular even though infrequent basis. TRW, for example, has an annual retreat where its top executives take such a look into the future.

Long-range planning further requires a much greater input of outside expertise. Because the firm is concerned about long-run changes in the economic, social, political, and technological areas, the necessary expertise usually will be well beyond the capability of the in-house staff. For example, *Business International* has published research reports on long-range international planning in which a large part of the material is supplied by scholars in political science, sociology, economics, and engineering.

The Link of Long to Short

Now that we have distinguished between long-range and short-range planning, we should note the link between them. At some point in time, the changes and strategies identified in a long-range plan must become part of a short-range plan. That is, the early warnings eventually must take shape and become specific marching orders. In this way, the long-range plan provides a framework within which to design the short-range plan. As the long-range planners point out changes in the environment and develop broad strategies appropriate to meet these changes, the short-range planners see that the required adjustments in products, technology, markets, organization, and level of involvement are made gradually through a series of short-range operating plans.

For example, if the company's long-range plan indicates a seven-year target entry into a particular new market with certain kinds of products and levels of involvement, short-range plans will be patterned in such a way that each one leads the company progressively closer to meeting these long-range goals. Thus the two kinds of planning stand in an important relationship to one another, the long range dominant over the short. This link, however, does not require that the two planning activities be closely related within the organization but only that appropriate communication exist between them.

The Long-Range Planning Process

Situation Analysis

Although the long-range and short-range planning processes include the same steps, these steps are carried out differently. The first step in long-range planning is again analysis of the situation, but here the situation has yet to take place, and in an environment well hidden from the planner. The rationale for long-range planning is that if the firm can get a picture of future developments, it can avoid being overtaken by events. Perhaps it can even gain a competitive advantage by being prepared for these events. Therefore, management must try to peer through the clouds that veil the future. Dimensions of the future are not difficult to define in general terms: They include every factor or variable that can have a significant influence on the firm's success. In effect, the planner tries to get a picture of the long-run situation as it encompasses all the variables we discussed in Part I of this book. In review, some of the principal variables are the following:

1. Population—global and in individual markets
2. Demography—education, literacy, health
3. Income—size and growth of foreign markets
4. World trade—growth and patterns
5. International relations—Cold War, regionalism, commercial policy
6. Technology—relating to the firm's products and operations
7. Political environment—nationalism, relations with host governments
8. International business—foreign operations and international competition

EXTRAPOLATION   How can the planner identify and evaluate the future environment? One common way to look ahead is through extrapolation of past trends. This is the easiest and most convenient method, but it has severe limitations. It requires the assumption that the future will be like the past, only more so, thereby eliminating possible forecast of breakthroughs and new developments. Nevertheless, extrapolation may well be one useful input to the planner's view of the future. Any projection of the future involves uncertainty, and the planner needs inputs, from all possible sources in order to make the most informed prediction. Thus he may want to have extrapolations to compare against other kinds of estimates. Of course, extrapolation works better for some kinds of variables than for others, being probably more useful for determining population or world-trade trends than political or technological developments. If extrapolations are used, it is important that they be developed according to sound statistical methods.

ANALYSIS OF PARAMETER DETERMINANTS   A more logical way of looking at the future than to extrapolate past trends is to analyze the underlying determinants of the major parameters to see how they will change. For example, rather than merely extrapolating population growth rates, the planner can look at the factors determining population changes. In a given country, he would look not only at birth rates and death rates but also at government population policies, family planning programs, and religious and cultural influences.

Such an approach taken to each of the important parameters of the future environment can yield a range of estimates for each parameter. Although this method is more satisfying from a logical point of view, it is not guaranteed to be more accurate than an extrapolation. For this reason, the planner will find it helpful to use both methods and compare the results. Such a dual approach will offer better understanding and insights. Mathematical and computer models can be built around this approach, but much of the data are hard to quantify, and the amount of conjecture and uncertainty increases, the farther one looks into the future. Therefore, if such models are to be operational, they may have to wait for advances in the state of the art.

OUTSIDE EXPERTISE   We have assumed that the first two approaches to divining the future are conducted by the planning manager or his staff, if he has one. In many cases of long-range planning, the use of outside expertise to supplement these efforts will be desirable. For many parameters of the external environment, the people most knowledgeable about the future are likely to be outside the firm, in academic or research organizations. For other parameters, executives from various company departments and from foreign operations will have the greatest expertise. In every instance, the best inputs should be obtained, assuming the cost is reasonable. One special technique is available for getting the best guess about the future of a given parameter from a group of experts. It is called the "Delphi technique."

GOING TO DELPHI   Although named after the Oracle of Delphi in ancient Greece, the Delphi technique was developed by the Rand Corporation in about 1950. Many hundreds of corporations are considering its use today for their long-range planning, and in view of this growing acceptance, we will give a brief description of the steps involved: First, a panel of experts on the particular problem at hand is drawn from both inside and outside the company. Second, each expert makes a forecast, anonymously. Third, each panelist gets a composite feedback of the other panelists' answers. Fourth, a second round of forecasting begins. From then on the cycle is repeated, perhaps continuing for several more rounds.

Because the forecasts are anonymous, each panelist feels more free to change his mind and less committed to defending his original idea. Successive iterations are considered to improve the individual answers and to add up to a better group judgment. It is basically a form of consensus forecasting. One American company using the Delphi technique is TRW, which has fourteen panels at work with an average of seventeen experts each. Such a sizeable effort would be impossible in smaller companies, but a similar approach could be used. One consultant says, "The most important thing in using the Delphi technique is that you obtain innovative items, not just an extrapolation of the past."[1]

Setting Objectives

Once the best possible estimate of the future environment has been made, setting company objectives is a much simpler task, and one that does not require complex approaches or outside expertise. In deciding on the company's international posture, management must consider not only its international involvement but also the desired relation or integration between its domestic and international operations. It must set long-range goals for finance, production, personnel, and R&D, as well as for marketing. We will confine our discussion to such long-range international marketing goals as the firm's international product line, the number of foreign markets, and the nature of the firm's involvement in them. Goals must be set for the whole company, as well as for product lines or divisions and for country subsidiaries.

COMPARATIVE ANALYSIS   In setting long-range international marketing objectives, comparative analysis again can be useful. Let us consider first the case of *planning for new market entry*. As a firm expands its international business, it will want to enter new markets. How should it choose these new markets? One way is to screen the potential markets, to rank them according to the relevant criteria for selection, and then to make a more detailed study of the better candidate markets. In this latter area, comparative analysis can help the evaluation.

Let us assume that the firm has been operating over the years in many different countries at different levels of development. A level of development in this context does not necessarily refer to economic development but rather to whatever market development or classification scheme is meaningful in terms of the company's experience. These countries are classified, for example, as A, B, C, or D countries according to criteria important to the firm. In the list of new market candidates, the countries probably also can be classified on an A, B, C, D basis.

As the planner analyzes the reasons for the firm's success or failure in present A, B, C, and D markets, he has a higher probability of success in

---

[1] See *Business Week*, March 14, 1970, pp. 130, 132.

identifying the better markets among the new candidates. They would be those most like successful existing markets. Of course, the comparisons between present and potential markets are never perfect because each country is unique in some respects. Nevertheless, a comparative analysis that organizes the experience of the firm in a meaningful way should yield a more complete evaluation than will an analysis based only on an ad hoc evaluation of individual countries.

A second situation where comparative analysis can help the planner is in setting objectives for *changing the firm's posture* in a market. This can mean changing from exports to local production, expanding or changing the product line, or changing the ownership pattern (expanding or contracting equity). Too often, a firm's change of posture results from government action or competitive pressure rather than from its own planning. A firm with experience in countries at different levels of development—say, A, B, C, and D countries again—should be better prepared. As it analyzes this experience, it should discover patterns in its own development.

Countries moving from a D level to a C level may be ripe for the introduction of a new product or line ahead of competition. For example, an executive with a large American food company developed just such an approach for planning his international product line. Countries moving from a C level to a B level might be ready for local production in place of exports, or a joint venture rather than a licensing operation. The point is that by studying its historical development in all of its markets, the firm should be able to formulate some "model" or understanding of its market development which will in turn enable its planners to predict important turning points when a change of posture is appropriate.

Formulating Strategies

The long-range plan is quite vague compared to the great detail of the short-range plan. This difference is especially evident in the area of strategy formulation. Long-range international marketing strategy includes plans for the variables in the marketing mix plus other company activities that relate to the marketing program. Among the major elements are the following: (1) the design of the product development activity that leads to the international product line of the future; (2) the laying out of steps for entering the new markets where the firm wants to involve itself in the future; (3) an outline of how the firm will change its level of involvement in present markets to that which it feels will be appropriate in some future period; (4) the design of the firm's international logistics to meet its future international market situation as well as the future level of technology and trade restrictions.

We will not go into the many other aspects of long-range strategy except to mention the international marketing intelligence operation. Long-range plans are made on the basis of data that are very "old" in terms of the seven- or ten-year target of the plan. To allow for appropriate mid-course adjustments and corrections (as in space exploration), a good monitoring system is necessary. With the growth of the firm's international involvement and a steadily changing environment, most companies need to improve their information system as part of their long-range strategy. Many firms have invested much in their information system for domestic operations. As their international business grows, the same kind of sophistication will be needed for international intelligence.

COMPARATIVE ANALYSIS AGAIN   Formulation of long-range strategies is another area where comparative analysis can help the planner. In preparing strategy for a foreign market, or group of markets, the planner can again draw on his multinational experience. International marketers frequently have observed patterns or stages of market development insofar as their firm's products are concerned. Thus it may be that European distribution patterns are following American developments of one or more decades ago. This knowledge can be of great help in planning company distribution strategy for European markets. One international marketing manager found that his firm's experience with the disappearance of resale price maintenance (rpm) in the United States was very helpful to him in planning his European strategy, because the same trend away from rpm was occurring in Europe. To the extent that American marketing practices are precursors of developments elsewhere, this kind of comparison gives the American firm an edge in planning foreign market strategy.

Not only in comparing foreign operations with those in the United States can lead-lag relationships be found. Often the more fruitful comparisons will be between the firm's experience in foreign markets at different levels of development. Experience in France might be useful in planning strategies for former French colonies, for example.

One firm found that consumption of some of its synthetic-fiber products in Argentina followed the pattern observed in its Italian operations, but with a several-year lag. This information obviously would aid planning product and marketing strategy for Argentina. Another firm, in its production planning for less developed countries, found that the best model was not the United States operation but the Brazilian. The operation in Brazil was not at an intermediate level, and its current or recent experience was much closer to the kinds of problems encountered in countries lower on the development scale.

These examples show that, in order to be most useful, comparative analysis must be truly multinational or global. If comparisons are made only on the basis of United States experience, or only within a geographic region—say, Latin America—the value of the analysis is lessened.

Organizational Participation

Long-range planning generally requires less participation by the national subsidiaries and more by the international division and corporate headquarters than does short-range planning. Three reasons for this are that long-range planning requires much less of a commitment by the national subsidiary, the kind of information required for long-range planning is of a different and broader nature than that ordinarily available to local operations, and that the long-range plan is strategic, not operational, and therefore requires centralization. Decisions must be made at the overall corporate level on certain basic questions: (1) What business should we be in tomorrow? (2) What markets should we be in? (3) What should be the division of our efforts between international and domestic? Once the corporation has answered these questions, the international division can plan within the guidelines given by the answers. The next step is to get some inputs from the regional headquarters and/or the national subsidiaries.

Even though country operations play the lesser role in long-range planning, they still should participate to some extent. By their participation they will not only add viewpoints from different environments, but they also may contribute valuable insights not forthcoming from the corporate level, where a certain intellectual conformity may exist. Furthermore, the firm will benefit from improved subsidiary morale if they have a voice in shaping their own future.

Conclusion: Examples

In closing our chapter on planning, we will present two examples of actual company international planning experience. The first example shows how one firm got its foreign managers' participation in long-range planning.

Foreign Management Participation in Long-Range Planning

Corn Products Company International, which had one-half its $1 billion sales in 1967 outside the United States, succeeded in bringing its international and domestic managers together in a long-range planning session. The company had six operating units: two for the United States; one each for Europe, Latin America, and the Far East; and one for R&D. In February 1968, CPC organized a long-range planning conference for fifty-eight top executives from the United States and overseas. The meetings were held at an Eastern resort town. Over twenty of the participants came from the subsidiaries and regional managements, and most of them were local nationals. The time horizon of the planning was 1968 to 1976, the year for which the company has set a sales target of $2 billion.

The agenda for the meeting was prepared by officers at corporate headquarters and based upon suggestions of operating executives of the different groups. It included discussions of environmental changes as well as internal company developments. At the conference, each operating executive outlined projections of his unit's problems, opportunities, and expectations to 1976. Only five noncompany people attended. They were there as special resource people to supply expertise not available within the company. The four-day conference resulted in the establishment of individual-unit and overall company goals for the period to 1976. After the conference, all the participants went to corporate headquarters for another week to formulate strategies and programs for the attainment of their 1976 goals.[2]

[2] *Business International*, April 5, 1968, p. 107.

International Planning at IBM

Our second example is a brief description of the overall international planning process, both long- and short-range, at IBM, which has been engaged in it seriously since the late 1950s. In 1968, IBM World Trade Corporation (WTC) operated in 106 countries, with plants in thirteen countries. WTC gross income was $2 billion of a corporate total of $6.9 billion. Planning has been a continuous process at IBM and results annually in two plans: a seven-year strategic plan and a two-year operating plan. Our discussion will show (1) the roles played by the corporate, international, and foreign subsidiary parts of the firm, and (2) the different aspects of the plans and planning process at IBM.

Role of IBM Corporate Organization

Each January, the corporate organization set targets for WTC for each year of a seven-year period. WTC responded with its goals for each of the seven years. This resulted in a review and eventual agreement between WTC and the corporation on goals that were a desirable and achievable level toward which to plan. The document included the major strategic problems and opportunities, the work to be done, decisions made, and a schedule for completion. This led to the strategic planning within WTC itself.

Relationship of WTC and Country Organizations

FORECASTING   *WTC received from the product divisions "assumption packages" which described future products as to technical and marketing aspects. These were forwarded to the major countries to get forecasts of sales over the life of the product. These country forecasts were consolidated at WTC and communicated to the product divisions. The forecasting was a continuous activity and provided input for all plans although not a plan in itself.*

COUNTRY STRATEGIC INPUT (SEVEN YEARS)   *During January through March, the major countries developed their seven-year strategic input. This was used at WTC to respond to the corporate targets agreed upon in January. This strategic input included a situation analysis, the country objectives, and the major strategies for the seven-year period. Note that the foreign subsidiaries participated in this way in the long-range plan. WTC experience had shown this to be necessary if the goals were to be more than a statistical extrapolation. The country input was more qualitative than quantitative in this long-range plan.*

Plan Guidance (Two Years)

In April, plan guidance was sent from WTC to the country organizations. This guidance was a catalog of suggestions on short-run strategies. It also made the countries aware of the international programs and resources on which they could draw, for example, a Marketing Support Center for tele-processing equipment in Belgium.

Country Two-Year Functional Plan

From May to July, the countries developed their own functional plans. They followed on the guidance received and prepared their initial two-year plan. Like the guidance, it was organized by function, that is, marketing, manufacturing, and so on. These initial plans were reviewed on site in the larger countries by WTC staff functional specialists.

Country Two-Year Operating Plans

Following the WTC review of the functional plan, the subsidiaries prepared their operating plan in August and September. These operating plans were reviewed on site by a WTC management team. This detailed plan then represented a commitment by the country operation to WTC. These plans, incidentally, were each fourteen pages in length: one page of summary and thirteen pages of supporting material.

WTC Seven-Year Plan

The WTC seven-year plan was prepared during the last quarter of the year. It had two distinct parts. The first was the operating plan period, or the first two years, and it included the country operating plans. The WTC operating plan represented a commitment of WTC to the corporation for the next two years.

The second part of the seven-year plan was the strategic plan period, or years three through seven. The strategic plan portion was open-ended, that is, never completed or finalized. The purpose of the plan was to set long-range goals and to consider the means for attaining them. The document was not bulky and the emphasis was on qualitative rather than quantitative statements. The importance was not in the plan document, but in the results obtained in the improvement of the quality of planning and business strategy.

This WTC seven-year plan was reviewed by IBM corporate staff and eventually accepted. It then became the base for budgets and performance analysis. This finished the annual planning cycle at IBM and led to the beginning of the next year's planning, with seven-year targets coming from the corporation to WTC, as outlined above.[3]

Questions

15.1 "It is through planning, organization, and control that the various elements of the marketing mix are blended to achieve an effective international marketing program." Discuss.

15.2 Identify some of the differences in the constraints affecting planning in the multinational company as compared with those affecting a purely domestic firm.

[3] See Hans Fryburg, "Modern Concepts of Planning for International Success," *Proceedings: American Marketing Association* (June 1969), pp. 53–60, and *Business International,* August 25, 1967, pp. 271, 272.

15.3   Any level of involvement that is less than a wholly owned subsidiary may present constraints and limitations to the firm's national market planning process. Discuss the influence of the firm's level of involvement in a market on its ability to plan for that market.

15.4   Discuss the organizational division of labor possible in international marketing planning. What should be the major contributions of corporate headquarters and the national subsidiaries?

15.5   How can the national plans of many foreign markets be coordinated into an effective overall international plan?

15.6   How can comparative analysis aid in the preparation of short-range marketing plans in foreign markets?

15.7   Identify some of the principal environmental constraints to be considered in international long-range planning.

15.8   Evaluate the use of extrapolations of past trends as a way of estimating the future international environment.

15.9   "Company executives, in effect, constitute a Delphi panel for purposes of long-range international planning." Discuss. Evaluate the use of this technique for international long-range planning.

15.10 Discuss the use of comparative analysis in setting long-range international marketing objectives.

15.11 Identify the major elements to be considered in formulating long-range international marketing strategies.

15.12 Discuss the relative roles of subsidiary and international headquarters in long-range marketing planning.

Further Readings

Books:

Business International, "Planning for Profits," A Business International Research Report, 1967.

International Management Association, Inc., *Planning Overseas Operations,* International Management Series No. 1 (New York, 1956).

Liander, Bertil, Vern Terpstra, M. Y. Yoshino, and A. A. Sherbini, *Comparative Analysis for International Marketing,* Marketing Science Institute (Boston: Allyn and Bacon, 1967), part 1.

Steiner, George A., and Warren M. Cannon, *Multinational Corporate Planning* (New York: Macmillan, 1966).

Articles:

Cain, William W., "International Planning: Mission Impossible?" *Columbia Journal of World Business* (July–August 1970), p. 58.

Fryburg, Hans, "Modern Concepts of Planning for International Success," *Proceedings: American Marketing Association* (June 1969), pp. 53–60.

Goldman, Irwin, "The Special Problems of International Long-Range Planning," *Management Review* (April 1965), pp. 34–40.

Pryor, Millard A., "Planning in a World-Wide Business," *Harvard Business Review* (January–February 1965), pp. 130–139.

16

ORGANIZATION AND CONTROL OF INTERNATIONAL MARKETING

In Chapter 15, we examined the function and nature of planning in the integration of international marketing. We will now turn to the role of organization and control. Whereas planning helps to *prepare the way* for the coordination of international marketing, the organizational structure and relationships *provide the framework* in which coordination can occur. The task of control, by contrast, involves implementing the plan, actually *assuring the coordination* of international marketing activities. In this sense, coordination equals control, although it is facilitated and made possible by planning and organization. We will first look at organization as it contributes to the coordination of international marketing. The chapter will conclude with a discussion of the control process.

ORGANIZATION

By organization we mean the way a company structures the relationships among the various members and parts of the enterprise. Here we are not concerned directly with the legal or tax aspects of organization but with the divsion of labor in the management of a multinational company. Organization is concerned with how people work together in managing an enterprise. Therefore, establishing an effective organization requires an understanding of the human relations involved. In its organization, a company must find the degree of specialization, departmentalization, and hierarchy that structures its management into a coordinated and effective group or team.[1] In an oversimplified sense, we are asking the question, Who does what, where?

[1] See Edmund P. Learned and Audrey T. Sproat, *Organization Theory and Policy* (Homewood, Ill.: Richard D. Irwin, 1966), pp. 7–57.

Organization is not an end in itself but a means to an end. The goals of the multinational company's organization, we will assume for present purposes, are long-run growth and profits. The *general* principles of effective organization are as valid in the multinational company as in the company operating in a single market. The *special* organizational problems in the multinational company arise from what Fayerweather calls the communications gaps.[2] The far-flung operations of the international company give special emphasis to the cultural, nationality, and distance gaps in organizational communication. The firm must organize to adapt to these gaps and overcome them if it is to be an effective integrated international company.

By definition, the international company has operations in several countries. The purpose of its organization is to integrate these separate national operations into a coordinated unit. The goal is not only to avoid duplication but also to achieve synergism. The organizational form and structure that is appropriate for a company is a function of many variables, and an individual case solution is necessary. Some of the variables affecting the firm's international organization are the following:

1. Size of its business—overall volume and foreign volume
2. Number of markets in which it is operating
3. Level of involvement in its foreign markets
4. Company goals for international business
5. Company's international experience
6. Nature of its products—technical complexity, service needs
7. Nature of its marketing task

Before considering organizational possibilities for international companies, we should note two qualifications to our discussion. First, we will not spend much time on organization charts, and second, since we have noted organizational implications in discussing international marketing management throughout Part II, we will not duplicate that coverage. We have already seen how the organizational division of labor applies to the individual marketing functions and to international marketing planning. The more general and technical aspects of organization for international business can be found elsewhere.[3]

Organizational Alternatives

Although each company's organization must be designed to fit its particular situation, certain basic alternatives are available. A company can either handle its international business in a separate and specialized way, or it can integrate

[2] John Fayerweather, *International Business Management* (New York: McGraw-Hill, 1969), pp. 173–181.

[3] See Endel J. Kolde, *International Business Enterprise* (New York: Prentice-Hall, 1968), pp. 240–258; Harold Stieglitz, *Organization Structures of International Companies* (New York: National Industrial Conference Board, 1965); and Business International, *Organizing the Worldwide Corporation* (New York, 1970). The last is a valuable overview which will round out our picture of organization as it applies to international marketing.

it with the domestic business. Separate treatment can range from selling abroad through a combination export manager (CEM) to using an in-house export manager to creating a full-fledged international division. Integrated treatment or the "world company" approach can take varied forms also, as we will see below.

Organizational Separation

When companies begin international marketing, they usually make some special arrangement for it because it is so different from their regular business. As international business grows, the special arrangement may change from export manager to export department to international division. The last usually is accompanied by overseas production (licensees, joint ventures, and subsidiaries), and becomes much more a general management operation. Whereas the export department is primarily a sales department, the international division is concerned with all the functions of the business abroad, for example, production, finance, personnel, and so on.

Some kind of separate organizational provision is by far the most common arrangement, partly because it is most appropriate for the small and medium-sized companies whose principal international business is through exporting. Even in large companies—for example, Pfizer and Pirelli, IBM and ICI (Imperial Chemical Industries)—however, a separate international division is the predominant arrangement. This is especially true for American companies, and it is common wherever the international sales are one-third or less of the total corporate volume.

ADVANTAGES   Handling international business through a separate organizational arrangement offers several advantages. It is possible, for instance, to centralize all the specialized skills and international expertise in one place. We have seen countless examples of the special knowledge needed for international business decisions. If this knowledge were scattered throughout the company, putting it to use would be both costly and inefficient. A firm with many product divisions, for example, would have to go through a great deal of duplication and expense if each division had to have its own international expertise.

Another advantage of separation is that international business is less likely to be ignored or lost in the press of a large domestic business. For most American firms, the United States market currently is more important than other world markets. If international business were not separated, many international opportunities might be overlooked. Recently, in fact, both Fiat and Bristol Myers created separate international divisions to zero in on growing markets outside their home countries (Italy and the United States).[4] They had previously operated as integrated global companies.

Yet another advantage of separating international business lies in the potential contribution to corporate management. Top management can get a better

[4] *Organizing the Worldwide Corporation*, p. 7.

idea of the global implications of their decisions because of the expertise available in the international division. Many top executives in American firms do not have extensive international know-how and must rely on in-house specialists for background material on which to base their decisions. Furthermore, the international division can take a company-wide look at international markets from a viewpoint that may offer more objective and valuable information than that offered by individual product divisions from their necessarily limited viewpoints.

DISADVANTAGES   Although it is undoubtedly advantageous to handle international business separately when it is a small part of company volume, problems may arise in using this approach as international business grows. For example, the international division may be separate—but not equal. It may receive less top management attention than its potential warrants. Producing divisions often place servicing of the international division very low on their list of priorities, and this subordinate position can be reinforced by transfer-pricing policies, as we saw in Chapter 14.

Another danger in the international division approach is that it can lead to suboptimization. Treating international business separately may segment corporate resources, preventing their optimal use from the viewpoint of the firm's global interest. Especially in American companies where the domestic market is so large, expertise available from domestic operations may not be fully transferred to the international division, making its performance less successful than it could be.

A further problem relates to internal company politics. When the international division is small, it usually has less power to influence company decisions than its potential would indicate. On the other hand, when the international division becomes large and important, the other divisions usually want to get control over their own international business. In this situation, the international division has developed from being relatively insignificant to rivaling other divisions.

The World Company

The world corporation or global company is an organizational form that makes no distinction between domestic and international business. In principle, top management discriminates against no market, although larger markets would, of course, receive more attention. This global outlook should apply not only to investment decisions, but also to sourcing, staffing, research, and other company activities. Operational and staff groups would have global responsibilities, handling both domestic and international business.

In theory, the world company optimizes performance and profits on a global basis. In reality, this goal is not always realized. As noted in *Organizing the Worldwide Corporation*, the global company cannot escape the imprint of its nationality: "It was founded, usually by a group of nationals of a single country, is still domiciled in that country and subject to its laws. . . . Foreign operations, even with a high degree of autonomy, realize that the final shots are called by a foreign parent—be it Swedish, Swiss, or U.S."[5] Furthermore, top executives in such a company do not always have the international experience and expertise to go with their international responsibilities. In such cases, international business may suffer in comparison with domestic. In domestic operations, the executives are less uncertain and therefore feel more comfortable making decisions. Thus they tend to emphasize domestic operations as more "their kind of game."

Figure 16–1 shows a simplified organizational chart for Dow Chemical Company, a firm that uses the global company approach. Although Dow is an American company, in its organization, the United States is but one of five major market areas in the world.

Area, Product, or Functional Orientation?

Whether a firm takes an international division or a world company approach to organization, it still must decide whether this organization should be structured along geographic, product, or functional lines. All international business decisions usually require these three kinds of input and expertise. For example, the question of whether to introduce a new product in Brazil obviously will require area knowledge. However, product knowledge and marketing expertise also will be necessary. The same kinds of expertise are needed for analyzing such questions as, How should we distribute our products in India? or What should be our level of involvement in France? Figure 16–1 shows how Dow provides for these three kinds of specialized knowledge.

Structuring by Area

When the international division or global company is structured by area, the primary basis for organization is by divisions or sections for major regions of the world. For example, when CPC International reorganized from an international division to a world company approach, it set up five operating companies—one for Europe, one for Latin America, one for the Far East, and two for North America (consumer products and industrial products).[6] Although this is primarily a regional form of organization, the North American area is divided into two parts on the basis of product. Some form of regional organization is the most popular among multinational companies, including such prominent examples as Dow, Unilever, Nestle, and Pfizer. Pfizer takes an international division approach to its area structure, whereas the other three are global companies with area organizations.

Several factors favor a regional approach to organization. The growth of regional groupings is one reason today. As nations within a region integrate economically, it makes more sense for the firm to treat them as a unit. A traditional reason for regional organization was that the countries in the region were close to each other but rather far from company headquarters. Modern communications render distance less important, but the proximity of countries still provides a rather logical and clear-cut base for organization.

[5] *Organizing the Worldwide Corporation*, p. 19.
[6] *Wall Street Journal*, October 25, 1967, p. 18.

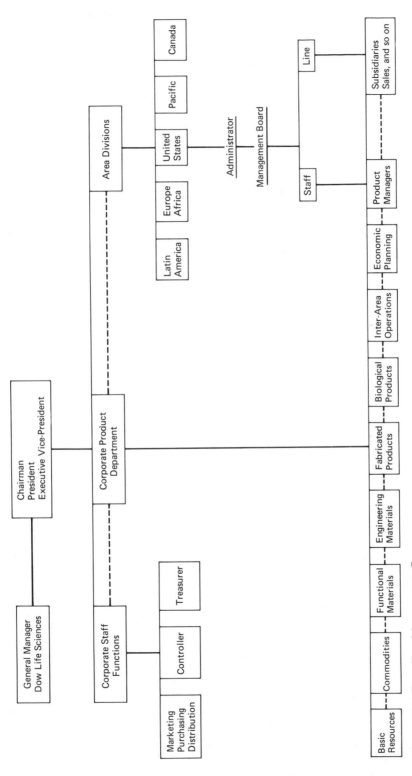

Figure 16–1 Dow Top Management Group

Certain kinds of expertise and resources can be grouped conveniently within the region for the benefit of individual country operations. Communications are easy and inexpensive. A narrow product line and similarity in technology and methods of operation also favor regional organization. The greater the international similarity of the firm's products and functions, obviously, the greater the importance of area knowledge.

In spite of its popularity, the regional approach to organization has its drawbacks. Although dividing an organization along regional lines assures the best use of the firm's regional expertise, it leads to a less than optimal allocation of product and functional expertise. If each regional group needs its own staff of product and functional specialists, costly duplication may result —and also inefficiency, if less than the best staff is available for each region. This inefficiency is most likely if the regional management is located away from corporate headquarters. If top regional management is located at corporate headquarters, expert centralized staff can serve all regional units, providing the firm some economies of scale. One large American firm recently brought back all its regional headquarters to corporate headquarters for this reason.[7] Of course, then the regional headquarters is not in such intimate contact with its region.

Structuring by Product

Organizing by product line usually means that product groups or divisions have global responsibilities for marketing their products; thus it is basically a world company approach by product division. An international division can be organized along product lines too, of course, but by its very nature it also includes area expertise as a principal organizational determinant. Structuring by product line is most common and most logical for companies with several unrelated product lines because their marketing task varies more by product line than by region. Diversified companies such as General Electric and Singer have had variations of the product structure. Firms that have expanded by merger and acquisition into unrelated fields—for example, Litton Industries— also favor a product approach to organization.

The Dutch company KZO markets world-wide through six product divisions: salt chemicals, fine chemicals, paints, pharmaceuticals, food products, and household goods.[8] KZO, through its mergers and acquisitions, is a good example of a European conglomerate. Because of the diversity of its acquired product lines, KZO chose a product structure for its world-wide operations. See Figure 16–2.

Structuring an organization along product lines is most appropriate for the diversified company. It also has the merit of flexibility, in that the firm can add a new product division if it enters another business quite unrelated to

[7] *Organizing the Worldwide Corporation*, p. 33.
[8] *Organizing the Worldwide Corporation*, p. 40.

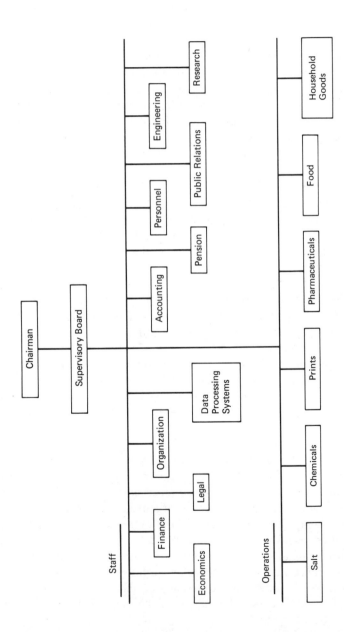

Figure 16–2 KZO Global Organization

its current lines. However, the product division approach has several potential limitations. Where the domestic market is more important to a product division, international market opportunities are likely to be missed, especially if the product division lacks the necessary international and regional expertise to exploit world markets.

Shortage of regional knowledge is a common weakness of product-structured organizations. Each product division cannot afford to maintain its own complete international staff. In lieu of such costly duplication, some firms maintain a mixed organization, including some elements of the international division or regional organization structure along with a basic product organization. Another problem in a product-structured approach is the difficulty of achieving company-wide coordination in international markets. If each product division goes its own way, the firm's international development will encounter conflicts and inefficiencies. The organization must provide for some kind of top-level global coordination to offset the sometimes contradictory international plans and programs of individual product divisions. For example, for each producing division to have its own advertising agency, service organization, and government relations staff in every market, is probably unnecessary.

Structuring by Function

A functional structure is a third way of organizing for international business whereby top executives in marketing, finance, production, and so on, all have global responsibilities. This form is most suitable for firms with narrow or homogeneous product lines, where product expertise is not a variable. It is also helpful if the regional variations in operations are not great, thus lessening the need for regional expertise. Because these conditions are not usually met, the functional form of organization is not common for American firms' international operations. Interestingly enough, however, it is the predominant form of organization for European companies' international operations. Because their domestic markets are smaller, they are in a different situation. Although functional executives in American firms often do have international responsibilities, as does the international marketing manager, these are usually in conjunction with a product or regional form of organization. Figure 16–3 shows the organization chart (by function) for one European company, SKF.

Choosing the Organizational Form

As our brief survey has shown, there is no perfect organizational form for conducting international business. Each kind of organizational structure has some weakness, usually in duplication of efforts and staff or in lack of coordination. Therefore, the appropriate organizational form for any company will be some compromise—a choice of the organization that best meets the firm's international and corporate goals but at the same time minimizes the inevitable problems arising from that form of organization. Since the organizational structure must also fit the particular variables of the individual company situation, it will be somewhat different in each company. It need not even be the same as those of other firms in the same industry. Indeed, when one

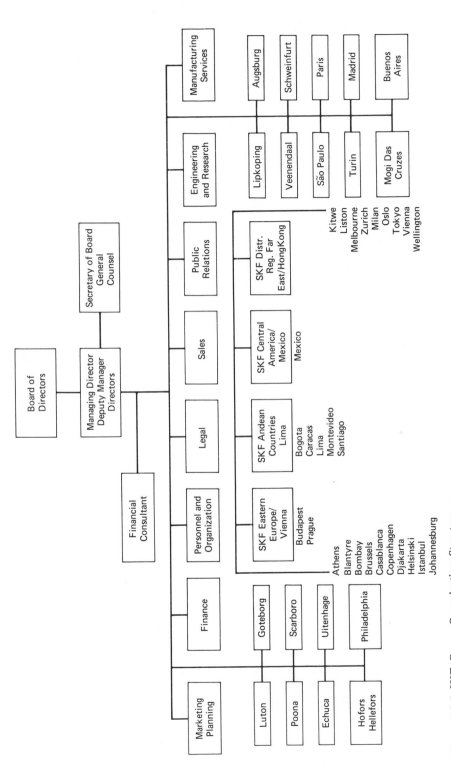

Figure 16–3 SKF Group Organization Structure
January 1969

examines the organization charts of international companies, the most striking fact that emerges is their diversity.[9]

Only rarely will a company's organization structure be a "pure" form according to the classifications we have used here. Almost always there is some blending of the regional, product, and functional elements. For example, the popular regional form of organization must allow for the necessary product and functional inputs. Similarly, the product or functional structure must allow for the other two inputs, because effective management requires all three, that is, the regional, product, and functional expertise. After all, the criterion is not how nice the structure looks on the organization chart but rather how well it facilitates the achievement of company goals.

The purpose of the international firm's organization is to eliminate or to minimize the communications gaps mentioned earlier and to blend the many country operations into an integrated, synergistic global company. Of course, the integration of multicountry operations will accomplish little if each national operation is inefficient. One way individual country operations are made efficient is through the provision of the resources and expertise of the whole multinational company. The organization should be designed to facilitate this. As Fayerweather notes: ". . . the objective of the organizational and administrative structure is to facilitate the flow of the necessary implementing skills and decisions toward the subsidiaries. Along with this is the secondary requirement that there be an adequate return flow of information, so that the skills and decisions transmitted to the field will be appropriate."[10]

A final word on organizational form concerns its temporary nature. Because of the dynamic environment, the determinants of a company's international organization structure, including company goals, are constantly changing. Therefore, organization planners never achieve the "ideal organization." At best, they can find one that works reasonably well for a given company situation and environment. Because organization is an evolutionary phenomenon, good organization planning will design it to be flexible so that it can adapt with the times. Then, when changes must occur, they can be accommodated without drastic consequences to the company and personnel involved. This is especially important for multinational companies that must organize and accommodate the nationals—and nationalism—of many countries.

International Marketing and Organization

We have looked at organization in terms of overall international business operations, but our interest is primarily in international marketing. How does marketing fit in with the overall organization? Marketing, as one function of the firm, obviously must follow the overall organizational patterns. It is not a question of one organization for marketing and another for the rest of the company operations. Organizational patterns and reporting relations in marketing must be consistent with those for other functions. One way marketing may differ from other functions is in the degree of decentralization. Since

---

[9] See Stieglitz, *Organization Structures of International Companies.*
[10] Fayerweather, *International Business Management*, p. 172.

marketing must relate intimately to the local market, marketing decisions usually have a greater degree of decentralization than do decisions in such functions as finance or production.

A study by Aylmer of several manufacturers of consumer durables gives a striking indication of the degree of decentralization of marketing decision making in this industry. The study covered twenty-six local affiliates and a total of eighty-six separate marketing programs.

The most striking pattern is the vital role played by local management in the development of marketing programs. Local management was primarily responsible for 86% of the advertising decisions, 74% of the pricing decisions, and 61% of the channel decisions. . . . The final task of developing viable local strategy was left to local management. . . . Only product design decisions were imposed upon local management in 55% of the cases observed.[11]

The *basic* task of international marketing management is the same regardless of the particular form of organization in a company. However, the scope of the international marketer's job may be somewhat restricted in a regional or product form of organization; that is, he may cover just one region or product group. Nevertheless, in every form of organization he must assure the transmission of marketing skills and resources from the corporation to the individual units. He also must act as a clearinghouse among the various national operations, an important function because the domestic operations do not have a monopoly on useful ideas and experience. Finally, he must coordinate and integrate the various national marketing programs, especially where the markets are interrelated in any way.

Where the firm follows a product or regional form of organization, it needs a corporate-wide international marketing manager or coordinator in addition to personnel with international marketing responsibilities in the product or regional divisions. Because the marketers in a product or regional group have only a partial view of the firm's international marketing, a corporate-wide coordinator is necessary to assure functional optimization at the overall corporate level.

That the organization form facilitate the task of international marketing management is important because marketing plays a critical role in the international company. First, because the firm is a foreigner in all but one of its markets, marketing as adaptation to the market helps the firm overcome the handicaps of its foreignness. Second, marketing skills are usually an important part of the competitive advantage of the international company. For example, studies by both the author and the OECD have shown marketing skills and orientation to be important advantages of American companies in Europe.[12]

[11] R. J. Aylmer, "Who Makes Marketing Decisions in the Multinational Firm?" *Journal of Marketing* (October 1970), pp. 26, 27. Emphasis added.

[12] Vern Terpstra, *American Marketing in the Common Market* (New York: Praeger, 1967); OECD, *General Report—Gaps in Technology*, 1968.

Ford Tractor provides a good example of how the organization form must reflect the marketing task to be performed.

Ford Tractor established two new marketing organizations for its markets outside North America and Europe. *Rather than organizing these markets (in Latin America, Eastern Europe, Africa, the Middle East, and the Far East) along product or geographic lines, the company grouped them by the nature of the marketing job. Overseas sales subsidiaries reported to the General Manager—Overseas Affiliates. Independent distributors reported to the General Manager—Overseas Direct Markets.*

The change was prompted by the recognition that the problems and opportunities of selling through independent distributors are quite different from those of marketing through subsidiaries. Hence, the company decided to streamline its international marketing, tailoring it to the specific needs of the different channels.[13]

Centralization and Decentralization

We have seen that organization reflects the specialization and division of labor in the management of a company. All our previous discussion, however, has considered the division of labor according to only three criteria—regions, products, and functions. The terms "centralization" and "decentralization" describe another kind of specialization within the international company, that is, the division of labor between corporate headquarters (the home office) and the operations in each national market. Before we were looking at horizontal specialization, or that between divisions or functions; now we will look at vertical specialization, or that between different levels of the company.

We have already noted that marketing decisions tend to be more decentralized than those in some other areas. What *organizational* factors affect the location of marketing decisions in the firm? The most important, according to Aylmer, are (1) the relative importance of the firm's international operations and (2) the relative importance of the local subsidiary within the firm.[14] The larger the firm's international business becomes, the more the home office participates in local marketing decision making. Working in the opposite direction is subsidiary size. The greater the subsidiary's relative size, the more autonomy it enjoys in marketing decisions.

Marketing management, obviously, must be largely carried out near the marketplace. But as we have seen repeatedly in Chapters 7 through 15, the international marketing manager at corporate headquarters also must play a big role. This role involves transmitting skills and resources to the subsidiaries, helping to plan and coordinate their activities, and acting as a clearinghouse for international marketing experience and know-how. We will summarize and review briefly the respective roles of corporate headquarters and the national subsidiary.

[13] *Business International*, November 20, 1970, p. 374.
[14] Aylmer, "Who Makes Marketing Decisions in the Multinational Firm?" p. 27.

Corporate Headquarters

Corporate headquarters must set overall objectives and policies for world markets and play the major role in long-range market planning. Another task of corporate headquarters is to provide ideas, techniques, and resources to help the local subsidiary management to market effectively. Finally, corporate headquarters must coordinate, beginning with the planning stage, the marketing programs of the various subsidiaries to avoid duplication and to help assure effective integration of the firm's international marketing. In fact, it is these activities at corporate headquarters that permit one to speak of "international marketing" rather than of a collection of national marketing programs.

The Local Subsidiary

The local subsidiary carries out most of the actual marketing management in its own country, within the guidelines and with the support of corporate headquarters. The local subsidiary conducts market research. It should have a voice in product policy, although it may have less control in this area than elsewhere. It will help to select, and then administer, distribution channels. It should have a voice in its pricing policies, if not control over them. It will manage the sales force and direct the promotional program. (Our chapters on these subjects have covered the organizational aspects of all these marketing tasks.) In terms of reporting relationships, the local marketing management probably would report to top management of the subsidiary. There should also be some reporting relationship between local marketing management and the international marketing manager at the corporate level.

Licensee and Distributor Markets

Even though corporate headquarters has no line authority over licensees and distributors, the firm needs effective marketing in licensee and distributor markets as well as in its own subsidiary markets. Thus the international marketing manager must, *insofar as possible*, play the same role in these markets that he plays in markets with subsidiaries; that is, he must assist licensees and distributors with ideas, materials, and guidance in marketing the firm's products. From the organizational standpoint, he does not even have a dotted-line relationship with these people, but he must try to achieve the same effect through maintaining good relations with them. We discussed some of the ways he can do this in Part II, especially in the chapters on distribution.

Regional Headquarters: A Halfway House

We have considered decentralization in terms of the managerial division of labor between corporate headquarters and the units in the foreign markets. Frequently, however, as the firm's business in a region such as Europe or Latin America grows larger, it becomes important enough to warrant separate special attention. This could lead to the establishment of a new level in the organization between corporate headquarters and the foreign markets, that is, a regional headquarters. A regional headquarters is not necessarily located within the region, although usually it is for the larger regions, such as Europe.

Many American companies, for example, have their Latin American headquarters in Coral Gables, Florida, truly a halfway location between corporate headquarters and country operations. Regardless of location, however, regional headquarters gives undivided attention to the affairs of the region.

As Adam Smith said, specialization is limited by the size of the market. As regional markets become large enough, they may warrant the firm's specialized attention and expertise. Whether the addition of a regional headquarters level leads to duplication depends on the division of labor between the corporate, regional, and subsidiary levels. For many companies, establishing a regional headquarters can increase overall efficiency.[15]

Regional headquarters often represents a useful halfway house in the decentralization of international business management. Although regional headquarters obviously fits in with a regional form of organization, it is often found with a product division form of organization, too. It can coordinate the activities of various product groups within the region and handle matters of common corporate interest. The rise of regional groupings reinforces its usefulness. Although modern communications and information systems encourage the centralization of international business management, we have seen that many management decisions and activities need to be decentralized, either to a regional level of management or to the country operations themselves.

CONTROLLING INTERNATIONAL MARKETING

Companies engage in international operations to attain certain corporate goals. We have assumed that their major goals are long-run growth and profits, but of course many intermediate and short-range goals lie along the road to achieving these major goals. The purpose of control is the regulation and direction of operations in order to achieve the desired objectives. Considered in this way, control is the essence of management. The basic control process involves the following three steps:

1. Establishing standards
2. Measuring performance against the standards
3. Correcting deviations from standards and plans[16]

Control is inextricably related to the two previous topics, planning and organization. Indeed, planning and organization can be considered steps or elements of the control process. Planning involves the setting of standards and goals, the first step in the control process. The organization of the firm establishes the hierarchy and division of labor in management control and structures the communications channels necessary to it. Not only that, the degree of decentralization practiced in a company determines the extent of

[15] See Charles R. Williams, "Regional Management Overseas," *Harvard Business Review* (January–February 1967), pp. 87–91.
[16] Harold Koontz and Cyril O'Donnell, *Principles of Management* (New York: McGraw-Hill Book Co., 1955), p. 550.

the control task. For example, a multinational company with a high degree of decentralization—that is, one with very self-sufficient subsidiaries—has very little control problem at the headquarters level. Much of the control is accomplished through self-control at the subsidiary level. On the other hand, a firm that tries to integrate many national subsidiaries into a coherent global operation has an extensive job of control at the headquarters level.

As we have noted frequently, general management principles are as valid internationally as they are domestically. This applies to control of international marketing operations as well. The differences and special problems arise, as usual, from the different environments in which these operations occur. The communications gaps already discussed are the major causes of difficulty— the distance between the firm's different markets and the differences in language, nationality, culture, and environment. Special technical problems also arise from differences in financial and monetary environments. For example, government supervision, exchange controls, and differing rates of inflation in international markets limit the firm's ability to control transfer prices, remittances, and the logistics of individual country operations, that is, where it will source and sell internationally.

The various communications gaps are also related to personal frictions in the control process. A study by C. Wickham Skinner revealed that many overseas managers had a strong feeling of resentment toward the home office. This resentment was reflected in charges of undue interference, inadequate delegation of authority, onerous reporting requirements, and lack of understanding and sympathy. On the other hand, "home office executives were often frustrated by possessing a sense of responsibility which is thwarted by having only paper authority over the field operations."[17] The inevitable frictions between the controllers and those being controlled are thus magnified in international business. The control system must be designed to minimize the international and intercultural conflicts but at the same time to retain effective direction of operations.

Our discussion of control will emphasize the role of international marketing management more than it will the issue of local control within an individual foreign market. The latter problem differs little from that in domestic marketing. We assume that the reader has already examined the subject of control in domestic marketing elsewhere. Our concern is the role of corporate headquarters and the international marketing manager in controlling the firm's international marketing.

For our purposes here, we take for granted an important role for the international marketing manager; that is, we assume that everything has not been decentralized to the national subsidiary. We have suggested repeatedly that unless corporate headquarters is active in its coordination efforts, there is likely to be a great deal of suboptimization in the firm's international opera-

---

[17] Cited in Richard D. Robinson, *International Management* (New York: Holt, Rinehart and Winston, 1967), p. 150.

tions. As Gianluigi Gabetti, president of Olivetti-Underwood, put it: "If a multinational firm is not centralized, at least for control and coordination, all the advantages of their worldwide association are lost."[18]

We will organize our discussion around the three aforementioned steps of the control process: (1) establishing standards, (2) measuring performance against the standards, and (3) correcting deviations from standards and plans. Within this framework, we will note the various tools and techniques available to facilitate the control of international marketing.

Establishment of Standards

The establishment of standards is critical because it determines the pattern of the whole control process. The number of standards and the way they are established and used will have a great impact, both on human relations within the organization and on the effectiveness of corporate control of international marketing. To be effective, standards must be not only clearly defined; they must be understood and accepted by those whose activities are being controlled.

What Standards?

The concern of the international marketing manager, of course, is with the firm's marketing performance in all of the various national markets. If corporate goals are growth and profits, the standards should relate to these goals, since the purpose of control is to achieve the firm's objectives. Overall growth and profits, however, are too broad and general to serve as operational standards. Therefore, specific intermediate standards must be established which further attainment of the larger goals.

Control standards for marketing should cover all aspects of marketing performance that are controllable, that is, those in which subsidiary management has power to affect results. Standards can be set for all the marketing functions performed locally (all those we discussed in Part II of this book). For example, marketing research standards can be set as to the number and kinds of research studies and how they are done. Targets can be established for sales volume by product line and perhaps by month or quarter; market-share targets are another possibility. In the product area, quality control standards can govern local production, targets can be set for product development, and service standards can apply where products require them.

In distribution, standards can be set for market coverage, dealer support, and performance of the channel. In pricing, standards can be established for price levels and margins on different products and for price flexibility or stability—including regular increases in markets with high rates of inflation. Pricing standards would apply to leasing and service charges, too. In promotion, standards can be set concerning the volume and nature of local advertising, the media used, and some measure of the effectiveness and impact of the advertising. Sales force development and management would be included under promotional standards.

Management, of course, is concerned not only with meeting targets but also

[18] *Business Abroad* (September 1969), p. 16.

with efficiency. Therefore the standards will include efficiency measures such as marketing cost ratios or return on sales or investment. In calculating profits, a special problem arises in international operations. Should they be calculated in the local currency where earned? Or should they be in the currency of remittance (dollars), that is, after devaluations and so on? Although the parent company may well want dollar profits, that places a burden on local management different from accountability for local currency earnings. This problem arises primarily where inflation and currency depreciation are common.

How Are Standards Determined?

The issue under discussion is corporate control of marketing within its foreign markets. The standards set, therefore, must be appropriate not only to corporate needs but also to the situation within each market. Corporate headquarters thus cannot impose standards arbitrarily but must use significant local input to establish local standards. Not only do nationals know the local market situation better, but also they will work harder to achieve goals they helped to determine.

Although local management plays an important role in determining local standards of performance, corporate interests are not best realized through a laissez-faire approach. The international marketing manager must help in establishing local marketing standards. Under a laissez-faire approach, local management tends to set standards and targets that are easy to meet. The international marketer must see that local standards are challenging enough to demand the best performance from the subsidiary. The standards finally incorporated into the operating plan for a given year thus will be some compromise and agreement between subsidiary and corporate management.

The actual methods and means of setting standards are several. The job descriptions of marketing personnel in the subsidiary should given preliminary ideas about the kind of performance required. However, the primary establishment of standards normally is done in the annual planning process, as we saw in Chapter 15. As the operating plan is finalized, many of the standards will be indicated in the annual budget. Although much of the planning communication between the subsidiary and corporate headquarters will be of an impersonal nature, personal contact sometime during the year is highly desirable. Such contact may be through the travel of the international marketing manager or through regional or corporate-wide meetings of the relevant managers. Personal meetings can help to minimize the misunderstandings and frictions that arise from purely impersonal and mechanical communications. The resentment noted by Skinner (see p. 491) can be offset partially by such face-to-face encounters.

COMPARATIVE ANALYSIS AGAIN   Comparative analysis once again can be a useful method for the international marketing manager to use in determining appropriate standards for individual national markets. The international marketer has the benefit of *local knowledge* in the inputs of the local subsidiary.

However, he is also familiar with all the *other international markets* of the firm, as well as with *domestic operations*. This experience helps him to recognize to what degree the market in question is like other markets of the firm and to what degree it is different. In the pricing area, for example, standards will be affected by competition, income levels, the role of government controls, and the rate of inflation. Experience with a group of markets that are similar on these parameters will aid the international marketer in finding appropriate standards for any one of them. If the comparisons are well made, the standards derived should be more appropriate and acceptable to the local market than standards drawn from, say, the firm's domestic operations or an ad hoc analysis of one country market by itself. Product sales quotas, sales force performance, and other local marketing standards and objectives can be determined by using a similar approach.

A survey by Butler and Dearden also emphasized the need for "common denominator yardsticks that can be applied around the world."

Companies that do not have tools to measure relative contributions to total profitability often get involved in costly communications problems. There are always differences in outlook between parent company and affiliate management, but these can become exaggerated when the results of a number of affiliates are judged by factors that will not stand comparison. Inevitably, this leads to detailed reporting which results in duplication and buildup of staff. It also places foreign national management at a disadvantage. Sometimes it means that too many people spend too much time defending yesterday's performance rather than focusing on today's operations and tomorrow's opportunities.

Wanted: Common denominator yardsticks that can be applied around the world.[19]

Measurement and Evaluation of Performance

Once management has decided on the appropriate standards of marketing performance in the local subsidiaries, it must establish a system for monitoring actual performance against those standards. Standards are not self-enforcing. They are adhered to only through the management control process. To achieve adherence to its standards, management first must be able to observe current performance. In international marketing, management's observation of subsidiary performance usually is not personal; rather it is indirect, through some kind of intelligence or information system.

Measurement = Feedback

Distance and communications gaps hinder the measurement process in international marketing. Two ways these gaps can be minimized are through the use of an effective information system for international operations and through decentralization of authority and control to regional headquarters or local

---

[19] W. Jack Butler and John Dearden, "Managing a Worldwide Business," *Harvard Business Review* (May–June 1965), p. 95.

subsidiaries. Both methods are used, but our discussion will concern primarily those areas of control that have not been decentralized. It should be noted that modern technology and communications have facilitated a more centralized control of international operations, as we saw earlier in the case of the firm's global logistics.

In today's world, many means of communication are available to headquarters to get feedback on subsidiary operations: mail, cable, telex, telephone, travel, and conferences and meetings. Satellites soon will enable companies to hold international closed-circuit televised meetings. The various international reports also can be tied in with a computerized management information system to expedite the processing of the data. When a firm has many foreign operations, it is obviously necessary that reports follow a standard format so that various subsidiaries can be analyzed and compared effectively. Reports also must use standard units and a common currency as well as a standard company language. Whereas American and British firms obviously use English, it is not uncommon for other multinational companies also to use English as the official company language. For example, Philips (Dutch) and SKF (Swedish) use English as the company language. Nestle (Swiss) uses both English and French.

REPORTS   A critical factor in the feedback system is the number, nature, and frequency of reports from the subsidiaries. The reports should cover all the factors over which corporate headquarters wants control and they should be regular enough so that management has time to react effectively in controlling or redirecting operations. These criteria are very general and need interpretation on a case-by-case basis. Some items or deviations may need to be reported immediately, others on a weekly, monthly, or quarterly basis. Despite the general nature of these criteria, however, they can be useful in helping to avoid some of the major problems of international reporting systems. These problems occur both on the corporate headquarters side and on the subsidiary side of operations.

From the corporate headquarters side, a frequent problem in the international reporting system is that too much information unnecessary for decision purposes is coming in at the same time that insufficient information is being received on certain variables which do trigger decisions. Many companies could make their information system more effective and less expensive by concentrating on the relevant decision variables, thereby saving executive time as well as data transmission and storage costs. Another problem is that information comes in too late for management to take effective action. It can be seen that the design of a streamlined, relevant reporting system can be an effective way of improving management's control of international operations. All these problems could be minimized or even eliminated by such a system. In the marketing area, it is the task of international marketing management to design its reporting system as part of the overall company system. A good design would incorporate the latest communications technology along with the principles of information system design.

As we saw earlier, the subsidiary side also has problems with the reporting system. Subsidiary management often feels that corporate reporting requirements are too numerous and onerous, represent undue interference and inadequate delegation of authority, and show a lack of understanding of the local situation. The reports often breed resentment and conflicts between subsidiary and parent. All these problems suggest a minimizing and streamlining of the reporting requirements. Corporate headquarters should not eliminate all reporting requirements for subsidiaries, however; some centralized control is necessary for effective international operations. Nevertheless, the reporting requirements can be limited to those *items on which corporate action is necessary*, for example, items in which headquarters has expertise not available to the subsidiary or items involving some aspect of international marketing, as opposed to purely domestic marketing questions in the subsidiary's market.

MEETINGS   In contrast to this impersonal method of written reporting is the personal approach to obtaining information through regular meetings of subsidiary management with regional or corporate executives. These gatherings provide a more intimate forum and permit a much more intensive examination and interchange. The major limitation on such meetings is the executive time and travel involved, but it is somewhat minimized if regional rather than headquarters executives attend the regular meetings. The costs involved are partially offset by the elimination of many of the regular mailed or cabled reports which instead are presented personally. Further benefits of this approach are that misunderstandings are reduced and the control process is more effective. Efficient use of this method requires that meetings be frequent enough to allow management to retain effective control of current operations. Even so, such meetings cannot be frequent enough to supply the continuing flow of information possible with more impersonal reporting methods. The advent of international closed-circuit television may lead to big changes here.

The most famous example of the meeting method of control is provided by International Telephone and Telegraph (ITT). President Harold Geneen instituted a monthly review of ITT's European operations. It was held in Brussels and was based on the company's "business plan," a two-year operating plan, rewritten annually and reviewed monthly. Subsidiary managements met monthly with top ITT executives. The company's performance suggested that this method of intensive probing and confrontation was an effective method of control.[20]

Sylvania International (of General Telephone and Electronics) wanted to improve its marketing trips abroad. It sent a "task force" consisting of a product specialist and an international marketing researcher to all its Latin American locations. They sat down with the local manager and together answered seventeen pages of carefully phrased questions. As a result, time required for the marketing trips was reduced by one-third, and more valuable information was obtained than in the previous approach.[21]

[20] *Business Week*, June 24, 1967, pp. 58–62.
[21] *Business International*, June 2, 1967, p. 171.

SPECIAL MEASUREMENT TECHNIQUES   In addition to the general and continuing information flows of the regular reporting system are various specialized techniques for measuring and evaluating marketing performance. Two of the most noteworthy are distribution cost analysis and the marketing audit. These are discussed in regular marketing texts and we assume that the reader is familiar with them. Here we wish merely to suggest their usefulness to the international marketing manager.

Distribution cost analysis is a technique for analyzing the costs and profitability of different parts of the marketing program. It can be used to study product lines, distribution channels, customers or territories, and so on. For several reasons the international marketer should introduce this control mechanism into his foreign markets. Not only will it help to improve the sophistication and efficiency of local marketing management, but also it will help the international marketer to get a better picture of local operations. Furthermore, by comparative studies of his markets, he can recognize specific weaknesses in marketing programs and find solutions to recommend for markets having particular problems.

The *marketing audit* has become somewhat popular recently, at least in the literature. There is no precise definition, but it usually implies a methodical and thorough examination or review of the total marketing effort, often by some outside expert. Such an audit perhaps could be done usefully by the international marketing manager for each of his markets every few years. If his staff is adequate and the necessary expertise is acquired, the cost involved would not be great. Certainly the audit would add to marketing management's understanding of the firm's foreign marketing and aid in improving it.

A marketing audit would be especially useful when the firm is changing the nature of its involvement or activity in a country. At a higher level, a marketing audit could be made of the total international marketing activity of the firm rather than just the marketing done by subsidiaries. Although some review of marketing effort presumably is carried out in connection with both short-range and long-range planning, it is probably not the same kind of careful, deliberate analysis done in a marketing audit. Considering the dynamic environment of international marketing, such a review could be useful in keeping marketing programs up-to-date.

Evaluation

The purpose of measuring subsidiary performance is to be able to take action (control) when things get out of line (deviate from standards). Therefore, performance not only must be measured but also must be evaluated. Management has to know what deviations from standards are unacceptable and require action, and thus the international marketer must have an understanding of the local situation as well as of corporate desires. For evaluation of subsidiaries, comparative analysis can again be useful. As Yoshino notes:

There are two ways whereby corporate headquarters can evaluate the performance of each foreign affiliate. One is to examine each unit against its own standards and goals, and the other is to assess each affiliate against the others. Of course, the two methods are complementary in nature. Comparability can also be achieved in two different ways. One is to reduce the data submitted by various affiliates to common denominators through technical adjustments. The other method is to limit comparison to those operations with similar operating characteristics.[22]

Controlling

To assure the attainment of corporate goals, management must correct performance that deviates from standards and plans; that is, mangement must control operations. The control process, therefore, culminates in actually making the necessary adjustments and directing operations. In international business, control is often difficult to achieve because of the distance and communication gaps already noted. However, it is very necessary if the far-flung country operations are to be an effective, integrated international operation. The multinational firm must be especially sensitive in establishing its control system; it is not merely an organizational problem, as in domestic operations, but has the added dimension of satisfying different national and cultural sensitivities.

Means of Maintaining Control

PLANNING   Planning is not usually considered part of the control process but actually it is. Goals are established in the planning process, but more important to the control function is commitment by the various parts of the organization to meeting the standards spelled out in the operating plan and budget. Planning is preventive medicine in that it minimizes the need for controls, as illustrated especially clearly in the case of contingency planning. When there is a significant deviation from the standards set up in the original operating plan, the control technique may be to shift to the contingency plan.

ORGANIZATION   The organization of an international firm sets the framework of the control process. Indeed, the purpose of organization is to facilitate managerial control of operations. Organization determines the relationships between different parts of the company and between different levels of management. It shows the lines of authority, the hierarchy of control. As we saw in the first part of this chapter, some organizational forms offer more effective control and coordination than others.

Organization determines the levels of management and the span of control. Perhaps only corporate headquarters and the subsidiaries comprise the company's structure, or perhaps there are intermediate levels such as regional headquarters or product coordinators. The degree of decentralization in the organization determines the division of labor in the task of control, including the role of the international marketing manager. Although not necessarily shown in the organizational structure, other organizational means can be used

---

[22] Bertil Liander et al., *Comparative Analysis for International Marketing*, Marketing Science Institute (Boston: Allyn and Bacon, 1967), p. 32.

to maintain control. One study found that European companies rely mainly on people—individual executives—as the elements of control and coordination. In fact, European companies tailor their organizations to fit the abilities and personalities of the executives, rather than choosing executives who fit the organization form. The report stated:

> *This is practical and possible due to the fact that executives in Europe are less mobile than in the U.S. They tend to grow with a firm, and stay with it a large portion of their working career. Because of tenure, executives in such firms tend to know each other well, and interpersonal relationships tend to be strong, giving validity to informal lines of reporting and communication.*[23]

Another organizational device for coordination and ·control is the management committee. A management committee may operate on a regional, product, or functional basis and have varying memberships. Such committees may be difficult to place on the organization chart, but they can be effective in monitoring and controlling operations. Yet another organizational approach to control is the management meeting, as in the ITT example already cited. This type of regular meeting of key managers is not only a reporting method. It can be a most effective means of controlling and correcting operations.

THE BUDGET   The budget is primarily a way of spelling out standards. To a lesser degree, it is an instrument of control in the sense of helping subsidiaries to meet those standards. The trouble is that the budget acts as a brake, when what is often needed is an accelerator. The nature of the control offered by the budget is essentially negative: it may prevent excessive expenditure in various areas, but it does not assure that the desired goals are reached. Furthermore, as Robinson notes, if the foreign subsidiary is substantially independent financially and in its operations, control from corporate headquarters can be very difficult.[24]

SUBSIDIARIES AS PROFIT CENTERS   One way of handling the control problem and minimizing the burden on corporate headquarters is to have each foreign subsidiary operate as a profit center. Profit centers can take on varying degrees of responsibility. Where there is a high degree of delegation and decentralization, the firm will place most control problems on the subsidiary. Headquarters may enter the scene only if profits are unsatisfactory. Of course, profits must be defined in terms of the time period—usually one year—and the currency—local currency or dollars; they also must be related to return on sales or investment. Most American companies operate their foreign subsidiaries as profit centers, but with differing degrees of decentralization.

The profit center approach to controlling subsidiaries has several advantages and disadvantages. It is good in that it maximizes the use of local knowledge and on-the-spot decision making and minimizes some of the frictions and public relations problems of absentee management. It is good for subsidiary

[23] *Organizing the Worldwide Corporation*, p. 69.
[24] Robinson, *International Management*, p. 160.

morale because local management likes to "run its own shop." Of course, competent local management is a necessity if there is to be decentralized control of operations.

On the negative side, local management, evaluated on short-run profitability, may act in ways that endanger long-run profits. Very autonomous subsidiaries are also more difficult to integrate into a coherent international operation. Therefore, a high degree of decentralization is most feasible when the local subsidiaries are most self-contained in buying and selling and have minimal reliance on the corporation for other inputs.

INTERDEPENDENCE AND COMMON INTEREST   We might say that control may take on aspects of both the carrot and the stick. It usually will employ both positive and negative incentives. The negative approach, which includes legal pressures and the threat of firing, is probably reasonably effective in getting minimum performance. Obtaining strong or outstanding performance in relation to goals, however, is more likely with a positive approach. Some of the positive motivations controlling subsidiary performance are the benefits the subsidiary receives from its interdependence and common interest with the international company. In contrast to the self-sufficiency of autonomous subsidiaries, interdependent subsidiaries are more or less heavily reliant on the parent corporation. Some of the benefits a subsidiary may receive from the parent corporation include the following:

1. Product inputs, from raw materials to finished products
2. An export marketing network for its production
3. Financial resources
4. Technological assistance in engineering and production
5. Marketing know-how, as discussed in Part II
6. Management development programs, which may be very important to the managers being controlled

Licensee and Distributor Markets

Most of the control techniques discussed do not apply to licensee and distributor markets. In these markets, the corporation has no ownership or organizational control. The principal legal tie is the contract or agreement relating them, but, as we have already seen, legal pressures or controls can only assure minimum performance at best. At worst, they can lead to a severing of relationships and, possibly, loss of the market. Therefore, the best "control" is to motivate licensees and distributors by making them realize that the corporate interest is also theirs. The company must make the relationship valuable to the licensee or distributor so that he also benefits from doing what the company wants done. We have examined several advantages he may obtain from the relationship, including good products well promoted and marketing, technical, and management support (see Chapter 11). The essential task of the firm is to make the nonfamily member feel a part of the family.

Coordinating International Sales

We have been looking at international control from the viewpoint of how corporate headquarters controls marketing operations within foreign subsidiaries. A separate and special problem common in international marketing is the coordination of international sales when several countries are possible sources for a given product. To avoid suboptimization from excessive competition between subsidiaries, some central control is necessary. Otherwise the corporation's global production and marketing facilities will be used less than optimally. For example, for each country operation to have its own export manager could be wasteful.

As we saw in our discussion of logistics, one way international companies handle this problem is through the establishment of a centralized export operation for world-wide markets. Because its primary purpose is to control subsidiary exports, this office not infrequently is located away from corporate headquarters. Hewlett-Packard is one company that has taken this approach. Interestingly, theirs is called an import marketing department, emphasizing the import rather than the export side. The principle is the same, however, because this department has the task of acting as the marketing interface between each of the overseas manufacturing subsidiaries and all other markets.[25]

Conclusions

We now conclude our discussion of organization and control, critical aspects of the management of international marketing. *Marketing* usually indicates a collection of activities pertaining to product, price, promotion, and so on. *Marketing management* involves the overall planning and coordination of these activities within the framework of the firm's organization. Thus one who would be a manager must go beyond the functional marketing activities discussed in Part II to learn how these can be integrated effectively in the international company. Our relatively brief discussion in Part III was intended to help round out the reader's perception of the task of international marketing management. It is fair to conclude that the marketing executive working in this field has responsibilities that are not only heavily *managerial* but also truly *international*.

Questions

16.1　"Organization is not an end in itself but a means to an end." What ends should be furthered by a firm's organization for international marketing?

16.2　Discuss the advantages and disadvantages of making separate organizational arrangements for international business.

16.3　What is a "world company"?

16.4　"A regional form of organization is better for a consumer-goods company than for an industrial-goods company." Discuss.

16.5　Why is a firm's organization rarely a "pure" area, product, or functional form of organization?

[25] *Business International,* November 21, 1969, p. 374.

16.6   What is the "ideal" organization for international business?

16.7   Should corporate headquarters and the international marketing manager have a role even in decentralized organizations?

16.8   Should the multinational company have regional headquarters?

16.9   Identify some of the problems peculiar to controlling international operations.

16.10 How can appropriate standards be determined for controlling international marketing?

16.11 Discuss the use of meetings as a way of monitoring performance in foreign markets.

16.12 Identify the various control techniques available in international marketing.

16.13 How can licensees and distributors be "controlled"?

Further Readings

Books:

Business International, *Organizing the Worldwide Corporation* (New York, 1970).

Fayerweather, John, *International Business Management* (New York: McGraw-Hill Book Co., 1969), chap. 6.

Kolde, Endel J., *International Business Enterprise* (Englewood Cliffs, N.J.: Prentice-Hall, 1968), chap. 16.

Lovell, E. B., *The Changing Role of the International Executive* (New York: National Industrial Conference Board, 1966).

Robinson, Richard D., *International Management* (New York: Holt, Rinehart and Winston, 1967), chap. 8.

Stieglitz, Harold, *Organization Structures of International Companies* (New York: National Industrial Conference Board, 1965).

Articles:

Aylmer, R. J., "Who Makes Marketing Decisions in the Multinational Firm?" *Journal of Marketing* (October 1970), pp. 26, 27.

Butler, W. Jack, and John Dearden, "Managing a Worldwide Business," *Harvard Business Review* (May–June 1965), pp. 93–102.

Clee, G. H., and W. M. Sachtjen, "Organizing a Worldwide Business," *Harvard Business Review* (November–December 1964), pp. 55–67.

Williams, Charles R., "Regional Management Overseas," *Harvard Business Review* (January–February 1967), pp. 87–91.

Zwick, Jack, "Is Top Management Really on Top?" *Columbia Journal of World Business* (Winter 1966), pp. 87–97.

SUBJECT INDEX

AUTHOR INDEX

512

COMPANY INDEX